S0-BIP-415

# GEOGRAPHICAL PERSPECTIVES ON THE ELDERLY

*Edited by*

A. M. WARNES
*Lecturer in Geography*
*King's College*
*University of London*

JOHN WILEY & SONS
Chichester · New York · Brisbane · Toronto

***British Library Cataloguing in Publication Data:***
Geographical perspectives on the elderly.
1. Aged—Congresses
I. Warnes, A.M.
305.2'6 HQ1061

ISBN 0 471 09976 7

Photosetting by Thomson Press (India) Limited, New Delhi
and printed in the United States of America

# Contributors

Roderick D. Allon-Smith, 56 High Street, Girton, Cambridge CB3 OPU, England.

Katherine C. Barnard, Research and Intelligence Unit, County Planning Department, Hampshire County Council, The Castle, Winchester, Hampshire SO23 8UE, England.

Andrew C. Bebbington, Personal Social Services Research Unit, University of Kent, Canterbury, Kent CT2 7NF, England.

James R. Bohland, Chairman, Environmental and Urban Systems—Urban Affairs, Virginia Polytechnic Institute and State University, Blacksburg, Viginia 24061, USA.

William R. Bytheway, Medical Sociology Research Centre, Department of Sociology and Anthropology, University College, Swansea SA2 8PP, Wales.

Paul Compton, Department of Geography, The Queen's University, Belfast BT7 1NN, Nothern Ireland.

Françoise Cribier, Laboratoire de Géographie Humaine de l'Université de Paris, 191 Rue Saint Jacques, 75005 Paris, France.

Bleddyn Davies, Director, Personal Social Services Research Unit, University of Kent, Canterbury, Kent CT2 7NF, England.

Patricia Frech, Department of Geography, University of Oklahoma, 455 West Lindsey, Norman, Oklahoma 73019, USA.

Robert Gant, School of Geography, Kingston Polytechnic, Penrhyn Road, Kingston upon Thames KT1 2EE, London, England.

Lawrence Greenberg, Department of the Environment, Becket House, Lambeth Palace Road, London SE1 7ER, England.

Christopher M. Law, Department of Geography, The University, Salford M5 4WT, England.

Charles F. Longino, Jr, Department of Sociology, University of Miami, Coral Gables, Florida 33124, USA.

Wiley P. Mangum, Department of Gerontology, University of South Florida, Tampa, Florida 33620, USA.

Russell Murray, Institute of Population Studies, University of Exeter, 101 Pennsylvania Road, Exeter EX4 6DT, England.

Sheila M. Peace, Survey Research Unit, Polytechnic of North London, Ladbroke House, Highbury Grove, London N5 2AD, England.

Paul Robson, formerly of 'Age Concern', Bernard Sunley House, 60 Pitcairn Road, Mitcham, Surrey CR4 3LL, England.

Nicki Skelton, Department of Civil Engineering, University of Aston, Gosta Green, Birmingham B4 7ET, England.

Christopher J. Smith, Department of Geography, State University of New York at Albany, 1400 Washington Avenue, Albany, New York 12222, USA.

Jose Smith, School of Geography, Kingston Polytechnic, Penrhyn Road, Kingston upon Thames KT1 2EE, London, England.

Louis Smith, Department of Geography, Portsmouth Polytechnic, Lion Terrace, Portsmouth, PO1 3HE, England.

Hedley Taylor, Senior Research Officer, Centre for Policy on Ageing, Nuffield Lodge, Regent's Park, London NWL 4RS, England.

Hilary Todd, Information Officer, Centre for Policy on Ageing, Nuffield Lodge, Regent's Park, London NWL 4RS, England.

Lexa Treps, Department of Geography, University of Oklahoma, 455 West Lindsey, Norman, Oklahoma 73019, USA.

Anthony M. Warnes, Department of Geography, King's College, University of London, Strand, London WC2R 2LS, England.

# Contents

# Preface

The stimulus to form this collection of geographical studies of the elderly population was a modest symposium on 'The Spatial Aspects of Ageing' at the 1979 Annual Conference of the Institute of British Geographers. Some of the speakers suggested the publication of its proceedings, and a subsequent short correspondence established that several young geographers had recently completed research in the subject area and that ample support would be found for an interesting book. I have also been given much support in my attempt to cohere the volume, both by the co-operation of colleagues from other disciplines who have filled a number of gaps, and by the willingness of the authors to alter the scope of their chapters.

My reading of the contributions has reaffirmed a view that a greater measure of the considerable research capacity of university geography departments would be profitably applied to the themes dealt with in this book. Apart from the obvious practical and humanitarian importance of many facets of social gerontology, the subject holds challenging intellectual and conceptual problems which would reward the ablest investigators. I also find that there are many geographical and spatial dimensions to the welfare of the elderly population, and that these would be more authoritatively described and understood if investigated by those with trained geographical insight and analytical ability. The making of the book has converted my intermittent interest in the field to a greater conviction of the merits and value of a geographical contribution to social gerontology. Like all converts, I am unabashed in encouraging others to take the same course.

While the majority of the book's chapters refer to Britain, a comparative element has been injected with the willing co-operation of colleagues from both the United States of America and from France. Another asset has been the contributions from sociologists, social administrators, a transport scientist, a civil servant and representatives of a lobby organization. Many geographical aspects of the condition of the elderly and their services are well appreciated by the planning and welfare professions, and many proficient studies of the effects of distance and location have been carried out by their practitioners. Geographers have much to learn from the existing literature by architects, planners, social administrators, and sociologists, but on the other hand the former's particular interests and techniques would supplement the capacity of social gerontology as an applied social science. Social gerontolgy is notable for its multi-disciplinary character, and it is believed that a contribution from human geography will produce mutual advantages.

This book was designed around five major themes which, as the introductory chapter explains further, are but a sample of those which could be explored under the book's title. They reflect the socio-spatial aspects of gerontology which have recently been taken up by human geographers in North America and in Europe. The first of the four substantive sections contains five chapters on the changing distribution of elderly people at the national and urban scales. Roderick Allon-Smith summarizes the changing regional and local distribution of pensioners in England and Wales during the twentieth century, while Christopher Law and myself examine the destination decision in retirement migration, the process which is increasingly important in altering the location of elderly people. Paul Compton and Russell Murray contribute an essay on Northern Ireland where, despite the many sad special circumstances, the distributional trends in Belfast and their policy implications show many parallels to those in English and American cities. Françoise Cribier has written about her latest study of retirement migration from Paris which, apart from its comparative value alongside related American and British studies, continues her innovatory and assiduous research on this topic. James Bohland and Lexa Treps's study of the inter-county patterns of elderly migration in the United States adds more detailed insights than have previously been available from inter-State analyses of migration. The five chapters supplement a growing literature in Britain, France, and the United States on the basic distributional trends of the elderly population, and illustrate a shifting focus to the underlying demographic and social processes.

The second section comprises four papers on spatial aspects of housing for the elderly, a field which has been studied little by European and American geographers. Indeed the only contribution here by a geographer is Katherine Barnard's chapter, developed from her doctoral thesis on housing for the elderly in England and Wales and more particularly in south-east Hampshire. William Bytheway's examination of the micro-spatial implications of the design of sheltered housing schemes upon the independence and social networks of their residents gives us the benefit of his long-standing interest in this distinctively European specialist housing. Two contributions from the United States indicate the substantial body of writing by sociologists, architects, and others on housing for the elderly. Wiley Mangum comprehensively reviews the present variety of housing types, tenures, and related services through the coterminous States, and Charles Longino also applies a sociological perspective to the diversity of retirement communities in contrasting environments through the United States. While there are deep cultural, institutional, and financial differences in housing supply and demand between the United States and Britain (and other European countries), the papers suggest that each nation's policies and practices have their own merits and limitations, and that they are mutually instructive. The issues raised in this section have considerable practical importance both for individuals and societies, and surely deserve and would reward much wider attention from geographers.

The third section examines the activity and travel patterns and problems of the elderly, generally at a more local geographical scale than the previous sections. Its four chapters reflect the interest in these topics evident for a decade in social-transport studies and among those concerned with the welfare and quality of life of elderly people. Paul Robson considers these issues at the national level and stresses the relationships between mobility and the variety, quality, and independence of old people's lives, while Nicola Skelton focuses on the wide range and variable effectiveness of public policy in this area. Sheila Peace, and José Smith with Robert Gant, in their respective urban and rural case studies point to the influence of residential location upon elderly people's accessibility to facilities, services, and social contacts. They also demonstrate the severity of spatial inequalities that arise from the combination of location, personal command of resources, individual physical ability, and the discretionary provision of services by local authorities. There is a clear call for more analysis of these variations and for better-informed planning and transport policies.

The last of the empirical sections deals with three aspects of service provision to the elderly. This subject has been pursued over many years in Britain by sociologists and social administrators, whose findings and recommendations were responsible in the 1950s and 1960s for several major changes and additions to the nation's welfare services. Andrew Bebbington and Bleddyn Davies, who have contributed frequently to these studies, discuss in their chapter the difficult concept of need, and analyse the massive variations in the provision of services among local authorities in England and Wales. Until recently, geographical expertise has not joined in these efforts. Two studies from Oklahoma City illustrate what is possible. James Bohland and Patricia Frech establish surprisingly strong distance-decay as well as socio-economic status relationships with the frequency and quality of primary health care, while Christopher Smith's innovatory action research project in the same city probes the practicality of stimulating home-based care of mentally ill elderly people by relatives and neighbours.

The book concludes with a short section of two overview chapters by authors who work outside of universities and who are concerned more directly with public policy in the field of old people's welfare. Lawrence Greenberg, formerly of the Ageing Studies Unit in the Department of the Environment, in a personal capacity writes an evaluation of the role of government in improving the quality of life of the elderly population and an assessment of applied research needs.

Equally instructive for geographers who are considering contributing to the subject is Hedley Taylor and Hilary Todd's chapter. As officers of the Centre for Policy on Ageing they are very well informed about current British social gerontological research, policy issues, and research needs, and their frank comments about a potential geographical contribution are both an encouragement and a challenge. The cross-disciplinary viewpoints of this final section, as well as those introduced earlier by Bebbington, Bytheway, Davies, Longino, Mangum, Robson, and Skelton should be of great assistance in integrating geographical research with the accomplished work of social gerontology.

Multi-authored volumes often suffer from incoherence, overlap, and inconsistent coverage of their subject matter. The authors have collaborated selflessly in altering their original emphases to reduce these evils to a modest level. My own efforts towards a coherent volume have been much helped by the recommendations of many people, among whom I wish to thank particularly Lawrence Greenberg, Hilary Todd, Wiley Mangum, and Celia Bird of John Wiley and Sons. Also of irreplaceable help was the opportunity to visit the University of South Florida, assisted by a grant from the Central Research Fund of the University of London.

The editorial task has been eased by the excellent secretarial and technical support at King's College. Bridget O'Donnell deserves particular thanks for her unstinting secretarial assistance, and Joy Barnett at King's College Hall and Roma Beaumont, Gordon Reynell, and Katherine Hopkirk of the Cartography Unit in the Department of Geography have been consistently enthusiastic helpers.

# List of tables

# List of figures

Geographical Perspectives on the Elderly
Edited by A. M. Warnes


Chapter 1

# Geographical perspectives on ageing

*Anthony Warnes*

## SOCIAL GERONTOLOGY AND SOCIAL GEOGRAPHY

Even among the proliferating and serial concerns of contemporary human geography, the study of ageing and of the elderly is novel. Following several decades of intermittent writing, which in Britain perhaps began with Gilbert's (1939) interest in the retirement function of seaside resorts, and after a crescendo of article publication following Golant's (1972) innovatory and influential research monograph on the elderly's travel and residential patterns in Toronto, this book joins other attempts of the last two years to take a broad view of the geographical aspects of ageing and of the elderly population (Golant, 1979; Paillat, 1979; Warnes, 1981; Wiseman, 1978). Neither the most productive research areas nor the potential of a geographical contribution to social gerontology have yet been determined, partly because hitherto there has been little exchange between geographers and other social scientists in the field. This book is a step in this direction, particularly in respect of the chapters by non-geographers whose opinions about worthwhile research and whose perception of the capabilities of geographers should be of much interest.

The academic study of old age and of ageing was founded in the late nineteenth century by medical research into the physiological and biochemical conditions of old age, or geriatrics. Gerontology emerged later, again mainly within the medical profession, as the study of the processes of growing old. Gradually these interests widened and merged with those of social statisticians, as exemplified at an early date by Booth (1894), to form social gerontology, which deals with the social, economic, and demographic conditions of the elderly, including such topics as government policy towards the aged and economic provision for retirement through insurance, pensions, and health and welfare services. Social gerontology is more often concerned with the circumstances of old people than with the processes of adult ageing. It has grown enormously since 1950, particularly in the United States and France, and has attained at least the threshold of a coherent independent social science discipline. This is shown by the quality and content of several fundamental texts and readers (Binstock and Shanas, 1977; Riley and Foner, 1968, 1969 and 1972; Shanas and Sussman, 1977; Tibbitts and Donahue, 1962; Woodruff and Birren, 1975).

Human geography has made comparable progress over recent decades and accomplished a substantial development of its research capacity and output, its theoretical underpinning, and its analytical ability and applied value. It has built a complementary relationship with other social sciences while enormously diversifying its subjects for study and, as an introductory text by one of its ablest practitioners shows, maintaining its age-old concerns with place, space, and man–environment relations (Haggett, 1972). It is therefore both remarkable and disappointing that the subject has given such slight attention to the many geographical aspects of social gerontology.

The reasons for this are undoubtedly related to the stunted growth of social geography as compared to either economic or urban geography. Human geography has always pursued distinguishable but related interests. While such diversity is by no means exceptional, in geography it confuses not only its own researchers and teachers but also most others. The most popularly understood interest can be described variously as the study of *place*, areal differentiation, or regional geography. An unprecedented feature since around 1960 has been the minority status of this interest, although more vigour has been evident in a closely related concern, the study of *man—environment relationships* in geographical context. A third broad interest has historically been less prevalent although it has existed from time out of mind. It is the study of *space*, distance, and location, or of spatial pattern or organization.

The history of human geography over the last half-century reveals a sequence of circumstances which have conspired to frustrate the 'study of the processes and patterns involved in an understanding of socially defined populations in their spatial setting' (Pahl, 1965b, p. 81). The antecedents and scope of the subject have been thoughtfully reviewed on several occasions (Buttimer, 1968, 1969; Eyles and Smith, 1978; Jones and Eyles, 1977, Chapter 1). Although Eyles and Smith are ambivalent about the desirability of furthering a distinctive social geography, most reviewers advocate this course, yet Buttimer's (1968, p. 134) assessment remains true: 'with some notable exceptions, for example, in Sweden and Holland, social geography can be considered a field created and cultivated by a number of individual scholars rather than an academic tradition built up within particular schools'.

Some of the principal handicaps to the development of the subject can be noted. Until the 1950s many geographers rejected the relevance of social facts to their studies of place because they are not normally expressed tangibly in the landscape. Others held a more sophisticated view derived from the French practitioners of regional study in the early decades of the century and associated particularly with Paul Vidal de la Blanche's emphasis upon 'the significance of social and cultural elements in the way certain regions had distinctive ways of life' (Jones and Eyles, 1977, p. 7). This view is evident in both the geographical contributions to British community studies and the small but creative group of American cultural geographers stimulated by Carl Sauer.

From the late 1950s the enthusiasm for dominantly idiographic studies of place was supplanted by one for explicitly nomothetic studies of spatial patterns. Both community studies and cultural geography became marginal concerns, and subsequently the furtherance of social geography was distorted if not restricted by the popularity of urban geography. The promise of several substantial research monographs in urban social geography (Jones, 1960; Robson, 1969; Timms, 1971) did not lead to a broader sociological inquisitiveness among human geographers, and their limitations and branding as urban ecology truncated that line of development. The 1970s witnessed some hibernation and some diversification of sociological and humanistic interests among geographers, the continuing activity being mainly in behavioural studies, the application of spatial analytic techniques to territorial social indicators, and further attempts to develop and synthesize knowledge of urban social patterns and problems (Herbert, 1972; Ley and Samuels, 1978; Robson, 1975; Smith, 1977). In Britain, few stood back from empirical studies to appraise the requirements of a more sociologically based and rounded social geography.

Finally, and in the last few years, social geography has come for many to be synonymous with radical human geography, inspired by a Marxist analysis of the spatial aspects of contemporary social structures or formations and their trends in contemporary capitalist nations. Its adherents tend to disclaim a particular interest in either space or place; proclaim an undifferentiated interest in society, economy, and polity; and assert the hegemony of class as the root of social differences and social problems. In part reacting to the most inept examples of spatial analytic studies, which attempted to account for spatial patterns with little reference to either the formative processes or the background circumstances, this view asserts the supremacy of macro-studies of political economy in accounting for spatial inequality. It has been argued that the recent focus on social problems

> is doing more to integrate geography—to create a new human geography—than to strengthen the various adjectival subfields.... Social geography has played as important a part as any subfield in opening up this wider view, within which social geography, like the other branches of the discipline, may well cease to justify an independent entity. Social geography's greatest achievement may yet turn out to be the acceleration of its own destruction (Eyles and Smith, 1978, p. 55).

While such a prescription is unlikely to be shared by many, there is widespread acceptance of the value of the study of political economy and of the importance of a more explicit ideological and methodological basis. This has been demonstrated most recently by the recommendations of a Social Science Research Council seminar on the Social Geography of the City (Herbert, 1980). While the group displayed commendable eclecticism and tolerance in their support of diverse existing studies in urban social geography, its purpose was also 'to add more significance to moves in some directions and less in others. The need for integrated studies and analysis of the interplay of structural and local effects, for example, has been consistently stressed' (p. 58). It advocates the application of different epistemologies to the same topical theme or research problem and argues that 'research which incorporates some focus on public policy and its implications should be encouraged' (p.60). One problem with the path that is now being followed is that sociological topics that are not manifestly associated with problems of equity are likely to be neglected by the growing emphases upon social relevance, philosophy, epistemology, and methodology. In an era of rapid social and cultural change, not least with respect to child-rearing, marriage, aspirations, and inter-generational roles and care, there *is* a strong case for studies in sociological geography as well as in a geography of society.

Coming back to the issues central to this book, many would argue that the quality of life of an elderly person is as much if not more related to their social isolation or integration and to their physical capacities as to their command of material resources. It is also widely asserted that the readiness of children to provide support, care, and contact to their elderly parents is declining: others deny the trend. Relevant to these questions are the increasing household independence of elderly people and the dispersing relative locations of parents and children. These topics have evident spatial dimensions and touch both on the social welfare of a large minority of the population and on an expensive area of social policy. The low commitment to sociological topics by human geography means that at present there is very little knowledge or advice that we can offer to inform those who are more directly concerned with the formulation or execution of social policies for the elderly. My own opinion is that the applied returns in this area from theoretical and structural emphases in social geography will be long in coming. This appears to be the view of academic social gerontologists also, for most display substantive concerns first and foremost, although as is shown in several chapters of the book, several specific theoretical issues have been vigorously pursued and have informed and stimulated the subject's dominantly empirical character.

Many geographers will nonetheless be intrigued by the idiosyncrasy of the book's substantive focus on a minority of the population who do not constitute a functional social group but are defined by age and, in most cases, by their inactive employment status. While the elderly are as heterogeneous as the younger adult population, most of them share characteristics and problems which distinguish them from younger people. These include lower income, declining income prospects, lower physical capacities, and a decaying social network as members of their generation die. There are important geographical aspects of their welfare, particularly their economic, social, housing, and health characteristics and requirements, and most of these have only been described in general terms. There are also profound welfare, resource, political, and humane issues associated with their situation. While these are increasingly claiming public attention in Europe, Japan, and North America—in Spring 1981 a much-delayed White Paper on the elderly was published in Britain, not only is social gerontology too understaffed to produce adequate information or sufficient recommendations, but the clear potential of a geographical contribution is unexplored and only a minute share of its now considerable research capacity is devoted to the tasks. The reader may be able to judge from this book whether more can usefully be done.

While very brief calls for geographical studies of ageing appeared in 1966 and 1974, it was not until the later 1970s that they were answered on any scale (Peet and Rowles, 1974; Zelinsky, 1966). Many research workers are now engaged in these studies, the majority in the United States of America. Several reviews have already appeared and these consistently name the same subject areas as having attracted research. Interest to date has reflected spatial rather than place interests, and one common characteristic is their association with readily available aggregate data. The principal chapters of Wiseman's (1978) review included, for example: the distribution of the elderly, migration, environment and ageing, and accessibility to and delivery of services. Golant's (1979) edited volume, and an annotated bibliography (Warnes, 1981) covered similar subjects but also reflected a growing literature on the relationships between elderly people and their geographical environments. It is not difficult to identify neglected topics among which housing is outstanding but others are international migration, access to medical services, leisure travel, and spatial aspects of employment in old age.

The recency of the publication of these research reviews removes any reason to repeat the task, so rather than looking back over completed studies, in the remainder of this introductory chapter the potential for new areas of study will be assessed. Three ageing topics which are believed to have practical importance and exceptional academic interest will be discussed. They are distinguished by their scales of aggregation and by the very different geographical perspectives, methodologies, theories, and empirical research designs that they invoke. A common characteristic, however, is that they set the social gerontological issue in its wider social, economic, and political context, rather than focusing exclusively on the elderly themselves.

The topics to be considered are: first, demographic ageing in national populations and the prospects for rapid ageing in those countries which have recently experienced substantial declines in fertility. The global and highly aggregated scale of this topic has not previously been adopted by geographers in their gerontological research, and is rare amongst gerontologists. Although there are considerable dangers of superficiality, cultural bias, and premature advocacy in any internationally comparative study, the potential value of the ageing experience of European countries to other parts of the world is considerable. Unmeasurable but far from negligible benefits may come from the study of the geography of the age structure transition.

This will be followed by a preliminary assessment of the importance of the relative locations of an old person's extended family members, particularly upon the material and emotional support that they provide and on the social or medical service dependency that arises if they are absent or ineffectual. The scale of this subject is that of the social group and the perspective focuses on the almost wholly neglected spatial or distributional aspects of consanguinity.

The third topic and geographical perspective is at the level of the individual, and concerns the study of the complex interrelationships between an individual's personality, competences, living arrangements and residential location, and the material and psychological satisfactions that they gain from their environment or place of residence. Such studies have been pioneered by Rowles (1978a, b) and represent an existential development of research into the spatial behaviour and individual activity patterns of elderly people; they also revive the study of the interrelationships of individual lifestyles, or in de la Blanche's term *genres de vie*, and the environment, in most cases in the challenging setting of almost totally man-made environments.

The reader will find that the later chapters in the book illustrate the contribution that geographers have already begun to make to the study of ageing and the elderly population's welfare. They do not represent, however, the full extent of geographical interest and concern with social gerontology, nor are the three perspectives discussed in this chapter claimed to close such an inventory. Rather it is hoped that this elaboration of personal interests will stimulate further ideas, encourage more research, and eventually lead to a useful contribution to the welfare of the elderly population.

## THE AGE STRUCTURE TRANSITION

Few studies in either social gerontology or social geography have been carried out at the international scale, and of these few add the temporal dimension. This is a lost opportunity, for the ageing of a population brings about predictable subsidiary demographic changes in the elderly population and in its relationship to other age groups. These in turn can be associated with social, economic, and political consequences that affect individuals, groups, organizations, and governments. Only a few countries of Europe have reached a high plateau in their relative elderly populations, one being the United Kingdom where the percentage of the population of pensionable age is not expected to increase for many decades. Comparative studies of the experience of ageing in these nations would be instructive and may carry lessons for countries at an earlier stage of demographic ageing.

A recent stimulus for such work is the mounting evidence of worldwide fertility declines on an unprecedented scale. 'If United Nations estimates are to be believed, modest fertility declines were widespread by 1970. . . the world crude birth had dropped by 12 per cent between 1950–5 and 1970–5' (Kirk, 1979, p. 396). Other estimates on more slender evidence have estimated that between 1968 and 1975 the world's total fertility rate dropped from 4.6 to 4.1 live births per woman (Tsui and Bogue, 1978, p. 9). If these declines are not exaggerated, and if they spread, most nations of the world will shortly experience an acceleration of ageing that *ceteris paribus* will continue for around two generations. The grounds for this assertion can be elaborated in three ways: empirically, theoretically by the elaboration of the demographic transition, and deductively by reference to the characteristics of stable populations with contrasting fertility and mortality levels.

Transition theory was first elaborated by Davis (1945) and Notestein (1945) and ever since has been a focus of research and debate about the trends of mortality and fertility in diverse settings. It is well summarized and evaluated in most demography and population studies texts (Bogue, 1969; Clarke, 1972; Petersen, 1975; Woods, 1979) and recent research contributions abound (e.g. Agyei, 1978; Beaver, 1975; Jakubowski, 1977; Knodel, 1977; Tilly, 1978). The following extract conveys its essentials:

> The essential demographic difference between traditional and modern societies is that in the former fertility and mortality rates are usually high while in the latter they are universally low, and that between them there is a temporal transition. Demographic transition theory postulated that as death rates declined urbanization and industrialization increased along with literacy, living standards, and social and occupational mobility. Decline in fertility awaited the obsolescence of traditional social and economic institutions and the emergence of the new ideal of the small family. . . . The clearest evidence for the theory is found in nineteenth century Britain and western Europe, especially if industrialization is equated with modernization, and it also found support, for example, from the evidence of demographic changes in eastern and southern Europe (Clarke, 1978, pp. 10–11).

A rarely emphasized concomitant of the transition is the ageing of the population. Mortality declines have usually been brought about initially by improving infant mortality, which for a time has increased the proportion of children in the population and depressed the elderly percentage. The generally more moderate improvements in mortality at adult ages have been less effective in raising average life expectancy but increased the absolute number of elderly people. As surprising as it may be on first inspection, improvements in mortality have generally been unable to bring about the ageing of a population. This has only begun some time after rapid population growth has been established when fertility has fallen. Demographic ageing has then continued beyond the end of the demographic transition, which is the notional date at which both fertility and mortality have stabilized at a low level. The period of the age structure transition therefore lags behind the period of transition in the population's vital rates, and the main engine of ageing is fertility decline. In England and

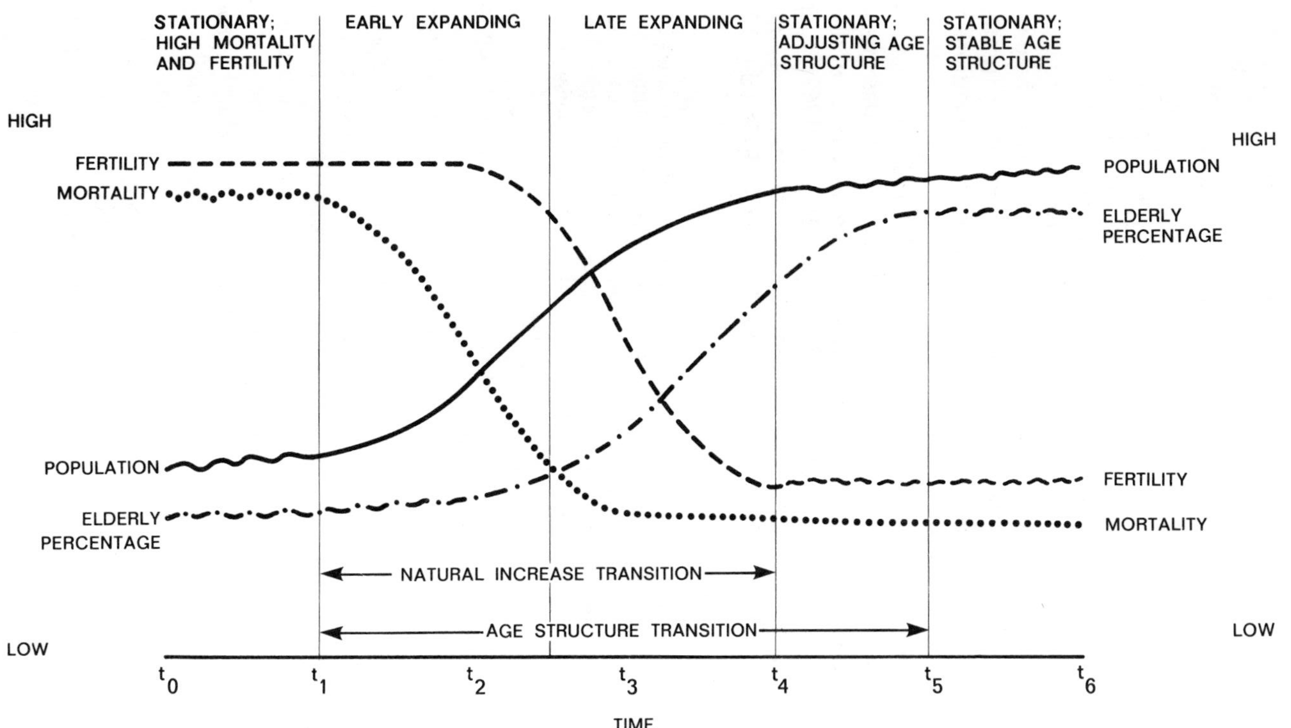


Figure 1.1 The age-structure transition

Wales, to take one example, the percentage elderly was remarkably stable from 1840 to 1900 and only subsequently began a sinusoidal increase which has recently reached a high plateau. Mortality began to fall from around 1770 and fertility from about 1870. The number of elderly people increased at a modest rate in the second half of the nineteenth century but at a much higher rate from 1910 to 1970.

A tentative and simplified representation of these descriptive hypotheses about the progress of ageing can be incorporated in conventional graphical representations of the demographic transition (Figure 1.1). Clarke's (1972) stages are adopted in the diagram, but his fourth and last stage is replaced by, first, a *stationary sub-stable* phase. This begins when fertility and mortality reach and maintain low if fluctuating levels, and continues as long as the age structure and population size adjust to the settled vital rates, and as long as the relative size of the elderly population increases. Only after two generations or more would the elderly percentage stabilize and a fifth stage of a *stable population* with stationary age structure be approached. It should be stressed that the final stage is an ideal abstraction, for most populations show too frequent disturbances for it to be realized. A stationary age structure is consistent with population growth, but in such a population the elderly fraction is reduced.

The lagged transition of the age structure can also be demonstrated by examining the age structures of theoretical stable populations under various stated fertility and mortality regimes (Hauser, 1976; Spengler, 1974). The feasible range of age-specific fertility and mortality conditions is represented in Table 1.1. The percentage of the associated stable population aged 60 years and more is given for each combination of fertility and mortality. At a given level of fertility this percentage varies little according to life expectancy, but at a given level of mortality the variation associated with fertility is substantial.

Table 1.1 Percentage of stable population aged 60 and over by life expectancy and fertility

| Gross Reproduction Ratio* | Average life expectancy (years) | | | | | |
|---|---|---|---|---|---|---|
| | 20 | 30 | 40 | 50 | 60.4 | 70.2 |
| 4.0 | 2.4 | 2.6 | 2.7 | 2.7 | 2.7 | 2.6 |
| 3.0 | 3.9 | 4.1 | 4.4 | 4.5 | 4.4 | 4.3 |
| 2.5 | 5.2 | 5.5 | 5.9 | 6.1 | 6.0 | 5.9 |
| 2.0 | 7.1 | 7.7 | 8.3 | 8.6 | 8.6 | 8.5 |
| 1.5 | 10.5 | 11.5 | 12.5 | 13.0 | 13.1 | 13.0 |
| 1.0 | 16.9 | 18.7 | 20.4 | 21.5 | 21.9 | 21.9 |

*Source*: United Nations Organization (1956). *The Ageing of Populations and its Economic and Social Implications*, New York; as extracted by J. J. Spengler (1974), Tables 1–1 and 1–2.

* The Gross Reproduction Ratio is the number of female children that will be borne by each newborn female child, assuming none die before the end of their reproductive period.

This paradoxical situation arises because high fertility continually expands the number of people reaching reproductive ages who themselves then display high fertility; the result is a very high proportion of the population in childhood and a very low proportion in old age. Not even the longest of life expectancies, or even an immortal population, can substantially change this position. More specifically, a striking demographic result of an instantaneous fall in fertility from a gross reproduction ratio (GRR) of 4.0 to the below replacement level of 1.0 would be an increase over half a century or more of the percentage of the population in the elderly age groups from around 2.5 per cent to between 16.9 and 21.9 per cent. As fertility levels below a GRR of 1.0 are difficult to envisage, and as life expectancy has little prospect of increasing substantially beyond 75 years, it is extremely unlikely that any population will ever report in the absence of substantial age-selective migration much more than a fifth of its numbers aged 60 years and more.

The 1970/71 vital rates of the world's nations range over a large proportion of the possible states, and the observed elderly fractions broadly accord with their predictions of the associated stable population (Table 1.2). The age

Table 1.2 Extremes and selected examples of vital statistics among the nations of the world, *c.* 1970

| Country | Population (millions) | Life expectancy at birth | | Crude vital rates per 1000 population | | Percentage of population | | |
|---|---|---|---|---|---|---|---|---|
| | | Male | Female | Births | Deaths | 0–15 | 15–64 | 65+ |
| East Germany | 17 | 69.2 | 74.4 | 13.9 | 14.1 | 23.3 | 61.1 | 15.6 |
| Austria | 7 | 66.5 | 73.3 | 15.1 | 13.2 | 24.5 | 61.3 | 14.2 |
| Sweden | 8 | 71.7 | 76.5 | 13.6 | 9.9 | 20.8 | 65.4 | 13.7 |
| West Germany | 61 | 67.6 | 73.6 | 13.3 | 11.6 | 23.0 | 63.6 | 13.4 |
| France | 51 | 68.6 | 76.1 | 16.7 | 10.6 | 24.0 | 62.7 | 13.4 |
| Belgium | 10 | 67.7 | 73.5 | 14.7 | 12.4 | 23.7 | 63.0 | 13.3 |
| England and Wales | 49 | 68.7 | 74.9 | 16.0 | 11.7 | 23.9 | 63.0 | 13.1 |
| United States | 203 | 66.6 | 74.0 | 18.2 | 9.4 | 28.5 | 61.6 | 9.9 |
| Australia | 13 | 67.9 | 74.2 | 20.5 | 9.0 | 28.8 | 62.9 | 8.3 |
| Canada | 22 | 68.8 | 75.2 | 17.0 | 7.3 | 29.6 | 62.3 | 8.1 |
| Soviet Union | 242 | 65.0 | 74.0 | 17.5 | 8.2 | 30.9 | 61.4 | 7.7 |
| Japan | 104 | 69.0 | 74.3 | 18.9 | 6.9 | 23.9 | 69.0 | 7.1 |
| India | 548 | 41.9 | 40.6 | 42.8 | 16.7 | 41.8 | 54.7 | 3.5 |
| Venezuela | 10 | 63.8 | | 40.9 | 7.8 | 47.1 | 50.5 | 2.4 |
| Honduras | 3 | 49.0 | | 49.0 | 17.1 | 46.8 | 50.8 | 2.4 |
| Zambia | 4 | 43.5 | | 49.8 | 20.7 | 46.3 | 51.5 | 2.2 |
| Mali | 5 | 37.2 | | 49.8 | 26.6 | 49.1 | 49.3 | 1.6 |

*Source*: United Nations Organization, *Demographic Yearbooks*.

structures of European countries vary with the recency of their industrialization and fertility decline. Some east and north-west European nations have exceptionally high relative elderly populations but the peripheral nations which have achieved low fertility more recently are characterized by lower relative elderly shares (Figure 1.2). Although many non-European industrialized nations have low mortality, their fertility remains generally higher, and so they have more youthful populations. It is in the poorest nations of the world with very high fertility and mortality that the smallest relative elderly populations

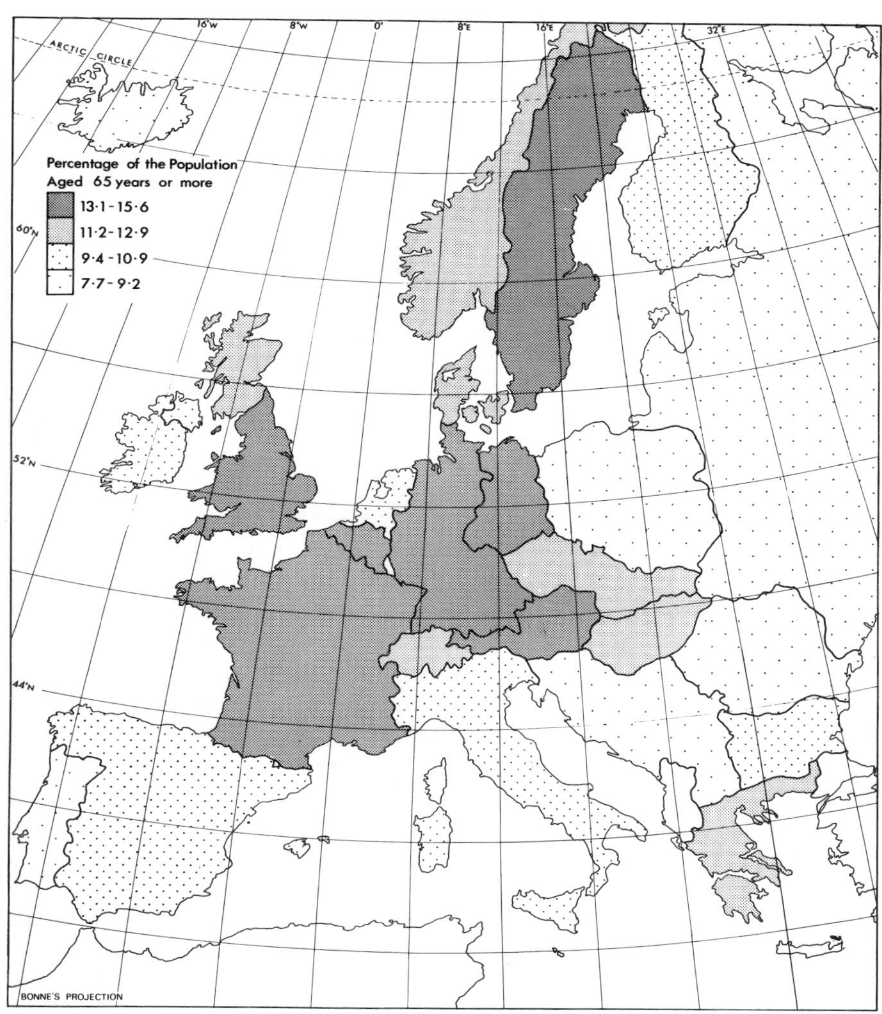


Figure 1.2 The relative elderly population of the major European countries

are found. The range of conditions can be considerable in a single continent or even more locally. In Latin America around 1970, for example, Argentina, Uruguay, and Chile showed almost European conditions with male life expectations of over 60 years and respectively 7.7, 9.9 (1975), and 6.0 per cent of their population aged 65 years or more, while neighbouring countries had the demographic characteristics of underdeveloped countries; e.g. Bolivia had only 3.5 per cent of its population in the elderly age group in 1975.

## Fertility declines and ageing in less developed countries

From this empirical and theoretical evidence it is concluded that the imminence and prospective rate of ageing in a nation are closely related to the scale of recent fertility decline and the attained level of fertility in its population. There is a complex relation between absolute and relative changes in fertility and the elderly share of the associated stable population (Table 1.1). For example, a 0.5 decline in the gross reproduction ratio from 3.0 leads to a maximum increase of 37 per cent in the elderly share (from 4.3 to 5.9 per cent of a population with a life expectancy of 70.2 years), whereas the same absolute decline from a GRR of 1.5 leads to an increase in the elderly share of from 61 to 69 per cent (from 13.0 to 21.9 per cent of the high life expectancy population). If the fertility decline is accompanied by improvements in mortality and life expectancy, as is the case in many parts of the world, the pace of ageing will be modestly accelerated. If it results in a no-growth state, the relative presence of the elderly will be increased further.

The mounting evidence of worldwide fertility decline should therefore be closely scrutinized by all concerned with the implications of ageing populations. As Kirk (1979, p. 401) has written: 'We are now at an exciting time in demographic history. We are well on the way to a new demographic transition among the developing areas, and this will occur much more rapidly than it did in the west'. The evidence of fertility changes must, however, be handled carefully. The most comprehensive and sophisticated estimates have been provided by Maudlin and Berelson (1978), and Tsui and Bogue's (1978) more dramatic estimates have attracted some scepticism, although as one critic points out, many of their conclusions are not revelatory and are consistent with other estimates (Demeny, 1979). They find that three sets of estimates, 'prepared independently and with different methodologies, suggest that fertility decline has occurred recently for at least three-quarters of the world's countries'. Their new estimates, based on very limited surveys for some countries, are that total fertility rates declined by 20 per cent or more from 1968 to 1975 in 31 of 148 countries, with a combined population of 1.6 thousand million in 1975, or 39 per cent of the world's total. The largest countries, with 35 million or more population, had the greatest declines on average at 13 per cent (pp. 10–11).

In Latin America, Tsui and Bogue estimate that 12 nations showed fertility

Table 1.4 Selected indicators of ageing populations

**A. Old age dependency**[a]

| | *1930/31* | *1950/51* | *1960/61* | *1970/71* | *Projections 2000/01* |
|---|---|---|---|---|---|
| United States | 97 | 133 | 167 | 177 | *177* |
| France | | 174 | 189 | 207 | |
| Sweden | | | | 181 | *212* |
| United Kingdom | | 160 | 190 | 203 | |
| United Kingdom[b] | 152 | 216 | 239 | 281 | *272* |
| West Germany | | 139 | 157 | 218 | |

**B. Age-specific death rates per 1000**

| *United Kingdom*[c] | *1930–32* | *1950–52* | *1960–62* | *1971* | *1977* |
|---|---|---|---|---|---|
| 65–74 years | | | | | |
| male | 58.7 | 55.3 | 54.7 | 52.1 | 49.3 |
| female | 43.4 | 34.8 | 30.4 | 26.4 | 25.1 |
| male : female | 1.35 | 1.59 | 1.80 | 1.97 | 1.96 |
| 75+ years | | | | | |
| male | 167.5 | 160.7 | 148.6 | 137.5 | 135.8 |
| female | 138.7 | 124.4 | 110.2 | 95.4 | 92.5 |
| male : female | 1.21 | 1.29 | 1.35 | 1.44 | 1.47 |

| *United States*[d] | *1900–02* | *1929–31* | *1949–51* | *1959–61* | *1964* |
|---|---|---|---|---|---|
| Age 65, whites | | | | | |
| male | 41.7 | 38.7 | 34.5 | 33.9 | 34.4 |
| female | 36.4 | 31.3 | 20.6 | 17.4 | 16.9 |
| male : female | 1.15 | 1.23 | 1.67 | 1.95 | 2.04 |

| *United States*[e] *Male : female* | *1900* | *1940* | *1954* | *1968* | *1976* |
|---|---|---|---|---|---|
| 55–64 years | 1.14 | 1.45 | 1.82 | 2.07 | 1.99 |
| 65–74 years | 1.11 | 1.29 | 1.57 | 1.88 | 1.97 |
| 75–84 years | 1.08 | 1.17 | 1.29 | 1.46 | 1.58 |
| 85 + years | 1.05 | 1.08 | 1.06 | 1.18 | 1.26 |

**C. Participation in the labour force**

| *United States*[f] | *1940* | *1950* | *1960* | *1970* | *1975* |
|---|---|---|---|---|---|
| Male | | | | | |
| 65–69 years | 59.4 | 59.7 | 44.0 | 39.3 | 33.3 |
| 70–74 years | 38.4 | 38.7 | 28.7 | 22.5 | } 14.9 |
| 75 + years | 18.2 | 18.7 | 15.6 | 12.1 | } |
| Female | | | | | |
| 65–69 years | 9.5 | 13.0 | 16.5 | 17.2 | 14.6 |
| 70–74 years | 5.1 | 6.4 | 9.6 | 9.1 | } 5.2 |
| 75 + years | 2.3 | 2.6 | 4.3 | 4.7 | } |

| *England and Wales*[g] *Male* | *1921* | *1931* | *1951* | *1961* | *1971* |
|---|---|---|---|---|---|
| 60–64 years | 88.7 | 87.2 | 87.5 | 92.0 | 86.6 |
| 65–69 years | 79.4 | 64.9 | 47.2 | 40.0 | 30.5 |
| 70–74 years | — | 41.7 | 27.4 | 21.0 | 15.9 |
| Over 65 | 58.9 | 47.5 | 31.1 | 24.4 | 19.1 |

Table 1.4 (*continued*)

**D. Sex ratios**

| *United States*[h] | *1930* | *1950* | *1960* | *1970* | *1980* (Projections) | *2000* (Projections) |
|---|---|---|---|---|---|---|
| 65 years and more | 101 | 89 | 83 | 72 | *68* | *67* |
| 75 years and more | | 83 | 75 | 63 | *56* | *54* |
| 85 years and more | | 70 | 64 | 53 | *45* | *39* |

*Great Britain*

*Males aged 65 + to Females aged 60 +*[i]

| *1911* | *1931* | *1951* | *1971* |
|---|---|---|---|
| 50 | 50 | 49 | 45 |

*Projections*[j]

| *Age* | *1976* | *1986* | *2006* |
|---|---|---|---|
| 65–69 | *80* | *82* | *89* |
| 70–74 | *69* | *71* | *78* |
| 75–79 | *53* | *58* | *62* |
| 80–84 | *42* | *46* | *47* |

[a]Ratio of population aged 65 or more years per 100 aged 15–64 years, except for United States where denominator aged 18–64. US figures from Cutler and Harootyan (1975), Table 3.7, p. 48. The Swedish figures refer to 1974 and 1990 and were calculated by the National Board of Health and Welfare, Stockholm: Bozzetti and Sherman (1977), Table 2, p. 137. Other national figures from Wirz (1977), Table 2, p. 47, except that:

[b]Ratio of population aged 65 + (male) and 60 + (female) per 100 aged 16–64 (male) and 16–59 (female): Central Statistical Office (1979), Table 3.9, 98.

[c]Central Statistical Office (1979), Table 1.2, p. 64.

[d]Figures calculated by Spiegelmann (1966) and reprinted in Riley and Foner (1968), Vol. 1, Table 2.10, p. 28.

[e]United States Bureau of the Census (1978), Table 7, p. 115.

[f]Percentage of the group economically active. Bouvier, Atlee and McVeigh (1975), Table 8, p. 13.

[g]Census reports of England and Wales.

[h]United States Bureau of the Census, *Current Population Reports*, Series P-25

[i]Recalculated from Wroe (1973), Table 1, p. 23.

[j]Recalculated from Age Concern (1977), Table 11, p. 13

The practical consequences of growing old age dependency are magnified by the population's rising expectations, the elderly's increasingly independent living arrangements, and their increasingly uneven geographical distribution. Locally distinctive age structures have always existed as a result both of the growth history of an individual settlement, parish or city block and of social class and areal differences in mortality, but in recent decades distinctive patterns of elderly migration have added to the variations. Many large metropolitan areas attract a net surplus of young migrants and generate a net emigration of people aged 50 years and more, but within them there are often areas of poorer housing that have a concentration of relatively poor and disadvantaged elderly people. As the public services most demanded by elderly people, such as residential care, domiciliary personal and medical services or public housing are normally funded partly by local property taxes, the local old age dependency ratio can have an important bearing on the range of support services that are provided, even when complex compensating 'needs' grants from central government operate.

Another complex and important realm of derivative demographic and social consequences of ageing stem from the substantially and increasingly lower mortality rates of women compared to men in old age (Table 1.4B). Between approximately 1930 and 1962, the ratio between the male and female age-specific death rates per 1000 increased in the United Kingdom for ages 65–74 years from 1.35 to 1.80, and in the United States for whites aged 65 years from 1.24 to 2.04. From 1950/51 to 1970/71 the ratio of elderly males to females dropped from 0.70 to 0.62 in the United Kingdom and from 0.89 to 0.72 in the United States (Table 1.4D). The United States Census Bureau expects the trend for a decreasing male sex ratio to slow during the next half-century (Siegel, 1978, p. 82; see also Bouvier, Atlee, and McVeigh, 1975). The differential improvement in mortality by sex is related to the socio-economic composition of a population, so there are marked regional effects which in Britain are only just being described (Gardner and Donnan, 1978). At this scale of analysis it is essential to identify the source of demographic and social changes; whether they are due to passing cohort effects, to the ageing of a local population, or to more durable 'period' changes in demographic and social behaviour (Blanchard, Bunker, and Wachs, 1977). There is immense scope for further research in those topics, for even at the level of national populations only an outline picture of the trends and their implications is available.

## THE GEOGRAPHY OF INTER-GENERATIONAL RELATIONS

The second gerontological topic which may be considerably illuminated by a geographical perspective is the changing composition and functioning of an elderly person's social group. There has been little study of the impacts of the changing social and spatial distances which separate an aged person from his or her relatives and friends. This subject is of considerable importance to the quality of life of elderly people and relates to their ability to maintain independent living arrangements and to their dependence upon public or voluntary social and caring services. Recent decades have seen a dispersion of the population within the decentralizing metropolitan areas of the country and this may be increasing the average separation between elderly people and their closest relatives: whether this is having an impact upon the frequency of visits or the range and quality of the tasks performed for each other is simply not known. By extension the implications of population movements for the medical and social services are not understood. There is therefore both a humanitarian and a material case for the study of the geography of inter-generational personal relationships and the associated mutual physical and emotional support and care.

Assertions that there have been changes both in the membership of the social groups most important to elderly people and the nature and quality of inter-generational relationships are founded upon evidence of recent social changes.

These range from the demographic aspects of social change associated particularly with changing marriage and fertility patterns, through the manifestations of affluence such as improving housing standards and the increased rate of household formation, to the social consequences of rapidly changing and diversifying cultural traits, which are indicated overtly by rising educational attainment and changing lifestyles but which have much broader impact.

**Socio-demographic trends**

The socio-demographic changes which have most influenced the household and living arrangements of the elderly include:

(1) the decline in the average age of marriage and the rise (at least until recently) in the popularity of marriage;
(2) the lowered average age at which the last child is born and the decreasing variation and average size of completed families;
(3) the closer spacing of surviving children as a result of lower infant mortality and smaller families; and
(4) modest improvements in life expectancy at all ages.

In effect these changes now mean that child-rearing is a more defined and shorter phase of the family cycle, that on average the generations follow each other in more rapid succession, and that there is a larger number of concurrent generations.

It is not the case, however, that on average an elderly person has fewer children to provide support, for the various trends compensate each other. Soldo (1978) has found for the United States population, for example, that in the fertility conditions of the 1920s a mother would have had 1.4 female children compared to 1.2 under the fertility conditions of the 1970s. Under the mortality conditions of the 1920s at age 70 years, however, only 73.5 per cent of the daughters, or 0.99 per mother, would be alive, compared with 90 per cent, or 1.1 daughters per mother under 1970s mortality conditions. The notable conclusion for the social geographer is that 'the congruence of intergenerational mobility paths will be a much better predictor of kin availability than fluctuations in the birth rate. Unfortunately, this is an area that we, as demographers and gerontologists, know very little about' (Soldo, 1978, p. 227). Social geographers would have to admit that they are no better informed.

As the nuclear family *qua* household has shortened in duration, the greater popularity of marriage, the decline of childlessness, and the reduced waste of births has produced an increasing probability of the existence during a person's old age of members of the second to fifth generations. Whether this multiplication of extant generations has resulted in either additional sources of support for the elderly or revised roles for elderly people is a matter of speculation; but various personal situations that have become relatively more common during the last 30 years can be described. For example, that of a married couple at retirement age with two residentially independent, widowed parents and a growing number of great-grandchildren—the latter may be the offspring of very young parents with high material expectations and like other members of the family call for support. Another more common situation is that of a widow aged 70 years whose child or children, having left the family home 25 years ago, now feel little responsibility or concern for the mother. Whether the aggregate effect of the host of changes that could be described upon the life satisfaction and material support of elderly people is positive or negative is another largely unanswered question.

### Changing lifestyles and inter-generational mutuality

As well as the temporal expansion of the family and its fission into a larger number of more scattered households, the roles of elderly people and the sources of their emotional and material support are being modified by an accelerated rate of cultural change. Superficially these can be demonstrated by changes in activity patterns or the more overt features of lifestyles, such as the occupational emancipation of women, rising occupational status, social mobility, and rising educational attainment. All of these are widening the differences between the generations and probably decreasing their mutual understanding.

Less demonstrable but frequently the subject of comment are revisions to personal beliefs and objectives. It is widely held that secularism, materialism, individualism, and even hedonism have become more dominant, and that religious belief, familism, collectivism, and social responsibility have become less common. These terms are ambiguous and it is normally difficult to support such opinions with convincing evidence. Whatever the exact shifts in attitudes or personal aims, I do support the view that cultural changes have accelerated and that this has increased the social distances between the generations. One area of social custom and practice that may be particularly divisive in this respect is child-care and rearing. As there is probably an inverse relationship between social distance and empathy, it would follow that individuals are progressively less willing to maintain inter-generational personal relationships or to provide emotional and material support across the generations.

The alleged decline of the extended family has been debated vigorously in sociology since the early 1950s and is now generally denied. Initially the argument was fuelled by the hypothesis, developed by both Tönnies (1887; translation 1955) and Parsons (1943, 1949), that industrialization and modernization entail: the decline of a traditional *folk* or *gemeinschaft* society, characterized by few, strong, multi-faceted, primary personal relationships; and their replacement by a looser *gesellschaft* society characterized by each individual having more, weaker, transitory, and functionally specialized secondary relationships.

Another aspect of the change is described by the terminology of closed and loose-knit social networks (Bott, 1957). Parsons and others went as far as suggesting that the decline of the extended family was a necessary condition of more rapid economic and social change, for it commonly obstructs occupational mobility and hence occupational and technical change.

This view quickly found widespread support (and is still the conventional wisdom in many circles). Townsend (1957; 1963 edn, p. 15) illustrated this point in the introduction to his study of the family life of old people in Bethnal Green, London, by quoting a former Permanent Secretary of the Ministry of Pensions and National Insurance:

> Provision for old age has emerged as a 'problem' largely because of the loosening of family ties and insistence on individual rights and privileges to the exclusion of obligations and duties. . . . The care and attention which the family used to provide for [the elderly] must be provided in some other way.

Very similar views have been expressed by the present and the immediate past Prime Ministers of the United Kingdom, and they tend to be implied by most supporters of allegedly traditional family forms.

Even in the early 1950s, however, the hypothesis was challenged. Townsend (*op. cit.*) pointed out that there was little evidence of decline and, referring to, among others, Sheldon's (1948) finding in Wolverhampton that frequent contact with younger relatives was common among old people, suggested that inter-generational support was rarely denied and often willingly given. Subsequently the sociological debate has deepened empirically and theoretically. Theories of inter-personal social exchange and linkage and of serial reciprocity through the generations have been elaborated (Bengtson, Olander, and Haddad, 1975), and most accounts now deny at least a simple representation of the change. The consensus now is that while the connections of most elderly people with their families and kin networks have been maintained despite industrialization and modernization and during the proliferation of family forms and lifestyles, there have been substantial changes in the role of the extended family (Rosow, 1967; Stehower, 1968; Sussman, 1965, 1975).

These are most commonly expressed in relation to the expanded role of public agencies in supplying housing, social services, and income in old age. Adapting to this change, and maybe partly bringing it about, the extended family members act increasingly both as agents for elderly people in seeking and gaining public services and as mediators with, and protectors from, the latter's bureaucracies (Shanas and Sussman, 1977). Litwak (1960a, 1960b) has examined the impact of residential re-location and social mobility on extended family cohesion and roles in an explicit challenge to Parson's thesis, and concluded that

> the extended family relationship which does not demand geographical propinquity (not examined by Parsons) is a significant form of social behaviour [and] that theoretically the

most efficient organisation combines the ability of large scale bureaucracy to handle uniform situations with the primary group's ability to deal with idiosyncratic situations' (1960b, p. 394).

A common sequence of strategies has evolved to delay as long as possible admitting elderly people to institutions which as ever is regarded by both the elderly themselves and the welfare agencies as the option of last resort. Members of the consanguineal family respond to the increasing dependence of an elderly member first by increasing the range and frequency of support that they provide at the latter's independent home; later they tend to seek and obtain the assistance of public or voluntary agencies, sometimes in association with the elderly person moving into another's household, sometimes by a residential move by one or other party to increase propinquity, but most often without any residential change.

Some sociological analysis has focused on the spatial aspects of kin networks. Kerckhoff (1965) has examined three functional types of extended family: the 'nuclear isolated' where the nuclear elements of the extended family are in close proximity but have few or no contacts; the 'modified extended' where family members are spatially dispersed but have strong contacts, interaction, and emotional and material exchange; and 'extended' where the members are residentially propinquitous and functionally strong. Several studies show that, despite residential dispersal, high levels of inter-generational activities between married children and older parents are maintained. The majority of older persons, between 84 and 89 per cent in the United States, Denmark, and Britain in the early 1960s, live less than an hour's distance away from a child, and almost 30 per cent in the United States were living in a child's household. Comparable statistics from Denmark and Britain suggested that respectively 20 and 42 per cent of all persons aged 65 years or more lived with a child (Stehower, 1968, pp. 193 and 222). The rapid change of living arrangements is revealed by more recent statistics, for in the 1976 Elderly at Home in England Survey only 12.5 per cent of those aged 65 years or more were living in a household with a child (Hunt, 1978, Table 4.6.1, p. 16), and Abrams (1978, Table 16, p. 21) found in his survey of 802 people aged 75 years or more in four English towns that only 10.2 per cent were living with their children. Another 36 per cent lived in the same neighbourhood, and a further 15 per cent within 6 miles.

It can be easily demonstrated that the conjugal and consanguineal family networks have adjusted to the greater dispersion of their nuclear units rather than simply declined in their emotional ties and functional exchanges. They have taken advantage of improved personal mobility and affluence, and in many cases have created a system of mutual assistance and involvement that is superior to sharing a home: its nuclear units retain greater independence and the strains of shared living arrangements are reduced. Part of the case for more studies to elaborate and refine this knowledge and for specifically

Table 1.5 Contributors to and recipients of occupational pensions: United Kingdom, 1936–75

| | Employees in pension schemes | | | | Pensions in payment | |
|---|---|---|---|---|---|---|
| | Men | Women | Private sector | Public sector | Former employees | Widows and dependents |
| 1936 | 2.1 | 0.5 | 1.6 | 1.0 | 0.2 | — |
| 1953 | 4.9 | 1.3 | 3.1 | 3.1 | 0.8 | 0.1 |
| 1963 | 9.4 | 1.7 | 7.2 | 3.9 | 1.5 | 0.3 |
| 1971 | 8.7 | 2.4 | 6.8 | 4.3 | 2.4 | 0.5 |
| 1975 | 8.7 | 2.8 | 6.1 | 5.4 | 2.8 | 0.6 |

*Source*: Government Actuary (1978), *Occupational Pension Schemes 1975*, London, HMSO, Table 3.2, p.9 and Table 4.1, p. 19.

spatial contributions is that these interpretations and understandings are so rare.

There is of course enormous variation among old people. Some are closely integrated with their children and make diverse exchanges from which they derive considerable satisfaction. Others prefer to develop their own activities, interests, and achievements with little reference to other members of their families, and their children would neither expect nor welcome them doing otherwise. Many are not only living independently, however, but also are socially isolated, lonely, and alienated. We do need to know more about this diversity. We would learn much from more study of the impact of the residential dispersal of extended family members on the elderly themselves and upon the demands for domiciliary services, housing with special design features or warden supervision, and residential care.

While the sociologists' continuing research into the family has deflated several erroneous ideas and made theoretical progress, studies with ecological or geographical emphasis have been few and have not progressed beyond isolated case-studies. In Britain for a short time around 1960, a promising line of enquiry into the social networks of different types of residential areas developed, following paths defined by Bott (1957) and Mogey (1955). Some geographical contributions elucidated the social consequences of both overspill (planned decentralization) and the invasion of extra-metropolitan villages by commuters (Blowers, 1970; Connell, 1974; Pahl, 1965a; Rodgers, 1965), but the interest unfortunately faded. When human geography turned to nomothetic spatial analysis and later began to adopt behavioural approaches to socio-spatial topics, the empirical community studies appeared to be concerned with unimportant and obsolescent themes. However, if they had been pursued, they would have laid the foundations for an informative social geography of consanguinity which we now see would be of applied value to several contemporary social issues. The re-adoption of the social group as a unit of study in social geography is one route that a geographical contribution to social gerontology can follow, and it could be unusually productive.

## AIMS AND ROLES OF THE STUDY OF INDIVIDUALS

To conclude the chapter some brief reflections are offered on a recent and interesting development in human geography in North America, namely the emergence of 'humanistic' geography. This is attracting attention and gaining advocates as an alternative to the neo-Marxist reaction against the crude form of logical positivism adopted by human geographers (most enthusiastically in the United States) in the late 1950s and 1960s. It is a truism that there are many forces of inertia and vested interests that oppose intellectual shifts, and it is not surprising therefore to find among their persuasive calls for a deeper philosophical and epistemological command among human geographers, that the humanists' writing is often evangelical and sometimes grandiose. A recent elucidation of the emergence and rationale of humanistic geography leans heavily on the intellectual heritage of humanism *per se* and tends to grasp at any evidence of sociological or cultural sensitivity in antecedent works to establish a humanistic tradition in geography (Ley and Samuels, 1978). These authors advocate a hugely ambitious and to my understanding somewhat mystical goal for the movement: 'the principal aim of modern humanism in geography is the reconciliation of social science and man, to accommodate understanding and wisdom, objectivity and subjectivity, and materialism and idealism' (p. 9). Humanistic geography has gained little ground in Britain to date, perhaps because of intellectual laziness or because of a pot-pourri of more respectable attitudes including scepticism (which has meant that probably never as many as a majority became convinced positivists and that only a small minority advocate neo-Marxist structuralism), a vaguely articulated adherence to 'realistic' philosophies of science or to the traditional academic values of the humanities, and to what might be described as a modest European eclecticism which has resulted in some aspects of humanism and existentialism long being part of the conceptual equipment of the human geographer.

The movement, however, claims our attention in this volume because within it Rowles (1978a, 1978b, 1979) has developed some most innovatory and interesting research into the relationships between elderly people and their locales. His experiential fieldwork explicitly adopted an astatistical approach to inference and to the furthering of understanding; it consisted of making close acquaintance with, and personal observations of, five elderly people living in a long-established inner area of an eastern United States city. His study was conceived within the geographical tradition of man–land enquiry and had the intention:

to clarify apparent confusion—existing in the literature and reflected in public policy—regarding the older individual's relationship with the environment. A prevalent image of a progressively shrinking geographical lifespace with advancing years attended by increasing attachment to a local setting was clearly a gross oversimplification.... It was clear, moreover, that the older person's changing relationship with space involved not only physical mobility dimensions but also perceptual and symbolic components. In-depth study of older persons was needed to explore their relationship with environment from an experiential perspective (Rowles, 1978a, p. 176).

From repeated meetings, extended conversations, and shared experiences with his subjects, Rowles demonstrated firmly that an individual's relationship with, and satisfaction from, the environment must be understood in terms of both the idiographic circumstances of an individual's character, experience, social network, and geographical location, and the degree and nature of constraints arising from physical disabilities, income, the accessibility of activity opportunities, the availability of different means of travel, and the friction of distance. His work demonstrates the complex influence of ageing on a person's use of his or her environment.

The question arises as to what extent this form of research should be recommended for wider adoption: it may be considered by examining the objectives, execution, and achievement of Rowles's work. Like many earlier sociological studies based on empirical studies including participant observation, focused interviews or in-depth conversations with few subjects, he demonstrates the enormous strides in understanding and theory that can come from a sympathetic consideration of individual cases. It is, however, enormously demanding in time; it demands exceptional tenacity, organization, and ability on the part of the researcher; and is prone to failure through the withdrawal of the subjects. Both the objectives and the achievement of the research emphasize epistemological or academic rather than practical or applied concerns, at least in the short term. The goals are to further understanding for third parties—whatever the empathy and assistance given and received in the inter-personal relationship between subject and investigator. Clearly this serves the proselytizing efforts of an emergent school of a social science but it may not be the best use of the scarce research capacity and commitment to the welfare of elderly people.

The humanistic approach and experiential fieldwork seem likely to overlap in intention and achievement with the creative arts, as with the recent novels and plays about the experience of old age written by Alan Bennett, Paul Scott, and Angus Wilson; and they will be an academic parallel to the learning experienced by every adult who builds a personal relationship with an elderly person. Most people learn to appreciate the actualities and problems of ageing through their older relatives; social scientists are likely to compare, relate, and conceptualize their observations more assiduously than others, and human geographers are most likely to appreciate the environmental constraints and satisfactions experienced by elderly people. One of Rowles's major achievements has been to elaborate more richly than hitherto the relationships between an elderly person and the environment, although psychologists, architects, and gerontologists in both Britain and America must be given the credit for leading the elucidation of specific features (Bytheway, Chapter 9 of this book; Lawton, 1970; Lawton, Newcomer, and Byerts, 1976; Lipman and Slater, 1977; Pastalan and Carson, 1970).

In practice no social scientist does, or wishes to completely, separate professional inquisitiveness from personal development and experience. For those involved in the study of the welfare of elderly people it is particularly appropriate consciously to develop these parallel experiences. Rowles's findings and views are recommended both to human geographers and to other interested social scientists, but following Madge's (1963) evaluation of sociological methodologies it is suggested that experiential fieldwork is appropriate principally either in the exploratory investigation of clearly specified topics or the development of tentative theory. The method complements others that are more suitable for the verification of hypotheses and theories or for applied and policy-oriented research.

Those motivated by a strong empathy with and concern for the welfare of elderly people may choose between several courses of action. They may invest more of themselves with their own elderly relatives or friends; they may give more of their time and emotional capacity to others through a caring profession, through the activities of churches or other voluntary associations, or through individual initiatives. Or they may reverse the asymmetry of these latter exchanges and deliberately attempt to conceptualize and interpret aspects of the elderly person's experience. The success of such an endeavour will bring personal fulfilment and professional esteem, but experiential fieldwork does encourage the combination of these legitimate ends with much giving on the investigator's part. Moreover the dissemination of the resulting understanding and insight in the long term may contribute considerably to the understanding of the position of elderly people in rapidly changing societies and environments. For a few it is a path that may greatly expand experience and existence: it may also through the power of ideas and concepts eventually improve the situation of old people.

## REFERENCES

Abrams, M. (1978). *Beyond Three-Score and Ten: A First Report on a Survey of the Elderly*. Age Concern England, Mitcham. Age Concern (1977). *Profiles of the Elderly*. Age Concern England, Mitcham.

Agyei, W. K. A. (1978). Modernisation and the theory of the demographic transition in the developing countries: the case of Jamaica. *Social and Economic Studies*, **27**, 44–68.

Beattie, W. M. (1978). 'Aging: a framework of characteristics and considerations for cooperative efforts between the developing and developed regions of the world.' Paper prepared for United Nations Expert Group Meeting on Aging, New York, 3–5 April,

All-University Gerontology Center, Syracuse University, Syracuse, New York.

Beaver, S. E. (1975). *Demographic Transition Theory Reinterpreted.* Lexington Books, Lexington, Massachusetts.

Bengston, V. L., Olander, E., and Haddad, A. (1975). The 'generation gap' and aged family members. In Gulbrium, J. (ed.), *Late Life: Recent Developments in the Sociology of Age.* Charles C. Thomas, Springfield, Mass.

Binstock, R. and Shanas, E. (1977). *Handbook of Aging and the Social Sciences.* Van Nostrand, New York.

Blanchard, R. D., Bunker, J. B., and Wachs, M. (1977). Distinguishing aging, period and cohort effects in longitudinal studies of elderly populations. *Socio-Economic Planning Sciences*, **11**, 137–46.

Blowers, A. T. (1970). Council housing: the social implications of layout and design in an urban fringe estate. *Town Planning Review*, **41**, 80–92.

Bogue, D. (1969). *Principles of Demography.* Wiley, New York.

Booth, C. (1894). *The Aged Poor in England and Wales.* Macmillan, London.

Bott, E. (1957). *Family and Social Network.* Tavistock, London.

Bouvier, L., Atlee, E., and McVeigh, F. (1975). The elderly in America. *Population Bulletin*, **30**, 36 pp.

Bozzetti, L. P. and Sherman, S. (1977). The aged in Sweden. 1. The country, its peoples and institutions. *Psychiatric Annals*, **7**, 128–39.

Buttimer, A. (1968). Social geography. In D. L. Sills (ed.), *International Encyclopaedia of the Social Sciences.* Macmillan, New York, pp. 134–45.

Buttimer, A. (1969). Social space in interdisciplinary perspective. *Geographical Review*, **59**, 417–26.

Central Statistical Office (1979). *Social Trends No. 10 1979*, HMSO, London.

Chile, Instituto Nacional de Estadisticas (1977). *Perfiles de la Poblacion de 65 y Mas Años de Edad, 1977.* INE, Santiago de Chile.

Clarke, J. I. (1972). *Population Geography.* Pergamon, Oxford.

Clarke, J. I. (1978). The more developed realm. In Trewartha, G. T. (ed.), *The More Developed Realm: A Geography of its Population*, pp. 1–22. Pergamon, Oxford.

Coale, A. J. and Hoover, E. M. (1958). *Population Growth and Economic Development in Low-Income Countries.* Princeton University Press, Princeton, NJ.

Connell, J. (1974). The metropolitan village: spatial and social processes in discontinuous suburbs. In Johnson, J. H. (ed.), *Suburban Growth*, pp. 77–100. Wiley, Chichester.

Cutler, N. E., and Harootyan, R. A. (1975). Demography of the aged. In Woodruff, D. S., and Birren, J. E. (eds), *Aging: Scientific Perspectives and Social Issues*, pp. 31–69. Van Nostrand, New York.

Davis, K. (1945). The world demographic transition. *Annals of the American Academy of Political and Social Science*, **273**, 1–11.

Demeny, P. (1979). On the end of the population explosion. *Population and Development Review*, **5**, 141–62.

Eyles, J. and Smith, D. M. (1978). Social geography. *American Behavioural Scientist*, **22**, 41–58.

Gardner, M. and Donnan, S. (1978). Life expectations: variations among Regional Health Authorities. *Population Trends*, **10**, 10–12.

Gilbert, E. W. (1939). The growth of inland and seaside health resorts in England. *Scottish Geographical Magazine*, **55**, 21–7.

Glass, D. (1963). Population growth and structure: a socio-demographic study. In Vries, E. de and Echavarria, J. M. (eds), *op. cit.*, pp. 94–111.

Golant, S. M. (1972). *The Residential Location and Spatial Behavior of the Elderly.* Research Paper No. 143, Department of Geography, University of Chicago, Chicago.

Golant, S. M. (ed.) (1979). *Location and Environment of Elderly Population*. Winston, Washington, DC.

Goldman, F. R. and Goldman, D. M. (1977). *Problemas Brasileiros: Alguns Aspectos Sobre o Processo de Envelhecer*. Franciscana do Lar Franciscano de Menores, São Paulo.

Goldman, F. R. and Goldman, D. M. (undated). Gerontology in Brazil. Typescript at International Federation of Aging, Washington, DC.

González, M. N. (ed.) (1974). *Primer Congreso Nacional de Jubilados, Retirados, Cesantes y Pensionistas*. Boletin No. 2, La Comercial, Arequipa.

Haggett, P. (1972). *Geography: A Modern Synthesis*. Harper & Row, New York.

Hauser, P. M. (1978). Aging and social structure. In Binstock, R. and Shanas, E. (eds), *op. cit.*, pp. 59–86.

Herbert, D. T. (1972). *Urban Geography: A Social Perspective*. David & Charles, Newton Abbot.

Herbert, D. T. (1980). *Social Geography and the City*. Report on a SSRC Seminar Series, Department of Geography, University College of Swansea, Swansea.

Herrick, B. (1976). Economic effects of fertility decline. In Keeley, M. C. (ed.), *Population, Public Policy and Economic Development*, pp. 49–84. Praeger, New York.

Hunt, A. (1978). *The Elderly at Home*. HMSO, London.

Jakubowski, M. (1977). The theory of demographic transition and studies on the spatial differentiation of population dynamics. *Geographica Polonica*, **35**, 73–89.

Jones, E. (1960). *Social Geography of Belfast*. Oxford University Press, Oxford.

Jones, E. and Eyles, J. (1977). *An Introduction to Social Geography*. Oxford University Press, Oxford.

Kasschau, P. L. (1978). Developing gerontology in a developing country: the case of São Paulo, Brazil. *International Journal of Aging and Human Development*, **8**, 325–37.

Kerckhoff, A. C. (1965). Nuclear and extended family relationships: normative and behavioral analysis. In Shanas, E. and Streib, G. (eds), *op. cit.*, pp. 93–112.

Kirk, D. (1979). World population and birth rates: agreements and disagreements. *Population and Development Review*, **5**, 479–94.

Knodel, J. E. (1977). Family limitation and the fertility transition: evidence from age patterns of fertility in Europe and Asia. *Population Studies*, **31**, 219–49.

Lawton, M. P. (1970). Planning environments for older people. *Journal of the American Institute of Planners*, **36**, 124–9.

Lawton, M. P., Newcomer, R. J., and Byerts, T. O. (eds) (1976). *Community Planning for an Aging Society*. Dowden, Hutchinson & Ross, Stroudsberg, Penn.

Ley, D. and Samuels, M. S. (eds) (1978). *Humanistic Geography: Prospects and Problems*. Croom Helm, Maaroofa, Chicago.

Lipman, A. and Slater, R. (1977). Homes for old people: toward a positive environment. *The Gerontologist*, **17**, 146–56.

Litwak, E. (1960a). Occupational mobility and extended family cohesion. *American Sociological Review*, **25**, 9–21.

Litwak, E. (1960b). Geographic mobility and extended family cohesion. *American Sociological Review*, **25**, 385–94.

Madge, J. (1963). *The Origins of Scientific Sociology*. Tavistock, London.

Maudlin, W. P. and Berelson, B. (1978). Patterns of fertility decline in developing countries 1950–75. *Studies in Family Planning*, **9**, 89–147.

Mogey, J. M. (1955). Changes in family life experienced by English workers moving from slums to housing estates. *Marriage and Family Living*, **17**, 123–8.

Notestein, F. W. (1945). Population: the long view. In Schultz, T. W. (ed.), *Food for the World*, pp. 36–57. University of Chicago Press, Chicago.

Pahl, R. E. (1965a). *Urbs in Rure: The Metropolitan Fringe in Hertfordshire*. Geographical

Paper 2, London School of Economics, London.
Pahl, R. E. (1965b). Trends in social geography. In Chorley, R. J. and Haggett, P. (eds), *Frontiers in Geographical Teaching*, pp. 81–100. Arnold, London.
Paillat, P. (ed.) (1979). Migrations de retraités. *Gérontologie et Société*, **8**, 213 pp.
Parsons, T. (1943). The kinship system of the contemporary United States. *American Anthropologist*, **45**, 22–38.
Parsons, T. (1949). The social structure of the family. In Anshen, R. N. (ed.), *The Family: Its Function and Destiny*, pp. 173–201. Harper, New York.
Pastalan, L. A. and Carson, D. H. (eds) (1970). *Spatial Behavior of Older People*. University of Michigan Press, Ann Arbor, Mich.
Peet, R. and Rowles, G. (1974). Geographical aspects of aging. *Geographical Review*, **56**, 445–47.
Petersen, W. (1975). *Population*. Macmillan, New York.
Riley, M. W. and Foner, A. (eds) (1968, 1969 and 1972). *Aging and Society*, 3 vols. Russell Sage, New York.
Robson, B. T. (1969). *Urban Analysis*. Cambridge University Press, Cambridge.
Robson, B. T. (1975). *Urban Social Areas*. Oxford University Press, London.
Rodgers, H. B. (1965). *Overspill in Winsford: A Social and Economic Survey of the Winsford Town Expansion Scheme*. Winsford Urban District Council, Winsford, Cheshire.
Rosen, B. C. and Berlinck, M. T. (1968). Modernisation and family structure in the region of São Paulo, Brazil. *America Latina*, **11**, 75–96.
Rosow, I. (1967). *Social Integration of the Aged*. Free Press, New York.
Rowles, G. D. (1978a). Reflections on experiential fieldwork. In Ley, D. and Samuels, M. (eds), *op. cit.*, pp. 173–93.
Rowles, G. D. (1978b). *Prisoners of Space? Exploring the Geographical Experience of Older People*. Westview, Boulder, Col.
Rowles, G. D. (1979). The last new home: facilitating the older person's adjustment to institutional space. In Golant, S. M. (ed.), *op. cit.*, pp. 81–94.
Shanas, E. and Streib, G. (eds) (1976). *Social Structure and Family: Generational Relations*. Prentice-Hall, Englewood Cliffs, NJ.
Shanas, E. and Sussman, M. B. (eds) (1977). *Family, Bureaucracy and the Elderly*. Duke University Press, Durham, NC.
Shanas E., Townsend, P., Wedderburn, D., Friss, H., Milhøj, P. and Stehower, J. (1968). *Old People in Three Industrial Societies*. Atherton, New York.
Sheldon, J. H. (1948). *The Social Medicine of Old Age: Report of an Inquiry in Wolverhampton*. Oxford University Press, London.
Siegel, J. S. (1978). Prospective trends in the size and structure of the elderly population, impact of mortality trends, and some implications. In US Bureau of the Census (1978), *op. cit.*, pp. 76–121.
Smith, D. M. (1977). *Human Geography: A Welfare Approach*. Arnold, London.
Soldo, B. J. (1978). Living arrangements of the elderly: future trends and implications. In United States Bureau of the Census, *op. cit.*, pp. 208–30.
Spengler, J. J. (1974). *Population Change, Modernization and Welfare*. Prentice-Hall, Englewood Cliffs, NJ.
Spiegelmann, M. (1966). *Significant Mortality and Morbidity Trends in the United States since 1900*, American College of Life Underwriters, Bryn Mawr, Penn.
Stehower, J. (1968). The household and family relations of old people. In Shanas, E. *et al.*, *op. cit.*, pp. 177–226.
Sussman, M. B. (1965). Relations of adult children with their parents in the United States. In Shanas, E. and Streib, G. (eds), *op. cit.*, pp. 62–92.
Sussman, M. B. (1975). The family life of old people. In Binstock, R. and Shanas, E. (eds), *op. cit.*, pp. 218–43.

Tibbitts, C. and Donahue, W. (eds) 1962. *Social and Psychological Aspects of Aging*. Columbia University Press, New York.

Tilly, C. (ed.) (1978). *Historical Studies of Changing Fertility*. Princeton University Press, Princeton, NJ.

Timms, D. W. G. (1971). *The Urban Mosaic*. Cambridge University Press, Cambridge.

Tönnies, F. (1887). *Community and Association*, (1955; translated by Loomis, C. P.), Routledge & Kegan Paul, London.

Townsend, P. (1957). *The Family Life of Old People*, Routledge & Kegan Paul, London; 1963 edn, Penguin, Harmondsworth, Middlesex.

Tsui, A. O. and Bogue, D. J. (1978). Declining world fertility: trends, causes, implications. *Population Bulletin*, **33**, 56 pp. (Population Reference Bureau, Inc., Washington, DC.)

United Nations (1977). *The Aging in Slums and Uncontrolled Settlements*. UNO, New York.

United States Bureau of the Census (1978). *Demographic Aspects of Aging and the Older Population*. Joint Hearing before the Select Committee on Population of the US House of Representatives and the Select Committee on Aging, 95th Congress, 2nd session, 24 May 1978, No. 9, vol. 1.

Uruguay, Social Documentation Service (1977). *Social Welfare for the Elderly*, **3**, part 6/7, August/September.

Vries, E. de and Echavarría, J. M. (1963). *Social Aspects of Economic Development in Latin America*, 2 vols. UNESCO, Paris.

Warnes, A. M. (1981). Towards a geographical contribution to gerontology. *Progress in Human Geography*, **5**, 317–41.

Wirz, H. (1977). Economics of welfare: the implications of demographic change for Europe. *Futures*, **9**, 45–51.

Wiseman, R. F. (1978). *Spatial Aspects of Aging*. Resource Paper 78–4. Association of American Geographers, Washington, DC.

Woodruff, D. S. and Birren, J. E. (eds) (1975). *Aging: Scientific Perspectives and Social Issues*. Van Nostrand, New York.

Woods, R. I. (1979). *Population Analysis in Geography*. Longman, London.

Wroe, D. C. L. (1973). The elderly. *Social Trends No. 4, 1973*, pp. 23–34. HMSO, London.

Zelinsky, W. (1966). Toward a geography of the aged. *Geographical Review*, **56**, 445–47.

PART 1

# THE DISTRIBUTION AND MIGRATION OF ELDERLY PEOPLE

Geographical Perspectives on the Elderly
Edited by A. M. Warnes


Chapter 2

# The evolving geography of the elderly in England and Wales

*Roderick D. Allon-Smith*

## INTRODUCTION

A distinctive geography of the elderly has been developing in England and Wales during the twentieth century. This essay explores the general evolution of the geographical patterns evident today, attempting to place those patterns within a contextual framework of demographic change across the population as a whole. The period of change covered is the half-century from 1921 to 1971. The essay will explore the changing geographical patterns during the period, identify phases of growth and change, and examine the basic processes of change. Where reference is made to 'the elderly', they are defined as all those over the standard pensionable ages of 65 (male) and 60 (female).

A context for considering the evolving geography of the elderly is suggested by the fact that the study period has witnessed rapid growth in both the numbers and proportions of elderly within the population. The total population of England and Wales rose from 37,886,700 in 1921 to 48,749,575 in 1971, an increase of 10,862,875 or 28.7 per cent. During the same period the number of elderly people in England and Wales rose from 2,971,900 to 7,813,350, a rise of 163 per cent. In 1921 the elderly accounted for 7.8 per cent of the population, a proportion that had risen to over 16 per cent in 1971. This rise in the number and proportion of the elderly has been one of the most distinctive demographic trends during the twentieth century, with repercussions throughout every aspect of society.

Many studies of retirement areas and the spatial aspects of ageing have been completed in recent years; for example, there have been studies of individual retirement areas (Moindrot, 1963; Law and Warnes, 1973); of the motivations for retirement migration (Golant, 1972; Karn, 1977; Law and Warnes, 1977; Allon-Smith, 1978) and the social consequences of migration to coastal retirement areas (Mellor, 1962; Barr, 1965; Hodge, 1969; Harrison, McKeown, and O'Shea, 1971; Lemon, 1973; South West Economic Planning Council, 1975). These studies have been mostly empirical, arising from local data and local population characteristics. A point has now been reached at which certain basic themes may be identified as characterizing both national and local patterns of change (Law and Warnes, 1976; Allon-Smith, 1978). First, concentrations of the elderly have been developing within well-defined geographical areas. These areas may be recognized at a national scale and within local, intra-urban areas. Secondly, a developing spatial polarization between the elderly and the rest of the population may be identified. Thirdly, a sequential or diffusion process of change is in operation through which the areas of concentration appear to be expanding and consolidating. This essay explores these themes as they apply to the evolving geography of the elderly in England and Wales. It is based on an analysis of published and unpublished census statistics for the years 1921–71. (References to administrative areas, therefore, do not take account of the local government re-organization of 1974.)

## PATTERNS OF CHANGE, 1921–71

It is important that changes in the geography of the elderly are examined not in isolation but within the context of changes in the general pattern of population distribution in England and Wales. These changes reflect various factors; natural gains and losses within the resident population being modified by processes of in- and out-migration. Population growth between 1921 and 1971, both absolutely and relatively, occurred principally in the counties of the South-East Region and in a belt reaching north-westwards from London through the Midlands to Cheshire and Nottinghamshire. The most dramatic changes were in the counties around London; for example, Essex, Hertfordshire, Buckinghamshire, Berkshire, and Surrey more than doubled their total populations as well as increasing their proportions of the total population of England and Wales. Many of these changes were encouraged by the adoption of new planning policies for the region, London itself losing population during the period. In contrast, proportional decline of population was experienced by almost all the regional rural fringes such as the South-West Region, Wales, the north-east and north-west coasts, Lincolnshire, and Norfolk. Total population increased in most counties, with the distinctive exception of several in mid-Wales. The general pattern of population change may be summarized as a steady drift towards concentrations in urban and south-eastern areas, with the rural peripheries experiencing decline. It is these latter areas which have special importance for the geography of the elderly.

The changing patterns of ageing differ sharply from those of the population as a whole and may be summarized by contrasting the distribution pattern for 1921 with that for 1971. The pattern in 1921 was characterized by above-average concentrations of the elderly in an axial belt across the centre of the country from the south-west to Norfolk, and two additional clusters of concentration in mid-Wales and Sussex (Figure 2.1). The axial belt reaching from the north-west through the Midlands to London and the home counties possessed below average proportions of the elderly.

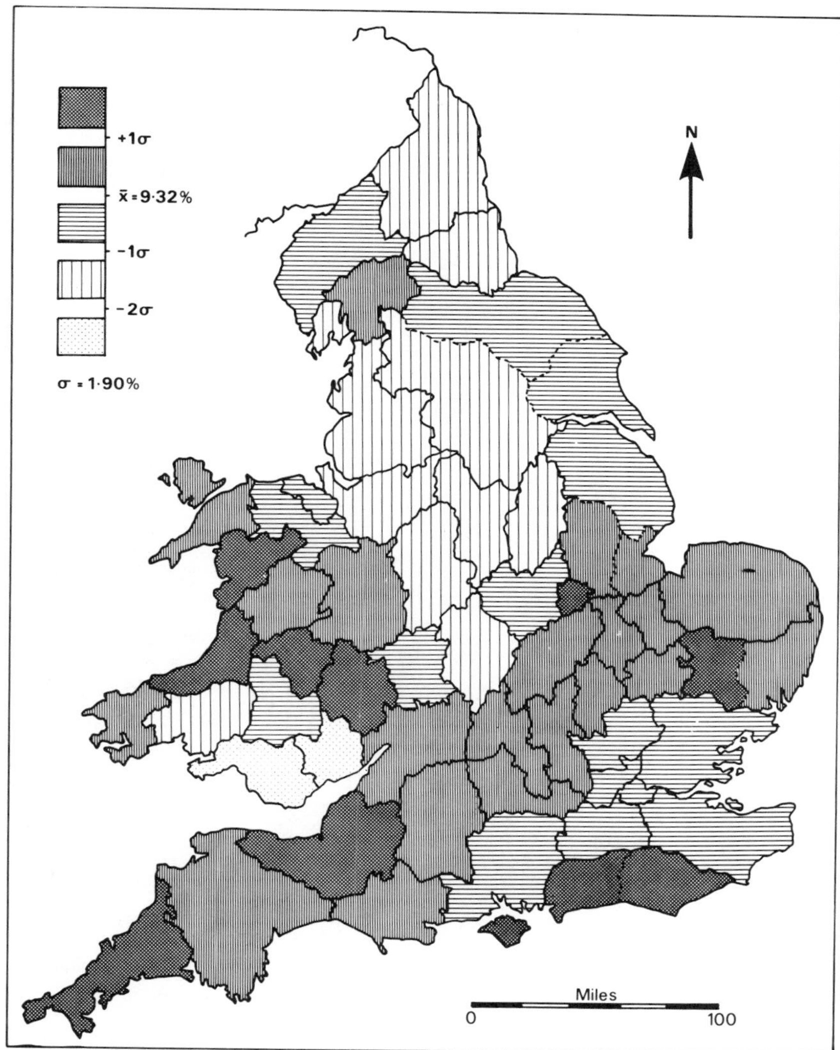


Figure 2.1 Percentage of elderly in the population: counties of England and Wales, 1921

By 1971 the pattern had altered to one in which the elderly had shifted, centrifugally, to dominate the coastal peripheries, with particular concentrations in Sussex, the South-West Region and Wales (Figure 2.2). The north-west coast and East Anglia were also prominent within the pattern. The shift towards an emphasis on the coastal peripheries was accompanied by a relative

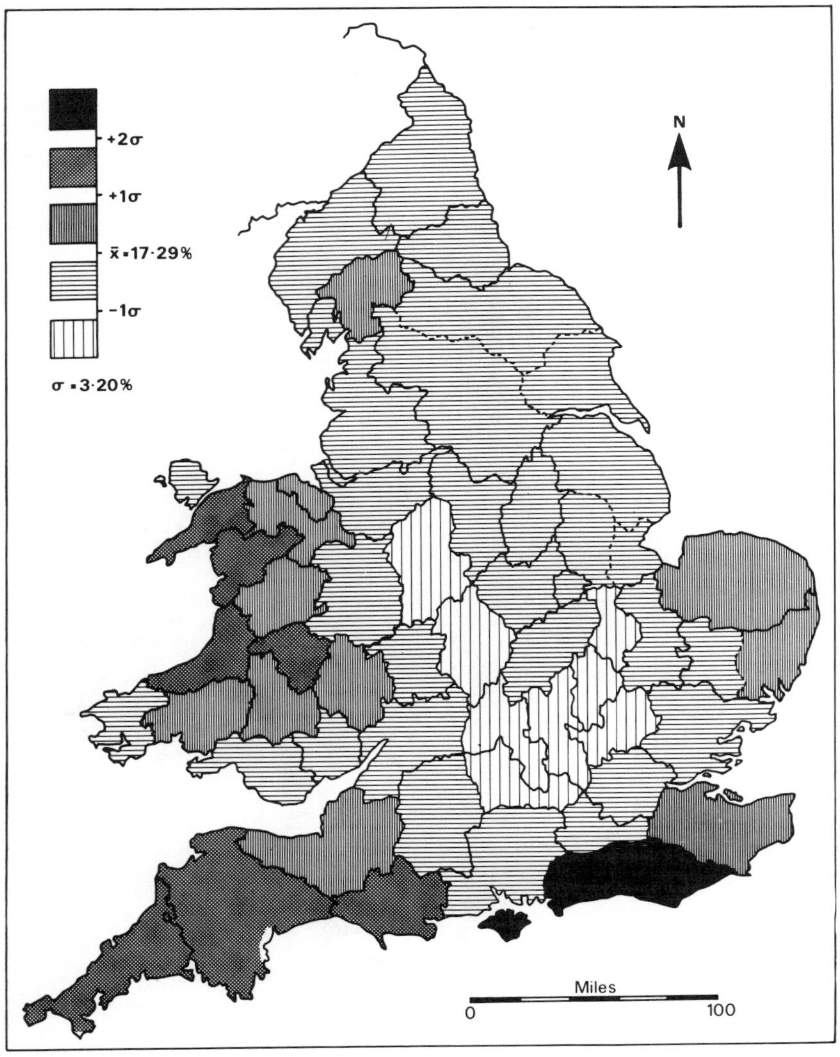


Figure 2.2 Percentage of elderly in the population: Counties of England and Wales, 1971

increase in the concentration of elderly people in areas of already high density; for example, Sussex and the Isle of Wight in 1971 registered densities of more than two standard deviations above the mean for England and Wales. It can be seen that there has been an evolving polarization between the areas of high and low density of the elderly, in terms of both age structure and spatial patterning.

A survey of the exact form of the geographical patterns of ageing in 1971, as summarized above, would be incomplete without noting the distinctive contribution of numerous individual coastal retirement areas to the overall pattern. From the 1971 Census an analysis of the proportion of elderly people in all administrative areas of England and Wales revealed that, of a total of some 1400 administrative divisions, 159 had a proportion of elderly people greater than one standard deviation from the mean of all areas. The mean for all areas was 17.5 per cent with a standard deviation of 5.1 per cent. Therefore, 159 areas had in excess of 22.6 per cent elderly within their population. These areas might be termed 'retirement areas' or 'areas of concentration of the elderly'.

With ten exceptions (three in England, seven in Wales) the pattern of distribution of these retirement areas was remarkably consistent, comprising mostly urban areas on the coast and their immediate rural hinterlands. Of the 159 areas, 45 were of County or Municipal Borough status, 75 were Urban Districts and 39 were Rural Districts. Seven had a proportion of the elderly in excess of 40 per cent and 39 areas had proportions of the elderly between 30 and 40 per cent. The population size of the areas varied considerably, from over 160,000 in Brighton and Southend-on-Sea to less than 500 in Llanwrtyd Wells. On balance, however, a distinctive feature was the relatively small size of the areas, only 15 areas having populations in excess of 50,000 and 81 areas having populations of less than 10,000 (Table 2.1).

One of the problems of interpreting the growth of individual retirement areas lies in trying to relate their growth to demographic changes taking place within the population as a whole. As has been noted, the elderly as a proportion of the population of England and Wales have increased from 7.8 per cent in 1921 to over 16 per cent in 1971, and this rise ideally should be taken into account when examining the proportions of elderly people within retirement areas. A means of resolving this problem is offered by index-linking the proportions of elderly people within individual areas to the national average of the elderly within the total population in any given census year. Thus, if the proportion of elderly within the total population of England and Wales for each and every census year is expressed as an index value of 100, the proportions of elderly within an individual areas may be expressed as a percentage of the national average, giving an index value tied to a national constant of 100. For example, in 1951 when the proportion of the elderly within the total population was 13.8 per cent the proportion in Worthing was 29.6 per cent, this being expressed

Table 2.1 Retirement areas 1971: the 25 areas with highest proportions of the elderly in England and Wales

| Rank | Administrative area | County | Population 1971 | Percentage of elderly |
|---|---|---|---|---|
| 1 | Grange UD | Lancashire | 3,475 | 45.5 |
| 2 | Sidmouth UD | Devon | 12,075 | 44.3 |
| 3 | Bexhill MB | East Sussex | 32,900 | 44.2 |
| 4 | Southwold MB | East Suffolk | 2,000 | 43.8 |
| 5 | Budleigh Salterton UD | Devon | 4,155 | 43.0 |
| 6 | Seaton UD | Devon | 4,140 | 42.1 |
| 7 | Frinton and Walton UD | Essex | 12,475 | 40.8 |
| 8 | Worthing MB | West Sussex | 88,405 | 38.8 |
| 9 | Preesall UD | Lancashire | 3,985 | 38.3 |
| 10 | Herne Bay UD | Kent | 25,200 | 36.8 |
| 11 | Newquay UD | Cardigan | 750 | 36.7 |
| 12 | Clacton UD | Essex | 38,070 | 36.4 |
| 13 | Minehead UD | Somerset | 8,055 | 35.3 |
| 14 | Lyme Regis MB | Dorset | 3,405 | 33.6 |
| 15 | Hove MB | East Sussex | 73,085 | 33.6 |
| 16 | Worthing RD | West Sussex | 50,560 | 33.6 |
| 17 | Filey UD | Yorkshire | 5,335 | 33.6 |
| 18 | Seaford UD | East Sussex | 16,225 | 33.4 |
| 19 | Eastbourne CB | East Sussex | 70,920 | 33.4 |
| 20 | Hailsham RD | East Sussex | 53,585 | 33.3 |
| 21 | Hunstanton UD | Norfolk | 3,910 | 32.7 |
| 22 | Broadstairs and St. Peters UD | Kent | 20,050 | 32.7 |
| 23 | Sheringham UD | Norfolk | 4,705 | 32.5 |
| 24 | Colwyn Bay MB | Denbigh | 25,565 | 32.4 |
| 25 | Prestatyn UD | Flint | 14,515 | 32.3 |

*Source*: Census 1971, County Reports.
*Abbreviation*: UD, urban district; MB, municipal borough; CB, county borough; RD, rural district (pre-1974 local administrative areas)

as an index value of 215.2. By 1971, when the proportion of the elderly in England and Wales was 16.1 per cent, the proportion in Worthing was 38.8 per cent, this giving an index value of 241.2. Thus, during the period 1951–71 Worthing experienced both an absolute and relative increase in its elderly population.

Application of this method (developed in Allon-Smith, 1978) gives rise to some interesting perspectives on the broad patterns of growth of retirement areas between 1921 and 1971. In general, while virtually every retirement area has been consistently gaining in its absolute proportions of the elderly the relative changes have not been so great and many areas have experienced a relative decline during specific inter-censal periods (for example, Llanwrytd Wells had an index value of 175.0 in 1921 and 165.0 in 1971; Liskeard—166.9

in 1921 and 153.0 in 1971). Of 159 retirement areas, 37 increased their index value by more than 50 points between 1921 and 1971 (Table 2.2). Although the majority of retirement areas lie on or near the coast there are some which may be classed as declining agricultural communities or inland spa towns (e.g. Llanwrtyd Wells and Builth Wells in Breconshire), and although population decline rather than population growth has been one of the causes of change in a minority of areas the majority of areas experienced substantial population growth, one of the major factors in this growth being migration.

The technique of examining the index of change may also be applied to the counties of England and Wales (Figure 2.3). In terms of absolute growth of the

Table 2.2 Retirement areas increasing their relative elderly population by 50 index points or more, 1921–71

| | Index change |
|---|---|
| *South-east Region* | |
| Frinton & Walton UD | 147.2 |
| Bexhill MB | 124.7 |
| Clacton UD | 103.2 |
| Seaford UD | 101.6 |
| Margate MB | 93.9 |
| Herne Bay UD | 81.0 |
| Eastbourne CB | 71.1 |
| Bognor Regis UD | 70.5 |
| Hailsham RD | 57.6 |
| Hythe MB | 56.8 |
| Worthing MB | 56.8 |
| Worthing RD | 54.1 |
| *South-west Region* | |
| Sidmouth UD | 110.5 |
| Minehead UD | 71.8 |
| Seaton UD | 71.7 |
| Budleigh Salterton UD | 65.1 |
| Swanage UD | 64.2 |
| Mere & Tisbury RD[a] | 55.6 |
| Dartmouth MB[a] | 53.4 |
| *East Anglia* | |
| Southwold MB[a] | 117.8 |
| Cromer UD[a] | 74.0 |
| Hunstanton UD[a] | 67.8 |
| Skegness UD[a] | 59.3 |
| Aldeburgh MB[a] | 53.3 |
| *North-west Region* | |
| Preesal UD | 114.5 |
| Grange UD | 105.1 |
| Thornton Cleveleys UD | 63.6 |
| Trawden UD[a] | 52.2 |
| *Yorkshire and Humberside* | |
| Filey UD | 86.2 |
| Mablethorpe and Sutton UD | 56.6 |
| Skegness UD | 53.5 |
| Bridlington MB | 52.8 |
| *Wales* | |
| Colwyn Bay MB | 57.2 |
| Abergele UD | 52.3 |
| Conway MB | 50.7 |
| Llandudno UD[a] | 80.6 |
| Narberth UD[a] | 54.6 |

[a]Authorities with a decline in total population
*Abbreviations*: See Table 2.1

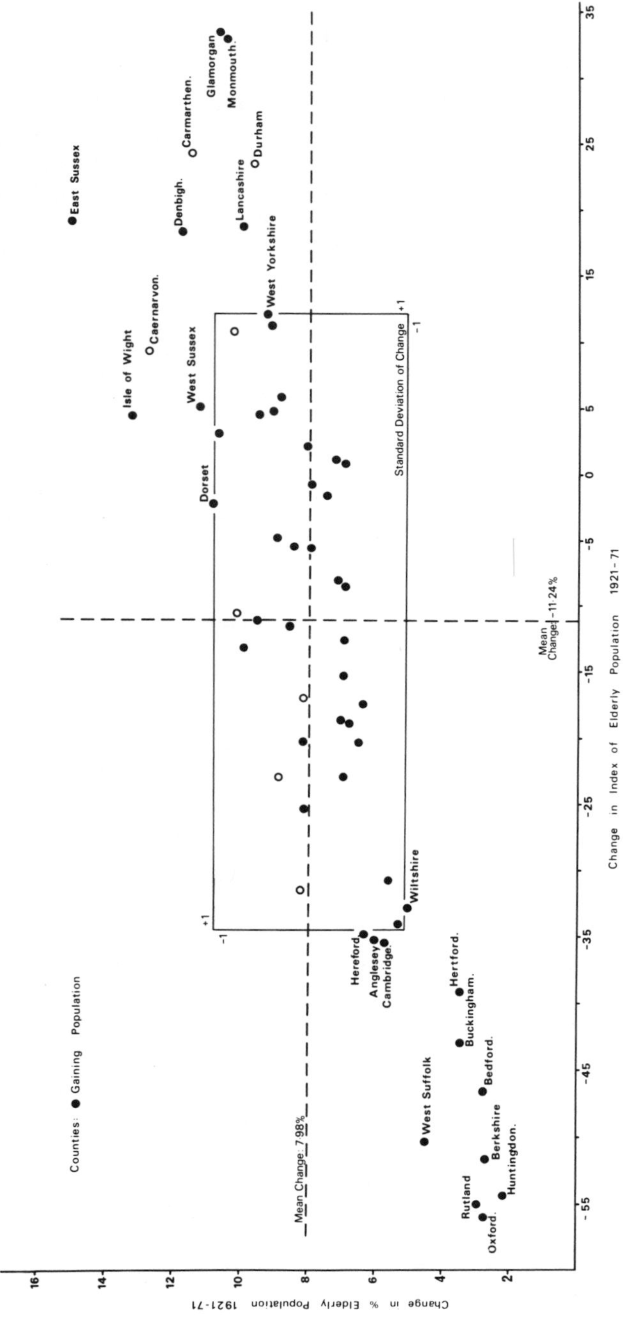


Figure 2.3 Changes in percentage of the elderly population: counties of England and Wales, 1921–71

percentage of the elderly within their populations, East Sussex, the Isle of Wight and Caernarvonshire saw the greatest change during the period 1921–71, but in relative terms, as measured by the change in index, the Isle of Wight did not show any exceptional increase, in contrast with several other counties such as the largely industrial areas of Durham, Lancashire, and Glamorgan. This contrasting geography of relative change illustrates the point that some of the major changes in the population geography of the elderly have taken place within stable, ageing communities and have not been produced by migration.

At the opposite end of the change spectrum the counties experiencing the largest decreases in the elderly population were clustered to the north-west of London, for example Berkshire, Oxfordshire, Bedfordshire, and Buckinghamshire. The present geographical pattern of ageing, then, contains a number of regional and thematic regularities within the overall pattern of change and growth. In particular, there are areas of developing concentration, and there has been a trend towards polarization between contrasting areas. Detailed examination reveals that not only some counties (e.g. Sussex and the Isle of Wight) but also individual retirement areas were already marked out as areas of concentration as early as 1921. The past 50 years have seen a confirmation and an accentuation of these trends and patterns.

## PHASES OF GROWTH AND CHANGE

There are two major levels of analysis to be considered when examining the development of the geographical patterns of the elderly in England and Wales, namely the local and the regional. The concern of this section is the regional level, but in the sense that the regional pattern reflects that of local areas 'writ large', and for the reason that similar features may be recognized at both levels of analysis, it is appropriate to introduce the themes of growth and change in the context of local areas. The basic patterns of change suggested by the evidence at both the regional and local scales are analogous to the pattern of spatial diffusion (e.g. Brown and Moore, 1969); that is, a pattern of scattered nodal centres had become evident by the 1930s and 1940s, since when there has been a growth in concentration of the elderly over time. In addition, there has been a spread of the concentration from the original nodes to adjacent areas. Growth has continued, to an apparent level of 'saturation' in particular areas. The process is best detected by examining the indices of change (i.e. the relative rather than the absolute statistics of change in the context of changing national patterns) for inter-censal periods.

A clear example may be seen in the pattern of growth for Sussex (summarized in Table 2.3). Particular areas were identified as innovators or 'primary adopters' of the retirement function during the years up to 1951. (An 'adopter' is defined as an area which experienced a rise of 15 or more index points during an inter-censal period.)' They were all characterized as coastal urban centres, for example,

Table 2.3 Sussex retirement areas: statistics of growth, 1921–71

| Local authority and decade | Population increase | Elderly population increase | Elderly index at end of period | Increase in index |
|---|---|---|---|---|
| *1921–31* | | | | |
| Bognor Regis UD | 219 | 687 | 151.1 | 28.6 |
| *1931–51* | | | | |
| Worthing MB | 23,207 | 11,961 | 215.2 | 21.2 |
| Worthing RD | 21,427 | 6,142 | 175.9 | 40.2 |
| Seaford UD | 2,431 | 1,264 | 173.4 | 33.2 |
| Eastbourne MB | 386 | 5,021 | 169.0 | 16.2 |
| Bexhill MB | 4,464 | 3,908 | 203.5 | 42.1 |
| Battle RD | 23,512 | 5,399 | 149.0 | 22.7 |
| *1951–61* | | | | |
| Bognor Regis UD | 2,417 | 2,222 | 191.2 | 28.2 |
| Arundel MB | 63 | 96 | 162.9 | 17.1 |
| Littlehampton UD | 1,760 | 1,168 | 148.8 | 28.7 |
| Worthing MB | 10,898 | 8,591 | 244.2 | 29.0 |
| Worthing RD | 8,512 | 4,939 | 213.2 | 37.3 |
| Hove MB | 3,238 | 4,272 | 207.5 | 17.6 |
| Seaford UD | 2,020 | 1,013 | 193.0 | 19.6 |
| Chailey RD | 2,760 | 1,542 | 162.7 | 17.7 |
| Eastbourne MB | 3,097 | 4,708 | 200.5 | 31.5 |
| Bexhill MB | 3,248 | 3,508 | 248.8 | 45.3 |
| Hailsham RD | 5,362 | 3,699 | 181.0 | 29.7 |
| Hastings CB | 956 | 3,402 | 192.7 | 19.3 |
| *1961–71* | | | | |
| Chichester RD | 13,708 | 5,786 | 146.7 | 22.9 |
| Chanctonbury RD | 5,228 | 2,821 | 171.4 | 26.2 |
| Bexhill MB | 3,959 | 3,844 | 275.2 | 26.4 |
| Hailsham RD | 11,165 | 6,430 | 207.2 | 26.2 |
| Rye MB | 12 | 231 | 150.3 | 22.0 |

*Abbreviations*: See Table 2.1

Worthing (index value of 215.2 in 1951), Eastbourne (169.0), Bexhill (203.5), and Seaford (173.4). In the years 1951–61 a number of additional adopters were identified which, with the exception of Hove, were adjacent to the primary adopters, for example, Chailey Rural District (RD) (index value of 162.7 in 1961), Hailsham RD (181.0), Arundel (162.9), and Littlehampton (148.8). During the decade 1961–71 further adopters such, as Chichester RD and Chanctonbury RD, further extended the contiguous belt of concentrations of the elderly. Thus, the early adopters may be seen to be the core centres from

of migration. Although a relatively minor feature within the overall pattern of national demographic change, migration of the elderly has been of great importance because of the relatively large numbers of elderly migrants being attracted to particular local destination areas, in particular the retirement areas discussed above.

The elderly form a small proportion of the total migration stream in any given period. If the number of migrants as a percentage of each quinquennial age group is examined, the pattern is one of a peak in mobility within the age groups 15–34, then a declining rate of mobility in each subsequent age group with the exception of ages 60–64, and 75 and above (Figure 2.4). Of about 5.6 million people in England and Wales who had moved within 1 year preceding the 1971 Census, only 453,670 (8 per cent) were elderly migrants. This was almost exactly half the proportion of the elderly within the total population of England and Wales in 1971 (16.1 per cent).

A similar pattern is revealed for the 5-year period, 1966–71. Of a total of 16.6 million migrants within or into England and Wales, elderly migrants constituted 1.7 million or 10.4 per cent of the total flow. Moves within regions and conurbations accounted for the majority of the elderly's migrations, for of a total of 1.7 million moves within England and Wales, 77.0 per cent did not cross regional or conurbation boundaries (Office of Population Censuses and Surveys, 1971).

The impression that elderly people dominate migration flows into retirement areas is not, on the whole, well founded. Certainly the proportions involved are higher than national averages, but not to the extent that is often believed. Between 1966 and 1971, for example, the highest proportions of elderly migrants

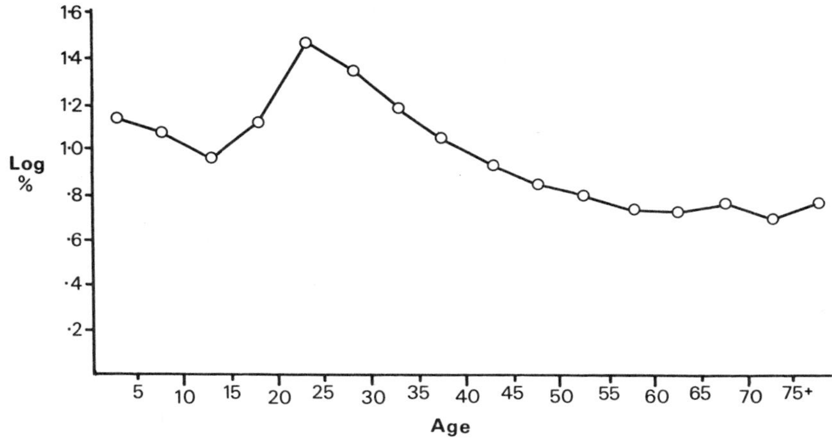


Figure 2.4 Percentage in each age group migrating: England and Wales, 1970–71

in any sub-regional flows were in the order of 27 per cent, e.g. migrants into the North Coast division of Wales and into the Sussex Coast division of the South-East Region. Obviously, more restricted retirement destinations would have received higher proportions.

The general pattern of retirement migration is of movement from cities and conurbations to coastal towns and resorts. In concurrence with interaction theories, the largest migration flows are usually to the nearest coastal areas, such as from London to the south coast and East Anglia, from Liverpool and Manchester to the Lancashire coast and Wales, and from the Midlands to Wales and the South-West Region.

One further feature is that the migration of the elderly has become more popular through time. Evidence from the retirement areas themselves, from the work of retirement associations, and from demographic and social sources suggests that the practice is spreading downwards through the social scale. Pre-war movement was mostly among the upper-middle and middle classes, whereas post-war movements have included less affluent classes, especially since the early 1960s. Improved pension schemes and more widespread compulsory retirement have encouraged this spread. One consequence of this development has been that individual retirement areas have become associated with particular socio-economic groups; for example, Frinton and Clacton each have a social distinctiveness, although geographically adjacent (Karn, 1977).

## CONCLUSION AND PROSPECTS

In recent years we have tended to become very concerned about the levels of concentration of the elderly within retirement areas and the seemingly unrelenting rise in those densities. This feature of retirement is best understood within the context of a national perspective which includes consideration of overall changes in demographic structure in addition to changes in the geography of the elderly. We have noted that the distortions of demographic structure which characterize some retirement areas are not new; in many instances the processes at work during this century have perpetuated and accentuated concentrations of the elderly which were already existent within the structure of an area. Nevertheless, during this century the geography of the elderly has changed to a pattern dominated by high densities of the elderly in some coastal peripheries. Levels of concentration, nationally and locally, are continuing to increase, as are measures of geographical and social polarization between the elderly and the rest of the population.

What of the prospects for the future? At one level the impetus to change supplied by rising numbers of the elderly in recent years will slacken as proportions of the elderly within the population stabilize in the last decades of the century; but stability in numbers does not necessarily imply a stability in geographical patterns. The reality of the diffusion dynamic which we have discussed briefly in this essay suggests that, economic and planning factors permitting, there will be continued pressure to sustain and develop the retirement function in certain coastal regions and in particular towns and villages. The potential for expanding the retirement function remains greatest in parts of the South-West and East Anglian Regions and in local areas adjacent to existing retirement centres. At a local scale, whether in urban, suburban or rural areas, the fact that residential stability characterizes the lives of the majority suggests that the nature and age of the housing market will determine those areas which, in the coming years, will become local pockets of concentration. For example, just as inter-war housing estates currently contain high concentrations of the elderly, post-war estates increasingly will develop similar characteristics.

There are, of course, considerable social and economic uncertainties facing the British population. As yet, we are uncertain of the net effects of inflation during the 1970s on the continued development of retirement areas. Similarly unclear are the prospects of even earlier retirement, or the consequences of economic depression upon the geography of the elderly. What can be stated with certainty is that the geography of the elderly is evolving, and that current and future change will be the result of increasing migration against a continued background of the majority ageing '*in-situ*'. Only recently have the major themes and dynamics of this evolution at a national level been identified, and it is within that context that our understanding of the evolving geography of the elderly can now deepen.

## REFERENCES

Allon-Smith, R. D. (1978). Migration of the Elderly: a Study in Social Geography. Unpublished PhD thesis, University of Leicester.

Barr, J. (1965). For old people only. *New Society*, 25 November.

Borough of Worthing (1956–72). *Worthing Town Council, Minutes of Proceedings*. Worthing.

Brown, L. A. and Moore, E. G. (1969). Diffusion research: a perspective. *Progress in Geography*, **1**, 120–57.

Golant, S. M. (1972). *The Residential Location and Spatial Behaviour of the Elderly*. Research Paper 143, Department of Geography, University of Chicago.

Harrison, E., McKeown, M., and O'Shea, T. (1971). Old age in Northern Ireland—a study of the elderly in a seaside town. *Economic and Social Review*, **3**, 53–72.

Hodge, E. W. (1969). Whose coast? *Town and Country Planning*, **38**, 99–102.

Hyman, G. (1974). *Cumulative Inertia and the Problem of Heterogeneity in the Analysis of Geographical Mobility*. Research Paper 11, Centre for Environmental Studies, London.

Karn, V. (1977). *Retiring to the Seaside*. Routledge & Kegan Paul, London.

Land, K. (1969). Duration of residence and prospective migration: further evidence. *Demography*, **6**, 133–40.

Law, C. M. and Warnes, A. M. (1973). The movement of retired people to seaside resorts—a study of Morecambe and Llandudno. *Town Planning Review*, **44**, 373–88.

Law, C. M. and Warnes, A. M. (1976). The changing geography of the elderly in England and Wales. *Institute of British Geographers, Transactions*, new series **1**, 453–71.

Law, C. M. and Warnes, A. M. (1977). *The Migration Decisions of Individuals at Retirement*. Report to the Social Science Research Council, London.

Lemon, A. (1973). Retirement and its effects on small towns. *Town Planning Review*, **44**, 254–61

Mellor, H. (1962). Retirement to the coast. *Town Planning Review*, **33**, 40–48.

Moindrot, C. (1963). Les villes de retraités de la côte de Sussex. *Population*, **18**, 364–6.

Morrison, P. A. (1967). Duration of residence and prospective migration; the evaluation of a stochastic model. *Demography*, **4**, 553–61.

Office of Population Censuses and Surveys (1971). *Migration Tables, Part I* and *Regional Reports*, Census 1971. HMSO, London.

Office of Population Censuses and Surveys (1972). *Population Projections*, **2**, *1971–2011*. HMSO, London.

Rogers, T. W. (1969). Migration prediction on the basis of prior migratory behaviour: a methodological note. *International Migration*, **7**, 13.

South West Economic Planning Council (1975). *Retirement to the South West*. HMSO, London.

Geographical Perspectives on the Elderly
Edited by A. M. Warnes


Chapter 3

# The destination decision in retirement migration

*Christopher M. Law* and *Anthony M. Warnes*

Migrations of elderly people around the time of their retirement are growing in number and occurring over increasing distances in most advanced countries. This is a product in part of the increasing number of elderly people, in part of their increasing longevity and improving health, but most of all of their ability to retire from gainful employment with reasonable continuing income. Before the establishment of private and state pension schemes most people continued working as long as it was physically possible since this was their only means of obtaining an income. As the real value of state pensions has increased and higher-yielding occupational pensions have spread, and as more people have accumulated property assets throughout their working lives, higher percentages of each succeeding generation have been able to cease paid work in their early sixties and to afford to move. Retirement has become a clear and distinctive stage in life to which many look forward, partly because of the opportunities to do things impossible during working life. One of these is the opportunity to live in another area, for accessibility to employment ceases to be a locational constraint. People can move to be nearer their relatives or friends, to return to their native or childhood areas, or to residentially, climatically, or socially more attractive areas. Such moves at or around retirement—from one suburb to another, from a large city to an adjacent rural area, or over greater distances to environmentally attractive areas—constitute the growing retirement migrations. These are supplementing the local residential moves that have always been made by elderly people either to adjust their housing expenditure to their means or for the companionship and care that is so often required following widowhood or in extreme old age. Our principal interest has been in the longer-distance retirement migrations that not only change the local area of residence but also the urban or metropolitan location.

In Britain retirement migration has been increasing rapidly in the post-war period, although it is still a minority characteristic and the potential for further increases is huge: it is, therefore, important to seek greater understanding of the determinants and likely patterns of retirement migration. Although the census does not tabulate the origins and destinations of migration by economic status, most moves of those aged 60 and over are by retired people. During the year 1970–71 about 60,000 people aged 60 and over moved between the eight Standard Regions of England and Wales, equivalent to 5.5 per cent of the age group, and representing an increase of 11 per cent over the figure recorded for 1965–66. However, this understates the phenomenon since often retirement migration is intra-Regional, as with the numerous movements from London to the south coast. As migration to environmentally attractive areas mainly takes place in the early years of retirement, an alternative census finding is of interest:in the year 1970-71, 56,470 people aged 60–69 moved out of the urban and industrial sub-regions of England and Wales, representing 10.8 per cent of the average number in the age group 60–69. Whilst some may have been short distance across the urban boundaries, these findings suggest that in 1971 a reasonable estimate of the proportion undertaking these total-displacement migrations at retirement was 10 per cent.

In Britain retirement migration has been predominantly to seaside resorts where the share of the elderly, defined here as the 60 + age group, has been rising faster than the national rate of increase (Law and Warnes, 1976; and Table 3.1). The most favoured receiving regions have been East Anglia, the South-West, the outer parts of the South-East region, and the North Wales, Lancashire, and Yorkshire coasts.

The growth of retirement migration is apparent to any casual visitor to the favoured destination areas. Characteristically the retired have settled in those seaside resorts which were developed in the second half of the nineteenth century following the arrival of railways. The peripheries of these resorts have acquired commonly during recent decades large estates of bungalows, the accommodation most favoured by the retired. Most recently, the wide possession of the motor car and the extension of public utilities to most rural areas have encouraged retired migrants to move to less accessible coastal areas and to inland villages. The inland retirement districts include areas remote from the coast like the Cotswolds, the Welsh Borders (Herefordshire and Salop) and the Yorkshire Dales. The sub-regional census statistics are of little value for measuring retirement migration to these districts since their retired communities are small and highly localized. Not only are retired migrants now searching more widely within Britain but there is evidence of increasing emigration. Such movements have been few, but the recent lifting of exchange controls, the slow harmonization of the EEC nations and the likely entry of Spain, and the development of the overseas property market in London (including a drive to sell Florida properties), will encourage larger numbers to retire abroad.

Retirement migrants are not drawn from all regions of the country but predominantly from the urban industrial areas (Table 3.2). In particular the Greater London area is by far the greatest source of retirement migrants and

Table 3.1 Percentage of population aged 60 or over: selected standard sub-divisions in England and Wales, 1951–71

| Sub-region | 1951 | 1961 | 1971 | Ratio 1971:1951 | Population (60+) 1971 |
|---|---|---|---|---|---|
| North Wales coast | 23.1 | 28.3 | 32.6 | 1.41 | 38,050 |
| Sussex coast | 24.1 | 28.8 | 32.1 | 1.33 | 308,000 |
| Fylde | 20.9 | 24.4 | 28.1 | 1.34 | 82,710 |
| Lancaster | 19.8 | 23.4 | 27.0 | 1.36 | 33,360 |
| South-West: south | 19.6 | 22.3 | 25.5 | 1.30 | 209,680 |
| South-West: west | 19.6 | 22.3 | 25.3 | 1.29 | 123,310 |
| Outer South-East: Kent | 19.8 | 23.3 | 25.2 | 1.27 | 157,025 |
| North Wales: remainder | 19.6 | 20.8 | 23.0 | 1.21 | 53,300 |
| Central Wales | 18.0 | 19.9 | 22.8 | 1.27 | 19,250 |
| East Anglia: north-east | 18.1 | 19.9 | 22.6 | 1.25 | 136,900 |
| Rural North-East: south | 16.9 | 19.9 | 22.5 | 1.33 | 55,770 |
| Outer South-East: Essex | 19.5 | 21.2 | 22.3 | 1.14 | 91,210 |
| South-West: central | 17.8 | 19.7 | 22.2 | 1.25 | 159,620 |
| Rural North-East: north | 17.0 | 18.7 | 22.0 | 1.29 | 30,260 |
| Wales: south-west | 17.7 | 19.0 | 21.4 | 1.21 | 49,110 |
| Outer South-East: Solent | 18.1 | 19.8 | 21.3 | 1.18 | 350,980 |
| North-West: Furness | 17.6 | 19.6 | 21.3 | 1.21 | 22,920 |
| East Anglia: south-east | 18.3 | 19.1 | 20.6 | 1.12 | 79,610 |
| West Midlands: rural west | 16.6 | 17.8 | 20.4 | 1.23 | 67,325 |
| Cumberland and Westmorland | 16.0 | 17.4 | 19.9 | 1.24 | 72,800 |
| England and Wales | 15.9 | 17.3 | 19.2 | 1.21 | |

*Source:* Census Reports, England and Wales.

Table 3.2 Origin areas of retired migrants, 1966–71

| | Population aged 60–69 | | | Rate | |
|---|---|---|---|---|---|
| Sub-region | Net loss 1966–71 ÷5 | Net loss 1970–71 | Total 1971 | per 1000 1966–71 ÷5 | 1970–71 |
| Greater London | 18,020 | 19,880 | 830,510 | 21.7 | 23.9 |
| West Midlands conurbation | 2,656 | 3,510 | 235,260 | 11.3 | 14.9 |
| Manchester | 2,028 | 1,970 | 267,025 | 7.6 | 7.4 |
| Outer Metropolitan north | 566 | 660 | 102,195 | 5.5 | 6.5 |
| South Yorkshire | 410 | 680 | 82,915 | 4.9 | 8.2 |
| Coventry | 264 | 460 | 62,740 | 4.2 | 7.3 |
| Outer Metropolitan south-west | 288 | 550 | 75,925 | 3.8 | 7.2 |
| West Yorkshire | 798 | 940 | 213,145 | 3.7 | 5.0 |
| Merseyside | 644 | 1,630 | 175,175 | 3.7 | 9.3 |
| North Staffs | 130 | 200 | 54,045 | 2.4 | 3.7 |
| Notts–Derby | 404 | 290 | 284,745 | 1.4 | 1.0 |
| Tyneside conurbation | 344 | 480 | 86,800 | 4.0 | 5.5 |

*Source*: Census Reports, England and Wales.

has the highest rate of outward movement. After London are ranked the Birmingham and Manchester areas, but it is clear that northwards the rate of outward migration falls. The different areal propensities to migrate may reflect durable characteristics, such as the size of urban areas, relative house prices, or the socio-economic composition of regional populations, but alternatively retirement migration may be diffusing through the population from London and from the higher levels of the income distribution. This is indicated by a comparison of the 1971 5- and 1-year census migration data for those aged 60–69 (Table 3.2). The comparison does not take into account the complications of return migration, deaths before the census date, or the changing base population over time, but if the average annual rate of out-migration over 1966–71 is compared with the rate recorded for 1970–71, then larger percentage increases characterized the northern than the southern sub-divisional and conurbation populations: Merseyside shows almost a threefold increase.

The limited evidence demonstrates that retirement migration is growing absolutely and relatively and that it is having an increasing impact on more diverse areas of the country. There are just over 10 million people in Great Britain aged 60 or more and they represent nearly one-fifth of the population. Their geographical distribution has become increasingly distinctive from that of the total population, to a large extent as a result of retirement migration. If the phenomenon continues to grow and the destinations remain restricted, the implications for housing and the social and medical services in the areas of concentration will ramify (Law and Warnes, 1981).

## THE RETIREMENT MIGRATION SURVEY

In order to study the influences upon the volume and geographical patterns of retirement migration, a survey of 201 retired migrants in North Wales and Dorset and 100 matching non-migrant households was undertaken during the summer of 1976 with support from the Social Science Research Council. Its objective was to supplement previous work by the authors and by Karn (1977), who had investigated the circumstances of migrants in Clacton and Bexhill. From these studies the basic characteristics of retired migrants were known: they were overwhelmingly owner–occupiers before and after the move, and were largely drawn from the Registrar General's Social Classes II and III, from white-collar occupations with medium to high incomes, and from small households. Married couples without others formed a large proportion of all retired migrants (Law and Warnes, 1973).

These characteristics were clear but not discriminating, for as has been discussed it is apparent from census and other sources that little more than 10 per cent of households with these characteristics migrated a long distance (over 40 kilometres) at or around the time of retirement. A prime objective of the 1976 survey was therefore to move further towards the identification of the distinctive personal, housing, or socio-economic circumstances of movers. This was pursued by a multi-stage sampling procedure which represented the regional origins and the occupational, household, and tenure characteristics of long-distance elderly migrants in England and Wales in 1970–71 as far as they could be ascertained from the census. These procedures are described in detail in the final research report to the SSRC (Law and Warnes, 1977, Chapter3). From the 201 migrant respondents were collected details of their housing, household, and socio-economic circumstances before retirement in their areas of origin. The profiles constructed in this way were then used in a sampling design to identify 100 non-movers in the London and Manchester metropolitan regions.

## The characteristics of retirement migrants

By comparing the two samples several characteristics were identified as distinguishing movers from non-movers. The results have been reported in more detail in earlier reports (Law and Warnes, 1977, 1980a) and here only a brief summary is repeated. The influence of the family on the migration decision was considered, for single people or married couples without children should in general be less constrained in their choice of residence than married couples with children, and moderate support for this hypothesis was found. Among married couples with children close ties were thought to inhibit movement and in fact where children were seen at least monthly movement was less likely.

Secondly, we considered the effect of pre-retirement mobility on the decision to migrate. Those who had not moved could well have developed strong links in an area, while those who had moved would not only have weaker links in an area but also a wider experience of other areas. A highly significant relationship was found of an interesting asymmetrical form. Retirement migrants were over-represented among both the small number of those who had not moved at all during their working ages, and more clearly among those who had experienced *non-local* moves. The former result may have been produced by imperfect recall of the movers' earlier short-distance moves in the origin area. It was also found that those who had cars, and thus were able to gain knowledge of other areas, were more likely to have moved than those who had never owned a car.

Since most migrants are drawn from the higher socio-economic groups it is unlikely that they would be living in poor, unsuitable houses or undesirable residential areas and thus be pushed to move. However, the replies to our questions about housing and environment suggested that movers placed a greater emphasis on getting the best, most suitable house in preferred kinds of areas than non-movers. We also investigated Karn's (1977) finding that retirement migrants were more likely to have retired at an early age compared to non-migrants and found this to be true. In general this was mainly because retired migrants were in jobs where retirement before 65 was normal and only slightly to the fact that retired migrants had chosen early retirement.

Overall it was found that the four variables having the strongest associations with migration were:

(1) the frequency and distance of residential mobility during working ages;
(2) like of pre-retirement house;
(3) the infrequency of seeing surviving children at the time of retirement; and
(4) relatively youthful ages of retirement.

All of these variables yielded contingency coefficients with moving or staying in the range of 0.27 to 0.35, so none were very powerful in their statistical explanation (Law and Warnes, 1980a, p. 209).

As well as studying the likely volume of migrations through a closer understanding of the characteristics that were positively associated with moves, the second major objective of the survey was to discover more about the factors which influenced the selection of a destination, in part to see if there is any basis for predicting a changing emphasis in the selection. The paper now focuses upon this element of the research, and begins with the empirical and conceptual background to our enquiries.

## ELEMENTS OF THE DESTINATION DECISION

The procedures involved in residential relocation are variable, complex, and subject to many different influences. The design of our own investigation was shaped, no doubt sometimes unconsciously, by the limited previous evidence concerning residential moves by elderly people, our previous studies and interest in the phenomenon, and by general conceptualizations of the mobility process of which the behavioural generalizations of Wolpert, Brown, and Moore are well known. They have recently been evaluated by Brown and Gilliard (1981). From these sources we had arrived at the view that any move can consist of the following elements:

(1) a decision (or an order) to leave the present dwelling;
(2) a decision to leave the present residential area;
(3) a decision to leave the region;
(4) decisions as to the (desired) size, tenure, amenities, and character of a replacement dwelling;
(5) decisions as to the location (national, regional, local, environmental, social) of the replacement dwelling;
(6) decisions as to how to seek or search for a replacement dwelling;
(7) selection of suitable residential area;

(8) selection of suitable dwelling;
(9) execution of transfer—selling, buying, making tenancy agreement;
(10) arranging physical move.

Not all of these elements are present in all cases, and some may be combined or joint decisions. Indeed in rare instances the process can be very much simpler than the list of elements suggests, as when a person owns two properties and decides to move from one to another upon retirement. Frequently, though, it seemed to us that many of the elements would be present, and the process would be further complicated by the fact that commonly more than one person would be involved in the decision, that in some cases the movers would be influenced by the advice, encouragement, or wishes of children or siblings and even friends and doctors. Furthermore it must be expected that to a varying extent individuals' preferences are not formed without reference to the opportunities available but that they can rarely be fulfilled completely because of each individual's less than perfect knowledge of the housing market. In other words, supply conditions or the constraints and directions stemming from the housing market also will influence individual decisions as to whether, when, how, and where to migrate at or around the age of retirement. Much more is involved, therefore, than an evaluation of comparative place and dwelling utilities, as Rossi (1980, pp. 10–50) has argued recently in his brief survey of mobility research since 1955.

## Previous evidence

Evidence from comprehensive studies of residential relocation had provided some insight into the search procedures employed by elderly households. The study by Murie (1974) of 3296 households in West Yorkshire who had moved during the electoral registration year 1967–68 included 556 heads aged 60 or more years of continuing households. They were much more likely than younger heads of continuing households to have applied to the local authority as their principal action in seeking accommodation, but much less likely to have sought owner occupation (Murie, 1974, Table 4.35, p. 74). Regarding the principal preferences in accommodation, house factors (amenities, garden, garage, design, modernity) were dominant (56 per cent), but the elderly were less likely than younger groups to be seeking larger, and more likely to be seeking smaller, accommodation. The price or value of the house was less often given (2 per cent) as a response to this question by the elderly than by younger age groups, but a similar proportion (13 per cent) cited the location or area as the most important quality (Murie, 1974, Table 4.39, p. 76). The principal contrasts with younger continuing households (divided respectively into those aged 25–44 and 45–49) in the main reason for moving were a higher incidence of their previous property being condemned or demolished (21 per cent against

8 and 13 per cent), and a higher return of health and otherwise unspecified personal reasons (37 against 9 and 17 per cent). On the other hand, the elderly less commonly cited reasons connected with the previous house being too small, a wish to change tenure or neighbourhood, or job-connected reasons (Table 3.3).

Murie demonstrated the importance of housing market factors both in initiating moves through redevelopment and in influencing the destination tenure through shortages of preferred private-renting accommodation. These considerations are well worth emphasis for, despite the consideration of all socio-economic groups and exclusion of inter-urban movers, his findings suggest that retirement migrations by relatively affluent groups may have been stimulated by the accelerated rate of residential redevelopment and by the shortage and high cost of small units of accommodation in the major urban areas of the country.

Our survey provided some evidence of the former, for 17 of the 201 (8.5 per cent) migrant households came from inner or industrial districts of large urban areas, and 13 (6.5 per cent) said of their former residential area that it was declining, obsolescent, blighted, or undergoing redevelopment. While this chapter is concerned principally with the selection of the destination area, Murie warns us that any consideration of the prospects for retirement migration or of likely shifts in destination must beware of too exclusive a concern with the 'pull' factors.

Other more explicit evidence was available before our survey commenced, from our own studies, from Karn's work, and from France and the United States. Karn's study of 503 migrant retirement households in Bexhill and 487 in Clacton was carried out in the winter of 1968 and reported in her thesis (1974). It included a few questions concerning the process of selection. She has recently summarized these results:

> The people who retired to Bexhill and Clacton had given little consideration in moving to any place other than coastal resorts and the Sussex coast stood out clearly as the most preferred retirement area, though many people had to reject moving there on grounds of cost. The presence of friends and relatives played a large role in influencing decisions about the choice of a retirement resort, but it was also clear that the majority of movers were fairly familiar with the towns from previous excursions and holidays there. Last, for the actual process of selecting a house, their sources of information were largely newspapers and estate agents, but help was given frequently by friends and relations, particularly in Clacton (Karn, 1977, pp. 60–1).

Another study, of the circumstances of retired people in Exmouth, had concerned itself particularly with 'the extent to which people had come from other parts of Britain and what made them decide to settle in Devon'. Information had been gathered from 54 over-65s who had moved into Devon or Exmouth over the age of 45, 11 of them before retirement. Almost one-half gave

Table 3.3 Main reason for wanting to move among continuing households who had moved, West Yorkshire 1968–69

| Age of head of household | Sample size | Condemned, demolished | Too expensive | Too large | Too small | Change tenure | Job | Neighbourhood | Heath and personal | Other |
|---|---|---|---|---|---|---|---|---|---|---|
| Under 25 | 153 | 11 | 7 | 1 | 15 | 14 | 11 | 8 | 5 | 29 |
| 25–44 | 1308 | 8 | 3 | 0 | 17 | 11 | 16 | 11 | 9 | 27 |
| 45–59 | 618 | 13 | 3 | 8 | 6 | 8 | 9 | 11 | 17 | 26 |
| Over 60 | 555 | 21 | 2 | 8 | 1 | 1 | 2 | 6 | 37 | 21 |

*Source*: Murie (1974), Table 4.7, p. 56.

as their main reason for moving that they or their spouse was of Devon or West Country origin (13) or that they were coming to join relations already there (13). Ten determined to return after spending holidays in Devon and 11 mentioned reasons connected with health or the climate as their chief motive (Glyn-Jones, 1975, pp. 19 and 22).

The few, partial other sources of information available to us tended to confirm that surprisingly short and limited searches were carried out (Beaver, 1979), few alternative destinations considered, and that the principal influences upon the selection of a destination area were:

(1) previous knowledge of the area, often through holidays or earlier residence; and
(2) the location of children and other relatives.

For example, it had been found from the 1971 survey of 121 retired migrant households in Llandudno that 70 per cent considered no other area for retirement. It was also found in Morecambe one year earlier that

> dissatisfaction with the previous area of residence—or push factors—were not a major influence in the decision to migrate. Only seven per cent of the retired migrants interviewed in Morecambe gave dissatisfaction with their previous residence as a factor in their decision to move, whereas 42 per cent mentioned the attractiveness of the resort and 27 per cent mentioned the proximity of friends and relations (Law and Warnes, 1973, p. 382).

## Scope of the questionnaire

The 1976 survey built upon this existing knowledge and was directed towards several themes that were least well understood. Its first subject was timing: decisions regarding a move at retirement are likely to be considered with increasing urgency as the transition date approaches, but the questionnaire sought to establish the duration of the consideration and decision. We expected that the longer the period of consideration the more complex would be the decision to move and the choice of destination. We tended to the assumption that people first decide to move and then decide where to move. In reality it may be that only when they have found somewhere to move is a decision made to move. As the list of the various elements of a decision to move shows, the structures, strategies, and tactics of the move may be innumerable. We hoped to go some way to establish at least the most common strategies.

Another set of questions concerned the factors affecting the choice of destination. Migrants normally move to areas which they know well and which therefore lie within what Wolpert has called a person's *action space*. Amongst the strongest factors shaping the action space will be the number and location of previous residences (including wartime moves). Of secondary importance, as reflected in earlier surveys, is the geographical knowledge gained during holidays, including those at second homes. In Britain only about 1 per cent of households have second homes, much lower than in most West European and North American countries, but ownership has been growing. Increases in leisure time, wealth, and motor car ownership have also made it easier to visit distant relatives and friends, while some individuals learn of areas through business and work trips and through the mass media. For a multitude of reasons there is usually a distance decay factor in the formation of the action space, with the adjacent areas being best known. However it is likely that the friction of distance has been reduced by greater affluence and the reduced inconvenience of travel. The survey attempted through a series of open-ended questions to explore more fully the relationship between individuals' action spaces and their destination decisions in retirement migration.

A third topic tackled by the questionnaire was the nature and importance of the characteristics of areas upon the selection of a destination. The obvious hypotheses from the pattern of retirement migration, which is dominated by movements from the largest urban areas and towards both small towns and rural coastal areas, are that the migrants seek environmental improvements. The movement towards the southern parts of the country appears to be related to milder and sunnier weather, but their social, aesthetic, and commercial characteristics may also be an attraction. Are migrants attracted by communities of predominantly the same age as themselves? Are they attracted by towns with good shops, fine buildings, and a cultural life? We hoped to assess the role of such environmental 'pull factors'.

Fourthly we sought to establish the influence of proximity or access to friends and relatives. We had already learnt that retired people who are childless or whose children are mobile were the most likely to move at retirement, but the variable deserved elaboration and further evaluation. Finally we examined the factors affecting the choice of property and residential area within a district. This implied that an individual or individuals first choose a retirement area, say North Wales, south Devon or Dorset, and then select a residential district or house. We therefore examined the availability of different types of both residential areas and dwellings in a potential destination area to explore more local spatial influences while recognizing that they would not always be independent of the selection of a destination area. Variations in house prices are likely to affect movement between different regions of the country and will certainly be influential at the local level. The questionnaire also examined the awareness and influence of the importance of accessibility to shops and services, and whether the individual's prospective circumstances, such as becoming more infirm or the surrender of a household car, affected the choice of residence.

## REVEALED CHARACTER OF THE SEARCH

This section summarizes findings about the structure and timing of the decision to migrate, the geographical extent and character of the search, and the influences upon the selection of a destination area. It is a necessarily selective digest of a greater quantity of results, relationships, and cross-tabulations, and reports numerical results to enable independent assessments of our qualitative judgements.

### The structure and timing of the decision

Information about the timing and duration of the decision was provided by the section of the questionnaire which dealt with attitudes to retirement. This had asked when people began to form plans for retirement. Undoubtedly the question was interpreted differently, not least in the degree to which the respondents associated saving and investment during working life with plans for retirement, but it was surprising to find that over 30 per cent of the movers claimed not to have begun thinking about retirement until within 5 years of its occurrence. On the other hand 22 per cent stated that they had made plans at least 10 years before retirement. As regards plans specifically to move, 56 per cent stated that they had not begun planning within 5 years of retirement, but on the other hand 19 per cent claimed to have had such plans for at least 10 years. Over a quarter stated that it was less than a year between the formation of the idea to move and the event (Table 3.4).

There were clear differences in the duration of plans among the sub-groups of the sample. They are best considered by excluding the exceptional circumstances of those in tied accommodation before the move. Married couple households (before the retirement move) were most likely to have planned over a long period, with 57 per cent claiming to have made plans over more than 2 years and 22 per cent over more than 10 years. This compares with only 38 per cent and 14 per cent respectively of one-person households. Larger households,

Table 3.4 Duration of plans for retirement and plans for moving: movers

| | Plans for retirement | | Plans to move | |
|---|---|---|---|---|
| | No. | % | No. | % |
| Less than 1 year | 28 | 13.9 | 53 | 26.4 |
| 1–1.9 years | 13 | 6.5 | 26 | 12.9 |
| 2–4.9 years | 23 | 11.4 | 35 | 17.4 |
| 5–9.9 years | 29 | 14.4 | 24 | 11.9 |
| More than 10 years | 45 | 22.4 | 39 | 19.4 |
| No plans | 48 | 23.9 | 7 | 3.5 |
| Tied house | | | 12 | 6.0 |
| Not relevant/other | 15 | 7.5 | 5 | 2.5 |
| TOTALS | 201 | 100.0 | 201 | 100.0 |

*Source*: Authors' Survey, 1976. As for all subsequent tables.

with three or more persons immediately before their retirement move, reported a similar distribution of planning-durations to two-person households, except that their plans were more likely to extend over 1–2 years and less likely to extend over 2–10 years (Table 3.5).

Educational attainment was found to be positively related to the duration of plans for moving, for 62 per cent of those with an academic qualification beyond GCE 'A' level (normally gained at 17/18 years of age) or with a vocational qualification had planned over more than 2 years, as compared to 47 per cent of those with lesser or no qualifications. Conversely, only 24 per cent of the higher educational attainment group began to plan less than a year before the event, compared to 38 per cent of the lower attainment group.

A clear relationship was also found between the duration of plans to move and attitudes towards retirement. Excluding those from tied accommodation, 31 respondents said that they had either never looked forward to, or were increasingly worried by, the approach of retirement. Only 7 (23 per cent) of these made plans extending longer than 5 years, and 11 (36 per cent) made plans less than a year before they moved. On the other hand, of the 73 respondents who always, or who increasingly, looked forward to retirement, 38 (52 per cent) made plans to move over 5 years before retirement, and only 15 (21 per cent) made plans over less than 1 year.

There were few other clear relationships with the duration of plans for moving, except that when as a result of bereavement or for other reasons the pre-retirement household did not move in its entirety, a relatively short duration of the plans to move were evident. Of the 30 cases in which this happened, 24 moved after less than 5 years of planning, compared to 87 of the 142 cases (61 per cent) of continuing households.

Table 3.5 Duration of plans to move and the size of household

| | Household size | | | | | |
|---|---|---|---|---|---|---|
| | One person | | Two person | | Three persons or more | |
| Duration in years | No. | % | No. | % | No. | % |
| Less than 1 | 10 | 34.5 | 33 | 26.8 | 10 | 27.0 |
| 1–1.9 | 5 | 17.2 | 13 | 10.6 | 8 | 21.6 |
| 2–4.9 | 4 | 13.8 | 25 | 20.3 | 6 | 16.2 |
| 5–9.9 | 3 | 10.3 | 18 | 14.6 | 3 | 8.1 |
| 10 or more | 4 | 13.8 | 27 | 22.0 | 8 | 21.6 |
| Other | 3 | 10.3 | 7 | 5.7 | 2 | 5.4 |
| TOTALS | 29 | 100.0 | 123 | 100.0 | 37 | 99.9 |

**The decision-makers**

It is possible that the distribution of retirement migration destinations is changing at the present time towards a more dispersed pattern, and that this is related to a changing pattern of influence upon the decision. The survey included questions about who first had the idea of moving and when the spouse (or other second member) agreed to move. There were 144 married couple (plus) households in the mover sample. When both husband and wife were present at the interview, our question about the initiator often prompted raised eyebrows and knowing or ironic smiles, and we believe that the 40 per cent who claimed 'both' exaggerates the prevalence of equal enthusiasm. The husband initiated the idea in 35 per cent and the wife in 26 per cent of the cases. Agreement was stated to be little delayed among the married-couple households: within 6 months in 69 per cent of the relevant cases, but on the other hand in 11 per cent of the cases it was admitted that agreement was never reached and the second member moved reluctantly. Among the 33 single-person pre-retirement households, 25 said that they themselves had first had the idea to move, the remainder being prompted by others.

Some interesting comparative findings from the non-mover sample are available. Among movers wives had first promoted the idea in 1 in 4 of the relevant cases, whereas among non-movers the ratio was 1 in 2.5. Only in 9 of 86 married-couple (plus) non-mover households did both members agree on the desirability of moving: not all of these were acutely disappointed at being unable to carry out their wishes. The expressed evidence—and even more our impressions from the interviews—suggest that for a retirement migration to occur among married couples, a period of discussion and consideration leading to the agreement of both parties normally occurs. Husbands' views were more likely to have prevailed and wives' more likely to have unsuccessfully recommended a move.

We did gain the impression that the following sequence of events was common if not universal. First, one member of the household would acquire a notion that it would be desirable to move a long distance at retirement. Often this idea would be adopted after observing a relative, work colleague or neighbour who had undertaken such a move; in other instances the formation of the idea was related to a specific area which was either the location of relatives and friends or the location of holidays or previous residence. Subsequently the idea would be discussed among the adult members of the household until, in most cases, a common determination was found. This would be followed by an active search for properties, although often it was preceded by a preliminary evaluation and sifting of potential areas.

**Extent of the search**

The unexpectedly short duration of the plans to move for a large proportion of the sample was reflected by the relatively restricted geographical pattern of the search and its short duration. Information was collected during the interviews about: the towns and districts which had been considered for a move; when and where property enquiries had been made; the information sources used to find vacant property; when and where properties were viewed; and the reasons for rejecting areas and properties.

A large number moved after extremely simple searches of short duration. Nearly 40 per cent considered only one area, and one in three of these made no house enquiries beyond the property to which they moved (Table 3.6). Another 4.5 per cent already owned a property in the retirement area, so virtually one-half of the respondents did not make any comparisons between alternative retirement areas; 16 per cent made house enquiries in one other area, and 26 per cent considered moving to, and enquired for, properties in two or more other areas. The remainder considered other areas but not to the extent of enquiring about properties.

When the sample is disaggregated, a difference again emerges between the single-person households (immediately before the retirement move) and the married-couple households (Table 3.6). Only one-quarter of the former (8 out of 34) made house enquiries in two or more areas, compared to one-half of the married couples (70 out of 145). Married couples without others were slightly more likely to make these extended searches than married couples with children or others (50.0 per cent as against 40.7 per cent), so the relationship is not simply

Table 3.6 Extent of the search and household marital composition at retirement

| Extent of search | Household at retirement | | | |
|---|---|---|---|---|
| | One-person: single, divorced or widowed persons | | Married couples with or without others | |
| | No. | % | No. | % |
| No search beyond the destination property | 9 | 26.5 | 16 | 11.0 |
| Other house enquiries in the eventual destination district | 12 | 35.3 | 31 | 21.4 |
| Other house enquiries in two or more districts | 8 | 23.5 | 70 | 48.3 |
| Other—including consideration of other areas but no house enquiries | 5 | 14.7 | 28 | 19.3 |
| TOTALS | 34 | 100.0 | 145 | 100.0 |

$\sum\frac{(O-E)^2}{E} = 11.18$; under null hypothesis $\chi^2$(d.f. $= 3$; $p = 0.025$) $= 9.35$.

a product of the numbers of people in the household. The relationship was symmetrical, with married couples also more likely than single-person households to have considered other areas without making enquiries (13 as against 8 per cent) but less likely to have had no search beyond the eventually occupied house (11 as against 26.5 per cent).

Further evidence of the relatively extensive search of married couples is implied when the sample is disaggregated by the number of people in the pre-retirement household, for contrary to our expectation three-plus-person households were less likely to have enquired about houses in two or more areas than two-person households. On the other hand, while 13 per cent of two-person households looked no further than the house they moved to, only 2 of the 33 three-plus-person households limited themselves to this most basic of searches.

There were some differences in the searches according to the origin area of the retirement household, with those from Greater London being particularly likely to have enquired about properties in two or more areas (52 per cent), and particularly unlikely not to have even considered a second area. Those from Greater Manchester, mainly surveyed in North Wales, showed the opposite propensities and engaged in less extensive searches than migrants from other large urban areas of the country—for 14 of the 23 did not even consider a second area.

There was no evidence from the data that there were different searches according to the household's earlier adult residential mobility, but a clear relationship was found with social class variables such as the educational attainment of the householder. Of those who had not achieved any educational qualifications beyond 'A' level (9 in 10 of whom claimed no qualifications at all) 45 per cent did not search in, or consider, areas other than that they retired to, as compared to 30 per cent of those with some further educational qualification. Conversely only 35 per cent of the low educational attainment group made house enquiries in two or more areas, compared to 54 per cent of those with further educational qualifications.

Interesting evidence for a trend towards more elaborate searches was derived from several of the variables. When the search pattern was cross-tabulated with the age of the oldest survivor in the household it was revealed that the more recently retired households had been more likely to search beyond the eventual retirement area. Thirty per cent of the households with the oldest survivor less than 70 years of age had been satisfied to consider only one area compared to 42 per cent of those aged 70–79 and 54 per cent of those aged 80 or over.

## Areas of search

Another aspect of the search was the character of the areas which were explored. Various strands of evidence had suggested a recent trend to search for retirement homes in inland rural areas as well as traditional coastal areas; these two categories of destination were distinguished as were areas close to the pre-retirement home and areas abroad. Nearly one-fifth of the sample were coded as effectively making no geographical search, sometimes because they already owned the property to which they moved, sometimes because the household head was joining another member already resident at the new address, or because the new home was inherited or acquired by others. One-third of the single-person households made no search, a surprisingly large fraction even given the small numbers involved (Table 3.7). Barrett (1976) has shown similarly restricted searches among an all-age sample from Toronto.

The most characteristic pattern was to search only among coastal areas, for 45 per cent confined themselves to such towns and rural districts. If the households who searched in coastal *and* inland areas are added, 69 per cent searched in coastal areas. The differences in the areas of search according to the size of the pre-retirement household were not considerable, but single people were the least likely to consider inland areas either exclusively or in combination with coastal areas and the most likely to have searched close to their pre-retirement home. Two-person households, who were predominantly married couples, were the most likely to have considered inland areas alone and, as found in the previous section, the most likely to have had the widest searches in inland as well as coastal districts. Only 1 in 20 of all household-size groups had searched abroad for a retirement home.

There were only modest relationships between social class measures and the geographical character of the search. For example, those in the higher of the

Table 3.7 Areas of search and the pre-retirement household

| | Single person | | Two person | | Three or more persons | | All households | | Married couples only | |
|---|---|---|---|---|---|---|---|---|---|---|
| Areas of search | No. | % | No. | % | No. | % | No. | % | No. | % |
| Coastal areas only | 12 | 40.0 | 56 | 42.7 | 21 | 53.8 | 89 | 44.5 | 53 | 44.9 |
| Inland areas only | 2 | 6.7 | 17 | 13.0 | 5 | 12.8 | 24 | 12.0 | 13 | 11.0 |
| Coastal and inland areas | 2 | 6.7 | 19 | 14.5 | 4 | 10.3 | 25 | 12.5 | 16 | 13.6 |
| Around pre-retirement home (and elsewhere) | 3 | 10.0 | 11 | 8.4 | 3 | 7.7 | 17 | 8.5 | 10 | 8.5 |
| Abroad (and elsewhere) | 1 | 3.3 | 6 | 4.6 | 2 | 5.1 | 9 | 4.5 | 6 | 5.1 |
| No search | 10 | 33.3 | 22 | 16.8 | 4 | 10.3 | 36 | 18.0 | 20 | 16.9 |
| TOTALS | 30 | 100.0 | 131 | 100.0 | 39 | 100.0 | 200 | 100.0 | 118 | 100.0 |

two educational attainment groups were less likely to have made no search and less likely to have searched exclusively in coastal areas, but were more likely to have searched in all other defined areas including the surroundings of their pre-retirement home (Table 3.8). Although the numbers were extremely small, the greatest difference between the relative frequencies of the two groups was in having searched abroad—a detail, but one which provides reassurance as to the realism of the data. While the frequencies displayed in Table 3.8 are not significantly different from those to be expected under a null hypothesis (of no difference in the search between the two educational attainment groups) at the 5 per cent level, if the categories of search are simplified to: coastal searches only, no search, and other areas of search, then a significant difference is found (calculated $\chi^2$ 7.25; $\chi^2$ (df = 2; $p = 0.05$), 5.99).

This association is corroborated by the differences in the areas of search by the social class of the (sometimes subsequently deceased) household head at the time of the move. Forty-two per cent of those in social classes I and II had searched only in coastal areas compared to 50 per cent of those in other classes, and the former were more likely to have searched only in inland areas and

Table 3.8 Areas of search and the educational attainment of the pre-retirement household head

| | Educational attainment | | | | | |
|---|---|---|---|---|---|---|
| | No qualifications or no more than 'A' level | | | Academic or vocational qualifications beyond 'A' level | | |
| Areas of search | No. | % | % | No. | % | % |
| Coastal areas only | 51 | 63.1 | 50.0 | 29 | 44.6 | 39.2 |
| Inland areas only | 9 | 11.1 | 8.8 | 11 | 16.9 | 14.9 |
| Coastal and inland areas | 10 | 12.4 | 9.8 | 11 | 16.9 | 14.9 |
| Around pre-retirement home (and elsewhere) | 8 | 9.8 | 7.8 | 9 | 13.8 | 12.2 |
| Abroad (and elsewhere) | 3 | 3.7 | 2.9 | 5 | 7.7 | 6.8 |
| SUB-TOTALS | 81 | 100.1[a] | 79.3 | 65 | 99.9[a] | 88.0 |
| No search | 21 | | 20.6 | 9 | | 12.2 |
| TOTALS | 102 | | 99.9[a] | 74 | | 100.2[a] |

[a]Rounding error.

The percentage distribution of types of search is given for all respondents in the third and sixth columns, and for those respondents who reported an active search in the second and fifth columns.

abroad. There were, however, only negligible differences among the social classes in the proportion not undertaking a search.

Some of the clearest differences in the geographical character of the search occurred in relation to the age of retirement of the household head and the social connections with the eventual retirement area. By and large those who retired at younger ages were more likely to have searched inland and more widely, and less likely not to have made an effective search. For example 28 per cent of those who retired before they reached 65 years of age searched in inland areas, compared to 18 per cent of older retirees. Later retirement was associated with no search, for 23 per cent of the older group fell in this category compared to 15 per cent of those under 65 years of age at retirement. These differences are probably interrelated with those arising from the presence or absence of relatives or friends in the eventual retirement area. Of those without such links, only 6 per cent did not undertake a comparative search compared to 25 per cent of those who knew people in the area. Conversely 37 per cent of those without connections searched in inland areas compared to 16 per cent of those with friends and relatives in the retirement area (Table 3.9). The differences between the two groups were highly significant according to a chi-squared test (calculated $\chi^2$ 31.6; $\chi^2$ (df $= 5; p = 0.001$), 20.5). The actual geography of a household's search was much influenced by the location of its origin and an accessibility effect. The people we interviewed in Dorset had predominantly searched along the south coast and few had considered northern regions of England. A similar emphasis upon adjacent holiday areas was

Table 3.9 Areas of search and social connections with the eventual retirement area

| | Relatives or friends in the retirement area | | | | | |
|---|---|---|---|---|---|---|
| | None | | Some | | Total | |
| Areas of search | No. | % | No. | % | No. | % |
| Coastal areas only | 33 | 42.3 | 56 | 45.9 | 89 | 44.5 |
| Inland areas only | 12 | 15.4 | 12 | 9.8 | 24 | 12.0 |
| Coastal and inland | 17 | 21.8 | 8 | 6.6 | 25 | 12.5 |
| Around pre-retirement home (and elsewhere) | 6 | 7.7 | 11 | 9.0 | 17 | 8.5 |
| Abroad (and elsewhere) | 5 | 6.4 | 4 | 3.3 | 9 | 4.5 |
| SUB-TOTAL | 73 | 93.6 | 91 | 74.6 | 164 | 82.0 |
| No search | 5 | 6.4 | 31 | 25.4 | 36 | 18.0 |
| TOTAL | 78 | 100.0 | 122 | 100.0 | 200 | 100.0 |

reported by the people interviewed in North Wales from Greater Manchester, although relatively more interest was found in distant areas, explained by the climatic and environmental attractions of southern England.

The accumulated results point to a clear distinction between the limited searches of single-person migrant households and the relatively extensive searches of married-couple (plus others) households. Of the 33 single, widowed and divorced households before the migration, 26 made no search or one confined to coastal areas, and only 4 (12 per cent) searched inland, compared to 41 (28 per cent) of the 149 married-couple (plus others) households. The majority of the single-person households were widows who were moving to strengthen by greater proximity a social link, and who made relatively attenuated searches which concentrated upon traditional coastal areas. Retirement migration among couples more frequently involved inland and more diverse searches, and was less influenced by the locations of friends and relatives. The long-term increase in life expectancy therefore has important implications, for it decreases the probability of widowhood at retirement age and this promotes the ability of the household to contemplate a move in search of environmental improvement rather than proximity to family. It is one factor producing a wider dispersal of relatively affluent old people, which in turn leads to concern about the extent to which migrants will be able to respond to bereavement or declining health by later moves either towards family support or to urban areas with superior health and social services.

Strong reasons exist, therefore, to study the trends in the destinations of retirement migration, but some suggestive evidence can be found from our cross-sectional survey by comparing the searches of older and younger people in the sample. These are taken to approximate respectively the less and the more recent retirement migrations. While their searches were similar in several respects, 20 per cent of the younger group (aged less than 70 years at the time of survey) had searched exclusively in inland areas compared to only 8 per cent of the older group. This difference was made up almost equally by the greater frequency among the older group in those making no search whatsoever, and by those searching exclusively in coastal areas. Admittedly this finding could be the result of the selection of inland areas for the survey, but as five separate locations around Shaftesbury in Dorset were used, it is reasonable evidence of the increase in interest in rural areas and provides support for Lemon's (1973) early observations in East Anglia.

### Information sources

When asked how they acquired information about the property to which they moved, the majority of the respondents referred to estate agents: 14 per cent said that they learnt that the property was for sale by the agent's board at the address, and 42 per cent were directed to the property by an agent's list. Just over a quarter acquired the information from relatives, friends or other personal acquaintances and one in eight found the property through newspaper small advertisements. The use of newspapers was positively related and of personal sources of information negatively related to the size of the household. For example, while one-person households rarely used newspapers, over one-fifth of three-plus-person households found their new home through this medium (Table 3.10).

There were marked differences in the information sources according to the type and tenure of the retirement property. Of the 22 respondents who took a privately rented house, bungalow, or flat as their first retirement home, 14 (64 per cent) did so after receiving information from a personal source, and only 3 made use of newspapers or estate agents' boards. On the other hand, for those moving into owner-occupied property, personal sources of information applied in only one-fifth of the cases (although in 6 of the 16 flat purchases), and in 102 (60 per cent) of the 171 cases information was received from estate agents, a quarter of these after identifying a vacancy by the agent's board at the address.

While no strong or readily interpretable relationships were found between the information source and social class, terminal educational age, or educational attainment, it was not surprising to find that the reliance on information from persons beyond the household was inversely related to the size of the pre-retirement household, and positively related both to the number of friends and relatives known in the eventually chosen retirement area and to the extent of previous acquaintance with the retirement area.

Broadly it appeared that while most migrants were ready to exploit all the common sources of information about property vacancies, the evinced variations in use of local newspapers, national newspapers, or estate agents reflected both their local availability and the individual's access to them. For example, people moving from London made most use of national and evening newspapers, whereas those moving from Manchester (mainly to North Wales)

Table 3.10 Sources of information for the new property by size of household

| | Persons in household | | | | | | | |
|---|---|---|---|---|---|---|---|---|
| | One | | Two | | Three or more | | All | |
| Source of information | No. | % | No. | % | No. | % | No. | % |
| Newspapers | 2 | 6.9 | 16 | 12.5 | 7 | 21.9 | 25 | 13.2 |
| Estate agents' lists | 12 | 41.4 | 52 | 40.6 | 15 | 46.9 | 79 | 41.8 |
| Agents' sign at address | 5 | 17.2 | 19 | 14.8 | 2 | 6.3 | 26 | 13.8 |
| Personal | 10 | 34.5 | 35 | 27.3 | 7 | 21.9 | 52 | 27.5 |
| Other | 0 | 0.0 | 6 | 4.7 | 1 | 3.1 | 7 | 3.7 |
| ALL | 29 | 100.0 | 128 | 99.9 | 32 | 100.1 | 189 | 100.0 |

most frequently cited personal sources—reflecting the long-established 'chain' of migrations in this direction. Migrant households without cars were more likely than car-owning households to have found their retirement home after receiving information from a personal source.

The availability of information about property vacancies was rarely a restriction on retirement migration. On the other hand in few cases did we discover a person who impressed us by the energy and thoroughness of their search. Where the pre-retirement household could exploit personal sources of information, these were clearly valued and heavily drawn upon. A least-effort principle was strongly operating in most cases; but most households drew information eclectically: certainly a comparison of properties and residential areas was much more common than a comparison of retirement areas. We found, in short, little support for the view that the selection of a migration destination area follows an elaborate comparative evaluation of place utilities (except perhaps at any early stage and in a subjective, inexplicit, and frequently ill-informed manner) but much evidence that property utilities and costs are compared, both between prospective homes and with the existing home.

### The influence of the location of children and relatives

The role of children in some aspects of the destination decision has already been raised. When asked the main reason for moving, 21 per cent of the respondents stated that it was to be nearer children or friends. However only 12 per cent said that this was the main advantage of the first retirement district over the pre-retirement location, even though 60 per cent said that some of their family or friends lived in the retirement area. For a minority, therefore, the move fulfilled a desire to be closer to children, relatives, or friends, while for a larger number this was said to be one advantage among others. It should be remembered that our sample was of a relatively healthy, independent, and young elderly group.

Some replies from the matched sample of 100 non-movers reinforce the importance of this factor in choosing a location for retirement. Forty-nine had considered moving upon retirement, a quarter giving as their main reason the wish to be near friends, relatives, and children. It emerged even more strongly, however, from the main reasons for *not* moving, for 22 said that they wished to remain near their children, and another 33 near to friends and relatives. Objective support for the importance of the proximity of children and relatives as a restraint on retirement migration came from a classification of their locations. Exactly one-half of the non-mover households said that the majority of their close family or one or more children were living in the same area as themselves, and one-fifth without such strong ties had relative(s) living in the area.

It has already been seen that where children or relatives lived in the eventually chosen retiremen area, they influenced the search. They often provided information about property vacancies and led to a more restricted (but perhaps intensive) search in their area of residence (Table 3.9). It appears that two groups were most influenced by family and friends in their choice of retirement location; unmarried, widowed or divorced single-person households seeking the proximity of relatives, friends, or children; and those married couples who enjoyed strong links with their children. Conversely it was those married couples without children or with weak family relationships that were least guided by the locations of children, relatives, or friends.

Other studies have confirmed the widespread residential proximity among the general population of elderly people and their children, revealed a substantial demand among the elderly to move nearer to their children, and indicated that such proximity is frequently associated with levels of family support that are essential if the elderly persons are not to require residential care (Hunt, 1978; DOE Housing Development Directorate (DOEHDD), 1976). Valuable studies are now in progress to find ways of facilitating moves by elderly people, often between tenures, so that they may live nearer the relatives willing to assist them (DOEHDD, 1980). Little information is available, however, on the trends in either family support, or the relative locations of parents and children. The last 30 years have brought a decline in average family size, a rapid lowering of the median age at which the last child is born, and clear trends towards more independent and careerist lifestyles among young people. Some improvement in the health and income of people at retirement age may be contributing to greater separation of the generations, in terms of both distance and the strength of contact. Contrary influences arise from increased holidays, reduced working hours, increased car ownership, and improved roads, all of which may be easing the restraints upon visiting or providing support. The variables to be considered are numerous and the diversity of practice is immense, but this subject is well worth much more intensive study from a geographical perspective, not just because of its implications for retirement housing but more generally for its importance in the quality and satisfaction of life among old people. As elaborated in the introductory chapter, a strong case can be made for initiating the study of the social geography of consanguinity, not only from the perspective of the welfare of the elderly but also to consider all inter-generational relationships and mutual support including such issues as the family sources of childcare and the support for mothers with young children and its interrelationship with the difficulties surrounding the entry of women into gainful employment and the quality of childcare.

## Geographical experience and the character of the search

Finally the destination decision is considered in relation to the earlier formation of geographical awareness and experience. Specific attention was given to the influences of a household's previous residential locations and mobility, its areas of holidaymaking and other connections with the retirement area. The area of childhood residence appears to have been of only weak influence on the selection of a destination area, for only 17 (8.5 per cent) of the 201 movers reported such a link, and in only 3 cases did more than one household member share the childhood link with the retirement area. Residence in the retirement area during working life was only slightly more common, being true for 12 (6 per cent) of the household heads at retirement and for 8 (4 per cent) of the second members of the households. This is in great contrast to the prevailing pattern in France, for Cribier's study of 265 retired households throughout France that had left Paris between 1970 and 1972 found that

> 43 per cent had returned to the region of origin of one of the spouses (including the 14 per cent of cases where husband and wife were both returning to their region of origin). 31 per cent gave this as the only reason for their departure from Paris, and most were now living in their native commune.... It is interesting to note that the retired people who wish to return to their areas or origin are most prevalent in the lower range of the social scale and among those born in rural areas (Cribier, 1979, p. 34; and Chapter 5 of this book).

Much more common among the British sample was a connection with the retirement area through holidays. A quarter of the sample claimed to have known the retirement area very well through seven or more visits, and conversely only one-fifth claimed no previous knowledge of the area before the retirement migration (Table 3.11). Of the mover sample 21 per cent said that they knew only one holiday area well through repeated visits; 32 per cent reported widely dispersed and varied holiday areas, and a further 30 per cent named three British areas that they knew well through holidays. A little less than 10 per cent of the sample reported negligible holiday experience. A holiday acquaintance with an area appears in most cases to have been a necessary rather than a sufficient condition of retirement residence. Within an individual's set of past holiday

Table 3.11 Holiday and social connections with the retirement area before migration (percentages)

| Holiday connections | | Social contacts | |
|---|---|---|---|
| None | 19.4 | None resident in the area | 39.3 |
| Up to three visits | 31.4 | Acquaintances only | 3.0 |
| Three to six visits | 14.9 | One plus friends | 24.9 |
| Seven or more visits | 24.9 | One plus relatives | 20.9 |
| Business or children's schools | 2.0 | One plus children | 5.0 |
| Second home or fixed caravan | 6.5 | Majority of close family | 7.0 |
| Other/no response | 1.0 | | |
| Number of respondents | 201 | Number of respondents | 201 |

areas, other influences operate in the selection of a retirement destination. The relative importance of such factors as earlier residence, the location of friends and relatives, or accessibility to children and other relatives varies in each case, but in aggregate there is a clear regional or distance decay effect. Migrants from Greater Manchester tended to favour northern and Welsh coastal areas, while those from the London metropolitan region tended to confine their searches south-east of a line between The Wash and the Bristol Channel. A pronounced metropolitan sectoral effect can also be shown, with East Anglia being considered particularly by residents of north-east London, and the Londoners among our respondents in Dorset having predominantly originated from the intermediate and peripheral southern and western suburbs of the London metropolitan region. Sectoral influences on the retirement migration search space would act both directly and indirectly through the leisure and holiday-trip pattern. Another influence on the awareness space is the location of relatives and friends who are visited. While only 14 respondents said that the majority of their close family were living in the retirement area, another 10 had children in the area, and a further 42 had relatives in the area. Others had acquaintances, friends, and relatives and only 39 per cent claimed no social connections with the retirement area (Table 3.11). While three-fifths of the sample claimed not to have been aware of others who had migrated for retirement, nearly three-tenths knew one or more households who had moved to the retirement area.

A simple model of the changing distribution of the destinations of retirement migrants can be posited from a comparison of French and English evidence. In the later stages of a period of rapid demographic urbanization involving substantial rural–urban migration, and for a generation or more afterwards, retirement migrations include many conservative, return migrations to widely dispersed rural destinations. This phase was weakly represented in Britain because it (*c.* 1870–1930) was a period of little affluence, relatively low life expectancy, restricted mobility, and political and economic disruption.

Later, as the urban population's connections with rural areas fade, retirement migration is guided more by innovatory motives connected with a widened search for improved residential environments. This tends to concentrate destinations on locations favoured either for their climatic attractions or for more general environmental reasons. In Britain this second phase of focused searches (*c.* 1930–70) was strongly represented by the retirement migrations to the coastal resorts nearest to each metropolitan area, although atypically extended migrations into Devon and Cornwall were also evident. This concentrated phase ends when a renewed widening of the destinations takes place. It is replaced, with the more affluent groups in the vanguard of change, by more varied searches in inland, rural, more distant, and more remote areas. The change is stimulated either by the increased mobility of the population as car ownership spreads or simply by the increasing scale of retirement migration.

This can be related to the transience of exceptional residential desirability, for this place characteristic often generates the instruments of its own destruction. Not only does a high demand for property raise local prices but in general there is an inverse relationship between the intensity of residential development and the attractiveness of an area for retirement. In Britain this third phase (*c*. 1970– ) is now well established as many residents from the northern regions of Britain move to South-West England, and areas such as north Northumberland and north Norfolk have become popular. It is also represented on a larger scale in the United States with interior destinations such as the Ozark hills now popular foci for retirement migration. In France lower income groups still demonstrate strong return migration while more affluent groups tend to a more varied search in environmentally attractive areas.

In the terms of this simple model, the evolution of the distribution of retirement migration destinations in a specific country will be affected by the relative timing of urbanization and its associated rural–urban migration, of the improvement of personal standards of life in old age, of the pace of residential development and development control in the most attractive environmental areas of a country, and of the spread of private means of travel. In Britain, the remote rural ancestry of the population, the growing affluence of people at retirement age, the relative rigour of development control in attractive areas, and the high level of car ownership are important factors promoting the current widening of the distribution of destinations.

## CHANGING DESTINATIONS AND PLANNING POLICY

Our description of the residential search has been based on a household survey of contemporary retirement migrants. All the migrants that we interviewed were born before the First World War and their formative years were in the first half of the present century. More than younger people, they lived in nucleated urban areas and had limited leisure travel patterns which were constrained by railway routes. It is also possible that these cohorts include a higher proportion of single people, partly reflecting the loss of men during the First World War and partly a lower rate of marriage. It is important to emphasize the distinct characteristics of each cohort since they are likely to influence both expectations and spatial behaviour in retirement. Since the 1950s the population of the conurbations and other large urban areas has been falling and an increased proportion of each succeeding middle-class cohort has settled in smaller towns and villages in or beyond the metropolitan fringes where they have enjoyed the benefits of non-industrial environments and pursued suburban lifestyles dependent on the motor car. Their holidays have become longer and more varied as repeated annual visits to neighbouring coastlines have tended to be supplemented and replaced by holidays in other regions of Britain and abroad.

The implications of these trends for retirement migration are not necessarily consistent. Some potential retirement migrants will have found desirable residential areas during their working life and feel little desire to move at retirement, while for others greater travel experiences will have heightened their appreciation of different environments and encouraged a move at retirement. The latter is believed to be more common as shown by our finding that the most recent retirement migrants are particularly discriminating in their choice between and within regions.

Our survey has also drawn attention to the differences in search patterns and behaviour between single-person households and married couples. Succeeding generations are more likely to have been married and declines in age-specific mortality have and will continue to reduce widowhood at pensionable age. The recent increase in divorce and re-divorce may in the long term lead to an increase in the number of single-person households at retirement age. Although single-person households are more likely than married couples to be influenced in their destination choice by other people, we have little evidence of a relationship between living arrangements and the spatial patterns of retirement migration. It is, however, mainly married couples who are choosing innovative destinations by moving to remote and formerly inaccessible places.

During the next 25 years the number of people reaching retirement age will fall, reflecting the low birth rate of the inter-war period and during the Second World War. In a previous paper we argued that the percentage of the age group moving at retirement is likely to increase because the characteristics which promote migration are increasing in the population (Law and Warnes, 1980a). These characteristics include greater lifetime mobility, greater home ownership, earlier retirement, and the more widespread location of children. This suggests that in spite of a falling age group the numbers moving at retirement will remain the same or increase. The great majority will of course continue to move relatively short distances (Golant, 1977).

The spatial origins of migrants are also likely to be stable. The London Region (rather than the London conurbation) is likely to remain the main source for retirement migrants, as a result of its concentrations of higher income groups, occupationally and geographically mobile population, and the incentive to leave produced by its atypically high house-prices. Like Parisians in France, Londoners already search more widely than migrants from other parts of the country, and this results in their selection of more distant areas. However their search still concentrates in southern and eastern England and neglects midland and northern areas. In contrast midland and northern retirement migrants appear recently to have broadened their search beyond the traditional resorts within easy reach of their new home areas. This has increased the pressure upon the South-West at the expense of such areas as the Lancashire and Yorkshire coasts and North Wales.

The movement of retired people overseas is likely to increase, encouraged by easier movements of capital, and wider holiday and work experience in

Europe. Recent newspaper articles suggest that many of those who have chosen to retire abroad, particularly in southern Europe, have previously experienced residence overseas. However for reasons related to culture and distance, we do not expect this to become a dominant feature of British retirement migration.

The favoured retirement areas of southern and eastern England, and particularly the South-West, are likely to come under increasing pressure for the development of retirement housing. These areas are attractive because of their perceived unspoilt environments and good climates, but continued expansion may pose problems for the provision of services and the maintenance of these good environments. Already some authorities, like Worthing, have refused to sanction more nursing homes, although this is unlikely to deter the newly retired and fit migrant. Elsewhere, as in Torbay, a strict limit has been placed on expansion to protect the physical environment. As a result retired migrant flows have been redirected to inland villages, which while suitable for the physically fit retired person often lack services for the disabled elderly.

There is a need for comprehensive planning in these areas which takes into account not just the short-term requirement for housing land but also the implications of the ageing of the retired population for specialist housing and social, nursing, and medical facilities. The prudent and realistic policy developed by some counties, to concentrate retirement settlement into larger villages or towns where services and facilities can be provided, should be more widey adopted and strengthened as far as the limited powers of development control allow. Two important elements of this strengthening would be the closer liaison of local authority planning, housing and social service departments, and the stimulus and education of private sector enterprise to anticipate and meet the demands of an ageing elderly population. If planning officers learn more of the huge demands made by elderly people on the housing and social service departments, and if they understand the problems faced by elderly, single-person households, they will be better able to co-ordinate, inform, and improve private and public sector development for elderly people.

## ACKNOWLEDGEMENTS

The research leading to this chapter was supported by the Social Science Research Council. During its course we received valuable assistance from the County Council Planning Departments of Clwyd and Gwynedd and the South-East Dorset Structure Plan Study Team at Bournemouth. The authors wish to thank Mrs Barbara Rough, the third member of the project team, for bringing her sociological knowledge and perspective to the research. We benefited at all stages from her suggestions, insights, and enthusiasm for the work. We also thank warmly Miss Bridget O'Donnell, Miss Sandra Lapsky and Mrs Joy Barnett for their typing and secretarial assistance at King's College.

## REFERENCES

Barrett, F. (1976). The search process in residential location. *Environment and Behavior*, **8**, 169–98.

Beaver, M. L. (1979). The decision making process and its relationship to relocation adjustment in old people. *Gerontologist*, **19**, 567–74.

Brown, L. A. and Gilliard, R. S. (1981). Towards a development paradigm of migration with particular reference to Third World settings. In DeJong, D. F. and Gardner, R. W. (eds), *Migration Decision Making*. Pergamon, Oxford (forthcoming).

Cribier, F. (1979). Des Parisiens se retirent en province: une étude de géographie sociale. *Gérontologie et Société*, **8**, 18–68.

Department of the Environment, Housing Development Directorate (DOEHDD) (1976). *Housing the Elderly: How Successful are Granny Annexes?* DOEHDD, London.

DOEHDD (1980). *Housing the Elderly Near Relatives: Moving and Other Options*. DOEHDD Occasional Paper 1/80. HMSO, London.

Glyn-Jones, A. (1975). *Growing Older in a South Devon Town*. University of Exeter, Exeter.

Golant, S. M. (1977). Spatial context of residential moves by elderly persons. *International Journal of Aging and Human Development*, **8**, 279–89.

Hunt, A. (1978). *The Elderly at Home*. HMSO, London.

Karn, V. A. (1974). Retiring to the Seaside: a Study of Retirement Migration in England and Wales. PhD thesis, University of Birmingham, Birmingham.

Karn, V. A. (1977). *Retiring to the Seaside*, Routledge & Kegan Paul, London,

Law, C. M. and Warnes, A. M. (1973). The movement of retired people to seaside resorts: a study of Morecambe and Llandudno. *Town Planning Review*, **44**, 373–90.

Law, C. M. and Warnes, A. M. (1976). The changing geography of the elderly in England Wales. *Transactions of the Institute of British Geographers*, New series, **1**, 453–71.

Law, C. M. and Warnes, A. M. (1977). *The Migration Decisions of Individuals at Retirement*. Final report to the Social Science Research Council, HR 3717.

Law, C. M. and Warnes, A. M. (1980a). The characteristics of retired migrants. In Herbert, D. T. and Johnston, R. J. (eds), *Geography and the Urban Environment*, vol. III pp. 175–222. Wiley, Chichester.

Law, C. M. and Warnes, A. M. (1981). Planning and retirement migration. *Town and Country Planning*, **50**, 44–6.

Lemon, A. (1973). Retirement and its effect on small towns. *Town Planning Review*, **44**, 254–62.

Murie, A. (1974). *Household Movement and Household Choice*. Occasional Paper 28, Centre for Urban and Regional Studies, University of Birmingham, Brimingham.

Rossi, P. H. (1980). *Why Families Move*, 2nd edn. Sage, Beverly Hills.

Geographical Perspectives on the Elderly
Edited by A. M. Warnes


Chapter 4

# The elderly in Northern Ireland with special reference to the city of Belfast

*Paul A. Compton* and *Russell C. Murray*

This chapter falls into two distinct but complementary sections. In the first part we concern ourselves with the elderly in Northern Ireland as a whole, their changing numbers through time, and their geographical distribution. Although one would expect many of the broad trends apparent in the rest of Britain also to be evident in Northern Ireland, significant divergences might also be expected due to the Province's distinctive demography dominated by emigration and a higher birth rate than in the rest of the country. In the second part of the chapter the position of the elderly in the Belfast urban area is examined in greater detail. Advantage is taken of the flexibility offered by the 1971 census to assess the degree of heterogeneity displayed by the population aged 60 and over with respect to spatial distribution, social composition and housing. An assessment is made of the extent to which the elderly form a special group within the city, generating their distinctive needs for the provision of facilities.

While a case can be argued for adopting a functional definition of the elderly, combining the two concepts of age and economic dependence, a more practical and convenient definition, certainly in terms of the analysis presented in this chapter, is one based solely on age. In this respect we had three clear choices: to define the elderly as the population of pensionable age (65 years for men and 60 for women), or as the population aged 65 years and over, or as the population aged 60 years and over. Our preference was to adopt the population aged 60 years and over as it avoids the difficulty of combining males and females of different ages. It also includes all the population of pensionable age, which the group aged 65 and over does not, as well as embracing the years immediately preceding male statutory retirement age when preparations for the impending retirement and changed lifestyle are being made. It is, however, useful to distinguish between the 'young' elderly and the 'old' elderly, the lower limit of the latter age group being taken as 75 years. It is around the age of 75 that the proportion of widowed persons first exceeds one-half of the total, an important threshold because at older ages the proportion of elderly one-person households rapidly increases with all the concomitant health and social problems. It is also to around the age of 75 that half the population now survives.

## THE ELDERLY IN NORTHERN IRELAND

### General considerations

General population growth and increasing longevity have generated a secular rise in the number of elderly not only in the British Isles but throughout the developed world. Moreover, low and declining birth rates have generated a faster expansion of the elderly component than of the population at large, with the result that the number of elderly as a proportion of the total population has risen steadily during the last few decades. The evolution of the age composition of the population of Northern Ireland conforms with these general trends. The number of people aged 60 and over rose from 145,000 in 1926, the year of the first Northern Ireland census, to 238,000 in 1971, an increase of just under two-thirds, while the number of 75-year-olds and over increased somewhat more strongly by around four-fifths during the same period (Figure 4.1). Compared with Great Britain, however, where the number of people over the age of 60 expanded more than two-fold, the advance of the elderly in Northern Ireland has been modest.

As elsewhere, the number of elderly females in Northern Ireland has risen substantially faster than has the number of males, a difference that becomes more strongly developed with advancing age. It is also clear that whereas most

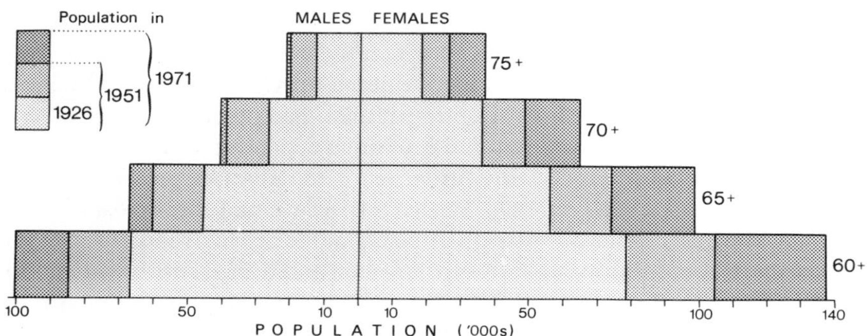


Figure 4.1 The number of elderly in Northern Ireland in 1926, 1951 and 1971 (number over the ages of 60, 65, 70 and 75). (*Source*: Government of Northern Ireland (1929, 1955); Northern Ireland General Register Office (1975).)

of the post-1926 advance in the number of elderly females has occurred since 1951, the bulk of the increase in the number of elderly males took place before 1951. Indeed the number of males over the age of 75 has remained virtually static for more than 25 years, although cohort analysis indicates that a substantial rise in the size of this group can be expected in the 1980s. The pattern of change for elderly females is thus one of accelerating growth, in which the rate of increase is a direct function of age. The elderly male population, on the other hand, grew more rapidly before than after 1951 at a rate which, unlike that of females, has tended to vary inversely with age.

The relative outcome of these changes is summarized in Figure 4.2. Overall

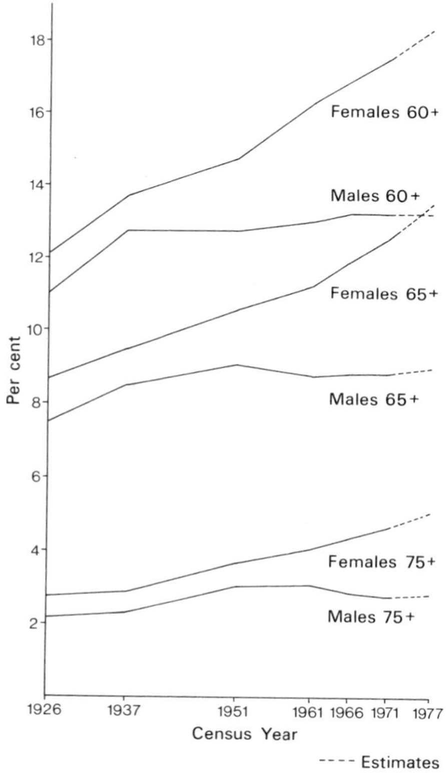


Figure 4.2 Change in the proportion of elderly people in Northern Ireland, 1926–77 (per cent over the ages of 60, 65 and 75). (*Source*: Government of Northern Ireland (1929, 1940, 1955, 1965, 1968); Northern Ireland General Register Office (1975).)

the elderly now comprise 15.5 per cent of the population of Northern Ireland compared with 11.5 per cent in 1926. Amongst females, the elderly make up 18 per cent of the total compared with 12 per cent in 1926, while the proportion aged 75 and over now stands at 5 per cent. By contrast, the proportion of elderly males, at around 13 per cent, has remained almost static, while the proportion over the age of 75 has in fact declined in recent years. The outcome of these changes has been a steady expansion of the elderly female surplus to a position where there are now more than 1300 females for every 1000 males in the over-60 age group, rising to more than 1450 per 1000 amongst those aged 75 and over. In marked contrast to this trend, the female surplus in the general population has fallen at each successive census since 1926.

The widening sex bias in mortality and in elderly life expectancy has clearly played an important role in bringing about the absolute changes discussed here, particularly the substantial increase in the number of elderly females. Taking age 65 for example, female life expectancy has improved markedly, rising from 12.7 years in 1926 to 15.3 years in 1977. By contrast, the life expectancy of the average 65-year-old male was 11.8 years in 1977, one-tenth of a year less than in 1926, and this lack of improvement, even regression, in life expectancy explains in large part why the number of elderly males has remained practically static during the last 25–30 years.

In addition, although difficult to assess because of deficient information and problems with the interpretation of the data that are available, the impact of many decades of migration on the number of elderly in the Province cannot be ignored. According to the 1971 census there was a fairly substantial inflow of 2250 elderly persons over the age of 60 to the Province in the year preceding the enumeration. Females are recorded as outnumbering males in a ratio approximately 5 to 4, but since census methods of collection are more likely to understate elderly male than elderly female migration because of higher male mortality it is likely that there was near equality between the two. Such a substantial inflow, if maintained over a period, would augment significantly the number of elderly in Northern Ireland but the influx was clearly moderated by out-migration. It is in this regard that our data are most deficient for although reasonable estimates of total out-movement are published by the Registrar General of Northern Ireland, no information linking out-migration and age is available either from the census or any other source.

In the absence of this age breakdown it is difficult to assess with any degree of assurance the precise numerical impact of migration on the size of the elderly population of Northern Ireland. The residual technique does, however, provide a method of estimating net migration by age, and its application to the last inter-censal period suggests a small net in-movement of approximately 300 males and a more substantial net inflow of around 1000 females aged 60 and over between 9 October 1966 and 26 April 1971. On an annual basis this amounts to a total net inflow of approximately 300 elderly people and on the assumption that the gross in-movement recorded for the year preceding the census is accurate would suggest an annual gross outflow of around 2000 elderly persons in the early 1970s.

Although great care was taken in their derivation, net migration estimates obtained from the residual method are subject to an unknown degree of error, not least in this case because of unavoidable inaccuracies associated with the application of the method to 5-year age cohorts over a $4\frac{1}{2}$-year period of time. Yet, although there may be doubts about the precise numbers involved, it is reasonably clear that the net inflow of elderly people suggested for the period 1966–71 is real, and contrasts strongly with the persistent net outflow of younger population. This finding is strengthened by the fact that residual computations for the inter-censal periods 1951–61 and 1961–66 reveal a similar pattern of 'return' migration of the elderly. Although on a comparatively small scale, it may therefore be concluded that 'return' migration has played a role in augmenting the number of elderly in Northern Ireland in the recent past.

The proportion, as opposed to the number, of elderly in a population is determined not only by the demographic processes bearing directly on the elderly but also by those which affect the number of people in younger age groups. Stable population analysis shows the birth rate to be considerably more important than the level of mortality in this respect and the lower the birth rate over a period the higher the proportion of elderly in the population. The essential point in this case is that the birth rate of the population of Northern Ireland has traditionally been higher than elsewhere in the United Kingdom. As a result, the proportion of elderly in the Province is substantially lower than in either England and Wales or in Scotland. The marginally lower life expectancy in Northern Ireland would act as a contributory rather than major factor in bringing this about.

Migration, of course, has also played a role. Since 1971 net emigration from the Province has averaged around 11,000 per annum, two-thirds of which is contributed by young adults under the age of 30. As a consequence, the proportion of the population falling within this age range is lower than would be the case under conditions of no emigration, while the proportion at other ages tends to be higher. This is particularly so with the elderly where the relative gain due to the emigration of young adults is augmented by the 'return' migration of the elderly discussed earlier. In Northern Ireland therefore, while a moderately high birth rate in United Kingdom terms has generated a comparatively youthful population, migration has had the effect of increasing the proportion of the elderly.

Stable population analysis enables us to demonstrate the differing impacts of fertility and migration on the proportion of elderly in more precise terms. Four stable populations have been derived by combining current birth and death rates with three different assumptions about net migration. For the purpose of the analysis the age distribution of net migration is assumed to be the same as that estimated by the residual method for 1966–71; it is treated identically to mortality in the sense that net emigration reduces and net immigration augments the number surviving from one age to another.

The stable populations demonstrate the long-run implications of the various combinations of fertility, mortality, and migration on the assumption that the respective rates remain unchanged through time (Table 4.1). Stable population A, based on the 1976 level of natural increase, provides a good index of the long-term implications of current fertility. It is the most youthful of the four populations and contains the lowest proportion of elderly, a proportion, incidentally, similar to that recorded at the 1971 census even though fertility is now lower than at any time this century. Stable population B takes account of the return migration of the elderly and is very similar to population A. It clearly demonstrates that a net inflow of elderly, by itself, has only a marginal effect on the proportion of people aged 60 and over. By contrast, building the average emigration rate for the 1970s into the stable model raises the proportion of elderly by approximately one-third (populations C and D).

It may therefore be concluded that while the return migration of people over the age of 60 plays no more than a marginal role, substantial emigration

Table 4.1 The percentage of elderly derived from various stable populations by age group

| Stable population | Males | | Females | |
|---|---|---|---|---|
| | Over the age of 60 | Over the age of 75 | Over the age of 60 | Over the age of 75 |
| A | 13.0 | 2.7 | 17.2 | 5.0 |
| B | 13.2 | 2.8 | 17.5 | 5.2 |
| C | 17.5 | 4.1 | 21.4 | 7.0 |
| D | 18.0 | 4.3 | 22.0 | 7.4 |
| E | 9.2 | 1.7 | 12.0 | 3.2 |
| 1971 Census | 13.3 | 2.8 | 17.6 | 4.7 |

* The stable populations are based on the following assumptions about fertility, mortality, and migration:

A the 1976 schedules of fertility and mortality excluding migration;

B the 1976 fertility and mortality schedules: net immigration to the 60 and over age group amounting to 150 males and 350 females;

C the 1976 fertility and mortality schedules: net emigration amounting to 11,000 persons but zero migration balance for the over-60s;

D the 1976 fertility and mortality schedules: net emigration amounting to 11,000 persons but including net inflow of 150 males and 350 females over the age of 60;

E the 1976 mortality schedule and a fertility schedule consistent with crude birth rate of 22 per 1000 population in 1976.

at younger ages has a considerable impact on the proportion of elderly in Northern Ireland. The one question that remains to be answered is what proportion of elderly would now pertain if there had been no net emigration this century. Although this question cannot be answered unequivocally, the stable population derived from the mortality rates of 1976 in combination with a fertility schedule consistent with a crude birth rate of 22 per 1000 in 1976 (the average annual birth rate for the last 50 years), must provide a close approximation to this. In fact just over 10.5 per cent of this population (stable population E) is made up of individuals over the age of 60 compared with 15.5 per cent in 1971. In other words, in the absence of emigration it seems probable that the population of Northern Ireland would contain relatively one-third fewer elderly people than it does at present.

### The religious composition of the elderly

A marked denominational disparity in fertility and emigration rates has generated an older Protestant than Roman Catholic age structure, a difference that has become more, rather than less, pronounced with time. Whereas Protestants aged 60 and over were almost one-third more numerous in 1971 than in 1951, the number of elderly Catholics grew by less than half that amount (Table 4.2). In both communities there are now substantially more elderly females of all ages than in 1951. In strong contrast, the number of very old Protestant males has only risen marginally, while the number of Roman Catholic males aged 65 and over has actually declined. There is no firm evidence of significant mortality disparities between the two denominations and these differences must largely be a function of the traditionally higher Catholic emigration rate which, over many decades, has severely depleted the size of that community.

Because of the very high Roman Catholic birth rate, the disparity in relative numbers is even more marked, and in 1971 barely 12 per cent of Roman Catholics were over the age of 60 compared with 17 per cent of Protestants. Of even more significance, however, is the change that has taken place since 1951, for whereas the percentage of elderly Protestants has advanced substantially the proportion of elderly Catholics was marginally lower in 1971 than in 1951 because of a marked fall in the proportion of elderly Catholic males.

Since the percentage of elderly Protestants differs little from the proportion of elderly in the population of England and Wales, the lower overall proportion of elderly in Northern Ireland is clearly a function of the youthful age structure of Roman Catholics. It follows that while the Catholic population creates a greater proportionate demand for education, maternity, and other services required by the young, their need for the facilities demanded by the old is lower than the Protestant community's. Indeed the trends since 1951 mean that Protestants now generate three-quarters of the demand for services for

Table 4.2 The distribution of elderly by religious persuasion: Northern Ireland, 1951–71

| | Number in 1971 (hundreds) | | | | Percentage change 1951–71 | | | | Percentage of all-age population | | | | | | | |
|---|---|---|---|---|---|---|---|---|---|---|---|---|---|---|---|---|
| | Protestants | | Roman Catholics | | Protestants | | Roman Catholics | | Protestants | | | | Roman Catholics | | | |
| | Males | Females | Males | Females | Males | Females | Males | Females | Males | | Females | | Males | | Females | |
| | | | | | | | | | 1951 | 1971 | 1951 | 1971 | 1951 | 1971 | 1951 | 1971 |
| 60 and over | 70.8 | 98.2 | 29.3 | 38.9 | 22.7 | 36.0 | 6.6 | 21.2 | 13.2 | 15.2 | 15.7 | 19.6 | 12.0 | 10.6 | 13.3 | 13.6 |
| 65 and over | 47.5 | 70.5 | 19.7 | 27.8 | 16.0 | 37.2 | −0.4 | 21.6 | 9.3 | 10.2 | 11.1 | 14.1 | 8.6 | 7.1 | 9.5 | 9.7 |
| 70 and over | 28.6 | 46.3 | 12.2 | 18.3 | 9.1 | 38.4 | −5.1 | 22.1 | 6.0 | 6.1 | 7.3 | 9.3 | 5.6 | 4.4 | 6.2 | 6.4 |
| 75 and over | 14.8 | 26.2 | 6.6 | 10.1 | 6.1 | 43.4 | −4.2 | 25.9 | 3.2 | 3.2 | 4.0 | 5.2 | 3.0 | 2.4 | 3.3 | 3.5 |
| All ages | 466.4 | 500.1 | 175.8 | 286.7 | 6.4 | 8.4 | 20.1 | 18.6 | 100.0 | 100.0 | 100.0 | 100.0 | 100.0 | 100.0 | 100.0 | 100.0 |

*Source*: Census of Population, 1951 and 1971.

the elderly, although the relative increase in the number of Roman Catholics in the general population suggests that this trend will move into reverse during the next decade.

### Distribution of the elderly in Northern Ireland

The spatial distribution of the elderly broadly corresponds with that of the general population. They are, however, somewhat over-represented in rural areas, a feature that becomes accentuated with advancing age. For example, 38 per cent of the elderly aged 60 and over, and 40 per cent of those over the age of 75, lived outside the recognized towns in 1971, compared with 36 per cent of the population of all ages (Table 4.3). In addition, there are broad regional differences and the elderly are over-represented in the south-west and in parts of counties Antrim and Down, but are under-represented in the north-west and in mid-Ulster where families have traditionally been large and the birth rate high. Yet there is an important distinction to be made between the two sexes for the comparative concentrations of elderly in rural areas and

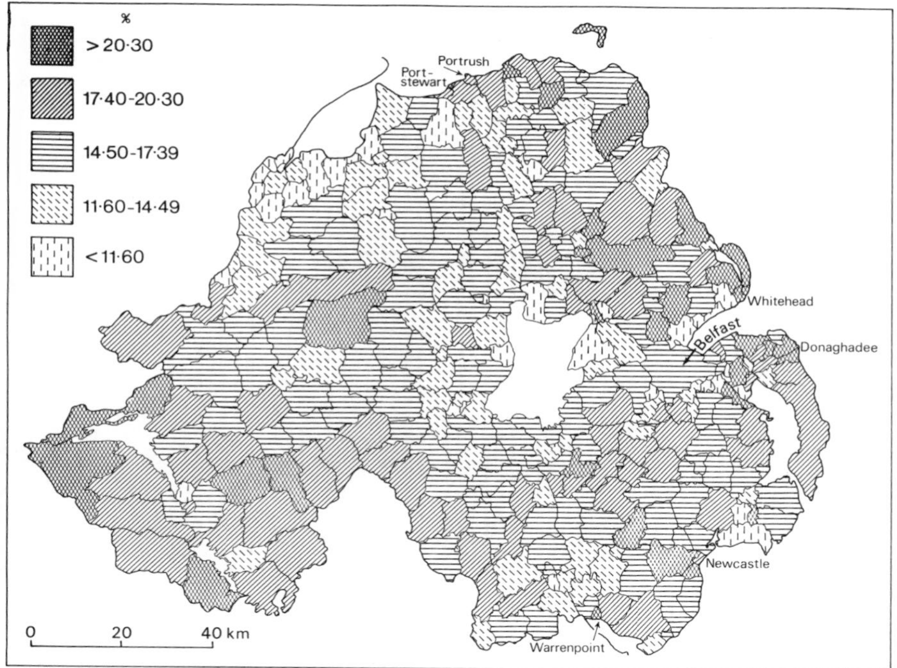


Figure 4.3 Distribution of the proportion of the population over the age of 60 in Northern Ireland in 1971. (*Source*: Northern Ireland General Register Office (1975).)

Table 4.3 Distribution of the elderly between rural and urban areas: Northern Ireland, 1971

| Age group | Population: Number (hundreds) | Population: Percentage in rural areas | Males: Number (hundreds) | Males: Percentage in rural areas | Females: Number (hundreds) | Females: Percentage in rural areas | Sex ratio: Urban areas | Sex ratio: Rural areas | Percentage of all-age population: Urban areas Males | Urban areas Females | Rural areas Males | Rural areas Females |
|---|---|---|---|---|---|---|---|---|---|---|---|---|
| 60 and over | 237.9 | 37.7 | 100.4 | 41.9 | 137.5 | 34.6 | 1542 | 1131 | 12.3 | 17.7 | 15.0 | 17.4 |
| 65 and over | 165.9 | 38.2 | 67.3 | 43.2 | 98.6 | 34.9 | 1677 | 1186 | 8.1 | 12.7 | 10.3 | 12.5 |
| 70 and over | 105.8 | 38.7 | 41.0 | 44.4 | 64.8 | 35.1 | 1848 | 1248 | 4.8 | 8.3 | 6.5 | 8.3 |
| 75 and over | 57.8 | 39.2 | 21.4 | 45.9 | 36.4 | 35.2 | 2033 | 1299 | 2.5 | 4.7 | 3.5 | 4.7 |
| All ages | 1,536.1 | 36.2 | 754.7 | 37.3 | 781.4 | 35.1 | 1071 | 976 | 100.0 | 100.0 | 100.0 | 100.0 |

*Source*: Census of Population, 1971.

in some regions of the Province is largely the result of an over-representation of elderly males (Table 4.3). The distribution of elderly females differs little from that of the population at large.

The percentage of people aged 60 and over in 1971 has been mapped in Figure 4.3 for each electoral ward. It reveals the intricacy of the spatial pattern of the elderly, including the high relative concentrations in many rural areas, especially in the south-west and in mid-Antrim where upwards of 20 per cent of the population were elderly. High percentages were also present in some of the small towns, notably the coastal resorts of Donaghadee, Newcastle, Portrush, Portstewart, Warrenpoint, and Whitehead. Together with parts of the north and east Antrim coast and most of the Ards Peninsula, these towns are the places most favoured for retirement migration. In addition, although the patterns are complex when examined in detail, as a general rule, the population of the towns and cities of the Province becomes progressively older as one moves from the suburban peripheries towards the urban cores. A simple grouping of urban places into inner core areas and surrounding suburbs revealed that over 20 per cent of the inhabitants of the inner areas were over the age of 60 in 1971 compared with no more than 10 per cent of the population living in the suburbs (Table 4.4). The areas in which the elderly form a substantially above-average proportion of the population can therefore be grouped into three main types, each distinguished by the processes that have brought about the comparatively high concentration. They are:

(1) inner districts of towns and cities,
(2) certain coastal resort towns with neighbouring rural areas, and
(3) certain rural agricultural communities.

The inner parts of the towns and cities constitute the oldest residential

Table 4.4 Distribution of elderly between urban cores and suburban peripheries: Northern Ireland, 1971

| | Percentage of all-age population | | | | Sex ratio | |
|---|---|---|---|---|---|---|
| | Urban cores | | Suburban peripheries | | | |
| Age group | Males | Females | Males | Females | Urban cores | Suburban peripheries |
| 60 and over | 16.9 | 24.2 | 8.9 | 12.7 | 1574 | 1478 |
| 65 and over | 11.2 | 17.4 | 5.8 | 8.9 | 1713 | 1593 |
| 70 and over | 6.6 | 11.3 | 3.4 | 5.8 | 1888 | 1759 |
| 75 and over | 3.3 | 6.4 | 1.7 | 3.2 | 2123 | 1937 |
| All ages | 100.0 | 100.0 | 100.0 | 100.0 | 1100 | 1031 |

*Source*: Census of Population, 1971, special tabulation.

districts from which the young and middle adult age population have tended to move, mostly to new housing areas in the suburban fringe. In consequence they are also areas of low fertility and few children. The elderly in these areas are therefore a residual community who have aged *in situ*. Nevertheless, they do participate in the removal to the suburbs but, for reasons such as inertia and low income, at a lesser rate than that of younger people. For instance, although the rate of elderly outflow from the inner parts of Belfast between 1966 and 1971 was less than half that of the general population, it still amounted to over 5000 people. In many inner parts of towns and cities it can therefore be the case that a high proportion of elderly comprises relatively few people in absolute terms. On the other hand, the reverse may be found in certain suburbs where a low proportion of elderly translates into substantial numbers. The situation in Belfast is discussed more fully in later sections.

The coastal resort towns and neighbouring rural areas, by contrast, contain both high absolute and relative numbers of elderly, mainly because of in-migration. In certain places, such as in Ballycastle, Donaghadee, Whitehead, and the rural areas of north and south Down, the elderly percentage is further augmented by a net outflow of younger people. They are also places where the birth rate is low and for this reason contain some of the highest proportions of elderly in the Province. A further variation is found in places such as Portrush, Portstewart, and Newcastle which receive a net inflow of both the elderly and people of working age. Although these places therefore have lower percentages, the absolute number of elderly is high.

Rural areas containing high proportions of elderly have all suffered from prolonged and heavy out-migration; the population of the south-west of the Province, for instance, is now less than one-third that enumerated in 1841. They also tend to be predominantly Protestant areas where fertility has traditionally been low. As with the inner districts of towns, their out-migration has involved population of all ages but unlike the urban case it has been highly selective of females, and their populations therefore contain high numbers and proportions of elderly males in strong contrast to inner urban areas where elderly females predominate. Although most rural communities of Roman Catholic complexion have comparatively low ratios of elderly people, there are exceptions. These are generally to be found in remote areas such as the Glens of Antrim and margins of the Mourne and Sperrin Mountains where the populations tend no longer to be demographically viable because of prolonged out-migration.

## THE ELDERLY IN BELFAST

We now turn to examine in greater detail the situation of old people in the Belfast urban area. This analysis will draw mainly on a set of special tabulations from the 1971 census covering all persons aged 60 and over. The emphasis in this section will be on variations amongst the elderly, by age and area, rather than on comparisons between the elderly and the rest of the population.

It is our contention that relatively little interest has been shown in the heterogeneity of old people. This is particularly important in the light of the growing problems of and for the elderly, particularly in the inner areas of cities (Association of Metropolitan Authorities, 1978; United States of America, White House Conference on Aging, 1971). The particular interest of the social geographer in this field is expressed by Kennedy and De Jong (1977):

> [An] interest in the residential distribution of the elderly in metropolitan communities stems in part from the social problems and policy implications of the possible emergence of ghettos of elderly. The general thesis is that within metropolitan regions the elderly population is more concentrated in the central city than in the suburbs, and within the central city, the elderly are segregated into certain sections of the city.

A large number of studies, mostly conducted in the USA, have investigated the residential distribution of the elderly in urban areas. Some have studied only one city at one point in time, while others have been longitudinal or comparative. All have demonstrated that the innermost areas of the city tend to have a high proportion of old people, the surrounding areas have the highest proportions, and the levels then fall away (more or less) steadily outwards. Over time, as a result both of the selective migration of younger people and of 'ageing in place' (Golant, 1972) proceeding against the background of general ageing, the levels in all the zones of a city tend to increase. This process may be more marked in the inner areas but the overall pattern is maintained in the absence of any widespread movement of the elderly.

The distribution of elderly people in the Belfast urban area in 1971 repeats the widespread pattern (Figure 4.4); the highest percentages are found not in the centre but in the adjacent pre-war suburbs of the city. These long-settled areas have a low turnover of population and their process of 'ageing in place' is accentuated by the predominantly middle-class population and the high quality of housing. This results in low levels of illness (such as bronchitis) and a higher life expectancy than in other areas (Boal, Doherty, and Pringle, 1974). The map also picks out high concentrations of the aged in the scattered centres of older towns now swallowed up by the growth of Belfast.

Table 4.5 Distribution of elderly in Belfast by area 1971 (as a percentage of the total population)

| | Inner city | Middle city | Suburbs | Total |
|---|---|---|---|---|
| Old people | 36.3 | 30.4 | 33.3 | 100 |
| All persons | 29.1 | 20.7 | 50.2 | 100 |

*Source*: Census of Northern Ireland, 1971.

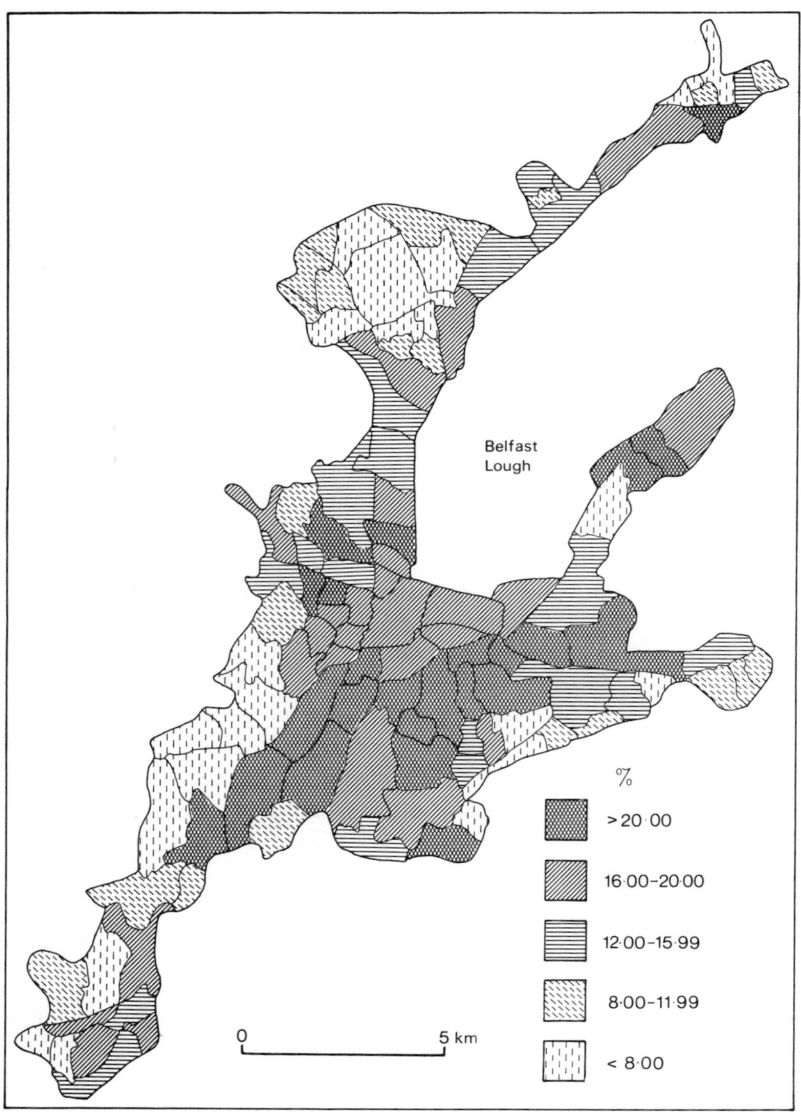


Figure 4.4 Distribution of the proportion of the population over the age of 60 in Belfast in 1971 (*Source*: Census of Population 1971, special tabulation.)

Temporal trends in the distribution of the elderly are hard to identify. The 1961 Census of Population employed an array of wards that was singularly unsuited to the study of essentially zonal patterns. Not only were they larger and more heterogeneous than in more recent censuses but many of them were elongated sectorally. Changes since 1971 can be studied with material from a 1978 sample survey (which interviewed approximately 1 household in 18, a total of 5066) carried out by the Northern Ireland Housing Executive which used the same wards as the 1971 Census (NIHE, 1979). Apart from its sample basis the main drawback to this study is that it was confined to the Belfast District Council area which comprises only 51 of the 113 wards that make up the urban area (Figure 4.4). The survey suggests that the proportion aged 60 years or more increased in 35 wards and decreased in the other 16; many of the changes, however, were within the range of the sampling error. In general, the increases tended to occur in the outer areas and the decreases towards the centre (Figure 4.5). It is often assumed that if the wards with the highest proportions of old people are found towards the centre of the city then this zone contains a high percentage of the elderly population, and that as the proportions

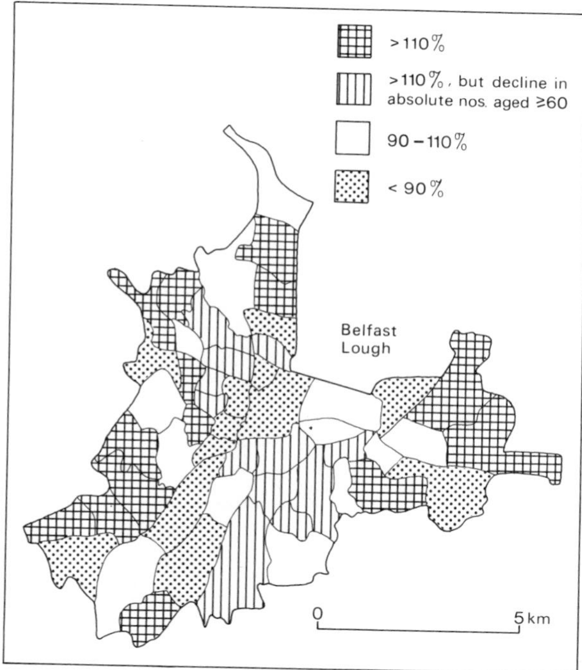


Figure 4.5 Percentage change in the elderly population proportion of Belfast District between 1971 and 1978. (*Source*: Northern Ireland Housing Executive (1979).)

rise in these wards so do the absolute numbers of old people. These twin beliefs underlie the concern expressed for the future problems of the elderly in the inner cities. It is important to stress that these conditions do not invariably occur but depend on a particular set of circumstances. We can examine the first for Belfast fairly simply by grouping the wards of the urban area into three groups on the basis of their predominant age and form of housing (Figure 4.6):

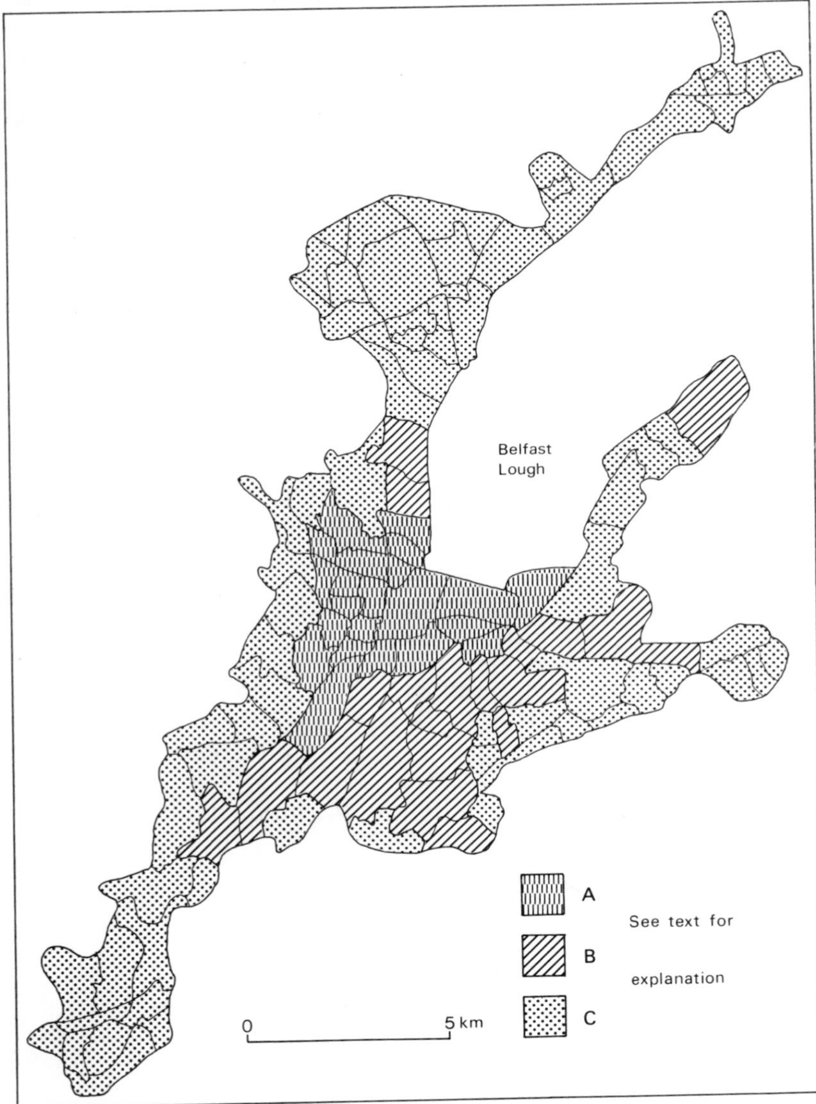


Figure 4.6 Inner, middle and outer city wards in Belfast

A inner city; predominantly nineteenth-century working-class terraced housing;

B middle city; mainly late nineteenth-century middle-class housing and pre-1945 twentieth-century housing;

C outer suburbs; mainly post-war housing, both public and private (but including some older settlements).

Table 4.5 shows what proportion of all old people (aged 65 and over) in the urban area, and of all persons, reside in each ward-group. The elderly were concentrated in the 'inner city' in comparison to the distribution of the population as a whole, but over-represented to a greater extent in the 'middle city'. Moreover, only slightly over one-third of the urban area's aged were in the inner city and nearly as many found in the peripheral suburban zone.

An increase in absolute numbers as the proportions in the wards rise only occurs if their populations remain roughly constant. Given the predominantly centrifugal migration flows of most cities this is unlikely to be the case. For example, Hiltner and Smith (1974) found that between 1940 and 1970 the proportion aged over 64 in the centre of Toledo rose from 10.7 per cent to 30.6 per cent but the absolute number in this age group increased by only 71. In Belfast many wards registered between 1971 and 1978 an increased proportion of people aged 60 or over, but these rises were often accompanied by decreases in their absolute numbers, particularly towards the centre of the city in wards which have been affected not only by redevelopment but also by the recent civil unrest and in the south-east of the city.

The second point made by Kennedy and De Jong concerning the distribution of the elderly is their segregation from the remainder of the population. Fears have been expressed that 'geriatric ghettos' may be created as a result of the out-migration of younger people. However, the fact that a ward has a high proportion of old people relative to other areas does not necessarily mean that its population is numerically dominated by them. An examination of the actual number of people of different ages in the various Belfast wards shows that the elderly are everywhere in a minority. For example, in the ward with the highest percentage of persons aged over 64 there were more children aged under 15 in 1971; these two age groups made up respectively 18.5 per cent and 20.6 per cent of the ward population. Even if all persons aged 60 or over are included there were, in 1971, only three wards in which the elderly constituted more than a quarter of the population.

The degree of segregation, measured at the scale of the wards, can be expressed quantitatively by means of the dissimilarity index (Duncun and Duncan, 1955). Table 4.6 presents dissimilarity indices calculated separately for the whole urban area and for the Belfast District Council area. This demonstrates that while the elderly are segregated from the rest of the population, this is to a much lesser degree than segregation by social class or religious denomination. Moreover, the NIHE survey suggests that the situation has changed little

Table 4.6 Dissimilarity indices by wards in Belfast, 1978

| | Populations compared | Area of study | Index |
|---|---|---|---|
| 1. | Persons aged 65 and over to the rest | Urban area | 21.5 |
| | | District Council area | 16.3 |
| 2. | Social class 1 to social classes 2–5 | Urban area | 43.4 |
| | | District Council area | 46.4 |
| 3. | Roman Catholics to other denominations | Urban area | 39.9 |
| | | District Council area | 43.8 |
| 4. | Persons aged 60 and over to the rest | 1971 District Council | 18.7 |
| | | 1978 District Council | 19.9 |

*Source*: Census of Northern Ireland, 1971; NIHE (1978).

since 1971. The index for all persons aged over 59 *versus* the rest of the population in Belfast District Council wards was 18.7 in 1971 and 19.9 in 1978. It may be that this relative lack of segregation at the ward level masks the presence of higher concentrations at a smaller scale.

This brief discussion of the residential distribution sets the scene for the more detailed analysis of the situation of the elderly within the Belfast urban area. The aims of this analysis are two-fold. First, to compare the characteristics and housing conditions of old people living in different residential environments. There is a tendency in discussions of the social geography of the elderly to concentrate on those living in the inner city. As we have seen, however, there are nearly as many old people living in the suburbs of Belfast as in the centre. Since the processes of residential location are not random it is reasonable to expect that there will be differences between the old who live in different areas. The second aim is to compare the characteristics and housing conditions of old people of different ages. In other studies of the elderly, particularly those of their health, marked differences have been found, particularly between the over-74s and the rest. As the proportion of the elderly in the population has increased, that of persons aged 75 years and over (mainly women) has risen most rapidly. In many aspects of social welfare, such as health or poverty, these 'old elderly' tend to be markedly worse off than the 'young elderly'. The first aim involves holding age constant and comparing areas; the second involves keeping area constant and comparing age groups within each area. In order to examine the characteristics of the elderly by age and area we obtained a special set of individual tabulations from the 1971 Census covering all persons aged 60 or over. Individuals were selected as the basic units of analysis in preference to households as providing a clearer measure of the relationship between age and other variables. For each individual, their age and their address was extracted from the Census records together with information on selected personal and housing characteristics. The first two variables were then categorized. Age was classified into three groups: 60–64; 65–74; 75 and over. The addresses were coded into the same system of three ward-groups described above (Figure 4.6).

The cross-tabulation of age and area yields Table 4.7. The composition of the elderly population does not show any marked differences between area; the middle city has the highest proportion of the 'old elderly' which is consistent with it containing the wards with the highest proportions of old people in general. It is difficult to generalize from this lack of variation in Belfast, for comparable studies have not disaggregated the elderly by age. Golant (1975) has suggested, however, that in future those aged over 74 will tend to move to metropolitan areas. It could be that the pattern observed for Belfast will prove to be characteristic of urban areas in areas such as the United Kingdom which have undertaken extensive urban redevelopment coupled with suburban public sector housing. The redistribution of population associated with these developments would tend to overcome the unwillingness or inability of elderly residents to relocate.

From the various tables generated by the three-way cross-tabulations of age, area, and the separate personal characteristics we have selected the information contained in Table 4.8. The three parts of this table, although each is of interest in its own right, were chosen to demonstrate three possible relationships. A variable, such as marital status, can vary by age but not by area. Conversely, as in the case of mobility, it can vary by area but not by age. Finally, the incidence of car ownership demonstrates variation by both age and area.

The personal variables, which included sex, social class, and employment status in addition to those in Table 4.8, were included in the analysis mainly to characterize the individuals, not to investigate any possible social issues. It should be noted, however, that even in the better-off wards outside the inner city most old people do not own a car and must therefore rely on public transport or the assistance of other people for trips beyond walking distance. The figures for mobility throw some light on our earlier observation (Table 4.7) concerning the even spatial spread of the elderly of different ages. They show that nearly one-third of all old people in the suburban wards had moved to

Table 4.7 Persons of different ages as a percentage of all elderly within each area: Belfast, 1971

| Age | Inner city | Middle city | Suburbs | All city |
|---|---|---|---|---|
| 60–64 | 32 | 30 | 34 | 32 |
| 65–74 | 47 | 46 | 46 | 46 |
| 75 + | 21 | 24 | 20 | 22 |
| All elderly | 100 | 100 | 100 | 100 |

*Source*: Census of Northern Ireland, 1971.

Table 4.8 Persons possessing certain personal attributes as a percentage of each age group by area: Belfast, 1971

| Age | Inner city | Middle city | Suburbs | All city |
|---|---|---|---|---|
| *A. Married* | | | | |
| 60–64 | 64 | 67 | 71 | 67 |
| 65–74 | 50 | 53 | 55 | 52 |
| 75 + | 28 | 32 | 29 | 30 |
| All aged | 50 | 52 | 55 | 52 |
| *B. Owning a car* | | | | |
| 60–64 | 21 | 53 | 49 | 39 |
| 65–74 | 13 | 38 | 36 | 27 |
| 75 + | 10 | 31 | 32 | 23 |
| All aged | 15 | 41 | 40 | 30 |
| *C. Moved since 1966* | | | | |
| 60–64 | 10 | 15 | 28 | 17 |
| 65–74 | 10 | 13 | 30 | 16 |
| 75 + | 10 | 13 | 28 | 15 |
| All aged | 10 | 14 | 29 | 16 |

*Source*: Census of Northern Ireland, 1971.

their present home between 1966 and 1971; it is very likely that most of them will have moved from more central wards.

The second subset of variables was concerned with housing conditions and these form the focus of our analysis. One theme that recurs constantly in discussions of the life of old people is that of bad housing. Poor housing conditions, apart from being a source of stress in their own right, can exacerbate other problems, particularly medical. Furthermore, such conditions can undermine the widely promoted policy of keeping the elderly at home wherever possible rather than admitting them to some form of institutional care. If the home is substandard the old person may be unable to cope satisfactorily, regardless of other factors; doctors are often reluctant to return an elderly person (particularly one living alone) to their home after hospital treatment if conditions there are unsatisfactory. It is important, therefore, to discover to what extent the aged are exposed to worse housing than the rest of the population. This applies especially to the over-74s who have much higher rates of illness.

There is no doubt that, as a group, the elderly in the United Kingdom live in worse housing than the general population. For example, the General Household Survey of Great Britain found in 1972 that 12.3 per cent of households with at least one person over 59, and 17.3 per cent of individuals aged 60 or over living alone, lacked any bath or shower; and also that 11.8 per cent of each lacked an inside WC compared with 8.2 per cent and 7.7 per cent respectively of all households (Office of Population Censuses and Surveys, 1975). Once again there is apparently no information about differences by age within the elderly group. Moreover, one cannot tell to what extent the bad housing conditions of the elderly derive from where they live rather than from their age. Many problems of the old are a direct consequence of their age. It seems likely, however, that in housing their problems may be due in part to their residential distribution. In short, more elderly people live in poor housing because more of them have continued to live in the inner city. If the spatial factor were controlled we may find that the aged, in respect of their housing at least, are no worse off than their younger neighbours.

To investigate the housing conditions of the elderly in Belfast measures were extracted for each person regarding the tenure of their dwellings; its size, and the presence or absence of the standard amenities. The differences between age groups and areas in these housing characteristics are shown in Table 4.9. Unfortunately, the published tables from the 1971 Census present figures for housing conditions only at the household level, not the individual, so straightforward comparisons of the housing of the elderly with other people are not possible. Indeed, since households containing old people tend to be smaller than average, household statistics will tend to exaggerate the extent to which the elderly, as individuals, are exposed to bad housing when compared with other individuals.

The figures presented here support the earlier suggestion that the housing difficulties of the aged derive primarily from where they live rather than from their age. We cannot determine their position relative to the rest of the population but it is clear that there are large variations between areas in contrast to the minor variations between age groups; the conditions of people in the suburbs would be even better were it not for the inclusion of some old county towns amongst this group. The relatively high incidence of small dwellings in the suburbs, however, is not necessarily an indicator of poor housing to the extent that it probably is in the inner city. In the latter they will tend to be nineteenth-century in origin whereas those in the former will be mostly modern council flats specifically intended for old people. One encouraging conclusion, from the viewpoint of social welfare, that can be drawn from these tables is that the 'old elderly' (those aged 75 and over) do not suffer from poor housing to any greater degree than their younger counterparts. In this respect, at least, they do not have to suffer an additional burden.

It may still be true that the elderly, even within a given area, will tend to live in the worst housing. Studies of attempts at inner city rehabilitation, through generous grants for home improvements, have found that the elderly householders are the least able or willing to take advantage of such opportunities to improve their housing. Nevertheless, it does seem that the housing problems of the elderly are essentially indistinguishable from those of the inner city in general. Vivrett's (1960) conclusions, although made in the context of housing in the USA are equally appropriate to the situation in Belfast:

in fact, many problems of the aging today relate directly to limitations in the supply of housing and in the physical framework of our communities. Thus, when we improve the supply or the quality of housing for the general population, we improve the situation for older people tomorrow (p. 601).

If we take Tables 4.8 and 4.9 and the tables of personal characteristics omitted because of lack of space collectively, then the variables fall into two groups. One comprises the housing variables together with the indices of social class and migration. These variables exhibit marked differences between areas but very little between age groups. The other consists of the measures of sex, marital status, and economic position. In this case the variations are between age groups and not between areas. The final variable, car ownership, is the only one to vary by both age and area. It seems reasonable to conclude that the second group, and to some extent car ownership, represent attributes of the population that will tend to alter as a direct consequence of the ageing process. Although one would expect slight variations from area to area, associated, for example, with greater longevity amongst certain social groups, the incidence of these attributes will be generally unaffected by other processes.

Table 4.9 Persons possessing certain housing attributes as a percentage of each age group by area: Belfast, 1971

| Age | Inner city | Middle city | Suburbs | All city |
|---|---|---|---|---|
| *A. Private rented* | | | | |
| 60–64 | 55 | 30 | 16 | 36 |
| 65–74 | 56 | 31 | 22 | 37 |
| 75 + | 56 | 30 | 18 | 37 |
| All aged | 55 | 30 | 19 | 38 |
| *B. Small dwelling (one to three rooms)* | | | | |
| 60–64 | 17 | 4 | 14 | 12 |
| 65–74 | 18 | 5 | 21 | 15 |
| 75 + | 16 | 5 | 22 | 13 |
| All aged | 17 | 4 | 19 | 14 |
| *C. Lacking exclusive use of all five basic amenities* | | | | |
| 60–64 | 69 | 23 | 14 | 39 |
| 65–74 | 71 | 25 | 17 | 42 |
| 75 + | 71 | 23 | 18 | 41 |
| All aged | 70 | 24 | 16 | 41 |

*Source*: Census of Northern Ireland, 1971.

The variables in the first group, however, represent attributes that derive not from the individual's age but primarily from the position in society that he or she attained before retirement. Given that there appears to be little voluntary movement within the urban area as a result of retirement (Boal *et al*, 1976; NIHE, 1979) (as opposed to movement out of the area), spatial variations in these attributes will reflect the action of general processes, such as the operation of the housing market or local government redevelopment policies, acting mainly independently of age. Thus the social geography of the elderly is, in many important respects, simply the social geography of the population at large.

There is, however, one final aspect of the geography of the elderly that we wish to examine that does reflect their special position. This is the location of facilities, such as old people's homes, which cater specifically for the elderly. As we have already seen, any talk of 'geriatric ghettos' in the Belfast urban area would be mistaken. Although some areas do exhibit higher proportions of old people than others, in general the aged are widely distributed throughout the metropolitan area. Our interest in this final section is to ascertain whether the facilities which cater for their needs are equally widespread. In general, the provision of facilities for the elderly within Northern Ireland has lagged behind that of Great Britain. For example, enrolment at day centres for the elderly in the Belfast District Council area in 1973 amounted to less than 2 per cent of the elderly population. Regional statistics collated by Evason, Darby, and Pearson (1976) demonstrated that by Northern Ireland standards Belfast was relatively well provided with residential accommodation for the elderly, although nearly half of the places were in the voluntary sector.

For this purpose we have selected three types of facility: old people's homes (state and voluntary), day centres (state and voluntary), and sheltered dwellings. In the urban area in 1978 there were 73 homes, 41 day centres, and 54 clusters of sheltered dwellings (Figure 4.7). The old people's homes and sheltered dwellings can be regarded as complementary to the normal housing of the elderly whose distribution was described earlier. The homes cater for those old people who can no longer manage in the community while the sheltered dwellings, where the residents have their own, specially designed homes but are supervised by a warden, represent a compromise between the private household and the residential institution. The day centres, on the other hand, cater for those old people still living at home who require or who want somewhere to meet other people, have a meal, and so on.

As can be seen from the map these three different facilities tend to have different spatial distributions. Very few old people's homes are new, purpose-built structures, they are mostly large, formerly privately owned dwellings. Their distribution, therefore, generally coincides with that of the pre-war upper middle-class areas of the city with very few located in what were or are working-class neighbourhoods. The sheltered dwellings, however, are provided by the Northern Ireland Housing Executive (the body responsible for all public-

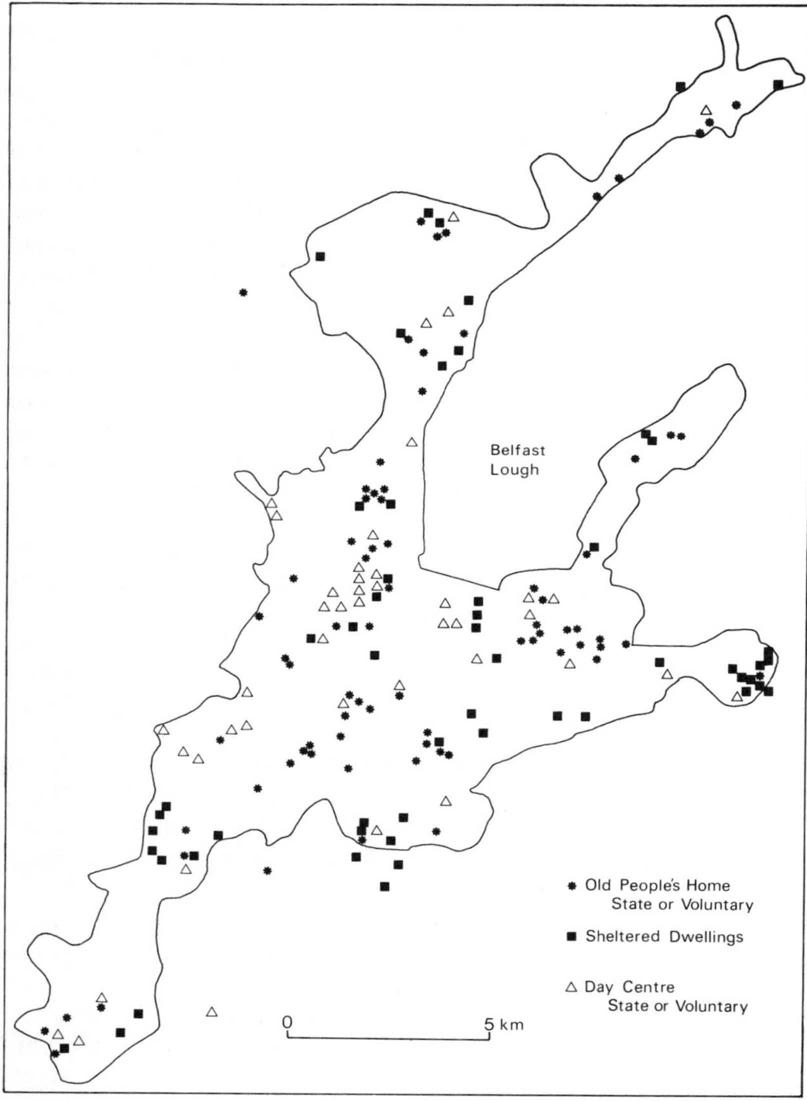


Figure 4.7 Distribution of facilities for the elderly in Belfast in 1978. (*Source*: Compiled by Geography Department, Queen's University, Belfast.)

sector housing in Northern Ireland), and it is their policy to integrate such dwellings with their general housing. As a result sheltered housing is found mainly in their new suburban estates and inner-city redevelopment schemes. They are noticeably lacking, however, from the extensive modern public estates in the west of the city. This distribution means that sheltered housing tends to be located in areas which otherwise have very low proportions of old people.

This is not entirely the case with the provision of day centres. These are clustered around the city centre to serve the areas with high proportions of old people but they are not found in all districts with a large elderly population (Figure 4.7). Almost without exception day centres are situated in mainly working-class areas. The middle-class areas of the city are markedly less well provided for, despite their often higher proportions of old people. This is partly offset, however, by the provision of transport to the centres by the social services. Unfortunately, we have no evidence to offer on the demand or need for these facilities and hence the suitability of their present distribution. If one assumes, however, that the need for their services will be greatest amongst those old people who live in the worst housing and amongst those with no car to take them elsewhere, then their distribution is logical.

## CONCLUSION

In this section we have examined certain aspects of the residential distribution of the elderly, of their housing conditions, and of the provision made for them. Unlike most studies in this field, which have generally treated the elderly as a homogeneous population, they have been disaggregated into different age groups. Special attention has been paid to those features of the aged, such as their segregation from the rest of the population and their poor housing, which have given rise to popular concern. On the basis of the material discussed above, however, it would appear that, at least in Belfast, much of that concern is unnecessary or misplaced.

Although it is true that some areas have markedly high proportions of old people in their populations than do others, and that such areas tend to lie near the city centre, it is totally misleading to speak of 'geriatric ghettos' or of areas dominated by the aged. They may be more dispersed in the suburbs than in the inner city but nearly as many old people now live in the former areas as in the latter and the indications are that they are increasing both absolutely and relatively in the suburbs, but declining in the inner city. Moreover, in many respects the greater density in the latter areas is an advantage as it enables services to be provided more efficiently. In the future it is the suburbs, with equal numbers of old people to be helped spread over a greater area, that may pose the major problems for those responsible for the provision of services for the elderly; the present distribution of day centres is clearly markedly unequal.

The main exception to this argument concerns the problems that arise from bad housing. Quite clearly, those old people who live in the inner city are markedly worse off than those who now live in the suburbs. Equally clearly, however, the quality of housing is not primarily a function of a person's age as is, for example, employment status. People are in bad housing because of where they are, not who they are; so the implication of some discussions of the problem, that the problems of housing in the inner city are, in some unexplained way the result of the large number of elderly residents, must be firmly repudiated. One important step in this matter would be to express measures of housing conditions on the basis of persons and not households.

The study of the differences between old people of different ages has pointed to the value of distinguishing those attributes which change with time, as a direct consequence of the ageing process, from those which in most cases remain fairly stable, such as social class or tenure. Old people carry into retirement many of the characteristics they acquire during middle age; it is not only in spatial terms that the elderly are relatively immobile. For the geographer the chief interest is that it is in these latter features, and not those such as employment, or marital status, that we will find significant spatial variations between the 'young old' and the 'old old'.

Although Northern Ireland differs in some details of its demography from the rest of the United Kingdom it represents, in respect of its major social and population processes, a microcosm of the whole. The more detailed examination which its size permits can therefore usefully illuminate the position of the elderly elsewhere. This is perhaps particularly true of the special analysis we have been able to undertake of the elderly in Belfast which has drawn attention to the heterogeneity which obtains within this group, both by age and by area.

## REFERENCES

Association of Metropolitan Authorities (1978). *Services for the Elderly A Metropolitan View.* AMA, London.

Boal, F. W., Doherty, P. and Pringle, D. G. (1974). *The Spatial Distribution of Some Social Problems in the Belfast Urban Area.* N. Ireland Community Relations Commission, Belfast.

Boal, F. W., Poole, M. A., Murray, R. and Kennedy, S. J. (1976). *Religious residential segregation and residential decision making in the Belfast urban area.* SSRC Final Report HR 1165 1/2.

Clark, M. (1971). Patterns of ageing among the elderly poor of the inner city. *Gerontoligist*, **11**, 59–66.

Compton, P. A. (1978). *Northern Ireland: A Census Atlas.* Gill & Macmillan, Dublin.

Duncan, O. D. and Duncan, B. (1955). Residential distribution and occupational stratification. *American Journal of Sociology*, **55**, 493–503.

Evason, E., Darby, J. P. and Pearson, M. (1976). *Social Need and Social Provision in N. Ireland.* Occasional Papers in Social Administration, The New University of Ulster, Coleraine.

Golant, S. M. (1972). *The Residential Location and Spatial Behaviour of the Elderly.* University of Chicago, Department of Geography, Research Paper 143, Chicago.

Golant, S. M. (1975). Residential concentrations of the future elderly. *Gerontologist*, **15**, 16–23.

Government of Northern Ireland (1929). *Census of Population of Northern Ireland 1926: General Report.* HMSO, Belfast.

Government of Northern Ireland (1940). *Census of Population of Northern Ireland 1937: General Summary.* HMSO, Belfast.

Government of Northern Ireland (1955). *Census of Population of Northern Ireland 1951: General Report.* HMSO, Belfast.

Government of Northern Ireland General Register Office (1965). *Census of Population 1961: General Report.* HMSO, Belfast.

Government of Northern Ireland General Register Office (1968). *Census of Population 1966: General Report.* HMSO, Belfast.

Hiltner, J. and Smith, B. W. (1974). Intra-urban residential location of the elderly. *Journal of Geography*, **73**, 23–33.

Kennedy, J. M. and De Jong, G. F. (1977). Aged in cities: residential segregation in 10 USA central cities. *Journal of Gerontology*, **32**, 97–102.

Northern Ireland General Register Office (1975). *Census of Population 1971: Summary Tables Northern Ireland.* HMSO, Belfast.

Northern Ireland Housing Executive (1979). *Belfast Household Survey 1978.* NIHE, Belfast.

Office of Population Censuses and Surveys (1975). *General Household Survey 1972.* HMSO, London.

United States of America, White House Conference on Aging (1971). *Housing the Elderly.* Government Printing Office, Washington, DC.

Vivrett, W. K. (1960). Housing and community settings for old people. In Tibbits, C. (ed) *Handbook of Social Gerontology.* University of Chicago Press, Chicago.

Geographical Perspectives on the Elderly
Edited by A. M. Warnes


Chapter 5

# Aspects of retired migration from Paris: an essay in social and cultural geography

*Françoise Cribier*

*Translated by Louis Smith* and *Anthony Warnes*

Every year a large number of retired people leave Paris (Paris refers in this chapter to the agglomeration of Greater Paris. The phrase City of Paris is used to distinguish the central city.) and settle into the provinces of France; 16,000 people aged 65 or more departed each year between 1962 and 1968, and between 1968 and 1975 the annual figure rose to 22,000. If the retired people (and their spouses) below the age of 65 who participate in this exodus are added, as well as those migrants who die before being included in the next census, then the annual average migration is nearer to 35,000 people. The departure rate of retired Parisians increased substantially during the 1960s and still more in the 1970s. In 1975 for every 100 non-migrants in the Paris agglomeration aged 60–69 there were 28 emigrants who had settled in the provinces in the previous 7 years and only three immigrants from either the provinces or abroad. The non-migrants include many people who had changed residence within the agglomeration, but in this paper the term migration is reserved for longer movements that alter the *milieu de vie*. As some Parisians born between 1906 and 1915 had left the agglomeration on retirement before 1968, and as others would have departed after 1975, around 30 per cent of the cohort reaching retirement left Paris to settle in the provinces. This proportion is approximately double the rate of departure from the Lille, Lyons, and Marseilles agglomerations.

Within Greater Paris, according to the 1975 census, there were 1.2 million people living on retirement pensions; 10 per cent more than in 1968. If the

220,000 retired emigrants had remained in Greater Paris, then this increase would have been around 30 per cent (partly accounted for by a lowered age at which people actually retired). Taking only the non-active population aged 65 and above in 1975 (about 1 million), the increase that would have been observed without a 25 per cent emigration was 8 per cent.

The retirement of Parisians to the provinces has had four important geographical consequences:

(1) Stability in the population size of Greater Paris after a long history of rapid growth. The 220,000 retired emigrants are balanced by the number of in-migrant workers and their families.
(2) A slow rate of growth of the aged population of the capital. Without retirement migration, Paris would be less able to provide the necessary care and services for its elderly.
(3) An ageing of its elderly population. Out-migrations over-represent the younger retired and those in best health. While retirement migration therefore slows down the ageing of the population of Paris, it accelerates the ageing of its elderly population.
(4) A redistribution of retired people throughout the regions and types of commune of France. Of all retired people who settle in the French countryside and seaside resorts, 40 per cent come from Greater Paris.

## THE CHARACTERISTICS OF MIGRATION TO THE PROVINCES

The characteristics of the migrants can be studied by comparison with non-migrant retired Parisians of the same age. We compiled special tables using data from the censuses of 1968 and 1975 and from sample surveys carried out by the Census Bureau concerning: the retired, non-employed wives of the retired, and widows living on a retirement pension. These three groups constitute the population living on retirement benefits (*de la retraite*). Records from the National Pension Fund also give details of previous employment as well as the income derived from various allowances. In addition, several surveys were carried out by the author. In 1973 a representative sample of 265 households (477 people) of retired Parisian migrants was surveyed (Cribier, 1975a). In 1979 a sample of 500 people recently settled in French seaside resorts were interviewed, 200 of them from Paris. Another survey, in 1975, of a representative sample of 700 recently retired Parisians remaining in Greater Paris made possible further comparisons of migrants and non-migrants (Cribier, 1978).

### Age structure

Migrants who retire to the provinces are particularly numerous among the younger retired. The migration normally takes place very soon after retirement itself and most Parisians who move to the provinces do so at the end of the career of the second marriage partner. We interviewed in 1974 a 10 per cent sample of (10,000) formerly salaried persons listed by the National Pension Fund of Greater Paris as having retired in 1972 and have followed up this sample in later surveys. Of these, 29 per cent had already moved to the provinces by 1974, while between 1974 and 1979 less than 5 per cent followed.

Among the minority group (less than 20 per cent) of retired migrants aged 75 and over, there were those who had continued working late in their lives, those who had chosen to remain in Paris for the first years of their retirement, and, most numerous, those for whom the migration was preceded by another significant event—most often widowhood. For the latter, this move is not a retirement migration in the strict sense of the word (Cribier, 1979a). In 1975, 30 per cent of retired Parisians who had settled in the provinces since the previous census were less than 65 years old, so many at the time of their move must have been less than the French male modal retirement age of 63. Further analysis of the census migration data shows that the rates of out-migration for people recently retired, or aged 55–69 years, are higher than those for all people aged 65 years and more which are more commonly described (Table 5.1).

Mobility is greatest among the younger retired because mobility is increasing in the cohorts which are now approaching retirement age and because out-migrations are most frequent amongst those who retire early. This is understandable because these people can hope for a longer period of agreeable

Table 5.1 Age-specific out-migration rates of non-active persons from Greater Paris, 1968–76

| Age group | Number of out-migrants | |
|---|---|---|
| | Per 100 of 1968 population | Per 100 of 1975 population |
| Quinquennial | | |
| 55–59 | 19.5 | 23.3 |
| 60–64 | 23.3 | 29.6 |
| 65–69 | 20.3 | 25.0 |
| 70–74 | 15.1 | 17.3 |
| 75 + | 9.4 | 10.3 |
| Other aggregates | | |
| 55–69 | 21.1 | 26.1 |
| 55 + | 16.0 | 18.7 |
| 65 + | 14.4 | 16.3 |

*Source*: France, General Census of Population and Housing, 1975.

retirement before becoming very old. The question arises whether the trend towards early retirement encourages mobility in all cases.

## Marital status, sex, and presence of children in the Paris region

The Parisians who leave to settle in the provinces are far more likely to be married that those who remain, but only slightly more likely to be married than those who change residence within Greater Paris. This applies for all age groups. The author's surveys show that the majority of widows and widowers lost their spouses after moving. The few widows who migrated alone mainly chose to settle where their husbands had planned to move and asked to be buried. As for spinsters and divorcees, very few leave Paris on retirement and these have higher than average incomes. This can be explained by the facts that these women have normally worked longer than other women, that they tend to have small incomes, and that their social network is well structured in Paris and more difficult to rebuild in the provinces. It may also be suggested that their social standing is less favourable in France than in the Anglo-Saxon countries and this means that they find it more difficult to integrate into the retirement area.

Typically, then, it is retired couples who leave for the provinces. Between the ages of 55 and 70 those who migrate are more likely to be married than those who stay behind. Among the unmarried, men are more likely to migrate than women. The few migrants over the age of 70 are often widows who are going to live near their children. The high migration rate for married couples has two causes. One is financial in that the couples have at least one male and frequently two retirement pensions, especially among working-class and lower middle-class migrants. The second is that those married couples for whom one partner provides the main companionship for the other can move readily in comparison to single people who are often worried that they will not be able to develop friendships elsewhere. We can relate the low migration rate of widows and widowers to the melancholia of bereavement, to their renunciation of the new life together which had been intended, and to a lack of confidence to set up alone elsewhere, except when this enables a move closer to children or other relatives.

Those who have one or more children living in the provinces frequently move to be with them. Couples without children were found more likely to leave Paris than those with children. The reasons for their high rate of migration are that they have few ties with the Paris region and that they are likely to have two pensions and sufficient savings for a comfortable retirement in the provinces. This reflects Karn's (1977) findings in two English coastal resorts, where 37 per cent and 30 per cent respectively of retired migrants had no children, whilst the national average for childlessness was around 15–20 per cent. For the obverse reasons parents of large families are under-represented among migrants.

## Place of birth of the retired

The majority of elderly Parisians today were not born in Greater Paris; 60 per cent were born in the provinces or abroad. Many had come to Paris in their youth and, when they reached the age of retirement, on average they had spent 40 years in the capital. While most Parisians native to the provinces stay in the Paris area, 30 per cent leave in the 2 years after retirement. Not all return to their native region. Among the natives of greater Paris the rate of departure is lower (27 per cent) but still very high. The greater out-migration rate among the provincial natives is related to their maintenance of strong ties with the locality, which is characteristic of all social classes in France. The opportunities to settle in their native area and their weak links with Paris are also important factors for the lower and lower middle classes of retired Parisians.

## Social status

One of the most remarkable features of the migration of Parisians to the provinces is that it affects all social levels. In 1975 the proportion registered for supplementary pensions was identical for non-migrant Parisians and for those settling in the provinces. The situation contrasts with that in Britain and the United States, because affluent Parisians live in its most desirable neighbourhoods and are very attached to the capital. They can also afford long holidays which may be regarded as a substitute for retirement migration (Cribier, 1980). Working-class Parisians, on the other hand, often live in small, uncomfortable houses and have insufficient resources to acquire better accommodation in the Paris region. They frequently live in the least pleasant neighbourhoods and in the decaying areas of the city where immigrant workers and the very poor have concentrated. They are also more likely than the upper classes to have originated from rural provinces with which they maintain close ties.

The French census does not yield data on either income or former occupation of the retired, but an analysis by social class has been carried out using educational attainment. For married couples aged 65–74 years the rate of out-migration increases slightly with educational attainment up to the third highest decile of the distribution. In this category, 31 per cent of the couples migrate away from Greater Paris. The higher 'social classes' resident in the central part of the agglomeration have a lower out-migration rate, but those living in the suburbs have even higher rates of departure than the lower decile groups. The best-educated people living in the *banlieue pavillonaire* (areas of inter-war, modest, owner-occupied, single-family detached dwellings) have much higher out-migration rates (27 per cent) than those of similar educational attainment generally (19 per cent).

The propensity to retirement migration is not only related to social class but also to the type of move. Return migrations to native areas are more frequent amongst the less well-off, while migrations to non-native provincial regions more often characterize the affluent.

### Location, dwelling type, and occupant's status

Of the French population aged between 55 and 74 in 1975, for every hundred who had remained in Paris since 1968, 25 had left the agglomeration for the provinces. Among residents of Central Paris living mainly in apartments the ratio was 29 : 100; among the residents of the inner suburbs, where a quarter of the retired lived in small houses, the ratio was 26:100; and among those in the outer suburbs, where three-fifths were thus housed, the ratio was 20:100. Relatively more flat-dwellers leave Paris than those who live in houses, largely because of the greater presence of renters. However this fact must be put into the context of the Paris housing situation: the social heterogeneity of both renters and owners is much higher than in Great Britain or the United States for many renters are wealthy and many owners very poor. The high out-migration rate of tenants can be related to worries about future rent increases, even though according to a 1973 Housing Survey 80 per cent of tenants above the age of 57 and living in Greater Paris had controlled rents; 17 per cent by municipal housing statutes and 63 per cent by 1948 legislation. The latter fixed rents at a very low level for private tenants and those still in the same flat continued to benefit. Many middle-class tenants, and even those in the working class earning good salaries, benefited from the low rents of the 1948 act which allowed them to purchase a second home outside Paris. Tenants also feared eviction or expropriation. In practice these affect only a small minority but the fear is not unfounded for among the 265 households in the 1973 survey, 29 had been evicted. Last but not least, many tenants had dreamed throughout their lives of becoming home-owners and after half a century of working life retirement migration achieves this ambition.

## REASONS FOR LEAVING PARIS

Retired migrants from Paris generally have no clear notion of the aggregate factors related to the urban system and changing society which have prompted their moves. Understandably they tend to perceive the causes of their migrations in terms of personal experiences. They perceive the personal effect of social conditions rather than the conditions themselves. Carefully conducted and analysed face-to-face surveys can identify the behaviour, attitudes, and values of people and transcend their false consciousness and rationalizations.

For every respondent the migration from Paris in their sixties represented one of the most important events and last major decisions of their lives. Most come to the decision without hesitation, but some give lengthy consideration to the move, and in the case of some couples, the view of one partner has prevailed. In the case of couples settling in the countryside the wish of the husband clearly prevails, whereas amongst those who stay in Paris the wife prevents the departure. Every migrant had at least one strong reason for leaving, even if this was only a desire to live in the provinces. For about a third of the respondents, who had nothing against Paris itself, the pull factors were greater than the push. Only for less than 10 per cent was it essential to leave Paris at all costs. For the remainder the reasons for leaving reinforced a desire to live elsewhere. The nine most commonly stated reasons given by either partner for leaving Paris in the 1973 survey of 265 households were:

(1) nothing to do in Paris after retirement (178 replies, 67 per cent);
(2) Paris had become unbearable (147; 55 per cent);
(3) Paris is unhealthy (140; 53 per cent);
(4) did not want to go on living in a flat (129; 49 per cent);
(5) wanted a change of climate (100; 38 per cent);
(6) wanted to go back home (82; 31 per cent);
(7) for family reasons other than reason (6) (82; 31 per cent);
(8) cost of living too high in Paris (57; 22 per cent);
(9) eviction (29; 11 per cent).

## Rejection of flat-life

A dislike of flats was expressed by half of the households, of all social classes and whether Paris- or provincial-born. It was, however, more often a masculine than a feminine response. On retirement men found themselves hemmed in a flat and unable to think of things to do between four walls. Unskilled workers were particularly likely to refer to being bored. The archetype conceived by many migrants was the retired Parisian who is restricted to an armchair and suffers an early death, with which inactivity and immobility were frequently identified. On the other hand, a house and a garden were seen as offering scope for activities, such as gardening or do-it-yourself jobs, as being compatible with keeping animals, as allowing one to go outside whilst remaining at home, and as allowing freedom with privacy.

Many people, both men and women, recognize that accommodation which was adequate 'when we were never in' can be both depressing and cramped when retired. The women complain of having their husbands under their feet, the men of not knowing where to put themselves, particularly when doing handicrafts. Street noise appears louder and is more intrusive when one is at home during the week. Climbing stairs becomes more difficult with the passing years and causes worry about the future.

The respondents (20 per cent) living in subsidized municipal accommodation complained a great deal despite their facilities. They referred to the blocks as 'rabbit hutches' where one could never feel at home and where relationships are those of mistrust and hostility, particularly with respect to the young. These feelings were accentuated where the aged feel themselves to be in a minority.

The complaints about life in flats often reflect an underlying dissatisfaction with the Parisian lifestyle. Many flat-dwellers, particularly men from the lower classes or born in rural areas, have a common perception of themselves as 'old codgers', *petits vieux*, who wander about the streets when not idling in cafés or squares or waiting for death in an armchair.

## There was nothing left to do in Paris

Two-thirds of the households expressed this view; men more than women although wives often said, 'my husband wouldn't have known what to do with himself'. In practice, the move to the provinces may not always reduce this problem, as many women live in small towns or rural areas in much the same style as in Paris. Only 28 per cent of women, but 53 per cent of men, had taken on a new hobby since moving. Higher rates of taking up new activities were found among predominantly middle-class migrants in the 1979 survey in coastal resorts but the male–female differential was repeated.

In all occupational groups, two-thirds of the men said that they would not have known what to do in Paris, but this reply was given a little more often by those who had grown up in the countryside. Among the older generation self-esteem is closely identified with work and perpetual idleness is reproachable. Many men talk about gardening and odd jobs as their work. How could they spend their days in Paris? They refuse to idle in cafés and streets with their cronies; they refuse to join a group of Parisians with such a stigmatized identity.

Retired men would like to go out in Paris but ask what they can do and where they can go. They say that its attractions are for the young; contemporary films do not interest them and indeed seven of ten migrants never went to see them. Neither do cultural activities and street life appeal. Their appetite for urban social life was not highly developed. Many hardly knew anyone outside an immediate circle at work, and this poverty of social relationships was regarded as quite normal; 'You know what its like in Paris: "Hullo", "Good-bye", "Good evening". One hardly speaks to anyone.' These frail social relationships also characterized the 1975 sample of retired people of the same age living in Paris, especially in the working classes.

These comments reveal the importance of the attitude of retired migrants towards Paris. For those who had never really adapted, Paris was just to work in (for 40 or so years!) and they could not see any other advantage in being there. This absence of interest in Paris, or of connection with the city, and the

Table 5.2 Attitudes towards Paris among retired migrants (percentages)

| | Men | Women | All |
|---|---|---|---|
| Never liked being there | 11 | 8 | 10 |
| Unhappy there after retirement | 26 | 20 | 23 |
| Happy in Paris despite inconveniences, but looked forward to leaving | 58 | 56 | 57 |
| Happy in Paris and regretted having left | 7 | 15 | 11 |
| TOTALS | 100 | 100 | 100 |

*Source*: Author's survey, 1975.

refusal to consider oneself Parisian is more widespread among migrants than stayers. The majority of the latter appreciate the capital, its ambience, the life they lead there, its wider social life, and their neighbourhood (Cribier, 1978).

This different attitude is not linked simply to a lower level of educational attainment as many less educated people love Paris. Neither is it necessarily related to provincial origins, though those who have never liked Paris invariably come from outside, because many adopted Parisians enjoy the city both before and after retirement (Table 5.2).

## Paris is intolerable

Half of the migrants described Greater Paris as intolerable and this view was most frequently expressed by those who lived in central Paris and the inner suburbs. The terms used were strong: unbearable, infernal, impossible, a cross to bear, insane, and murderous. The complaints were based on noise, traffic, pollution, the pace of life, the young, the immigrant worker—one can identify here the racism of poor whites aware of the mediocrity of their own social position. Some even went as far as saying that to stay in Paris would have meant death and that leaving has prolonged their life. The opposite view was occasionally encountered among stayers in our Paris survey of 1975; in one instance expressed as: 'to leave Paris is to die a little, in any case to age more quickly'.

It has already been reported that most migrants had had few social activities and few personal relationships beyond their families. Common statements were that: 'we don't know anyone', meaning also that no-one knew them; 'people don't take any notice of us, they push us about', meaning that others deny their existence. The lack of care and consideration hurts old people and makes them feel insignificant. *Invivable* is often used to imply that in Paris people don't know how to live or what role to play. Negative aspects of social intercourse occupy a prominent place in their discussions and they feel deeply the low status of the elderly in an urban society.

Many deprecate the changes that have occurred in Paris, and regard the city as intolerable because it is not as it used to be. Only a minority believe that Paris life has not changed. Increasing noise, traffic, and pollution are regarded as unbearable, and changes in people stimulate unfavourable comments; Parisians are described as having become more touchy and quick to argue, unfriendly, and inconsiderate. Some residents of working-class neighbourhoods are nostalgic for bygone social fabrics and forms (Chevalier, 1967). Several spoke of the transformation of their quarter, of the new blocks of flats and of property speculation, which they see as directed against weaker individuals and as increasing their insecurity. After having lived in Greater Paris for 30 years with security of tenure and rent-control, many were afraid of being evicted or higher rents when they retired in the early 1970s.

### Health and climate

Paris as described by many of the respondents is unhealthy and bad for one's 'nerves' (which in France may refer euphemistically to alcoholism). They said that in other parts of the country, life is calmer, more tranquil, the air is purer, and the food fresher. Half of the respondents from all walks of life admitted seeking a healthier life when they left Paris. Two-fifths claimed that they had moved to a better climate; all those who were living in the Midi and many of the migrants to other regions made this assertion. We were told even in Calais that the air was cleaner and the town more lively than Paris; in Picardy that the crispness of the air improved the circulation of the blood.

### Return to one's native region

Although 43 per cent of the sample returned to the native region of either husband and wife (and 14 per cent to the home of both), only 31 per cent of all interviewed households offered this as a reason for leaving Paris. Most actually retired to the commune which they had left; for these people few other reasons for the migration were expressed and the move had been planned long before. The elderly who are particularly anxious to return to their native region predominate at the lower end of the social scale: 42 per cent of unskilled workers; 32 per cent of skilled workers; and 9 per cent of technicians and managers. They are also more numerous amongst those who had originated in rural areas (46 per cent) than among those from towns (22 per cent) and cities (14 per cent). This bears out the strong relationship between the rural background of so many Parisians and retirement migration.

### Eviction

The process of urban renewal in Paris, as elsewhere, brings in a new population partly by expelling the old. One in ten of the 1973 respondents had been evicted from their Paris accommodation. Some said that they would have moved to the provinces anyway; others had thought that they would not be able to stay and began looking for a house in the countryside several years before retirement. Eight of the 29 households that had been evicted remained in unsatisfactory conditions; badly housed, isolated, and remote from Paris and their families. Some had refused subsidized municipal housing but it had not been offered to most.

Few migrants said that bad relations with children had prompted the migration although in actuality it may have been more common. The very high rate of out-migration of the few remarried retirees may indicate a desire to escape family problems. All in all, the majority of migrants left the capital of their own accord and for positive reasons. Retirement migration was normally found to be a considered strategy and a deliberate means of achieving a new way of life. However, as we have suggested, the husbands had a more decisive role than the wives in the decision to leave Paris. The decision was mutually taken in 61 per cent of the couples, but taken by the husband in 31 per cent and by the wife in 8 per cent.

## DESTINATION AREAS AND THE CHOICE OF THE LOCALITY

### Dispersal throughout France

While every French town has a sphere of dispersal for its retired population, that of Paris is distinguished by its very great extent within the nation (Figures 5.1 and 5.2, and Cribier, Duffau and Kych, 1974). Only a third of provincial migrants settle more than 120 km from the town they leave, but three-quarters move this far from Paris. The different behaviour of Parisians is partly explained by the fact that those in the provinces usually live less than 130 km from their place of birth, while half of the Parisians from the provinces were born more than 350 km from Paris. This greater diffusion has three major causes. Paris recruits its population from the whole of France and particularly from the rural areas. Just after the 1914–18 war, when today's retired people were arriving in Paris, a national labour market had been established, and young people throughout the country were moving to find work. Most of the retired people of the 1970s who were born outside Paris arrived in the city between 1918 and 1938; more than half were born in the countryside and most others in small or very small towns. Other reasons for the wide dispersal of Parisians are that they have higher retirement pensions than the national average and they collectively become familiar with the whole of France through holidays (Cribier, 1969) and relationships at work with people from all parts of the country. Furthermore, reflecting an element of the cultural geography of France, Parisians feel that they have the right to make use of the whole national territory, whilst provincials tend to retire within their own region, in the holiday

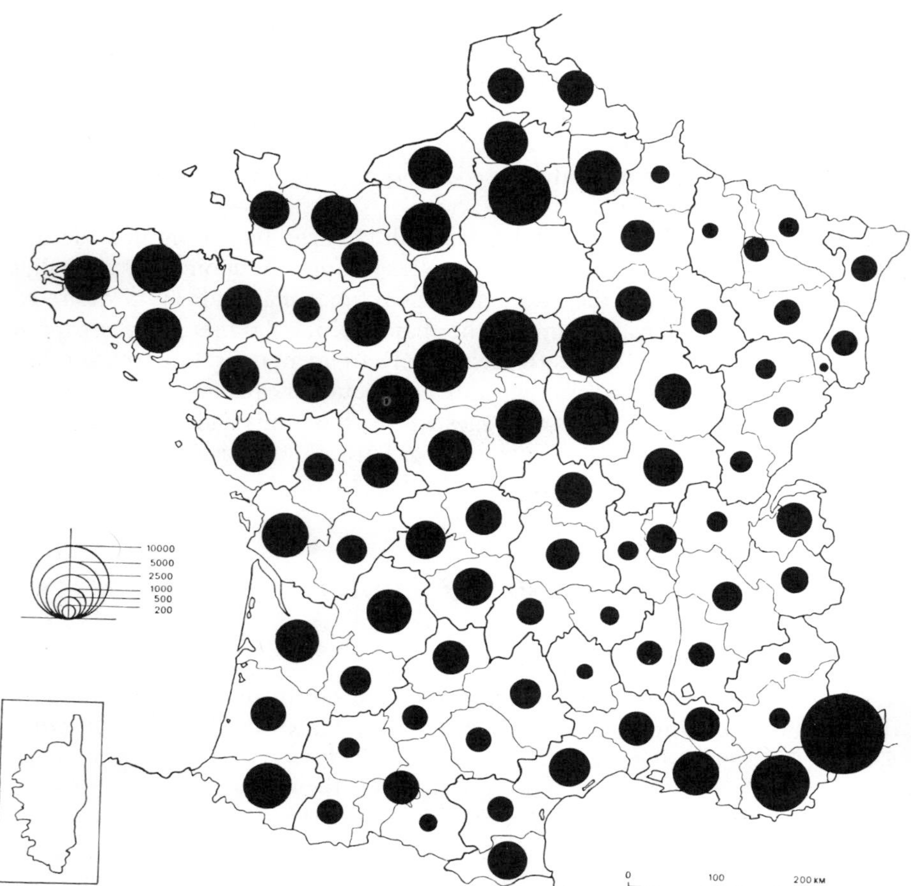


Figure 5.1 Distribution in 1975 of 145, 435 people aged 65 years or more who have left the Paris region since 1968. Data for Corsica are unreliable. (*Source*: 1975 Population and Housing Census of France; F. Cribier (1979) *Gérontologie et Société*, No. 8, Carte 8, p. 36.)

region most favoured by their own town, or in a prominent national retirement centre such as the Côte d'Azur.

The distribution by department of the migrants aged 65 years and more moving out of Paris is shown in Figure 5.1. The distribution is similar to that of all retirement migrants, even though 40 per cent of them are below 65. Another view of the distribution is given by the locations of residence of the 265 households from Paris interviewed in 1973 (Figure 5.2). Because these were former industrial workers, the regions from which Paris civil servants originate (e.g. the south-west) were under-represented, as were places which attract the non-salaried retired (e.g. some areas of the Massif Central, the

Figure 5.2 Distribution of 262 former salaried workers in Paris, having left Paris between 1970 and 1972. (*Source*: Author's survey.). ● Those who returned to their 'départment' of origin; ○ others

south-east and the coast in general). The unattractiveness of the upland areas with their cold winters and the popularity of the Paris Basin and Brittany are common to both patterns. To elucidate the distribution of retirement areas from Paris, a first step is to set aside the decision to return to one's place or origin from all other locational reasons.

## Return *versus* other types of migration

We must distinguish two types of migration. In the first, the retired migrant returns to his native region using the term in a broad, historical sense (e.g.

Brittany, Perigord, Languedoc). Most returns are to the very same canton, but it still seems appropriate to talk of 'homecoming' even when a person returns to another part of the same region. If a return migration is not undertaken a wider range of criteria are evoked to select a destination area.

Return migrations are more prevalent in France (from Paris and elsewhere) than in either Britain or North America (Law and Warnes, 1980; Longino, 1980). Every year thousands of retired people move back to the regions with which they have remained attached and familiar. We have estimated from census data and the National Pension Fund dossiers that 70 per cent of the residents of provincial towns who move on retirement return home, compared to only 45 per cent of Parisians.

Return migrations can be distinguished from other retirement migrations from Paris by the characteristics of the migrants and of the destination regions. They are most common among less affluent Parisians. Their prevalence exceeds 50 per cent at the bottom of the social scale (unskilled workers, women domestics, and poorly qualified employees), as compared with around one-third for managers and businessmen. For households with modest incomes, returning home is often the only way of leaving Paris. In addition these people have more limited horizons than other Parisians and, having rarely taken holidays outside their native regions, they are less prepared to integrate themselves into hitherto unknown places. The fact that these poorer people have less choice does not mean that they are any less happy in their retirement locality. Many are keen to end their days in these familiar places, most decided to move more than 10 years in advance, and some always intended to return. They are often profoundly happy when re-established in their native district.

As for the destination areas, the provinces of France have contributed unequally to the population of Paris and are of unequal attractiveness for return migrants. The North, East and Massif Central only attract a quarter of their natives who have become Parisians, whereas the South-West, Brittany, Burgundy, and provinces close to Paris attract at least one-half. The fraction reaches two-thirds in Provence. As the regions received varying numbers of non-native retired, the proportion of natives among the retirees from Paris varies from 7 per cent in Provence and Côte d'Azur to 67 per cent in the Nord. Around Paris and on the Côte d'Azur where large numbers of retired Parisians settle, natives can only be a minority among the arrivals even when they exhibit a high rate of return.

While all regions of France receive a socially diverse population through the migration of retired Parisians, the differences between regions are significant, even among return migrants. For example, when affluent Parisians return to their native region they often settle in coastal areas, from Normandy to the Basque region and from Roussillon to the Côte d'Azur. Favoured inland regions include the whole of the south, parts of the south-west (Quercy, Perigord,

Pays d'Adour, Pays Basque), and the areas surrounding Paris. On the other hand, the Parisians who return to the north (Champagne, Lorraine, Franche-Comté) and to the uplands of the Massif Central are generally of more modest means.

These differences are even more marked for those who migrate to non-native regions. Some regions (North, North-East, and upland zones) attract hardly anyone, while the Paris Basin and the coastal areas from Picardie to the Basque region and to the east of the Rhone attract Parisians in great numbers. It is with non-return migration that the income of the retired person exerts the most influence on the choice of region and commune. The median latitude of the distribution of those with below median-income passes through the Basse Loire, but for those with above median income it passes 340 km further south through Toulouse (Cribier, 1975b).

## Evolution of the distribution pattern

The changing distribution of retiring Parisians can be described over a period of 20 years. There has been an annual increase of retired Parisians in all departments but much variation in their shares; the north-eastern third of the country has experienced a relative decline in its share; the regions with an increasing share have included the western coastal and rural areas including the small towns of the interior, the Midi, and the southern and western parts of the Paris Basin. Elsewhere, the relative share of each department has shown little change.

These trends result from the stability of the total numbers involved, a decline in the relative shares of the settlement of retired people who are native to the north and north-east third of the country, and an increase in the settlement of non-natives in the departments close to Paris, in the coastal areas and in Mediterranean inland areas.

## Characteristics of communes selected for retirement

In 1975 half of the retired people who had left Greater Paris since 1968 had settled in a rural commune and only one-tenth in a major agglomeration of 200,000 inhabitants or more. The countryside and the towns with less than 15,000 inhabitants welcome two-thirds of migrants aged 65 and more. Amongst the younger retired the proportion is even higher, whilst for those aged 70 or more moves to urban districts become more frequent, whether these migrants come directly from Paris or are making a second retirement move. Second moves lead most often to settlement in a larger and better-serviced centre.

An analysis of pension files, which give the place of birth of the retired person and in many cases also the spouse, has enabled returns to native communes to be distinguished from other retirement migrations. A clear result is that natives of a region are more likely than the Parisian-born to settle in a rural commune; the majority of the former were born in the countryside and do not fear its isolation because they know many people who never left or who have themselves returned. However an increasing number, particularly from those rural districts which have witnessed a massive exodus, no longer have a house or relatives in their native commune. It should be remembered that the average retired Parisian from the countryside comes from a family of 4.6 children, and that half of them are children of tenant farmers, agricultural labourers, or domestics who did not own a house. Returns to the locality of childhood account for three-quarters of return migrations to communes with less than 15,000 people, but only 40 per cent in towns with a population of 5000–50,000. Out of every 10 people returning to the department of their birth, 5 choose the commune of their childhood, 3 settle in a larger commune, generally the administrative centre of the canton, and 2 settle in a smaller one. The last are usually those who were born in a town and retired from Paris to the nearby countryside, often the birthplace of their parents.

The non-native retired are more likely to settle in an urban area, selected for its lifestyle and services. This is particularly evident in the towns of the Mediterranean Midi, the Loire valley and south-western France. They are also numerous in the villages and hamlets surrounding Paris. Within the Paris Basin many retirement homes are former second homes, often bought with retirement in mind (Cribier, 1973). Being fairly close to Paris, contact can be maintained with children and friends in the city while enjoying a rural setting, pleasant scenery, and lower house prices than in the immediate environs of Paris. Lastly, non-natives are numerous in the coastal resorts; one in three has retired to a former holiday home whilst one in four remains a tenant. The average size of the chosen communes is the same for natives and for others but, as has already been seen, their distribution is different. The latter have more frequently settled in coastal resorts, inland residential towns, and in very small localities in the countryside around Paris. The social ambience, landscape, type of accommodation, facilities, and services all depend upon the size of the residential centre. On average the quality of facilities improves up to a threshold with increasing size of commune. For those seeking a 'human scale' and a small commune, the optimum size is undoubtedly the large village or small market town; but the more mobile retired with greater affluence and better health may prefer even smaller communes, where they have the advantages of living in the countryside but having access to a small market town. For these people their orbit transcends the commune as long as their mobility is maintained.

A dispersed settlement pattern is characteristic of a great part of the French countryside. Both census and pension fund records give information only on the total population of a commune but the size of the settlement is equally important and this can be discovered only through a survey. Such a survey enables the classification of retirement localities by the type of habitat (Table 5.3).

More than one household in four is situated in a hamlet or *ecart* (isolated settlement outside the main commune and administrative centre). Most have inadequate facilities and are isolated and poorly served by public transport. Of the retired people living there, some are natives but of modest means, others are affluent and have taken up residence in their former second home. So long as they remain in good health and have access to a car they encounter few problems, but most wives do not drive and four out of five will be widowed. An additional third of the households settle in very small communes, with few good facilities and often an ageing population as a result of the out-migration of young people. The new housing estates where 15 per cent of retired people settle are neither reserved for the elderly nor even inhabited by a majority of old people. Retirement villages on the North American pattern do not exist in France.

Most households are located in a rural commune which is too small to administer municipal services to the elderly. On the other hand towns of over 10,000 inhabitants attract only one household in seven. Many of them have populations little above 10,000 and constitute a similar social milieu to smaller towns, although they usually have better facilities—they always have a hospital. Coastal resorts received around 15 per cent of the retired Parisian 1973 respondents and nearer 20 per cent of the younger retired leaving the

Table 5.3 Types of areas selected by retirement migrants

| Type of commune | Percentage of sample |
|---|---|
| *Urban communes* | |
| Central areas (*quartiers*) | 12 |
| Old suburbs | 3 |
| New suburbs | 5 |
| Housing estates within towns | 6 |
| TOTAL | 26 |
| *Rural communes*[a] | |
| Housing estates in villages | 9 |
| Old village cores or centres | 26 |
| Village peripheries | 12 |
| Hamlets of at least four households | 20 |
| Isolated dwellings (one to three households) | 7 |
| TOTAL | 74 |

[a] Isolated developments outside the built-up area of a town are classified as rural communes.
*Source*: Author's survey of 265 households, 1973.

capital. Out of season the municipal and leisure services of these towns are disappointing but the larger proportion of elderly people is stimulating a social life in the form of clubs for the elderly and spontaneous personal relations.

## Reasons for the choice of commune

Two settings attract the majority of Parisian migrants on retirement; the countryside receives three-quarters and the coast nearly one in five. These two milieux have a special appeal for Parisians. Appreciation of the countryside has been a well-established cultural trait among Parisians since the early nineteenth century and reflects a love of nature as modified by man in woods, meadows, fields, hamlets, and villages. The social life of villages is also valued, reflecting a desire for simpler and warmer human relationships. Those who retire expect to integrate easily into this idealized community and they understate its internal tensions, giving it a fictional unity and cohesion. A move to the countryside is expected to satisfy deep-rooted but often contradictory human needs: privacy and ties with the community; solitude and human contact; rest and activity; traditional pleasures; and a new way of life.

Hostility towards cities is a more recent cultural trait in France. For many migrants Paris represents restrictions, disturbance, and noise from the street or from neighbourhoods which is all the more unbearable because it represents an active life from which the elderly are excluded, and youth of which they are jealous. The countryside is seen as the antithesis of the town, giving freedom, independence, nature, and the tranquillity which ensures good health; it is associated with fresh air, real bread, fresh vegetables, pure water, and most of all peace. It is also an environment where the elderly person is given more respect, a recognized social status, and the prestige accorded to Parisians. It is indeed a paradox that migrants are often here treated as 'real' Parisians, whereas in Paris they tended to lose their status (Cribier, 1979b).

From the earliest days of tourism the seaside provided the ideal setting for seasonal holidays; the Parisian has normally stayed on the coast on holiday. Many resorts have attracted sufficient retired people to support the social facilities they favour, and to some extent an elderly sub-culture and group identity has developed.

Whether they move to the countryside, a seaside resort, or to another town, three in four Parisian households settle in a region which they knew before retirement. Half of the migrants of the 1973 survey had previously stayed either during holidays or for weekends in a second home. Half of the households had members of their family in the chosen region and one-third had been born here. Many spoke of the strength of their attachment to the region and of the inner satisfaction they drew from living harmoniously with places and people in their native place where they would end their days as their parents had done. The 1979 survey in seaside resorts found that three-quarters of Parisians had known the resort before retirement and one-third had owned a house in the area. Another pattern, less expected, was found in these seaside resorts: one-third of Parisians had family links in the neighbouring region and one household in four was born there. Among a British sample, only 8.5 per cent of retirement migrants had a childhood link with the destination area (Law and Warnes, Chapter 3 in this book).

Also important were the climatic reasons cited by 38 per cent of the sample. These are most influential among those affluent enough to be able to choose a destination. The search for a better climate is often related to ideas about health: sea and country air are widely regarded in France as good for one's health, particularly among the working class.

Shopping facilities, health and other services such as public transport are cited as reasons for the selection of a commune. However, people also tended to select a locality characterized by a particular ambience—a town or market town 'full of life' in contrast to quiet backwaters. The atmosphere of the small town is contrasted with that of Paris; it is more tranquil, people know one another, the pace of life is less tiring, life seems more conservative, and old age attracts respect. Many of these small towns are not industrialized and have a population which is ageing and growing only slowly.

Those interviewed seldom presented their choice of neighbourhood or locality as part of a coherent social strategy but social status reasons for their choice appeared to be important in some cases. For many Parisians, settling in a country village or in a seaside resort gave the positive social status of someone who 'lives on income' or of a *villégiateur*. For some, the act of settling into a fashionable resort represents the acme of social mobility.

Lastly 16 per cent of households settled outside their native region but still went either to be near relatives (brothers, sisters, cousins) who had already retired or went to join a son or daughter who had left Paris to work or marry in the provinces.

## RETIREMENT ACCOMMODATION

Many migrants acquired a dwelling so that they could live in the locality of their choice; others left for the provinces to find the home they had dreamed about. They generally wanted either a clean new apartment or a house with a garden; neither could be afforded in the Paris region. The survey showed that one migrant household in five would have preferred to settle in Greater Paris near their children, but house prices and rents forced them further afield. There are many interesting comparisons between the previous and new accommodation, and information was also collected on the search for a new home.

### Previous accommodation in Paris

Eighty per cent of retirement migrants were flat-dwellers compared to 65 per cent of Parisians aged 60–69. Seventy per cent were tenants compared to 50 per cent of the general population in the same age group. The accommodation they vacated was usually old (only 16 per cent was less than 30 years old), small (half had only two main rooms), and of slight comfort (two-thirds did not have a bathroom, two-fifths no inside lavatory, half were heated only by a stove, and most had no lift); six dwellings in ten were situated in a noisy street. Complaints were directed at the noise, the number of floors, and sometimes at the social composition of the neighbourhood or flat block; it was less often directed towards poor facilities. The retired people who remain in Paris are little better accommodated, but amongst the retired who had moved away from the capital the proportion living on top floors, in noisy streets, and in neighbourhoods with a large number of immigrants had been higher. These factors undoubtedly prompted migration among those who had the ability to move.

A surprising proportion of the poorly housed from Paris belong to either middle-class or more affluent working-class groups such as skilled workers and some self-employed. Good-quality Parisian housing was beyond their means, but retirement migration enabled them to acquire better accommodation in better districts more in keeping with their income level and social status.

Finally one should note the fact that most former Parisian tenants had paid very low rents, accounting often for only 10 per cent of expenditure just before retirement. Many were able to invest what they had saved on rent in a new residence for retirement. The 1948 rent control act thus contributed to the growth of second homes and in turn to retirement migration.

## Acquiring accommodation for retirement

A house with its own garden has long been the nostalgic dream of city-dwellers. It represents the common ideal of Parisians raised in the provinces, most of whom came from the countryside or small towns. Seven out of ten of the Parisian migrants had spent their childhood in a house. A house means security, intimacy in its nooks and crannies, independence in its more spacious rooms, and provides purposeful occupation. Most men who were interviewed had dreamed of having a house with a garden. The women aspired towards a more comfortable home which was less confined and which they could arrange the way they wanted. For many women of the working class, this was their first comfortable home. Most tenants, having spent 40 years in a flat, wanted one day to become home-owners: its achievement would give them one of the last great joys of their lives.

Of the households leaving Paris 85 per cent settled in houses but several tenants lacked the means to buy the house they wanted and had to buy or rent a flat (very few houses are for renting). Others, living in a house in communes they did not like, envied those who could afford a flat in a pleasant and lively town, but it was usually the type of commune rather than the accommodation which was criticized. Two-thirds moved to a house and nine out of ten moved to a dwelling with a garden. Another characteristic of the new residence was that 80 per cent were owner-occupied, compared to only 25 per cent of their homes in Paris. To own one's home gives the older generation a feeling of security. This is not always justified in the sense that if widowed or handicapped many of the migrants can no longer remain in their homes. They also gain a sense of social achievement: as one old sick man related 'At least I will die a landowner'. The remaining migrants moved to accommodation provided by their children (5 per cent) or became tenants (15 per cent), usually in coastal or other residential towns where new comfortable rented homes at lower prices than in Paris, or cheap uncomfortable older homes were available.

What search procedures have Parisian tenants undergone to become the owners of their retirement homes. Inherited properties are less common (16 per cent) than one expects from the prevalence of return migrations, and one-third of these had had to buy the shares of co-inheritors. The majority of new dwellings were either bought (55 per cent) or constructed (29 per cent). Three-quarters of the purchases were completed before retirement, one-quarter at least 10 years before, 30 per cent 3–9 years before, and 24 per cent in the year of retirement.

Whether purchasing, constructing, or renovating old property, finance was a major constraint. For most migrants it was the most important purchase of their life and as only one in five had sold a property in the Paris region, accumulated savings played a fundamental role. Over decades, many of these families had had to sacrifice excursions, taking holidays, improving their Paris accommodation, and many sacrificed owning a car. To the question 'Did you go to the cinema when you lived in Paris', Madame X replied, 'Two cinema seats make one bag of cement'.

## Degree of comfort and facilities

One-third of the dwellings were less than 10 years old, but half dated from before the 1914–18 war, this figure rising to two-thirds in the countryside. Forty per cent were old country houses and in this way migrants contribute to the conservation and rehabilitation of housing abandoned by the exodus to the towns. Most owners of old houses appreciate their antiquity (73 per cent) but others remark on their discomfort (17 per cent) or the cost and effort of maintenance (9 per cent).

Most retirement accommodation is more spacious than that in Paris; the average room size increases from 2.7 to 3.8 and the percentage of those with only two main rooms falls from 47 to 10. Two-thirds of households had more room than in Paris; only one in ten had less, usually after leaving accommodation regarded as too spacious. In almost all cases, therefore, the changed number of rooms is appreciated. After the move most households can accommodate an overnight guest, for their rooms are not only more numerous but also more spacious. Lastly, those who moved from a flat to a house usually acquired a garden, various nooks and crannies, a basement, a garage, an attic, and a utility room: at last they have room for all their possessions and for stores, wine, tools, a winter greenhouse, and space for drying clothes. The men gained a corner for their handicrafts and many gained a proper workshop.

Great improvements were also achieved in the degree of comfort. The percentage of houses with their own bathroom increased from 32 to 77, and of those without an inside lavatory decreased from 37 to 14. A few poor people continue to live with very little comfort as they had done all their lives. Taking an overall view of comfort (heating, sanitation, condition of the property), half of the households were better off than in Paris; amongst the 45 per cent who first acquired a bathroom when they retired, half had lived in homes without an inside lavatory.

Of the migrant households in the 1973 survey only one in four had a telephone, but two-thirds had not had one in Paris. Relative isolation and the separation from children in retirement makes a telephone more valuable; 50 per cent lived in communes without a resident doctor. More recently the installation of telephones has greatly increased, as shown by almost universal possession among the 1979 respondents in resorts.

Most of the retired migrants were satisfied with their accommodation, some because they are well accommodated, others because they are easily pleased. This is especially the case with the lower third of the income distribution; most are better-housed than in Paris or at any other time in their life. This is the positive contribution of retirement migration (Table 5.4). Although they did not mind being without comforts in Paris, all say that now they could not be without them. In nearly every home one finds fresh paintwork, bright and cheerful wallpaper, trinkets, photos, art reproductions, and house plants. The occupants have obviously derived great pleasure from arranging these things and from the organization of their new homes. Almost all gardens have flowers, shrubs, and well-tended paths and hedges. The retired people are justifiably proud of the way they maintain their homes which they see as a reward for half a century of work.

Table 5.4 Self-expressed comparison of retirement with pre-retirement accommodation

| Attribute | Better | Similar | Worse | Total |
|---|---|---|---|---|
| Quietness, tranquillity | 86 | 10 | 4 | 100 |
| Size | 82 | 12 | 4 | 100 |
| Natural light | 68 | 25 | 7 | 100 |
| Heating | 54 | 34 | 12 | 100 |
| Overall | 90 | 4 | 6 | 100 |

*Source*: Author's survey of retired migrants (1973).

## A FIRST ASSESSMENT OF RETIREMENT MIGRATION

It was logical to describe their new circumstances before asking the respondents whether they were satisfied with their life and environment. However, an analysis of *modes de vie* was an important component of the surveys. Only the most important aspects of retirement lifestyle will be reported here before proceeding to a preliminary evaluation of retirement migration.

According to the migrant's own perceptions and expression, retirement is more active away from Paris than in the city. Using one's time gainfully gives a feeling that things are being achieved, reinforces one's self-esteem, structures the day, and helps to ensure continuity with the patterns and values cherished before retirement. Secondly, migration promotes a feeling of freedom in time and space, and allows more seasonal variation of activities than in Paris. There are also many important continuities, particularly in the cultural life of the migrants. Television, newspapers, little other reading, few social encounters, little participation in clubs, few exchanges with neighbours, and the occasional café meetings for the men are as true in the provinces as in Paris.

Despite the distance, family relationships were normally well maintained, close, and warm; but the frequency of visits was strongly related to distance. Half the parents were more than 200 km from their children and about the same fraction saw them less than once a month. Twenty-five per cent of migrant families had no children at all; 18 per cent had none in the Paris region; 16 per cent moved closer to their children; and 57 left children behind in Paris. For many elderly parents, moving to the provinces may be interpreted as a sign of independence and a display of modern individualism; for others it represents an adjustment to their children's independence and a distancing so as not to be a burden. Only one-third of the individuals and 20 per cent of married couples had many friends and acquaintances in the destination commune. These poor social relationships reflected their previous sociability during working life: only 20 per cent of migrants had entertained friends at home in Paris. About two-thirds of the native settlers and half the non-native migrants said that they were made welcome in the retirement locality. With the exception of returning natives, former Parisians had few relationships with the local elderly population and tended to associate with other ex-urban dwellers of the same social class.

Those interviewed on average had been in the provinces for 2 years. The migrants were asked whether they were happier than in the Paris region, why this was the case, what they were missing, whether they were healthier, whether they had a better life, whether they would recommend the move to others, and if they were settled permanently. As in any survey of this type, the answers to open questions need to be analysed and interpreted carefully. For example, the discontent due to inadequate adjustment to retirement, ill health, or family problems is sometimes presented as due to the environment. The great majority of the 477 interviewees were very pleased with their move. Only 16 per cent of women and 12 per cent of men admitted that they were disappointed, and 7 per cent of women and 4 per cent of men refused to answer the question. Thus 80 per cent expressed no disappointment, with a slightly higher percentage among men. The women has less frequently chosen the commune for retirement, they gained fewer new activities, missed their children more, were more affected by the inadequate shopping facilities, and some missed the social life of their Paris neighbourhood or suburb more than men.

People who retired to their native region were less likely to be disappointed (6 per cent) than others (18 per cent), and not suprisingly disillusion was most common among those with only slight previous acquaintance with their new commune. Most thought that they were in better health than when they arrived and attributed this improvement to rest and the new environment. This improvement was reported most frequently among working-class people.

To the question, 'Lastly, are you happy here', three-quarters of men and two-thirds of women replied with a straight 'Yes', but three in ten were only partially or not contented, although many of them began by answering 'Yes of course'. This was most commonly the case among those in poor health, particularly among the non-natives and women. The least contented in the retirement area were usually those who were not very happy in Paris; 82 per cent of those who were happy in Paris were equally so in the provinces, but only 65 per cent of the discontented in Paris. Most migrants (77 per cent) thought that if they had remained in Paris their life would have been less pleasant. This view was held more often by men than women; 17 per cent of the latter thought the opposite. As many of these women were brought to the retirement area by their husbands, one wonders how contented and socially integrated they will be if they are widowed.

One question asked if anything was missed in the new commune in comparison to Paris: 34 per cent cited shops and facilities, 19 per cent (often the same people) a lively atmosphere, and 17 per cent cited social relations. Women more often said that they missed their children and the shops, while the few discontented men most missed their work. It is worth noting that the majority of the former Parisians (60 per cent) did not express any loss.

The majority (77 per cent) said that they would make the same choice again, men (82 per cent) more frequently reaffirming their decision than women (71 per cent); but 4 per cent of men and 9 per cent of women admitted that they wished they had remained in Paris and 14 per cent of men and 20 per cent of women wished they had moved elsewhere. The latter are more numerous among the migrants living in a commune with poor facilities (35 per cent) and among the respondents who had few friends (20 per cent) than among those who had many (4 per cent). They are over-represented in the poorest group, who considered somewhat naively that they had just 'had bad luck in settling in such a poorly equipped locality'. Those who wished that they had stayed in Paris were often those in poor health, women with children in Paris, or those who missed the lively atmosphere of Paris. None of the many migrants who had lived in noisy accommodation would have preferred to have stayed in Paris.

Overall, 80 per cent of the sample were not disappointed with the move; 77 per cent thought that life was better as a result, and 71 per cent were unreservedly happy. Asked what they would do if they won the jackpot on the National Lottery, 64 per cent said they would stay in the same commune, but others said that they would move to the Midi (21 per cent), nearer Paris, or to a town. Most said that they were now settled for good, but in both the 1973 and the 1979 surveys 12 per cent of households envisaged another move. The places where they hoped to settle were invariably larger, better-equipped, less remote, and with better communications. The few households which had made a second move had all moved to a better-equipped commune. Some people were considering moving nearer to their children as the years advanced.

The surveys had concentrated upon the move itself, the reasons for leaving Paris, the choice of retirement area, and the new lifestyle rather than on the unfulfilled needs of the migrants, which mainly relate to social life, entertainment, facilities, and services. These unmet needs will increase with advancing years when inadequate shopping and medical facilities and poor local services will be exacerbated by widowhood, deteriorating health, and isolation. Even 2 years after the move one person in ten would have been better off elsewhere. Many were widows who would have preferred to stay in Paris; the death of their husband left them with a reduced income and few if any reasons to remain in a village where their husband came for fishing and gardening. A few will be able to return to Paris but most will stay on regardless of their vulnerability and aimlessness. They are bored, have few friends, and are isolated in the countryside or in small towns.

Other respondents were disappointed by the move, and had found that the countryside did not meet their expectations even if it had been visited during weekends and summer holidays. In the noise of Paris, they craved tranquillity, but now the countryside is too quiet. Some hoped to make new friends but this had not happend; some had relied on the facilities in the local town but the bus service had been discontinued; some came because of local friends who had died soon after they arrived. A few respondents said that they had hoped that their children would visit them more frequently than had been the case. Some had come for the fishing, but every year the river seemed further away.

Seaside resorts with their long winter season (except in the Midi) had deceived some of their new inhabitants. But the situation of the retired Parisians interviewed in 1979 in coastal resorts did appear more favourable than that of the migrants of the 1973 survey. Half of them belonged to the middle classes; thus they were more affluent, had better-defined goals and were more at ease in their social relationships. The resorts are often well provided with shopping facilities and services and have a lifestyle more adapted to middle-class tastes;

but the 1973 sample was more representative of Parisian retirement migrants because it was selected at the origin. It demonstrated that the majority of migrants are drawn from the working and lower middle classes which constitute the vast majority of the Paris population; approximately half move to the countryside and eight out of ten move further away from their children. These two principal characteristics of the moves each underlie problems that will worsen with a migrant's advancing years.

The inadequate shopping facilities and medical services in rural areas are sources of fatigue, worry, and eventually distress. There is a considerable difference in this respect between France and England where most retirement migration is directed towards the coast. Although I agree with Karn (1977) when she states that because the old want to retire at the seaside these towns must be equipped with the necessary facilities for supporting old people, the cost and practical difficulty of providing services in rural areas suggests that their facilities in France or elsewhere are unlikely to be greatly improved.

The second problem of retirement migration is social and family isolation. Many retired couples rely on each other for companionship; other friends are few and themselves elderly. Who will look after a widow or widower if they do not have a network of supportive friends? Two-thirds of the migrants have either no family or very few near them and half of these have very few friends. An impoverished social network in Paris is commonly replaced by a life still deficient of social relationships. The clubs which have multiplied in recent years (more in the towns and cities than in the countryside) do substitute to some extent, at least as long as the migrants are 'young' old people.

The migration of retired Parisians raises problems almost everywhere in France, not excluding Paris. How can those who are languishing far away from their children return to Paris? How can those in Paris who are being pushed out by the threat of eviction or the deterioration of their neighbourhood be helped to find better replacement housing? Retirement migration is also partly a consequence of a wider urban crisis. Many people leave Paris of their own will, or so they think, because after half a century of work they have insufficient incomes or capital to live comfortably in Paris. As nearly a third of older Parisians leave, housing is opened up for those young workers who take their place: so retirement migration can be seen as a means of maintaining the urban system.

The purpose of this study was not to investigate the consequences of retirement migration in either the sending or receiving areas. It sought a better understanding of the factors of retirement migration, its spatial and social characteristics, and of the behaviour and the attitudes of the Parisians who move to the provinces. I have tried to demonstrate that in order to understand the relationship between people and places, it is necessary to take into consideration not only the material and social characteristics of the places, but also a set of social facts of all kinds—economic, cultural, historical, legal, and psychological.

We have seen that the great majority of migrants are satisfied and the reasons for this. We have observed the difficulties encountered by the younger retirees and their reasons for dissatisfaction, and suggested that not all these difficulties are related to retirement migration itself or to the locality of residence. The study represents a first assessment. A fuller examination requires a longitudinal study to assess the responses to widowhood, to the bereavement of parents and friends of the same age, to declining health and the loss of autonomy, and above all to advancing age.

## REFERENCES

Chevalier, L. (1967). *Les Parisiens*. Hachette, Paris.

Cribier, F. (1969). *La Grande Migration d'Eté des Citadins en France*. Centre National de la Recherche Scientifique (CNRS), Paris.

Cribier, F. (1973). Les résidences secondaires des citadins dans les campagnes françaises. *Etudes Rurales*, No. 49–50, 181–204.

Cribier, F. (1975a). *La Migration de Retraite des Parisiens*. Laboratoire de Geographie Humaine, Paris.

Cribier, F. (1975b). Retirement migration in France. In Mansell Prothero, R. and Koszinski, E. (Eds), *People on the Move*, pp. 360–73. Methuen, London.

Cribier, F. (1978). *Une Génération de Parisiens Arrive à la Retraite*. CNRS, Paris.

Cribier, F. (1979a). La migration de retraite: définitions et problèmes. *Gerontologie et Société*, No. 30, 7–17.

Cribier, F. (1979b). Relations à Paris et images de Paris: Les Parisiens qui se retirent en Province. In Frémont, A. (Ed.), *L' Espace Vécu*, pp. 59–68. CNRS, Paris.

Cribier, F. (1980). A European assessment of aged migration. *Research on Aging*, **2**, 255–70.

Cribier, F., Duffau, M. L., and Kych, A. (1974). *La Migration de Retraite en France*, 2 vols. Laboratoire de Geographie Humaine, Paris.

Karn, V. (1977). *Retiring to the Seaside*. Routledge & Kegan Paul, London.

Law, C. M. and Warnes, A. M. (1980). The characteristics of retirement migrants. In Herbert, D. T. and Johnston, R. J. (Eds), *Geography and the Urban Environment*, vol. 3, pp. 223–56. Wiley, Chichester.

Longino, C. F. (1979). Going home: aged return migration in the United States 1965–70. *Journal of Gerontology*, **34**, 736–45.

Geographical Perspectives on the Elderly
Edited by A. M. Warnes


Chapter 6

# County patterns of elderly migration in the United States

*James R. Bohland* and *Lexa Treps*

The increased relative size of the elderly population in post-industrial societies such as the United States or Great Britain is well documented in demographic statistics. Recent census figures for the United States indicate both an absolute and a relative growth in the population 65 years or older. In 1920 less than 5 per cent of the population was older than 65; in 1970 it was almost 10 per cent; and it is projected to be nearly 20 per cent by 2000 (US Bureau of the Census, 1976). While summarizing national trends these figures conceal important regional differences in the dynamics of elderly population growth. In some regions of the country the portion of the population 65 years and older exceeds 14 per cent, while in other areas the elderly constitute a very small percentage of the total population. Moreover, regional variations are continually shifting. In 1950 the counties with high concentrations of elderly were in New England and the Middle West, while in 1970 concentrations were highest in the Plains states and Florida (Graff and Wiseman, 1978).

The dynamics of elderly redistribution are a function of fertility, mortality, and migration. While the movement of all age cohorts influences the relative size of the elderly population, the migration of older persons is a major force in changing the distribution of elderly population. Yet, research in migration has only recently begun to focus on the movement of the elderly.

The research presented in this essay adds to the current literature on elderly migration in two ways. First, using county net migration data for two time-periods we have identified and described changes in the spatial pattern of elderly migration. In the last section relationships between elderly net migration rates and selected county attributes are analysed in order to test hypotheses concerning the significance of both economic and non-economic variables to elderly migration. Previous research is ambivalent on whether economic conditions in an area influence elderly migration. We believe our research establishes that economic as well as social factors do influence elderly migration.

## ELDERLY MIGRATION RESEARCH

Research on elderly migration is sparse in comparison with the literature on the migration of other sub-populations, but the volume has been increasing recently. The quickening pace of research on the elderly reflects two factors:

(1) the demographic structure of industrial societies and the importance of elderly cohorts in that structure; and
(2) the poor predictive and explanatory power of most existing migration models when applied to elderly migration.

Despite the recent research on the migration of the elderly explanation is still based primarily on postulates and suppositions rather than fact or theory.

To explain the migration behaviour of any group two issues must be considered. What Morrison (1973) terms the 'Who moves?' question, and the 'Where do people who move go?' question. While the two are interrelated, for the selection of a destination is a function of the motivations for moving, distinguishing between the two does provide a useful framework for considering the migration behaviour of a group such as the aged.

In a recent review Murphy (1979) concluded that precious little is known about what group of elderly has a higher propensity to move, or why they move. The elderly are known to be less mobile than younger age cohorts, but differentiating between movers and stayers on the basis of personal characteristics such as income or occupation has proven to be difficult. Neo-classical economic models that assume inter-regional migration to be function of employment differentials also seem to be inappropriate for explaining elderly migration. Both Barsby and Cox (1975), who used state aggregate migration data, and Chevan and Fischer (1979), who used disaggregate data, concluded that employment variables were unimportant in explaining differences in elderly migration. Cebula's (1970) analysis of the migration behaviour of different age cohorts showed income and employment variables to be insignificant in explaining the migration of persons 65 and older. Because most individuals leave the labour force between the ages of 60 and 65 the lack of correspondence of elderly migration and employment variables is not surprising. However, since employment variations are indicators of the general economic well-being of an area, it is surprising that some type of relationship, even a spurious one, does not exist.

While we agree that employment conditions are unimportant to elderly migration decisions, we do believe that certain economic factors are important. At present considerable disagreement exists on this point. On the one hand

rates and attributes influencing migration within a state. The assumption is unrealistic, of course. Even in Florida, the state with the highest rate of in-migration by the elderly, a number of counties experience a net loss of elderly through migration.

To avoid the problems associated with using state aggregates, county data for all counties within the conterminous United States were used in this analysis. Unfortunately, the use of county data is not without its own limitations. Origin and destination information is unavailable at this scale. Consequently, patterns of flow cannot be identified, nor can place utility differentials be calculated. Only net migration totals and rates are available for 5-year age cohorts at the county level. Net rates conceal information on gross movements as well as on origins and destinations; however, the advantages of using the finer geographical data network outweigh the disadvantages of relying on net values in our opinion.

County net migration totals and rates for 5-year age cohorts for two decades, 1950–60 and 1960–70 have been published by the US Department of Agriculture (Bowles and Tarver, 1965; Bowles, Beale, and Lee, 1975). Net migration totals for individual age cohorts ($N_a$) were estimated by the differentials between cohort expected populations ($E_a$) and end-of-decade census totals for the cohort ($A_a$). Expected populations for elderly cohorts were determined by simply subtracting the number of deaths of persons in the cohort during the decade from the population at the beginning of the period. In the USDA report age-specific net migration rates were calculated as the ratio between net total and expected population in an age cohort ($R_a = N_a/E_a$). When standardized by a constant ($k$), e.g. 100, the rate can be interpreted as the number of net migrants (+ or −) per 100 of the expected population.

Since we used several cohorts in defining our elderly population, all cohorts 60 years and older were aggregated to obtain elderly net totals ($N_e$) and net rates ($R_e$). Equations (1) and (2) show the calculations used to determine the values for each county. Rates were multipled by a constant ($k$) to aid the interpretation.

$$N_{e,i} = \sum_{a=1}^{4} (A_{a,i} - E_{a,i}) \tag{1}$$

$$R_{e,i} = \left( N_{e,i} \Big/ \sum_{a=1}^{4} E_{a,i} \right) \cdot k \tag{2}$$

where $a = 1, 2, 3, 4$ represents the age groups: 1, 60–4 years; 2, 65–9 years; 3, 70–4 years; and 4, 75 and more years.

Sixty rather than 65 was the threshold age used to define the elderly because of the increased number of retirements in the cohort 60–65. The use of 60 rather than 65 as the threshold does not appear to change significantly the results, for the correlation of the 60–64 age cohort rates with those in the cohort immediately post-dating it (65–69) was very high (0.82), indicating considerable similarity in the migration behaviour of the two groups.

## SPATIAL STRUCTURE OF ELDERLY MIGRATIONS

In order to describe the geographical pattern of elderly migration, counties with elderly migrant surpluses and deficits were identified for the two decades. The totals for the two periods indicate a marked change in the spatial pattern of elderly migration (Table 6.1). In the earlier decade the majority of the counties (69 per cent) lost more elderly residents through migration than were gained. In contrast, in the 1960s the number of counties with a net surplus of elderly migrants increased by 87 per cent and the average rate increased from — 1.59 to 3.25.

Although the average rate increased' the variability in rates, as measured by the standard deviations, was similar for the two periods. This consistency in conjunction with the change in the average rate would occur if the pattern of increase was general and uniformly distributed rather than confined to a small number of counties. The areal comprehensiveness of the increase between the decades is clearly evident from the change in the spatial distributions (Figure 6.1 and 6.2).

In the earlier decade only three areas of any size had concentrations of counties with net surpluses greater than 500 (Figure 6.1). Peninsular Florida and southern California–western Arizona not surprisingly were two of the areas with a large number of counties with elderly surpluses. The third, consisting of counties in the metropolitan corridor along the mid-Atlantic coasts, is an area not usually considered as an important destination for elderly migrants.

These three areas were also clearly evident on the map of net rates (Figure 6.2).

Table 6.1 Summary statistics for elderly net migration rates: USA, 1950–60 and 1960–70

| Summary statistic | Decade 1950–60 | Decade 1960–70 | Decadal change |
|---|---|---|---|
| Average number of elderly migrants per county ($N_e - E_e$) | 0.35 | 50.63 | + 50.28 |
| Average county elderly net migration rates (net migrants per 100) | − 1.59 | 3.25 | + 4.85 |
| Standard deviation of net migration rate | 17.79 | 17.34 | − 0.45 |
| Total number of counties | 3065 | 3065 | 0 |
| Number of counties with net rate $\geq$ 2.5 | 950 | 1778 | + 828 |
| Percentage of counties with net rate $\geq$ 2.5 | 31.3 | 58.0 | + 26.7 |

In addition to these three, three other areas could be identified that had concentrations of counties with net rates about 2.5. The three included the Ozark area of Arkansas, Missouri and Oklahoma, eastern Texas, and western Oregon. Although the rates here were 20 per cent higher than the median value for the two decades, in none of the three was the total number of elderly migrants comparable to that in the Florida, California, or mid-Atlantic areas.

Three generalizations concerning the geographical pattern of elderly migration during the earlier decade can be noted. First, there was an urban focus to much of the elderly migration. The larger surpluses were not, however, necessarily in large metropolitan areas, but rather were in the adjacent suburban counties. This trend was most evident in the mid-Atlantic area, but it was prevalent throughout the county, except possibly peninsular Florida. A second characteristic was the southerly and peripheral orientation to the pattern. Few counties in the interior or northern portions of the country experienced net surpluses of elderly migrants during the decade. Finally, the spatial structure of the elderly migration can be characterized as 'origin extensive–destination intensive' on the basis of the pattern of surpluses. Migrant deficits were evident throughout the country while surpluses were concentrated in a relatively small number of counties. Such county distributions reinforce the conclusion of other authors about the focal nature of elderly migration (Flynn, 1978).

The number and geographical coverage of counties with a surplus of elderly migrants increased substantially in the latter decade (Figure 6.1). Almost every section of the country experienced increases in the rate and number of excess elderly migrants (Figure 6.3). The major exception was in a large area stretching from Pennsylvania through Ohio, Indiana, southern Michigan, and Illinois into Iowa; here most counties actually had a decrease in net figures. In the 1960s this area, along with counties in the western Great Plains and intermontane region of the West, were the areas where the majority of the counties had negative rates.

While in the 1950s the focal aspect of elderly migrant was quite evident, in the 1960s it was less pronounced. For example, 51 per cent of the counties with surpluses in excess of 500 were located in three areas in the 1950s, whereas in the later decade only 23 per cent of the surplus counties were within the same three.

Peninsular Florida, southern California–western Arizona and the mid-Atlantic surplus areas were still much in evidence in the 1960s, and in fact had expanded in size (Figure 6.1). However, several new concentrations of counties with large surpluses appeared. Many counties in the Ozark and eastern Texas areas, which in the earlier decade had positive rates but small numbers, now had absolute totals in excess of 500. An increased number of counties along the Gulf coast in Louisiana, Mississippi, and Alabama, in the upper South, in the Pacific North-West and in the upper middle West also had sizable surpluses. With the addition of these new surplus areas' by the end of the decade the

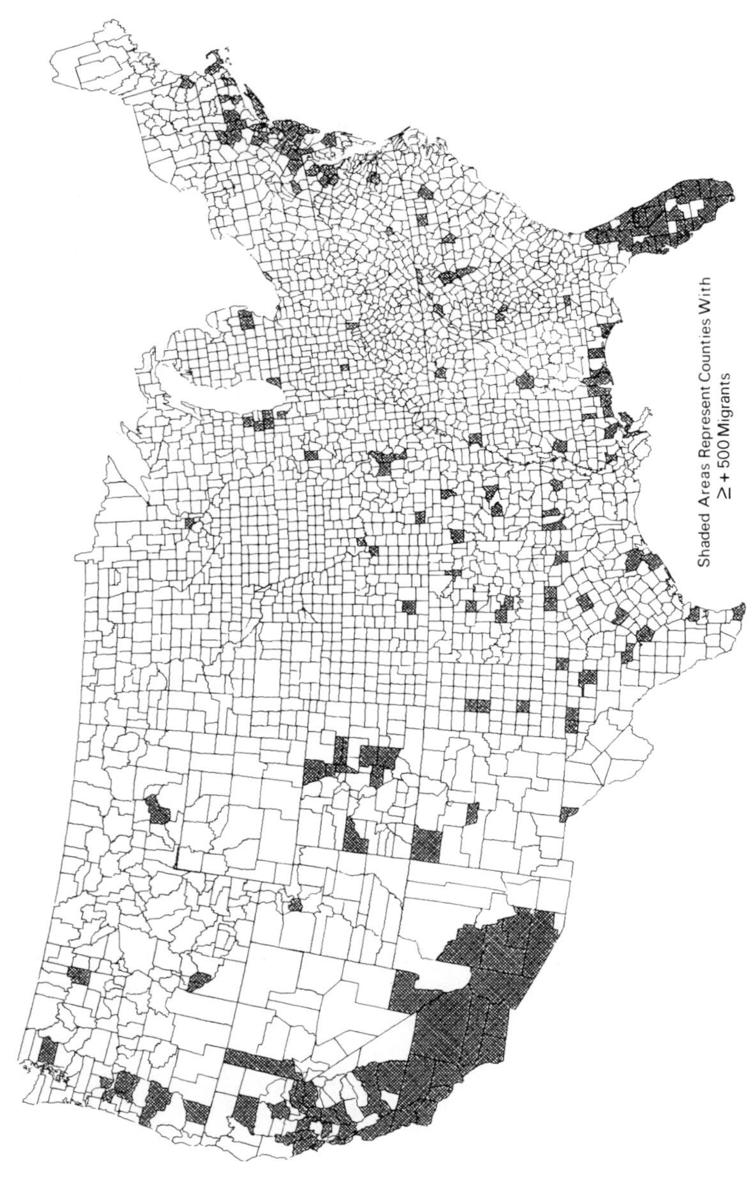
Shaded Areas Represent Counties With
≥ + 500 Migrants

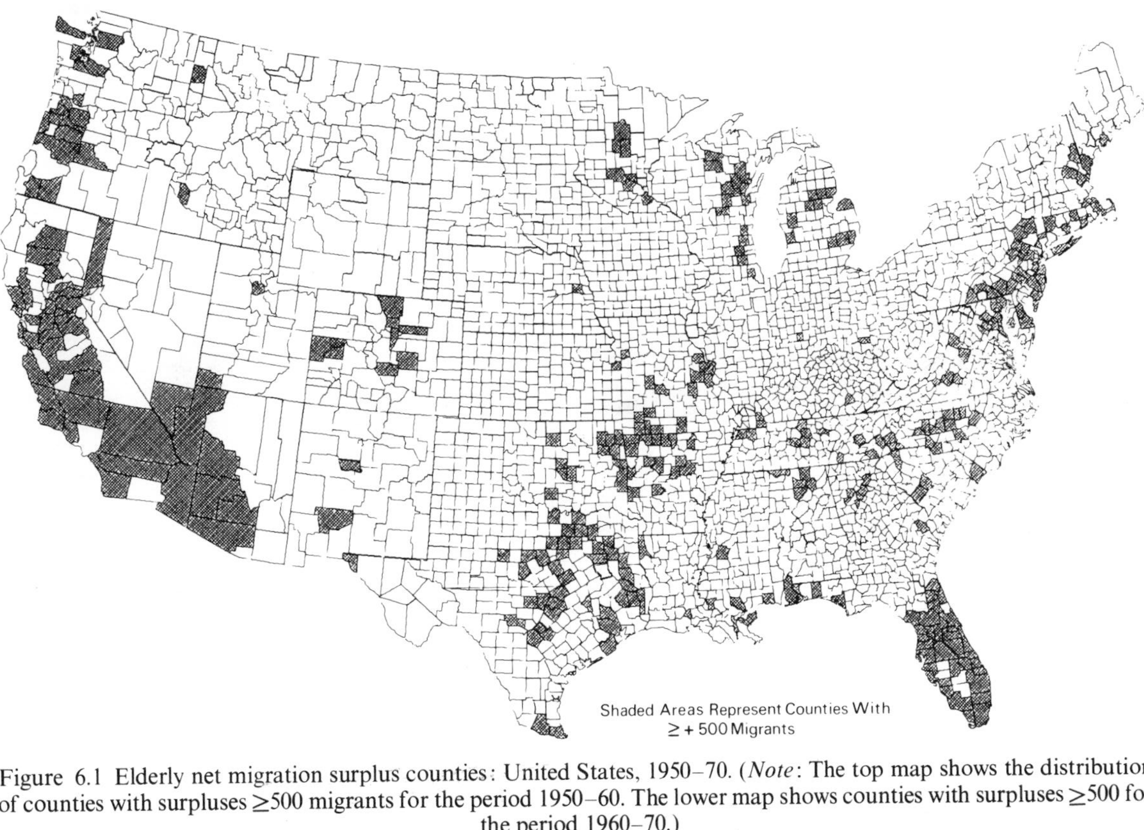


Figure 6.1 Elderly net migration surplus counties: United States, 1950–70. (*Note*: The top map shows the distribution of counties with surpluses ≥500 migrants for the period 1950–60. The lower map shows counties with surpluses ≥500 for the period 1960–70.)

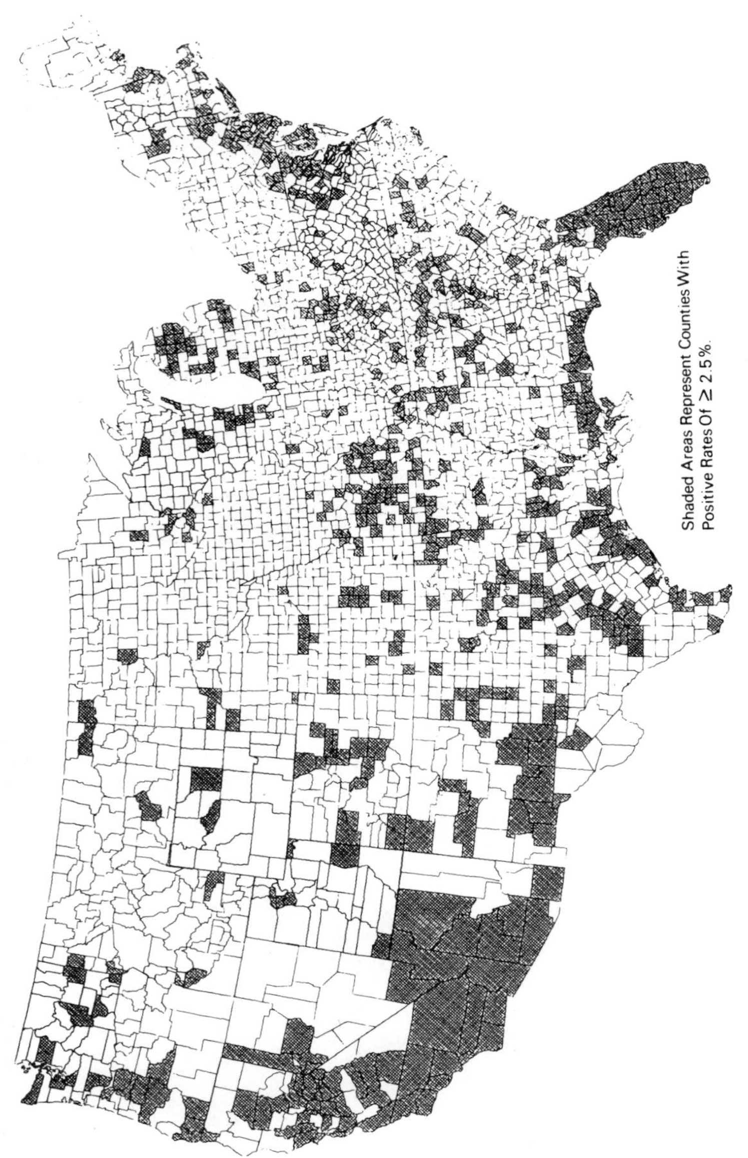
Shaded Areas Represent Counties With
Positive Rates Of ≥ 2.5%.

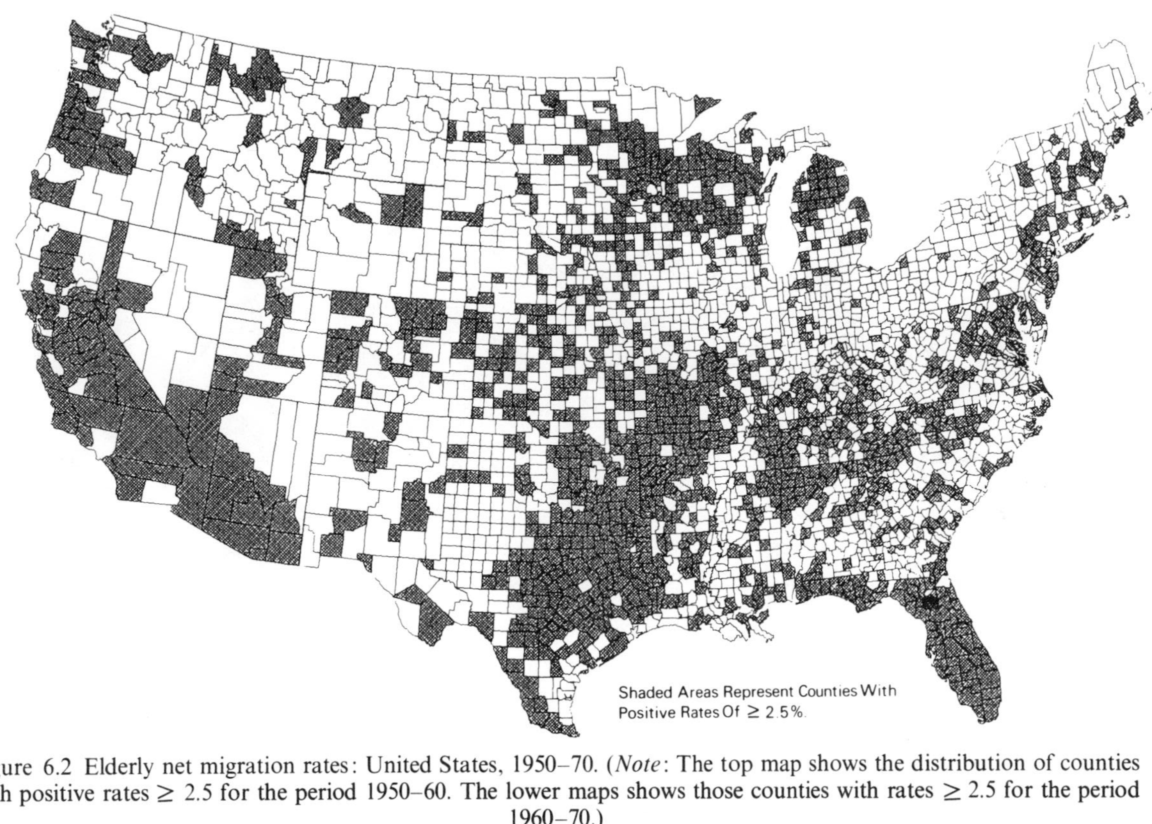


Figure 6.2 Elderly net migration rates: United States, 1950–70. (*Note*: The top map shows the distribution of counties with positive rates ≥ 2.5 for the period 1950–60. The lower maps shows those counties with rates ≥ 2.5 for the period 1960–70.)

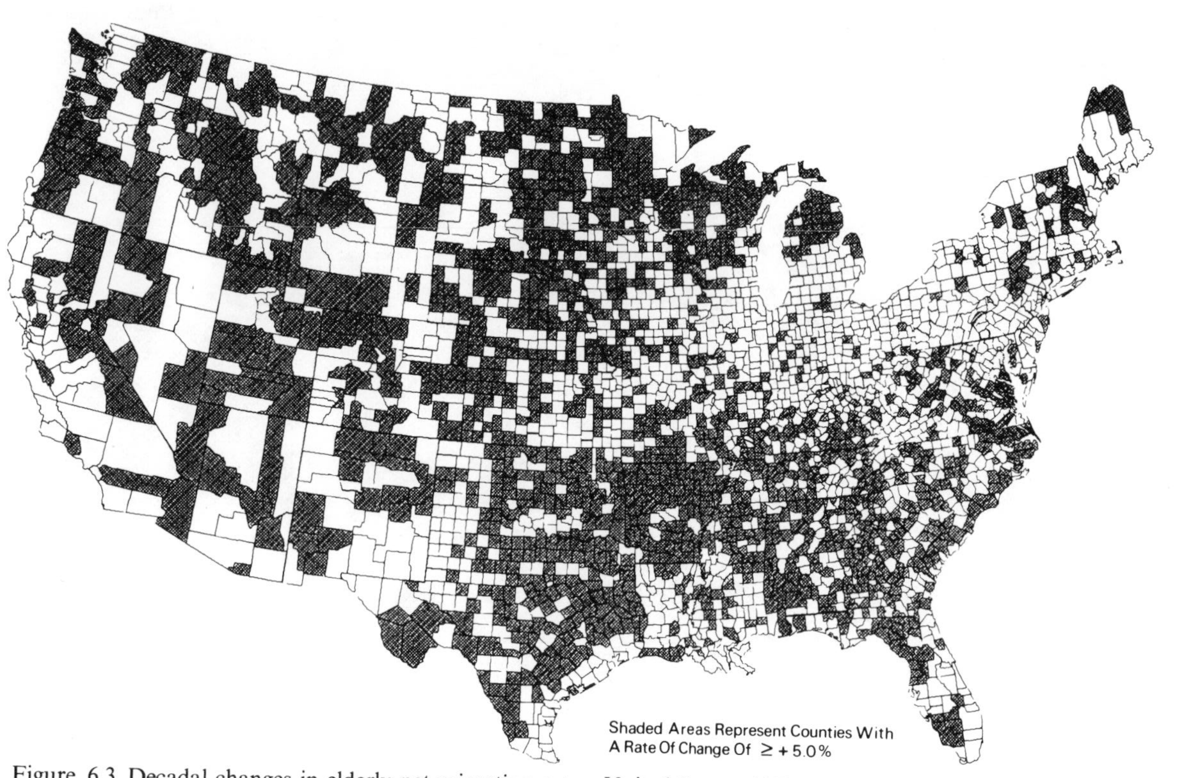


Figure 6.3 Decadal changes in elderly net migration rates: United States, 1950–60 to 1960–70. (*Note*: Counties with values ≥ 5.0 percentage points increase in the 1960–70 rate compared with the 1950–60 are shaded.)

southern, peripheral orientation to elderly movement so evident in the 1950s had been significantly altered and the movement pattern was more national in scope.

The magnitude of the change in the geographical pattern of elderly migration is best illustrated by the areal expansion of counties with positive net rates (Figure 6.2). The distribution of counties with positive rates differs radically from that of the 1950s.

The complexity of the distribution of surplus counties makes it difficult to identify those areas which constitute important foci of elderly movement. To clarify the county patterns and to identify those areas which are major concentrations of elderly surplus migrants, an algorithm was used to group counties into what we have termed 'elderly net migration regions'. To establish the basis for a region and to define its geographical extent the following criteria were used. For a region to be defined, a minimum of ten contiguous counties with positive rates in excess of 2.5 had to exist. Moreover, at least five of these had to have absolute surpluses of 500 or more, Once the core was identified counties were added if their net rates were greater than 2.5, and they shared a common border with at least one county within the region.

Using these criteria eight regions were identified (Figure 6.4). The eight re-

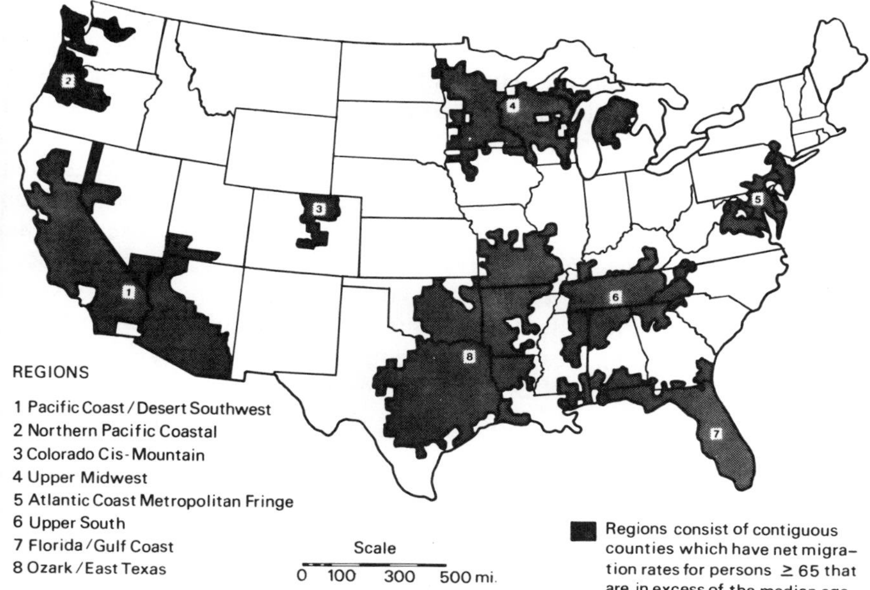


Figure 6.4 Elderly net migration regions: United States, 1960–70. (*Note*: Regions are based on county elderly net migration rates for the decade 1960–70. The regions constitute contiguous counties which have net migration rates for persons aged 65 years or more that are in excess of the median.)

present those areas in the United States that were destination areas for a significant number of elderly migrants during the decade. While they shared this in common, each was distinctive in its own right. The salient characteristics of each are briefly described.

(1) Pacific Coast/Desert South-West. This region consisted primarily of counties in California and Arizona and ranked second in terms of absolute numbers of migrants. Although many of the counties had surpluses in the earlier decade, the extent of the region had increased primarily because of the addition of counties in northern California.
(2) Northern Pacific Coast. The region was formed by the coalescing of two smaller county concentrations evident in the earlier decade. By the 1960s a sufficient number of counties with positive rates had emerged to form the larger areal unit. The area with the highest surplus was in northern Oregon.
(3) Colorado Cis–Mountain. This region met the minimum criteria and constituted the smallest region. It was composed primarily of counties adjacent to the Front Range of the Rockies with the largest surpluses being in the metropolitan counties of Denver and El Paso (Colorado Springs).
(4) Upper Midwest. The Great Lakes interrupt the continuity of the region; however, the similarities between Michigan and western section warranted their being considered a single region. Despite its size the region had few counties with large numeric surpluses; most were in the northern portion of the Michigan Peninsula. The positive rates were due in large measure to a slowing down in the rate of out-migration of the elderly which was prevalent in the earlier decade.
(5) Atlantic Coast Metropolitan Fringe. The region was a major surplus area in the 1950s. The surpluses here were apparently the result of movement by the elderly into the suburbs and non-metropolitan counties surrounding the large cities in the region.
(6) Upper South. A sufficient number of counties in the upper South reversed a trend of negative net rates to form this extensive region of surplus. In fact, only a few remaining areas of negative rates prevented a coalescing of this region with the Atlantic, Ozark and Florida areas to form a very large region of elderly surplus migration that would have encompassed most of the South.
(7) Florida/Gulf Coast. The traditional area of elderly surpluses, peninsular Florida, was combined with the Gulf coast counties in adjacent states to form this new region. The region ranked first in terms of total number of surplus migrants, although as the map illustrates many counties in Florida actually had a reduction in the number of surplus migrants (Figure 6.3).
(8) Ozark/East Texas. This region was the largest in areal extent and ranked third in total number of migrants. The increase in rates between decades

was highest. All of these indicators attest to the fact that the region had become an important new destination for the elderly migrants in the United States.

Both the numeric and rate distributions illustrate the point made earlier about the advantages of using county rather than state data. In most surplus areas counties were concentrated in specific sections of a state, particularly in the earlier decade. Intra-state migration also appeared to be the dominant process in some areas, particularly in the upper Middle West and in the mid-Atlantic regions. Had state aggregates been used this dimension of elderly movement would have been obfuscated.

## MODEL OF ELDERLY MIGRATION

Although the spatial structure of elderly net migration rates provides some clues as to why the elderly are moving to particular areas, the patterns are too complex to sort out easily the various factors responsible for the movement. Moreover, it is impossible to determine the relative importance of different factors from the maps.

To test the hypothesis that certain county attributes are favoured by elderly migrants, the net migration rates for the last decade were used as the dependent variable along with county attributes as independent variables in a multiple-regression model. Predictor variables were selected to test hypotheses concerning the relative importance of economic and social conditions in directing elderly migration.

The economic variables used in the model were unemployment rates, median income, percentage of the elderly living below the poverty level, average monthly old age assistance benefits, and average property tax. The 1960 and 1970 county data were averaged to estimate mid-decade values, and thus to reduce the problems associated with using predictor variables that pre-date or post-date the migration process. All counties in the coterminous United States were included in the model with two exceptions. Because of the lack of correspondence between data units all counties in Virginia were excluded from the analysis. Also, several counties (seven) scattered throughout the country were excluded because of missing data.

The unemployment rate was included despite earlier studies reporting on its insignificance. We have it as a measure of the economic viability of an area, and to determine whether changing the geographical scale of the analysis gives results different from those associated with state data. We did anticipate that the four other economic variables would be significantly related with the rates.

Our hypotheses are based on the assumption that some elderly migrants have moved in response to cost of living factors, and consequently have selected destinations where the standard of living is reasonably high, but where the living costs are lower. We also assume that public contributions to old age assistance constitute an important part of the real income of many elderly, and that they would seek to maximize these benefits where possible.

On the basis of these assumptions we have hypothesized that net rates would be negatively associated with the county property tax, for the taxes constitute an indicator of cost of living. Median income was anticipated to have a positive association with rates as it is a measure of standard of living. The poverty measure, in contrast, should be negatively associated with migration rates because a high percentage of elderly below the poverty level would indicate a low standard of living and an inadequate commitment by the local government to assisting the elderly. Since we have included contributions by local governments to the old age assistance variable, it should be positively associated with net rates.

To test for a rural bias in elderly migration the percentage of population living in urban areas was included in the model. It was hypothesized to have an inverse relationship with elderly migration. To measure social agglomeration and information effects the rate of net migration was hypothesized to be positively associated with the relative size of the resident elderly population.

Finally, to measure for a 'sunbelt' orientation to migration a dichotomous regional variable was included in the model. Southern counties were identified as those within the South as defined by the US Bureau of the Census and were coded one. Non-southern counties were coded zero. Regression coefficients were estimated using ordinary least square procedures (Table 6.2). Partial correlation coefficients were also estimated to measure the association of each variable with net migration rates holding all other variables constant.

In the original model only the urbanization variable was insignificant. All others, including the unemployment variable, were significant at least at the 0.05 level, although not always in the direction hypothesized. Although all but one variable was statistically significant, the overall predictive value of the model was low ($r = 0.43$), and the partials for most variables were also quite low.

Of the eight variables in the national model the percentage elderly and the regional variables had the strongest association with net rates when the effects of the other variables were controlled. The strength of the regional variable is significant for not only does it indicate a definite regional bias to the movement, it also raises the question as to whether there are regional differences in the nature of the relationships between dependent and predictor variables. To test for a regional effect, coefficients were estimated for southern and non-southern models. If regional effects exist, the predictive qualities of the model should be improved by the differentiation for the relationships between net rates and the predictor variables may differ from those in the national model.

Segmenting the models improved the predictive quality of the model for

Table 6.2 Regression and partial correlation coefficients for elderly net migration rates, USA, 1960–70

| Independent variables[a] | Regression coefficients and partial correlation coefficients (in parentheses) | | |
|---|---|---|---|
| | National | Southern | Non-southern |
| Percentage urban | 0.019<br>(.028)[b] | – 0.007<br>(– 0.009) | 0.023[c]<br>(0.045) |
| Percentage of population 65 years or older | 2.61[d]<br>(0.329) | 3.36[d]<br>(0.333) | 1.66[c]<br>(0.271) |
| Percentage unemployed | 0.55[d]<br>(0.078) | – 0.35<br>(– 0.038) | 0.83[d]<br>(0.153) |
| Median income | 0.002[d]<br>(0.010) | 0.002[d]<br>(0.073) | 0.002[d]<br>(0.131) |
| Percentage of elderly below poverty level | – 0.405[d]<br>(– 0.125) | – 0.655[d]<br>(– 0.137) | – 0.232[d]<br>(– 0.103) |
| Average monthly public assistance payment | 0.218[d]<br>(0.093) | 0.469[d]<br>(0.170) | 0.044<br>(0.025) |
| Property tax | 0.0001[c]<br>(0.041) | – 0.55[d]<br>(– 0.133) | 0.0001<br>(0.057) |
| Region | 11.36[d]<br>(0.272) | | |
| Constant | – 69.54 | – 79.84 | – 39.28 |
| $R$ value | 0.43 | 0.51 | 0.32 |
| $R^2$ | 0.19 | 0.26 | 0.10 |
| Number of counties | 2967 | 1369 | 1598 |

[a]Value for all independent variables represent an average of the 1960 and 1970 census figures
[b](0.028) represents 7th or 6th order partial correlation coefficients.
[c]Beta coefficient significant at the 0.05 level.
[d]Beta coefficient significant at the 0.01 level.

the southern counties ($r = 0.51$), but reduced it in the non-southern case ($r = 0.32$) (Table 6.2). Differentiating the models also changed the nature of the some of the relationships. For southern counties neither the urbanization nor the unemployment coefficients were significant. The urbanization variable did, however, have the hypothesized negative relationship, indicating a tendency in the South for rural counties to have higher positive rates. The property tax variable also reversed its sign in the hypothesized direction, and its partial correlation coefficient increased from the national model. The relative size of the resident elderly population was still the most important predictor of elderly rates; however, the monthly benefits variable, relatively unimportant in the US model, had the next highest partial in the southern counties. At least in the South those counties with the higher public assistance benefits had the greater net surplus of elderly migrants.

The relationships in the non-southern model were similar to those in the national model; however, two exceptions are noteworthy. First, the urbanization variable had a positive and significant association with elderly rates. Urbanization proved to be significantly associated with elderly net migration only in this model, but in the positive direction. Thus, in the non-southern counties the trend was for urban counties to have higher net surpluses of elderly migrants, a reversal of the southern situation.

The second exception of note was the reduced significance of average assistance payments as a predictor of net migration rates. This variable proved to be the only one without a significant relationship with the dependent variable in the non-southern case. Thus, outside the South county public assistance differentials did not have an influence on the rate of elderly net migration.

## CONCLUSIONS

Our purpose was to describe and to analyze the spatial structure of elderly migration for two decades. The cartographic analysis clearly indicated major changes in the geographical pattern of elderly migration in the United States. The number and areal extent of net surplus areas increased substantially through time as new foci for elderly migration emerged. Accompanying this expansion was a restructuring of net migration surplus areas. The southern foci to net surpluses which dominated the 1950s was less evident in the next decade.

Modification of the spatial structure of elderly net migration totals and rates indicated that new factors had emerged to influence elderly migration behaviour. Using regression analysis we attempted to determine what some of these factors were. In comparing the results of the regression models three conclusions can be drawn. First, economic conditions within a county do, in fact, have a relationship to elderly migration. Not all economic variables were significant, nor were economic variables the more important predictors; however, income, poverty, level and property taxes proved to be significantly associated with elderly net migration rates in all three models. A fourth variable, monthly average benefits, was also significant in the South; whereas unemployment rates were associated with net migration rates primarily in the non-southern counties.

Second, a regional effect definitely exists which alters the relationships between migration rates and structural variables. Counties with higher, positive net rates differ structurally by region. In the South they tend to be rural counties with lower living costs, higher public benefits, and large resident elderly populations. In non-southern counties the pattern of the relationships suggests suburbanization rather than long-distance movement, and those with the higher positive net rates tend to be the most urbanized, to have higher living costs and large resident elderly populations. Public welfare benefits appear to have no influence on elderly rates outside the South.

Our analysis has demonstrated the complexity and the dynamic quality of elderly migration. New areas are emerging as concentrations of elderly migrants. It is important that we be able to identify these areas and try to understand the factors responsible for their growth. Not only will this provide greater understanding concerning the motivations and preferences of the elderly, but it will also allow us to divert resources to these areas to help maintain or improve the quality of life enjoyed by their elderly populations.

## REFERENCES

Barsby, S. L. and Cox, D. R. (1975). *Interstate Migration of the Elderly*. Heath-Lexington, Toronto.

Bowles, G. K. and Tarver, J. D. (1965). *Net Migration of the Population, 1950–70 by Age, Sex and, Color*. Parts 1–6. Economic Research Service, USDA, Washington, DC.

Bowles, G. K., Beale, C. L., and Lee, E. S. (1975). *Net Migration of the Population, 1960–70 by Age, Sex, and Color*. Parts 1–6. Economic Research Service, USDA and Institute for Behavioral Research, Athens, Ga.

Cebula, R. J. (1970). Interstate migration and the Tiebout hypothesis: an analysis according to race, age, and sex. *Journal of the American Statistical Association*, **69**, 876–9.

Cebula, R. J. (1974). The quality of life and migration of the elderly. *Review of Regional Studies*, **4**, 62–68.

Chevan, A. and Fischer, L. R. (1979). Retirement and inter-state migration *Social Forces*, **57**, 1365–80.

Flynn, C. G. (1978). A comparison of interstate migration patterns for the elderly and general United States populations. Paper presented at the annual meeting of the Gerontology Society, Dallas, Texas.

Golant, S. M. (1978). Spatial context of residential moves by elderly persons. *International Journal of Aging and Human Development*, **8**, 279–89.

Golant, S. M. (1979). Central city, suburban, and nonmetropolitan area migration patterns of the elderly. In Golant, S. M. (ed.), *Location and Environment of Elderly Population*, pp. 37–54. V. H. Winston & Sons, Washington, DC.

Goldstein, S. (1967). Socio-economic and migration differentials between the aged in the labour force and in the labor reserve. *Gerontologist*, **7**, 31–40.

Graff, T. O. and Wiseman, R. F. (1978). Changing concentrations of older Americans. *The Geographical Review*, **63**, 379–93.

Lewis, C. W. (1977). The role of age in the decision to migrate. *Annals of Regional Science*, **11**, 51–60

Lundy, G. R. (1978). Nonmetropolitan Migration: A Study of Age Specific Net Migration Rates in the Ozarks–Ouachita Area. Unpublished MSc. thesis, University of Oklahoma, Department of Geography.

Morrison, P. A. (1973). Theoretical issues in the design of population mobility models. *Environment and Planning*, **5**, 125–34.

Murphy, P. A. (1979). Migration of the elderly. *Town Planning Review*, **50**, 84–93.

Rudzitis, G. (1979). Determinants of the central city migration patterns of older persons. In Golant, S. M. (ed.), *Location and Environment of Elderly Population*, pp. 55–63. V. H. Winston & Sons, Washington, DC.

Serow, W. J. (1978). Return migration of the elderly in the USA: 1955–1960 and 1965–1970. *Journal of Gerontology*, **33**, 288–95.

Svart, L. M. (1976). Environmental preference migration: a review. *The Geographical Review*, **66**, 314–30.

US Bureau of the Census (1976). *Current Population Reports, Special Studies, Demographic Aspects of Aging and Older Population in the United States*. US Government Printing Office, Series P.823, No. 59, Washington, DC.

Walker, J. and Price, K. (1975). Retirement choice and retirement satisfaction. *Gerontologist*, **15**, 50.

Wiseman, R. F. (1978). *Spatial Aspects of Aging*. Association of American Geographers, Washington, DC.

Wiseman, R. F. (1979). Regional patterns of elderly concentration and migration. In Golant, S. M. (ed.), *Location and Environment of Elderly Population*, pp. 21–36. V. H. Winston & Sons, Washington, DC.

PART 2

# SPATIAL ASPECTS OF THE ELDERLY'S HOUSING

Geographical Perspectives on the Elderly
Edited by A. M. Warnes


Chapter 7

# Retirement housing in the United Kingdom: a geographical appraisal

*Katherine C. Barnard*

## THE BACKGROUND TO THE STUDY

The recent upsurge of geographical interest in social gerontology covers many facets of the ageing process, not least of which is the changing residential behaviour of individuals as they grow older (Riley and Foner, 1968). Retirement from work frees many households from residential ties to local employment while, in later life, the ageing process produces specific needs with regard to housing stemming mainly from growing spatial dependence on the local environment and reduced income. The public response to such needs centres around the provision of sheltered dwelling schemes, purpose-built exclusively for old people (Department of the Environment (DOE), 1970, 1972) although more recently, alternative forms of housing have been introduced such as 'granny annexes' (Tinker, 1976). In addition, the continuing decrease in the average size of households within the United Kingdom has encouraged the conversion of standard family houses into smaller residential units many for occupation by older households (DOE, 1975a). This chapter explores these developments, monitoring the growth of a housing sub-market which provides dwellings for elderly households.

The agencies supplying retirement dwellings and the policies affecting their supply merit attention and, following a general discussion of the national provision of housing for the elderly, structural and spatial variations in the level of provision will be examined in this context. Detailed investigation of the housing policies adopted by local housing authorities reveals interesting contrasts in the priority attached to housing old people, and different housing strategies produce contrasting residential opportunities for local elderly people. Moreover, the activities of private developers and charitable organizations, including housing associations, have influenced the spread of retirement housing in different parts of the country. Both public and private sector housing developments over the last few years will therefore be examined in the context of growing central government interest in housing the elderly.

In order to obtain a clearer picture of the factors affecting the level of housing provision for old people, mention will be made of the housing strategies adopted by selected local authorities both towards their own dwelling stock and with regard to other housing developments within their boundaries. In this context, two districts in south-west Hampshire—Southampton and the New Forest—have been singled out for detailed study. Information collected from recent household and mobility surveys of the elderly residents in these local authorities provides a useful backcloth against which to observe the growth of retirement housing in the area. This part of the investigation highlights the effects that an expanding housing sub-market geared towards the needs of old people can have on their residential behaviour, a fact warranting further discussion in general terms. These relationships are taken up towards the end of the paper but the initial objective is to examine the physical extent of an elderly housing sub-market within the United Kingdom. The first part of the chapter prefaces this examination with a brief consideration of the growing demand for retirement housing.

## THE NEED FOR RETIREMENT HOUSING

The provision of specialized accommodation for old people has been government policy since the Second World War and various agencies now provide this accommodation which is either specifically designed for the elderly or of the type, size, and price to appeal to older people. The growing number of retirement homes can be seen, at least in part, as a response to the substantial increase in the number of elderly households. The population over the statutory retirement age has quadrupled since the turn of the century, forming one-sixth of the total population in 1971 (Wroe, 1973). Three-quarters of these elderly people were living in small pensionable households at the start of the 1970s, a proportion that has increased significantly in recent years in line with changing social and familial structures. As a result, one and two-person households containing at least one pensioner accounted for over one-third of the household total in 1971 (Table 7.1).

The numerical importance of elderly households has focused attention on their general housing situation. A great deal is known about the housing circumstances of retired people (Age Concern, 1977; Rose, 1978), recent surveys showing that elderly households are not evenly distributed throughout the available housing stock (Office of Population Censuses and Surveys (OPCS), Social Survey Division, 1973; Central Statistical Office, 1979). In terms of dwelling type, old people are over-represented in subdivided property, especially

Table 7.1 Small pensionable households as a percentage of all households: England and Wales, 1971

| | Both pensioners | At least one pensioner |
|---|---|---|
| Tyneside Conurbation | 28.3 | 35.1 |
| Remainder of North Region | 27.5 | 34.0 |
| West Yorkshire Conurbation | 31.1 | 37.7 |
| Remainder of Yorks and Humberside Region | 29.1 | 35.5 |
| Merseyside Conurbation | 26.5 | 33.4 |
| South-east Lancashire Conurbation | 28.4 | 35.2 |
| Remainder of North-West Region | 30.1 | 36.8 |
| East Midlands Region | 28.2 | 34.5 |
| West Midlands Conurbation | 25.0 | 31.4 |
| Remainder of West Midlands Region | 24.7 | 30.8 |
| East Anglia | 31.6 | 38.2 |
| Greater London | 26.3 | 33.0 |
| Outer Metropolitan Area | 24.1 | 30.0 |
| Outer South-East Region | 36.5 | 43.4 |
| South-West Region | 32.9 | 39.9 |
| Wales | 28.5 | 35.3 |
| England and Wales | 28:8 | 35.3 |

*Source*: England and Wales Census, 1971: *Persons of Pensionable Age* (1974), Table 1; *Housing: Part 1, Households* (1974), Table 1.
Office of Population Censuses and Surveys (1974a), *Census of England and Wales 1971, Person of Pensionable Age*, HMSO, London, Table 1; (1974b) *Census of England and Wales 1971, Housing: Part 1, Households*, HMSO, London, Table 1.

in purpose-built, as opposed to converted, flats (Table 7.2). Conversely, they are under-represented in both detached and semi-detached housing. Nationally, aged households are twice as likely to be living in unfurnished rented accommodation and are far less likely to own their dwellings than households generally. Residential inertia is strong among older households with over one-third having occupied the same accommodation for 30 or more years and nearly two-fifths still living in dwellings built before 1914. This means that old people occupy dwellings which are less likely to possess the modern amenities now regarded as standard fittings in newly constructed accommodation. The majority of households lacking at least one of these basic amenities in 1977 were elderly households, one-third being single-person households aged 60 or over and a further quarter consisting of a couple at least one of whom was aged over 60 (Central Statistical Office, 1979).

This growing number of elderly households, many under-occupying dwellings in a poor state of repair, has encouraged the construction of purpose-built dwellings and the conversion of large houses. The increased provision of small accommodation is intended to improve the housing condition of many older

Table 7.2 Elderly households by dwelling type and tenure: England and Wales, 1971 (percentages)

| | Head of household, 60+ | All households |
|---|---|---|
| Detached house | 10.9 | 15.8 |
| Semi-detached house | 22.8 | 32.9 |
| Terraced house | 30.9 | 30.0 |
| Purpose-built flat or maisonette | 23.3 | 12.6 |
| Converted flat or maisonette | 10.7 | 6.5 |
| | | |
| Owner-occupiers | 38.8 | 49.2 |
| Rented from local authority or new town | 34.6 | 31.0 |
| Rented from housing association | 1.3 | 0.6 |
| Rented from private landlord—unfurnished | 22.1 | 11.7 |
| Rented from private landlord—furnished | 2.3 | 2.7 |

*Source*: OPCS, Social Survey Division, 1973, Table 2.2(b).

people while encouraging a more efficient use of the existing dwelling stock by freeing family-sized homes for occupation by younger households. Nor is it thought likely that the demand for smaller dwellings will lessen in the near future (DOE, 1975a). While the number of old people will rise only slightly over the next 20 years, the number of elderly households into which this population is divided is expected to increase (Central Statistical Office, 1979). The social and economic factors, including the rising disposable incomes of older people (Law and Warnes, 1980), which have encouraged the formation of elderly households in the past, are likely to continue to do so at least until the end of the century. Moreover, the number of single-person households (who are most likely to demand small dwellings) is much higher among the over-75s, a group which is expected to increase in size during the 1980s. Thus, by 1991, over 6 million elderly households will require accommodation within Great Britain and over one-half of these households will be formed by an elderly person living alone (Central Statistical Office, 1979).

It should not be assumed of course that all the small elderly households currently competing on the housing market wish to live in one- or two-bedroomed dwellings. Ample evidence exists to show that old people exhibit a variety of housing preferences (for example, Tinker, 1977; MacGuire, 1977). Yet there is no denying the increasing demand for small, easily maintained accommodation if not at the first retirement move, then perhaps at subsequent moves such as those necessitated by widowhood or failing health (Karn, 1974). Many of the small older households presently living in three or more bedroomed properties may be deterred from moving into smaller accommodation for personal or financial reasons. Few elderly owner-occupiers for example will have purchased their house recently except for those migrating on retirement.

Rather they are likely to have remained in the family house following the departure of childern. Even though their current expenditure on housing may put pressure on a reduced family budget, the substantial costs, inconveniences, and disruption of moving house may encourage residential inertia. Moreover, there may be limited alternative accommodation at an appropriate price available to them. Thus, while the family life-cycle theory predicts that moves to smaller dwellings in accessible locations may occur in later retirement (Robson, 1975), limited residential opportunities, combined with other factors, may inhibit this mobility (Murie, 1974).

Small dwellings which may or may not include design features for older households are in demand wherever they are to be found. Local authorities interviewed by the Housing Development Directorate commented on a rise in the number of offers of owner-occupied family houses in exchange for their limited supplies of small local authority flats while private developers have waiting lists for any small dwellings under construction or yet to be built (Housing Development Directorate, 1976). The demand for retirement housing will continue to increase into the 1980s for a variety of demographic, social, and economic reasons. In looking at the current supply of dwellings for older households it is pertinent to consider the extent to which the housing sector has met the existing demand for retirement housing and whether it can meet the anticipated increase in this demand.

## THE SUPPLY OF RETIREMENT HOUSING

Before looking at the degree to which certain accommodation has been made available to older households in the United Kingdom, it is useful to clarify what exactly is meant by the phrase 'retirement housing'. As was suggested in the preceding section, retirement accommodation can either be taken to mean dwellings purpose-built for occupation by elderly people and allocated exclusively to them, or it can be viewed in a wider context including small, low-cost properties which match the reduced size and incomes of older households. Mention too has been made of an elderly housing sub-market, a phrase that can itself be interpreted in a variety of ways. The housing system comprises a series of sub-systems or sub-markets but no consistent approach to, or criteria for, the definition of a housing sub-market has gained universal acceptance (Bourne, 1976). Indeed, any division of the housing system incorporated into a particular study often depends on its orientation and main area of concern. To identify an elderly housing sub-market implies the existence of dwellings available exclusively to elderly households, separated from the rest of the housing stock. This type of housing can certainly be found in the sheltered housing schemes promoted by local authorities and housing associations. Yet while not actually labelled 'retirement' housing, it is clear that may of the flats and and bungalows built both by private developers and local authorities all over the country are expected to be occupied by elderly people. To ensure that these dwellings can also be included in the present investigation, a wide definition of retirement housing is adopted. The term 'elderly housing sub-market' for the moment therefore includes that part of the housing market geared to the provision of small dwellings as well as purpose-built accommodation.

The housing system's complexity complicates the production of a model which identifies and quantifies all the relationships and interactions determining the housing situation. As the definition of retirement housing incorporates more than purpose-built accommodation it is not proposed to offer a detailed model of an exclusive elderly housing sub-market but rather to consider the activities of the many institutions and organizations controlling the supply and allocation of housing for older households. Following this point, it is helpful to look at the supply of dwellings for old people by tenurial group, not least because public intervention in the British housing system tends to be tenure-specific. Looking first at the supply of retirement housing for purchase, the investigation will move on to consider the amount of local authority accommodation provided for elderly tenants followed by a comment on the activities of other agencies operating in this area of the housing market.

Attempts to monitor change within any part of the housing system are complicated by inconsistencies and omissions in published information describing the national housing stock. England, Wales, Scotland and Northern Ireland each have responsibilities for their own housing policy and tend to collect data on different bases. The resulting variation in coverage within the United Kingdom means that the supply of retirement housing cannot be easily measured outside England and Wales. Even here difficulties arise because of the lack of appropriate information. Nationally the Census provides details on both households and dwellings but does not include measures of housing age, type, and cost or the rate of dwelling construction. The number of new dwellings started, in progress, and completed in local housing authorities is recorded in *Local Housing Statistics* for both public and private sector developments but, again, this is not disaggregated by dwelling type for individual districts. No explicit information is provided concerning the number of flats or bungalows built in each area by private developers and no indication of the number of dwellings provided for elderly households appears in the section relating to housing association construction. The only national data which specifically record the tenure and condition of housing occupied by pensionable households are not disaggregated beyond the Standard Region (OPCS, 1974) and the *General Household Survey* inevitably monitors national rather than local trends. One is left with data published annually by the Chartered Institute of Public Finance and Accountancy (CIPFA, 1978) concerning public sector housing provision. Even this poses problems, as not all housing authorities complete returns. Moreover, the information fails to specify the number of dwellings specifically designed for elderly people or allocated to them. Given these difficulties it is impossible to quantify exactly any changes in the supply of small properties or purpose-built dwellings by housing sector. Rather, by piecing the available information together, one can establish the degree of involvement of the different parts of the housing market in providing retirement housing.

## RETIREMENT HOUSING FOR OWNER-OCCUPATION

In the United Kingdom as a whole, over one-half of all households own or are buying their houses (Central Statistical Office, 1979). Owner-occupied dwellings include properties of varying size, type, and condition although the vast majority comprise family-sized houses. The private sector has always been extremely conservative in its approach to housing type and size and, throughout the post-war period, three-bedroomed houses have monopolized private residential developments. This contrasts markedly with public sector building as shown by recent construction figures (Table 7.3).

In the short term, the supply of housing for purchase is relatively static. From the consideration of whether to build more houses or not to the time they are finished and ready for sale takes at least a year, and often longer. Apart from the long time required to increase the housing supply and the consequent importance in the market of the existing stock, the supply of housing is similar to other goods in that it depends on the conditions under which a producer has access to the factors of production—capital, land, materials, and labour. Supply is rarely related to demand within the private sector, private house construction responding less than proportionately to increases in housing requirements (DOE, 1975b). Increased demand is likely to be seen through a rise in house prices or the multi-occupancy rate, with only a limited and delayed effect on new construction. So, despite a growing demand for retirement housing within the market, there has been no widespread increase in the provision of one- or two-bedroomed properties for purchase.

This is not to deny a marked trend within the private sector towards the construction of smaller houses. However, smaller dwellings are not necessarily intended for small households. Rising production costs have encouraged builders to economize on residential developments often by a reduction in the size of living areas within individual units or by building at higher densities. Such measures are preferred to a reduction in the number of bedrooms, for where one- or two-bedroomed properties have been included in private residential developments a substantial reduction in costs per dwelling unit is not guaranteed. A recent survey of private developers building small dwellings in different parts of the country underlined their unpopularity among the building profession, not only for financial reasons but also because of the practical difficulties of operating in confined spaces and of meeting different building regulations (Housing Development Directorate, 1976). The switch to one- and two-bedroomed properties had been necessary to maintain a relatively low selling price following the difficulties experienced by first-time purchasers in obtaining sufficient capital. It was not a response to the growing demand

Table 7.3 New dwellings completed in 1978 within England and Wales

| Number of bedrooms | Percentage of new dwellings | | | | | |
|---|---|---|---|---|---|---|
| | Houses | | Flats | | All dwellings | |
| | For local authorities and new towns | For private owners | For local authorities and new towns | For private owners | For local authorities and new towns | For private owners |
| One | 4.0 | 1.1 | 28.7 | 2.6 | 32.7 | 3.7 |
| Two | 14.1 | 16.2 | 12.4 | 5.7 | 26.5 | 21.9 |
| Three | 32.9 | 56.4 | 3.3 | 0.7 | 36.2 | 57.1 |
| Four of more | 4.0 | 17.2 | 0.6 | 0.1 | 4.6 | 17.3 |
| Total percentage | 55.0 | 90.9 | 45.0 | 9.1 | 100.0 | 100.0 |
| Number completed | 53,164 | 121,920 | 43,588 | 12,222 | 96,752 | 134,142 |

*Source*: Housing and Construction Statistics, 1979, Table 18.

for purpose-built flats by older households. Most of the design modifications, where included, were intended to cut costs rather than to introduce special features to attract particular consumer groups. Indeed, the developers included in the sample were looking forward to returning to the more familiar three-bedroomed house as soon as market conditions permitted.

Of course there are parts of the country where private developers are keen to include the design features and build the type of property attractive to retiring households. Dwellings aimed specifically at the elderly house-buyer are being built in both coastal and inland locations (Mellor, 1962; Barbolet, 1969; Grant, 1971; Lemon, 1972). Karn (1974) describes the numerous estates of bungalows so typical of British seaside towns claiming that such resorts offer more housing suitable to the needs of younger retired people than any other type of town. The suitability of these dwellings usually relates to their design on one storey rather than to their location (Skrimshire, 1973; Glyn-Jones, 1975) but, despite often hilly terrain and positions distant from town centres, they retain their attraction for older people. More recently, similar residential developments have prospered in inland locations, usually in areas of scenic attraction. Lemon (1972) identified an emerging local retirement housing market in small, inland Norfolk towns following the initiative of a local building firm in constructing bungalows and advertising them in London newspapers as retirement homes.

There is nothing in Britain yet to compare with the exclusive retirement towns of the United States of America such as Sun City, Arizona, where several thousand elderly people purchase properties in which to spend their last years (Walkley *et al.*, 1966). Another feature of the American housing market for the elderly is the retirement condominium where supporting services are available to elderly residents. In Britain, sheltered housing schemes provide an equivalent type of dwelling but, until fairly recently, developments of this kind have not appeared in the private sector. While it is impossible to know the precise number of these dwellings now in existence within Britain, details of retirement houses are advertised in local and national newspapers where included in the purchase price and maintenance charge of the property may be sports, restaurant, and cleaning facilities, together with a security service. One further type of retirement housing in this sector, popular for many years in Britain with older households, is the mobile home. Permanent caravan parks providing accommodation for elderly people proliferate in seaside locations but their exact contribution to the supply of owner-occupied accommodation for elderly people is at present unclear.

## LOCAL AUTHORITY HOUSING FOR THE ELDERLY

While the special housing needs of elderly people have been recognized from the earliest years of local authority housing (Mellor, 1973), the public sector continued to concentrate on the provision of family dwellings until the late 1970s. In the early post-war period the national housing shortage necessitated the construction of standard family accommodation in all parts of the country (Central Statistical Office, 1979). More recently, however, the surplus of dwellings over households within the United Kingdom has meant that increased attention could be paid to improvement policies and the adaptation of existing dwellings to meet the changing needs of council tenants (DOE, 1977). A series of government circulars issued in the early 1970s, culminating in the 1977 Green Paper on Housing, emphasized the importance of providing public housing for elderly people given the unresponsiveness of the private sector to meet the growing demand for smaller housing. Concentrating first on sheltered housing schemes and latterly on more general provision, central government has clearly put high priority on this part of the housing market.

Spurred on both by the under-occupation of public housing by older tenants and the increasing number of elderly households within the housing stock, local authorities have substantially increased their supply of small properties over the last few years. Table 7.3 shows clearly that virtually all the new building of one-bedroomed dwellings takes place within the public sector, local housing authorities building eight one-bedroomed flats to each one in the private sector. This emphasis on small dwellings has meant a relative decline in the amount of three-bedroomed housing added to the public dwelling stock since the mid-1960s (Table 7.4). Before 1945, only 3 per cent of council house building was of one-bedroomed flats, but this increased to over 10 per cent in the two decades following the war. Since 1965, the construction of one-bedroomed flats has accounted for over one-quarter of all new council building and, at present, 13 per cent of the total council stock in England and Wales is composed of this type of dwelling.

The changing emphasis in favour of small dwellings increases the likelihood of small pensionable households continuing an autonomous existence within the community. If an elderly household has to leave its former residence for cost or size reasons, these smaller dwellings offer a viable alternative within a housing market still composed predominantly of larger dwellings. Not all small accommodation in the public sector is allocated to pensioner households, with many two-bedroomed flats being offered to younger families. One-bedroomed council dwellings, on the other hand, are more likely to be occupied by elderly people given the present allocation policies of many housing authorities. It would be wrong, however, to equate one-bedroomed properties with specialized dwellings for the elderly as has been done in the past by successive government departments (Mellor, 1973). Mellor's sample of 19 local authorities revealed that many one-bedroomed dwellings lacked the special design features suggested for inclusion in old people's accommodation and that the number of dwellings actually designated for elderly households failed to correspond to the number of one-bedroomed properties. In some districts elderly households were

Table 7.4 Local authority dwellings: age and size distribution: England and Wales, April 1978

| | All local authorities (excluding new towns). Percentages | | | | | | | |
|---|---|---|---|---|---|---|---|---|
| | Completed pre-1945 | | Completed 1945–64 inclusive | | Completed after 1964 | | Total stock 1978 | |
| | Houses[a] | Flats | Houses | Flats | Houses | Flats | Houses | Flats |
| One bedroom | 0.4 | 0.8 | 1.7 | 4.6 | 1.4 | 7.7 | 3.5 | 13.1 |
| Two bedrooms | 3.8 | 1.0 | 7.1 | 6.6 | 3.5 | 5.6 | 14.4 | 13.2 |
| Three bedrooms | 15.4 | 0.5 | 20.3 | 2.1 | 8.1 | 2.2 | 43.8 | 4.8 |
| Four or more bedrooms | 1.0 | | 1.1 | | 0.9 | | 3.0 | |
| Other | 3.3 | | 0.5 | | 0.4 | | 4.2 | |
| Total percentage | 26.2 | | 44.0 | | 29.8 | | 100.0 | |
| Number completed | 1,056,315 | | 1,767,001 | | 1,199,408 | | 4,022,724 | |

[a]And bungalows.

*Source*: Chartered Institute of Public Finance and Accountancy (1978). *Housing Statistics (England and Wales), Part 1*, CIPFA, London.

allocated to two-bedroomed flats or bungalows while, elsewhere, some one-bedroomed dwellings were deemed unsuitable for occupation by elderly people, usually because of their location.

To be certain of the actual number of sheltered dwellings presently let by local authorities to elderly tenants requires additional information to that published in *Housing and Construction Statistics*. With the inception in 1978 of Housing Investment Programmes (HIP) as the method of grant allocation to local housing authorities, they are now required to include such information within the numerical return accompanying a Strategy Statement. Should HIP information be made available, it would be possible to ascertain the number of sheltered units already built and those planned by local authorities, housing associations, and private developers within each district, along with an estimate of the local need for such accommodation. The Department of Health and Social Security has suggested that a rate of 25 places per 1000 resident elderly might be a reasonable level of provision, although this could well be below the actual need for sheltered units (Mellor, 1973; MacGuire, 1978). With the publication of specific figures for individual local housing authorities it would be possible to monitor more clearly how far demand for this specialized form of retirement housing is being matched by supply.

## THE SUPPLY OF RETIREMENT HOUSING WITHIN THE PRIVATE RENTED SECTOR

It is both convenient and traditional to identify one residual tenure group within the British housing market and to include households renting from private landlords. A distinction is often made between furnished and unfurnished rented accommodation although revised legislation concerning rent controls and regulations has reduced the relevance of such a division. Elderly households in this sector normally occupy unfurnished premises (Table 7.2) which often lack the standard amenities. For these pensioners, few opportunities have existed in the past to change tenancies or finance house purchase. Moves to flats or rooms within this sector have become increasingly difficult with the declining number of private rented properties on the market (DOE, 1977), and elderly people have been looking to the public sector to provide accommodation suitable for their needs.

There has been little enthusiasm on the part of private landlords, with the notable exception of housing associations, to become involved in an exclusive retirement housing market. As an attempt to counter the decline of the private rented sector, both central and local government have encouraged housing associations during the 1970s (DOE, 1973, 1977). Officially linked to the public sector in government statistics and usually working closely with local government departments, housing associations have acted as private landlords to an increasing number of elderly households. Over one-third of the total stock of dwellings controlled by housing associations is let to elderly households

(Stallybrass, 1976) and these associations are currently responsible for 8 per cent of all new housing construction (CIPFA, 1978). It is still the case, however, that only a small proportion of elderly people find accommodation in this part of the housing market. In addition, a few elderly owner-occupiers are entering the rented sector following the initiative of charitable organizations other than housing associations. Groups such as *Help the Aged* offer to convert large dwellings occupied by elderly people to multi-occupation. The owner of the property continues to occupy a self-contained flat within part of the dwelling while elderly tenants are accommodated in other sections of the house. Schemes such as these, which are increasing the amount of rented accommodation available to old people within the private rented sector, are still few in number and require considerable managerial and financial inputs at the initial stages (Help the Aged, 1978—personal communication).

Descriptions of the current housing situation are of limited value in the absence of any explanation of why the situation exists and of what factors determine the distribution of housing resources. Nationally, marked variation exists in the provision of retirement housing and, in studying this variation, much can be learnt concerning those processes controlling the supply of dwellings for old people.

## VARIATION IN THE PROVISION OF RETIREMENT HOUSING

The construction rate in all sectors of the housing market has varied through time following the phases of expansion and stagnation within the economy as a whole. Factors which have affected the supply of housing include central budgetary policy, the activities of the various housing agencies, and the fluctuating fortunes of the construction industry (Needleman, 1965). Central government provides a legislative framework for housing with supporting finance, advice, and guidance to encourage the implementation of its national housing policy but locally this policy is in the hands of local authorities, housing associations, builders, building societies, landlords, and individual property-owners who may interpret it in a variety of ways (Niner, 1975). Having direct links with local authorities and, through the Housing Corporation, with housing associations, government policy is most clearly outlined for public sector housing. For example, the recent Green Paper on Housing (DOE, 1977) argues that local authorities along with other public sector bodies have a statutory duty to review the housing conditions in their areas and make assessments of the full range of housing requirements. Dwellings which complement private sector provision should be provided so that the local stock is of a satisfactory quality and matches the needs of local people in terms of house size, type, and location. The emphasis on building family homes in the private sector inevitably places much of the burden of retirement housing provision onto the public sector.

Variation in the number of dwellings provided for older households in different parts of the country has much to do with the policies of local authorities. They have exercised a wide range of powers to influence the housing situation within their boundaries, powers which reflect the pattern of public involvement in housing and extend beyond the construction of new council properties. Specific encouragement can be given to housing associations operating within their areas while development control policies can influence the amount and type of private dwellings built locally. The nature of both public and private housing can be altered through clearance, improvement, and conversion schemes. As landlords, local authorities may seek a more efficient use of public housing through revised allocation and transfer policies while, less directly, the attractiveness of areas for retired people can be affected through the enhanced or reduced provision of local government-controlled services.

Traditionally, *ad hoc* arrangements were established in an individual authority reflecting its definition of local housing needs. Few authorities took account of all the factors influencing the local housing situation, particularly the output of private builders and housing associations. With regard to retirement housing within the private sector, little control was exercised over the type and size of development taking place in their areas. However, the localized nature of the private retirement house construction industry in the popular destination areas for retirement migration has put increasing pressure on selected authorities to monitor these residential developments. The development control policies adopted for private construction will not be independent of planned local authority housing projects in the area. Evidence exists that some authorities look directly to private developers to provide more houses for elderly people and occasionally make land available to retiring migrants for the construction of individual retirement homes, as at North Walsham in East Anglia (Lemon, 1972). Alternatively, some district councils inhibit residential development of a kind likely to attract the elderly (as we shall see in the New Forest area of Hampshire) while others operate indirect policies which act to divert speculative builders to other areas. Law and Warnes (1980) have studied these zoning policies at the sub-regional level revealing how both market forces and planning controls operate to divert new housing away from the most popular resorts. In East Sussex the high proportions of elderly residents in coastal areas evoked a policy statement from local planners that retiring migrants should be directed inland to Uckfield and Battle by the construction of retirement-type housing in these inland centres and the banning of such developments on the coast (National Parks Commission, 1966).

Policies such as these are not always successful in practice. Brindley and Hole (1978) show how private builders in Torbay concentrated on the buoyant retirement market dominated by inward migrants despite pressure from the local council to provide for the needs of lower-income residents. One difficulty obviously faced by development control officers is to distinguish retirement housing schemes at the application stage in that these first retirement homes may well contain two or three bedrooms which could meet the needs of many younger households.

As it was difficult to do more than indicate the degree of involvement shown by private developers in the retirement housing market, so too is it hard to determine the actual supply of private housing in particular retirement areas. A clearer picture emerges, however, with regard to public sector provision. Interesting variations are found when the supply of small dwellings and sheltered accommodation is compared over different parts of the country.

Since before the war, small dwelling construction has been most common in London and the larger conurbations (Table 7.5). Restricted land availability in these cities has encouraged residential building at high densities resulting in the high-rise developments of small flats in the 1960s and early 1970s. In addition, the growing age-polarization of urban populations (Barnard, 1978) has increased the proportion of elderly households on council waiting lists in central city areas underlining the need to step up the provision of one- and two-bedroomed properties. Yet it seems that demand factors on their own do not explain local variation in the provision of public sector retirement housing. While Boaden (1971) thought that a population's age structure might influence the size and type of dwelling built by local authorities, Mellor (1973) could find no straightforward supply–demand association between the proportion of elderly people and the incidence of one-bedroomed council properties at the local authority level.

Recent statistics recording the proportion of one-bedroomed dwellings present in each authority's dwelling stock summarize the amount of variation between districts within England and Wales (Table 7.6). Twenty of the housing authorities submitting returns to CIPFA currently have one-quarter or more of their total stock as one-bedroomed properties as a result of construction and conversion policies, while 47 authorities have less than 10 per cent. If these differences do not relate to the number of elderly residents, alternative explanations are required. Possible reasons are suggested where detailed studies of local housing authority practices reveal the different priority given to the housing of old people (Niner, 1975; Brindley and Hole, 1978). An authority with a positive disposition towards the housing needs of its elderly population would be likely to place particular emphasis on the provision of small-dwelling units. In the West Midlands for example, Niner (1975) cites the case of Halesowen which operates an allocation policy favouring households under-occupying their accommodation and those aged 70 or more, and maintains a short housing queue for small elderly households by the construction of one-bedroomed units. Districts noting a particularly low supply of small properties in the private sector may also increase their stock of one- and two-bedroomed units while areas with large numbers of very old people might give priority to sheltered housing schemes with warden supervision.

Table 7.5 Age and size distribution of local authority dwellings in 1978 by type of district

| Percentage of one-bedroomed dwellings built | GLC and London boroughs | Metropolitan districts | Non-metropolitan districts | All local authorities[a] |
|---|---|---|---|---|
| Pre-1945 | 7.4 | 4.9 | 3.5 | 4.8 |
| 1945–64 | 20.1 | 16.2 | 11.8 | 14.3 |
| Post-1965 | 33.7 | 32.0 | 28.6 | 30.7 |
| TOTALS | 20.9 | 17.3 | 14.9 | 16.7 |

[a]Excluding New Towns.
*Source*: CIPFA, *Housing Statistics (England and Wales)*, *Part 1*, 1978.

Table 7.6 Percentage of one-bedroomed properties in the public housing stock, 1978

| | Mean | Coefficient of variation | Number of authorities[a] |
|---|---|---|---|
| London boroughs | 22.3 | 29.6 | 27 |
| Metropolitan districts | 18.1 | 28.2 | 34 |
| Non-metropolitan districts | 14.4 | 34.7 | 267 |

[a]Excluding authorities with incomplete returns.
*Source*: CIPFA, Housing Statistics (England and Wales), Part 1, 1978.

Brindley and Hole's (1978) survey of selected local housing authorities highlighted the importance attached to providing small dwellings for elderly people in the majority of districts. Yet where broad agreement exists on the need for this accommodation, some authorities seem less able than others to increase their numbers of small dwellings and purpose-built sheltered schemes. MacGuire (1978) suggests that the reasons why some established urban areas have difficulty in meeting the demand for specialised retirement housing are the length of time taken to respond to change and the small scale of building programmes that are tied to long-standing waiting lists. Brindley and Hole (1978), on the other hand, found that some larger urban authorities were better organised than smaller districts in terms of housing projects for the elderly. An authority's ability to put policy into practice depends both on the resources available to it and the way in which these resources are managed. In Brindley and Hole's sample, the larger housing authorities were dealing with sufficiently large numbers of elderly people to warrant special sub-programmes within the overall housing strategy. These programmes were planned in detail taking account of the requirements for different types of retirement housing in contrast to the rather *ad hoc* arrangements made for housing elderly tenants in small authorities. So, while the housing policies of the large, long-established authorities may be constrained by the nature and condition of the existing stock and traditional management practices and policies, the sheer number of elderly households affected by their actions helps to ensure both the constant monitoring of old people's housing conditions and the careful planning of their future requirements. Certainly the examples of a few metropolitan districts and London boroughs in this field emphasize the advantages of a detailed corporate approach to the preparation of housing policies for elderly people (Stockport Metropolitan Borough, 1976).

Turning finally to the contribution of housing associations, their activities like those of the other housing agencies vary markedly from area to area affecting the supply of retirement housing. The amount of housing association accommodation built in an area is dependent on a variety of factors, not least of which is the responsiveness of the local housing authority in the provision of both sites and long-term capital funding. In the United Kingdom, the supply of these properties in recent years has been limited in many cases to areas with large housing allocations. In the late 1960s development could only proceed if the local authority in question would agree to commit the new property against its own allocation. Consequently it often proved difficult for associations to operate actively anywhere except where an authority had a large enough allocation to include housing association projects without prejudice to local authority schemes. Also, areas were favoured by housing associations where loan facilities were available. These conditions resulted in a concentration of building in northern and industrial Midland authorities and in inner-city areas (Barnard, 1978).

In the absence of information recording recent details of housing association activity throughtout the United Kingdom, it is possible to obtain some idea of inter-authority variation in the provision of retirement housing by these agencies through studying figures for Hampshire. Relating only to sheltered housing schemes, Table 7.7 reveals how the number of specialized dwellings varies from district to district within the county. The local housing authorities of Southampton and Portsmouth provide considerably more of this accommodation than the other districts in line with the relative size of their populations and housing stock. Yet the figures suggest that housing associations have been most successful in Winchester, resulting in an exceptionally high level of

Table 7.7 Sheltered dwelling units within Hampshire, 1979

| | Local authority | | Housing association | |
|---|---|---|---|---|
| District | Total number of units | Units per 1000 elderly[a] | Total number of units | Units per 1000 elderly |
| Southampton | 1422 | 44.9 | 311 | 9.8 |
| Portsmouth | 1384 | 37.6 | 178 | 4.8 |
| Winchester | 508 | 38.8 | 358 | 36.0 |
| Havant | 454 | 29.5 | 32 | 2.1 |
| Basingstoke | 448 | 33.8 | 125 | 9.4 |
| Test Valley | 445 | 35.4 | 99 | 14.5 |
| New Forest | 408 | 14.8 | 188 | 6.8 |
| Fareham | 363 | 30.9 | 58 | 4.9 |
| East Hampshire | 343 | 25.7 | 63 | 4.7 |
| Rushmoor | 316 | 32.4 | 84 | 8.6 |
| Eastleigh | 306 | 27.9 | 253 | 23.0 |
| Gosport | 237 | 25.4 | 205 | 22.0 |
| Hart | 188 | 26.1 | 146 | 20.3 |
| County | 6822 | 32.1 | 2100 | 10.8 |

[a]Estimated population 65+, 1979.
*Source*: Hampshire County Council, Social Services Department. Unpublished table.

provision there in relation to the size of the resident elderly population. When viewed in relation to the size of the population aged 65 and over, housing association provision varies much more than the local authority supply. In looking for explanations, differences in attitude towards housing association schemes may be found amongst the district housing authorities while special local conditions might attract associations to particular areas. It would be interesting, for example, to examine the effects of religious affiliations between certain housing associations and the cathedral city of Winchester as an influence on dwelling location.

These figures for Hampshire provide an introduction to the detailed study of two local housing authorities—a study which will attempt to develop many of the points raised in the general discussion. This discussion suggests that the activities of a local housing authority are of central importance to an understanding of the supply of retirement housing in an area not only through the manipulation of its own stock but also in the control that it can exercise over other housing agencies. Attention will be focused therefore on local housing policy within the two districts of Southampton and the New Forest, alongside more general local government planning policies affecting residential development. Private developers and housing associations operating in the area will be affected by these policies and it will be interesting to note the extent and effects of local government intervention on the provision of retirement housing within the private sector. Finally, the impact of this type of accommodation on the residential location and mobility of local elderly households will receive attention, these relationships being of increasing concern both to those working in the field of retirement housing and to those concerned more generally with the welfare of older people.

## HOUSING FOR RETIREMENT IN SOUTH-WEST HAMPSHIRE

Southampton and the New Forest local authorities cover much of south-west Hampshire, an area of considerable residential variety. The New Forest District Council includes industrial and commuter suburbs fringing the New Forest, one of the leading recreational areas in southern England (Figure 7.1). Southampton City to the north-east contrasts with these suburban, rural, and seaside areas. With a population just exceeding 200,000, the City forms its own residential mosaic of twilight immigrant areas, fast-growing outer suburbs, inner city high-rise developments and extensive inter-war private and public housing estates (Taylor, 1974).

Over 63,000 elderly people currently live in south-west Hampshire, forming 18 per cent of its total population. Concentrations of older households are found in selected coastal and rural communities as well as certain inner-city areas while younger families predominate in Southampton's outer suburbs and the dormitory suburbs of the New Forest's waterside area. Factors associat-

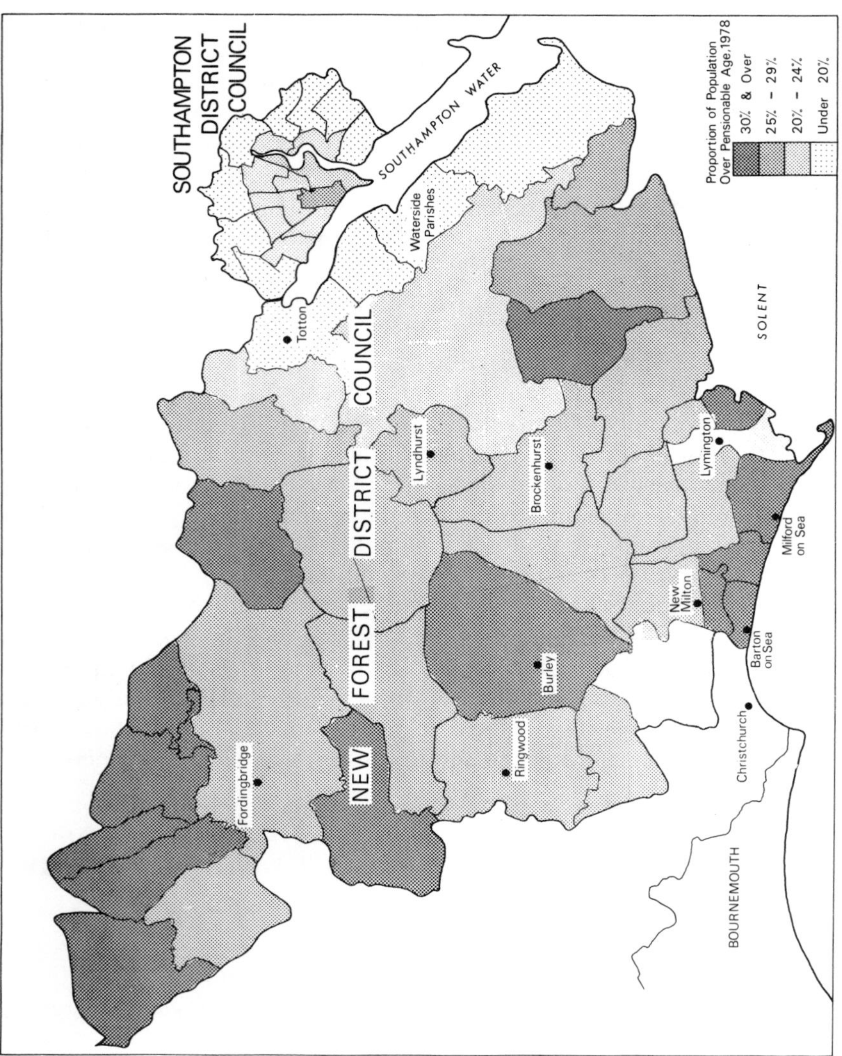


Figure 7.1 The elderly population of the local authorities of south-west Hampshire, 1978

ed with the residential distribution of this elderly population differ for migrant areas and those where the elderly have long been local residents. In the former, sea-front locations and areas containing flats and bungalows attract retiring migrants while, in the resident retirement areas, the elderly are concentrated in both inter-war housing estates and developments of purpose-built flats (Barnard, 1978).

The presence in south-west Hampshire of both incoming retiring migrants and local elderly people makes this area of particular interest to an investigation of retirement housing. Here we expect and find various housing agencies combining to provide dwellings for elderly households. Yet the degree of involvement by the public and private sectors varies considerably between the two Districts reflecting the different nature of their local housing markets and the different residential preferences and opportunities of their elderly residents. Only 14 per cent of dwellings in the New Forest are owned by the District Council in contrast to Southampton's public housing which represents almost one-third of the total stock. This balance is reflected in the tenure of properties occupied by small elderly households, less than half owning their dwellings in Southampton compared with over 70 per cent in the New Forest (Table 7.8). On the other hand, over one-third of the city's pensioners look to the local authority to provide their accommodation while, in the New Forest, private rented dwellings are more important than council properties in housing elderly people. Retiring migrants normally seek dwellings for purchase and, in any case, seldom qualify for local authority housing in a new area (Karn, 1974; Law and Warnes, 1980). Thus private developers in the New Forest have a

Table 7.8 Size and tenure of property occupied by elderly households in south-west Hampshire, 1978

| | Percentage of elderly households | | | | | |
|---|---|---|---|---|---|---|
| | Owner-occupied | | Local authority | | Other tenures | |
| Number of bedrooms | One person[a] | Two persons[b] | One person | Two persons | One person | Two persons |
| *Southampton* | | | | | | |
| One | 1.6 | 1.0 | 17.0 | 5.5 | 3.9 | 1.4 |
| Two | 7.3 | 10.1 | 2.0 | 3.8 | 2.0 | 2.8 |
| Three | 10.5 | 16.8 | 2.4 | 3.8 | 0.6 | 5.3 |
| Four or more | 0.4 | 1.4 | 0.0 | 0.0 | 0.2 | 0.2 |
| TOTAL ($N = 495$) | 19.8 | 29.3 | 21.4 | 13.1 | 6.7 | 9.7 |
| *New Forest* | | | | | | |
| One | 0.9 | 0.9 | 3.6 | 1.6 | 0.7 | 0.7 |
| Two | 13.9 | 19.8 | 2.3 | 3.0 | 2.3 | 2.9 |
| Three | 7.7 | 22.5 | 0.9 | 1.8 | 2.7 | 2.9 |
| Four or more | 0.7 | 5.0 | 0.0 | 0.0 | 2.7 | 0.5 |
| TOTAL ($N = 440$) | 23.2 | 48.2 | 6.8 | 6.4 | 8.4 | 7.0 |

[a] Aged 65 and over.
[b] At least one person aged 65 and over.
*Source*: As for Table 7.7.

good opportunity to meet the demand for retirement housing from elderly people, many of whom would be able to find the purchase price from their own funds, an important attraction in times of economic restraint. Alternatively, in Southampton, private sector agencies are likely to be overshadowed by the local authority in providing housing for retirement given the size of its dwelling stock and the recent upsurge of interest in public housing policies for local elderly residents.

Looking first at the private sector, retirement housing for purchase should be widespread in certain parts of the New Forest assuming that conditions here are similar to other destination areas for retiring migrants. Indeed, the estates of bungalows built along the coast at Milford-on-Sea and Barton-on-Sea during the 1950s mark the beginning of a continuing private retirement housing industry. More recently, multi-storey blocks of luxury retirement flats in similar seaside locations have replaced lower-density residential developments as less land is made available to the construction industry. The New Forest District Council (1976) operates an informal development control policy in the area by encouraging the construction of family dwellings, a policy which it seems has met with limited success. As in other areas, the only definition of retirement housing available is a 'non-family home', built in an area known to be attractive to elderly people. The flats and bungalows of this coastal area are certainly marketed as retirement homes by local estate agents but as this label is attached to nearly every property of four bedrooms or less in the more attractive parts of the area, this is not necessarily a reliable indicator. Elsewhere in south west Hampshire, with the exception of a limited number of minor developments in central Southampton, the construction industry reflects the preference for three- and four-bedroomed houses. As a result, many of the elderly owner-occupiers in Southampton and those selecting to live in the New Forest itself rather than on the coast are faced with few alternatives to the family-sized house.

The limited supply of small privately owned dwellings is reflected in the size of property occupied by elderly house-owners in the area (Table 7.8). Most of these Southampton households will still be living in the house they have occupied for most of their adult lives (Barnard, 1978), and their potential mobility may well be constrained by the lack of smaller property. In the New Forest too, the preponderance of larger housing may frustrate the attempts of retiring migrants to purchase a small dwelling should this be their wish. Whatever the reason, less than half the elderly households owning a dwelling in south-west Hampshire occupy one- or two-bedroomed properties, a fact that has important implications for public housing policy.

The under-occupation of housing found in the private sector is far less common in local authority housing. Only 25 per cent of elderly council tenants have an extra bedroom and, in Southampton, three-quarters of elderly people living alone in council accommodation occupy one-bedroomed properties.

Generally, there is less under-occupation of council housing in Southampton than the New Forest although the very different scale of public sector provision should be borne in mind when making comparisons. For instance, the New Forest supply of 41 one-bedroomed properties per 1000 elderly residents contrasts with an equivalent figure of 172 for Southampton. Table 7.7 reveals the marked difference in sheltered housing provision between the two Districts, Southampton's supply being the highest in Hampshire, the New Forest's the lowest. The contrasting supply of council properties means that 28.3 per cent of the city's elderly population can currently find accommodation in small council dwellings in contrast to 10.5 per cent in the New Forest (Table 7.8).

Important reasons lie behind these differences both in the rate of supply of public sector retirement housing and in the relationship between that supply and the number of elderly residents. Clearly, in the New Forest, the number of elderly households is inflated by retiring migrants resulting in low overall rates of provision in comparison to Southampton. Yet what is perhaps surprising is the relatively low proportion of small dwellings within a limited public sector stock in an area likely to generate considerable housing demand from small households (Table 7.9). To understand, at least in part, the present levels of supply within the public sector it is necessary to investigate past and present council housing policy.

Both districts attach great importance to the provision of dwellings for elderly people but, with a limited stock, the New Forest District Council feels it must also meet the needs of those younger households who have long been resident within the area. In a part of Hampshire where house prices are exceptionally high, inflated by retiring migrants and commuters seeking the village life, young couples find it difficult to enter private sector accommodation and thus turn to the council for help. Many older households, on the other hand, are financially secure and only in their latter years approach the local authority for domiciliary services or maybe a place in a sheltered scheme. For, while

Table 7.9 The size of local authority-owned dwellings in south-west Hampshire, 1978

| | Southampton | | New Forest | |
|---|---|---|---|---|
| Dwellings containing | Number | Cumulative percentage | Number | Cumulative percentage |
| One bedroom | 5,450 | 22.8 | 1,120 | 14.3 |
| Two bedrooms | 7,674 | 55.0 | 2,131 | 41.5 |
| Three bedrooms | 8,892 | 92.3 | 4,373 | 97.0 |
| Four or more bedrooms | 1,841 | 100.0 | 220 | 100.0 |
| TOTAL | 23,857 | | 7,844 | |

*Source:* CIPFA, *Housing Statistics (England and Wales), Part 1*, 1978

neither needing or qualifying for council accommodation on arrival in the area, retiring migrants do form an important group of residents qualifying for specialized housing as they grow older. With failing health and reduced incomes, these are the elderly people who may have bought a large house on moving to the area in their sixties and now find, as they approach their eighties, no alternative retirement accommodation outside the public sector. Certainly a main housing priority of the District Council in recent years has been the expansion of specialized sheltered housing schemes for these very old people rather than increasing the general supply of small council dwellings.

Southampton's housing practices run along different lines as here more emphasis has been placed on the provision of sheltered accommodation. Within the city, those council estates built between the wars and in the early 1950s were found to contain many older households by the early 1970s, the tenants growing older with their housing. While no official pressure was brought to bear on these tenants to exchange their properties for smaller dwellings, the substantial increase in the number of one- and two-bedroomed flats has led to a more rational distribution of household and dwelling sizes within the public sector. This policy continues, with over half of the council dwelling stock now consisting of small dwellings (Table 7.9) and a new building programme almost totally geared to this type of property. The demand for sheltered housing has also grown during the 1970s alongside the increased provision of wardened housing schemes. Over half of the current housing waiting list is composed of people over pensionable age and the proportion of elderly applicants is expected to increase in future years. At present the city provides just short of 1500 sheltered dwellings in 26 different schemes. In addition, 974 one-bedroomed flats are categorized as *Part 1* accommodation for the elderly, containing design modifications but not overseen by a resident warden. The result is a relatively high level of provision when judged against other Hampshire districts, but the supply is still exceeded by local demand.

Both Southampton and the New Forest foster housing association activity, recognizing the potential contribution that these agencies can make to an expanding local retirement housing market. Currently four housing associations in the New Forest and nine in Southampton provide sheltered accommodation for local elderly people, usually allowing the local housing authority nomination rights to half of the places in each scheme. A major difficulty found by individual associations working in conjunction with Southampton has been the shortage of residential land suitably located for old people's dwellings. One solution has been the use of small infill sites within the older parts of the city; another has involved the acquisition of land outside the city boundary. In terms of overall provision, housing associations have still only made a marginal impact on the retirement housing market. In 1978, only 2 per cent of small elderly households were renting accommodation from the various associations operating in south-west Hampshire. Yet, in both districts, future housing strategies seek to encourage housing association developments, particularly of sheltered schemes for frail elderly people, through the provision of building land and capital funding.

In the two districts, further support for the provision of sheltered housing has been elicited from Hampshire County Council Social Services Department and the Area Health Authority. This marks a growing interest within the county in planning retirement housing on a corporate basis and involves projects where different levels of housing need can be accommodated on one site. Thus at developments in Lordshill, Southampton, and Lyndhurst in the New Forest, disabled elderly people requiring continuous support are able to live independently within the community through the provision of specialized sheltered units. Adjacent to these schemes, elderly residents in more familiar wardened dwellings are secure in the knowledge that, should their housing needs increase, enhanced support is close at hand.

Other innovative schemes planned to improve the housing situation of local elderly residents include the introduction of peripatetic wardens within the New Forest to visit people living in unsupervised sheltered schemes and the provision of communal facilities within a council-owned tower block in Southampton for the use of local people as well as elderly and middle-aged residents. Both housing authorities therefore show signs of extending and improving their services for elderly people. In terms of overall supply, however, it must be acknowledged that Southampton far outstrips its neighbour in the provision of retirement housing. The large scale of Southampton's general housing involvement may have itself proved beneficial as Brindley and Hole (1978) intimated from their study of other local housing authorities. The need for careful planning of public sector housing in Southampton is clear, and those officers involved in estimating the need for retirement dwellings use their detailed knowledge and understanding of the local housing situation to good effect. In the New Forest, on the other hand, the housing activities of the District Council are necessarily constrained by limited resources, a small stock of dwellings and vigorous conservation policies. The housing need of elderly residents has to be viewed against that of other local people and much effort has been concentrated recently on the rehabilitation of existing dwellings for family occupation in addition to the provision of sheltered housing. Moreover, the merging in 1974 of three former local authorities (New Forest Rural District, Ringwood and Fordingbridge RD, and Lymington Municipal Borough) to form the New Forest District Council obviously created short-term organizational difficulties and the need to re-assess housing policy. Southampton's housing plans for its elderly population, uninterrupted by local government reorganization, supported by an enthusiastic community health department and free of the additional problems posed by incoming elderly migrants, can only have benefited in comparison.

## THE IMPACT OF RETIREMENT HOUSING

Any attempt to describe the current housing situation of elderly people requires some assessment of the nature and extent of the opportunities older households have to change their residential circumstances. To conclude this consideration of retirement housing it is pertinent therefore to evaluate the effects that an expanding retirement housing market might have on the residential opportunities open to older people.

Evidence from south-west Hampshire and the United Kingdom generally confirms that it is in the public sector that most retirement housing is found. This does not mean, however, that only elderly council tenants are affected by changes in the nature of the dwelling stock. More movement takes place between housing sectors amongst local elderly migrants than other mover groups (Murie, 1974). The National Dwelling and Housing Survey revealed the two most common types of residential mobility amongst pensioner households to be moves within the private sector for two-person households and council exchanges for elderly people living alone (Central Statistical Office, 1979). However, relatively more elderly households moved from the private to the public sector than households generally, a finding supported by movement patterns in Southampton. Examining a sample of intra-city movers drawn from concessionary bus pass application forms (Barnard, 1978), one-quarter of these elderly households moved into council accommodation from other tenures (Table 7.10). Where such a move took place, the destination was most commonly to sheltered accommodation.

These findings suggest that the increasing provision of suitable council accom-

Table 7.10 Origin–destination matrix of elderly movers in Southampton, 1973–76 (percentage of all moves by type of dwelling)

| Type of dwelling | Destinations | | | | | | |
|---|---|---|---|---|---|---|---|
| | 1 | 2 | 3 | 4 | 5 | 6 | All |
| *Origins* | | | | | | | |
| 1. Privately rented and owner-occupied | 34.6 | 8.3 | 5.7 | 4.5 | 10.7 | 1.2 | 65.0 |
| 2. Local authority | 0.3 | 10.7 | 0.6 | 5.1 | 8.7 | 0.9 | 26.3 |
| 3. Private sheltered | — | — | — | — | — | — | — |
| 4. Local authority, Part I | 0.3 | — | — | — | 2.4 | 0.6 | 3.3 |
| 5. Local authority, Part II | 0.3 | 2.1 | — | — | 2.4 | 0.3 | 5.1 |
| 6. Public and private old people's homes, Part III | — | — | — | — | — | 0.3 | 0.3 |
| ALL | 35.5 | 21.1 | 6.3 | 9.6 | 24.2 | 3.3 | 100.0 |

*Source*: Barnard (1978).

modation may have broadened the residential opportunities of old people generally. Given the dearth of retirement housing within the private sector, however, to place the burden of housing those elderly people who are only able to manage or afford small properties on to the public sector inevitably means that demand will exceed supply. In the present circumstances, there is no way that local housing authorities, even with the assistance of housing associations, can cope with providing a sufficient number of dwellings to meet this demand. Moreover, for authorities like Southampton working hard to increase their stock of small and sheltered dwellings, a 'Catch 22' situation is developing, whereby the more that is built, the more people are attracted to the idea of living in retirement housing. It seems that many more elderly households would form if suitable accommodation were made available and these potential households should be taken into account in any assessment of housing need.

The enhanced residential opportunities of elderly households following the increased provision of retirement housing in the United Kingdom may be marginal or even non-existent for elderly people wishing to remain in owner-occupation. If the lack of choice in the housing market forces the over-75s to remain in family-sized housing long after they feel they can manage such accommodation, then the housing condition of an increasing sector of the elderly population may deteriorate in the years to come.

The locational effects of retirement housing should also be reviewed when assessing its impact on the residential situation of older households. For those elderly people offered retirement homes within the public sector, the benefits of purpose-built accommodation may be offset by the need to move to a different area. Returning to the Southampton sample, those elderly people entering public sheltered housing schemes often had to move several kilometres from their old district and away from the city centre (Barnard, 1978). The shortage of building land within the city during the early 1970s necessitated the building of many of these schemes on the outskirts of Southampton and, at that time, no neighbourhood allocation policy was in operation. Thus, as a dwelling became vacant in a particular scheme, so it was filled by the individual most in need of rehousing at the time, irrespective of where that person might be living in the city.

The effects of these actions are obvious. In the outer parts of most cities, journeys to bus stops, shops, and urban services tend to be longer while moves in old age away from well-established social ties may heighten the physical isolation felt by old people. In the designation of areas for residential development, approvals for retirement housing, whether in the public or private sector, should take account of the elderly's locational requirements and activity patterns so as to increase rather than decrease their spatial opportunities. Southampton's housing policy now aims at providing a variety of retirement dwellings in each part of the city to allow elderly people the option of remaining within one neighbourhood as their housing needs change.

The effects of retirement housing location can also be viewed at the regional level and highlight further policy implications. The concentration of private sector retirement housing in coastal resorts and, more recently, in scenically attractive inland areas, may limit the number of destination areas considered by potential migrants, particularly if they are set on purchasing a retirement bungalow or luxury flat. The more equitable distribution of this accommodation would widen the choice of retirement areas; Law and Warnes (1980) have suggested that the increased provision of smaller housing in towns and cities might encourage local moves in late middle age rather than long-distance moves on retirement. This would certainly reduce the development pressures currently affecting environmentally attractive areas such as the New Forest.

Tinker (1977) claims that few authorities are willing to indulge in theoretical discussions about retirement housing. Yet the future size of the elderly population, the reasons behind the formation and dissolution of elderly households, and the changing residential preferences of elderly people are only a few of the topics pertinent to the formulation of housing strategies. These topics should be viewed both nationally and locally, in the context of a changing housing system which has led for so long to a reduction of residential opportunities in old age. Only when this is done will retirement housing become a major element within the United Kingdom's housing market.

## ACKNOWLEDGEMENTS

The research leading to this paper was supported by the Social Science Research Council while the author was registered as a postgraduate student at Southampton University. Valuable assistance was received from many local government officers in the Planning, Housing, Social Services, and Transport Departments of both Southampton City Council and the New Forest District Council, and all must be thanked for their information and time, so generously given. In addition, members of the Social Services Research Section and the Research and Intelligence Unit of Hampshire County Council made available the results of recent surveys which have proved useful in updating local information.

The views expressed throughout this paper are those of the author.

## REFERENCES

Age Concern (1977). *Profiles of the Elderly*. Age Concern, Mitcham.

Barbolet, R. H. (1969). *Housing Classes and the Socio-Ecological System*. Centre for Environmental Studies, University Working Paper 4, London.

Barnard, K. C. (1978). The Residential Geography of the Elderly: a Multiple-scale Approach. Unpublished PhD. thesis, University of Southampton.

Boaden, N. J. (1971). *Urban Policy Making: Influences on County Boroughs in England and Wales*. Cambridge University Press, Cambridge.

Bourne, L. S. (1976). Housing supply and housing market behaviour in residential development. In Herbert, D. T. and Johnston, R. J. (eds), *Social Areas in Cities*, Vol. 1: *Spatial Processes and Form*, pp. 111–58, Wiley, London.

Brindley, T. S. and Hole, W. V. (1978). *Progress towards Local Housing Strategies: A Review of Local Authority Housing Planning in 1976*. Building Research Establishment Current Paper 77/78. Garston, Watford.

Central Statistical Office (1979). *Social Trends No. 10, 1980*. HMSO, London.

Chartered Institute of Public Finance and Accountancy (1978). *Housing Statistics* (*England and Wales*), Part 1. CIPFA, London.

Department of the Environment (1970). *Housing for Old People*. HMSO, London.

Department of the Environment (1972). *Sheltered Housing for the Elderly*. HMSO, London.

Department of the Environment (1973). *Widening the Choice—The Next Step in Housing*. HMSO, London.

Department of the Environment (1975a). *Housing Needs and Actions*. HMSO, London.

Department of the Environment (1975b). *The Retirement Industry in the South West*, by I. R. Gordon. HMSO, London.

Department of the Environment (1977). *Housing Policy: A Consultative Document*. HMSO, London.

Glyn-Jones, A. (1975). *Growing Older in a South Devon Town*. University of Exeter, Exeter.

Grant, W. (1971). Old people's towns. *New Society*, **25**, 817–18.

Housing Development Directorate (1976). The need for smaller homes. *The Architects Journal*, **164**, 925–30.

Karn, V. (1974). Retiring to the Seaside—a Study of Retirement Migration in England and Wales. Unpublished PhD thesis, University of Birmingham.

Law, C. M. and Warnes, A. M. (1980). The prospects for increasing retirement migration: an appraisal based on the characteristics of retired migrants. In Herbert, D. T. and Johnston, R. J. (eds), *Geography and the Urban Environment III*, Wiley, Chichester, pp. 175–222.

Lemon, A. (1972). The Small Town: a study of changing functions with special reference to the smaller urban settlements of Norfolk and Suffolk. Unpublished DPhil. thesis, University of Oxford.

MacGuire, J. (1977). The elderly in a new town: a case study of Telford. *Housing Review*, **6**, 132–6.

Mellor, H. W. (1962). Retirement to the coast. *Town Planning Review*, **33**, 40–8.

Mellor, H. W. (1973). Special housing for the elderly. In Mellor, H. W. (Ed.), *Housing in Retirement*, pp. 15–26. National Corporation for the Care of Old People, London.

Murie, A. (1974). *Household Movement and Household Choice*. Occasional Paper No. 28, Centre for Urban and Regional Studies, University of Birmingham.

National Parks Commission (1966). *The Coasts of Kent and Sussex*. HMSO, London.

Needleman, L. (1965). *The Economics of Housing*. Staple Press, Hertford.

New Forest District Council (1976). Untitled, Housing Seminar. Unpublished paper, 30 January.

Niner, P. (1975). *Local Authority Housing Policy and Practice—A Case Study Approach*. Occasional Paper No. 31, Centre for Urban and Regional Studies, University of Birmingham.

Office of Population Censuses and Surveys (1974). *Census of England and Wales, 1971: Persons of Pensionable Age*. HMSO, London.

Office of Population Censuses and Surveys, Social Survey Division (1973). *General Household Survey*. HMSO, London.

Riley, M. W. and Foner, A. (1968). *Ageing and Society: An Inventory of Research Findings*. Russell Sage, New York.

Robson, B. T. (1975). *Urban Social Areas*. Oxford University Press, Oxford.

Rose, E. A. (1978). *Housing for the Aged.* Saxon House, Farnborough.

Skrimshire, J. (1973). Retiring to the seaside. *Built Environment*, **2**, 494–5.

Stallybrass, A. (1976). Housing the elderly. *The Times*, 6 April; special report.

Stockport Metropolitan Borough (1976). The elderly: an interim report. Unpublished paper.

Taylor, S. D. (1974). The Geography and Epidemiology of Psychiatric Illness in Southampton. Unpublished PhD thesis, University of Southampton.

Tinker, A. (1976). *Housing the Elderly: How Successful are Granny Annexes?* Department of the Environment, Housing Development Directorate, London.

Tinker, A. (1977). Time for rethink on housing the elderly. *Local Government Chronicle*, 20 May, pp. 415 and 428.

Walkley, R. B., Mangum, W. P., Sherman, S. R., Dodds, S. and Wilner, D. M. (1966). The California survey of retirement housing. *The Gerontologist*, **6**, 28–34.

Wroe, D. C. L. (1973). The elderly. *Social Trends*, **4**, 23–34.

Geographical Perspectives on the Elderly
Edited by A. M. Warnes


Chapter 8

# Housing for the elderly in the United States

*Wiley P. Mangum*

Housing for the elderly has been an object of societal and gerontological concern in the United States since the end of World War II. As a result, much has been published on the topic, including several major review articles (Carp, 1976; Lawton, 1979; Robbins, 1971; Vivrett, 1960). Rather than attempting to provide a more recent general review, this chapter will focus on a limited number of topics, some of which are especially germane to the spatial theme of this book. These include a brief account of the history of societal concern with housing for the elderly, the current housing situation of older Americans, the nature and geographical distribution of special housing for the elderly, major theoretical and applied issues in housing for the elderly, a review of studies of the impact of special housing on older persons, and, finally, some speculation on the prospects of housing for the elderly in the United States.

## HISTORY OF SOCIETAL CONCERN WITH HOUSING FOR THE ELDERLY

Since the end of World War II an increasing amount of attention has been devoted to the housing of older persons in industrial societies. This is particularly true of western European nations, Great Britain, and the United States where approaches to the problem have involved considerable professional and lay speculation, governmental arousal and intervention, and private and public construction of various types of housing (Carp, 1976; Donahue, 1960; McRae, 1975; Vivrett, 1960; Wilner and Walkley, 1966). A major assumption has been that adequate housing is problematic for older persons in industrial societies. This assumption and the related effort stem from a variety of common and unique societal events and processes.

In some European nations the bombings and evacuations of World War II revealed the unsuitable living conditions of many older persons and provided fresh impetus to the improvement of existing housing and the construction of new types of facilities (Donahue, 1960). In addition, many of these nations have long had some form of social policy on the housing of low-income older persons and had been experimenting with different types of residential settings for many years prior to the war. Even though governmental involvement in housing for the elderly in France, the Netherlands, and the United Kingdom is fairly recent, it is also quite extensive (Rubenstein, 1979).

In the United States other factors, such as the depression of the 1930s which served to reveal the general socio-economic plight and vulnerability of older persons, precipitated some concern for their housing and initiated its redefinition from an individual to a social problem. However, organized concern is strictly a post-war development and such Federal housing policy as exists dates back only to 1956 (Gozonsky, 1965; Robbins, 1971). According to Robbins (1971, p. 44):

> Special Federal programs for elderly housing started with the Housing Act of 1956. Previously, the only specialized housing for the elderly had been such facilities as the county homes, church-supported homes, Federal and State homes for veterans, and privately endowed institutions. The Federal programs recognized that government resources should be made available if the housing needs of the elderly were to be met.

In 1956 the US Government explicitly sought to improve the housing of poor older Americans by amending the US Housing Act of 1937 so as to make older individuals (i.e. 62 and over) eligible for low-rent public housing. Prior to 1956, older persons had only been able to live in public housing as members of families. This legislation recognized some major demographic facts: most older persons in the United States are women—13.9 million as compared with 9.6 million men in mid-1977; most older women are widows and many live alone; and older women are heavily over-represented among the aged poor (US Senate Special Committee on Aging, 1979).

Public housing has been the single largest Federally assisted housing programme for older persons—providing 529,900 dwelling units as of 30 June 1978 (US Senate Special Committee on Aging, 1980). However, in 1959 two other rental housing programmes for the elderly began: Section 202 of the Housing Act of 1959, a direct loan programme for non-profit sponsors, and Section 231, a mortgage insurance programme for profit-oriented or non-profit sponsors. As of the late 1970s, these programmes (with the later Section 236 programme) had resulted in an additional 156,000 units of housing for the elderly (US Senate Special Committee on Aging, 1980). In addition to stimulating the development of rental housing for the elderly, the Federal government has also attempted to make it possible for older persons to become home-owners by insuring their mortgages from private lenders.

For those familiar with the history of old age legislation in the United States, it should not be surprising that government activity in housing for the elderly was late in coming. After all, it was not until 1935 that the Social Security Act was passed—making this country the last of the major industrialized nations to provide supplementary income for the elderly (Fischer, 1977). The housing efforts of the government thus far would probably be characterized by a neutral observer as modest and by a critical observer, such as Estes (1979), as woefully inadequate. However, it has typically shown a reluctance to move into an area which is regarded as a matter of private enterprise and housing has traditionally been such an area.

The term 'housing for the elderly' will be used to refer to conventional housing as well as to retirement housing. Conventional housing consists of detached houses, apartments, and mobile homes located in urban, suburban, and rural settings while retirement housing is specially planned for or caters more or less exclusively to older and/or retired persons. Retirement housing may also involve detached houses, apartments, and mobile homes but is distinguished from conventional housing by its planned, age-segregated nature.

Unless otherwise noted, the terms elderly, older American, or older person refer to someone who is 65 years of age or older. Age 65 has become designated as the official threshold of old age in the United States in connection with the Social Security Act, with 65 being the statutorily defined age at which an individual can begin to draw maximum benefits. However, other ages now have official significance: to qualify for various services under the Older Americans Act, a person must be at least 60 while to qualify for Federally assisted housing for the elderly, a person must be at least 62 years of age.

## THE GENERAL HOUSING SITUATION OF OLDER AMERICANS

Despite the increasing attention focused upon special housing for the elderly over the past 25 years, most older persons in this country continue to live in their own homes. Table 8.1 shows some characteristics of households with heads 65 and over from 1950 to 1973. In 1973 there were 69,337,000 occupied housing units in the United States, approximately one-fifth (19.2 per cent) of which were households headed by persons 65 or older (US Department of Housing and Urban Development, 1979a). The number of older households has more than doubled since 1950, reflecting general increases in the older population of the United States.

Of particular geographical interest is the urban–rural location of older households. The majority are in urban areas and most have long been inside Standard Metropolitan Statistical Areas. For rural households there has been a clear decline from a substantial percentage (14 per cent) of farm households in 1950 to only 5 per cent in 1973. During the same time the percentage of older non-farm rural households has increased. Recently an informative account of the housing of the rural aged in the United States has been presented by Atchley and Miller (1979).

Table 8.1 Selected characteristics of households with heads 65 and over in the United States, 1950–73

| | 1950[a] | 1960[b] | 1970[c] | 1973[d] |
|---|---|---|---|---|
| Number of households | 6,362,560 | 9,244,944 | 12,367,380 | 13,332,000 |
| Geographical distribution of households | | (percentage distribution) | | |
| Urban | 67 | 70 | 73 | 71 |
| Inside SMSA | 49 | 58 | 55 | 55 |
| Outside SMSA | 18 | 12 | 18 | 16 |
| Rural | 33 | 30 | 27 | 29 |
| Farm | 14 | 8 | 4 | 5 |
| Non-farm | 19 | 22 | 23 | 24 |
| Occupant status | | | | |
| Owner | 67 | 69 | 68 | 70 |
| Renter | 33 | 31 | 32 | 30 |
| Financial characteristics | | | | |
| Median home value ($) | 5500 | 9490 | 12,600[e] | 18,531[e] |
| Median gross rent | 45 | 60 | 87[e] | 101[e] |
| Year structure built | | | | |
| Since 1970 | — | — | — | 3 |
| 1965–69 | — | — | — | 10 |
| 1960–64 | — | — | — | 7 |
| 1950–59 | — | — | — | 15 |
| 1940–49 | — | — | — | 12 |
| before 1940 | — | — | — | 53 |

*Sources*:

[a]US Bureau of the Census (1953 and 1954).
[b]US Bureau of the Census (1963).
[c]US Bureau of the Census (1973).
[d]Struyk (1977).
[e]US Department of Housing and Urban Development (1979a).

For the past quarter of a century around 70 per cent of older Americans have owned their own homes and one-third or fewer have rented. Many older persons entered the housing market when homes were relatively inexpensive. Even in 1973 the median value of homes owned by older persons was only $18,531, a modest sum in comparison to the current median cost of around $70,000 for a new single-family home. However, the majority of structures inhabited by older persons were built before 1940 and fewer than 15 per cent would be considered relatively modern housing.

Table 8.2 shows the composition of households with heads 65 and over in the United States in 1977. Most households involve families and those with husband–wife families are the modal type (45.3 per cent). A large minority of households (45.1 per cent), however, involves older persons, mainly women

Table 8.2 Composition of households with heads 65 and over in the United States, 1977

| Type of household | No. | Percentage |
|---|---|---|
| All households | 14,816,000 | 100.0 |
| Households with primary families | 8,129,000 | 54.9 |
| Husband–wife families | 6,703,000 | 45.3 |
| Other families with male head | 282,000 | 1.9 |
| Families with female head | 1,144,000 | 7.7 |
| Households with primary individuals | 6,687,000 | 45.1 |

*Source*: Adapted from *Statistical Bulletin of the Metropolitan Life Insurance Company* (Oct.–Dec. 1978), Table 1.

living alone or with other unrelated individuals. In 1978, more than eight of every ten older men, but less than six of every ten older women lived in family settings. The remainder lived alone or with non-relatives, except the one in twenty who lived in an institution (US Senate Special Committee on Aging, 1979).

## Housing need and housing satisfaction

Housing has long been viewed as a major area of need among older persons in the United States. This belief received its most emphatic statement at the 1971 White House Conference on Aging which declared that education, employment and retirement, physical and mental health, housing, income, nutrition, retirement roles and activities, spiritual well-being, and transportation were the most important needs for the attention of national policy (White House Conference on Aging of 1971, 1973). However, the extent to which housing represents a problem for older Americans has been a matter of some contention among gerontologists. Rosow (1967, p. 5) argued that

> among practitioners in the field of housing and gerontology a tremendous amount of work is. . .devoted to housing as a major problem of older people. For the age group as a whole, this is certainly a serious error. Only a small minority of the aged has a housing problem even though it may be acute in some cases. Seldom do even 5 per cent of old respondents in various surveys spontaneously mention housing as a problem. When they are explicitly asked about housing, usually less than 15 per cent express any dissatisfaction with their living arrangements.

Rosow's view is supported by findings from a major national survey in which only eleven per cent of the respondents 65 and over indicated that housing represented a 'very serious or somewhat serious' problem (National Council on the Aging, 1975).

Other gerontologists are less willing than Rosow (1967) to accept older persons' own evaluations of the adequacy of their housing. A suggestion by Keller (1968) that people may say they are satisfied with their surroundings but then move when an opportunity presents itself prompted Carp (1976) to question the validity of older persons' stated evaluations of their living situations. Similarly, seeming discrepancies between objective indicators of housing quality and a relatively high degree of satisfaction expressed by the elderly in a number of surveys led Lawton (1979, p. 64) to aver that, 'one cannot accept at face value the conclusion that older people can necessarily tell us better than objective indicators can how well their housing needs are being met'.

Objective indicators of housing quality show that the housing of older persons is quite comparable to that of other age groups and of generally good quality. Nevertheless, for certain sub-groups of the aged such as blacks, Hispanics, and those in rural areas, housing quality tends to be objectively much poorer (Lawton, 1979). This has recently been affirmed by the US Department of Housing and Urban Development (1979b) which found that the physical adequacy of older persons' housing matches that of the total population: only about one-tenth of these living units are physically deficient. The probability of the elderly living in inadequate housing is related to such factors as income, sex, and household size (men living alone have a substantial chance of residing in flawed housing), ethnicity (poor Hispanic men who live alone have the highest chance of being ill-housed), and tenure (renters have poorer housing).

## NATURE AND DISTRIBUTION OF SPECIAL HOUSING

### The nature of special housing for the elderly

The housing of older persons in the United States has been viewed as a social problem and several types of special housing have been built as part of the solution. Such housing has been referred to as specially designed housing for the elderly, special group housing for the elderly, senior citizens' housing, age-segregated housing, planned retirement housing, or retirement housing. Retirement housing includes mobile-home parks, retirement villages, retirement apartments, retirement hotels and life-care facilities. These vary considerably in design, sponsorship, cost, location, on-site services, and characteristics of residents. Another important dimension of variation is *supportiveness*, which refers to the degree to which the housing environment provides for the routine and special needs of the resident, as well as the extent to which the resident is freed of responsibility for maintaining the housing environment (Mangum, 1979). This concept provides an ordering principle in terms of which all major forms of non-institutional housing, both conventional and retirement, can be viewed. The resulting ordering is shown in Figure 8.1.

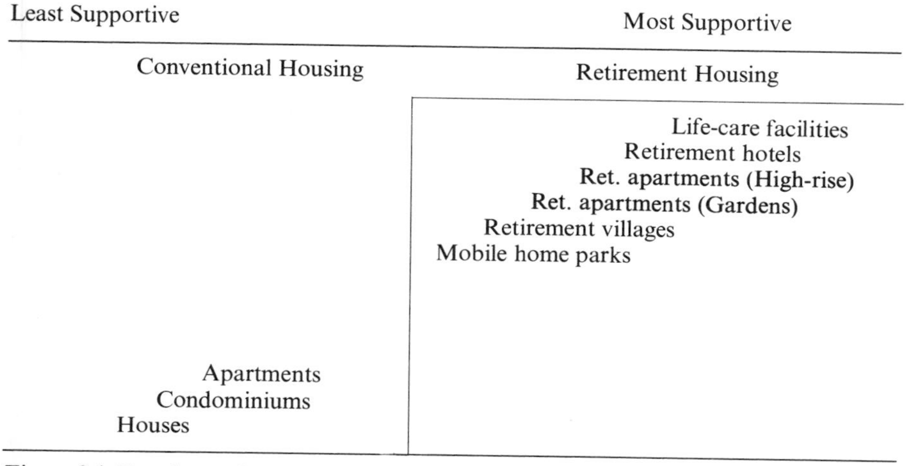

| Least Supportive | Most Supportive |
|---|---|
| Conventional Housing | Retirement Housing |
| | Life-care facilities<br>Retirement hotels<br>Ret. apartments (High-rise)<br>Ret. apartments (Gardens)<br>Retirement villages<br>Mobile home parks |
| Apartments<br>Condominiums<br>Houses | |

Figure 8.1 Typology of non-institutional housing for older persons in the United States (*Source*: W. P. Mangum (1979). Retirement villages: past, present and future issues. In P. A. Wagner and J. M. McRae (Eds) *Back to Basics: Food and Shelter for the Elderly*, Center for Gerontological studies, University of Florida, Gainesville, Fig. 1, p. 90)

An owned or rented *conventional* house is usually the least supportive in that the resident must not only cook meals and satisfy other personal needs but also perform or arrange home and yard maintenance. *Condominiums* are somewhat more supportive in that the resident is responsible typically only for housekeeping and interior maintenance, with exterior maintenance being provided by the condominium association. *Apartments* are theoretically somewhat more supportive than condominiums because the management is responsible for providing all maintenance while the resident is responsible only for housekeeping. The vast majority of older persons in the United States live in these low-support types of conventional housing, particularly houses and rental apartments.

Turning to the supportiveness of different types of retirement housing, the least is provided by mobile home parks. Not all mobile home parks cater exclusively to retired persons but at least 700 capable of accommodating almost 350,000 older persons have such an orientation (Woodall Publishing Company, 1977). Park owners view older persons as very desirable residents because of their financial responsibility, quiet and orderly nature, and their lower mobility than younger persons.

*Mobile home parks* range from modest 'mom and pop trailer parks' renting spaces for \$30–40 a month to sumptuous 'mobile home estates' which rent spaces for \$200–300 a month and provide a large number of amenities. Some of the larger ones sell lots and require that the mobile home meet certain standards. Mobile home parks are usually more supportive than conventional housing because of mutual aid among park residents, such as light duty nursing during an illness. However, mobile home parks are the least supportive form of retirement housing because residents are expected to live independently and park managements provide few services other than recreational. Most mobile home parks are commercially operated and are in and around urban areas. Their residents range from those with working-class backgrounds to affluent retired professionals who have chosen the country club atmosphere of some parks. Unlike other forms of retirement housing, which often stipulate a minimum age (e.g. 50, 62, or 65) for occupancy, retirement-oriented mobile home parks rarely do. However, it is usually clear from their advertising, e.g., 'shuffleboard, potlucks, no children under 18', that the parks welcome only older or retired persons.

The next most supportive type of retirement housing is the *retirement village* which has been defined as, '. . . a small community, relatively independent, segregated, and non-institutional, whose residents are mainly older people separated more or less completely from their regular or career opportunities in gainful or non-paid employment' (Webber and Osterbind, 1961, p. 4). Although this definition was formulated almost 20 years ago it is still valid today and applies to a typical large retirement village such as Sun City Center, near Tampa, Florida. Sun City Center has approximately 5000 largely middle and upper middle income residents living mainly in detached houses which are owned by the residents and in some rental and condominium apartments. The purchase price of homes ranges from $30,000 to $50,000 although some 'custom' homes which cost $100,000 or more have been offered recently. In a retirement village such as Sun City Center perhaps 90 per cent of the residents pay cash for their homes. However, most were home-owners before moving to Sun City Center and simply reinvest in the village. Large retirement villages normally contain a multitude of stores, services, and recreational facilities. Sun City Center has several churches, a supermarket, drug store, variety stores, beauty salons, barber shops, auto service centre, furniture store, theatre, bowling alley, two 18-hole golf courses and several swimming pools and man-made lakes, and over 80 different clubs, groups, and organizations which accommodate an extremely wide variety of interests. In keeping with the prevailing leisure ethic, particular emphasis is placed upon recreation but, increasingly, health care services are being offered or expanded as the average age of residents and their health care needs increase.

To the extent that the term 'housing for the elderly' implies housing which is specially provided for older persons who cannot adequately provide for themselves, mobile home parks and retirement villages cannot truly be considered housing for the elderly. Rather, such facilities are aimed at a relatively affluent segment of the older population for whom housing *per se* is not usually a problem but who are interested in the package of housing, recreational facilities, health services, sociability, and other lifestyle features that retirement villages and large mobile home parks can provide. True planned housing for the elderly begins with the two types of retirement apartments shown in Figure 8.1.

Garden apartments, usually one- or two-storey structures, are considered to be less supportive than *high-rise apartments* because any services, in addition to housing, that they offer are more dispersed and less readily accessible to residents. Most retirement apartments were built under various Federal programmes. Section 202 of the 1959 Housing Act was originally a direct loan programme of housing for the elderly or handicapped in which low interest rate loans were made by the Federal Government to private non-profit corporations, certain public agencies and bodies, and consumer cooperatives for the construction of multi-family rental housing projects. Occupancy is restricted to the handicapped and those persons, or families, over age 62. About two-thirds of the projects are high-rise apartment buildings and most of the residents are older persons rather than handicapped persons. About 60 per cent of the projects have central dining and most have activity areas. The projects are subject to income limits of, for example, a minimum family income of $7200 and a maximum of $10,500. Typical rents are from $130 to $215 for unfurnished apartments ranging in size from 'efficiency' (one-room fully serviced bed-sitters) to two or three rooms with one bedroom. Section 202 operated from 1959 to 1972 when it was discontinued. It resumed operation in 1974, partly in connection with the Section 8 rental assistance programme. Section 202/8 is a direct loan programme of housing for the elderly or handicapped combined with Section 8 rent supplement assistance to low-income residents. The housing project attempts to provide necessary services for the occupant, which may include dining services, transportation, health, continuing education, welfare information, and a counselling and referral service. Section 231 provides mortage insurance to finance new or rehabilitated rental housing of eight or more dwelling units specifically designed for persons over age 62 or those who are handicapped. Some projects are eligible for rent supplements. Developers may be public agencies, non-profit sponsors, or profit-motivated groups. There are no income limits restricting occupancy, except in the case of persons receiving rent supplement assistance. The units may include kitchens or there may be central dining facilities.

Low-rent *public housing* for the elderly represents the major Federally assisted programme for rental housing: 529,900 units were provided throughout the United States as of 30 June 1978 (US Senate Special Committee on Aging, 1980). Most cities, towns, and rural areas in the United States fall under the jurisdiction of one of the 2500 local housing authorities which administer this housing. Elderly housing units are generally found in three types of settings:

(1) public housing projects not designated or designed for the elderly. Units containing older persons are mixed in with the units of all families and have no age restrictions.
(2) Housing projects serving all ages but with units designated for the elderly.

Such units may be composed of a building, one floor of a building, or one section of a floor and may contain special design features.

(3) Entire projects designated for the elderly which, in addition to housing, may include group dining facilities, recreation areas, and special design features.

Tenant eligibility is based upon income limits and asset ceilings which may vary slightly between cities and regions. No one may be charged more than 25 per cent of his income. The Department of Housing and Urban Development pays to the local housing authority the difference between the project's operating expenses and the tenant's rent (US Department of Housing and Urban Development, 1979c).

*Retirement hotels* occupy the next level of supportiveness largely because the residents are freed of housekeeping responsibilities. Typically they are older, commercially non-competitive hotels which cater to lower middle income older persons by providing meals in a central dining room, weekly maid service, and light recreation. However, most retirement hotels offer few other services and they tend to be the least adequate type of retirement housing, both physically and socially (Mangum, 1973).

Finally, the most supportive type of non-institutional retirement housing is the *life care facility*. In addition to providing a diversity of accommodations (for example, small houses, apartments, and rooms with maid service) keyed to the functional capabilities and desires of the residents, they offer a full range of supportive services, including meals in a central dining room, health care, and light recreation. Life-care facilities are expensive, however, with accommodation fees of $35,000 or more and monthly fees of $300–500.

Only the most visible, well-known and prevalent types of retirement housing have been described. One additional type which captures the imagination of some people is the communal or quasi-communal living arrangement. Streib and Streib (1975) have presented a thoughtful account of the prospects and problems involved in developing such living arrangements for older persons in the United States and have concluded that the problems (principally, social values opposed to communal living) generally outweigh the prospects. One exception may be a concept in Winter Park, Florida, known as Share A Home. Share A Home involves seven to twenty older unrelated individuals sharing a large older home under the general guidance of a paid manager. At the present time few such homes exist, and the number of older persons they accommodate is negligible.

## The geographical distribution of special housing for the elderly

Table 8.3 shows the geographical distribution of dwelling units of Federally assisted housing (Section 202, 202/8, 231, 236—a discontinued programme—

Table 8.3 Units of Federally assisted housing for the elderly in relation to population 60 years of age and over by major regions of the United States, c. 1975

| | Units[a] | | Population 60 +[b] | |
|---|---|---|---|---|
| | No. | % | No. | % |
| *Northeast* | 118,091 | 25.79 | 8,027,400 | 24.89 |
| New England | 44,095 | 9.63 | 1,959,100 | 6.07 |
| Middle Atlantic | 73,996 | 16.16 | 6,068,300 | 18.82 |
| *North Central* | 125,743 | 27.45 | 8,680,200 | 26.92 |
| East North Central | 75,355 | 16.45 | 5,875,400 | 18.22 |
| West North Central | 50,388 | 11.00 | 2,804,800 | 8.70 |
| *South* | 138,287 | 30.20 | 10,245,700 | 31.78 |
| South Atlantic | 70,512 | 15.40 | 5,171,100 | 16.04 |
| East South Central | 29,670 | 6.48 | 2,054,300 | 6.37 |
| West South Central | 38,105 | 8.32 | 3,020,300 | 9.37 |
| *West* | 75,863 | 16.56 | 5,292,000 | 16.41 |
| Mountain | 21,005 | 4.59 | 1,268,000 | 3.93 |
| Pacific | 54,858 | 11.98 | 4,024,000 | 12.48 |
| TOTALS | 457,984 | | 32,245,300 | |

*Sources*:

[a]US Department of Housing and Urban Development (1979c).
[b]US Department of Health, Education and Welfare (1978).

and public housing for the elderly). The largest number and percentage of dwelling units is found in the South and the smallest is found in the West and one might readily conclude that there are fairly large differences between the regions and sub-regions. However, when the percentage of dwelling units is viewed in relation to the apposite percentage of population aged 60 and over, there is generally a close correspondence between the two sets of figures. This relationship is not unexpected since the construction of a given Federally assisted housing project is based, in part, on the number of potentially eligible older occupants in the target area. However, other factors enter into the actual building of projects, such as the interest and availability of sponsoring organizations and lending institutions. In view of this, it seems remarkable that there is such a high degree of correspondence between the older population and the number of dwelling units, and it is concluded that the distribution of Federally assisted housing throughout the various regions of the United States is quite even and apparently equitable.

Information on the quantity and geographical distribution of non-Federally assisted retirement housing is much more difficult to obtain. The major sources of such information currently available are the *National Directory on Housing for Older People* (National Council on the Aging, 1969), the *National Directory of Retirement Residences: Best Places to Live When You Retire* (Musson, 1973), and *Woodall's 1978 Retirement and Resort Communities, National Edition* (Woodall Publishing Company, 1977). Each of these directories has its own strengths and weaknesses and all are concerned with helping older persons select retirement housing rather than merely providing a list of existing housing facilities. Beyond the fact that they are all more or less dated, their greatest weakness is the incomprehensiveness of lists. Some facilities, such as Sun City Center, have not been included in any of the directories; other facilities which are listed may no longer be operating as retirement housing. Nevertheless, in combination, the directories permit the development of quantitative estimates of the relative geographical distribution of retirement mobile home parks, retirement villages, retirement hotels, and life-care facilities. In addition, they provide a basis for conservatively estimating the amount of such non-Federally assisted retirement housing and the number of residents. Findings based on the directories are shown in Table 8.4.

In terms of total dwelling units, non-Federally assisted retirement housing is unevenly distributed throughout the United States. Most dwelling units are in the southern and western regions while relatively few are in the northwest and north central regions. This is in marked contrast to the distribution of Federally assisted housing for the elderly, particularly mobile home parks and retirement villages, which is concentrated in Florida, California, and Arizona. The four types of housing also tend to be differentially geographically distributed. Mobile home parks and retirement villages are mainly located in the South and West—primarily in the states of Florida, California, and Arizona, while life care facilities are concentrated in the north central region. Only retirement hotels match the population distribution of persons aged 60 and over across the various regions. Altogether there are 589,118 non-Federally assisted dwelling units, 96,782 fewer than the Federally assisted dwelling units.

Among older persons the median number of occupants in owned homes is 1.8 while the median number in rented homes is 1.3 (US Department of Housing and Urban Development, 1979a). If the higher occupancy factor is applied to the number of dwelling units associated with mobile home parks and retirement villages, which predominantly involve ownership, and the lower occupancy factor to retirement hotels and life-care facilities, which approximate a rental situation, it can be estimated that 1,018,637 older persons reside in the four types of non-Federally assisted retirement housing. This represents 3.2 per cent of the population 60 and over. Applying the rental occupancy factor to the 685,900 dwelling units of Federally assisted housing leads to an estimate of 891,670 residents or 2.8 per cent of the population 60 and over. In total, these figures indicate that 1,910,307 persons or 5.9 per cent of the population 60 and over reside in retirement housing in the United States.

Table 8.4 Number of non-Federally assisted retirement housing facilities and residents by major regions of the United States, *c.* 1975

| | Mobile Home Parks | | | Retirement Villages | | | Retirement Hotels | | | Life-care Facilities | | | Total Dwelling Units | | Population 60+ | |
|---|---|---|---|---|---|---|---|---|---|---|---|---|---|---|---|---|
| | No. parks | No. spaces | % spaces | No. villages | No. DU's | % DU's | No. hotels | No. rooms | % rooms | No. facilities | No. DU's | % DU's | No. | % | No. | % |
| *Northeast* (NE) | 30 | 5,932 | 3.07 | 9 | 8,100 | 2.60 | 27 | 4,050 | 20.30 | 16 | 4,800 | 7.55 | 22,882 | 3.88 | 8,027,400 | 24.89 |
| New England | 6 | 847 | 0.44 | 1 | 900 | 0.29 | 5 | 750 | 3.76 | 4 | 1,200 | 1.89 | 3,697 | 0.63 | 1,959,100 | 6.07 |
| Middle Atlantic | 24 | 5,085 | 2.63 | 8 | 7,200 | 2.31 | 22 | 3,300 | 16.54 | 12 | 3,600 | 5.66 | 19.185 | 3.25 | 6,068,300 | 18.82 |
| *North Central* (NC) | 44 | 7,509 | 3.88 | 5 | 4,500 | 1.44 | 29 | 4,350 | 21.80 | 82 | 24,600 | 38.68 | 40,959 | 6.95 | 8,680,200 | 26.92 |
| East North Central | 28 | 4,881 | 2.52 | 4 | 3,600 | 1.15 | 22 | 3,300 | 16.84 | 53 | 15,900 | 25.00 | 27,681 | 4.70 | 5,875,400 | 18.22 |
| West North Central | 16 | 2,628 | 1.36 | 1 | 900 | 0.29 | 7 | 1.050 | 5.26 | 29 | 8,700 | 13.68 | 13,278 | 2.25 | 2,804,800 | 8.70 |
| *South* (S) | 343 | 124,414 | 64.30 | 31 | 168,795 | 54.09 | 37 | 5,550 | 27.82 | 48 | 14,400 | 22.64 | 313,159 | 53.16 | 10,245,700 | 31.78 |
| South Atlantic | 313 | 95,583 | 49.40 | 27 | 147,015 | 47.11 | 25 | 3,750 | 18.80 | 39 | 11,700 | 18.40 | 258,048 | 43.80 | 5,171,100 | 16.04 |
| East South Central | 10 | 1,447 | 0.75 | 0 | 0 | 0.00 | 2 | 300 | 1.50 | 3 | 900 | 1.41 | 2,647 | 0.45 | 2,054,300 | 6.37 |
| West South Central | 20 | 27,384 | 14.15 | 4 | 21,780 | 6.98 | 10 | 1,500 | 7.52 | 6 | 1,800 | 2.83 | 52,464 | 8.91 | 3,020,300 | 9.37 |
| *West* (W) | 304 | 55,683 | 28.75 | 24 | 130,680 | 41.87 | 40 | 6,000 | 30.08 | 66 | 19,800 | 31.13 | 212,118 | 36.01 | 5,292,000 | 16.41 |
| Mountain | 100 | 21,720 | 11.23 | 9 | 49,005 | 15.70 | 7 | 1,050 | 5.26 | 6 | 1,800 | 2.83 | 73,575 | 12.49 | 1,268,000 | 3.93 |
| Pacific | 204 | 33,918 | 17.52 | 15 | 81,675 | 26.17 | 33 | 4,950 | 24.82 | 60 | 18,000 | 28.30 | 138,543 | 23.52 | 4,024,000 | 12.48 |
| TOTAL | 721 | 193,493 | 100.00 | 69 | 312,075 | 100.00 | 133 | 19,950 | 100.00 | 212 | 63,600 | 100.00 | 589,118 | 100.00 | 32,245,300 | 100.00 |
| Assumed $\bar{x}$ No. of DUs per site | | Actual No. of spaces | | | NE & NC = 900<br>S & W = 5,445 | | | 150 | | | 300 | | | | | |
| Assumed median No. of persons per DU | | 1.8 | | | 1.8 | | | 1.3 | | | 1.3 | | | | | |
| Estimated total No. of residents | | 348,287 | | | 561,735 | | | 25,935 | | | 82,680 | | 1,018,637 | | | |

*Source*: Basic housing data derived from National Council on the Aging (1969), Musson (1973), and Woodall Publishing Co. (1977). Population data derived from US Department of Health, Education, and Welfare (1978).

DU = dwelling unit.

## MAJOR THEORETICAL ISSUES IN HOUSING FOR THE ELDERLY

Perhaps because of its physical nature, a great many isolated facts about the housing of older persons have been assembled. This may suggest that the field is essentially one of simple empiricism, but there are a number of theoretical issues and considerations which have substantially influenced discourse and research. These include the causes and consequences of high concentrations of older persons in planned or unplanned residential settings, ageing and the environment, the psycho-social needs of older persons in relation to housing, and planning and design aspects of housing and environments for older persons.

### Age concentration

For many years the concept of age concentration has occupied a prominent and often controversial place in the literature of gerontology. Age concentration refers to a relatively high proportion or population density of older persons in a given population or other analytic unit and may come about through ageing in place, the out-migration of younger persons from an area, or the in-migration of older persons to an area (Wiseman, 1978). It has been studied on levels ranging from national societies to small environments such as apartment buildings for the elderly (Cowgill, 1974; Rosow, 1967).

The controversy regarding age concentration has usually centred upon residential integration *versus* residential segregation of older persons, or age segregation *versus* age integration. Since at least the mid-1950s, critics of age-segregated residential settings have advocated residential integration on the grounds that it promotes social integration (Bohn, 1961; Mumford, 1956). It has been argued that older persons' accessibility to younger age groups fosters sociability and socialization, maintains continuity in the lives of older persons, and prevents a narrowing of interests and other possibly deleterious psychological consequences. Other critics have opposed age-segregated residential settings on the grounds that the majority of older persons prefer to remain in their old homes. More recently, Butler (1975, p. 120) has stated that 'retirement communities do serve as a useful option to those elderly who prefer them'. However, he is very critical of age segregation in general, viewing it as a significant element in negative attitudes towards the old and as having reached such an extreme degree in American society that it has become non-functional.

Age segregation is rarely viewed as a positive and functional social phenomenon but there are theoretical as well as empirical grounds for believing that it may be more advantageous than disadvantageous to many older persons. Rosow (1967) has developed this position most forcefully. He has argued that in modern, industrialized societies such as the United States, older persons are devalued, stereotyped, excluded from social participation and societal rewards enjoyed by younger persons, suffer from role loss and role ambiguity, and cling to ego-defensive youthful self-images. Thus, he has concluded that there is little basis in present-day society for the social integration of older persons—except among their own age peers. Although not all gerontologists agree with Rosow's characterization of older persons' alienation in American society (Atchley, 1980), his findings of a positive relationship between the degree of age concentration in apartment buildings in Cleveland and the social integration of older residents lend support to his arguments in favour of age-segregated settings, particularly for older persons who are dependent on the local environment for social interaction.

Another early study which shed light on the age-integration–age-segregation issue was one by Messer (1967), who hypothesized that:

(1) in an age-segregated environment high morale is a function of the normative milieu rather than the higher rate of interaction; and
(2) in a mixed-age setting morale is more dependent on a high rate of social interaction.

To test these hypotheses a probability sample of 88 tenants of Chicago public housing projects occupied exclusively by the elderly was compared with a similar sample of 155 elderly tenants living in public housing of mixed-age composition. The hypotheses were supported by the findings: a high level of interaction was associated with high morale among older persons living in mixed-age settings. However, the relationship disappeared in the age-segregated sample and was, in fact, slightly reversed. Messer (1967) concluded that his findings were consistent with the activity theory of ageing for the sample of older persons living in the environment with a normal age distribution *and* with the position of disengagement theorists that interaction and morale are independent of one another for the age-concentrated sample.

More recently Teaff *et al.* (1978) studied the relations between age-mixing and indicators of well-being in a national probability sample of 2000 elderly residents in 103 public housing sites. Age segregation was shown to be positively associated with amount of participation in on-site activities, morale, housing satisfaction, and neighbourhood motility.

A review of all studies of age-segregated housing would probably show that most but not all older residents endorse it. The general nature of the situation has recently been well expressed by Lawton (1980, p. 92):

> How do older people themselves feel about the integration issue? Data from two large-scale research studies (Lawton, in press; Lawton and Nahemow, 1975) show that older people now living in age-segregated projects overwhelmingly approve of this style of living and a large proportion of those who are uncertain how they might like living only

with age peers before they moved into such housing came to approve of it after a year of residence. In addition to the greater security perceived in age-segregated settings, a number also cited the lack of bother from noise and boisterous behavior as factors in their preference. A minority (31 per cent) would have preferred having among their neighbors younger adults with children. Thus, although the majority were satisfied, the needs of some were not fulfilled by the age-segregation pattern.

## Ageing and the environment

One of the fastest growing sub-fields within gerontology in recent years has been ageing and the environment, particularly the behavioural implications of the environment. It has attracted the interests and efforts of a variety of professionals including architects and those with architectural perspectives (Byerts, Howell, and Pastalan, 1979; Pastalan and Carson, 1970), geographers (Golant, 1979; Wiseman, 1978), psychologists (Carp, 1976; Kahana, 1980; Lawton, 1977, 1980; Lawton and Nahemow, 1973) and sociologists (Gubrium, 1973, 1974). According to Lawton (1980, p. 2): 'The basic assertion underlying the study of the environment and behavior is that *a person's behavioral and psychological state can be better understood with knowledge of the context in which the person behaves*' (italics his). This context may be broad or narrow, stimulus-rich or stimulus-deprived, making it exceptionally difficult to develop a taxonomy of environment. Lawton (1980) has, however, identified a number of important aspects of environment which may impinge on an individual and influence behaviour. These include the personal, physical, social, group, and the suprapersonal environments, the last consisting of the characteristics of the aggregate of individuals in physical proximity to the subject. Information has been summarized for these aspects of environment by Lawton (1977, 1980) but perhaps his most important contribution has been his and Nahemow's ecological theory of adaptive behaviour and ageing (Lawton and Nahemow, 1973).

According to Lawton and Nahemow, the adaptive behaviour of an individual is a function of the interaction between the individual's general competence and the degree of environmental press he is experiencing. Competence is not a unitary characteristic but a set of competencies in the domains of biological health, sensorimotor functioning, cognitive skill, and ego strength (Lawton, 1980). Environmental press were defined by Murray (1938) as forces in the environment that, together with an individual nead evoke a response. Press may be viewed in terms of such characteristics as their stress-producing properties, problematic qualities, demand character, and supportive character. Furthermore, press are neutral in that their positive or negative quality is defined by the interacting individual rather than residing intrinsically in the environment (Lawton and Nahemow, 1973).

The relationship between competence and press and their joint effect on behaviour, as well as affect, are shown schematically in Figure 8.2. As can be

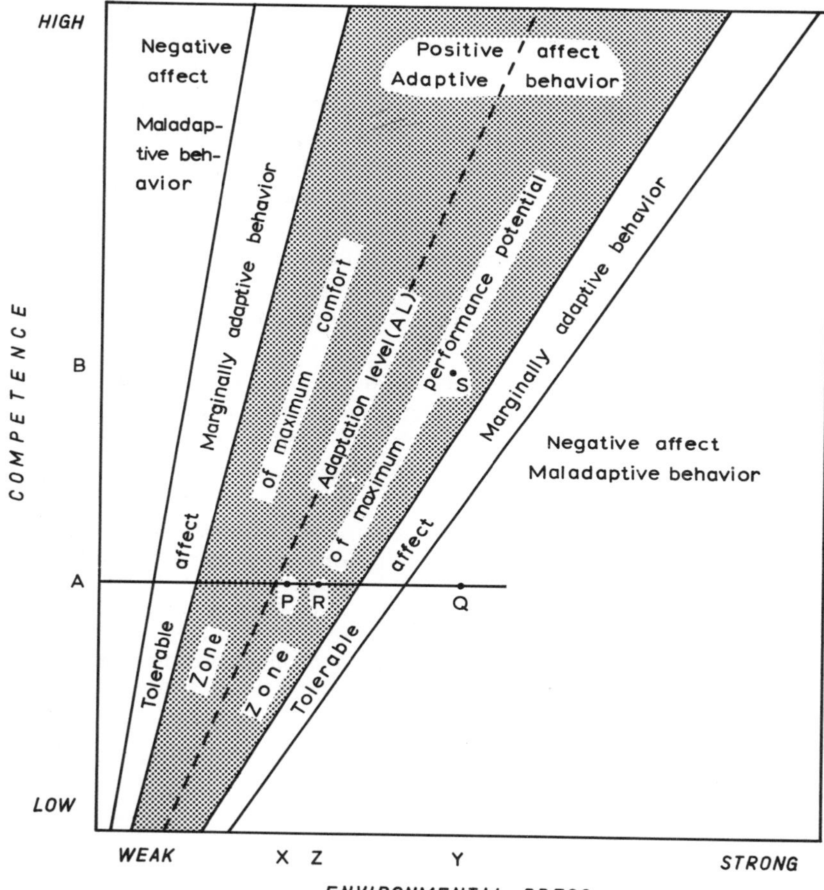


Figure 8.2 Relationship between competence and environmental press. (*Source*: M.P. Lawton (1980). *Environment and Aging*. Brooks/Cole, Monterey, California, Fig. 1–4, p. 12.) Copyright 1973 by the American Psychological Association. (Reprinted by permission)

inferred, the intersection of any degree of individual competence with any degree of environmental press result in behaviour and affect which may range from adaptive and positive to maladaptive and negative. If, for example, a person of low competence is subjected to moderate to strong press, the outcome will be negative affect and maladaptive behaviour. However, if a person of high competence experiences a similar degree of press, his behaviour and affect are much more likely to be positive. The dashed line labelled 'adaptation level' represents points where environmental press are average for whatever level of competence the person in question has. When a given individual is at adaptation level, appropriate behaviour and affect go on as normal. To the right of the adaptation level is the zone of maximum performance potential which is based on the proposition that as environmental press increase, persons are challenged to behave at a higher level. As press continues to increase, however, adaptive behaviour begins to become marginal and affect becomes merely tolerable and, eventually, if press become strong enough, the result is negative affect and maladaptive behaviour. Conversely, to the left of the adaptation level line, as press decrease an individual enters first a zone of maximum comfort, experienced perhaps as a feeling of unharried well-being. Beyond this, however, lies the possibility of boredom and frustration if press become too weak.

A major applied implication of the model is that it should be possible to maximize the adaptive behaviour of older persons in housing settings by making appropriate adjustments between their levels of competence and degree of press or, as Lawton and Nahemow (1973, p. 666) have expressed it:

> Environmental programming is seen as an effective means of elevating behavior and affect, particularly if it is carefully adjusted in its demand quality to the functional level of people who utilize it. Conversely, 'downward' environmental programming, or increased support, is seen to be appropriate as poor health, social rejection, or emotional distress intrude. [They caution however that]...the net balance of positive outcome may be maximized only by careful assessment of the individual, his environment, his active and passive needs, and the potential behavior and affective states that may eventuate from the transaction.

## Psycho-social needs of older persons in relation to housing

Hansen (1971) has estimated that persons aged over 65 spend 80–90 per cent of their time in the home. Housing helps to satisfy a number of fundamental needs of older persons: independence, safety and comfort, a wholesome self-concept, a sense of place, relatedness, environmental mastery, psychological stimulation, and privacy (Montgomery, 1972). The desirability of matching the characteristics of settings to the needs of older individuals has been a recurrent theme in gerontology and one group of investigators has attempted to develop a system for assigning them to appropriate residential settings. Sherwood, Morris, and Barnhart (1975) have conducted preliminary work on the use of discriminant function analysis in determining whether older persons would be most appropriately housed in a sheltered setting, a semi-sheltered setting, or a non-sheltered setting. They found that their procedure replicated the independent judgements of clinical teams in a large percentage of cases. Work of this sort should eventually enable older persons seeking housing to be counselled on the basis of their responses to certain critical items as to the most appropriate residential settings.

### Planning and design aspects of housing and environments

To maximize the satisfaction of older persons' needs, psychologists, architects, and other professionals have suggested various principles and procedures of planning and design. Many years ago the need for special design features such as grab bars in the shower and waist-high electrical outlets engaged the interest of housing developers and gerontologists. Some argued that such features were absolutely essential to the well-being of an older person; others argued that such special features might undermine an older person's sense of independence. Many of these features have been incorporated into existing planned housing for the elderly and are now standard items.

Stimulated by the concern in recent years with creating barrier-free environments for the handicapped, such environments have also been recommended for older persons (Costa and Sweet, 1976). Beattie (1970) argued that we should develop supportive environments throughout the lifespan and has noted some of the necessary design features. Chapanis (1974) suggested that human engineering concepts be applied to environments for the aged, and described design features which would facilitate mobility. Similarly, Tucker, Combs, and Woolrich (1975) have discussed design features such as closet storage. The level of interest is evinced by a number of volumes which present issues and principles of design (Byerts, Howell, and Pastalan, 1979; Gelwicks and Newcomer, 1974; Lawton, 1975, 1980; Lawton, Newcomer, and Byerts, 1976).

## STUDIES OF THE IMPACT OF SPECIAL HOUSING FOR THE ELDERLY

### Mobile home parks

Only a few studies of older persons residing in mobile home parks have been published and perhaps the earliest investigation was Hoyt's (1954) study of residents of a large retirement mobile home park in Florida. Hoyt explored the question: 'To what extent, and in what sense, does this type of community meet the needs and interests of older, retired persons?' (Hoyt, 1954, p. 362). A sample of 194 residents (from a park population of over 1000) with a median age of 64 years was interviewed. Approximately 88 per cent preferred to live in a community where everyone was retired rather than one in which most people were working; 4 per cent preferred a working community; and 8 per cent were undecided. When asked their reasons for preferring a retirement park, 48 per cent mentioned possibilities for association with others as the chief reason, 43 per cent referred to mutual aid between residents in times of illness and on other occasions, and 9 per cent preferred the retirement park because there was less disturbance from children and people going to work. Among the chief advantages attributed to mobile home living were sociability and activities, economy, less work, and less worry. Only 49 respondents reported any disadvantages of mobile home living—size being the most frequently cited. Hoyt concluded that 'Personal adjustment in retirement and old age is facilitated by the attitudes and institutional practices of mobile home communities. Social roles which are congruent with the needs and interests of the retired person are sanctioned' (Hoyt, 1954, p. 370).

Johnson's (1971) study of Idle Haven, a mobile home park in the San Francisco Bay Area containing mainly working-class retired persons, was mainly concerned with the means by which and the extent to which the residents were able to develop a sense of community in the park. It appears that they were generally satisfied with mobile home park living. Hamovitch, Peterson, and Larson (undated) studied three lower-income mobile home parks in and around Los Angeles. While a majority of the respondents were generally satisfied with such features of the parks as location, design, and cost, they generally had a lower degree of overall housing fulfilment than did residents of other types of housing.

In the absence of further research it is impossible to evaluate the impact of mobile home parks on the psycho-social well-being of older persons. However, as mobile homes become more prevalent for older persons, research is in order to determine whether they are suitable as a regular form of housing or whether they should be regarded merely as a stop-gap (Butler, 1974).

## Retirement villages

Retirement villages are a well-established type of housing for older persons. However, from their inception they have been the most controversial type of retirement housing available in the United States and they have often been treated with contempt and suspicion both by professionals and non-professionals. Margaret Mead once labelled them golden ghettos; Maggie Kuhn often alludes to them as playpens for the elderly; and Louis Mumford (1956) long ago argued that such large-scale organized living quarters for older persons are socially unnatural and should be avoided. The bulk of the evidence indicates, however, that retirement villages generally provide satisfying living environments.

A major question surrounding retirement villages as they were beginning to develop concerned why older persons chose to live in them and the first investigators to deal with this topic were Peterson and Larson (1966). Interviewing a sample of 411 prospective in-movers to Leisure World, Laguna Hills, California, they found that contrary to prevailing assumptions, 27 per cent were between 65 and 75, and 15 per cent were aged 75 and over. This bears on a point made by Kleemeier (1961, p. 294) that, 'to the uncritical, a group composed of persons above the age of 60 would appear highly age segregated, yet it could contain persons separated in age by one or even two generations'.

In addition, 27 per cent of the in-movers were not yet retired; 12 per cent of those presently employed were blue-collar workers while 30 per cent were professionals; median educational attainment was 12 years; 81 per cent of the in-moving group were married; 14 per cent were widowed; 2 per cent were divorced; and 2 per cent had never been married. Peterson and Larson noted that life was contracting in various areas of participation for the sample, that there was some distress over role discontinuity consequent to retirement, and there was some evidence of alienation from the groups and activities which gave meaning to their lives. They also pointed out that 'the expectation that moving into the retirement community would bring a new life is almost universal', and that 'many apparently assumed that moving into this community would end their worries, concerns, responsibilities and ennui' (Peterson and Larson, 1966, pp. 136–7).

Approximately 1 year after the 411 respondents had moved into the retirement village they were re-interviewed ($N = 366$) to determine any changes in attitudes and to ascertain satisfactions and dissatisfactions associated with the move (Hamovitch and Larson, 1966). Seventy-three per cent were very pleased with the retirement village, 16 per cent were mildly pleased, and 11 per cent were mildly or very displeased. Twice as many women as men were displeased (15 to 7 per cent). Respondents were also asked how the retirement village measured up to their original expectations. Forty-four per cent indicated that it was about as expected, 45 per cent stated that they found it even better than expected, and 11 per cent were disappointed.

As part of a larger research project on retirement housing, residents of three California retirement villages (a lower-income rental village, a middle-income purchase village, and an upper middle-income purchase village) and matched control samples of residents of ordinary, community housing were studied by Wilner and Associates at the University of California, Los Angeles (UCLA). Findings to be presented for the retirement village residents were originally reported by Sherman *et al.* (1968) while those for the control residents are based on data analysed independently by Mangum (1971). Of particular interest to the present review are comparative findings on residents' attitudes towards age-segregated residential settings, interaction with younger persons, particularly their own children, general residential satisfaction, and morale. Forty-two per cent of the respondents at each of the retirement villages agreed with the statement 'I like living in a place where there are no younger (i.e. under 40) people', approximately 45 per cent in each disagreed with it, and the remainder were undecided. Among the control respondents, however, disagreement with a similar statement ranged from 61 per cent of the lower-income rental village control group to 89 per cent of that of the upper-income purchase village. A Guttman-type scale of attitude towards age-segregated housing revealed statistically significant differences between residents of the retirement villages and their matched controls. While the control respondents were preponderantly opposed to age-segregated housing, the retirement village respondents' significantly greater approval was by no means universal. Residents in the lower- and middle-income retirement villages saw their children significantly less often than did their matched controls but there was no statistically significant difference for residents of the upper middle-income village. Although there was a slight tendency for retirement village residents to desire more contact with their children there were no significant differences between village residents and their controls. Residential satisfaction of the retirement villagers and their controls was very high, with over 90 per cent of all groups reporting they liked the village or neighbourhood 'a lot or quite a bit'. Lastly, the morale of the respondents in the three retirement villages was significantly higher than that of the controls for the lower and upper middle-income villages but not for the middle-income village.

Data from the UCLA study of retirement housing have also been used by Sherman (1972) to study reactions of retirement village residents and their control groups to their living situations. Results were presented for three points in time: a retrospective account of how much residents liked the village when they first resided, their degree of liking at the time of a first interview which was conducted after they had lived in the villages for a while, and at a second interview 2 years later. At each time the level of reported satisfaction was high. Retirement village residents strongly recommended special housing for older persons and controls strongly recommended ordinary housing. The vast majority of retirement village residents also indicated that they would move to the villages again and only 20 per cent had given serious thought to moving out.

Bultena and Wood (1969) sought to assess the role of retirement villages in American life by comparing retired men who had migrated either to retirement villages or ordinary age-integrated communities in Arizona. When asked about retirement living in Arizona, more than two-thirds indicated that they were very satisfied. However, satisfaction was significantly higher for those in retirement villages (75 per cent) than in regular communities (57 per cent). Morale was also higher for the village residents. Bultena and Wood concluded that, while retirement communities are not a universal solution for older persons, they were not the ghettos of ill-adjusted, frustrated, and alienated old people that they have sometimes been characterized.

One study which departed from the usual survey research tradition was that of Jacobs (1974), who did an ethnographic study of a retirement village he termed 'Fun City'. Social scientists often disguise the names of communities they study by substituting a name that characterizes, as well as masks, the object of study. 'Fun City', in this sense, seems to have been meant to denigrate the lifestyle that Jacobs purported to study. His discussion of the retirement village is generally disdainful and he clearly prefers older persons to live under more 'natural' circumstances. However, as Lawton (1980, pp. 89–90) has pointed out, 'his conclusions are not consistent with those from the data-based studies that a positive overall effect on the well being of tenants was associated with residence in planned housing for the elderly'.

Two further studies of retirement villages identify other features. Sherman (1975) reported that mutual assistance involving neighbours was substantially higher among residents of two of the retirement villages studied in comparison to their matched controls, while it was approximately the same between the third retirement village and its matched control; and Marshall (1975) has indicated that retirement villages may prepare their residents for impending death through a process of socialization.

All of the studies of retirement villages noted thus far have been concerned with the impact of the village on the lives of the residents. A final study by Heintz (1976) examined the impact of retirement villages in New Jersey on institutions of the larger community such as the economy, political structure, and health-care system. In general, she concluded that retirement villages had no adverse impact and several positive effects.

### Retirement apartments

One of the earliest and most intensive studies of retirement apartments was Carp's (1966) before and after study of the first cohort of older persons to move into Victoria Plaza—a rental public housing apartment building. She sought:

(1) to assess the impact of changed and physically more adequate housing for older persons;
(2) to identify background and personality characteristics associated with differences in adjustment to life in Victoria Plaza; and
(3) to investigate processess of interpersonal contact, group formation, and leadership among residents.

The general conclusion was that:

> Evidence of the dramatic effect of improved life setting on this group of older people was overwhelming. It appeared not only in increased satisfaction with the residential situation but also in more favorable attitudes toward self and others, in improved physical and mental health, and in more active and sociable patterns of life (Carp, 1966, p. 223).

In a follow-up study 8 years later of Victoria Plaza residents and a comparison group who had remained in ordinary housing, Carp (1975) found that the residents were not only more satisfied with their housing but also happier. On several indicators of morale there were statistically significant differences in the expected direction between the two groups. Carp concluded that the benefits to older persons from improved housing were long-lasting and not merely a honeymoon reaction.

Partly to test the generality of these findings, Lawton and Cohen (1974) compared persons moving into five different high-rise apartment buildings for the elderly with similar persons remaining in their old homes. The former had higher morale, greater perceived change for the better, more housing satisfaction, more external involvement, and greater satisfaction with the *status quo*. A relative decline in functional health was associated with the new housing but no differences were found in 'loner' status, orientation to children, or activity breadth.

In an even larger study, Lawton, Nahemow and Teaff (1975) gathered data from 2457 respondents in 154 Federally assisted housing projects to examine the relationship between housing sponsorship, community size, building size and height of building, and various measures of well-being. Private, non-profit sponsorship was associated with higher friendship scores and greater activity participation. Residents of smaller buildings had higher friendship scores, greater housing satisfaction, and greater activity participation. Housing satisfaction was negatively related to the total number of units but not to size when size was defined in terms of elderly designated units. Finally, height of building was negatively associated with housing satisfaction and neighbourhood motility.

In a different vein, Lawton (1976) contrasted a retirement apartment project with many on-site services with one which had very few. The service-rich residents showed relative improvement in morale, housing satisfaction, and available social network, but poorer external involvement, supporting the hypothesis that service-rich housing lowers behavioural competence while increasing positive affect.

A recent variant of retirement apartments is *congregate housing*. Arising from the 1970 Housing Act which authorized Federal housing assistance programmes to provide space and fixed equipment for services in addition to basic social space, and partially funded under the 1978 Housing Act, congregate housing has evolved as age-segregated housing with an integrated housing and services package and a non-institutional living environment (Lawton, 1980). It is generally intended to enable older persons to remain in a semi-independent living situation as long as possible and a recent nationwide evaluation concluded that:

> congregate housing is highly useful for a broad spectrum of elderly with an accompanying array of needs. It effectively provides the elderly with shelter and services once they no longer want to live independently, and before their physical capabilities decline to the point of needing constant surveillance and intensive health care (Urban Systems Research and Engineering Inc., 1976, p. 255).

## Retirement hotels

In contrast to the intense study and evaluation of Federally assisted apartments, the appraisal of retirement hotels has been deficient. For two decades the literature has contained mainly descriptive accounts of the hotels and their residents. The picture that emerges is one of socially marginal older persons living in older hotels which may or may not be physically adequate (Albrecht, 1969; Cohen and Sokolovsky, 1979; Eckert, 1979; Lake, 1962; Mangum, 1973; Sherman *et al.*, 1968).

### Life-care facilities

The last type of retirement housing to be considered is the life-care facility. As with mobile home parks and retirement hotels, there have been few studies of their impact on residents' well-being but such evidence as exists is favourable. Sherman *et al.* (1968) and Sherman (1972) found that relative to older residents of three retirement villages, a retirement apartment, and a retirement hotel, those in a life-care facility expressed the highest degree of overall satisfaction. They also had the second-highest level of morale (only slightly below that of the residents of an upper middle-income retirement village), ranked highest in endorsing special housing for older people and willingness to move to the site again, and lowest in having thought seriously about moving out. Hamovitch, Peterson, and Larson (undated) reported that their life-care respondents expressed a high degree of housing fulfilment.

While differences in satisfaction and morale between residents of the various types of retirement housing have been identified, there are major differences in background characteristics among the groups. For example, residents of life-care facilities tend to be relatively healthy, wealthy, and well-educated; those in retirement hotels tend to be just the opposite. Until a study successfully controls for these personal variations, the differential impact of various types of retirement housing will not be clearly established.

## PROSPECTS OF HOUSING FOR THE ELDERLY

This chapter has focused upon housing specially planned for or oriented to older persons in the United States as a major organized societal response to their perceived housing problems. However, whether planned housing for the elderly will continue to be emphasized in public policy is uncertain.

It appears that both Federally assisted and non-Federally assisted housing has been generally satisfying and beneficial to the estimated 5.9 per cent of persons 60 and over who live in it. A continued increase in the number of older Americans—from an estimated 24,927,000 persons 65 and over in 1980 to a projected 50,920,000 in 2025 (US Senate Special Committee on Aging, 1980)—will probably sustain the growth of non-Federally assisted facilities.

Federally assisted housing should also continue to show modest gains. Not only has it been popular with older consumers; it has also been very popular with members of Congress (US Senate Special Committee on Aging, 1980). Unlike non-Federally assisted housing, however, it is subject to public policy debate and, possibly re-direction. Struyk and Soldo (1980) for example, have argued that the Federal Government has devoted too much attention and money to providing special housing for relatively small numbers of older renters and not enough to the 90 per cent of older Americans who reside in ordinary housing. Housing assistance for the substantial number of the latter who need it would, in their view, not only upgrade the housing of the majority of the elderly but also serve to stabilize and revitalize urban neighborhoods. Rabushka and Jacobs (1980) have argued that the housing (and other) problems of older Americans have been grossly exaggerated. In their judgement modest housing assistance should be targeted on the small minority of older persons who need and want it, and the country should move on to other problems. It will be interesting to see how these disparate points of view become resolved in the public policy arena.

What lies ahead for the majority of older Americans living in ordinary, community housing? Kiplinger (1979), analysing data from *The Annual Housing Surveys* of 1973 and 1976 (a joint product of the US Department of Housing and Urban Development and the US Bureau of the Census) and *Current Population Reports* of the US Bureau of the Census, has produced projections dealing with housings conditions and demographic characteristics of older household heads who will be 55 years of age or older in 1990. Her major conclusions are that in 1990 there should be more older persons living independently, particularly women; a large percentage of home-owners among the elderly, although rental housing will become more common with advancing age; a reduction in both the size of the housing unit and the size of the household, although older persons will continue to be over-housed in terms of space; an increase in the number of older persons living in mobile homes and multi-unit structures, particularly for those aged 75 and over, although single-unit houses and apartments will continue to be the most popular form of housing for older Americans; continued growth of the number of households headed by older persons in southern states; and continued residence of the majority of older persons in metropolitan areas, although they will be increasingly likely to live in non-metropolitan areas.

These general characteristics, being the eventual product of already established demographic and social trends, are susceptible only at the margin to public policy and are more likely to be affected by such forces as the state of the economy. Whatever the Federal role in improving the housing of older persons may be, there is no doubt that much remains to be learned about the implications of different types of housing for their independence and quality of life.

## REFERENCES

Albrecht, R. (1969). Retirement hotels in Florida. In Osterbind, C. C. (ed.), *Feasible Planning for Social Change in the Field of Aging*, pp. 71–82. University of Florida Press, Gainesville.

Atchley, R. C. (1980). *The Social Forces in Later Life: An Introduction to Social Gerontology*, 3rd edn. Wadsworth, Belmont, California.

Atchley, R. C. and Miller, S. J. (1979). Housing and households of the rural aged. In Byerts, T. O., Howell, S. C., and Pastalan, L. A. (eds), *Environmental Context of Aging: Life-Styles, Environmental Quality, and Living Arrangements*, pp. 62–79. Garland, New York.

Beattie, W. M. (1970). The design of supportive environments for the lifespan. *The Gerontologist*, **10**, 190–3.

Bohn, E. J. (1961). Prepared statement, in *United States Senate Special Committee on Aging, Housing Problems of the Elderly*. US Government Printing Office, Washington.

Bultena, G. L. and Wood, V. (1969). The American retirement community: bane or blessing? *Journal of Gerontology*, **24**, 209–17.

Burgess, E. W. (1961). *Retirement Villages*. Division of Gerontology, University of Michigan, Ann Arbor.

Butler, R. N. (1974). Mobile homes—stop gaps or permanent shelters? Public interest report no. 12. *International Journal of Aging and Human Development*, **5**, 213–14.

Butler, R. N. (1975). *Why Survive?: Being Old in America*. Harper & Row, New York.

Byerts, T. O., Howell, S. C., and L. A. Pastalan, (eds) (1979). *Environmental Context of Aging: Life-styles, Environmental Quality, and Living Arrangements*. Garland, New York.

Carp, F. M. (1966). *A Future for the Aged: Victoria Plaza and Its Residents*. University of Texas Press, Austin.

Carp, F. M. (1975). Impact of improved housing on morale and life satisfaction. *The Gerontologist*, **15**, 511–15.

Carp, F. M. (1976). Housing and living environments of older people. In Binstock, R. H. and Shanas, E. (eds), *Handbook of Aging and the Social Sciences*, pp. 244–71. Van Nostrand Reinhold, New York.

Chapanis, A. (1974). Human engineering environments for the aged. *The Gerontologist*, **14**, 228–35.

Cohen, C. I. and Sokolovsky, J. (1979). Health-seeking behavior and social networks of the aged living in single room occupancy hotels. *Journal of the American Geriatrics Society*, **27**, 270–8.

Costa, F. J. and Sweet, M. (1976). Barrier-free environments for older Americans. *The Gerontologist*, **16**, 404–9.

Cowgill, D. O. (1974). The aging of populations and societies. *Annals of the American Academy of Political and Social Science*, **415**, 1–18.

Donahue, W. (1960). Housing and community services. In Burgess, E. W. (ed.), *Aging in Western Societies*, pp. 106–55. University of Chicago Press, Chicago.

Eckert, J. K. (1979). The unseen community: understanding the older hotel dweller. *Aging*, 28–35.

Estes, C. L. (1979). *The Aging Enterprise*. Jossey–Bass, San Francisco.

Fischer, D. H. (1977). *Growing Old in America*. Oxford University Press, New York.

Gelwicks, L. E. and Newcomer, R. J. (1974). *Planning Housing Environments for the Elderly*. The National Council on the Aging, Inc., Washington, DC.

Golant, S. M. (1975). Residential concentration of the future elderly. *The Gerontologist*, **15**, 16–23.

Golant, S. M. (ed.) (1979). *Location and Environment of Elderly Population*. Winston, Washington, DC.

Gozonsky, M. J. (1965). Preface. In Carp, F. M. and Burnett, W. M. (eds), *Patterns of Living and Housing of Middle-Aged and Older People*. U. S. Government Printing Office, Washington.

Gubrium, J. F. (1973). *The Myth of the Golden Years: A Socio-Environmental Theory of Aging*. Charles C Thomas, Springfield.

Gubrium, J. F. (1974). *Late Life: Communities and Environmental Policy*. Charles C Thomas, Springfield.

Gutman, G. M. (1978). Issues and findings relating to multilevel accommodations for seniors. *Journal of Gerontology*, **33**, 592–600.

Hamovitch, M. B. and Larson, A. E. (1966). The retirement village. Paper presented at the Institute for State Executives in Aging at the University of Southern California, Idyllwild Campus, 3 February.

Hamovitch, M. B., Peterson, J. A., and Larson, A. E. (undated). *Housing Needs of the Elderly*. Andrus Gerontology Center, University of Southern California, Los Angeles.

Hansen, G. B. (1971). Meeting housing challenges: involvement—the elderly. In *Housing Issues. Proceedings of the Fifth Annual Meeting, American Association of Housing Educators*. University of Nebraska Press.

Heintz, K. M. (1976). *Retirement Communities: For Adults Only*. Center for Urban Policy Research, Rutgers, the State University, New Brunswick, New Jersey.

Herbert, N. M. (1966). *The Older Adult: Life in a Retirement Community Compared to Life in a City*. Bureau of Community Research, Berkeley, California.

Hoyt, G. C. (1954). The life of the retired in a trailer park. *American Journal of Sociology*, **59**, 361–370.

Jacobs, J. (1974). *Fun City: An Ethnographic Study of a Retirement Community*. Holt, Rinehart & Winston, New York.

Johnson, S. K. (1971). *Idle Haven: Community Building Among the Working-Class Retired*. University of California Press, Berkeley.

Kahana, E. (1980). A congruence model of person-environment interaction. In Lawton, M. P., Windley, P. G. and Byerts, T. O. (eds), *Aging and the Environment: Directions and Perspectives*. Garland, New York.

Keller, S. (1968). *The Urban Neighborhood: A Sociological Perspective*. Random House, New York.

Kiplinger, V. L. (1979). The future of elderly housing: 1990. Paper presented at the meeting of the Gerontological Society, Washington, 25–29 November.

Kleemeier, R. W. (1961). The use and meaning of time in special settings: retirement communities, homes for the aged, hospitals and group settings. In Kleemeier, R. W. (ed.), *Aging and Leisure*. Oxford University Press, New York.

Kutner, B., Fanshel, D., Togo, A. M. and Langer, T. S. (1956). *Five Hundred Over Sixty*. Russell Sage Foundation, New York.

Lake, W. S. (1962). Housing preferences and social patterns. In Tibbitts, C. and Donahue, W. (eds), *Social and Psychological Aspects of Aging*, pp. 341–7. Columbia University Press, New York.

Lawton, M. P. (1975). *Planning and Managing Housing for the Elderly*. Wiley-Interscience, New York.

Lawton, M. P. (1976). The relative impact of congregate and traditional housing on elderly tenants. *The Gerontologist*, **16**, 237–42.

Lawton, M. P. (1977). The impact of the environment on aging and behavior. In Birren, J. E., and Warner Schaie, K. (eds), *Handbook of the Psychology of Aging*, pp. 276–301. Van Nostrand Reinhold, New York.

Lawton, M. P. (1979). The housing status of the elderly: report on a national study. In Wagner, P. A. and McRae, J. M. (eds), *Back to Basics: Food and Shelter for the Elderly*. University of Florida Center for Gerontological Studies and Programs, Gainesville, Florida.

Lawton, M. P. (1980). *Environment and Aging*. Brooks/Cole, Monterey, California.

Lawton, M. P. (in press). *Social and Medical Services in Housing for the Elderly*, US Government Printing Office, Washington, D. C.

Lawton, M. P. and Cohen, J. (1974). The generality of housing impact on the well-being of older people. *Journal of Gerontology*, **29**, 194–204.

Lawton, M. P. and Nahemow, L. (1973). Ecology and the aging process. In Eisdorfer, C. and Lawton, M. P. (eds), *The Psychology of Adult Development and Aging*. American Psychological Association, Washington, D. C.

Lawton, M. P. and Nahemow, L. (1975). *Cost, Structure, and Social Aspects of Housing for the Aged.* Final Report to the Administration on Aging, U. S. Department of Health, Education and Welfare. Philadelphia Geriatric Center, Philadelphia, Pens.

Lawton, M. P., Nahemow, L. and Teaff, J. (1975). Housing characteristics and the well-being of elderly tenants in federally-assisted housing. *Journal of Gerontology*, **30**, 601–7.

Lawton, M. P., Newcomer, R. J. and Byerts, T. O. (eds) (1976). *Community Planning for an Aging Society: Designing Services and Facilities.* Dowden, Hutchinson & Ross, Stroudsburg, Pennsylvania.

Mangum, W. P. (1971). *Adjustment in special Residential settings for the aged: an inquiry based on the Kleemeier conceptualization.* Unpublished doctoral dissertation, University of Southern California, Los Angeles.

Mangum, W. P. (1973). Retirement hotels and mobile home parks as alternative living arrangements for older persons. In *Housing and Environment for the Elderly: Proceedings from a Conference on Behavioral Research Utilization and Environmental Policy, December, 1971, San Juan, Puerto Rico*. Gerontological Society, Washington.

Mangum, W. P. (1979). Retirement villages: past, present, and future issues. In Wagner, P. A. and McRae J. M. (eds), *Back to Basics: Food and Shelter for the Elderly*, pp. 88–97. University of Florida Center for Gerontological Studies and Programs, Gainesville.

Marshall, V. W. (1975). Socialization for impending death in a retirement village. *American Journal of Sociology*, **80**, 1124–44.

McRae, J. (1975). *Elderly in the Environment of Northern Europe*. University of Florida Center for Gerontological Studies and Programs.

Messer, J. (1967). The possibility of an age-concentrated environment becoming a normative system. *The Gerontologist*, **7**, 247–51, Gainesville.

Montgomery, J. E. (1972). The housing patterns of older families. *The Family Coordinator*, **21**, 37–46.

Mumford, L. (1956). For older people: not segregation but integration. *Architectural Record*, **119**, 191–4.

Murray, H. A. (1938). *Explorations in Personality*. Oxford University Press, New York.

Musson, N. (1973). *The National Directory of Retirement Residences: Best Places to Live When You Retire*. Frederick Fell, New York.

National Council on the Aging (1969). *A National Directory on Housing for Older People.* The National Council on the Aging, New York.

National Council on the Aging, Inc. (1975). *The Myth and Reality of Aging in America.* The National Council on the Aging, Inc., Washington.

Pastalan, L. A. and Carson, D. H. (1970). *Spatial Behavior of Older People*. The University of Michigan–Wayne State University, Ann Arbor.

Peterson, J. A. and Larson, A. E. (1966). Social–psychological factors in selecting retirement housing. In *Patterns of Living and Housing of Middle Age and Older People.* US Government Printing Office, Public Health Service Publication No. 1496, Washington.

Rabushka, A. and Jacobs, B. (1980). *Old Folks at Home*. Free Press, New York.

Robbins, I. S. (1971). *Housing the Elderly: Background and Issues.* White House Conference on Aging, Washington.

Rosow, I. (1967). *Social Integration of the Aged.* Free Press, New York.

Rubenstein, J. M. (1979). Housing the elderly in Europe. *The East Lakes Geographer*, **14**, 50–9.

Sherman, S. R. (1972). Satisfaction with retirement housing: attitudes, recommendations and moves. *Aging and Human Development*, **3**, 339–66.

Sherman, S. R. (1975). Mutual assistance and support in retirement housing. *Journal of* Gerontology, **30**, 479–83.

Sherman, S. R., Mangum, W. P., Dodds, S., Walkley, R. P., and Wilner, D. M. (1968). Psychological effects of retirement housing. *The Gerontologist*, **8**, 170–5.

Sherwood, S., Morris, J. N., and Barnhart, E. (1975). Developing a system for assigning individuals into an appropriate residential setting. *Journal of Gerontology*, **30**, 331–42.

Streib, G. F. and Streib, R. B. (1975). Communes and the aging: utopian dream and gerontological reality. *American Behavioral Scientist*, **19**, 176–89.

Struyk, R. J. (1977). The housing situation of elderly Americans. *The Gerontologist*, **17**, 130–9.

Struyk, R. J. and Soldo, B. J. (1980). *Improving the Elderly's Housing: A Key to Preserving the Nation's Housing Stock and Neighborhoods.* Ballinger, Cambridge, Massachusetts.

Teaff, J. D., Lawton, M. P., Nahemow, L., and Carlson, D. (1978). Impact of age integration on the well-being of elderly tenants in public housing. *Journal of Gerontology*, **33**, 126–33.

Tucker, S. M., Combs, M. E., and Woolrich, A. N. (1975). Independent housing for the elderly: the human element in design. *The Gerontologist*, **15**, 73–6.

Urban Systems Research and Engineering, Inc. (1976). *Evaluation of the Effectiveness of Congregate Housing for the Elderly: Final Report.* Prepared for US Department of Housing and Urban Development, US Government Printing Office, Washington D. C.

US Bureau of the Census (1953). *US Census of Housing: 1950, Vol. III, Farm Housing Characteristics.* US Government Printing Office, Washington D. C.

US Bureau of the Census (1954). *US Census of Housing: 1950, Vol. II, Nonfarm Housing Characteristics, Part 1: United States and Divisions*, U. S. Government Printing Office, Washington D. C.

US Bureau of the Census (1963). *US Census of Housing: 1960, Vol. II, Metropolitan Housing. Part 1, United States and Divisions.* Also, *Vol. VI, Rural Housing*, US Government Printing Office, Washington D. C.

US Bureau of the Census (1973). *Census of Housing: 1970, Subject Reports, Final Report HC(7)–7, Geographic Aspects of the Housing Inventory.* US Government Printing Office, Washington D. C.

US Department of Health, Education, and Welfare (1978). *The Elderly Population: Estimates by County, 1976.* Administration on Aging, National Clearinghouse on Aging, US Department of Health, Education, and Welfare, Washington D. C.

US Department of Housing and Urban Development (1979a). *Annual Housing Survey: 1973, Housing Characteristics of Older Americans in the United States.* US Government Printing Office, Washington D. C.

US Department of Housing and Urban Development (1979b). *How Well Are We Housed?* US Government Printing Office, Washington D. C.

US Department of Housing and Urban Development (1979c). *US Housing Developments for the Elderly or Handicapped.* Office of Multifamily Housing Development, US Department of Housing and Urban Development, Washington D. C.

US Senate Special Committee on Aging (1979). *Developments in Aging, Part 1—1978.* US Government Printing Office, Washington D. C.

US Senate Special Committee on Aging (1980). *Developments in Aging, Part 1—1979.* US Government Printing Office, Washington D. C.

Vivrett, W. K. (1960). Housing and community settings for older people. In Tibbitts, C. (ed.), *Handbook of Social Gerontology*, pp. 549–623. University of Chicago Press, Chicago.

Webber, I. L. and Osterbind, Carter (1961). Types of retirement villages. In Burgess, E. W. (ed.), *Retirement Villages*. pp. 3–10. University of Michigan, Division of Gerontology, Ann Arbor.

White House Conference on Aging of 1971 (1973). *Toward a National Policy on Aging, Final Report, Vol. 2*, US Government Printing Office, Washington D. C.

Wilner, D. M. and Walkley, R. P. (1966). Some special problems and alternatives in housing for older persons. In McKinney, J. C. and DeVyvrer, F. P. (eds), *Aging and Social Policy*, pp. 221–59. Appleton-Century-Crofts, New York.

Wiseman, R. F. (1978). *Spatial Aspects of Aging*. Association of American Geographers, Washington.

Woodall Publishing Company (1977). *Woodall's 1978 Retirement and Resort Communities, National Edition*. Woodall Publishing Company, Highland Park, Illinois.

Geographical Perspectives on the Elderly
Edited by A. M. Warnes


Chapter 9

# Living under an umbrella: problems of identity in sheltered housing

*William R. Bytheway*

## INTRODUCTION

Many people in Britain are now familiar with the idea and look of sheltered housing schemes for the elderly. Schemes regularly feature in local newspapers as examples of the exciting new developments of local housing authorities. More generally sheltered housing is something which the general public has come to believe to be an essential component of the answer to the problems of old age. This is well illustrated by a letter published in the *Radio Times* in 1977 regarding a BBC 'Man Alive' programme which reviewed the range of special accommodation available for the elderly:

> It seems to me that of all the valuable social services offered to the elderly the most worthwhile development is the sheltered home. The couple who spoke from their flat in one of these said they had never been so happy before coming here, and I have heard this said by many such residents. If, between the ages of 60 and 70, while they are still reasonably fit, we could let people escape from their big, old houses—now a physical and often financial burden to them—and take up residence in sheltered homes, we should give them companionship and warden-help when they want it, and yet allow them to retain privacy, and some domestic occupations in labour-saving accommodation. For many the move to an old people's home or a geriatric ward would never be needed.

Such enthusiasm has characterized many of those who have written on the subject of housing for the elderly, particularly since Townsend (1962) recommended that a long-term objective should be the replacement of local authority old people's homes (usually known as Part III homes) by sheltered housing. The critical government circular which led to the establishment of sheltered housing came out in 1957 (Ministry of Housing and Local Government, 1957).

Several schemes had been established well before this date but the main period of expansion did not follow until the mid and late 1960s (see Butler, Oldman, and Wright, 1979).

Throughout its development a primary concern has been that sheltered housing should provide an environment in which elderly people can feel secure and independent; one in which they can engage in social activities with some of their contemporaries and also one from which they can participate in ordinary community life. Such objectives, which can easily conflict, have led local authorities and central government to be particularly sensitive to the size and location of schemes. Such environmental characteristics are seen to be critical in the selection of sites and in the subsequent success or failure of schemes.

One way in which these concerns have come to affect the design and provision of sheltered schemes is through the establishment in 1969 of two distinct types

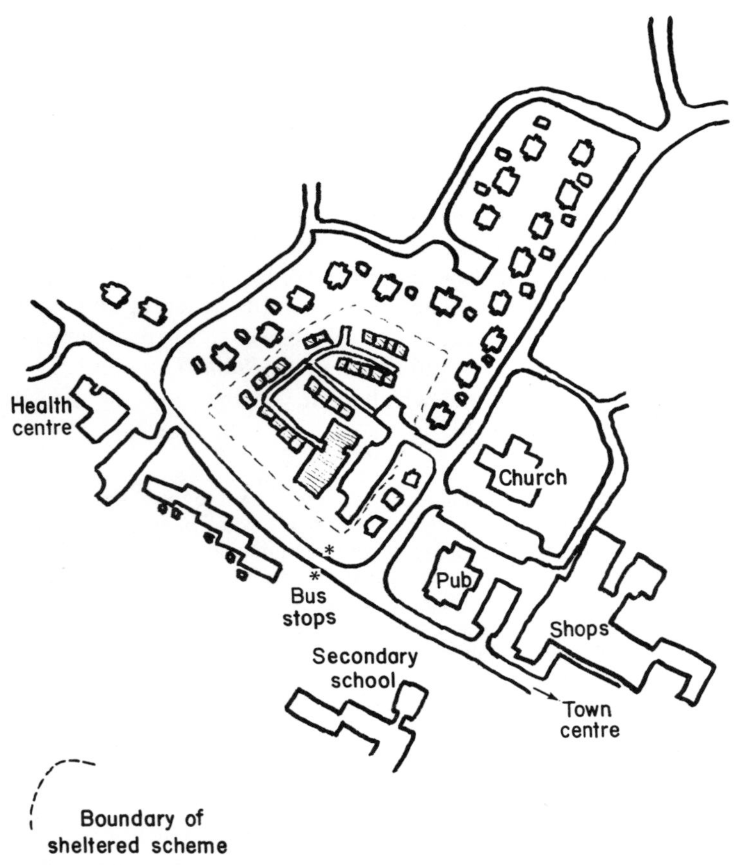


Figure 9.1 Characteristic plan of a Category I elderly persons' housing scheme

of sheltered housing schemes known as Category I and Category II schemes. These categories were instituted in a Ministry of Housing and Local Government circular of 1969 which set out different means of distributing subsidies to local authorities: these still apply in 1979. The key difference between their specifications is that Category I is intended to serve 'old people of the more active kind'. It only includes communal facilities such as a common room as optional extras. Typically a scheme in this category may include several blocks of flats, or it may be little more than a small estate of bungalows, as illustrated in Figure 9.1.

In contrast, Category II is provided 'to meet the needs of less active elderly people'. A scheme usually includes small flats, and communal facilities are a requirement. The most important distinction is that 'all accommodation shall be accessible by enclosed and heated circulation areas'. As a result of this simple and brief specification a Category II sheltered housing scheme necessarily amounts to just one building. Its plan will resemble the example shown in

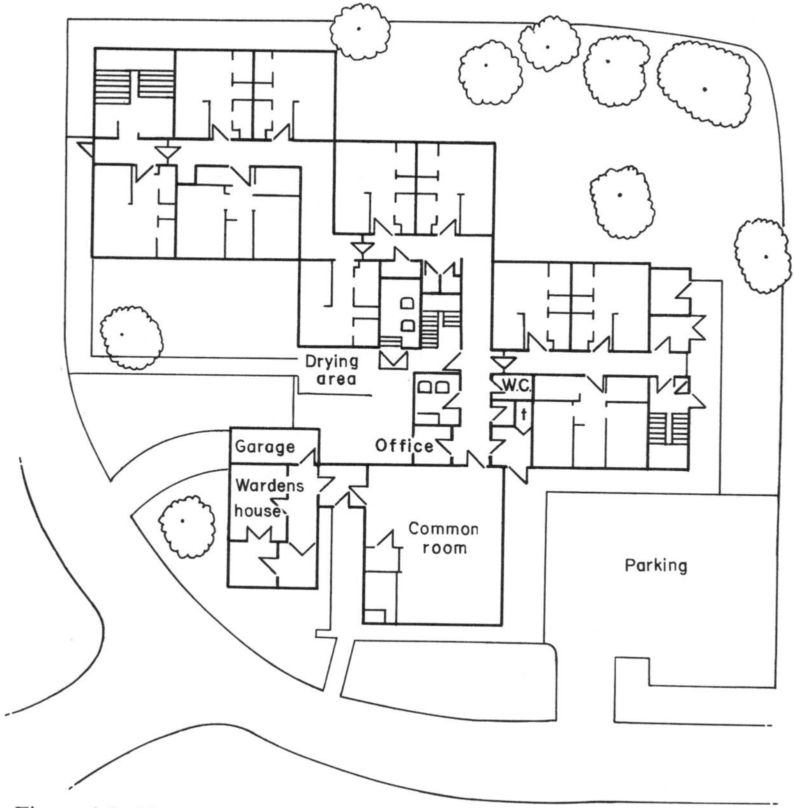


Figure 9.2 Characteristic plan of a Category II sheltered housing scheme

Figure 9.2. All the residents share an enclosed and heated circulation area, as well as the common room, laundry, drying area, and paved sitting area. Of more importance, the lobby area with the warden's office, toilets, coin-operated telephone box, and communal entrance adjacent to the car park are physical manifestations of the group identity that all those who live within will share. As sheltered housing will continue to form a significant element in the nation's effort to improve the provision of housing for the elderly, it is appropriate to evaluate its effectiveness. This chapter will therefore review the extensive debate concerning the design of sheltered housing, and then specifically examine the relationship between the design and environmental features of existing schemes and perceptions of the status and social identity that the residents feel they gain from their membership of these community settings. In other words, the valuation of sheltered housing by the residents will be considered as a guide to their success and possible modification in future schemes.

## ACCESS

The principal geographical feature to have been emphasized by planners in government publications and in the literature of architects and housing managers is access to shops—particularly post offices, surgeries, and chemists—and bus stops. The critical factor is, of course, simple proximity; other factors which are occasionally mentioned are the gradients which pedestrians might face in the course of such journeys, and the problems posed by busy roads. Thus the Anchor Housing Association, one of the largest of the Housing Associations in the United Kingdom that specializes in sheltered housing for the elderly, claims in a recent publication that:

> The satisfactory location of a sheltered housing scheme is probably the most important factor in determining the extent to which tenants are able to retain maximum independence within the community. Free and easy access to shops, bus and other facilities encourages tenants not only to keep up their own housekeeping, but also to make and maintain fruitful contact with people and interests outside the scheme (Anchor Housing Association, 1977, para. 2.6.1).

The same emphasis is shown in a well-known Department of the Environment (DOE) study of a scheme in Stevenage which describes the site as suitable because the 'shops were close enough for old people to do their own shopping with a minimum of travelling' (MHLG, 1966, p. 7). It also approves the location for its proximity to the church and the pub and for the frequency of local buses to the town centre.

In these recommendations and evaluations the emphasis has been upon proximity rather than upon ease of access. It is certainly the case that when tenants enter a scheme and find that, in contrast to their previous location, it is sufficiently near a retail centre to permit them to shop independently, they enjoy a new lease of life. Invariably, however, there will be some residents who will be unable to shop no matter how close the local retail centre might be. This may be due to a handicap that is only temporary, but even then the common presumption that the tenants should and are able to lead independent lives, may cause the handicapped tenant to feel inadequate and stigmatized when help is sought. In contrast to the fact that sites may 'fail' in this way despite being centrally placed, I have noted that a compensation of many isolated schemes comes from the services of mobile shops and other peripatetic retail enterprises.

## OUTLOOK

The second spatial attribute which has recurred in policy discussions on sheltered housing is outlook. The 1966 DOE report on the Stevenage scheme, for instance, suggests that the nearby school and shopping centre provide a varied and lively outlook. A photograph shows that of the fourteen units which overlook the church and the school, ten have bay windows, and that the enclosed sitting areas between the blocks of flats have floor-to-ceiling windows. The popular belief is that a tenant should have an interesting view from the window: not necessarily a pretty view but rather one overlooking some kind of social activity, such as a shopping street, a road junction, or a playground. A government Bulletin on the design of accommodation suggests that 'since old people spend a great deal of time sitting at the window watching the world go by, they generally prefer windows which give an outlook of activity and life as well as a pleasant and sunny environment' (Ministry of Housing and Local Government, 1968, p. 6).

The image of lonely old people gazing out of windows, however, is frequently disparaged as representing all that is wrong with the lives of elderly people. The intervening pane of glass is seen to symbolize the segregation of the inactive elderly viewer from the world outside. Moreover, while commentators have on occasions cited the territories of schoolchildren such as parks, playing fields, and playgrounds as appropriate outlooks, they have felt obliged to warn planners against sites which are so close that the elderly tenants will be disturbed by noise and other intrusions.

## PRIVACY

The problem of intrusive behaviour leads to a third attribute, privacy, about which there is some confusion. Firstly there is the problem of relationships with immediate neighbours *within* the scheme. The author of another government study reported that:

> It emerged that the phrase 'visit your neighbour' had an unfortunate connotation. A good neighbour was not given to visiting or to being visited by her neighbours in the home,

while one who made a habit of popping in to see her neighbour was socially disapproved. . . . It was not uncommon for an informant to say that she never received visits from neighbours even though a neighbour had just left the flat in the presence of the interviewer (DOE, 1968, p. 21).

These observations reflect an ideological commitment on the part of the respondents to the privacy of the home. Privacy, however, is threatened by endeavours to foster mutual support. The Anchor Extra Care Study for example, suggested that

no source of help for a tenant is more immediately accessible than that of other tenants within the scheme. . . . Evidence seems to confirm that the existence of the communal facilities is an important factor in generating a fresh outlook on life among tenants which in turn creates an atmosphere of neighbourliness and mutual support without which a warden would require much more paid help (Anchor Housing Association, 1977, para. 3.4.5).

Privacy within the scheme reflects the problem of privacy from groups *outside* the scheme. This concern of commentators on sheltered housing is most evident in the problem of children. Some tenants love children, others hate them; but in either case children are liable to be noisy, dangerous and tiring. Empson and Sheppard (1967, p. 67) argue the case for a balance between these conflicting interests:

It is often said that old people are disturbed and worried by having children near them and this is certainly true of some though by no means all old people. While it would be undesirable to site a playground too near housing for the elderly, many old people enjoy the sight of children going to and from school, and very pleasant relationships have developed in some cases between the tenants of old people's flats and bungalows and the staff and children of nearby schools. It is as well, however, not to lay out the space immediately in front of old people's windows in such a way to tempt children to play there.

To children many schemes are sheltered *cul de sacs* with under-used tarmaced and grassed areas highly suitable for play. The design of schemes may also encourage short cuts, when the centrally placed site occupies an area between other housing estates and local shopping facilities. Children come not just from adjacent schools or housing estates but also with adult visitors. In the cramped internal spaces of a sheltered housing unit it is inevitable that visiting children will venture out and play in the corridors and common room or, when weather permits, in the grounds of the sheltered scheme.

The desirability of providing outdoor space such as private gardens has also been considered, and it has been suggested that the absence of such space can be compensated 'if there is real seclusion within the scheme, such as produced by the frequently disfavoured inward-looking layouts' (Page and Muir, 1971). In these designs the outdoor space is shared by all the tenants. It provides a private area often including a paved path, flowers or bushes, young trees, seats, lamps, as well as the comings and goings of neighbours and visitors. In other words the scheme can be designed so that a large part of the outside space is seemingly private and provides the tenants both with interesting outlooks and certain ill-defined tenurial rights of access.

## EXTERNAL SOCIAL LINKS

The fourth factor prominent in planners' discussions has been the desire to ensure that external links and contacts are developed or maintained (over and above those which accrue from functional expeditions such as those to the shops), including those with the tenant's family, previous social contacts, and local bodies such as churches and clubs which the tenant might join after moving to the scheme. All of these links are seen to be the means by which the tenants can remain independent and active members of the local community. For example, Empson and Sheppard (1967, p. 178), presenting the official view of the Ministry of Housing and Local Government in 1967, stated that 'housing for old people will be needed in all housing areas so that elderly parents may be housed near their children living there, or so that tenants who have grown old in a place may move to smaller houses without being obliged to leave a familiar neighbourhood'. Indeed, one reason for emphasizing the upper limit of 30 or 40 units per scheme is that this will tend to disperse sheltered units more widely within a local authority's area, and the same objective explains the location of many schemes within larger council housing estates. Certain conflicts of priority arise, however.

> The locations which enable the elderly to live close to their relatives tend to be peripheral rather than central, because this kind of scheme can best be developed on a package deal basis as part of a new estate. There are enormous advantages in this arrangement.... but in terms of other social contacts and activities the tenants may fare relatively badly (Page and Muir, 1971, p. 50).

A difficulty in defining desirable locations is that an ideal site for most old people may not be the best for the less mobile. The Anchor Extra Care Study Group specifically considered the needs of the very old and the very frail and suggested that 'their degree of external contact and support is often particularly high where a scheme has been built adjoining a church or similar community group with whom excellent relations can often be established' (Anchor Housing Association, 1977, para. 2.6.1). Although there are many difficulties in specifying the precise nature of external social links, their maintenance and development is critical to the successful establishment and performance of sheltered housing. It is significant that discussions of the design and location of sheltered schemes should include such topics. To be a distinctive alternative to Part III homes, the conditions must be created which encourage the elderly person neither to withdraw from the wider community nor to become dependent upon a variety of services for his or her daily needs, but rather to remain involved and even to enhance their roles and activities. In this way sheltered housing is not just an effective form of housing, it can be seen to be a successful example of welfare intervention.

The life that Part III offers is considered by many to be undesirable, and is frequently described as institutional. The Anchor Group, for example, reported that 'most of our respondents thought that the normal housing aspects of sheltered housing should be emphasised and that any steps likely to create an institutional pattern of life should be avoided' (Anchor Housing Association, 1977, para. 2.3.). Townsend's 1962 study, by describing the conditions and life of many older residential homes as institutional, has established and labelled a model against which the designers of sheltered housing have been able to react.

## GROUP IDENTITY

These then are some of the spatial factors which planners have taken into account. Although some concern the location of the site in relation to other features of the neighbourhood, all of the identified factors have been ascribed significance only because of their direct relevance to the circumstances of the typical elderly tenant rather than to those of the tenants as a group. Thus accessibility is considered important because 'the tenant' maintains his or her independence by being able to shop; outlook is important because 'the tenant' spends much time at the window; privacy is important because 'the independent tenant' must be free to choose to participate or withdraw from social activities; and links with the community are important because 'the tenant' should not be isolated from external social groups.

At no point do the commentators directly adopt the idea that the scheme is a unit which has a social identity of its own. In my view one of the critical features of sheltered housing is the creation of a group identity. It can be argued that many of the characteristics of life in a scheme arise from the existence, and widespread awareness, of a collective identity among the tenants.

It is instructive to contrast a sheltered housing scheme with a group of old people's bungalows without a resident warden. In the latter case a group identity may develop, but it is not organizationally maintained; the tenants of the bungalows do not share any kind of personal service which is allocated to the group of bungalows. As a result their group identity is derived socially from within the neighbourhood rather than administratively generated from outside.

In the case of a typical sheltered housing scheme, however, all the tenants share exclusive access to the services of the resident warden. This imposed group identity is not easily concealed and rarely denied. No matter how persistently the housing authorities argue that a sheltered scheme is just ordinary housing with a few extra features to meet the special needs of the elderly, the widespread recognition of the group's identity and its origins has considerable significance within the wider community. It is the fact that they are a group of people who are permanently in exclusive receipt of government-funded services and facilities which can set them apart. The consequences of this are not necessarily undesirable, but the view that they are just ordinary tenants in ordinary housing is clearly unjustified.

## THE TENANTS' PERCEPTIONS

The discussion that follows draws upon a 1973 study of a voluntary scheme in Birmingham, a 1978 study of allocation procedures, and a current study of the extent and characteristics of sheltered housing in Wales. Every tenant occupies a sheltered dwelling because at some point he or she either applied for a tenancy or was offered one in emergency circumstances. Whatever the details, the experience of applying, waiting, and moving in is much more complicated than an ordinary transfer of local authority tenancies, not least because housing, social, and medical needs are given much more attention. Housing officers, doctors, home helps, relatives, and neighbours make official or unofficial enquiries in which the special features, advantages, and disadvantages of sheltered housing are mentioned. Visits to view may be arranged and the warden may be introduced to the prospective tenant at an early stage. Even after acceptance, the organizational aspects of the transfer will be distinctive because it is expected to be the tenant's move to his or her last home. Personal possessions will often be released since the sheltered unit will be small and compact, and the tenant's attitudes will also be distinctive: last looks at the previous home may take on the significance of a life review and often prompt reflections upon past experiences. The transfer is not just a transfer between two equivalent settings for the new tenancy is reserved for old people, is specially designed, and has a resident warden. The new tenant is expected to settle quickly into the scheme. More particularly, the tenant is expected to establish active new social relationships, not just with neighbours as with any move to a new house or flat, but rather with the other tenants and, most important of all, with the warden. People who inquire—visitors, old friends and relatives, the warden and other tenants themselves—can refer to the scheme and warden by name or to the other tenants as your neighbours, the other residents or the old people here, knowing that no ambiguities arise. In these ways the social identity of the scheme is learnt by the new tenant.

The tenant recognizes that this will have been experienced by every other tenant; arrival may have been either disorienting, poignant, or a long-awaited release from inadequate housing; it may have been anticipated well in advance or the result of a brief, alarming, and confusing emergency. Despite the wide variation in circumstances, all will see themselves as having taken the same step, for the very admission itself introduces the group experience and identity to the tenant. All must be aware of it even before meeting another tenant.

## THE SIGNIFICANCE OF THE BOUNDARY

A sheltered scheme is usually located on a single site and the plot's boundary specifies the limits of the scheme. Within this boundary there are all the buildings of the scheme and within these the homes of the members of the scheme. The group identity is recognized *socially* and maintained *administratively*, and is identified *spatially* either within a single building as in the case of most Category II schemes, or more commonly within a bounded geographical area. The varied impact of different boundary arrangements may be considered by reference to specific schemes. In the case of the scheme illustrated in Figure 9.1 there is just one legitimate entrance in the form of an ordinary residential road and its accompanying pavements. This is the only break in a continuous boundary marked by hedging, walls, or fencing. The scheme's spatial identity, reinforced by a well-maintained communal identity, can lead to a strong sense of territoriality.

In larger more open schemes with more than one entrance or less clearly marked boundaries, the tenants, through their group identity and desire for exclusive outdoor space, often develop a clear and shared perception of the location of the scheme's boundary and about the public's rights of entry. Outsiders appear to be divided into three categories. Firstly there are visitors with business in the scheme. Although it is normally accepted that they have indisputable rights of access, informal rules governing their entry are commonly established. For example, motorists are expected not to park in bays which have become part of the scheme's informal system of paths. Similarly the visiting pedestrian should follow these paths and not take short cuts. Secondly there are the outsiders who will pass through without any business in the scheme. If some footpaths are recognized as public rights of way then this may be accepted, although sometimes begrudgingly; but there are also frequent expectations about the standards of behaviour that can be tolerated, and failings in these are often the source of serious problems for the warden and the tenants. Even when there is no accepted right of way, certain people may be permitted passage, usually ones who are acquainted with the tenants. They will hold a relationship which may give substance to the belief that the tenants remain a part of the wider community.

The third category of outsiders are the immediate neighbours whose territories are contiguous to the scheme. These may be ordinary householders or the residents and employees of schools, pubs, garages, shops, churches, and industrial concerns. The tenants or the warden will inevitably relate to such neighbours on matters such as the maintenance and repair of the boundary fence, and the view that each presents the other. Often it is the immediate neighbours who most wish to use the scheme as a right of way since access to other facilities is most likely to be obstructed by the plot, and access into the scheme is often easier for these neighbours since they need do no more than cross the back-garden wall. It should also be appreciated that a neighbour will relate most directly with those tenants whose flats or bungalows are immediately adjacent to the shared boundary. As a result, problems that arise with immediate neighbours may be divisive because they are particularly felt by a minority of the tenants.

Designers of sheltered housing begin with the unique feature of a site and a neighbourhood. They must take into account the need of tenants to walk to local facilities and the requirement of satisfactory access for motor vehicles, and therefore they first plan the point or points of entry. Having established the pattern of entry, the design then tends to focus on the communal facilities and the warden's house, since these will generally be serviced by motorized traffic, and only thereafter to the individual units. Many other factors are involved, of course, but this sequence means that the boundary is frequently dissociated from the entrance. As a result the entrance may be visually very open but the remaining boundaries marked by substantial fences or walls. The visitor may appreciate the sense of integration suggested by the open entrance, but the tenants may feel enclosed and isolated by the nature of the remaining boundaries.

The appearance of the entrance is critical for the image of the scheme. Many members of the public, including ratepayers and voters, are unlikely to have any acquaintance with the scheme other than its aspect from the public highway. If this is characterized by an open access-road and pavements with no apparent checks such as gates or restrictive notices, then there will be no differentiations from any other small housing development. The general impression will be of a non-institutional milieu in which the elderly are able to lead independent and socially integrated lives.

Thus one disadvantage of an open entrance may be that it beguiles the general public. Another is that some people will mistakenly assume it to be public territory and therefore use it, for example, to park cars to do business elsewhere or to look for a route to the public park beyond, while others who do have business at the housing scheme will not recognize it for what it is. As a result many schemes over time acquire a collection of *ad hoc* signs which prohibit parking, cycling, or ball games, identify the scheme, or direct the visitor to the warden's office. Some even acquire trip fences to mark conspicuously the boundary, and reduce the possibility of embarrassment.

The spatial attributes of each scheme also influence the range and manner of execution of the warden's duties as well as the quality of his/her private life. Wardens have complex job specifications to fulfil, as shown by the examples examined during the course of the study of the allocation of local authority sheltered housing (Bytheway and James, 1978). The written duties of wardens issued by one local authority housing department, for example, include:

(1) To be accountable to the Housing Officer for the care and good management of the property and its occupants.
(2) To do all that is possible to foster among the tenants the spirit of a neighbourly and mutually supportive community.
(3) To be alert to the degree of ill-health and dependence of each tenant and to take appropriate action, whether through direct or indirect supervision, to ensure that all is well with a particular person.
(4) To give emergency help and general assistance of a neighbourly kind in case of accident or illness until the help of local services and/or relatives can be obtained.
(5) To promote and encourage, but not necessarily to organize, communal activities within the scheme and the participation by individual tenants in neighbourhood organizations.
(6) Regularly to inspect all communal equipment (heating installations, lighting, communication system, communal laundry and drying facilities, lifts, etc.) and promptly to report all defects and breakdowns and to make sure that action follows.
(7) To carry out cleansing of the communal areas, with additional domestic help where provided.
(8) To take responsibility for the security of the communal areas within the scheme and to enforce any local rules as to their use.
(9) To advise and instruct tenants on the proper use of fixtures and fittings provided in the flats or in the common areas.

It is clear from these that the warden has a specific responsibility to each and every tenant. The warden's duties are in effect the administrative source of the group identity. Regardless of both the warden's and the tenants' inclinations, a good neighbourly relationship is expected to exist. Like publicans, janitors, or matrons, they have been appointed to live in a particular place to fulfil specified functions, and as with all figures of residential responsibility they are faced with considerable difficulties in coping with their conflicting roles. On the one hand they are neighbours in the everyday sense of the term; on the other they are expected by employers, friends, neighbours and relatives to fulfil their duties by acting as good neighbours.

The siting and design of the warden's flat or house within the scheme is therefore generally carefully planned. For example, the common room may be placed between the warden's house and the dwelling units, and the warden may be given a separate office, to distinguish official and private lives. Nevertheless, from a 'segregated' house, the warden may still overlook the main entrance and s(he) is normally able to survey much of the scheme from a first-floor bedroom window. When s(he) sees that his or her services are required or requested s(he) will have to walk further than would be the case from a more centrally located house. The designers, by attempting to protect the privacy of the warden's domestic life, assume that s(he) will not be tempted to keep an eye on things outside.

Wardens adjust to this situation slowly and in different ways. One sought relief by regularly leaving the site to participate in a keep-fit club in the town; others cope by withdrawing for lengthly periods from the public areas of the scheme except for a daily round of calls upon tenants. Most, however, adjust by adopting the group leader/organizer role so that instead of living as an ordinary person in an ordinary house, they adopt the role of a resident worker. For example, many wardens regularly exhort tenants into activities that are representative of a full, independent, and happy life.

The warden may also acquire a representative role on behalf of the group of residents. When a housing officer took me to view a scheme that had received architectural awards, he was vigorously harangued by the warden because the grass had not been cut for several weeks as a result of industrial action. This role is indicated in public telephone directories where the warden's home telephone is generally found under the list of the warden-supervised schemes of the housing authority. So the warden handles all enquiries ranging from people who wish to visit the scheme through local groups offering voluntary services to enquiries from the distant relatives of the tenants.

Many more examples can be given of the consequences of the group's identity for the actual work and life of the warden. Like the tenants, the warden will regard the scheme's site as personal territory and consequently will attend to its boundaries, entrances and appearance as well as its relations with immediate neighbours in much the same way as any household head. Like anybody who has invested much time and effort in the life and fabric of their households, wardens will claim that they cannot really relax when away from home, particularly when they have left their charges in the hands of a temporary replacement. Consider the implications for wardens of the following Condition of Employment in one local authority:

> The Warden need not be in constant attendance. Should she be absent from the block overnight and the service of the relief warden is not available, the Warden will then be responsible for ensuring that the unit is under supervision by a suitable person and for the renumeration, if necessary, of her relief.

## DISCUSSION

Social science research has tended to polarize around micro and macro issues. As a result the elderly have come to be seen as either a substantial and deprived section of society or as a population of individuals characterized only by age.

The latter individualistic approach has led to a view of an elderly person as someone who, as a result of the passage of time and the ageing process, accumulates a wide range of deficient and problematic characteristics or circumstances. In this way the provision of sheltered housing has generally been seen to be an answer to meet individual needs. Some needs are perceived to be social: companionship, mutual support, and shared activities, for example, but the assumption that they originate within the individual has meant that little attention has been given to the milieu of sheltered housing. It is for this reason that the influence of environmental design upon old people's lives has been underestimated, and that attention has concentrated on the amelioration of the tenants' individual problems.

Through both Townsend's seminal study and subsequent research (e.g. Lipman and Slater, 1976) on the subject of old people's homes, it has been clearly established that the residential environment or milieu does indeed have an effect upon residents. A wide range of personal characteristics have been attributed to the experiences of moving into and living in a home, and these tend to be summarized (and disparaged) in the word institutionalization. Similar phenomena are identified elsewhere as the consequences of hospitalization. The consensus of castigation has produced a reaction in further research to examine this relationship between milieux and human responses.

In a large part this development has been accompanied by the acceptance of the view that the consequences of institutionalization and hospitalization are undesirable. The further studies have sought to identify ways in which these consequences could be avoided. This history of ideas brings us to the present emphasis on sheltered housing and a narrowed view of the role of old people's homes.

Among the tenants of sheltered housing, most do express satisfaction and report that their lives are much better than in their previous accommodation. The objective of creating a better alternative to institutional life is generally thought to have been achieved. The unfortunate aspect of this happy result is that the effects of the new milieu have been neglected. Instead it is claimed or assumed that sheltered housing is no different from ordinary housing. It is apparent, however, that a scheme does have a social identity: the tenants and the local community are able to distinguish it from adjacent general-purpose housing. This identity is administratively maintained through the distinctive features of the scheme's management. Moreover, it has a geographical boundary and this means that the sheltered group has to relate to its neighbours. The boundaries within the scheme are absent or ill-defined, apart from those of the individual dwelling unit itself, and its entrance or entrances are socially recognized to give access to the whole scheme rather than to individual dwelling units.

It is also apparent that this social identity does have consequences. The warden, in organizing social activities, has to distinguish between 'his or her' tenants and other elderly members of the local community. Gifts are received from local voluntary groups for the tenants as whole. The warden visits every tenant every day and maintains a record, while the administrators worry about the balance between the more dependent and the less dependent tenants of the scheme.

That all is not well is shown in two ways. Some wardens complain about the concept of being a good neighbour: 'one moment you are paid *to work* as a good neighbour, the next you knock off and are expected *to be* a good neighbour!' ... 'How can you be a good neighbour to forty old people?' ... 'The trouble with them is that they want all the benefits and comforts of an old people's home without it being one.'

On the other hand tenants may complain about 'vandals': 'They come and make faces through the windows' ... 'This used to be a field they used to fool about in on their way to the woods. They don't seem to realise that people live here now' ... 'They have no respect and make so much noise'. Although such complaints may be the exception rather than the rule, the fact that they are repeatedly expressed indicates that sheltered housing does create an unfamiliar environment. If the better understanding of the consequences of accommodating people in sheltered housing is to be achieved, then it will be necessary to study much more closely the relationship between social spaces, group identities, and the beliefs and actions of individuals.

## REFERENCES

Anchor Housing Association (1977). *Caring for the Elderly in Sheltered Housing*. AHA, London.

Butler, A., Oldman, C., and Wright, R. (1978). *Sheltered Housing for the Elderly: A Critical Review*. University of Leeds, Leeds.

Bytheway, W. R. (1973). *Suggestions for Sheltered Housing*. Centre for Social Science Research, University of Keele, Keele.

Bytheway, W. R. (1974). *Possible Trends in Sheltered Housing*. Centre for Social Science Research, University of Keele, Keele.

Bytheway, W. R. and James L. (1978). *The Allocation of Sheltered Housing: A Study of Theory, Practice and Liaison*. Research Report of Medical Sociology Research Centre, University College of Swansea, Swansea.

Department of the Environment (1968). *Grouped Flatlets for Old People*. Design Bulletin 2. HMSO, London.

Empson, M. and Sheppard, N. J. (1967). Housing for Old People. *The Architects Journal*, **19**,

Lipman, A. and Slater, R. (1976). *Homes for Old People: Towards a Positive Environment*. Social Science Research Council.

Ministry of Housing and Local Government (1957). *Housing Old People*. Circular 181/57. HMSO, London.

Ministry of Housing and Local Government (1966). *Old People's Flatlets at Stevenage.* Design Bulletin 11. HMSO, London.

Ministry of Housing and Local Government (1968). *Some Aspects of Designing for Old People.* Design Bulletin 1. HMSO, London.

Page, D. and Muir, T. (1971). *New Housing for the Elderly.* Bedford Square Press, London.

Townsend, P. (1962). *The Last Refuge.* Routledge & Kegan Paul, London.

Geographical Perspectives on the Elderly
Edited by A. M. Warnes


Chapter 10

# American retirement communities and residential relocation

*Charles F. Longino, Jr*

Retirement communities in the United States are not necessarily municipalities. While their boundaries are sometimes civic and political in nature, they are more often like those of ethnic neighbourhoods or those of condominium complexes or housing developments rather than municipalities; and they vary in the degree to which they are permeable. Some are very closed; the residents seldom venture outside and the sense of community as a separate place is strong (Sherman, 1979). Many others are about as permeable as most suburban towns, where the sense of community is much less. Retirement communities are defined more by their membership than their geographical boundaries (Webber and Osterbind, 1968). *A retirement community is any living environment to which most residents have moved since they retired.* This does not mean that no residents are full- or part-time employees. In fact, Long and Hansen (1979) found that nearly one-eighth of 'retired' household heads who had moved between states in the mid-1970s in the United States had re-entered the labour force. On the other hand, some retirement community residents have never been employed outside the home. Nonetheless, nearly all who have worked have also retired from full-time employment at least once. The above definition excludes communities of retirement-aged people who have 'aged in place' and which result from the out-migration of the young, for retirement communities are settings to which retired people move. Retirement and relocation, therefore, are the essential elements of the definition.

American retirement communities are middle-range living environments. The largest are like small towns with several thousand residents, having a complex institutional structure which meets a variety of the residents' personal and household needs. The smallest ones are groupings of a few households of retired people who identify themselves as members of a living environment, a small neighbourhood or apartment house.

## *DE JURE* AND *DE FACTO* RETIREMENT COMMUNITIES

The major dimension along which retirement communities can be differentiated is the degree to which they are consciously planned for retired people (Walkley *et al.*, 1966). Some communities, for example, deliberately limit housing eligibility to persons who have reached a certain age. These are retirement communities *de jure*, for they are designed as such. Others place no age restrictions upon new residents but overwhelmingly attract people who are retired (Golant, 1979). These are not designed as retirement communities, but in them a series of organizations and services may arise which cater to older people. Retirement hotels, as well as some seaside communities in England, fit into this category. These are *de facto* retirement communities.

A minimum age limit for housing eligibility, of course, is one element of planned retirement communities. By consciously limiting residence to those aged 60 or more, however, it is possible to design both community and dwelling environments which take into account some of the more common needs of the oldest of these residents. In this way, the communities can hope to be more than temporary residences for young retired people (Walkley *et al.*, 1966). Service and social opportunities, such as transportation, shopping and medical services, social and recreational opportunities, can be built into the living environment. Thus, the most planned communities would be those which meet the greatest range of resident needs most fully. Planned communities in the United States may be divided into two sub-types: subsidized and non-subsidized. The subsidized planned community, in its most common form, is congregate housing provided by various programmes of the United States Department of Housing and Urban Development (HUD). This type of housing has been well described in a number of works (Donahue, 1966; Hochschild, 1973; Lawton and Cohen, 1975; Lipman, 1968). (See Chapter 9 of this book for Mangum's discussion of subsidized housing types in the United States).

There is also a variety of non-subsidized planned communities for older people. They range along a continuum from planning limited to housing provision alone, to life-care communities which attempt to provide a full range of services including medical care. The cost of residence, of course, tends to increase with the level of services (Hamovitch, 1968; Bultena and Wood, 1969; Sherman, 1971, 1972).

The Social Security Administration of the US government in 1975 funded an ambitious comparative study of midwestern retirement communities. This 3-year project involved ethnographic fieldwork and extensive interview surveys in eight retirement communities. Both *de facto* and *de jure*, and both subsidized and non-subsidized planned communities were studied by a team of social scientists representing the disciplines of sociology, anthropology, psychology and economics.[1] Three communities were chosen from the files of this project for use as examples of the theoretical and research findings. In the following paragraphs these example communities are briefly described, emphasizing their physical setting, development and ambiance, and the profiles of their residents.

## *De facto* retirement communities: the Ozark Lakes Country

There are several places in the United States which have become popular locations for retirement migration since 1945. One of these is the Ozark region connecting the states of Missouri, Arkansas, and Oklahoma. The major influx has been into Arkansas, but migration into the south-west Missouri counties is also substantial. These mountainous counties, like most of rural America, recorded a population loss each decade in this century until after World War II when several dams were built which created miles of fishing lakes and fresh-water reservoirs among the wooded peaks. The lakes provide outdoor recreation opportunities which attract summer tourists. Local residents, and some entrepreneurs from elsewhere, quickly capitalized on the natural environment and the hillbilly mystique of the area. The result was the rapid development of a major tourist and resort industry.

In Taney County, the heart of the Missouri Ozarks, Branson grew from 2175 in 1970 to an estimated 3000 in 1980, while the nearby village of Forsythe grew from 803 to 2500 (Eckerman, 1979). The migrants to these and many other mountain towns and villages come primarily from the suburbs of mid-western cities. Most pay cash for their single-family homes in the Ozarks, although some live in mobile homes and a few live in condominiums and apartments. They are not inclined to purchase the scattered farm houses in the countryside, but rather to cluster in towns or in newer housing developments outside the towns. Typical of such new developments is Kimberling City, a settlement of 1000 people 40 minutes by car west of Branson. It resembles an upper middle-class suburb such as one would expect to find near Chicago with three-bedroom split-level homes built around an attractive shopping mall and social clubhouse. However, it occupies a mountain ridge, each house having an inspiring view of the serpentine Table Rock Lake below, and it is a difficult 20 minute drive over narrow mountain roads from the nearest town.

The population of the Missouri part of the Ozark Lakes Country has been estimated at 30,000. A land-development boom has contributed to the economic growth of the area. The median resident age of the old mountain towns climbed as the number of retired migrants exceeded that of native-born residents. There was some resentment towards the outsiders at first, but they brought many resources into the area. By the mid-1970s older migrants represented the dominant group in most of the area's churches, civic and community organizations, and neighbourhoods. The towns in the Ozark Lakes Country had become retirement communities *de facto*.

The characteristics of the retired migrants in Branson, Forsythe, and Kimberling City, from which the Ozark sample of the retirement community study was drawn, are similar to those of retired migrants on the West Sussex coast of England and the French Côte d'Azur (Cribier, 1980). They are relatively young, with a mean age of 68. The average age at migration, of course, would be younger. Most of them (86 per cent) are married and virtually all (99 per cent) are white. The median household income of all inter-state migrants in the United States who gave retirement as their reason for moving was nearly $12,000 (Long and Hansen, 1979), comparable to that of all retired migrant households in the Ozarks. Not surprisingly, therefore, almost three-quarters of these Ozark residents rated their health as good.

The Ozark communities are not age-restricted. Young families do move there, attracted by the economic expansion in the area, but it is clear that community institutions cater for the old. This may not be so evident to the community visitor but is shown by an adult community centre doing a booming business, the large number of daytime bridge clubs, a public library whose management and clientele are mostly retired, a new cardiac unit in the Branson hospital, and an expanded trust department in a local bank. Otherwise the round of community life would strike an outsider as similar to other small communities in resort areas. The predominance of older people in the population is hardly apparent to the casual observer, especially during the summer tourist season when the towns are swollen and crowded with family holidaymakers.

The Ozark Lakes Country is thus an inland resort area in the heart of the United States; one of outstanding beauty. It is more accessible to the major midwestern metropolitan areas than the other popular destinations of retired midwestern migrants such as those found on the Pacific, Gulf, and Atlantic coasts or in the south-western desert. The migrants attracted to the *de facto* retirement communities in this area tend to be young, healthy, married retirees with good incomes.

## A subsidized planned retirement community: Horizon Heights

Horizon Heights is part of a network of public housing facilities in a midwestern city with a population of 170,000. The network consists of 19 buildings with 2000 individual units. Seven of these buildings are specified for elderly tenants and 12 for low-income families. They were initially funded by the United States Department of Housing and Urban Development (HUD) under a 40-year bond, and the Department subsidizes their operation and maintenance.

Constructed in 1969, Horizon Heights was the first facility in the city's public housing network exclusively for people over age 60. It is located in a deteriorated neighbourhood five blocks from the central business district. In

1970 the racial composition of the census tract in which Horizon Heights is located was 43 per cent black, and 16 per cent of the households were classified as below the poverty level. Over two-thirds of the residents have lived in the greater metropolitan area all their lives and many had lived in the immediate neighbourhood.

This subsidized planned community is housed in a sixteen-storey poured-concrete building and has 18 apartments on each of the 15 residential floors. An additional area contains 33 garden apartments, built primarily with exterior brick construction. The entire project resembles a city park with walks connecting the apartments to one another and to the high-rise building. Residents give personal touches to the apartments by adorning their yards with bird baths, rose trellises, and flower and vegetable gardens. It faces a busy city street and houses 300 people.

The tenants of this subsidized community pay only 25 per cent of their adjusted income towards the rent. The residential profile of Horizon Heights stands in sharp contrast to that of the Ozark Lakes Country. Most of its residents are over age 70 and the mean age is 78; 83 per cent are female, 18 per cent are married, and 59 per cent are black. The median household income for these residents in 1976 was $2608. Only half rated themselves as in good health. They are mostly older working-class widowed women in their 70s and 80s.

A number of formal services and activities are provided to the residents by the Horizon Heights staff as well as by groups from outside the community. There are social activities, voluntary service groups, and religious and educational programmes; but the most prominent service to residents is the weekday lunch programme provided by the US Administration on Aging, attended by approximately 115 residents daily. Staff members refer residents to several publicly and privately funded service agencies designed to help people with financial, physiological, and psychological problems. Resident–staff communication difficulties, however, hamper the dissemination of information about community services, and the system works better on paper than in reality. The overall impression of Horizon Heights is one of social vitality, reflected in a high frequency of social exchanges and the alertness of residents to the ebb and flow of daily activity.

The physical layout of Horizon Heights contributes to one's impressions of the community. The stark, modernistic building appears stately and imposing. Wall decorations and houseplants are few and vinyl upholstered chairs contribute to the starkness. There is a paucity of adornment in the public spaces. The black- and-white colour scheme encourages a feeling of detachment and coldness. In contrast, the institutionalized atmosphere is balanced by the heavy use made of the lobby and other common spaces, and the warm, friendly sound of laughter and small talk. The building seems to conspire against an insistent community.

The staff are pervasive, as is their message that the residents had better toe the mark. They are easy to identify for they walk faster than the residents and have an air of authority, yet they are friendly and reasonably approachable, if always busy. As one walks through the front doors a sign reads 'Wipe your Feet'. On the television set a note says 'Do not adjust'. 'Please' and 'thank you' are conspicuously absent in these messages. Residents commonly complain that they are patronized like children.

A prevalent symbol in the community is the lock. While physical security in this central city location is an issue of great concern, the lock also symbolizes staff control. The security guard locks the outside doors, the lights, and the apartments; he carefully watches persons entering, and requests that each one signs in and out. There is a small padlocked case on one side of the lobby displaying for sale hand-made items that the residents have made. A small bulletin board posts death notices and the thank you cards from hospitalized residents who have been sent flowers. Even the bulletin board is encased and securely locked.

The ambiance of Horizon Heights is institutional. The staff keep the rules enforced and everything in order to make their work manageable. As in many institutions in Horizon Heights one senses that the institution is run to meet staff rather than client needs. Yet there is an equally strong feeling of vitality and of cheerful community envolvement tempered by realism and tenacity. There is a toughness about the residents, most of whom are women born between 1890 and 1910. The tempo, warmth, and interaction of their genuine community survives amidst the signs, locks, and polished tile floors. The institutional character of Horizon Heights does not escape comment, but the residents tend to view it as a problem to be lived with, to be ignored when possible, and to be overcome. 'It might have been hard to adjust to this place', asserted one resident thoughtfully, 'but I didn't let it be.' The lady at the left, with the two tall grocery bags in her arms turned as she entered the lift: 'The first hundred years are the hardest, you know', she said, and smiled as the door closed.

### A non-subsidized planned retirement community: Carefree Village

Carefree Village resulted from post-World War II Protestant denominational expansion in the suburbs. It was launched as a church-related project but as it grew it became less dependent upon church support. Since 1961 its management organization has established over 40 life-care retirement communities in 17 states. Carefree Village, with over 3000 residents, is the largest and the prototype.

Its residents are similar to those in Horizon Heights in their gender, marital status, and age but quite different in their socio-economic status, health, and race. The mean age is 76, nearly three-quarters (72 per cent) are women, two-fifths are married, and they are all white. The median household income of $7700 in 1976 was triple that at Horizon Heights, and nearly two-thirds (64 per cent) rated their health as good. Thus, the Carefree Village resident profile falls between that of the Ozark Lakes Country and that of Horizon Heights. They are less frequently young, married, healthy, and wealthy than the retired migrants to the Ozarks, but more so than those in Horizon Heights. Most are older middle-class white women.

The Village lies in a suburban community near a midwestern metropolitan centre. Single- and two bedroom apartments and cottage-style houses dominate its housing. All the wings of the apartment complexes are interconnected by enclosed passageways so residents in these areas are protected from outside heat or cold. In the middle of the village stands a health centre serving the housebound and doctor's, dentist's, psychologists's, and the chaplains' offices. A short distance away at an unobtrusive location is the skilled nursing facility for bedfast residents. Throughout the village there are varied activity settings including dining rooms and cafeterias, the swimming pool, a bowling alley; gift, plant, craft, barber and beauty shops; a bank, a chapel, an ice cream parlour, and a cavernous community auditorium. Carefree Village as a whole, then, is a sprawling suburban settlement of houses, apartments, cottages, public buildings, recreation areas, and health-care operations. It is a middle-class planned community, populated by retired people and managed for a profit by a large service organization.

Carefree Village sells itself as a specialized provider of supportive services, and of health care in particular. 'Life care' is the name of the package which includes freedom from maintenance worries, ultimate health care, and a wide range of formal services. The Human Services Division is responsible for these services and is staffed by a dentist, physician, optometrist, audiologist, social worker, nurses, and several chaplains. Meals are taken to people who are unable to prepare their own, and housekeeping services are available for brief periods twice a month. Villagers confined to wheelchairs are pushed to meals or other places by young staff members. Buildings and lawns are maintained by the Village, and a visible security force, wearing distinctive uniforms, is always on patrol. Residents moving into Carefree Village have to acclimatize themselves to this service-oriented environment.

The initial impression that one gets from Carefree Village is of genteel affluence. There is a sense of newness. The residents dress as if on their way to club or church meetings. The architecture and landscaping remind one of southern California. It is relatively easy to identify the professional staff for they are young, immaculately groomed in conservative clothes, and speak softly and deliberately. The entire feeling of Carefree Village is one of enclosure. It is an indoor environment in which the climate is controlled all year and everyone speaks in low tones.

There are different levels of physical access to health care and to other services according to residential location. People in the outlying cottages tend to be younger and healthier than those in the apartment complexes, while those nearer the Health Center are older and in greater need of health care access. The nursing home, at the centre of the Village, is only used for residents who can no longer live in their apartments even with outpatient and home-delivered health care. As their dependence increases, residents are moved from one level of care to the next until ultimately they may be cared for in the nursing facility. This process aims to prolong independent living and to minimize the costs of institutionalization.

Unless death intervenes there invariably comes a time when a decision to institutionalize must be made. In a community of 3000 old people, this is a recurring event. The resident, his or her physician, the management, and family members when possible, are all involved in this decision. After the patient is transferred to the nursing home the door of his or her apartment is padlocked until the relatives claim the personal belongings. The unit is then sold to another buyer. This final institutionalization is usually brief. Life care has been completed.

## AGE AND HOUSING RELOCATION IN THE UNITED STATES

In order to assess the potential for retirement community development it is important to review what is known about the patterns of aged migration and the characteristics of the aged migrants. The United States Bureau of the Census uses a set of terms to summarize the mobility of the population (Shryock and Siegel, 1976; Rives, 1980). These terms refer to a question concerning where the person lived exactly five years earlier:

I. Same house (non-movers)
II. Different house in the same county (intra-county movers)
III. Migrants (inter-county movers)
  A. Different county, same state (inter-county migrants)
  B. Different state (inter-state migrants)
    1. Between contiguous states
    2. Between non-contiguous states
IV. Movers from abroad

There are two major problems arising from the census question. Firstly, it leads to an underestimate of population mobility for a person may have moved several times in 5 years. Furthermore, those who moved only once but have resided in the same house for more than 5 years will be recorded as non-movers. The question underestimates population movement in the United States because more people relocate within 5 years than at longer intervals.

Secondly, the categories provide an extremely crude measure of distance.

It cannot be assumed that all inter-state migrants move farther than all intra-state movers, nor that within states the intra-county movers make the shortest moves. These assumptions hold only when all the people in each category are averaged together. It has become an axiom in US migration research that for the general population local (intra-county) moves tend to be housing motivated and long-distance (inter-state) moves are most often job-related. But a person can move across a street in Kansas City and become an interstate migrant. The fact that neither states nor counties within states are of uniform size produces exceptions to the distance assumption attached to mover categories. For example, Elko County in the north-east of Nevada is larger than the combined New England states of Connecticut and Rhode Island. Caution is always required, therefore, when working with census data.

Older people are less likely to move than is the general US population. In 1970 slightly over half (53 per cent) of the population over age 5 reported living at the same address 5 years earlier, but for those aged 65 or more the figure was 72 per cent. The fact that over a quarter of these older people had moved in this 5-year period strikes many as surprisingly high. Occupational opportunities, the major migration motivator for the general population, are less relevant for the older population, but as there are more households per thousand older migrants there is a smaller differential in mobility between older and younger mobility units or households.

Not only does the absolute amount of residential movement differ for older people, but they are more likely to move shorter distances (Golant, 1977). In 1970, over one-fifth (21 per cent) of movers of all ages were interstate migrants as compared with one-sixth (16 per cent) of older movers. While a majority (58 per cent) of all movers are relocating within the same county, the percentage for older people approaches two-thirds (65 per cent). In this regard, it is instructive to treat age as a continuous, rather than as a categorical, variable and to compare mobility rates for successive age cohorts (Wiseman and Roseman, 1979). Seen in this way, there is a middle age plateau at which the rates of residential relocation do not change from one decade to the next. In the age 65–70 cohort there is a jump in the inter-state migration rate, especially for men. This is the time when older people are most inclined to make long-distance moves. On the other hand, local moves gradually decline during the middle and later years, increasing (especially for women) only after age 75. If these trends are reflected in retirement community residential populations, we would expect the communities more attractive to inter-state migrants to have different distributions of resident characteristics than those attracting mostly local movers.

What can be learned from the Census about the distributional patterns of older people in the United States? Where do they move? A recent study extracted from the 1 per cent Public Use Sample of the 1970 US Census tapes all persons 60 years or older and analysed their migration behaviour (Flynn *et al.*, 1979). Inter-state flows were found to be quite channelized (Wiseman, 1979). That is, half of the inter-state migrants, regardless of their origin, were flowing into only 7 of the 50 states. Of all the people who were 60 years or older in April, 1970, and who lived in another state 5 years earlier, nearly one-quarter of them filled out their census form in Florida. California attracted another one-tenth (9.5 per cent). After these two states, the percentages plummeted. Arizona, a south-western desert state, and New Jersey, an Atlantic coast state just south of New York, both drew 4 per cent from the migrant pool. Other states drew even fewer (Flynn, 1980).

This study examined not only the destinations, but the origins of the migrants as well, making it possible to describe the state-to-state streams of these long-distance movers. While only Florida, California, and Arizona attracted several unusually large flows from non-contiguous states, the major recruitment areas were different. It is as though a Great Divide stretching in a line south from Lake Michigan created two drainage systems of aged inter-state migration, eastwards to Florida and westwards to Arizona and California (Flynn, 1980). Several regional migration centres also were identified, attracting older migrants disproportionately from surrounding states. These were the Olympic Peninsula in the north-west coast state of Washington, the Ozarks area in Missouri and Arkansas, and the southern coastal counties of New Jersey. The story of the Ozark Lakes Country, told above, could be repeated with variations in each of these regional migration centres. All three have strong tourist industries (Flynn *et al.*, 1979).

Retirement migration to the coastal towns of southern France and of southern England, together with the location of the national destination states in the southern United States reinforces the notion that aged migration is a Sunbelt phenomenon. Sunbelt migration, however, is neither that simple nor that uniform in the United States. A state-by-state analysis (Biggar, 1979) shows that only 9 of the 15 states in the southern and coastal rim of the United States attract older migrants out of proportion to all migrants. Furthermore, only 4 of the top 10 receiving states in 1970 were located in this warmer area. Finally, nearly one-third (32 per cent) of the older migrants to the northern states came from the Sunbelt. Care should be taken, therefore, when the term Sunbelt is used not to exaggerate the elderly migration influx into the entire southern area of the United States (Biggar, 1980). It is a far more focused phenomenon.

There is a sense in which one has not made a major residential relocation if one moves from a certain three-bedroom house to a similar house in a similar suburb, even if it is on the other side of the country. The environment has been essentially preserved, at least in type (Cribier, 1980). The issue of environmental exchange has recently been examined for migrants age 60 and over using 1970 US census data, but limited to movement between and within metropolitan and non-metropolitan settings, admittedly broad environmental categories (Longino, 1980a). A Standard Metropolitan Statistical Area (SMSA) in the United States includes a central city of 50,000 or more, the county in which it is located, and any surrounding heavily suburban counties. Most local moves take place in such environments (Cleland, 1965; Golant, 1977, 1980a, 1980b). This observation is compounded by the fact that, even among migrants, the overwhelming tendency is to move within types of environmental settings. Over half of all older migrants in 1970 were SMSA residents who moved from another SMSA. If those who made within-type moves outside of SMSAs are added, the percentage rises to 70 for intra-state and 62 for inter-state migrants. Within-type moves clearly dominate the migration pattern of older American migrants (Longino, 1980a).

More people were moving away from SMSA settings (18.4 per cent) than into them (11.7 per cent), but the difference amounts to only about 6 points, hardly a major outpouring. Nor is there any rural renaissance here, narrowly viewed. The greater flow to non-SMSA settings was destined for towns ranging in size from 2500 to 50,000 people. Rural areas attract less than half as many SMSA residents among intra-state migrants (5.5 per cent) as do urban settings (12.8 per cent). The rural areas do better among inter-state migrants but even so attract less than half (9.6 to 21.7 per cent) of all SMSA out-migrants.

Interesting variations appear when the types of moves are examined state by state. Certain states in 1970 experienced a greater than average intra-state migration from non-metropolitan settings to locations within the central cities and suburbs of SMSAs. These were primarily rural states but others were the noted centres of regional inter-state migration. Rural settings attract a disproportionate number of older intra-state migrants in states with well-known rural recreational areas. Missouri, the location of the Ozark Lakes Country, was in this group, as well as Michigan, the home of a large northern forest camping and recreation area (Longino, 1980a).

## RESIDENTIAL RELOCATION TO RETIREMENT COMMUNITIES

Retirement communities have different fields of recruitment, like colleges and universities. Some recruit locally and others recruit from a larger area (Sherman, 1971, 1972). This may be demonstrated by comparing the three example retirement communities previously described (Table 10.1). Subsidized planned communities tend to recruit from the local area. Horizon Heights is typical, drawing four-fifths of its residents from the same county. Non-subsidized planned communities vary in their recruitment range depending upon the size, sophistication, and vitality of their sales staff and upon the availability of local persons who fit their market profile. More restrictive entrance requirements tend to widen the market area. For non-subsidized planned communities offering extensive service packages at substantial cost, like Carefree Village, local recruitment may not be sufficient to sustain growth or maintain necessary residence levels. Therefore, the more complex and

Table 10.1 Places of origin of residents of three sample retirement communities in the United States

| Percentage of residents who moved from: | Horizon Heights (%) | Carefree Village (%) | Ozark Lakes Country (%) |
|---|---|---|---|
| Same county | 81 | 48 | 5 |
| Different county | 7 | 28 | 31 |
| Different state | 12 | 24 | 64 |
| TOTALS | 100 | 100 | 100 |

complete the service levels in planned communities of this type, the larger the proportion of inter-state migrants one could expect to find among the residents. *De facto* retirement communities, in settings such as the Ozark Lakes Country, could be expected to attract high proportions of inter-state migrants. It is not surprising, therefore, to see that a majority of the older Ozark residents came from out of state.

### *Why people move to retirement communities*

For an explanation of the different patterns of residential relocation found in the different types of retirement communities, our attention now turns to the question of why older people move. Just wanting to move is no guarantee that the move will take place. It may be too costly, too risky, or the idea may not be congenial to other household members. There is a growing consensus among American thinkers that the decision process is multi-staged. It involves a cluster of decisions about whether to move, where to move, and where to live in the new location (Brown and Moore, 1970; Sherman, 1979; Wiseman, 1978, 1980).

People in Horizon Heights, Carefree Village, and the Ozarks came to these communities for a variety of reasons. It must be remembered that each community has its own special attractions and its own built-in inhibitors which, taken together, will tend to select certain kinds of potential residents. Horizon Heights, for example, offers services and safety. Cost of residence is not inhibitive if one is poor, since it is there to serve the poor; but if an applicant's income is too high, he or she will be excluded. Carefree Village advertises its life-care plan, emphasizing health care in particular. The cost of residence would be an obstacle to an applicant without substantial assets with which to make a down payment. The payment is called an 'endowment fee' and remains with the Village after the person's death. The Ozark Lakes Country offers a beautiful natural setting, but does not have many of the specialized services of Carefree Village. The potential migrant who is in his 70s might consider this location too risky.

People in all of these communities were asked for the single most important reason for their move. There is indeed a congruence between personal needs and community selection (Table 10.2). The financial advantage of subsidized housing is not overlooked by Horizon Heights residents. Over half of the Carefree Village residents listed health needs as the major reason for their selecting this life-care community. Finally, there is a congruence between the outstanding natural beauty of the Ozarks and the motivation for moving there. We must remember that such answers only tap the most obvious reasons for moving. The underlying processes that bring a person to the migration decision are subtle, complex, and often not well understood by the person being questioned (Cribier, 1980).

People in the three communities were asked 'How did you come to be living here?' The number of positive and negative reasons for the move were counted and coded for each respondent. It is not surprising that positive qualities of the place they left were seldom mentioned and the negative aspects of the retirement community did not figure into their reasons for coming. The minuses had to do with negative features of their former home and neighbourhood, their inability to cope with their environment because of declining health, their fears and insecurities, and negative experiences ranging from loneliness and unpleasant relations with neighbours or landlords to being assaulted. The pluses of their new community had to do with their positive feelings of being accepted, being secure, or being a useful member of the community. It had to do also with being able to do those things that were enjoyed and which fulfilled fantasies of the good life, such as being associated with a place of

Table 10.2 Stated reasons for moving to the three retirement communities

| Reasons | Horizon Heights (%) | Carefree Village (%) | Ozark Lakes Country (%) |
|---|---|---|---|
| Financial | 23 | 2 | 5 |
| Health needs | 4 | 51 | 2 |
| Physical incapacity; manageable environment | 4 | 2 | 1 |
| Security | 8 | 8 | 0 |
| Services | 14 | 19 | 13 |
| To leave old neighbourhood | 25 | 2 | 2 |
| Role loss | 6 | 3 | 1 |
| Social needs | 16 | 13 | 21 |
| Natural environment | 0 | 1 | 54 |
| TOTALS | 100 | 101[a] | 99[a] |

[a] Rounding error

beauty, strength, and occasionally even purpose, being nearer to people and things that were loved or desired, and being in a more controllable and convenient environment where their needs could be met without frustration, worry, or delay. There were many residents in each community who gave both positive and negative reasons for moving. However, more minus responses were given by Horizon Heights residents, plus and minus responses were almost evenly balanced in Carefree Village but with the latter having the edge, and among the Ozark residents the plus responses overwhelmingly outweighed the minus responses (Longino, 1978).

We have seen that the Ozarks attracts people from farther away than the two planned communities; that they tend to be younger, married, and in better physical and financial health. Their reasons for moving are also positive like retired migrants who move to seaside communities in France and England. Planned communities, on the other hand, tend to attract people who, like the very old or poor, due to critical events in their lives or unhappy situations feel that they must move.

### *Selective recruitment*

The process of matching migrants to environments involves the individual who makes the decision to move, or 'self-selection', and the 'selective recruitment' efforts of the community itself. In Horizon Heights there is a waiting list. Little open recruitment goes on by the Housing Authority which manages the community. Rather, social service agencies, particularly those who have as clients people of modest means, refer clients with pressing housing problems to Horizon Heights.

In Carefree Village there is a large sales force which aggressively recruits new residents, using skilled newspaper, radio, and television campaigns. Unlike Horizon Heights, the selectivity process filters into the community those who *can* afford the entrance fee and monthly maintenance payments. In the Ozarks, land developers acquire and use large mailing lists of people nearing retirement age. These mailings proclaim the pleasures of picturesque mountain life, and offer an invitation to visit.

Retirement communities therefore selectively search with varying degrees of success for new residents, just as people self-selectively search for destinations that will meet their perceived needs. Over one-third of the Horizon Heights residents said that community social service providers first told them about Horizon Heights; almost one-third of Carefree Village residents said that community sales representatives first talked with them about the Village; and in the Ozarks, over one-fifth said that developers and realtors first approached them. Selective recruitment, then, cannot be ignored when considering the migration decision process of older people. In addition to people who are involved in official recruitment efforts, there are many informal recruiters in retirement communities, and their efforts also facilitate self-selection on the part of their friends or family members considering a move.

### *Network recruitment*

When retired migrants move into an area a common pattern is the establishment of a visiting routine with other retired family members and friends, especially if the migrant lives near a resort. Visits often precede a move to the area, after which the chain of visits begins anew.

Residents of the three example communities were asked if they had known anyone in the community before they themselves moved. In each, about half had known someone before they moved. For both intra-county and inter-state migrants the proportion remained about half. On average they had known five people in Horizon Heights and seven in both Carefree Village and the Ozarks. Most residents characterized these prior acquaintances as friends, and nearly all the Ozark and Carefree Village residents had visited their communities as least twice before moving. Network recruitment, like selective recruitment, is part of a filtering process which results in a general similarity of migrant backgrounds in each community. Network recruitment, however, has a greater long-term impact because it initiates and then maintains the migration stream.

### *The final decision to move*

When migration to planned retirement communities is discussed, a frequent question is how many residents are 'put there' by their children. Carefree Village, Horizon Heights, and Ozark residents were asked several questions about who participated in the final decision. It was surprising to learn that only about half acknowledged help from anyone. When others did participate in the decision, they did so primarily by giving advice, and practically no-one felt coerced by others. As regards the person who made the final decision a few women said their husbands, but most couples said they made the decision jointly and the unmarried made the final decision alone. In Horizon Heights, some residents had been residentially displaced by urban renewal projects and admitted that the final decision was not entirely theirs. A few retirement community residents are placed there by their children but the proportion is negligible in comparison to the vast majority who make the final decision themselves or with their spouses. Most do not involve their children in the decision at all. In England and France this social and psychological independence from children is evidence of a modern rather than a traditional lifestyle, and a middle- rather than working-class pattern (Cribier, 1980; Law and

Warnes, Chapter 3 in this book). What may have been measured, inadvertently, is the resident's pride and desire for independence, rather than actual freedom from the influence of others. Nonetheless, the degree of expressed independence in making the final decision to move is substantial.

## CARE AND SUPPORT IN THE COMMUNITIES

### Person–environment interaction: support systems

The processes by which retirement communities recruit new members and by which retired migrants choose residential locations should result in compatibility between the person and his or her new living environment (Carp, 1968). The details of how various living environments, including retirement communities, meet the needs of their residents are not fully understood. Before this problem can be discussed in relation to the example communities it is necessary to define some terms and concepts.

#### *The support system concept*

Support is defined in terms of the physical, emotional, psychic, intellectual, and spiritual maintenance provided to a person by individuals, groups or institutions (Robertson, 1978). There are two approaches to the description of support systems depending upon whether one's interest centres on its provision or its appropriation (Longino, 1979a).

Service providers tend to see support for the elderly in systemic terms and to speak of the family, the neighbourhood, the village, the religious, or the ethnic support system. There is also the support system made up of a network of agencies and organizations aimed at meeting service needs. An individual can be the client of several systems at once. It is possible to examine the structural relationships between systems, as is done in market research for the service-providing companies and agencies.

When descriptive emphasis is placed upon the recipients of support appropriation, it is the relationship between the provider and the recipient that is of interest. The relationship is primary if the relationship is personal, as between close friends or family members. On the other hand, the relationship is secondary if it is segmental and impersonal and applies only to particular services, as in the case of a formal agency or tradesman.

The need for support increases with age and declining health, but one of the threats to the elderly is the progressive loss of primary support. Parents, uncles, and aunts die, then older siblings and one's spouse, and later still younger siblings and even older children. This reduces primary support during a period when increasing support is needed. The response is a quest for new resources and an increased reliance on secondary support.

## Retirement communities and support systems

Residents of Horizon Heights, Carefree Village, and the Ozark Lakes Country were asked to list the people who currently meant a lot to them and who were important in their lives. Then they were asked what each person did for them on a more of less regular basis. In coding these open-ended responses, support activities were placed into three categories: emotional, social, and instrumental. 'She is kind to me, listens to my problems, encourages me', would be coded as evidence of emotional support; 'she calls, writes, visits, goes places with me', would be an indicator of social support; and 'she takes me places, helps me shop and repairs things around the house', would be coded as instrumental, task-oriented support.

A list of the daily needs that might require help from others was then reviewed, and the resident asked who did each of these things. Most retirement community residents were found to be primarily self-supporting. Often it was not a person that was mentioned but a role, such as the bus driver, the maintenance man, or the nurse, for example. The residents finally were asked if anyone else helped regularly in any way.

It is clear that people in both planned and unplanned communities were similar in the number of people giving support which was characteristically between eight and ten, although the balance between primary resources and secondary resources varied. Ozark in-migrants, on the whole, had more primary supporters than did Carefree Village residents, while Horizon Heights residents had least. People living in the planned communities, however, most relied on secondary resources, although there were more available in Carefree Village than in Horizon Heights. Of those providing secondary support, the number who lived or worked in the community was highest in Carefree Village and lowest in the Ozark Lakes Country, but the number living outside was similar in all three areas.

Instrumental support is task-oriented. In all three communities about half of the residents' primary contacts provided no instrumental support. Many lived too far away to help on a regular basis, and this was particularly true of the Ozarks residents.

### *Support and self-selection to retirement communities*

Declining primary support in the face of rising needs can powerfully affect the decision to move. Both the subsidized and non-subsidized planned communities were designed in accordance with the particular needs of very old people and it is therefore not surprising that many who move to these environments were local rather than long-distance movers, and emphasized in their reasons for moving those very areas of support which are the strengths of the planned community. Nor is it surprising that the retirement-aged people who were attracted to planned communities tended to have greater need and vulnerability as they were older, more often widowed, and less healthy than the retired people who moved to the unplanned *de facto* retirement community. The fit between the living environment and individual needs was therefore reasonably well matched among the three retirement communities; people with a greater need for instrumental support do tend to be attracted to communities built to meet those needs.

## RELATIVE BENEFITS OF PLANNED RETIREMENT COMMUNITY RESIDENCE

The foregoing implies that residents of planned retirement communities are better off than they would have been had they not moved there. Almost all voluntary movers, including those to retirement communities, felt better off in their new surroundings than at their former address (Britton, 1966; Bultena and Wood, 1969; Hamovitch, 1968; Sherman, 1972; Winiecke, 1973).

Further evidence of this result was produced by the larger study of mid-western retirement communities, which compared retirement community residents with matched sub-groups of a national sample of older people (Harris and Associates, 1975). The sub-groups controlled for the effect of self-selection into the retirement communities.[2] The results of this study provide a basis for assessing the relative benefits of moving to different retirement communities.

### *The non-subsidized planned community*

Carefree Village provides medical care, freedom from fear of crime, and social support. Nearly nine-tenths of Carefree Village residents had no problem in getting enough medical care. Their counterparts in the general population were more likely to say that sufficient medical care was a problem. Carefree Village residents also benefited from the uniformed security guards and sub-urban location which give the Village a low crime rate. While nine-tenths of the residents perceived crime as no problem, only half of their counterparts from the national sample made the same claim. When their social support problems are compared, Carefree Village residents, again, were clearly better off. They were less likely to be troubled with loneliness, lack of friends, feeling un-needed, or being bored. While it is clear that in many respects residents of the non-subsidized planned community are better off, it must be recalled that it is expensive to live in Carefree Village.

### *The subsidized planned community*

Beneficial living environments are not reserved for the affluent, for even though medical care is much less extensive in Horizon Heights than in Carefree Village, at the former over four-fifths of the residents said sufficient medical care was not a problem. The matched sub-group of the general population were more troubled by insufficient medical care. Over three-quarters of the people in Horizon Heights said that crime was not a problem, while only two-fifths of their counterparts said the same. Many residents had moved from high crime areas into Horizon Heights, whose security guards and exclusiveness made them feel safe. Social support was less problematic in Horizon Heights as well. While a quarter of the residents said that loneliness was a problem this was the case for over half of the national sub-group. Community residents were also more likely to feel that they had enough friends to keep busy, and less than one-tenth felt that poor housing was a problem compared to over one-quarter of their national counterparts. Elderly public housing is clearly beneficial for the people it attracts when they are compared to others with similar characteristics.

The only study of a group before and after they entered planned living environments in the United States was conducted by Carp (1966). She compared non-movers with movers to subsidized public housing communities and not only measured the adjustment of the move after a year (Carp, 1968), but also conducted final interviews after 8 years (Carp, 1974). She found positive benefits similar to those reported for Horizon Heights; that satisfaction with both housing and living environment increased after the move; and that it was higher for retirement community residents even after 8 years. She concluded that 'the factors which predict short-term adjustment in elderly-designed public housing tend to predict long-range adjustment, implying that the new environment will benefit the same people in the long run as in the short run' (Carp, 1976, p. 248).

It remains to assess the advantage of unplanned *de facto* communities like the Ozark settlements and of planned communities which offer very low levels of services, such as hotels and some Florida condominiums which cater to the elderly. One would expect that the residents of such unplanned, or at least unserviced, communities would be increasingly burdened over time with health and service needs. The absence of built-in services promotes secondary moves away from such communities (Longino, 1979b). The 1970 census showed that the counter-flows of people age 60 and over from Florida to New York and Ohio were heavily laden with widows, the poor, and the very old. Many were returning to their state of birth, and large numbers went to live with their children and siblings.

## POSITIVE OUTCOMES OF AGE-HOMOGENEITY

Retirement community research in the United States has been concerned with the social outcome of age homogeneity in community settings and with the relationship between the ageing individual and his or her living environment.

Sociologists have been more interested in the former and environmental psychologists in the latter (Mangum, Chapter 9 of this book). Rose (1962, 1965) proposed a theoretical framework for examining the relationship between social interaction and definitions of reality among older people. He suggested that there was developing in America a subculture of the ageing, which when fully developed produced 'aged group consciousness', the replacement of negative stereotypes of ageing by group pride. Participation in the aged subculture should mean for the older person an increase in interaction with other elders, changes in values and attitudes, and increased morale or feelings of self-worth.

While this suggestion is still debated, the subculture hypothesis can be supported with modifications. The impression of retirement community residents that emerges from the example communities is not one of activism or aggressiveness, as Rose predicated, but one of withdrawal or retreatism. The type of retreatism is different in the three environments (Longino, McClelland, and Peterson, 1980). Retirees moving to the Ozark settings tend to be younger, richer couples who are retreating on an extended vacation. They have earned it and are enjoying themselves and do not feel a strong need to be socially active or useful community members. Their levels of activity are no higher than for a similar group in the general population and in some community samples lower. Their morale is high, and they practise what Parsons (1963) called a 'consumatory' phase of life. Those who seek out age-segregated settings tend, however to be older, more often widowed, and in public housing, poorer. They seek shelter from the troubles of later life, a more manageable environment, more appropriate and accessible services, and companionship. Indicators of subcultural activity are higher for residents of these environments than in the general population.

It appears that residents of all the communities find what they are looking for. Their levels of social activity may not be especially high, but neither are their expectations. Their social contacts are more likely to be with other elders or with the younger people who serve them. In this context, a type of gerontophilia does develop, though it is not as combative as Rose expected. Residents believed that older people in general were sufficiently respected by younger people; they also perceived them as being useful members of their communities. The clear implication is that older people are seen as deserving the respect they get, and that the residents feel no lack of respect themselves.

## CONCLUSIONS

A retirement community is any living environment to which most residents have moved since they retired. Planned communities may be subsidized, like elderly public housing sites, or non-subsidized, like the growing variety of private communities. The range of supportive services built into these living environments varies greatly. In addition to planned communities, there are *de facto* retirement communities resulting from concentrated migration into popular retirement settings.

Subsidized planned communities in the United States tend to attract from the local area residents who are seeking to escape from an unsuitable environment. Planned non-subsidized communities with extensive service packages tend to exclude the poor. Their residents are more likely than public housing residents to give positive reasons for their relocation, but both types attract the widowed and the very old. American *de facto* retirement communities, which do not offer rich service environments, attract younger and wealthier retirees from greater distances. This 'fit' between individual needs and living environments results from three interrelated migration processes: self-selection, selective recruitment, and network recruitment. Few retirement community residents have moved involuntarily. Are people in planned communities really better off for having moved there? A definite answer to this deceptively simple question is methodologically difficult. The best recent studies, however, suggest that residents of service-enriched living environments benefit measurably from them.

The American tendency towards voluntary age segregation, when coupled with the trends of early retirement and greater pension security, encourage the speculation that retirement communities will continue to multiply in both number and variety. Network recruitment will maintain migration streams to established *de facto* retirement areas and within them planned communities will continue to develop. These trends are well established. The growing American dependency upon foreign oil supplies and their rapidly escalating costs have had the effect of taxing those who live in cold climates through the cost of heating-fuel in the winter. This trend should swell the migration streams to warmer climates even further. Federal and state contributions to the welfare of older people over the past decade have greatly expanded social and health service programmes. In a recessionary economy, such programmes are likely to be curtailed in an attempt to bring government spending under tighter inflationary control. The result may be unfortunate for poor older people. An increased attractiveness of non-subsidized planned retirement communities may be an unanticipated result of declining government services for the economically comfortable older persons since there is an economy of scale in such communities so that many services can be offered at less cost to community members than would be possible under the condition of scattered residence and less certain consumer market conditions. Therefore, both residential relocation and community planning are research topics in American social gerontology that are likely to receive more attention in the 1980s than heretofore.

## NOTES

[1] Drs Warren A. Peterson and Charles F. Longino, Jr, the project's Principal and Co-Principal Investigators, are both sociologists and social gerontologists. Sociologists David B. Oliver, Jill S. Quadagno, David R. Dickens, Michael G. Lacy, Linda W. Phelps, and Jocelyn M. Eckerman worked on various phases of the project. Psychologist Thomas Blank and economist Mark Evans contributed their expertise. Anthropologist Robert C. Smith, with the assistance of Ruth G. Kuhar, conducted the ethnographic community studies.

[2] Standardization procedures evolved (after other methods were tried) into a system of shadow sampling. Shadow samples were drawn from the Harris and Associates (1975) survey sample in the following manner: (1) a matrix of five or six background variables was created for each community. Each cell in the community matrix represented one particular combination of the background variables of age, gender, marital status, education, and income. Race was also used in the public housing samples where there was racial diversity. (2) Cases in the national sample which conformed to the combination of characteristics in each cell were selected randomly and in the same proportion as in the retirement community sample. The result of this matching technique is that for every widowed black woman over age 75 with an elementary-school education living on less than $2000 a year in Horizon Heights, a person with the same profile of characteristics was drawn from the general population sample and placed in the Horizon Heights shadow sample. The process was repeated for every other combination of the background variables. Shadow samples were drawn to be as large as possible consistent with preserving the correct proportions of respondents with the specified background characteristics. In this way the study deals with the problem of the unrepresentativeness of retirement community populations and attempts to control for the effect of selective recruitment—at least as far as it relates to background variables. Shadow sampling and some other points discussed in this chapter are discussed further elsewhere (Longino, 1980b).

## REFERENCES

Biggar, J. C. (1979). The sunning of America: migration to the Sunbelt. *Population Bulletin*, **32**, 1–43.

Biggar, J. C. (1980). Reassessing elderly Sunbelt migration. *Research on Aging*, **2**, 177–190.

Britton, J. H. (1966). Living in a rural Pennsylvania community in old age. In Carp, F. M. and Burnett, W. M. (eds), *Patterns of Living and Housing of Middle-Aged and Older people*, pp. 99–105. Government Printing Office, Washington, DC.

Brown, L. A. and Moore, E. G. (1970). The intraurban migration process: a perspective. *Geografiska Annaler*, **52** (Series B), 1–13.

Bultena, G. L. and Wood, V. (1969). The American retirement community: bane or blessing? *Journal of Gerontology*, **24**, 209–17.

Carp, F. M. (1966). Effects of impoverished housing on the lives of older people. In Carp, F. M. and Burnett, W. M. (eds), *Patterns of Living and Housing of Middle-aged and Older People*, pp. 147–67. Government Printing Office, Washington, DC.

Carp, F. M. (1968). Person–situation congruence in engagement. *Gerontologist*, **8**, 184–8.

Carp, F. M. (1974). Short-term and long-term prediction of adjustment to a new environment. *Journal of Gerontology*, **29**, 444–53.

Carp, F. M. (1976). Living environments of older people. In Binstock, R. H. and Shanas, E. (eds), *Handbook of Aging and the Social Sciences*, pp. 244–71. Van Nostrand Reinhold Company, New York.

Cleland, C. B. (1965). Mobility of older people. In Rose, A. M. and Peterson, W. A. (eds), *Older People and Their Social World*, pp. 191–96. F. A. Davis, Philadelphia.

Cribier, F. (1980). A European assessment of aged migration. *Research on Aging*, **2**, 255–270.

Donahue, W. (1966). Impact of living arrangements on ego development in the elderly. In Carp, F. and Burnett, W. M. (eds), *Patterns of Living and Housing of Middle-Aged and Older People*, pp. 1–9. Government Printing Office, Washington, DC.

Eckerman, J. M. (1979). An Exploratory Study of Age-integrated Retirement Communities in the Ozarks. Unpublished MA thesis, Trinity University, San Antonio, Texas.

Flynn, C. B. (1980). General versus aged interstate migration, 1965–1970. *Research on Aging*, **2**, 165–176.

Flynn, C. B., Biggar, J. C., Longino, C. F. Jr and Wiseman, R. F. (1979). *Aged Migration in the United States, 1965–1970: Final Report*. National Institute on Aging, Washington, DC.

Golant, S. M. (1977). Spatial context of residential moves by elderly persons. *International Journal Aging and Human Development*, **8**, 279–89.

Golant, S. M. (1980a). Locational–environmental perspectives on old-age-segregated residential areas in the United States. In Johnson, R. J. and Herbert, D. T. (eds), *Geography and the Urban Environment*, vol. 3. Wiley, Chichester.

Golant, S. M. (1980b). Future directions for elderly migration research. *Research on Aging*, **2**, 271–280.

Hamovitch, M. B. (1968). Social and psychological factors in adjustment in a retirement community. In Carp, F. M. (ed.), *The Reitrement Process*, pp. 53–65. Government Printing Office, Washington, DC.

Harris, L. and Associates (1975). *The Myth and Reality of Aging in America*. National Council on the Aging, Washington, DC.

Hochschild, A. R. (1973). *The Unexpected Community*. Prentice Hall, Englewood Cliffs, New Jersey.

Lawton, M. P. and Cohen, J. (1975). The generality of housing impacts on the wellbeing of older people. *Journal of Gerontology*, **29**, 194–204.

Lee, E. S. (1966). A theory of migration. *Demography*, **3**, 47–57.

Lipman, A. (1968). Public housing and attitude adjustment in old age. *Journal of Geriatric Psychiatry*, **2**, 88–101.

Long, L. H. and Hansen, K. A. (1979) Reasons for interestate migration. *Current Population Reports*, p–23, 81.

Longino, C. F. Jr (1978). Pushes and pulls: migration selectivity and retirement relocation. Paper presented at the annual meeting of the Southern Regional Demographic Group, San Antonio, Texas.

Longino, C. F. Jr (1979a). The unit of analysis problem and network measures of changing support. Symposium on recent orientations to the study of support networks and residential relocation. Gerontological Society 32nd Annual Scientific Meeting. Washington, DC.

Longino, C. F. Jr (1979b). Going home: aged return migration in the United States, 1965–1970. *Journal of Gerontology*, **34**, 736–45.

Longino, C. F. Jr (1980a). Residential relocation of older people: metropolitan and non-metropolitan. *Research on Aging*, **2**, 205–216.

Longino, C. F. Jr (1980b). The retirement community. In Berghorn, F. J. and Schafer, D. E. (eds), *The Dynamics of Aging : Original Essays on the Experience and Process of Growing Old*. Westview Press, Boulder, Colorado, pp. 391–417

Longino, C. F. Jr, McClelland, K. A. and Peterson, W. A. (1980). The aged subculture hypothesis: social integration, gerontophilia and self-regard. *Journal of Gerontology*, **34**, 758–767.

Parsons, T. (1963). Old age as a consumatory phase of life. *Gerontologist*, **3**, 53–4.

Rives, N. W. Jr (1980). Conducting research on the migration of the elderly: sources of statistical information. *Research on Aging*, **2**, 155–164.

Robertson, J. F. (1978). Women in midlife: crisis, reverberations, and social support. *The Family Coordinator*, **27**, 375–81.

Rose, A. M. (1962). The subculture of the aging, a topic of sociological research. *Gerontologist*, **2**, 123–7.

Rose, A. M. (1965). The subculture of the aging: a framework for research in social gerontology. In Rose, A. M. and Peterson, W. A. (eds), *Older People and Their Social World*, pp. 3–16. F. A. Davis Co., Philadelphia.

Sherman, S. R. (1971). The choice of retirement housing among the well-elderly. *Aging and Human Development*, **2**, 118–38.

Sherman, S. R. (1972). Satisfaction with retirement housing: attitudes, recommendations and moves. *Aging and Human Development*, **3**, 339–66.

Sherman, S. R. (1979). Site permeability, service availability and perceived community support in crisis. *Journal of Social Service Research*, **3**, 139–57.

Shryock, H. and Siegel, J. (1976). *The Methods and Materials of Demography*. Academic Press, New York.

Walkley, R. P., Mangum Jr, W. P., Sherman, S. R., Doods, S., and Wilner, D. M. (1966). The California survey of retirement housing. *Gerontologist*, **6**, 28–34.

Webber, I. and Osterbind, C. C. (1968). Types of retirement villages. In Burgess, E. W. (ed.), *Retirement Villages*, pp. 157–71. University of Michigan Press, Ann Arbor.

Winiecke, L. (1973). The appeal of age-segregated housing to the elderly poor. *Aging and Human Development*, **4**, 293–306.

Wiseman, R. F. (1978). *Spatial Aspects of Aging*. Resource Papers for College Geography, 78–4. Association of American Geographers, Washington, DC.

Wiseman, R. F. (1979). National patterns of elderly concentration and migration. In Golant, S. M. (ed.), *The Locational and Environmental Context of the Elderly Population*, pp. 25–39. Halsted Press, New York.

Wiseman, R. F. (1980). Why older people move: theoretical issues. *Research on Aging*, **2**, 141–154.

Wiseman, R. F. and Roseman, C. C. (1979). A typology of elderly migration based on the decision making process. *Economic Geography*, **55**, 324–37.

PART 3

# ACTIVITY PATTERNS AND TRAVEL DIFFICULTIES

Geographical Perspectives on the Elderly
Edited by A. M. Warnes


Chapter 11

# Patterns of activity and mobility among the elderly

*Paul Robson*

This chapter is concerned with the day-to-day activity that old people are engaged in, and the travel that this involves. We are mainly concerned with the activities that old people find necessary for daily living or for a satisfying old age, such as doing their shopping, visiting their friends, collecting their pension, and obtaining medical services. These are usually carried out by travelling to a particular place from home and returning later the same day. We are interested in the effects that travelling and its associated difficulties have on the activity pattern', the way that these activities are distributed in sequence, time, and space (Chapin and Hightower, 1965), and conversely how the travelling that old people do is determined by the activities that old people want and need to be involved in. The importance of the travel lies in the importance of the activity. Even if it is only routine activity, it may be vital for their quality of life, and even for them to maintain any independence and self-respect.

Until about 100 years ago travel was not an important part of people's lives, which were rarely influenced by the need to travel or by its associated problems. In the medieval city, for example, the majority of people had nothing but their own energy to rely on for transport, so all the necessities of daily life had to be located within walking distance. Shops, markets, work-places, and dwellings were clustered together with a minimum wastage of space. Since then society has harnessed new sources of energy for transport, and these have been increasingly relied upon for personal transport (Foley, 1976, p. 19). It is increasingly possible for facilities to be widely separated from one another, e.g. in Britain 13 per cent of workers live more than 10 miles away from their work and 7 per cent of children live more than 5 miles away from their school (Rigby, 1977). It has been suggested that those who are responsible for marketing energy resources have been keen to promote a wider spatial separation of the facilities necessary for daily life to increase the use of their products (Foley, 1976, p. 60). The type of activities that people can engage in, and their quality of life, now depend heavily on travel, and therefore upon both access to different energy sources and ways of using them.

Until recently this interdependence of mobility and the daily activities of older people has been a neglected area of study. On the one hand gerontologists have avoided studying the mobility of old people, and have concerned themselves more with the health services, the personal social services, and housing as policy areas which affect the quality of life of old people. On the other hand geographers, and those in related disciplines such as town planning and transport planning, have neglected the effects that their work might have on the activities and quality of life of particular sections of the population, such as old people. There are a number of aspects of most planning studies which make them insensitive to the needs of particular groups.

Firstly, many transport studies use only highly aggregated data of travel patterns, which do not differentiate between different types of people. They observe statistical regularities in patterns of human behaviour without recognizing that there are differences in travel needs and abilities which produce contrasts between the travel of different groups of people. Many studies use zonally aggregated data on the assumption that 'geographical proximity results in similarity of households with respect to trip making and socio-economic characteristics', even though it has been demonstrated that 'relationships or correlations developed between variables representing aggregated data will be inaccurate, because there is a considerably larger portion of variation within zones than between zones' (McCarthy, 1969). Another very common form of aggregation is the use of data for households rather than individuals. As Kutter (1973, p. 246) has shown, travel characteristics vary most with stages in the life-cycle and with sex roles, and are therefore likely to be greater between members of a household than between households. It has also been shown that 'the implicit assumption of most planning studies that the household car necessarily enables all its members to be mobile runs counter to reality' (Hillman, Henderson and Whalley, 1973), as a single household car is used mainly by one household member whose travel needs are often different from those of other household members.

Secondly, many transport studies use descriptions of present behaviour to predict future behaviour without investigating constraints on behaviour. In this vein the present British Minister of Transport has said that policy 'will be directed to ensuring for everyone a reasonable level of personal mobility, accepting that the car is likely to be the dominant form of transport in the foreseeable future' (Fowler, 1979). This would seem to be based on the fact that 40 per cent of all journeys are made by car, but this average results from the frequent use of cars by the half of the population that has a household car, while the other half travel only rarely by car (Rigby, 1977). Planning on the basis of high car usage ignores that portion of the population that cannot use a car, and could well replicate and intensify the constraints on that portion of the population.

Thirdly, travel is commonly studied in isolation without considering the needs and preferences for activities that make travel necessary. In short, travel is often looked at as an end in itself. There is very little attempt to check whether particular groups of people are able to reach particular activities, and therefore whether their needs can be met. This approach also tends to equate increasing amounts of travel with increased satisfaction, without recognizing that it may well be a sign of failure of a policy if people are having to travel further to satisfy their needs. Chapin has pointed out that we need to understand people's activities to understand their travel and vice-versa, and called for more research into people's motivations and preferences for activities (Chapin, 1974). Kutter has shown that it is the differences in people's needs which are the major determinants of differences in travel and activity patterns (Kutter, 1973, p. 251).

Fourthly, transport planning often evaluates its projects by calculating and valuing the time savings that they give to travellers. This approach ignores the complexity of the relationship between time and travel. The value of time is by no means a constant between people or throughout the day. Journeys and activities fit into an individual's time budget which may require rapid travel at a particular time, and place a lower evaluation on time at another. It should also be noted that estimates of time savings usually leave out measures of the quality of the journey which may be important to some people, such as whether the journey can be made at all, the physical difficulty involved in making the journey, and whether the journey permits the desired activity to be carried out (Moseley *et al.*, 1977, p. 88).

Fifthly, planners tend to allow themselves only one variable that they can control through policy; that is the provision of more, or less, transport. If it is agreed, however, that the ultimate goal of policy is to enable people to carry out particular activities then there is a vast range of policy options; in the spatial dimension concerned with the location of activities in relation to the people who use them, and in the temporal dimension with such matters as the opening hours of facilities and the more careful co-ordination of public transport timings and opening hours (Moseley *et al.*, 1977, p. 120). It is sometimes found that improving transport encourages further dispersion of land uses to the benefit of those people with the best access to means of transport, but to the detriment of those with the least access (Hamer, 1979). The best illustration is the spread of out-of-down leisure centres and hypermarkets which are accessible only to car-travellers and which have been seen as responsible for the closure of more accessible town centre facilities (Hillman, 1973).

The last feature to note of certain transport studies is their under-recording, or even total neglect, of walking as a method of transport. Old people make over half their journeys on foot (Hopkin, Robson and Town, 1978a), so their omission in some surveys (Ashford and Holloway, 1970; Markovitz, 1971; Wachs, 1978) will mislead us.

The intention here is to overcome these problems by working towards an understanding of the interdependence of activities and mobility among elderly people. This will involve examining how mobility by all modes changes with age, and so how old people may differ from other people, and why they behave as they do. Other aspects involved in accessibility and the effect of land-use policies on old people will be discussed; their characteristic activities and use of time, the most important barriers to an active life by old people, and some of the policy options that are available.

## MOBILITY

Mobility is sometimes used to mean the amount of travelling that people do (Skelton, 1978). By this definition a mobile person travels a lot; an immobile one travels only a little. However, as noted above, we are not so much interested in what old people do, as why they do it, and the constraints that exist on their travel. Some old people may travel a lot because they have to, but find travelling difficult. Others may travel very little because they have few needs to travel, but could do so easily. An alternative definition will therefore be used, which describes mobility as the ability to travel, whether or not this ability is used (Hopkin, Robson and Town, 1978b). In this context mobility is the sum of the ability to use different methods of transport and of their availability. The mobility of old people is a topic that has been extensively researched in the past few years (Hopkin, Robson and Town, 1978a; Hillman, Henderson, and Whalley, 1976; Robson, 1978; see also Hanson, 1977 for an annotated bibliography of American studies).

Among people aged between about 20 and 65, the most important determinant of mobility is car availability, which in turn is very closely related to social class, income, and sex. In Britain 60 per cent of people in households headed by a professional or managerial worker have one car and 27 per cent two or more cars. In contrast only 31 per cent of people in households headed by a semi-skilled or unskilled manual worker have one car, and less than 4 per cent two or more cars (Rigby, 1977). As an illustration of the effect that this has on travel, only 14 per cent of journeys by people with no household cars are further than 5 miles, compared to 24 per cent by those in households with one car, and 31 per cent by those in households with two or more cars (Rigby, 1977). Within a household, however, it is men who are more likely to have the use of a car. Sixty-four per cent of men have a licence to drive a car, but only 21 per cent of women (Mitchell and Town, 1977). In some western countries (especially the United States and Canada) there are many more people with independent access to cars.

Ageing adds further dimensions to these differences in mobility. Firstly health and personal capabilities decline with age. In 1968/69 the proportion of people in Great Britain who had some impairment was less than 1 per cent among people aged 16–29; 22 per cent in the 65–74 age group; and 38 per cent among people aged 75 and over (Harris, 1971). The most common complaints suffered by old people are arthritis, rheumatism, and cardiac conditions (Hunt, 1978). This has consequences for the use of all methods of travel. Driving a car becomes more dangerous; climbing into a bus becomes more difficult; hills, steps, ramps, and road crossings become more difficult when walking. Secondly, retirement from work brings a reduction in income. Further reductions in real income may occur if an old person is relying on a pension which does not keep pace with the increase in prices, or for widows if the spouse's private pension does not make provision for them. In these circumstances it is difficult to maintain and run a car or to replace it when its life expires. It also becomes expensive to travel by bus unless concessionary fares are available.

Thirdly, widowhood means the loss of a partner to help with travelling. Most common is the death of a husband, leaving a widow who is unable to drive. A typical sequence of changes in old age would be first to give up a car and to rely on buses and walking (bus use does increase early in retirement), followed by increasing difficulty with using buses and with walking which tends to limit travel to short distances on foot unless special arrangements are made to use taxis, other people's cars, or special car schemes. A recent survey in Britain found that one-third of the over-65s were in a household with a car, another one-third had no household car and no difficulty with walking. Over half of women aged over 80 were in this last group (Hopkin, Robson and Town, 1978a). It should be emphasized that this decline in mobility does not necessarily mean a decline in the number of journeys, for this is determined more by the needs that have to be satisfied. The more likely results of declining mobility are shorter journeys and a greater effort of travel. Other studies have found no decline in the number of journeys with age but this does not mean that increasing age does not restrict the freedom to go where one wants.

It should also be noted that mobility in old age relies considerably on the availability of public transport services. Public bus services are less frequent and accessible in rural areas than urban areas, and the number of bus miles operated in Britain fell by 20 per cent between 1967 and 1977. Voluntary and local authority transport are unevenly available, depending on local initiative and voluntary activity. Most forms of public transport are less common in North America than in Britain.

## ACCESSIBILITY

When people are mobile they are able to travel more easily, but this is just one factor in determining whether people are able to reach where they want to go. The term accessibility describes how easy it is to get to particular places. It takes into account the spatial separation of people from a potential destination, and the mobility of the people concerned. In geographical studies accessibility has usually been seen in terms of how many people can get to particular destinations from their catchment areas. The concern of this paper is rather with individuals' accessibilities or the range of opportunities available to them. This requires greater sensitivity to the variation in mobility among people, which means that accessibility cannot be measured solely in terms of distance. A more satisfactory measure may be the time that journeys take which reflects their difficulty. For old people, however, time may not be the most important resource, and the effort of a journey may be related more to particular barriers, such as boarding a bus, using a subway, or climbing a hill. Journey time also tells us very little if a person is unable to make the journey at all, and later in this section we will examine measures of accessibility that cope with this. These are more complicated and have been little used so to illustrate old people's accessibility it is necessary to use journey-time measurements.

It has been found that people over 65 in Britain travel 22 per cent fewer miles than the population as a whole, but spend 12 per cent more time doing so (Hopkin, Robson and Town, 1978b). This reflects the fact that fewer of them have cars available. Accessibility varies markedly between geographical areas. In the centre of towns housing and facilities are close by, but in the suburbs housing density is lower and facilities more widely dispersed. In rural areas this dispersion is even greater. For car-users this dispersion may not create many difficulties as driving and parking is easier where facilities are more widely dispersed, but there is a marked effect on old people without a car. For example, in London over 40 per cent of people over the age of 65 could reach a chemist's shop within 5 minutes, but less than 20 per cent could do so in the rural counties of England. This was despite the fact that only 10 per cent of old people in London used motorized transport compared to half of the elderly in the rural counties (Hunt, 1978). That people with cars are not penalized in their accessibility by dispersed facilities may have disguised the effects on those without cars, particularly as planners and decision-makers are more likely to fall into the former group.

Planning has tended to assume universal car availability and to produce land-use patterns in which housing and facilities are more widely separated. This process is more advanced in the United States but is beginning in Britain. The overall density of housing has fallen from 3720 people per square kilometre in 1901 to 2310 in 1971, and it is expected to fall to 2010 by the year 2001. There has also been a redesign of urban housing areas, from being built around main traffic routes with shops and a public transport service, to housing estates segregated from main roads and heavy traffic. This makes them much harder to serve by public transport and tends to isolate them from certain facilities (Tyneside Passenger Transport Executive, 1973). There is a slight over-representation of old people in older neighbourhoods in the inner areas of towns, yet special housing for old people tends to be built on the outskirts of towns where land is cheaper. This produces a noticeable effect on travelling. Old people who lived between 1 and 3 miles from the centre of one town made only three-quarters of the journeys undertaken by those living within $\frac{1}{2}$ of its centre, and the effect was most pronounced among those without cars (Hopkin, Robson, and Town, 1978a). In another town half of the elderly who suffered from arthritis could not walk more than 100 yards, but only one-third of those living in its outer areas had a shop or bus within this range (Buchanan and Chamberlain, 1978a).

There is clear evidence of the dispersion of facilities which exacerbate the consequences of planning trends. The number of retail outlets in Britain fell by 17 per cent between 1950 and 1971 (Hamer, 1976). Some types of shops have been more likely to close; fishmongers and greengrocers have about halved in number, while off-licences have increased in number. The number of small, local shops which can easily be reached on foot has declined, while supermarkets in shopping parades or town centres have increased in size and number. More recently, large shopping centres on the outskirts of towns, which can only be reached by car, have been built. One of the types of shop which has disappeared most quickly is the dispensing chemist, which old people with poor health are likely to require frequently. In 1965 there were 14,137 but by 1975 only 11,162; a fall of over 20 per cent in 10 years (Robson, 1978, p. 31). There has also been a notable decrease in the accessibility of other medical services. General medical practitioners have concentrated their surgeries into larger practices and their number has fallen by 15 per cent in 15 years. Concentration has also meant relocation into new buildings, often in less accessible places where land is cheaper. The distribution of hospitals has changed less quickly than that of general medical practitioners, but there is a trend towards the closure of old hospitals and the construction of the few new large hospitals on sites with poor access by foot or public transport (Robson, 1978, p. 32; Rigby, 1978). These trends have gone nowhere near as far as those in North America, though, where cases are cited of only one public hospital out-patient department serving a major urban region, with a catchment area over 20 miles in radius (de Vise, 1971).

To assess the effect of policies of this type on different groups of people such as old people, we need fairly sophisticated measures of accessibility. Hagerstrand has developed a method of analysis called 'space–time geography' which attempts to define what activities particular individuals and groups can reach, bearing in mind the distances involved, mobility, the amount of free time available for the trip and the activity, and whether this coincides with the times when the facility and the transport to it are available (Hagerstrand, 1973). This detailed approach has been used in one area in Norfolk to record the opportunities for different activities that are available to different types of people in particular locations (Moseley *et al.*, 1977). This required a large amount of

Table 11.1 Inaccessibility of various facilities in rural Norfolk, 1976

| Facility | Percentage of the retired population unable to travel to the facility |
|---|---|
| Hospitals | 70 |
| General medical practitioner | 41 |
| Dentist | 48 |
| Chemist | 44 |
| Evening classes | 70 |
| Leisure facilities | 55 |
| Public house | 27 |
| Shops (excluding local 'corner' shop) | 46 |

*Source*: Moseley *et al.* (1977).

information including: individual car ownership and use, the distribution of different population groups, the ability to walk, the ability to use buses, when people want and are free to visit a facility, and facility opening times. The survey found that there was a large number of people to whom many facilities were inaccessible and that old people made up a high proportion of this group (Table 11.1). The differences in accessibility among the facilities reflects their degree of centralization although the inaccessibility both of evening classes and hospitals is also due to timing constraints for hospital visiting hours and evening classes are at times infrequent or there are no suitable bus services. The proportion of economically active men who cannot get to these facilities is very much less because more of them are in households with a car. Only a quarter of economically active men cannot get to a hospital or evening classes.

## TIME, NEEDS AND ACTIVITIES

Apart from poor accessibility, there are a number of factors which may stop someone doing something; lack of time, lack of income, physical incapacity, or lack of motivation. Before examining the relationship between mobility and activity patterns, it is helpful to assess these other factors in more detail.

Lack of time should rarely affect old people, as free time is a major feature of old age. After children have left home or no longer need looking after, and particularly after retirement from paid employment, many of the constraints that structured people's days disappear: working, preparing for work, travelling to and from work, meeting children from school, preparing other people's meals. Old people should be free to do very much as they like. Table 11.2 illustrates how ageing affects the use of time. The loss of the work role is the major change in the time budget. The loss of work activity is compensated for by increases in rest and relaxation time, watching television, home-making and eating. It is not compensated for by any increases in the time spent on recreation, family activities and socializing (which in fact decreased).

Table 11.2 Mean duration (in hours) of selected activities by heads of household and their spouses on weekdays, Washington, DC, 1968

| Activity | Aged < 35 with no children < 19 | Aged > 65 with no children < 19 living with them |
|---|---|---|
| Main job | 6.65 | 1.26 |
| Eating | 1.48 | 1.89 |
| Home-making | 1.02 | 3.42 |
| Family activities and socializing | 1.57 | 1.35 |
| Watching television | 1.27 | 2.44 |
| Rest and relaxation | 0.71 | 1.94 |

*Source*: Chapin, 1974, p. 114.

This use of time by old people on passive activities is confirmed by many other studies. One reported that two-thirds of its respondents' waking time was spent in activities described as 'passing the time' (Skelton, 1978). Another found that the average person aged 65 or more spent 3 hours each day watching television, $1\frac{1}{2}$ hours listening to the radio, $1\frac{1}{4}$ hours reading, and two hours 'just resting'. Nearly two-thirds would not venture outside for a walk on an average day (Abrams, 1978b).

This type of evidence has led gerontologists to hypothesize that growing old involves a process of disengagement (Cumming and Henry, 1961). This hypothesis suggests that the older one gets, the fewer activities one wishes to undertake. It implies that people voluntarily give up activities. If this were accepted it would be pointless to devise policies to improve the accessibility of facilities to old people. Before accepting this conclusion the other constraints need to be checked, for otherwise we might be unwittingly ignoring old people's needs.

Old people carry out those activities which meet their needs, but we cannot assume as some writers implicitly have that current activities will demonstrate all old people's needs. This would ignore the barriers which prevent the pursuit of an activity, and in fact would define the problem away. In addition, some needs such as access to medical advice may be urgent at particular times but hardly appear in the general activity pattern. Needs must be identified in another way. People may be asked for their own opinion as to their needs to determine *expressed need*. This will give no more than a partial picture of *felt needs*. Alternatively one group may be compared with another to define *comparative needs*, or an individual or group may be compared to previously defined standards to indicate *normative needs* (Bradshaw, 1972). None of these is entirely satisfactory, especially as very little information is available about the expectations of old people. In practice the elderly often adapt to problems by lowering their expectations and by making themselves content with what they have. Most of today's old people grew up during years when material conditions were harder and so expect less from life than younger people. Perhaps we should be asking ourselves in 1980: 'What sort of access to facilities would we like when we are old in 20, 30, or 40 years?'

Despite the difficulties of identification a number of needs seem clear for old people in their retirement. They should have the essentials for material survival, such as food and household goods, and most need to collect their pension. This can be acquired either by shopping themselves or by asking someone else to do it. Access to medical advice and supplies is essential for many, particularly in advanced old age; 21 per cent of those aged 75 or more consulted their doctor in a 2-week period, compared to 17 per cent of those aged 65–74 years and 11 per cent of those aged 15–44 years (Office of Population Censuses and Surveys, 1973). Access to social contacts and recreational facilities is also more important in old age as old people tend to be cut off from social contacts made at work and are more likely to be living alone. Loneliness is known to be a considerable problem among old people (Abrams, 1978a).

## MOBILITY AND ACTIVITY

In this section we will try to assess whether old people's need for activities are being met and whether any lack of these is due to mobility problems. It has been reported that the average number of journeys made declines steadily with age (Kutter, 1973, p. 252; Hopkin, Robson, and Town, 1978b, p. 13). This relationship is produced by intermediate variables rather than by age itself. As is shown in Table 11.3, age by itself appears to have a marked effect on the average number of journeys made; more so than the effect of household car ownership. However it has been shown that if journeys to and from work are excluded from this analysis, the difference between the age groups narrows considerably: considering those with no household car, people aged 17–64 made an average of 1.53 journeys per day, those aged 65 or more 1.34 journeys per day (Hopkin, Robson, and Town, 1978b, p. 3). In other words, much of the difference which

Table 11.3 Effect of age and household car ownership on number and length of journeys: England and Wales, 1975–76

| | Aged 17–64 | | Aged 65 or over | |
|---|---|---|---|---|
| | No car | Car-owner | No car | Car-owner |
| Average number of journeys per person per day | 2.33 | 2.90 | 1.49 | 1.87 |
| Percentage of journeys less than 1 mile long | 38 | 22 | 48 | 26 |

*Source*: Robson, 1978, p. 23.

might be attributed to age is due to retirement from work without taking up other activities. This supports the views of Kutter, who sees the life-cycle or age and sex roles as the primary variables in structuring activity and travel patterns, and who suggests that mobility affects only how the journey is made (Kutter, 1973). However, as Table 11.3 shows, the availability of a car does have an effect on the number of journeys made, and an even greater effect on length of journeys. A closer look at travel for different activities indicates some of the reasons for these changes.

Shopping is an essential journey purpose except for the small proportion of old people who are able to find someone else to do it for them. Shopping facilities are normally widely available in urban areas, even though there may be the penalties of higher prices and lack of choice in using local shops. The less mobile elderly usually cope but only by considerable adjustments to a normal shopping pattern. In one town it was found that 75 per cent of the retired had their main source of groceries within 0.8 km ($\frac{1}{2}$ mile), compared to only 61 per cent of all shoppers (Daws and Bruce, 1971). In another it was found that the more mobile old people (who drove and had no difficulty with walking) travelled an average of 1.3 km to shops, while the less mobile (who had no car and found difficulty with walking) travelled 1.0 km (Hopkin, Robson and Town, 1978b). So shopping activity does not change with age but the distance travelled to shops does change.

There are other essential activities which are less ubiquitous and therefore present fewer choices of location. A good example of these is medical facilities such as chemists' shops, doctors' surgeries, and hospitals. Journeys to these facilities are normally unavoidable and the penalties of declining mobility are increased effort and difficulty.

Social and recreational activity is desirable if not essential for the elderly, but with ageing there is a marked decline in travelling for these purposes as well as on the activities themselves (Hopkin, Robson and Town, 1978b, p.3; Chapin, 1974). The differences among the elderly are probably greater than would be found in younger age groups (Abrams, 1978b). The release from the constraints of time set by paid employment leads to diversity in their 'inessential' activities, and by no means always to routine of passive, home-based activities. Some spend considerable amounts of time on social and recreational activity outside the home. The variation in the use of free time is related to social class and is most pronounced among men. After the statutory retirement age of 65, men who have had white-collar jobs are more likely to continue to work than those who have had manual jobs. The former are also more likely to be involved in active, and less likely to have passive, leisure interests. Abrams cites some research which interviewed 152 retired teachers and 81 retired steelworkers in Europe and the United States and which was able to describe contrasting lifestyles. The most common was a *general slowing-down*, which showed no increase of replacement activities for work. Another common response was continued *interest in work*, either by maintaining the previous employment or in a new job; the other was involvement in *non-work activities* such as clubs, church, community or political activities. More than half the retired steel-workers had adopted the slowing-down style of life while only 15 per cent had continued to work or become involved in new social activities. Among retired teachers the position was very different, however, with 30 per cent having chosen to slow down, nearly one-quarter still working and nearly one-fifth having taken up new social activities.

Social class differences in adaptation to retirement may of course be due to mobility differences (especially car ownership levels) or to other factors. Abrams claims that working-class men may not have had the opportunity during working life to make the contacts and generate the interests that allow middle-class men to move into an active retirement, and they do not have the same opportunities to stay in paid employment, especially where the work is physically demanding. He goes on the suggest both that this may account for the fact that the average middle-class man outlives the average working-class man by nearly 10 years, and that in the future increased redundancies among middle-aged working-class men will increase the problem of forced inactivity in retirement.

The transition from middle age to old age is less abrupt for women. They usually continue to carry out household tasks but need to adjust to the increased presence in the home of their husband, and very often to the discontinuation of part-time work. Older women spend as much time as working-age women on housework but they experience a sharp reduction in social contacts (Abrams, 1978b).

Some research in France has examined in more detail class-based variations in response to retirement and their links with travel behaviour (Matalon and Averous, 1978). They showed that the apparent decline of travel with age is often accounted for by the failure to record short-distance journeys, and that a typical response to ageing is to make fewer journeys outside the immediate neighbourhood, and more within it, although there is much diversity and complexity in the response. As Matalon and Averous point out, this does not mean that all needs can be served within the neighbourhood. Open-ended discussions revealed that the use of increased free time depended greatly on the way of life before retirement, both at and away from work. If the pre-retirement lifestyle included activities that could be expanded after retirement, such as leisure interests or professional activities that could be used in another capacity, then retirement could be an opportunity to explore new possibilities. If, on the other hand, work was repetitive, and lacked initiative and interest, or if it was too tiring to allow other activities or any preparation for retirement, then few activities would be pursued after retirement and empty time would be merely passed away. Matalon and Averous found that if there were poor conditions before retirement such as repetitive work, no opportunity to organize one's own work, low position in the organizational hierarchy, or tiring work, then these were strongly linked to expressions of hopelessness and withdrawal in retirement (not being able to meet people to talk to, not feeling it worthwhile to make plans, not making an effort to be well-dressed, not being able to rely on other people, and feeling that events are too difficult to cope with). The effect of working conditions on activity patterns is in a sense stronger for those who have ceased work than for those still in employment. Paradoxically, their effect becomes more apparent when work has been left behind because time is less of a constraint.

## CONCLUSIONS AND IMPLICATIONS FOR POLICIES

Old age has become an important stage in the life-cycle. People are giving up full-time work at an earlier age and are living longer. It would seem important that this stage in the lifestyle is an active one, and that we should be concerned to promote the conditions which permit an active old age. Old age is a stage in the life-cycle where needs and abilities are different from earlier stages, and it is often found that these different needs and abilities are not very well catered for. Barker and Bury (1978) point out that old age is often regarded as a problem, with, for example, old people regarded as being similar to handicapped people. The help that they receive feels patronizing, whereas what they would like is not 'helping', but a recognition that their needs and abilities are different and planning to take into account these differences.

At present we are hampered in our study of old people's activities, needs, and abilities by rather crude data, which concentrate on easily observed features of behaviour and which force old people into our preconceived ideas about old age (Johnson, 1978). Johnson has therefore made a plea for more interviews which allow an old person to describe fully and to explain how they feel about ageing, what their aspirations are, and whether and how these aspirations are frustrated. This would help us in this case to see what part travel problems play in determining the activity patterns of old people.

An interdisciplinary approach is obviously required to this problem. The solutions lies as much with the geographer and planner as the gerontologist. Policy measures which could help old people to lead a more active life lie in a number of fields. The last section has shown that we need to improve middle-age life by creating less alienating work and making available more preparation for retirement. This might prevent people accepting inactivity as an appropriate image of old age. However if old people do start participating more in activities, it is likely that they will more often come up against the barriers that have been identified in this chapter. We need to promote policies that will increase people's accessibility to potential activities. There are a wide variety of types of policy that can be adopted to do this. Mobility can be facilitated in a number of ways, for example by a better pedestrian environment, through subsidies for bus or taxi travel, better bus services, assistance with maintaining a car, or by the provision of special bus services. Other policies need to be concerned with location. For example we could incorporate into planning policies an objective to ensure the provision and maintenance of localized facilities, or another to ensure that housing is built where people could easily reach facilities. Greater provision of mobile facilities could also be considered. Finally policy should tackle time constraints, either by adjusting opening hours or through careful revision of train and bus service times.

Only a few of these possibilities have been tried; mainly concessionary bus fares and special transport facilities. Many others have complications, but the principal barrier to their consideration seems to be that they rarely fit neatly into disciplinary, departmental, or institutional areas of concern. For example, a report by consultants to the National Bus Company on the future of rural bus services drew attention to the fact that no-one has responsibility for ensuring that public facilities are located where they can be reached by public transport (Peat, Marwick, Mitchell and Co., 1977). In the case of the health services it has been stated that 'the planning process does not incorporate any formal mechanism or procedure for ensuring that public facilities are located at sties which are more accessible to the public' (Johnson, 1977). The institutional barriers to altering timing and location in the private sector are probably much greater, but as the authors of the study of accessibility in East Anglia point out, these policies may be much more effective (Moseley *et al.*, 1977). They call for 'assessibility planning' by local authorities who would devise and evaluate plans to promote the accessibility to a range of facilities of different types of people in different locations. Local authorities are in a position to co-ordinate the various institutions which influence accessibility.

If such action is not taken the barriers to activity for old people will not be dismantled. Ageing will continue to cause activity rates to decline and involvement to decrease, and we will say that this is simply a result of old age; a voluntary withdrawal. This is until we come upon the barriers ourselves.

## REFERENCES


Abrams, M. (1978a). *Beyond Three-Score and Ten.* Age Concern England, Mitcham.

Abrams, M. (1978b). Time and the elderly. *New Society*, **46**, 685–6.

Ashford, N. and Holloway, F. M. (1970). *The Effect of Age on Urban Travel Behaviour.* Florida State University, Transportation Centre Research Report 1, Tallahassee.

Barker, J. and Bury, M. (1978). Mobility and the elderly: a community challenge. In Carver, V. and Liddiard, P. (eds), *An Ageing Population*, pp. 179–92. Hodder & Stoughton in association with the Open University Press, London.

Bradshaw, J. 1972). A taxonomy of social need. In McLachlan, G. (ed.), *Problems and Progress in Medical Care*, pp. 69–82. Oxford University Press, London.

Buchanan, J. and Chamberlain, M. A. (1978). Mobility of the disabled in an urban environment. In Ashford, N. and Bell, W. (eds), *Mobility for the Elderly and Handicapped*, pp. 239–42. Loughborough University of Technology, Loughborough.

Chapin, F. S. (1974). *Human Activity Patterns in the City; Things People Do in Space and Time*. Wiley, New York.

Chapin, F. S. and Hightower, H. C. (1965). Household activity patterns and land use. *Journal of American Institute of Planners*, **31**, 222–31.

Cumming, E. and Henry, W. E. (1961). *Growing Old: the Process of Disengagement*. Basic Books, New York.

Daws, L. F. and Bruce, A. J. (1971). *Shopping in Watford*. Building Research Station, Watford.

De Vise, P. (1971). Cook County Hospital: bulwark of Chicago's apartheid health system and prototype of the nation's public hospitals. *Antipode*, **3** (1), 9–20.

Foley, G. (1976). *The Energy Question*. Penguin, Harmondsworth.

Fowler, N. (1979). Interim road policy statement. *Transport Retort*, **3** (9), 4–5.

Hagerstrand, T. (1973). The domain of human geography. In Chorley, R. J. (ed.), *New Directions in Geography*. Methuen, London.

Hamer, M. (1976). *Getting Nowhere Fast*. Friends of the Earth, London.

Hamer, M. (1979). On space, time and transport. *Transport Retort*, **3** (7), 4–5.

Hanson, P. (1977). The activity patterns of elderly households. *Geografiska Annaler*, **59B**, 109–24.

Harris, A. I. (1971). *Handicapped and Impaired in Great Britain*. HMSO, London

Hillman, M. (1973). The social costs of hypermarket development. *Built Environment*, **2**, 88–91.

Hillman, M., Henderson, I., and Whalley, A. (1973). *Personal Mobility and Transport Policy*. Political and Economic Planning, Broadsheet 542, London.

Hillman, M., Henderson, I., and Whalley, A. (1976). *Transport Realities and Planning Policy*. Political and Economic Planning, Broadsheet 567, London.

Hillman, M. and Whalley, A. (1979). *Walking is Transport*. Policy Studies Institute, London.

Hopkin, J. M., Robson, P., and Town, S. W. (1978a). *The Mobility of Old People; a Study in Guildford*. Transport and Road Research Laboratory Report LR 850, Crowthorne.

Hopkin, J. M., Robson, P., and Town S. W. (1978b). *Transport and the Elderly: Requirements, Problems and Possible Solutions*. Transport and Road Research Laboratory Supplementary Report SR 419, Crowthorne.

Hunt, A. (1978). *The Elderly at Home*. HMSO, London.

Johnson, J. (1977). When a node is as good as a link in improving access. *Health and Social Services Journal*, **87**, 1374–5.

Kutter, E. (1973). A model for individual travel behaviour. *Urban Studies*, **10**, 235–58.

Markovitz, J. (1971). Transportation needs of the elderly. *Traffic Quarterly*, **25**, 237–53.

Matalon, B. and Averous, B. (1978). The mobility of elderly people: the influence of retirement and former life style. In Ashford, N. and Bell, W. (eds), *Mobility for the Elderly and Handicapped*, pp. 122–29. Loughborough University of Technology, Loughborough.

McCarthy, G. M. (1969). Multiple regression analysis of household trip generation—a critique. In Highway Research Board, *Transportation Planning Process*, pp. 31–43. Highway Research Report 297, Washington.

Mitchell, C. G. B. and Town, S. W. (1977). *Accessibility of Various Social Groups to Different Activities*. Transport and Road Research Laboratory Supplementary Report SR 258, Crowthorne.

Moseley, M. J., Harman, R. G., Coles, O. B., and Spencer, M. B. (1977). *Rural Transport and Accessibility*, vol. 1. Centre of East Anglian Studies, University of East Anglia, Norwich.

Office of Population Censuses and Surveys (1973). *The General Household Survey: Introductory Report*. HMSO, London.

Peat, Marwick, Mitchell and Co. (1977). *An Interim Report on Minimum Levels of Service for Rural Public Transport*. Report to the National Bus Company. Peat, Marwick, Mitchell and Co., London.

Rigby, J. P. (1977). *An Analysis of Travel Patterns Using the 1972/73 National Travel Survey*. Transport and Road Research Laboratory Report LR 790, Crowthorne.

Rigby, J. P. (1978). *Access to Hospitals: a Literature Review*. Transport and Road Research Laboratory Report LR 853, Crowthorne.

Robson, P. (1978). *Profiles of the Elderly: their Mobility and Transport*. Age Concern England, Mitcham.

Skelton, N. G. (1978). Understanding travel. In Ashford, N. and Bell, W. (eds), *Mobility for the Elderly and Handicapped*, pp. 106–13. Loughborough University of Technology, Loughborough.

Tyneside Passenger Transport Executive (1973). *A Plan for the People*. Tyneside Passenger Transport Executive, Newcastle.

Wachs, M. (1978). Lifestyles and changing transportation needs of the elderly in Los Angeles. In Ashford, N. and Bell, W. (eds), *Mobility for the Elderly and Handicapped*, pp. 130–9. Loughborough University of Technology, Loughborough.

Geographical Perspectives on the Elderly
Edited by A. M. Warnes


Chapter 12

# The activity patterns of elderly people in Swansea, South Wales, and South-East England

*Sheila M. Peace*

Our understanding of the social meaning of growing old depends for much of its theoretical development on the work of American social gerontologists. When seen from a behavioural geographical perspective, therefore, certain concepts hold precedence. This chapter examines whether the activity patterns of certain groups of elderly people are moulded by the environment in which they live. Thus, the setting for such a study demands a discussion of activity and environment as seen through the eyes of the gerontologist and the geographer alike.

The two major social gerontological theories of *activity* and *disengagement* have given rise to a great deal of debate both in the United States and more recently in Britain. The *activity theory* maintains that normal ageing involves the maintenance for as long as possible of the activities and attitudes of middle age, and that for those activities and roles which the individual is forced to give up, new substitutes should be found (Cavan, *et al.*, 1949). In contrast the *disengagement theory* describes normal ageing as the 'mutual withdrawal' or 'disengagement' between the ageing person and others in his or her social system, a withdrawal initiated by the individual himself, or by others in the system (Cumming and Henry, 1961). In short the theory emphasizes that accompanying the later stages of the ageing process is a physical, social, and psychological constriction of the life-space. This may be reflected in such terms or behaviour as alienation, dissatisfaction with life, withdrawal from social activities, a recognition of the need for reduced activities, and perhaps increased willingness to acknowledge the problems of the young as having greater priority.

Both theories are therefore concerned with activity, and proponents of either viewpoint have supported their position through empirical studies which show that their own theory of the ageing process is conducive to high morale and general satisfaction with life (Maddox and Eisdorfer, 1962; Maddox, 1963; Tallmer and Kutner, 1970). However, these particular sociological perspectives neglect the environmental factors which may influence, albeit indirectly, the social construction of old age, and it is the study of environment which provides the link between the geographer and the social gerontologist.

One can look at activity through the concepts of *activity* or *action space* and the notions of *revealed* and *repressed preference*. The action space of the individual has been defined by Wolpert as that area with which he has contact and within which his activities take place (Wolpert, 1965). The extent of this interaction is directly affected by an individual's access to environmental information. Thus, the degree to which an individual's behaviour in his action space reflects his objective depends upon his effectiveness in collecting and assimilating pertinent information. Perceptions and action spaces are to a degree individualistic, but, as noted by Horton and Reynolds (1969), there is reason to suggest that they are shared by groups of people, and that this homogeneity can be differentiated by stage in the life-cycle, position in social networks, and spatial location with respect to potential trip destinations.

Given the opportunity for certain courses of action, the individual can make a choice; that is he reveals a preference. However, the opportunities available are directly affected by socio-economic status, perception of the urban environment, length of residence, and other factors. Because of this Eyles (1970) suggests that a more important concept is that of repressed preference. He suggests that the concept of revealed preference is not enough, since if an individual does not have the opportunity to behave in a certain way then his preference is repressed. Eyles shows that repressed preferences may be representative of the poor, who constitute a distinctive culture within society. This study argues that the elderly also form a sub-group in society whose activities exemplify this concept. Obvious factors such as low income are common to both groups, but the elderly possess many other characteristics which identify them as a unique group (Figure 12.1). How society moulds this identity lies outside the scope of this paper, but is no less important and should always be borne in mind.

A preference for certain activities within the urban environment is determined, therefore, by the individual's position in the social and spatial structure; and is reflected in his image structure and in change over time. As a result of their decline in purchasing power, often coupled with declining physical and mental health, the elderly are forced to be dependent, and this dependency can be intensified by the environment in which they live.

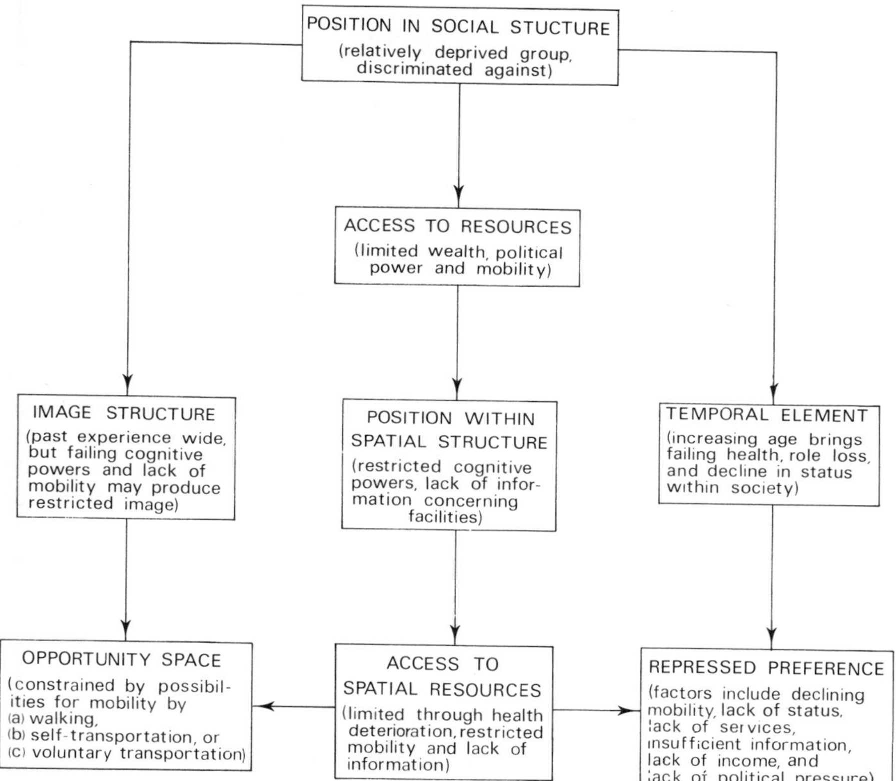


Figure 12.1 The concept of repressed preference. (*Source*: Peace (1977); after Eyles (1970) *Space, Territory and Conflict*, Geographical Paper 1, Dept of Geography, University of Reading.)

The concepts underlying repressed preference are similar to those put forward by those American gerontologists who sought to understand the ageing person's interaction with his environment within the ecological tradition. Lawton and Simon suggested the *environmental docility hypothesis* which states that

> there is a relationship between the state of the organism and its docility in the face of environmental restrictions . . . the more competent the organism—in terms of health, ego strength, social role performance, or cultural evolution—the less will be the proportion of variance in behaviour attributable to physical objects or conditions around him (Lawton and Simon, 1968, p. 108).

They argue that the decline in competence associated with the ageing process increases environmental dependence. Subsequent studies undertaken by Lawton and others have looked at the relationship between environment and morale, and give some positive evidence for the importance of environment within the social construction of old age (Lawton, 1970; Schooler, 1969).

On the other hand Bohland and Davis (1978, p. 1) argue that the evidence for environmental influence has been based on 'intuition, speculation and limited empirical evidence'. They stress the need to investigate how the neighbourhood sustains and diminishes the well-being of persons of all ages, and conclude that there is little difference between age groups in the construction of neighbourhood satisfaction.

The present study takes up a number of these interrelated issues within a British context. Given the importance placed upon activity in the social theories of old age, it asks: are there any relationships between activity and morale for elderly people living in different environmental settings? Do environmental influences have a direct effect upon activity patterns or are such patterns determined by the socio-economic characteristics of the individual? How do the activity patterns of elderly people living within an institutional setting differ from those living in the community, and to what extent do such residents interact with their local environment? The answers to such questions will help to explain whether the environment influences the activity patterns of elderly people or whether, as Lawton suggests, it is 'merely the screen against which the dynamic aspects of human behaviour are played' (Schooler, 1969, p.25).

## THE ELDERLY IN AN URBAN ENVIRONMENT

Data concerning elderly community residents were collected in a study of elderly people living in the city of Swansea, South Wales (Peace, 1977). Interviews were undertaken with 226 individuals over the age of 65 years who were living in five contrasting neighbourhoods within the city. Initial mapping from the 1971 census small area statistics of the distribution of the elderly revealed that they are over-represented in central and western parts of the city. Local concentrations occur in the higher status districts of Mumbles, Sketty, and Uplands; in the council estates of West Cross, Sketty Park, and Townhill; and in the older lower-status neighbourhoods of St Helens, Manselton, Brynhyfryd, Landore, Hafod and Morriston (Figure 12.2).

An area sampling procedure was followed in order to select five residential neighbourhoods in which to conduct the questionnaire survey. This procedure was guided by an initial analysis of the overall social geography of Swansea and by indicators which identified the local concentrations of the elderly. The five survey areas selected were:

(1) Mumbles/West Cross—an old fishing village which is now a tourist and retirement area. Parts of the West Cross council estate are also included.

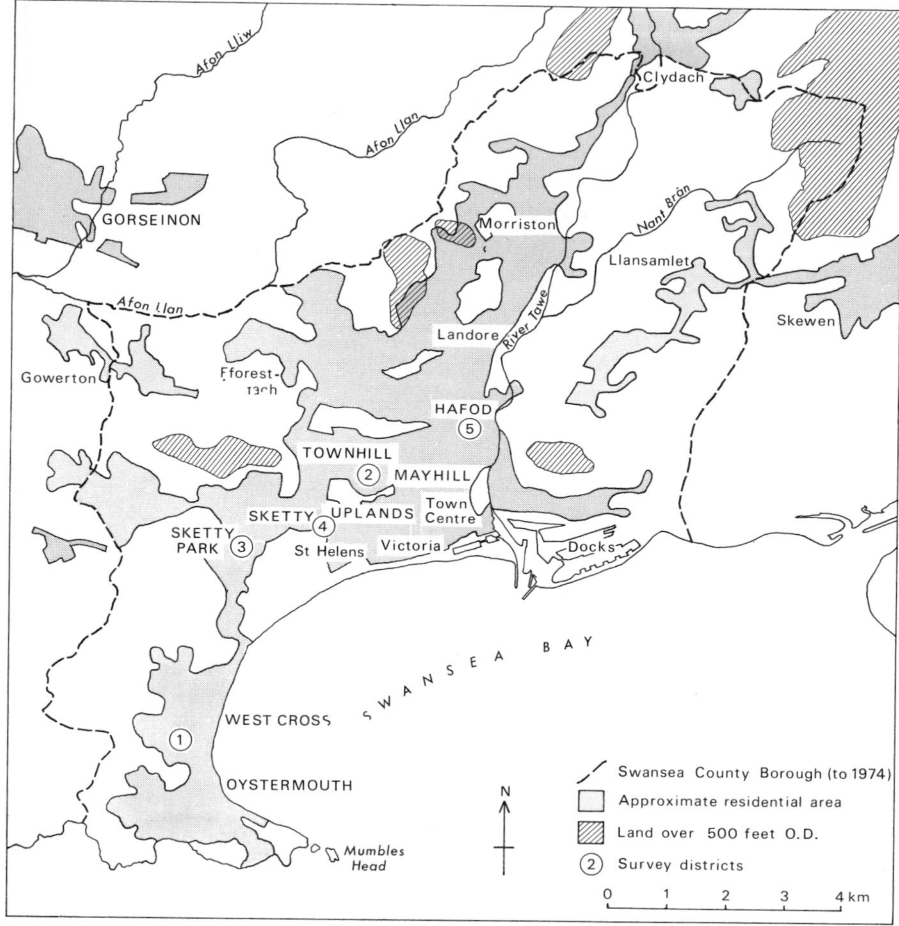


Figure 12.2 Swansea: built-up area and survey districts

(2) Townhill/Mayhill—an inter-war council estate severely run down in many streets.
(3) Sketty Park—a modern post-war council estate with many planned features such as single-person dwellings for the elderly.
(4) Sketty/Uplands—a predominantly middle-class, owner-occupied residential area.
(5) Hafod—a traditionally working-class valley community, dominated by terraced housing.

The interview covered the characteristics of the residential environment, details of activity patterns and social relationships, self-reported physical

Table 12.1 Personal characteristics of the sample by area: Swansea

| Characteristics and categories | Mumbles/ West Cross | Townhill/ Mayhill | Sketty Park | Sketty/ Uplands | Hafod |
|---|---|---|---|---|---|
| *Sex* | | | | | |
| Male | 19 | 23 | 28 | 31 | 38 |
| Female | 81 | 77 | 72 | 69 | 62 |
| *Age (years)* | | | | | |
| 60–70 | 27 | 23 | 32 | 24 | 33 |
| 71–80 | 56 | 59 | 53 | 62 | 39 |
| 81–90 | 13 | 18 | 15 | 14 | 25 |
| Over 90 | 4 | — | — | — | — |
| *Marital status* | | | | | |
| Married | 34 | 37 | 35 | 40 | 33 |
| Single | 8 | 2 | 15 | 17 | 6 |
| Widowed/divorced | 58 | 59 | 50 | 43 | 61 |
| Other | — | 2 | — | — | — |
| *Social class*[a] | | | | | |
| 1 | 15 | — | — | 17 | — |
| 2 | 38 | 11 | 28 | 45 | 2 |
| 3 | 35 | 48 | 43 | 29 | 52 |
| 4 | 12 | 32 | 27 | 7 | 44 |
| 5 | — | 9 | 2 | 2 | 2 |
| *Health*[b] | | | | | |
| Very poor | — | 2 | — | 2 | 2 |
| Poor | 6 | 36 | 25 | 12 | 29 |
| Fair | 46 | 39 | 40 | 53 | 50 |
| Good | 25 | 14 | 22 | 29 | 19 |
| Very good | 21 | 9 | 13 | 2 | — |
| Excellent | 2 | — | — | 2 | — |
| *Morale*[c] | | | | | |
| Low 0–3 | 2 | 7 | 7 | 2 | 4 |
| 4–6 | 40 | 54 | 48 | 55 | 52 |
| High 7–9 | 58 | 39 | 45 | 43 | 44 |
| Number of respondents | 48 | 44 | 40 | 42 | 52 |

Each figure records the percentage of the sample in the district in each category

[a]Social class uses the classification of the Registrar General into five classes.
[b]Health scores are based on self-assessment.
[c]Morale score is an index of three questions relating to loneliness, boredom and contentment. Max. score 9, Min. score 0.

health, and certain aspects of emotional well-being or morale (Table 12.1). Female respondents outnumber males in the sample and in all areas a high proportion are widowed. The Sketty/Uplands area stands out as having a higher proportion of married and single respondents.

Six factors of particular importance to the study require explanation. The measure of activity is termed *spatial mobility*. The Swansea study sought only to measure mobility outside the home, to give an indication of interaction with the external environment of the neighbourhood and its environs. For this reason the study is concerned with individual journeys and trips made *by* the respondent rather than journeys and trips made *to* the respondent by others. Thus one unit was scored for each journey made, whether per day or per week. Journeys included shopping visits, outings, visits to family and friends, attendance at meetings, and any other outside activities. No differentiation was made for the different durations of individual trips (Table 12.2).

Two measures concerning social interaction were also defined. The number of *social roles* which the individual possesses strongly affects his/her potential level of both social contact and spatial mobility. In this study nine major roles are distinguished which range from spouse to organization member, and respondents score one unit for each role. Each role offers a potential for interaction, and loss of role can lead to a depletion of potential activity. However, role substitution may occur, as in the case of the widowed respondent who takes on new organizational roles. The effects or role substitution in terms of psychological well-being are, however, beyond the subject of this account.

Social role directly affects *social contact*, the definition and measurement of which has concerned many writers in the field. Both Townsend (1957) and Tunstall (1966) assumed that most individuals would have a well-defined weekly routine of 'social contacts'. A contact was defined as 'a meeting with another person, usually pre-arranged or customary, at home or outside,

Table 12.2 The construction of the spatial mobility index: example of a widow living alone

| Travel activity | Score |
|---|---|
| Daily trips to local corner shops | 6 |
| Visits to neighbourhood shops (twice a week) | 2 |
| Visits to town centre (weekly) | 1 |
| Church attendance (weekly) | 1 |
| Visit to old people's club (weekly) | 1 |
| Weekly visits to each of her four sisters | 4 |
| Visits to a neighbour twice a week | 2 |
| Irregular visits (doctors, hospital, holidays and trips) averaged weekly | 1 |
| TOTAL | 18 |

which involves more than a casual exchange of greetings between, say, two neighbours in the street' (Townsend, 1957, p. 35). A similar scoring system was adopted in the present study and the average number of social contacts made per week was calculated for each individual. Although this system does not give any indication of intensity or duration of contact it does give a single measure of social interaction.

The fourth factor concerns the *health* of the respondent. Despite the problems of validity associated with purely attitudinal self-assessment, the Swansea study asked respondents to give a personal evaluation of their own state of health. The question asked was 'How is your health nowadays?' and responses were graded on a scale from 1 (very poor) to 5 (very good). This basic assessment was supplemented by questions concerning personal mobility.

As with the state of health, the *morale* of the individual figures strongly in much social gerontological research. Numerous measures of life satisfaction and psychological well-being exist, a number of which have been specifically designed for use with elderly people (Bradburn and Caplovitz, 1965; Lawton, 1975; Neugarten, Havighurst and Tobin, 1961). Such scales are concerned with enjoyment, involvement, boredom, day-to-day worries and fears, feelings about life accomplishments, unhappiness, and dissatisfaction. The Swansea study developed an index of morale based on questions relating to the three constructs of loneliness, boredom, and contentment.

Finally, of key importance, an *environmental index* was derived, the most complex of all the indices developed in the study. Guidelines were taken from the work of Lawton and Kleban (1971) and Schooler (1969, 1970), both of whom sought to distinguish an environmental factor applicable to the elderly and representative of the important conditions of the neighbourhoods in which they live. Thus three facets of environment were distinguished:

(1) the built physical environment—derived from questions relating to housing conditions and the attractiveness of the area;
(2) a subjective measure of attitude to the community, defined in terms of the degree of friendliness;
(3) the social environment—as defined by distance to and provision of local facilities and services (Peace, 1977).

These measures are in some way similar to Bohland and Davis's four dimensions of neighbourhood—neighbourliness, physical condition, convenience, and safety (Bohland and Davis, 1978).

## THE SPATIAL PATTERNS OF ACTIVITY OF THE ELDERLY IN SWANSEA

The survey focused upon lifestyles as revealed by spatial activity patterns outside the home. A number of commonly held travel preferences emerged for the elderly in Swansea. The importance of links with friends and neighbours was seen in all areas, such contacts being more frequent than those with family and kin. This does not mean that family and kinship do not form important sources of contact, but rather that the proximity of neighbours and friends in walking distance facilitates access. Essential trips, mainly for shopping and to medical facilities, were another substantial element of spatial activity, whilst discretionary trips, reported by most of the sample, were related to a variety of special interests such as the church, a social club, or some form of recreation. All activities through necessity must either be within walking distance or reached via informal (family, relatives, friends), voluntary (organized) or public transport. Within each area sample, a classification of respondents in terms of potential mobility was possible (i.e. unlimited, limited due to disability, and housebound). When comparing the type of transport used for activity with the potential for mobility it was interesting that even of those with 'unlimited mobility', very few had access to their own transport, and the majority either walked or relied on public transport.

## Family and friends

Of the total sample between 30 and 40 per cent in each area did not visit their children. Most visits to children were made in Townhill/Mayhill and Hafod, least in Mumbles/West Cross. The pattern of visiting varied but the majority were made weekly and usually involved the elderly person being collected by a son or daughter. Thus without assistance most waited to be visited. Only in Sketty/Uplands, one of the higher-status areas, was there a pronounced pattern of visiting two or three times a year; trips were often beyond Wales and give an indication of the occupational mobility of this type of family. Whereas family may be dispersed, friends are more likely to be local. Visits to friends and neighbours were more frequent than to family and kin; usually on at least a weekly basis. The importance of neighbouring to the elderly person was particularly strong, especially where family and friends did not live in the immediate vicinity.

## Shopping patterns

Shopping patterns were classified into three levels which reflected the retail hierarchy of local stores, neighbourhood centres, and the town centre. Local shopping patterns clearly reflected the availability and proximity of the different levels, and the rates of shopping activity could be systematically linked with level of provision within the areas (Figure 12.3). In Mumbles/West Cross and Hafod, for example, there were many local shops within walking distance and these were well used, despite their drawbacks of higher prices.

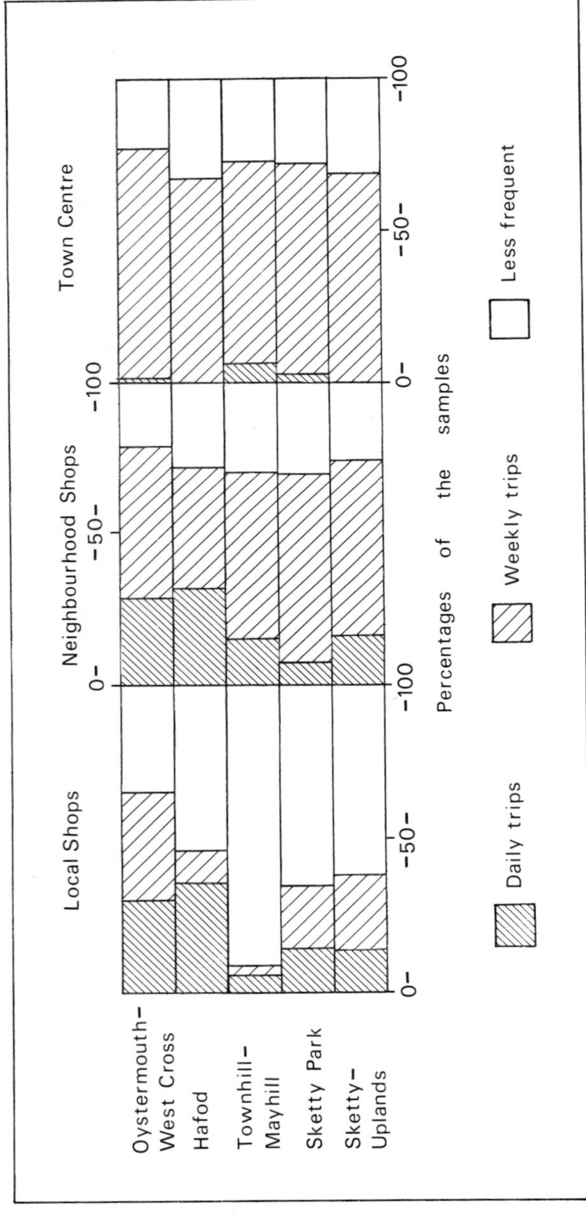


Figure 12.3 Swansea: aspects of the elderly's shopping by district of the town

Neighbourhood shops in these areas were observed to play an important role in the lifestyle of the elderly both for historical and locational reasons. In every survey area there was a neighbourhood centre no further than $\frac{1}{2}$ mile from any respondent but there were marked variations in their use. Frequency of neighbourhood shopping was greatest in Mumbles/West Cross and Hafod. In the former the relative remoteness from the town centre appeared to intensify the use of local facilities, whereas in the latter a strong level of allegiance to local traders was apparent. Town-centre trips were infrequent and generally irregular. Over one-quarter of all respondents never went to the town centre; these were in most cases people classed as housebound or possessing limited mobility. Of the remainder only 40 per cent made the journey weekly or more than weekly, and in the majority of cases (80 per cent) respondents relied upon the local bus service for transport. Local travel costs were clearly an important factor in relation to frequency of travel. Trips to the town centre were most infrequent from Mumbles/West Cross and Sketty Park, reflecting their accessibility. Hafod is the nearest survey area to the centre, though in fact respondents tended to use the older part of the centre rather than its modern extension, reflecting a maintenance of traditional shopping patterns. Also in Hafod, the greater availability of local family support made it more common for children to take over the shopping needs of the elderly.

## Other activities

Over a range of other activities there were considerable variations in levels of mobility amongst the areas. In the Mumbles/West Cross and Sketty/Uplands areas levels of activity were relatively high with 25–50 per cent of respondents both using several local facilities such as the library and church and participating in organizations and meetings. By contrast the Townhill/Mayhill estate possessed the least active residents in terms of these activities; only 7 per cent regularly use the library and only 9 per cent are church-goers. This low level of use is partly explained by the fact that both facilities were relatively inaccessible to at least half of the sample in this area. Finally, in Sketty Park and Hafod only the old age pensioners' clubs attracted any members and in both cases a convenient location facilitated access. In summary, a number of differences were noted between the areas, all of which offered a whole range of activities outside the home, although it must be stressed that overall the general level of activity was low.

## Activity patterns of elderly sub-groups

Apart from the differences in type of activity between areas, a number of sociodemographic factors were seen to have a direct effect on activity patterns. These included age, sex, marital status, health, social class, and the degree of social role and social contact. The age of the elderly respondent was one clear basis for variation and an inverse relationship was found between age and level of mobility for the sample as a whole ($r = -0.25$, sig. 0.001) and for each district except Sketty Park. Differences in sex did not appear to have any significant effect upon mobility in any of the areas. Indeed the effect of role loss experienced by widows and widowers alike generates new patterns of activity.

Marital status had variable effects upon mobility. The highest rates of participation occurred among the widowed respondents, and is attributable to their new roles which substitute for those recently lost; married respondents were relatively less active while single respondents, a small element in the overall sample, were the most immobile of all. The close expected relationship with health was confirmed, with activity decreasing with declining health ($r = 0.28$, sig. 0.001). This result provides some validation of the accuracy of the self-reported health index. There was also a consistent and direct relationship between the degree of morale and the level of spatial activity ($r = 0.23$, sig. 0.001).

Although there was little difference among the social classes in the overall level of mobility, each tended to pursue different activities. Whereas the visiting patterns of the lower social classes included not only friends and relatives but also the local old age pensioner clubs, those of the middle class included not only friends and relatives but also a wider variety of organizations and interests. It seems clear that the marked differences in behaviour due to social class, which have frequently been noted for the population as a whole (Carey and Mapes, 1972) remain but in a 'diluted' form amongst the elderly. Thus the general hypothesis suggested by Smith Blau that

> there is reason to suggest that the social life of working class women is largely visits to relatives and some joint participation with her spouse in activities. The social life of the woman in higher classes, on the other hand, is more likely to include extensive association with other women—due to organisational activities and social pastimes' (Smith Blau, 1961, p. 435).

can be supported from the Swansea study.

Two remaining variables were seen to have particular effect on the generation of activity patterns amongst the elderly sample. These were social role and social contact. Marital status has the most profound affect on role formation, and married respondents, followed by widowed respondents, possessed the greatest number of social roles. The most active elderly respondents were those with the greatest diversity of social role, those who led an active life as parent and grandparent, whilst performing other roles such as church-goer or organization member.

Social role and social contact are clearly interdependent, although some roles generate more contacts than others. However, it is important to remember that the respondent need not be mobile in order to engage in social contact.

Social contacts include visits made to an elderly person within his or her own home; mobility only increases the opportunity for visiting and making contact outside the home environment. Both female and married respondents possessed the highest degree of social contact both inside and outside the household. No relationship was seen between age and degree of contact.

However, a number of differences were noted between the various survey areas. In Mumbles/West Cross single respondents possessed the highest number of social contacts, and widows and widowers least. This was an unusual pattern which may have been due to the number of professional single people in this area who were active in community life. In Townhill/Mayhill high social contact scores for married respondents indicated the degree of interaction amongst families on a local authority estate. In contrast, married respondents in Sketty/Uplands had low social contact scores.

## THE EFFECTS OF ENVIRONMENT UPON ACTIVITY PATTERNS

The elements of the environmental factor—housing conditions, attractiveness, friendliness, level of service provision, and distance to facilities—have already been described. They form the basis of the environmental influence which in this study denotes both the built environment and the social milieu. Table 12.3 shows the various environmental components of each area within the Swansea study. The picturesque former fishing village of the Mumbles, and its neighbouring area West Cross, possessed the highest environmental score. Although predominantly a middle-class area with a retirement function, the area still retains much of its 'village' life which, together with good local facilities, account for its high overall score.

The study of activity patterns revealed that distance was a major constraint on mobility especially as the majority of respondents walked to their destination. A quarter of a mile was seen to be a critical distance for elderly respondents on foot. In Mumbles West Cross all facilities and services studied were $\frac{1}{4}$–$\frac{1}{2}$ mile away from all respondents. This was not the case in any other area, so some respondents had to travel further. This was particularly true of the Townhill/Mayhill estate where services were located eccentrically to much of the estate, and also of Hafod where certain local services were lacking, e.g. a chemist. The trip from Hafod to the adjacent town centre was too difficult for many respondents who therefore had to rely on relatives and friends.

Because of the various problems of access and provision of services, a direct relationship between the 'social environmental factor' and mobility was revealed ($\chi^2 = 31.3$, df $= 9$, sig. 0.001) indicating that increased distance to facilities and lack of vital services affects activity patterns. However, this relationship was stronger in some areas than in others. Townhill/Mayhill showed the highest degree of correlation due to the poor siting of facilities to one side of the council estate ($r = 0.46$, sig. 0.001).

Table 12.3 Spatial mobility and the environmental factor among the districts in Swansea

| Districts and factors | Minimum | Maximum | Mean |
|---|---|---|---|
| *Mumbles/West Cross* | | | |
| Spatial mobility | 0 | 17 | 8.2 |
| Social environmental factor | 36 | 67 | 57.3 |
| Community attitude factor | 3 | 5 | 4.6 |
| Physical environmental factor | 10 | 24 | 17.8 |
| Environmental factor | 57 | 92 | 79.7 |
| *Townhill/Mayhill* | | | |
| Spatial mobility | 0 | 13 | 5.9 |
| Social environmental factor | 37 | 60 | 52.7 |
| Community attitude factor | 2 | 5 | 3.7 |
| Physical environmental factor | 9 | 19 | 13.5 |
| Environmental factor | 50 | 80 | 69.9 |
| *Sketty Park* | | | |
| Spatial mobility | 0 | 15 | 7.0 |
| Social environmental factor | 36 | 61 | 52.2 |
| Community attitude factor | 2 | 5 | 4.0 |
| Physical environmental factor | 11 | 20 | 16.4 |
| Environmental factor | 53 | 86 | 72.6 |
| *Uplands* | | | |
| Spatial mobility | 0 | 14 | 7.3 |
| Social environmental factor | 44 | 68 | 52.9 |
| Community attitude factor | 2 | 5 | 3.6 |
| Physical environmental factor | 14 | 23 | 17.6 |
| Environmental factor | 66 | 93 | 74.1 |
| *Hafod* | | | |
| Spatial mobility | 0 | 23 | 9.6 |
| Social environmental factor | 27 | 41 | 33.6 |
| Community attitude factor | 3 | 5 | 4.5 |
| Physical environmental factor | 9 | 15 | 13.0 |
| Environmental factor | 43 | 58 | 51.1 |
| *Extreme values (all districts)* | | | |
| Social environmental factor | 0 | 71 | |
| Community attitude factor | 0 | 5 | |
| Physical environmental factor | 0 | 25 | |
| Environmental factor | 0 | 101 | |

The factor relating to the built physical environment was concerned with the state of repair and attractiveness in terms of architectural design, layout, and the maintenance of the area. In terms of the overall sample little relationship was seen between the physical environmental factor and activity patterns. However, a relationship was noted in Sketty Park ($r = 0.35$, sig. 0.01). The relative newness of the Sketty Park estate with its planned facilities for the elderly, e.g. single-person flats and local community centre, shows how the built environment can be influential in fostering the development of the social system. In other areas the advantages and disadvantages of the physical environment have been overshadowed by the importance of established social networks, even though individual cases of hardship were noted, e.g. in Hafod the siting of a community centre at the top of a slope with a steep gradient prevented many respondents from using this facility.

The final aspect of the environmental factor concerned the degree of friendliness within the neighbourhood, which to some extent gives an indication of how safe a person feels within his or her environment. Indeed, some relationship was seen between this 'community attitude factor' and spatial mobility ($r = 0.29$, sig. 0.001). This relationship was most intense on the two council estates, Townhill/Mayhill and Sketty Park, and suggests that activity patterns amongst the elderly are more likely to be affected by attitude to community in lower rather than higher status areas.

When all scores were combined to form the 'environmental factor', environmental influence in relation to activity diminishes, and little relationship is seen with respect to the overall sample. However, there is some evidence to support the initial hypothesis that environmental influences have an effect on the activity patterns of the elderly, and the study has demonstrated how different dimensions of environment can be influential.

## THE ACTIVITY PATTERNS OF THE ELDERLY IN RESIDENTIAL CARE

Community integration has up to now been a basic aim of all planning policies concerned with residential homes for elderly people. Indeed, the Department of Health and Social Security's (DHSS) advice for the siting of homes states that 'a home should serve and be planned to form part of its neighbourhood so that it becomes accepted as a participating element in the local community' (DHSS, 1973, p. 2).

The ideology behind such planned accommodation is one of integration with the local neighbourhood; but just how far do residents interact with their immediate surroundings? In looking at the activity patterns of elderly residents in residential homes, two samples will be discussed. Firstly, a sample of 47 elderly respondents living in local authority old people's homes in Swansea, South Wales (Peace, 1977), and secondly, a sample of 155 elderly respondents also living in local authority accommodation in the South East of England (Peace, Hall and Hamblin, 1979). The first sample was interviewed as part of the larger study already discussed, whilst the second formed the basis of a feasibility study of 'The Quality of Life of the Elderly in Residential Care', carried out for the Personal Social Services Council in 1978–79.

Some basic characteristic of the two samples are given in Table 12.4 and figures for the Swansea community sample are included for comparison. A number of factors distinguish those elderly people living in residential accommodation from those living in the community. Respondents were older than those in the community, and there was a significant difference between the two Swansea samples ($\chi^2 = 19.97$, df = 6, sig. 0.01). A higher percentage were either widowed or single, and this is an important factor when considering the potential for social contact. Indeed in many cases admission to a residential home had been precipitated by a combination of failing health and the fact that they were living alone. The move into care often meant a move away from their home area. For many of the respondents in both residential samples, the home they were now living in was not situated in the area in which they had lived all their lives; they therefore had few contacts locally, and were less likely to keep up any form of organised activity.

Table 12.4 Personal characteristics of both residential and community samples: Swansea and South-East England, 1976-8 (percentages)

| | Elderly in care, Swansea, 1976 | Elderly in care, South-East England, 1978 | Elderly in community, Swansea, 1976 |
|---|---|---|---|
| *Sex* | | | |
| Male | 38 | 48[a] | 28 |
| Female | 62 | 52 | 72 |
| *Marital status* | | | |
| Married | 0 | 6 | 35 |
| Widowed | 68 | 60 | 55 |
| Single/Divorced | 28 | 24 | 9 |
| Other | 4 | 6 | 1 |
| Not available | 0 | 4 | 0 |
| *Age (years)* | | | |
| 66–70 | 8 | | 22 |
| 71–75 | 23 | Average age, 80 years | 30 |
| 76–80 | 21 | Males, 79 years | 23 |
| Over 80 | 43 | Females, 82 years | 17 |
| Over 90 | 2 | | 2 |
| Not available | 3 | | 6 |
| *Social class* | | | |
| 1 | 8 | | 6 |
| 2 | 19 | | 24 |
| 3 | 21 | Information not comparable | 42 |
| 4 | 43 | | 25 |
| 5 | 9 | | 3 |

[a] Males over-sampled for statistical purposes.

So what kinds of activity patterns are typical of those in residential care? The characteristics described above do not bode well for continued interaction within the local community and indeed an immediately striking finding is the lack of any activity outside the home environment. There was a significant difference in terms of spatial mobility between the two Swansea samples ($\chi^2 = 27.0$, df $= 3$, sig. 0.001). Apart from those factors already discussed a partial explanation is that in general residents in care are mentally and physically more frail. Yet the respondents' subjective views of health differed little between the samples, with residents actually showing a more favourable view of their own health (Table 12.5). Lack of activity must therefore be explained by something other than ill health, and in many cases the problem lies in the lack of opportunities for activity outside the home.

A large number of basic activities are no longer necessary for those in residential accommodation. Shopping becomes a special occasion, nurtured by the 'pocket-money' system which is run in many homes. Medical visits, with the exception of hospital visits, cease to exist as all medical attention is taken care of in the home. Church services are often a regular part of home life, and facilities such as a library are usually provided. In Swansea 19 per cent of the community sample made use of library facilities whilst none of the residential sample showed this type of activity pattern.

Social interaction in terms of visits to family and friends outside the home is also at a low level. Of those in the community 60–70 per cent visited their children, however infrequently, but only 30 per cent did so in the Swansea residential sample. In terms of friends this figure falls to 24 per cent. This pattern reflects the greater number of single and widowed respondents, the lack of attachment between family members, the death of friends, and the increased distance to family and relatives. When visiting is no longer a case of just walking down the road, the elderly person waits to be visited.

This lack of any form of outside activity was confirmed by the more recent study in South-East England. Respondents were asked to state whether they took part in several different indoor and outdoor activities, and in reply to the

Table 12.5 Health scores: Swansea and South-East England 1976-8 (percentages)

| | Elderly in care, Swansea, 1976 | Elderly in care, South-East England, 1978 | Elderly in community, Swansea, 1976 |
|---|---|---|---|
| Very poor | 0 | 1 | 1 |
| Poor | 6 | 5 | 22 |
| Fair | 38 | 30 | 46 |
| Good | 43 | 35 | 22 |
| Very good | 13 | 23 | 9 |
| Excellent | 0 | 0 | 1 |
| Not available | 0 | 6 | 0 |

outdoor activities there was a resounding 80 per cent 'No'. Of the indoor activities, passive pastimes such as watching television, listening to the radio, and reading proved most popular, and organized indoor activities were far less popular. In order to assess the life satisfaction of respondents, Bradburn's Affect Balance Scale—a measure of psychological well-being—was included in the questionnaire (Bradburn and Caplovitz, 1965). The positive relationship that was found between activity and psychological well-being (indoor activity $r = 0.33$, sig. 0.001; overall activity $r = 0.37$, sig. 0.001) gives some support for the activity theory of ageing.

Whether the lives of residents in residential accommodation would be enhanced if they made more use of the neighbourhood in which they live, and how this could be achieved, should be more widely considered. The lack of activity outside the homes is a striking finding from the survey, and an initial subjective reaction is that it must severely reduce the quality of the residents' lives. The degree of segregation of residential accommodation for the elderly from the wider community should not be accepted as inevitable, as a manifestation of preference, or as independent from the design, management, and organization of other residential schemes.

## CONCLUSIONS

One of the initial emphases of this paper was that the elderly as a relatively deprived group within society are forced into a situation of 'repressed preference' whereby their choices concerning daily living are constrained and they are made ultimately to feel dependent. Dependence in this study was viewed in relation to environment, and was discussed with respect to the individual's level of mobility within his/her environment.

Initially factors other than environment were discussed. In relation to levels of spatial mobility amongst the elderly it is a clear finding that the health of the individual, which is closely related to age, is the most pervasive influence. However, given this influence, other factors such as marital status and social class are relevant to an understanding of mobility patterns. In the community sample, widowed respondents were the most active, whilst married respondents were more content to centre activity around the family unit, and the single were the least mobile. Social class affected the type of activity in that the higher status elderly were more likely than those in lower status groups to travel further though less frequently to visit their relatives and to participate in a wider range of social activities.

Environment can be seen as just another factor which has a direct influence on activity patterns. However, whereas social class and marital status affect individuals in different ways, environment, like health, is all-pervading. Declining health means that a large number of elderly people are forced to become more dependent on their local environment. Yet older people, who are no longer in a position to exercise a wide choice, are commonly constricted by environments which no longer match their needs. For all groups in this study distance was found to be a major constraint, and the limits of personal mobility were critical. Walking was the principal means of travel yet few could walk more than $\frac{1}{2}$ mile. The problem of access is most serious with regard to medical services. Community facilities were used in inverse proportion to the distance individuals were from them, and organized transport is clearly the necessary complement of organized facilities. The prohibitive cost of local transport also produced increased reliance on the local area as Golant (1972) and Seymour (1973) found in Canadian cities.

This study has also shown evidence of the extent to which planned environments with special facilities for elderly people affect mobility patterns, and the consequences of the poor planning of service locations. All the factors add support to Lawton's environmental docility hypothesis and the conclusions of other authors (Lawton and Simon, 1968; Schooler, 1969). Indeed, the environment was by no means found to be merely a 'screen against which the dynamic aspects of human behaviour are played' (Schooler, 1969, p. 25). Increased dependence on a local environment which fails to meet the needs of the elderly increases deprivation.

The interrelations between morale, mobility, and environment are therefore important. This study has shown that a positive relationship exists between morale and mobility/activity both in the community and for those in residential care, and therefore offers support for the activity theory of ageing. However, as environmental factors are also found to influence activity, a greater emphasis is needed on the interrelationship between activity and/or disengagement and life satisfaction with respect to a number of controlling factors such as environment. Theories of ageing also restrict themselves to a study of the elderly, and if, as Bohland and Davis (1978) have shown, environmental factors have an important bearing on the life satisfaction of all age groups, then perhaps a longitudinal approach to the social construction of old age would be especially productive.

The greater the decline in mobility among the elderly the greater the dependence upon domiciliary and residential care. The influence of environmental factors must therefore become an important dimension in any policy which encourages elderly people to live in the community as long as possible. The degree to which the local statutory, voluntary, and informal care facilities and services can meet the needs of an elderly person is directly related to how long the individual can remain living in the community. Thus to pursue a policy of community care there is a need to maintain the system of social contacts within which the elderly person is placed, and to provide easily accessible services and facilities within the immediate neighbourhood environment. The elderly, though often labelled as a homogeneous group, are as heterogeneous as any other age group, and because of this the local environment must be seen as a dynamic entity able to cope with the needs of all its members.

## REFERENCES

Bohland, J. R. and Davis, L. (1978). Sources of residential satisfaction amongst the elderly: an age comparative study. Unpublished paper, Department of Geography, University of Oklahoma, Norman, Oklahoma.

Bradburn, N. M. and Caplovitz, D. (1965). *Reports on Happiness: a Pilot Study of Behaviour Related to Mental Health.* Aldine, Chicago.

Carey, L. and Mapes, R. (1972). *The Sociology of Planning.* Batsford, London.

Cavan, R. S., Burgess, E. W., Havighurst, R. J. and Goldhammer, H. (1949). *Personal Adjustment in Old Age.* Science Research Associates, Chicago.

Cumming, E. and Henry, W. E. (1961). *Growing Old.* Basic Books, New York.

Department of Health and Social Security and Welsh Office (1973). *Residential Care for Elderly People.* Local Authority Building Note 2. HMSO, London.

Eyles, J. (1970). *Space, Territory and Conflict.* University of Reading, Department of Geography, Geographical Papers No. 1, Reading.

Golant, S. M. (1972). *The Residential Location and Spatial Behaviour of the Elderly.* University of Chicago, Department of Geography, Research Paper No. 143, Chicago.

Horton, F. E. and Reynolds, D. R. (1969). An investigation of individual action spaces: a progress report. *Proceedings, Association of American Geographers*, **1**, 70–5.

Lawton, M. P. (1970). Ecology and ageing. In Pastalan, L. A. and Carson, D. H. (eds), *Spatial Behaviour of Older People*, pp. 40–67. University of Michigan, Ann Arbor.

Lawton, M. P. (1975). The Philadelphia Geriatric Centre morale scale: a revision. *Journal of Gerontology*, **30**, 85–9.

Lawton, M. P. and Kleban, M. H. (1971). The aged resident in the inner city. *The Gerontologist*, **2**, 277–83.

Lawton, M. P. and Simon, B. (1968). The ecology of social relationships in housing for the elderly. *The Gerontologist*, **8**, 108–15.

Maddox, G. (1963). Activity and morale—a longitudinal study of selected elderly subjects. *Social Forces*, **42**, 195–204.

Maddox, G. and Eisdorfer, C. (1962). Some correlates of activity and morale among the elderly. *Social Forces*, **60**, 254–60.

Neugarten, B. L., Havighurst, R. J. and Tobin, S. S. (1961). Measurement of life satisfaction. *Journal of Gerontology*, **16**, 134–43.

Peace, S. M. (1977). The Elderly in an Urban Environment. Unpublished PhD Thesis. University of Wales.

Peace, S. M., Hall, J. F. and Hamblin, G. (1979). *The Quality of Life of the Elderly in Residential Care.* Polytechnic of North London, Survey Research Unit, Research Report No. 1, London.

Schooler, K. K. (1969). The relationship between social interaction and morale of the elderly as a function of environmental characteristics. *The Gerontologist*, **9**, 25–9.

Schooler, K. K. (1970). Effect of environment on morale. *The Gerontologist*, **10**, 194–7.

Seymour, L. (1973). Social Interaction of Senior Citizens in St. Mary's, Ontario. Unpublished MA thesis, University of Western Ontario, Ontario.

Smith Blau, Z. (1961). Structural constraints on friendships in old age. *American Sociological Review*, **26**, 429–39.

Tallmer, M. and Kutner, B. (1970). Desengagement and morale. *The Gerontologist*, **10**, 317–20.

Townsend, P. (1957). *The Family Life of Old People*. Routledge & Kegan Paul, London.

Tunstall, J. (1966). *Old and Alone*. Routledge & Kegan Paul, London.

Wolpert, J. (1965). Behavioural aspects of the decision to migrate. *Papers and Proceedings of the Regional Science Association*, **15**, 159–69.

Geographical Perspectives on the Elderly
Edited by A. M. Warnes


## Chapter 13

# Transport policies and the elderly

*Nicki Skelton*

If one defines 'travel' as personal movements from one place to another, then virtually everyone travels, including the elderly, One may ask, then, how the elderly differ with respect to travelling, and whether transport policies do, could, or should discriminate in their favour. Patterns of land-use and transport systems, and people's expectations from them, evolve continuously. Most people have 'reasonable' access to opportunities for at least those activities that are considered essential but some are clearly less fortunate. In Britain these are generally people without regular access to a car and for whom public transport is unavailable, inaccessible, or prohibitively expensive, including many people in rural areas, many physically handicapped, and, to some extent, those with low incomes.

During the last decade there have been increases both in the awareness of personal transport problems and in practical measures taken on behalf of those recognized as transport-disadvantaged. In Britain the work of Hillman, Henderson, and Whalley (1973) highlighted the fallacy that the majority have independent access to cars. They focused on the roles of walking and bus use, and on the constraints and problems of people with only limited access to cars. The elderly were one group of a number that they considered in this way, the others being children, teenagers, and mothers with pre-school children.

Since then there has been widespread recognition of the transport disadvantages of the elderly—to the point, indeed, where it has been assumed that all the elderly have problems, and that the only people with problems are elderly—both of which are manifestly untrue. However, taken as a group the elderly do have a number of characteristics which indicate potential difficulties with travel. In particular, the 'typical' elderly person has a low income, and is less physically able than younger people. It is difficult to determine the proportion of the elderly whose mobility is limited by health, since it depends heavily on the definitions used: estimates have been 20 per cent (Wachs and Blanchard, 1975), 41 per cent (Office of Population Censuses and Surveys, 1973), and even higher (Skelton, 1978). Under any definition, handicap increases with age, as decreasing income and declining abilities lead to low levels of car ownership. Many of the current older generation do not hold a driving licence since, when they were younger, car ownership was very much a luxury.

The ingredients are present, therefore, for many elderly people to be considered transport-disadvantaged. Comparison of the travel patterns of elderly and younger people shows, too, that the elderly travel less frequently and over shorter distances than younger people. But caution must be exercised before concluding that the elderly's mobility limitations are the main direct cause of their lower propensity to travel. A number of other factors may also be at work. For example, in many cases those things that limit mobility—low income, poor health—are likely also to limit the willingness or ability to engage in activities, and a lower propensity to engage in activities will be reflected in less travel. The validity of direct comparisons between the elderly and younger people is itself dubious, because of the great differences in their lifestyles, reflecting both the ageing process and the conditions and opportunities experienced when each generation's basic activity and travel habits were being shaped.

Nevertheless, the difficulties which elderly people do experience with the transport system must tend to limit their choice of activities, sometimes drastically. Transport policies can sometimes alleviate this situation; but they are not always the most appropriate solution. In many cases more thought also needs to be given to planning policies (Hillman, Henderson and Whalley,1976); while in others, needs can best be met by taking facilities to a person, rather than *vice versa* (e.g. Meals On Wheels, mobile libraries). In the majority of cases, particularly in the shorter term, transport policies can increase or prolong people's ability to live independently and to get themselves to places and facilities. This also accommodates one of the less understood benefits from travel—satisfaction of the need just to get out, sometimes to get away from the restrictions of four walls, to have a change of scene and see what else is happening in the world.

Although the 'average' elderly person may have relative disadvantages with respect to transport, the elderly are a large and diverse section of the population and the ranges of their locations, attributes, preferences, and requirements are nearly as broad of those of the whole population. So almost all policies relating to the transport of people have some impact on the elderly. Most policies relate to a specific mode of transport or situation, and as such may have a greater or lesser effect on the elderly as a group, in proportion to their use of that mode or participation in that situation. In addition, some policies (such as the provision of some concessionary fares schemes) are aimed directly and exclusively at the elderly. Others, for example the provision of social services transport, have very specific aims and cater for a tightly defined clientele; the majority of the elderly may be ineligible for such services, but elderly people may nevertheless comprise the bulk of clients. This chapter provides a brief review of some of the most important transport policy issues for the elderly in Britain.

## POLICIES FOR THE OLDER PEDESTRIAN

Nearly all elderly people get about on foot to some extent. Defining a trip as a one-way movement from one location to another for one main purpose, according to the 1972/73 National Travel Survey (conducted by the Department of the Environment), more than half of all elderly people's trips are made on foot. Walking is of similar importance to other members of the population, and yet policies for the pedestrian of any age were conspicuously absent from the (previous) Government's Transport Policy Green Paper (Department of the Environment, 1976), its White Paper (Department of Transport, 1977) and the 1978 Transport Act. This would seem to result from a lack of recognition of the importance of walking, rather than the lack of scope for improvement. For walking to be an effective mode of transport requires proximate facilities, the provision of adequate pathways, and suitable arrangements for the pedestrian to cross intersecting roads.

That walking is so common indicates that in many situations the requirements of the pedestrian are met adequately. Yet many problems have been identified, such as those associated with the trends towards lower housing densities, for new housing estates to have few or no communal facilities, and towards a greater concentration of shops and medical facilities. All tend to increase the distance between homes and the location of facilities and so reduce the possibilities for travel on foot.

Many elderly people are as able to walk as the average member of the population, and there are octogenarians who think nothing of walking 5 miles. But increasing age is associated with many physical and psychological changes which increase the difficulties associated with walking—reduced agility, strength and stamina; greater frailty; higher probability of disabilities such as rheumatism, arthritis, or heart disease; reductions in the acuity of vision and hearing; deteriorating judgement of traffic speeds, and increased reaction times; increasing difficulty in adapting to changes in road layout or traffic management measures (traffic lights, pedestrian crossings); increasing fear of traffic or personal attack; and the greater frequency of needing access to a toilet or somewhere to sit and rest.

For the policy-maker, the importance of these difficulties is related to the number of people affected and their ability to use other modes of travel or means of access. The proportion of elderly people with a health-related difficulty in walking is substantial, although hard to define or to measure precisely. Hopkin, Robson and Town (1978) found that 44 per cent of a sample of people aged over 65 said they had such difficulty.

The scope for elderly people to substitute other modes of transport for walking is limited. People of pensionable age are rarely the owners and drivers of cars, and with the degeneration of health, those who had cars are likely to give them up. Some, of course, have access to lifts in other people's cars. The majority of pensioners, however, are dependent on public transport for vehicular travel. But it has been found for the elderly (Hopkin, Robson and Town, 1978) and the handicapped (Feeney *et al.*, 1979) that walking difficulties are strongly related to problems with using public transport, because walking is invariably involved and because many health problems that curtail movement on foot limit even further the use of public transport vehicles.

The problems of the elderly pedestrian are considerable therefore, and have led to strong calls for policy responses (Norman, 1977; Hillman and Whalley, 1979). The relevant policies are largely in the domain of the local authorities, who are responsible for the design and maintenance of pedestrian facilities, but central government through the Departments of Transport and of the Environment sets standards, requirements, and limitations on many aspects of the facilities.

Particular calls have been made for the minimization of changes of pavement level (kerbs, steps), and for the greater avoidance of uneven surfaces (e.g. loose paving stones). The required attention to detail and vigilance in maintenance depends upon an understanding of the desirability of these measures, which is rare among able-bodied younger people. Such measures benefit many apart from the less able elderly: those with temporary or permanent health problems, people with prams or pushchairs, and those carrying heavy shopping or luggage—as well as any women wearing fashionable shoes; nobody is actually inconvenienced by such measures.

In the provision of facilities for pedestrians to cross trafficked roads, however, there is clearly an element of conflict between the interests of people on foot and those in vehicles—each class of road-user tends to impose delay, inconvenience, and a degree of danger to the other. The road accident figures demonstrate the danger to pedestrians: in Britain, typically some 20 per cent of all casualties resulting from road accidents (reported to the police) are pedestrians, but pedestrians comprise more than one in three of all fatalities. The two groups with particularly high pedestrian accident rates are children and the elderly.

Pedestrian crossing facilities consist of bridges and subways, offering complete segregation from vehicles, and at-grade crossings—pedestrian phases at junction traffic lights, zebra and pelican crossings—which allow pedestrians periods with right-of-way over the road space. Bridges and subways are expensive to construct, take up much space, and are generally only provided where at-grade crossings would be inappropriate. Since they require the pedestrian to go up and down steps or ramps, and to deviate from the straight-line route from one side of a road to the other, they can be very difficult for precisely those people—the less fit and able—who most need protection in crossing the road. Subways also discomfort many people, especially the elderly, who fear personal attack.

At-grade crossing facilities have evolved over many years. Crossings with pedestrian rights-of-way were first introduced in Britain in 1935 following the Road Traffic Act 1934. By the early 1950s they had developed to the familiar zebra crossing, but these have been found inadequate where flows of either pedestrians or vehicles are high. Pelican crossings were consequently introduced in 1969, and after 4 years' experience their installation was recommended under a wider range of conditions. Pelicans are light-controlled crossings where pedestrian right-of-way is requested by a push-button. Their distinctive feature is a phase where the pedestrian lights show a flashing 'green man' while the vehicle lights show flashing amber: during this phase, any pedestrian already on the crossing has right-of-way over vehicles, but pedestrians are not supposed to start to cross, and if the crossing is clear then vehicles may move. The logic of this phase is to allow pedestrians adequate time to cross with right-of-way, without delaying vehicles unnecessarily. The timings of the signal cycle are laid down in regulations issued by the Department of Transport.

Attempts have been made to compare the accident rates of zebra and pelican crossings (Inwood and Grayson, 1979) but without conclusive results so far. Many users of pelican crossings nevertheless feel them to be unsafe—this is particularly true of the elderly, and there have been many calls to increase the right-of-way times for the pedestrian (Association of Metropolitan Authorities, 1977; Help the Aged, 1975; Greater London Council, 1976). This perceived lack of safety has been linked to a general lack of understanding among both drivers and pedestrians of who has right-of-way during the flashing stage, which accounts for the small proportion of drivers who attempt to move off when pedestrians are on the crossing (Bruce and Skelton, 1977). This may be a problem that decreases with time as all road users become more aware of their required behaviour; in the meantime, the Greater London Council has been allowed to experiment with slightly longer times for the full pedestrian right-of-way phase.

The provision for pedestrians to cross roads at signalled junctions is often less adequate than at pelicans, even when a pedestrian phase is incorporated into the signal cycle. The time allowed for the pedestrian phase seems to be based on the assumptions, first, that pedestrians cross at a speed of 4 feet per second—which a significant proportion of the elderly cannot attain—and, second, that pedestrians start to cross when the pedestrian right-of-way begins, which assumes fast reactions. Because in their early years zebra crossings proliferated to the point where drivers were failing to observe them, zebra and pelican crossings are now subject to a quota of one per 2000 population in urban areas (one per 10,000 in rural areas). Their siting is also controlled e.g. they are not allowed close to junctions or other traffic control measures. The majority of sites where pedestrians wish to cross roads can therefore have no crossing facility installed. The Highway Code states that pedestrians should be given right-of-way by drivers turning at junctions, but few drivers are aware of this.

Although most pedestrians cross roads quite easily in most circumstances, the less able elderly pedestrian can suffer considerable difficulty, anxiety, and danger. There is a need for the continuing development of policies relating to the pedestrian, with the limitations and needs of some elderly pedestrians kept clearly in mind.

## BUSES AND THE ELDERLY

For the majority of elderly people with low access to cars, to reach a destination beyond walking distance requires the use of public transport—usually the familiar stage carriage bus service. According to the 1972/73 National Travel Survey one in six of all trips made by the over-65s was by bus, and although a higher fraction (nearly a quarter) was made by car, the use of cars and buses by individuals varies considerably. For example, in an urban area with good public transport and free bus passes for the elderly, of a sample of people over pensionable age, four out of five used buses during one week, while only half travelled anywhere by car (Skelton, 1977). The distribution of car use was much more skewed than that of bus use: while a few respondents made car trips, 90 per cent made no more than five car trips, whereas more than half made more than five bus trips in the week. On the basis of National Travel Survey figures, elderly people make about 15 per cent of all bus passenger trips. In off-peak periods, about a quarter of all bus journeys are made by the elderly.

For buses to provide an adequate means of getting about, three requirements must be met. First, there must actually be a bus service at suitable times and with adequate reliability between, or near to, the locations where people are and those they want to get to. Second, the fare must be reasonable given a person's income. Third, a person must be able to walk to and from the bus stop, to sustain the necessary wait often while standing and without shelter from the weather, to be able to get on and off the bus, and to have the capacity to stand and move around inside the vehicle even while it is moving. These three factors pinpoint the areas that cause difficulty to many elderly bus users (and potential users), and also serve to illustrate the limitations of the policies used to alleviate the problems.

### The rural transport problem

In many rural areas bus services are non-existent or very infrequent, but many dwellings are distant from all or most facilities, so that some vehicular travel is needed: these factors are at the root of 'the rural transport problem'. Public transport is easiest to provide—or at least, it can be run on a more viable economic basis—when there are larger numbers of people who want to travel either between the same points, or along the same travel corridor. The sparsity of settlement in rural areas means that frequent, inexpensive bus services to a wide variety of destinations cannot be provided in most circumstances without enormous levels of subsidy. So people tend to buy and to use cars whenever they can. Car ownership in rural areas is higher for a given level of income and for all age groups than it is in urban areas; driving licence holding is also higher (though still, in absolute terms, low for the older age groups). As more people own cars, so there may be more opportunities for those without one to get a lift, sometimes sharing or paying the costs. For these reasons, public transport patronage declines further and the provision of services becomes less viable.

The rural transport problem has been widely discussed and researched in recent years (Moseley *et al.*, 1977), but it is usually seen as a general problem for the carless, not as a particular problem for the elderly. The policies that have been adopted reflect this attitude; and concessionary fares schemes for the elderly are less common and often less generous in rural areas than they are in urban areas. Public transport initiatives are not the only way to reduce the rural transport problem. Car-sharing is encouraged, for example, by the Transport Act 1978 which legalized passengers' payment of contributions towards the cost of car journeys. However, more efforts seem to have been put into policies relating both to conventional and unconventional rural public transport schemes, with initiatives coming from many directions including the politicians, the operators, and the community.

The provision of conventional stage carriage bus services is bolstered in some areas by subsidies to the operator granted by the local authority. Despite, or more likely because of the difficulties inherent in running public transport in rural areas, its subsidy tends to be low or non-existent in contrast to the major urban areas. In all areas where subsidies are given, the amount needed to run the same level of service tends to rise year by year. Many local authorities are increasingly reluctant to meet rising subisidy bills, questioning the cost-effectiveness of this expenditure. The National Bus Company, which controls the large majority of bus operators in rural areas, has been responding to this situation with its Market Analysis Project (Barrett and Buchanan, 1979). Among other objectives, this seeks to identify those parts of its network which are financially self-supporting, and to control the deficit on loss-making routes, so that the company's resources can be used more effectively and to provide a local authority with a clearer idea of the returns from a proposed subsidy.

Central government too has an interest in rural transport, and in 1980 there were proposals before Parliament to relax the regulations governing the licensing of public transport operations. The stated intentions of this Bill were to encourage initiative and innovation in the provision of public transport in rural areas (Pickering, 1980); critics feared, however, that it would allow the profitable routes of a system to be creamed off and so reduce the cross-subsidization of less viable ones. The 1980 Transport Act in fact only relaxed the regulations for longer distance bus services.

In many remote rural areas of Britain there are no conventional bus services at all, but some unconventional services have been initiated during the last ten years. The postbus, for example, was first introduced by the Scottish Postal Board in an attempt to reduce its very heavy and increasing losses on the provision of postal services to remote rural areas. There are now more than 125 postbus services throughout Britain (Watts, Stark and Hawthorne, 1978). Postbuses carry passengers as well as the mail, in vehicles ranging in size from a Land Rover to a minibus. The carriage of passengers, at a low additional cost, has helped to reduce the cost to the Post Office of providing rural postal services, but it is the mail services that are its prime function and this inevitably limits the level of public transport provision that it is able to offer.

A number of remote rural areas now have co-operative schemes providing some public transport. Each community bus scheme is different, but the North Norfolk Village Bus, the first such scheme (Madgett, 1977), is fairly typical and is still a considerable success in its fifth year of operation. This scheme is based on six villages with no conventional public transport and few amenities, and uses minibuses driven by volunteers from the local community, operating some regular scheduled trips and numerous excursions. The vehicles are maintained by Eastern Counties, the local bus operator, who also train the drivers to public service vehicle licence standards. A committee of the community runs the scheme. The target financial objective is to meet the week-to-week operating costs; North Norfolk District Council pays for the remainder. With goodwill and enthusiasm on all sides, the scheme has been popular and effective, and a number of other communities have since started their own schemes. A guide to such provision has now been produced by the Department of Transport (1978). A third example of a very versatile rural public transport service is the Border Courier scheme in southern Scotland (Crockford, 1980). It combines a goods delivery service for the Regional Health Board, stage carriage services, and school and social services contract work.

All these schemes have been set up for the benefit of the rural population in general and not only the elderly. While popular and often successful within their terms of reference, not a great deal is known about the contribution they make to the population's travel and activity patterns. An exception is the Transport and Road Research Laboratory's Rural Transport Experiments (Rutex) demonstration projects, which set up a variety of unconventional public transport schemes in rural areas and monitored their effects (Balcombe, 1979). Each Rutex scheme was unique, and response to the schemes was very varied. Patronage ranged from 210 one-way trips per week on a basically conventional bus service with certain route diversions when required, to two trips per week for a community car scheme provided only for hospital visits. The investigators concluded that only a very small amount of Rutex travel had actually been generated by the new service provision.

It is difficult to judge from the literature how effective these rural transport schemes have been from the point of view of the elderly. The limited evidence suggests that the elderly do not predominate among the users of unconventional services (Crockford, 1980; North Yorkshire Rutex Working Group, 1979; Scottish Rutex Working Group, 1979). Even where public transport is provided the elderly in rural areas are likely to be constrained by the cost of fares (which are usually high in rural areas because of the unit operating costs per passenger carried, the low levels of subsidy, and the longer distances that have to be travelled by the passenger), and by bus design, just as they are in urban areas.

## Concessionary bus fares

Even where an adequate or good bus service exists, a potential passenger must be able and willing to afford the fare. Fares are well-recognized as a deterrent to travel by public transport; in general about 3 per cent of patronage is lost for every 10 per cent rise in fares. In addition, the propensity to travel by bus increases with income. Webster (1977) showed that among households without cars the average number of bus trips made by individuals varied by a factor of three among groups whose income varied by a factor of about four.

Given the low income of the 'typical' elderly person, bus fares can be expected to be a significant deterrent to travel. In a nationwide survey conducted in 1971, Age Concern (1973) found that fare increases were the greatest problem in bus use by elderly people in urban areas. In rural areas fares, though important, caused less concern to the elderly than inadequate or non-existent services.

The provision during the last decade of concessionary fares on buses (and sometimes on local rail services) has been the major public effort which has been made to increase the mobility of the elderly. Concessions come in many forms, including a pass allowing free travel at all times throughout a county or a conurbation, eligibility for children's fares, and tickets or tokens with a set value. The nature of a scheme, and its cost, is negotiated between the local authority (at the county, district or parish level) and the relevant public transport operators.

Enabling legislation for concessionary fares was initially contained in the Travel Concessions Acts of 1955 and 1964, then on a much wider basis in the Transport Act 1968 and the Transport (London) Act 1969. The schemes proliferated in the early 1970s, and the 1970 expenditure of £6 millions escalated rapidly (Table 13.1). Concerned at the rate of increase in concessionary fares expenditure, the Government declared in late 1974 (Department of the Environment, 1974) that the situation should be frozen, with no new schemes to be introduced and no existing schemes to be expanded until further notice. However, following widespread response to the Green Paper on Transport

Table 13.1 Trends in public expenditure on concessionary fares and other aspects of transport

| | £million at current prices | Indices at constant prices (1976/77 = 100) | | | | |
|---|---|---|---|---|---|---|
| | 1976–77 | 1972–73 | 1975–76 | 1976–77 | 1977–78 | 1978–79 |
| Total public expenditure on roads and transport (4% of all public expenditure) | 2757 | 91 | 114 | 100 | 93 | 92 |
| Total public expenditure on public transport | 1069 | 51 | 111 | 100 | 101 | 98 |
| Support to British Rail | 482 | 44 | 122 | 100 | 106 | 102 |
| Subsidies to local bus, Underground, and ferry services | 184 | 7 | 112 | 100 | 80 | 80 |
| Public transport investment | 179 | 92 | 102 | 100 | 105 | 104 |
| Other public transport industries including ports and shipping | 127 | 102 | 87 | 100 | 111 | 89 |
| Concessionary fares | 97 | 27 | 102 | 100 | 101 | 110 |

*Source*: Central Statistical Office (1978), Table 10.13, p. 166.

Policy (Department of the Environment, 1976), the ensuing White Paper (Department of Transport, 1977) recognized the popularity of concessionary fares schemes and reversed this decision. A subsequent Green Paper (Department of Transport, 1979) went further, and put forward proposals for a minimum, nationwide scheme of half-fare concessions, with local authorities retaining the option of providing more generous schemes if they wished. There was, however, yet another reversal of policy in August 1979, when the newly elected Conservative Government scrapped this proposal as part of wide-ranging cuts in public expenditure.

The current situation is still one of enormous variation in the generosity, power, eligibility, cost and method of costing of concessionary fares schemes for the elderly. This situation was well documented by McTavish and Mullen (1977) and, in its inequality, severely castigated by Norman (1977). McTavish and Mullen illustrate the geographical diversity of schemes in England and Wales. They show that the most generous schemes tend to be found in the major conurbations, where public transport provision is often at its best, while many rural areas have no concessionary schemes and sometimes very little or no public transport. This reflects the inherent limitations of the provision of concessionary fares to enhance the mobility of the elderly. Existing schemes have produced considerable inequality, and commonly result in anomalies at the borders between areas with different schemes. Equally clearly, the benefits which concessionary fares are able to provide are fundamentally limited by the existence and level of public transport service that is available.

Despite the popularity, high cost and controversies surrounding concessionary fares, very little objective evidence has been sought of their effects, although many local authorities have investigated the level of use for costing purposes. An exception was the work carried out by London Transport (Day, 1973; Freeman, 1975), which although predominantly a costing exercise also sought understanding of the benefits provided by concessionary travel. Detailed assessments of the benefits accruing from concessionary fares have also been made by Benwell (1976, 1977) and by Skelton (1977).

For the recipients of concessionary fares, benefits arise in three ways. First, there is the saving of the money that would have been paid in the absence of concessions. Second, there are the benefits from the additional travel that is made. An investigation on Tyneside (Skelton, 1977) concluded that these additional trips were broadly similar to those previously made by bus, and that they were mainly 'new' trips rather than diversions from other modes of transport. A change in the Tyneside concessionary fares scheme from half fare to free travel led to an increase of a third in the numbers of bus trips, and the Passenger Transport Executive estimated that if full fare were charged, fewer than half of the elderly's free bus trips would continue to be made. The third benefit of concessionary fares is that, with the more powerful schemes at least, a bus pass can give the holder a great feeling of freedom to get about, whatever the amount of travel actually undertaken (Skelton, 1978). The public transport operator can also benefit from concessionary fares: they provide a predictable and easily collected source of revenue, and in general the extra travel that is generated is during the off-peak daytime periods, when most services have spare capacity. Indeed, in many areas concessionary fares have been a considerable success and have demonstrated that the flagging demand for public transport can sometimes be reversed.

## Bus design

In all the debates over the provision of public transport in rural areas and concessionary fares, one sector of the elderly population is often forgotten: the least physically able. Even when they live in areas with both excellent bus services and generous concessionary fares schemes, their physical disabilities make it difficult or impossible for them to use public transport. Nearly four million people in the United Kingdom are probably unable to negotiate the maximum legal bus step height, and the majority of such people are elderly (Brooks, Ruffell-Smith and Ward, 1974). The medical causes of difficulty, and the aspects of bus design that cause most problems, have been quite thoroughly investigated (Buchanan and Chamberlain, 1978; Brooks, Ruffell-

Smith and Ward, 1974; Leyland Vehicles Human Factors Group, 1978). Following their research, British Leyland have developed a new double-decker bus—the Titan—which they claim can be used by a larger proportion of the less able population. Their first major order, to supply 250 vehicles to London Transport, should be completed by June 1980.

South Yorkshire Passenger Transport Executive is one of the few operators to improve the accessibility of their buses to the less able. Their fleet includes 18 'kneeling buses' which are Leyland National vehicles converted at low cost so that the suspension over the front nearside wheel can be lowered at stops, to reduce the step height. They are also experimenting with 'Cityliners'—articulated single-deck buses, which achieve a high passenger capacity while avoiding stairs. Despite the efforts of British Leyland and sympathetic operators such as South Yorkshire, most public transport concerns show little interest in improving their fleet design for the benefit of the less able passenger. A typical attitude is that their financial and operating difficulties prevent investment or effort to relieve the problems of a small minority of the travelling public. Before a major improvement is seen in the extent to which the less able members of the population are able to use service buses, vast changes in public and political attitudes will be necessary.

There are in any case limitations on the extent to which vehicle design can enhance mobility. People who are less able must be sure that when they go to catch a bus, then the vehicle that arrives will be accessible to them. This means that all the buses on a route or corridor should be of suitable design, including any vehicles injected as duplicates or as replacements for breakdowns. Since the serviceable life of a bus can exceed 20 years, it would obviously take a long time before an entire bus fleet consisted of 'accessible' buses.

Although the height of bus steps is a major barrier to bus travel, personal physical limitations lead to difficulty with many other aspects of bus travel. Feeney *et al.* (1979), for example, identified several operational practices which generate impediments, such as vehicles failing to draw right up to the kerb and the necessity to get to and from a seat (assuming one is available) while the bus is in motion. To change these practices would require a change in the priorities of operators, since they result mainly from a desire to minimize the dead time in bus schedules. Apart from the difficulties of getting on to and moving inside a bus, the less able passenger is likely to have problems in walking to and from a bus stop and in waiting for a bus—waiting a long time is irksome for anyone, but may become physically impossible for the less able. Improvements in the walking environment, and the provision of bus shelters and seats, can do much to help. The extent to which the demand for bus travel would be increased by improved vehicle design alone is, therefore, likely to be small. Nevertheless, improvements will benefit those who use buses but only with difficulty and may improve buses' safety record: although bus travel has always been regarded as relatively safe because there are relatively few bus passenger casualties according to the official road accident statistics, recent research indicates that there is a larger number of casualties occurring to passengers, only rarely resulting from collision with another vehicle (Leyland Vehicles Human Factors Group, 1978).

## THE IMPACT OF SOCIAL SERVICES AND VOLUNTARY TRANSPORT SCHEMES

While the vast majority of elderly people's trips are made on foot, by bus, or by private car, in recent years there has been growing awareness of the contribution made to personal mobility by social services and voluntary transport schemes (Garden, 1980). Bailey (1979, 1980) has investigated the provision of these schemes. Local authorities have an obligation under the Chronically Sick and Disabled Persons Act 1970 to provide transport services to enable clients to reach facilities provided by the local authority. Their services tend therefore to be destination-specific, e.g. to adult training centres for the mentally handicapped (87 per cent of all social services journeys in Birmingham), or to social welfare centres (10 per cent of all journeys in Birmingham) (Bailey, 1979). The Ambulance Service also provides transport to hospitals—91 per cent of all ambulance passenger journeys are routine non-emergency cases (Howell, 1979). Few other personal trips are made by social services transport, except for clients in residential establishments to visit the doctor or dentist (Bailey, 1979).

Local authorities often run a fleet of vehicles for these services, including minibuses adapted to carry wheelchairs. They also make use of hired taxis, and private cars whose drivers are remunerated for their running costs. Some authorities are also willing to provide at cost their own vehicles and drivers to voluntary organizations at weekends or in the evening. Many voluntary agencies run their own vehicles, typically a minibus, and organize lift-giving schemes in private cars; a contribution to the costs is asked for in some cases. As with the social services, the major emphasis of voluntary schemes is on getting people to a specific activity or place such as a hospital appointment, a day centre, or a lunch club, or providing home-based services such as Meals on Wheels.

With both social services and voluntary transport, the elderly—or subsets of the elderly such as the frail or those inclined towards going to lunch clubs—are the major client group. Little is known, however, about the contribution of these transport schemes to the lifestyles of individuals, for concern is currently focused on supply problems. Bailey (1979) estimated that social services or voluntary transport made on average six trips per household per year. The distribution of such trips among the population is highly skewed, and for some individuals such schemes provide most or all of their travel opportunities. In the light of both the costs of providing these services and the severe mobility limitations of many of their clients, it would seem well worthwhile to identify their beneficiaries and the differences between them and others, and to assess the distribution of benefits geographically, socially, and against some criterion of 'need'.

The policy issues on the supply side of social service and voluntary transport schemes seem to be common to all parts of this sector, and not just to those serving the elderly. The main issues relate to efficiency, legislation, and vehicle design. During the last decade there has been a considerable increase in the provision of transport services both by the social services and the voluntary sector. The number of vehicles has escalated, in some cases leading to inefficiency in operation (Oram, 1979). The scheduling of fleets may leave vehicles unused for long periods of time. Hospitals may impose unnecessary strains and peaks in the demand for transport services, e.g. by concentrating out-patient appointments at 9 a.m. It is common for separate voluntary organizations each to own one or two minibuses, but to use them only occasionally; there is clearly scope for greater co-ordination and co-operation between organizations, but many other considerations constrain such attempts.

Legislation also imposes constraints on the operation of voluntary transport services. Some services are defined as public service vehicle (p.s.v.) operations and are subject to all the relevant legislation; drivers then need to hold a p.s.v. driver's licence (Dods, 1978). Recent legislation such as the Minibus Act 1977, intended to improve the situation for voluntary organizations running minibuses, has at the same time introduced additional constraints and complexities (Dods, 1978).

Many organizations have also found considerable difficulties in getting suitably designed vehicles for the carriage of frail, severely disabled or wheelchair-bound passengers. The problems arise with both purchasing the basic vehicle and commissioning adaptations (Garden, 1979b; Wadley, 1979).

All in all, there is much scope for the further development of social services and voluntary transport for the elderly and for research into and policies relating to their provision. In terms of the elderly population's travel, the contribution of these schemes is small but their actual and potential value may be great for those sections of the population who, through frailty or disability, are most in need of assistance. This is particularly so as the Government's Mobility Allowance (£12 per week in March 1980) discriminates directly against the elderly and is granted only to disabled people of normal working age.

## LONG-DISTANCE TRAVEL

While the vast majority of elderly people's trips are local, holidays or visits to distant friends or relatives may require long-distance travel. This often entails complicated trips with the main part of the journey by coach or train and local travel at either end of the trip. Such journeys compound the problems

Table 13.2 Sales of British Rail Senior Citizen Railcards

| Financial year | Sales (thousands) |
|---|---|
| 1975/76 | 227 |
| 1976/77 | 481 |
| 1977/78 | 818 |
| 1978/79 | 874 |
| 1979/80 | 950 (estimated) |

*Source*: British Rail Press Office.

inherent in the use of separate modes, together with others such as getting travel information, carrying luggage, and coping with unfamiliar situations.

This has not been a matter of great public concern, but it has been the subject of some commercial initiatives. Some firms offer package holidays and day trips either specifically for the pensioner or under conditions attractive to the older person. Intense competition has also developed between long-distance public transport operators, to attract revenue from the elderly using spare capacity at off-peak times. British Rail, for example, sells a Senior Citizen Railcard which allows travel at half the standard fare on nearly all trains in Britain and on certain ferries and some European railways. The increasing popularity of these Railcards is indicated by their sales figures (Table 13.2).

## SUMMARY AND CONCLUSION

There is a diversity both in the problems that elderly people have in getting about in their daily lives and in the policies that have developed as a response. Elderly people have more than average difficulty in making use of the transport system, particularly through their low income and reduced physical ability, but sometimes compounded by inconvenient geographical location. While some elderly people have insuperable problems with getting about, not all have any more difficulty than many younger people. Although the transport problems of the elderly are well-documented, their effects are not easily evaluated—in Britain, mobility limitations generally affect the quality of life rather than raising questions of life and death.

Nearly all passenger transport and related policies are relevant to the elderly. Some discriminate in favour of the elderly as a whole, e.g. concessionary fares; others for a subset of the elderly, e.g. transport to old people's clubs; others for a set of people of whom the elderly form a major part, e.g. social services transport; and one policy at least—the Mobility Allowance for the disabled—discriminates against the elderly.

Policies arise from many sources. Central government has introduced both statutory obligations to provide transport as with the Chronically Sick and

Disabled Persons Act, and enabling legislation such as the Minibus Act, and it has laid down standards and guidelines for pedestrian crossing design and location. Local authorities of all levels are involved in policies relating to transport and the elderly, e.g. in negotiating and supporting concessionary fares schemes and in maintaining pavements. Their departments of social services, highway and transport engineering, and land-use planning are all involved. Some charities devote much time, money, and effort towards, for example, providing transport to hospitals or to old people's centres. Community action also plays a part, as in the setting up and running of community bus schemes in rural areas.

Some policies are wide-ranging and powerful, such as the provision of unlimited free bus travel for all pensioners throughout a major conurbation; others are small-scale. Many require great attention to detail, e.g. in the design of pedestrian crossing facilities, or in the interior design of buses and minibuses. Other policy areas need a broad perspective to determine the most effective course of action, as in the evaluation of the alternatives of transporting people to facilities or of delivering goods and services.

Given that this diversity exists without an overall, centrally guided policy, it is not surprising that many of the broadest issues are not confronted. These include: the relative priorities that should be given to the elderly and to other disadvantaged groups; the concentration on urban or on rural problems; the stimulation given to each mode of transport; and the relative emphasis upon either the improvement of transport opportunities or changes in land-use to reduce the need to travel. In Britain now, the main policy issues concerning elderly people's travel are the inequitable provision of concessionary bus travel, the provision of unconventional public transport in rural areas, the quality of the pedestrian environment, the continuing needs of the least able section of the elderly population, and the effective and efficient provision of social services and voluntary transport schemes. Of overriding importance is finance, for in a situation of economic depression, with large cuts in public spending, the costs and effectiveness of all policies are closely scrutinized and the competition for scarce resources is increased; no policy can be considered sacrosanct.

More information is needed on the effects and importance of travel difficulties: what effects do they have on the lifestyles and the quality of life of the elderly (and other people)? What are the alternative policy options—how efficient and how effective can each of these be? Who will gain, who will lose, and who will pay? Over the longer term patterns of land-use and transport provision will undoubtedly change; so too will the lifestyles, habits, and expectations of the elderly. Some trends are predictable. Increasing proportions of the younger section of the elderly population will be car drivers: while this will enhance their own travel opportunities, it will also mean that a larger percentage of elderly people will eventually have to give up the use of their own car, which may lead to different demands. There will anyway always be a substantial proportion of the elderly who, through income, ability, or preference, will not have a car available, and for whom the provisions for travel on foot or by bus will be crucially important.

It is to be hoped that the future makers of transport policies will be increasingly aware of the human impacts of their decisions, and that continuing research will allow them to be informed by a better understanding of the range and interconnection of the issues. By reducing the insensitivity, inequity, and lack of co-ordination of some current transport policies, both the elderly beneficiaries and the taxpayer may see a more effective distribution of expenditure in the future.

## REFERENCES


Age Concern (1973). *Age Concern on Transport*. Age Concern England, Mitcham.

Association of Metropolitan Authorities (1977). *Pedestrian Behaviour at Pelican Crossings*, P&T 77 37 Item 24. Association of Metropolitan Authorities, London.

Bailey, J. M. (1979). *Voluntary and Social Services Transport in Birmingham, Redditch and Bromsgrove*. Supplementary Report 467. Transport and Road Research Laboratory, Crowthorne.

Bailey, J. M. (1980). Community transport—an overview. In Garden, J. (ed.), *Community Transport*. The Beth Johnson Foundation, Stoke-on-Trent.

Balcombe, R. J. (1979). *The Rural Transport Experiments: A Mid-Term Review*. Supplementary Report 492. Transport and Road Research Laboratory, Crowthorne.

Barrett, B. and Buchanan, M. (1979). The National Bus Company 'MAP' Market Analysis Project. *Traffic Engineering and Control*, **21** (6), 471–4.

Benwell, M. (1976). Bus passes and the elderly—a need for more informed policy making? *Local Government Studies*, **2**, 51–7.

Benwell, M. (1977) *An Examination of the Extent and Welfare Implications of Bus Use by the Elderly in Harlow*. Memorandum 22, Centre for Transport Studies, Cranfield Institute of Technology, Cranfield.

Brooks, B. M., Ruffell-Smith, H. P., and Ward, J. S. (1974). *An Investigation of Factors Affecting the Use of Buses by Both Elderly and Ambulant Disabled Persons*. Transport and Road Research Laboratory Contract Report, British Leyland UK Ltd, Leyland.

Bruce, S. and Skelton, N. G. (1977). Pedestrian-vehicle conflict at Pelican crossings. Proc. PTRC Summer Annual Meeting, University of Warwick, June 1977.

Buchanan, J. M. and Chamberlain, M. A. (1978). *Survey of the Mobility of the Disabled in an Urban Environment*. The Royal Association for Disability and Rehabilitation, London.

Central Statistical Office (1978). *Social Trends No. 9–1979*. HMSO, London.

Crockford, D. (1980). The Border Courier. In Garden, J. (ed.), *Community Transport*. The Beth Johnson Foundation, Stoke-on-Trent.

Day, D. J. (1973). *1973 Concessionary Fares Survey*, Operational Research Report R200. London Transport Executive, London.

Department of the Environment (1974). *Rate Fund Expenditure and Rate Calls in 1975–76*, Circular No. 171/74, DOE, London.

Department of the Environment (1976). *Transport Policy: a Consultation Document*. HMSO, London.

Department of Transport (1977). *Transport Policy*. Cmnd. 6836, HMSO, London.

Department of Transport (1978). *A Guide to Community Transport*. HMSO, London.

Department of Transport (1979). *Concessionary Fares for Elderly, Blind and Disabled People*. Cmnd. 7475, HMSO, London.

Dods, J. (1978). Lost opportunities: passenger vehicle licensing and the law. In Garden, J. (ed.), *Solving the Transport Problems of the Elderly: the Use of Resources*, pp. 25–36. The Beth Johnson Foundation, Stoke-on-Trent.

Feeney, R. J., Ashford, N. J., Morris, A., and Gazely, D. (1979). *Travel and the Handicapped: a Project Summary*. Supplementary Report 480, Transport and Road Research Laboratory, Crowthorne.

Freeman, J. D. (1975). *Free Travel for the Elderly in Greater London—1974 Survey*. Operational Research Report R208, London Transport Executive, London.

Garden, J. (ed.) (1979a). *Social Services Transport and the Elderly*. The Beth Johnson Foundation, Stoke-on-Trent.

Garden, J. (1979b). A specialised vehicle for the transport of the elderly. In Garden, J. (ed.) *Social Services Transport and the Elderly*. The Beth Johnson Foundation, Stoke-on-Trent.

Garden, J. (ed.) (1980). *Community Transport*. The Beth Johnson Foundation, Stoke-on-Trent.

Greater London Council (1976). *GLC Acts Over Pelican Crossings*. Press release No. 476, 22.11.1976. Greater London Council, London.

Help the Aged (1975). *Old People Frightened to Use Crossings*. Press release, November. Help the Aged, London.

Hillman, M., Henderson, I., and Whalley, A. (1973). *Personal Mobility and Transport Policy*, Broadsheet 542, Political and Economic Planning, London.

Hillman, M., Henderson, I., and Whalley, A. (1976). *Transport Realities and Planning Policy*. Broadsheet 567, Political and Economic Planning, London.

Hillman, M. and Whalley, A. (1979). *Walking* is *Transport*. Broadsheet 583, Policy Studies Institute, London.

Hopkin, J. M., Robson, P., and Town, S. W. (1978). *The Mobility of Old People: a Study in Guildford*. Laboratory Report 850, Transport and Road Research Laboratory, Crowthorne.

Howell, R. G. (1979). Planning in an ambulance service. In Garden, J. (ed.), *Social Services Transport and the Elderly*. The Beth Johnson Foundation, Stoke-on-Trent.

Inwood, J. and Grayson, G. (1979). *The Comparative Safety of Pedestrian Crossings*. Laboratory Report 859, Transport and Road Research Laboratory, Crowthorne.

Leyland Vehicles Human Factors Group (1978). *Passenger Problems on Moving Buses*, Transport and Road Research Laboratory Contract Report, Leyland Vehicles Ltd, Leyland.

McTavish, A. D. and Mullen, P. (1977). *Survey of Concessionary Bus Fares for the Elderly, Blind and Disabled in England and Wales*. Local Transport Note 1/77, Department of Transport, London.

Madgett, J. S. (1977). Village bus service : report on the first ten months of operation. In *Proc. Symposium on Unconventional Bus Services*. Supplementary Report 336, Transport and Road Research Laboratory, Crowthorne.

Moseley, M. J., Harman, R. G., Coles, O. B., and Spencer, M. B. (1977). *Rural Transport and Accessibility*. Vol. 1: Main Report. Centre for East Anglian Studies, University of East Anglia, Norwich.

Norman, A. (1977). *Transport and the Elderly: Problems and Possible Action*. National Corporation for the Care of Old People, London.

North Yorkshire Rutex Working Group (1979). *Rural Transport Experiments: the Ripon Flexibus*. Supplementary Report 491, Transport and Road Research Laboratory, Crowthorne.

Office of Population Censuses and Surveys, Social Survey Division (1973). *The General Household Survey: Introductory Report*. HMSO, London.

Oram, J. (1979). Social services transport: efficient and effective use of resources. In Garden, J. (ed.), *Social Services Transport and the Elderly*. The Beth Johnson Foundation, Stoke-on-Trent.

Pickering, P. (1980). Changes in the law—a plain man's guide. In Garden, J. (ed.) *Community Transport*. The Beth Johnson Foundation, Stoke-on-Trent.

Scottish Rutex Working Group (1979). *Rural Transport Experiments: Blackmount Services*. Supplementary Report 446, Transport and Road Research Laboratory, Crowthorne.

Skelton, N. G. (1977). *Travel Patterns of Elderly People Under a Concessionary Fares Scheme*, Supplementary Report 280, Transport and Road Research Laboratory, Crowthorne.

Skelton, N. G. (1978). An Investigation into the Travel of Elderly People in Urban Areas. Unpublished PhD thesis, University of Newcastle upon Tyne.

Wachs, M. and Blanchard, R. D. (1975). *Lifestyles and Transportation Needs of the Elderly in the Future*. Report for the Urban Mass Transit Administration, Washington, DC.

Wadley, D. (1979). Vehicles for use in social service fleets. In Garden, J. (ed.), *Social Services Transport and the Elderly*, pp. 29–43. The Beth Johnson Foundation, Stoke-on-Trent.

Watts, P. F., Stark, D. C., and Hawthorne, I. H. (1978). *British Postbuses—a Review*. Supplementary Report 840, Transport and Road Research Laboratory, Crowthorne.

Webster, F. V. (1977). *Urban Passenger Transport: Some Trends and Prospects*. Laboratory Report 771, Transport and Road Research Laboratory, Crowthorne.

Geographical Perspectives on the Elderly
Edited by A. M. Warnes


Chapter 14

# The elderly's travel in the Cotswolds

*José Smith* and *Robert Gant*

The travel patterns of the residents of rural Britain have changed considerably over the past 25 years. Increased car ownership has led to greater personal mobility and been largely responsible for decline in public transport. Furthermore, with increased centralization of services into the larger settlements, the means to reach these facilities has become more important. Inevitably these many interlinked changes in travel and transport have had a varied impact on rural communities. The elderly, for example, have benefited less than working-age people from increased car ownership and have been more disadvantaged by the reorganization and reduction of rural public transport services.

Recent research by national bodies (Association of District Councils, 1978; Standing Conference of Rural Community Councils, 1978; National Association of Local Councils, 1980), local authorities (for example, Hereford and Worcester County Council, 1978; Hertfordshire County Council Transport Co-ordination Unit, 1977) and academics (Moseley *et al.*, 1977; Moseley, 1978a, 1979; Shaw, 1979) has demonstrated the multidimensional nature of rural change and explored the interrelationships between transport provision and population structure, employment opportunities, and public and commercial services. In this context of intricate change, the elderly are usually identified as a vulnerable group in rural society, but few studies have concentrated specifically on their movement patterns or attempted to evaluate the extent of their mobility and accessibility problems (Hillman, Henderson, and Whalley, 1973; Moseley, 1978b).

This chapter analyses the transport needs and travel patterns of elderly households in the Cotswolds in relation to the availability of private and public transport, the size of settlements, and in comparison with those of non-elderly households. The object of this analysis is to identify the extent of the rural transport problem and to comment on the policy implications of relating transport services to the specific needs of the elderly in the study area.

## SURVEY AREA AND METHODS

The population of the Cotswold District Council area displays many of the characteristics of the less remote and poorer parts of rural Britain (Jackson, 1968; Dunn, 1976). Its employment in agriculture and related services has declined substantially since 1880 (Robinson, 1963; Clout, 1972). In many of its areas selective migration from the countryside has produced an advanced age structure in the residual population (Dunn, 1976; Cloke, 1977). Elsewhere, commuters and retired households have moved into the parishes most accessible to urban centres (Best and Rogers, 1973; Hale and Hale, 1976). As a result of these trends, a considerable number of pensioner households are found in the Cotswold District and marked contrasts are a feature of the social, demographic, and economic profiles of neighbouring parishes (Rawson, 1978; Gant and Smith, 1979).

Twenty-two parishes were selected for study (Figure 14.1) and were grouped into three categories on the basis of their 1971 populations and the range of facilities and amenities available in March 1979. Northleach and Stow-on-the-Wold were the large parishes with respective populations of 1150 and 1560; eight medium-sized parishes had a median population of 403; and twelve small parishes a median population of 113. Most of the parishes in each group had similar histories of population change. In the period 1921–71, for example, the combined populations of Northleach and Stow-on-the-Wold increased by 32 per cent, while among the medium-size parishes, only Andoversford, Bibury, and Chedworth increased their populations. Without exception, the small parishes lost population, the overall decline being 18 per cent. Not unexpectedly, by 1971 there were contrasts in the proportion of pensioner households: the median was 30 per cent and the range extended from 13 per cent at Hampnett to 53 per cent at Clapton.

Survey data were collected by interview and postal questionnaire from 511 households; 86 in a pilot survey conducted in March 1978 and 425 in the main survey of March 1979. The random sample covered 10 per cent of the households in the large settlements, 20 per cent in the medium and 50 per cent in the small. Thirty-seven per cent of the survey households were classified as elderly. All one- and two-pensioner households, and those where the male head had retired before the age of 65, were included but not those three-generation households containing one elderly member. The elderly and non-elderly households were similar with regard to their housing tenure and migration histories. Sixty-five per cent of the elderly households were owner occupiers, 16 per cent lived in private rented accommodation, 5 per cent in tied housing, and 14 per cent were local authority tenants. One-third of the elderly households

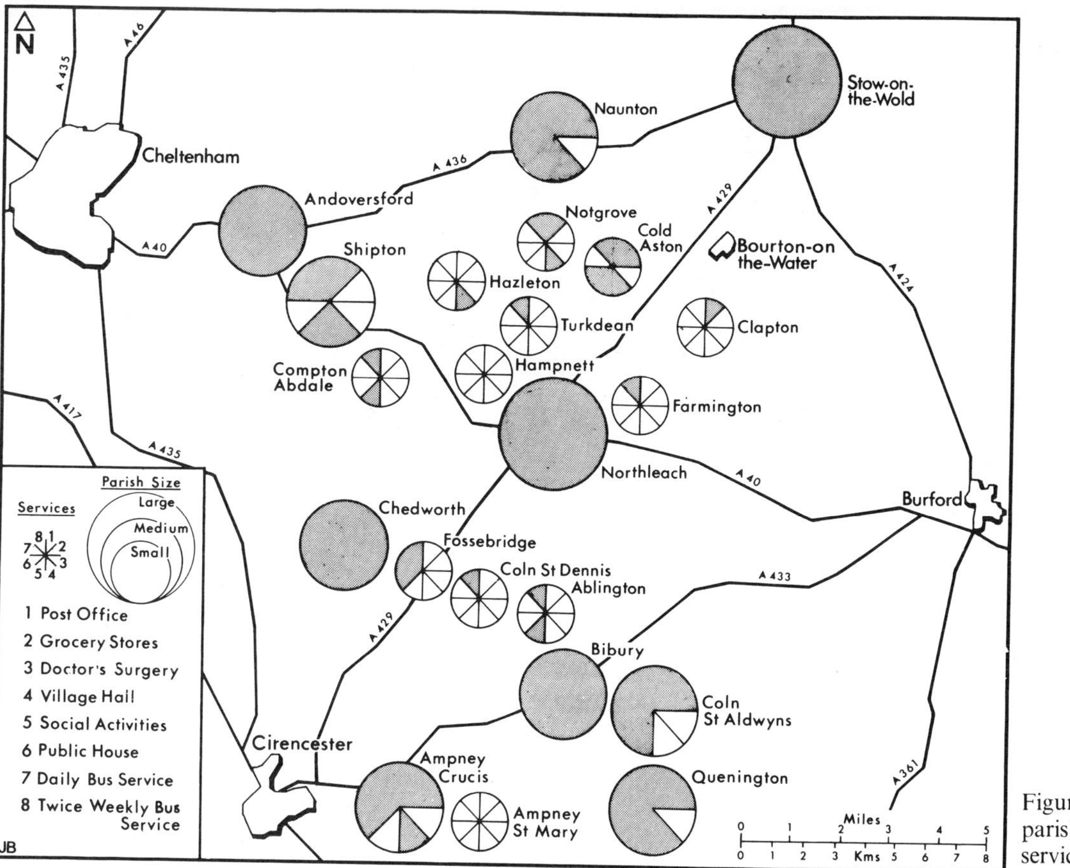


Figure 14.1 Cotswold survey parishes: distribution of services and facilities

had lived in their homes for less than 10 years, including both local households who had moved into council bungalows in Northleach, Bibury, and Quenington and outsiders who on their retirement had bought property in one of the villages.

## CHANGES IN THE LEVEL OF SERVICE PROVISION AND TRANSPORT

Since 1900 the elderly have been severely affected by the considerable changes which have occurred in the pattern and organization of rural services (Gloucestershire County Council, 1979). This pace of change has accelerated since 1945 and in the period 1972–77, for example, 8 per cent of Gloucestershire villages lost their sub-Post Offices; 13 per cent a shop; and 3 per cent a doctor's surgery (Standing Conference of Rural Community Councils, 1978). Small and medium-sized parishes in the study area have experienced the greatest decline. For example, Naunton lost its garage, Shipton a grocer's shop and bakery, and Hazleton its sub-Post Office (Whiteley, 1971). Fortunately for the elderly there have only been minor changes in the organization of health-care facilities and in the distribution of dispensing chemists (Gloucestershire County and City Executive Council, 1966, 1968). Figure 14.1 summarizes the availability in 1979 of eight services and facilities which the survey showed were important to the elderly. Stow-on-the-Wold and Northleach offer the full selection. With the exception of doctors' surgeries and some social activities, most medium-size parishes offered a comparable level of services but the small parishes supported few services, some lacking even a weekly bus service.

One of the most far-reaching changes, however, has been the reduction and withdrawal of the public transport services. In the 1950s the survey area was served by work, shopping, and weekend bus services and several parishes had a rail service. By 1979 all rail services had been withdrawn and the bus services had contracted. All remaining routes in the survey area were licensed to small independent operators who have been more successful in maintaining services than the National Bus Company subsidiaries operating in other rural areas of Gloucestershire (Figure 14.1). Nevertheless, since 1970, services have been completely withdrawn from two parishes, some routes have been amalgamated, and others seen a reduced frequency of operation. Although the costs of the independent operators have risen less than those of the regional companies, fares increased by 80–100 per cent between 1975 and 1979 (Traffic Commissioners, Western Traffic Area, 1975–79 ).

The survey showed that car ownership levels were substantially lower in elderly than younger households and that the members of the former were less likely to own a driving licence (Table 14.1 and 14.2). Notwithstanding, there were marked contrasts in accessibility to private transport among the elderly. In the small parishes elderly households were most likely to have cars and car ownership was also high (83 per cent) in the 'early retired' house-

Table 14.1 Household car ownership

| | Number of cars (%) | | | Number of households (100%) |
|---|---|---|---|---|
| | 0 | 1 | 2+ | |
| *Elderly* | | | | |
| Large parishes | 54 | 44 | 2 | 39 |
| Medium parishes | 53 | 35 | 12 | 94 |
| Small parishes | 25 | 50 | 25 | 59 |
| TOTAL | 45 | 41 | 14 | 192 |
| *Non-elderly* | | | | |
| Large parishes | 10 | 68 | 22 | 71 |
| Medium parishes | 12 | 52 | 36 | 158 |
| Small parishes | 15 | 42 | 43 | 90 |
| TOTAL | 12 | 53 | 35 | 319 |

*Source*: Authors' survey (as for all tables).

Table 14.2 Driving licences owned (percentage of respondents with a licence)

| | Male heads | Female heads |
|---|---|---|
| *Elderly* | | |
| Large parishes | 58 | 30 |
| Medium parishes | 55 | 37 |
| Small parishes | 85 | 52 |
| TOTAL | 65 ($N = 118$) | 41 ($N = 160$) |
| *Non-elderly* | | |
| Large parishes | 92 | 42 |
| Medium parishes | 93 | 57 |
| Small parishes | 92 | 58 |
| TOTAL | 93 ($N = 218$) | 55 ($N = 231$) |

holds. The level of car ownership was low where the household head was over 70 years of age (36 per cent) and in single-female households (30 per cent). Thus certain groups of elderly were severely disadvantaged by the limited availability of transport.

## HOUSEHOLD TRAVEL PATTERNS

Trips to and from Post Offices, grocery stores, doctors' surgeries and for social activities were selected for analysis as representing the main purposes of the

Table 14.3 Household journeys for selected goods and services

| Purpose and origin | Destinations (percentages) | | | | Number of households (100%) |
|---|---|---|---|---|---|
| | Same parish | Small centres | Cheltenham/ Cirencester | Other | |
| POST OFFICE | | | | | |
| *Elderly* | | | | | |
| Large parishes | 100 | — | — | — | 39 |
| Medium parishes | 86 | 11 | 3 | — | 94 |
| Small parishes | 16 | 75 | 9 | — | 59 |
| *Non-elderly* | | | | | |
| Large parishes | 94 | 3 | 3 | — | 71 |
| Medium parishes | 63 | 12 | 23 | 2 | 158 |
| Small parishes | 15 | 52 | 27 | 6 | 90 |
| DOCTOR'S SURGERY | | | | | |
| *Elderly* | | | | | |
| Large parishes | 92 | 8 | — | — | 39 |
| Medium parishes | 11 | 66 | 22 | 1 | 94 |
| Small parishes | — | 73 | 27 | — | 59 |
| *Non-elderly* | | | | | |
| Large parishes | 90 | 3 | 1 | 6 | 71 |
| Medium parishes | 16 | 47 | 37 | — | 158 |
| Small parishes | — | 81 | 16 | 3 | 90 |
| WEEKLY GROCERIES | | | | | |
| *Elderly* | | | | | |
| Large parishes | 77 | — | 23 | — | 39 |
| Medium parishes | 25 | 19 | 55 | 1 | 94 |
| Small parishes | 2 | 59 | 39 | — | 59 |
| *Non-elderly* | | | | | |
| Large parishes | 54 | 1 | 35 | 10 | 71 |
| Medium parishes | 15 | 6 | 77 | 2 | 158 |
| Small parishes | — | 18 | 78 | 4 | 90 |
| SOCIAL ACTIVITIES | | | | | |
| *Elderly* | | | | | |
| Large parishes | 91 | 9 | — | — | 35 |
| Medium parishes | 75 | 16 | 9 | — | 80 |
| Small parishes | 79 | 12 | 9 | — | 33 |
| *Non-elderly* | | | | | |
| Large parishes | 74 | 22 | 4 | — | 49 |
| Medium parishes | 41 | 15 | 44 | — | 104 |
| Small parishes | 44 | 22 | 34 | — | 67 |

*Note*: The small centres were Bourton-on-the-Water, Burford, Fairford, Northleach and Stow-on-the-Wold. Individual journeys were recorded for social activities.

elderly's essential and discretionary travel (Dods, 1978). The travel patterns revealed by the survey broadly reflected the spatial distribution of facilities. The elderly were more likely to use the nearest available facilities while the non-elderly more commonly travelled to a wider range of centres, but this contrast was more marked for travel to some facilities than to others.

Post Offices were the most widely available facility and their distribution was associated with the most restricted travel patterns (Hillman and Whalley, 1979). Fifty-five per cent of all journeys made to a Post Office were on foot, compared to 24 per cent of journeys for groceries and 19 per cent of those to a chemist's shop. The journeys made to the Post Office by the elderly households were also extremely localized: only 4 per cent used facilities outside their own parish or neighbouring small centre (Table 14.3). In contrast, a larger percentage of the non-elderly, especially from small and medium-size parishes, chose to use the Post Offices in Cheltenham or Cirencester.

The travel patterns to doctors' surgeries illustrated the effect of a more centralized service (Table 14.3). The surgeries in Northleach and Stow-on-the-Wold were used by nearly all households in those parishes but the residents of other parishes travelled into larger centres. Although part-time surgeries were held in Andoversford, Bibury and Chedworth, they were used by only a small proportion of the residents. Both elderly and non-elderly households in all parishes tended to use the nearest available surgery. The restricted distribution of surgeries undoubtedly led to a problem of access to medical advice, but the difficulties of acquiring a prescription were more severe as only Northleach and Stow-on-the-Wold had dispensing chemists. This had been overcome in some parishes by dispensing prescriptions from the surgery, and alleviated elsewhere by a prescription postal delivery service from Northleach.

Weekly grocery shopping produced one of the greatest contrasts in the travel patterns between elderly and non-elderly households. Village stores were patronized by only 28 per cent of the non-elderly households, the majority of whom preferred to shop in Cheltenham or Cirencester. In contrast, 56 per cent of elderly households used either their village stores or the grocers in small centres. A detailed survey further illustrated this contrast, especially among the populations of the small and medium parishes (Table 14.4). The main reason given for the infrequent use of village shops was high prices, being mentioned by 53 per cent of the elderly and 49 per cent of non-elderly households. When 20 grocery items were priced in the village stores and in the supermarkets of Cheltenham and Cirencester, the existence of a declining price gradient from the medium and small village stores, most of which were independently owned, through those of Northleach and Stow-on-the-Wold, with shops affiliated to national purchasing chains, to the supermarkets of Cheltenham and Cirencester was confirmed (Table 14.5). It is this gradient which generates the relative disadvantage among those elderly households who rely on village

Table 14.4 Frequency of use of village stores

| | Frequent (%) | Occasional (%) | Rarely/never (%) | Number of respondents (100%) |
|---|---|---|---|---|
| *Elderly* | | | | |
| Large parishes | 73 | 24 | 3 | 37 |
| Small/medium parishes | 56 | 31 | 13 | 77 |
| TOTAL | 61 | 29 | 10 | 114 |
| *Non-elderly* | | | | |
| Large parishes | 66 | 25 | 9 | 53 |
| Small/medium parishes | 32 | 45 | 23 | 110 |
| TOTAL | 44 | 38 | 18 | 163 |

*Note*: Based on household data from ten parishes with village stores.

Table 14.5 Cost of a 'basket' of grocery items (average cost)

| Store location | Named brands (£) | Cheapest alternatives (£) |
|---|---|---|
| Small/medium parish | 7.09 | 6.65 |
| Large parish | 6.96 | 6.38 |
| Cheltenham/Cirencester | 5.94 | 5.22 |

stores. Some of the contrasts between the travel patterns of elderly and non-elderly households reflect their different shopping needs. Elderly households tend to have lesser requirements and will not necessarily benefit from, for example, buying food in bulk. Only 43 per cent of the elderly households owned a freezer compared to 68 per cent of the non-elderly households. Some differences derive, however, from the lower levels of car ownership among the elderly households and, consequently, their more limited access to large urban centres.

An active involvement in social organizations represents one aspect of discretionary travel. While the participation rates of both the elderly and non-elderly were generally low, the elderly in small parishes were less active socially than both their non-elderly neighbours and their peers in larger parishes. The elderly were heavily dependent on social organizations based on their home and neighbouring parishes while many of the younger households were attracted to social organizations in Cheltenham and Cirencester (Table 14.3). Furthermore, the joint sponsorship of social organizations by neighbouring parishes inevitably led to an increase in the journeys made from small to larger parishes (Macgregor, 1972).

## RURAL BUS PASSENGER SURVEY

The extent to which the elderly's use of public transport differed from that of the non-elderly was examined in a bus passenger survey made on the routes linking the survey villages with Cheltenham and Cirencester on Friday 23 March 1979. The journey origins of both the elderly and non-elderly passengers showed a widely scattered pattern of demand with each parish generating a few passengers broadly in proportion to its population (Smith and Gant, 1979). The low-paid, teenagers, and housewives accounted for the majority of the non-elderly passengers. The dependence on public transport of these groups was anticipated, but the survey showed that the elderly were the most reliant (Table 14.6). A very large proportion of elderly passengers came from households without cars and only 3 per cent came from households which had no dependence on public transport. Seventy-seven per cent of the elderly passengers, and 67 per cent of the non-elderly, used the bus service once a week or less. While 80 per cent of journeys by the elderly were for shopping, the non-elderly travelled for a greater variety of purposes (Table 14.7). As the ownership of cars and driving licences among the elderly is unlikely to increase

Table 14.6 Bus passenger survey: dependence on public transport

| Passengers' dependence on public transport | Elderly (%) | Non-elderly (%) |
|---|---|---|
| Completely dependent: no car | 68 | 40 |
| Partially dependent: car/no licence | 20 | 24 |
| Partially dependent: licence/limited access to car | 9 | 22 |
| Not dependent: licence/access to car | 3 | 14 |
| TOTAL | 100 ($N = 75$) | 100 ($N = 110$) |

Table 14.7 Bus passenger survey: purpose of travel

| Purpose | Elderly (%) | Non-elderly (%) |
|---|---|---|
| Employment | 1 | 11 |
| Shopping | 80 | 59 |
| School/education | — | 3 |
| Medical | 5 | 5 |
| Visiting friends | 9 | 11 |
| Recreation | 5 | 7 |
| Other | — | 4 |
| TOTAL | 100 ($N = 78$) | 100 ($N = 117$) |

*Note*: Multi-purpose journeys are included under each purpose.

substantially, a further decline in the bus service will have severe repercussions on the group's accessibility to essential facilities.

Concessionary travel schemes for pensioners have become an important factor in meeting the social need for transport in many rural areas (Norman, 1977; Department of Transport, 1977; Garden, 1978). However, the survey indicated the limited impact of the scheme operated by the Cotswold District Council, for only 62 per cent of the elderly passengers entitled to a concession had taken advantage of the scheme. The remainder were either unaware of the existence of the scheme (12 per cent) or had chosen not to use it (26 per cent). Of greater significance to both the elderly and non-elderly passengers was the quality of the service provided. Although the pattern and frequency of public transport services have declined in recent years, 88 per cent of the elderly and 84 per cent of the non-elderly passengers expressed satisfaction with the existing bus routes and timetables. The services still play a vital role in the life of the countryside and enable the elderly to travel from scattered communities to the facilities and services of Cheltenham and Cirencester.

## CONCLUSIONS

Although the level of private and public transport is higher in the Cotswolds than in most other rural areas of Britain, the mobility of many elderly households in the area gives cause for concern. They have low car ownership, high dependence on public transport and parish facilities, and their travel patterns are far more localized than those of younger adults. As it is likely without intervention that the withdrawal and rationalization of public and commercial facilities will continue in the Cotswolds, existing mobility difficulties will be aggravated. The elderly's special and irregular needs for transport must be met if they are to cope effectively with life in the countryside and the growing relative and absolute number of elderly persons will place an increasing demand on the area's social and welfare services (Dods, 1978).

Many of the elderly who were interviewed were acutely conscious of the problems having experienced the consequences of decline in rural facilities. The worst affected were those who had never owned, or had lost the use of, a car. Prominent among them were the very old, single females, widows, the handicapped, and those with the most limited income: they most frequently expressed concern about the further decline of facilities and services and the cost of using village shops and public transport. Car owners were concerned, however, by the cost of driving to more distant facilities.

The reduction of facilities and declining accessibility must be viewed within a wider perspective of village life (Willis, 1974). The household survey had asked respondents to identify the main disadvantages and advantages of their environment, and about one third of both elderly and non-elderly residents expressed no dissatisfaction with their environment. In addition, almost all households perceived one or more of the advantages of peace and quiet, a high-quality environment, and the opportunity to engage in community life (Table 14.8). There was much evidence that the elderly had adjusted their lives to the pattern of available services. In the small parishes, a higher level of personal mobility and a variety of mobile services compensated for the lack of local facilities. Households with a handicapped member often received considerable assistance from neighbours and welfare organizations. Above all, the elderly without cars had adapted their journeys to the limited public transport system and expressed a high degree of satisfaction with the service. For the majority, at least, there are fewer problems in practice than one might expect from an *a priori* consideration of the availability of facilities and means of transport.

With the prospect of further declines in transport and local facilities, policies to cater for the special needs of the elderly have been proposed in the Gloucestershire Draft Structure Plan (Gloucestershire County Council, 1978). This advocates the dispersal of residential development among the main villages and their supporting settlements to stabilize population levels and to maintain local services. Special units of accommodation for small households, including the elderly, would be provided as part of this strategy. The County Council also encourages the reinstatement of basic services in the main villages. This policy cuts across the trend towards the centralization of services in the larger

Table 14.8 Satisfaction with rural life: disadvantages and advantages

| | Elderly (%) | Non-elderly (%) |
|---|---|---|
| *Disadvantages* | | |
| Public transport | 31 | 25 |
| Retail/service provision | 17 | 26 |
| Isolation/remoteness | 17 | 13 |
| Prices of goods | 9 | 5 |
| Traffic problems | 8 | 3 |
| Social life | 8 | 20 |
| General problems | 10 | 8 |
| TOTAL | 100 ($N = 157$) | 100 ($N = 296$) |
| *Advantages* | | |
| Peace/quiet | 30 | 29 |
| Rural environment | 26 | 32 |
| Village life/community | 34 | 24 |
| Health | 6 | 10 |
| Accessibility | 3 | 4 |
| Facilities/services | 1 | 1 |
| TOTAL | 100 ($N = 271$) | 100 ($N = 353$) |

centres, but if achieved would reduce the distances travelled by the elderly. Whereas public services might be reintroduced at public expense, some form of financial incentive might be required from Gloucestershire County Council to encourage commercial services to operate with lower threshold populations (Gilder, 1979).

This settlement strategy can only be implemented successfully if public transport can be maintained to serve the scattered pattern of infrequent demand and thereby links clusters of settlements to the market towns. It is therefore essential that present levels of public transport are maintained and, where possible, improved (Gloucestershire County Council, 1979). This will inevitably involve Gloucestershire County Council in determining and awarding further subsidies to rural bus operators. As in other rural areas they may also have to consider the greater use of unconventional forms of public transport and further support for voluntary schemes (Creswell, 1977; Moseley, 1978b). Any reduction in the real level of financial support will have serious implications for those elderly households in parishes which lack basic services.

The accessibility problems of the elderly vary in different localities and solutions will only be found at a local scale (Banister, 1979). Meeting their demands at a time of financial restraint will require the co-operation of all agencies concerned with the welfare of the elderly. In particular, their transport needs will be most effectively met by the greater co-ordination of public services, voluntary organizations, and the local community.

## ACKNOWLEDGEMENTS

We acknowledge the assistance of the geography students at Kingston Polytechnic who conducted the interviews; Tony Redpath, who helped with the analysis of survey material; Peter Ashcroft and Roger Macklin of the County Surveyor's Department, Gloucestershire County Council; and Nigel Payne of the Planning Department, Cotswold District Council.

## REFERENCES

Association of District Councils (1978). *Rural Recovery: Strategy for Survival.* Association of District Councils, London.

Banister, D. (1979). A method for investigating consumer preferences for certain transport policy alternatives. In Goodall, B. and Kirby, A. (eds), *Resources and Planning*, pp. 325–41. Pergamon, London.

Best, R. H. and Rogers, A. W. (1973). *The Urban Countryside.* Faber, London.

Cloke, P. (1977). An index of rurality for England and Wales. *Regional Studies*, **11**, 31–46.

Clout, H. D. (1972). *Rural Geography.* Pergamon, London.

Creswell, R. (Ed.) (1977). *Rural Transport and Country Planning.* Leonard Hill, London.

Department of Transport (1977). *Survey of Concessionary Bus Fares for the Elderly, Blind and Disabled in England and Wales*, Local Transport Note 1/77. Department of Transport, London.

Dods, J. (1978). Lost opportunities: passenger vehicle licensing and the law. In Garden, J. (ed.), *Solving the Transport Problems of the Elderly: The Use of Resources*, pp. 25–36. Beth Johnson Foundation, Keele.

Dunn, M. C. (1976). Population change and the settlement pattern. In Cherry, G. (ed.), *Rural Planning Problems*, pp. 13–46. Leonard Hill, London.

Gant, R. L. and Smith, J. A. (1979). *Changes in the Occupation Structure of Six Cotswold Villages 1939–1979: A Consideration of Information Sources and Fieldwork Practice*. School of Geography, Kingston Polytechnic, Kingston upon Thames.

Garden, J. (ed.) (1978). *Solving the Transport Problems of the Elderly: The Use of Resources*. Beth Johnson Foundation, Keele.

Gilder, I. (1979). Rural planning policies: an economic appraisal. *Progress in Planning*, **11**, 213–71.

Gloucestershire County and City Executive Council (1966). *Pharmaceutical List*. GCCEC, Gloucester.

Gloucestershire County and City Executive Council (1968). *List of Doctors Who Have Undertaken to Provide General Medical Services*, 11th issue. GCCEC, Gloucester.

Gloucestershire County Council (1978). *Draft Structure Plan*. GCC, Gloucester.

Gloucestershire County Council (1979). *Public Transport Plan*. GCC, Gloucester.

Hale, S. and Hale, M. (1976). *Rural Depopulation in England*. Community Council of Hereford and Worcester, Worcester.

Hereford and Worcester County Council (1978). *Rural Community Development Project*, Report of the Working Party, October 1975 to June 1978. HWCC, Worcester.

Hertfordshire County Council Transport Co-ordination Unit (1977). *Public Transport for Rural Communities*, Report No. 2. HCC, Hertford.

Hillman, M., Henderson, I., and Whalley, A. (1973). *Personal Mobility and Transport Policy*, Broadsheet 542. Political and Economic Planning, London.

Hillman, M. and Whalley, A. (1979). *Walking is Transport*, Report 45. Policy Studies Institute, London.

Jackson, V. J. (1968). *Population in the Countyside*. Frank Cass, London.

Macgregor, M. (1972). The rural culture. *New Society*, 9 March, pp. 486–9.

Moseley, M. J. (ed.) (1978a). *Social Issues in Rural Norfolk*. Centre for East Anglian Studies, University of East Anglia, Norwich.

Moseley, M. J. (1978b). The mobility and accessibility problems of the rural elderly: some evidence from Norfolk and possible policies. In Garden, J. (ed.), *Solving the Transport Problems of the Elderly: The Use of Resources*, pp. 51–62. Beth Johnson Foundation, Keele.

Moseley, M. J. (1979). *Accessibility: The Rural Challenge*. Methuen, London.

Moseley, M. J., Harman, R. G., Coles, O. B., and Spencer, M. B. (1977). *Rural Transport and Accessibility*, Centre for East Anglian Studies, University of East Anglia, Norwich.

National Association of Local Councils (1980). *Rural Life: Change or Decay*. NALC London.

Norman, A. (1977). *Transport and the Elderly*. National Corporation for the Care of Old People, London.

Rawson, M. (1978). *Rural Housing and Population in Cotswold District*, Working Paper 5. Wye College, University of London, Wye, Kent.

Robinson, M. (1963). The north Cotswolds. *Town and Country Planning*, **31**, 177–83.

Shaw, J. M. (ed.) (1979). *Rural Deprivation and Planning*. Geo Abstracts Ltd, Norwich.

Smith, J. A. and Gant, R. L. (1979). *Rural Transport in the Cotswolds: A Bus Passenger Survey*. School of Geography, Kingston Polytechnic, Kingston upon Thames.

Standing Conference of Rural Community Councils (1978). *The Decline of Rural Services*. National Council of Social Service, London.

Traffic Commissioners, Western Traffic Area (1975–79), *Notices and Proceedings*. TCWTA, Bristol.

Whiteley, P. F. (1971). Cheltenham as a Central Place. Unpublished MSc thesis, University of Bristol, Bristol.

Willis, K. G. (1974). Transport in rural areas. In Whitby, M. C., Robbins, D. L. J., Tansey, A. W. and Willis, K. G. (eds), *Rural Resource Development*, pp. 177–97. Methuen, London.

PART 4

# SPATIAL ASPECTS OF SERVICE PROVISION

Geographical Perspectives on the Elderly
Edited by A. M. Warnes


Chapter 15

# Spatial aspects of primary health care for the elderly

*James R. Bohland* and *Patricia Frech*

The topic of this chapter is primary health care for the aged. Health care is but one of the many services the elderly must obtain from the public and private sectors of the urban economy. Because a finite number of health care providers exist within any city, competition for access is so keen that a majority of the population believes a crisis in health care exists within the United States (Lewis, Rashi and Mechanic, 1976). The competitive aspect of health services is particularly critical for elderly residents, for they compete for health care resources against persons whose personal mobility and financial resources are greater. While public programmes provide alternative health care settings for the elderly, other forces constrain their access to health care. One such factor may be the locational arrangement of health services, its influence upon access and service performance, and its relationship to the type and quality of health care available to the elderly. Previously this has not been analysed and in this chapter we take a small step towards reducing this void.

We have considered only two primary medical care providers: private physicians and hospital emergency rooms. We have chosen to ignore those services restricted to the elderly, such as home-bound services for the aged or special clinics for the aged. These programmes exist in part because of the failure of the existing private and public sector health care systems to meet the needs of the elderly. Our interest is to determine whether the spatial arrangement of those health care facilities which are available to the entire urban population influences their use by the aged.

The empirical portion of the chapter has two components. First, the relative location of the elderly to primary care physicians is analysed. Because of higher morbidity rates the health care needs of the elderly are greater than those of younger persons, yet medical services are not always distributed on the basis of need (see deVise, 1973; Knox, 1978). Too frequently an 'inverse law' of service distribution exists; that is, the greatest resources are in areas of lesser need (Phillips, 1979). Whether this is true for the elderly has not been evaluated thoroughly, although a recent study by Pinch (1979) indicated that in London resources for the elderly were distributed generally in accord with need.

The use of emergency rooms for primary health care by the elderly is the second topic analysed. In many American cities emergency rooms have become important as primary care settings for all age groups. Several surveys report that as many as 50 per cent of all patients admitted for care in an emergency room are non-urgent, primary care patients (Jonas and Rimer, 1977; Noble *et al.*, 1971). Little is known, however, about how this treatment setting is used by the elderly.

## PRIMARY CARE FOR THE AGED

Good health is essential to the personal well-being of all ages. The primary care physician is the first link in the chain of care, and as such, typically provides:

> medical attention to the great majority of ills, provided continuously over a significant period of time by the same appropriately trained individual . . . who is as capable of keeping people as well as he is of returning them to health when they fall ill (Jonas, 1973, p. 177).

A simpler yet more practical definition is that he or she is the physician of 'first contact' (Lewis, Rashi and Mechanic, 1976). At the time of illness he is the person who evaluates the complaint, diagnoses the cause, and prescribes the treatment. If more specialized curative services are necessary, a specialist may be required.

Such a definition places primary care outside the sole domain of the professional medical person. In fact, in the truest sense of the concept, much that can be considered primary care is provided by the family or by other informal sources which may be very important as in the case of children.

The availability of primary care services is particularly important to the elderly, as increased morbidity and chronic illness are the realities that too frequently accompany old age. For many, increased morbidity means reduced mobility, loss of discretionary time, increased dependency, or even institutionalization. Although Medicare has alleviated the financial burdens of most elderly patients, in some cases the costs are severe. The average per capital health costs for persons 65 or older is three times the figure for younger persons and it has been increasing at alarming rates (Mueller and Gibson, 1975).

The increasing cost of care for the elderly has important public policy repercussions because the greatest share of these costs (approximately 60 per cent) are charged against Medicare and Medicaid. As a result, the bill for health care for the aged reached $45 billion in 1978 (Sommers, 1978). Costs such as these have caused some public officials to voice concern about the goals and the expense of special social service programmes for the elderly; a trend that could have serious consequences for future service levels (see Golant and McCaslin, 1979 for a summary of the arguments on this issue).

Even as costs escalated the elderly were accused of being a favoured class with respect to health care: 'if you are either very poor, disabled, *over 65* [emphasis mine], white, or live in a middle-upper class neighborhood, you belong to a privileged class of health care recipients...' (deVise, 1973, p. 1). Although it is true that with the advent of Medicare in 1965 many of the financial constraints on health care for the aged were removed, increased visits do not necessarily produce better health care. Moreover, while the financial burden of professional care was removed for most aged residents, costs associated with travel and access remained.

One indication that health care behaviour changes with old age is the distinctive treatment settings used by the elderly. The aged rely more on public clinics, hospital out-patient services and home-bound care programmes, while for younger people private physicians and the family are the major sources of care (Auerbach *et al.*, 1977; Solon and Rigg, 1972; Shanas, 1979).

The reasons for these differences include widowhood in old age, the unwillingness of some physicians to honour Medicare, and the special health care needs of the elderly. Whether accessibility also influences the choice of a treatment setting has yet to be established, but the reduction in physical mobility and loss in personal income that occurs with increased age suggests its importance. However, empirical evidence indicates that the elderly are willing to travel further for medical care than for other types of services (Cantor, 1975; Neibanck, 1965).

Despite a sizable body of literature in geography on the relationship between distance and intensity of use of health care facilities the evidence is unclear (Earickson, 1970; Morrill, Earickson and Ress, 1970; Shannon and Spurlock, 1976; Shannon, Spurlock and Skinner, 1975). After reviewing the literature on distance and health care, Hodgart (1978) concluded that frequency of use appeared to be inelastic with distance, but, and perhaps more importantly, the selection of the health care settings did appear to be influenced by access. Thus, the spatial structure of health care facilities appears to be more influential in determining the type of setting used than the rate at which a particular alternative is used.

For the elderly the choices available for primary care may be considerable. Figure 15.1 illustrates some of these which can typically be found in an urban setting. The most accessible forms of care are associated with the home and the local environment. Most are informal, non-professional and used regularly, but only if the illness is not perceived as being serious. However, for some older residents the lack of a family constrains their use of these more immediate choices.

At the next level are community-supported forms of care. Some are formal

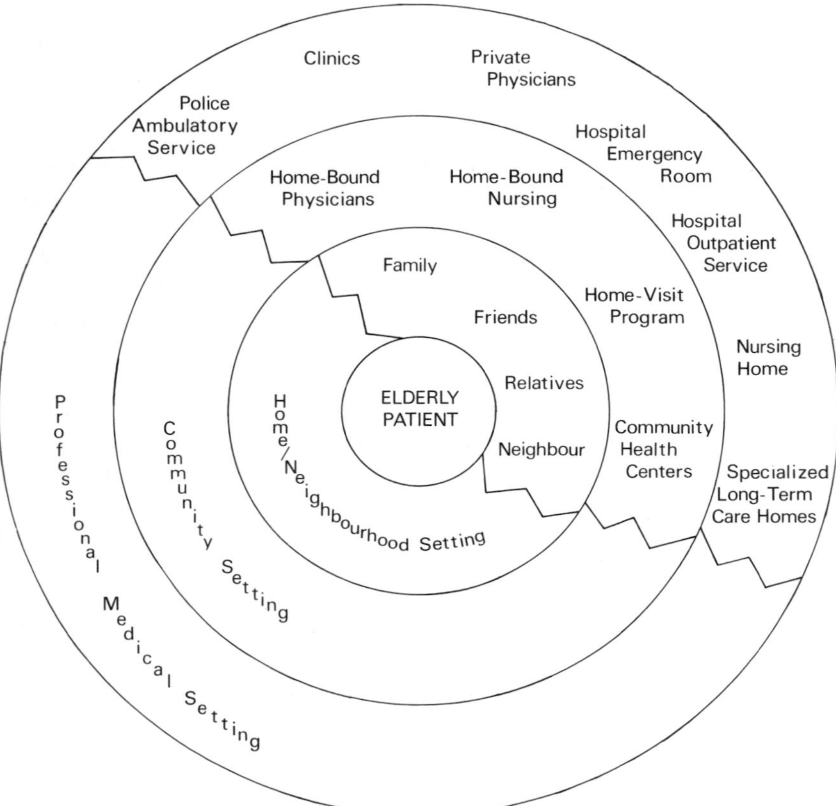


Figure 15.1 Primary care treatment facilities in an urban environment (*Note*: The categorization of settings is a modification of the taxonomy of mental health settings proposed by Dear and Wolch, 1979.)

in structure, such as home-bound programmes run by professional medical groups, while others are informal. Some informal services are available only through membership to particular groups, e.g. church or retirement groups, while others are open to all. Community programmes are becoming increasingly important, particularly with the trends towards decentralization of medical facilities (Tobin, 1975; Oktay and Sheppard, 1978).

Traditional medical settings constitute the last set of alternatives. Care in such settings is professional and more formal in its patient–provider relationship, but is typically less responsive to the specific needs of a particular group.

The total number and character of the available alternatives in each type of care is determined by forces in both the private and public sector. The choice of facility is, however, a personal decision and is a function of both personal factors and the attributes of the various alternatives. Among the influential attributes are the degree to which care is personalized, the immediacy of access, the continuity of care, and the ability of the client to participate in decisions affecting their health (Lewis, Rashi and Mechanic, 1976).

If choice is influenced by access, then the spatial arrangement of primary care facilities will influence which treatment settings are used by the elderly and therefore the quality of care provided them. While our data do not permit an analysis of individual choices, it is possible to analyze the relative location of the elderly with respect to specific primary care alternatives, and to evaluate whether their location places them at a disadvantage in comparison to younger residents.

## INTRA-URBAN DISTRIBUTION OF THE AGED

The study area included most of Oklahoma City and all of two large suburbs, Midwest City and Del City (Figure 15.2). In 1970 the Oklahoma City SMSA (Standard Metropolitan Statistical Area) had a population in excess of 640,000, of which 85 per cent was within the study area. In 1970 persons 65 and over constituted 7.2 per cent of the population in the study area. Whether the

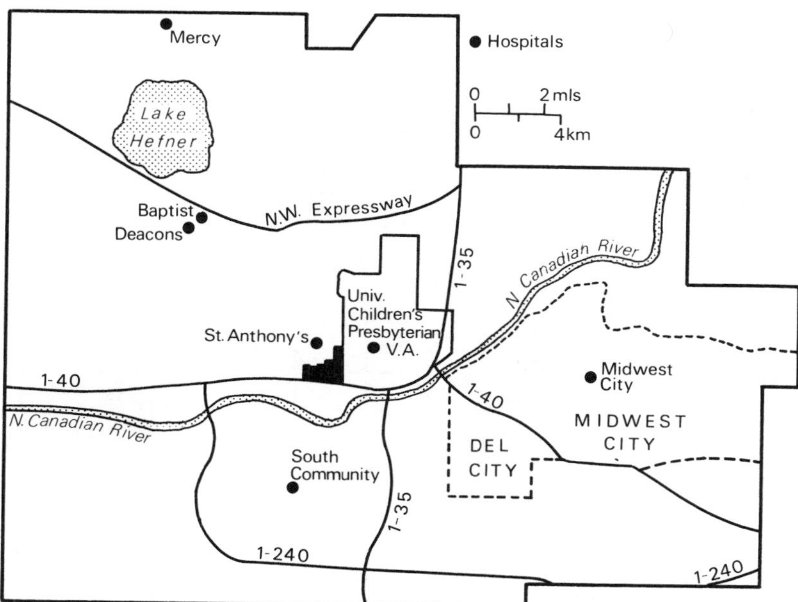


Figure 15.2 The study area of Oklahoma City. (*Note*: The central business district is indicated by the solid black area. The major suburbs of Del City and Midwest City are shown.)

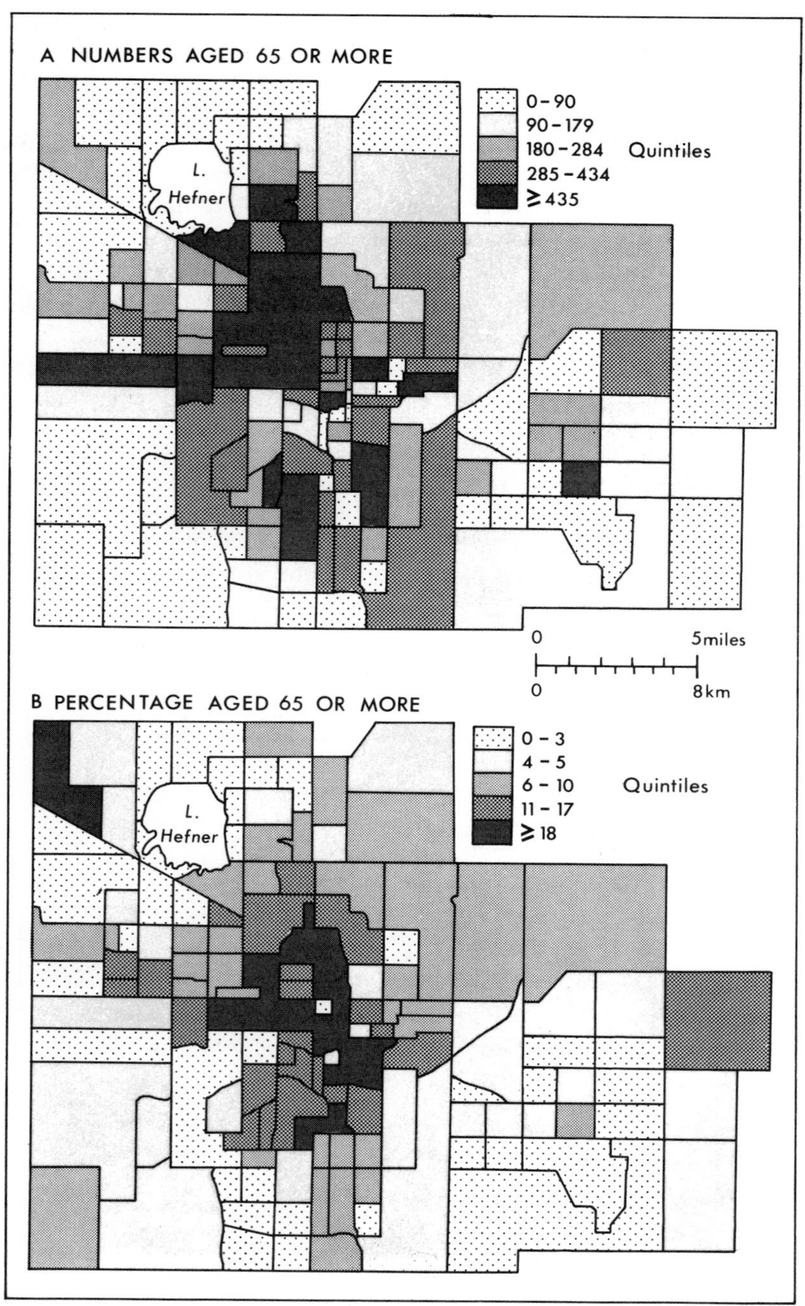


Figure. 15.3 Distribution of the elderly (65 + ) population in Oklahoma City, 1970

elderly are more poorly situated than younger residents for securing primary care is in part a function of their segregation. If the elderly are evenly distributed amongst the population, age differentials in access would be minimal. The extent of age segregation has been analysed in several cities. Wiseman (1978) provides a good summary and shows that the empirical evidence is ambivalent. Age segregation does occur in some cities, though not at the levels associated with racial segregation, but in others it is not found. Concentrations of elderly residents are generally in the older neighbourhoods surrounding the city core (Cowgill and Ostertag, 1962). In 1970 the elderly in Oklahoma City were clearly concentrated in inner city neighbourhoods (Figure 15.3). The largest absolute numbers were located immediately to the west of the CBD (Central Business District) and in some of the more distant neighbourhoods to the north and west. The distribution of elderly percentages was similar, although the large number of younger persons in the outer tracts caused a decline in percentages outward from the core. South of the CBD percentages were high, although the absolute numbers were modest. The absence of sizable numbers of elderly east of the CBD reflected racial differences in neighbourhood composition for the Black neighbourhoods extend north and east of the core (Figure 15.2). The western edge of the Black residential areas corresponded closely with the eastern boundary of areas of elderly concentration.

The index of dissimilarity was used to measure the level of age segregation in the city (see Timms, 1971 for a discussion of the index). The index can be interpreted as the proportion of the elderly population that would have to be redistributed to achieve the same distribution as the younger population. According to the index value (39.1), the elderly were only moderately segregated in comparison to ethnic groups but more segregated than in most cities; 32 was the highest index value reported by Kennedy and DeJong (1977) in their study of age segregation in metropolitan areas. The level of age segregation in Oklahoma was therefore high enough to expect age differentials in access to primary health care locations if these were non-randomly distributed.

## DISTRIBUTION OF PRIMARY CARE PHYSICIANS

A maldistribution of physicians has plagued the health care delivery system in the United States for several decades. Public interest and public policy has focused on rural deficiencies, but maldistribution within cities is equally severe. The problem seems to exist even in countries with more centrally planned health care systems (Giggs, 1979; Knox, 1978; Shannon and Dever, 1974).

The distribution of primary care physicians within a city is typically clustered. There is a tendency for many to locate in the higher income suburban areas and an equally strong tendency to cluster around hospitals. Since large hospitals are often in the inner city, many physicians are located in close proximity to its population (Bashshur, Shannon and Metzner, 1970). Another consequence is that those living in the fringe areas have to drastically alter their travel behaviour in order to secure health services (Shannon and Spurlock, 1976). If inner city hospitals are poorly situated, or if a hospital is not a focus for primary care physicians, then inner city residents are deprived of easy access (Norman, 1969).

Data from the Oklahoma State Medical Association were used to locate the offices of all primary physicians in the study area (Oklahoma State Medical Association, 1979). For this study primary physicians were defined as doctors with specialities in family practice, general practice, general preventive medicine, geriatrics, gynaecology and obstetrics, pediatrics, and internal medicine. Thirty-five per cent of all doctors in the area listed specialities in primary care. This figure was well below the national average of 46 per cent, but the per capita ratio of 2.9 per 3500 was well above the standard of 1 per 3500 established by the federal government to designate depressed areas (Department of Health, Education and Welfare, 1978).

Although the entire city had an acceptable ratio, considerable areas within the study area were under-served (Figure 15.4). In fact, most census tracts

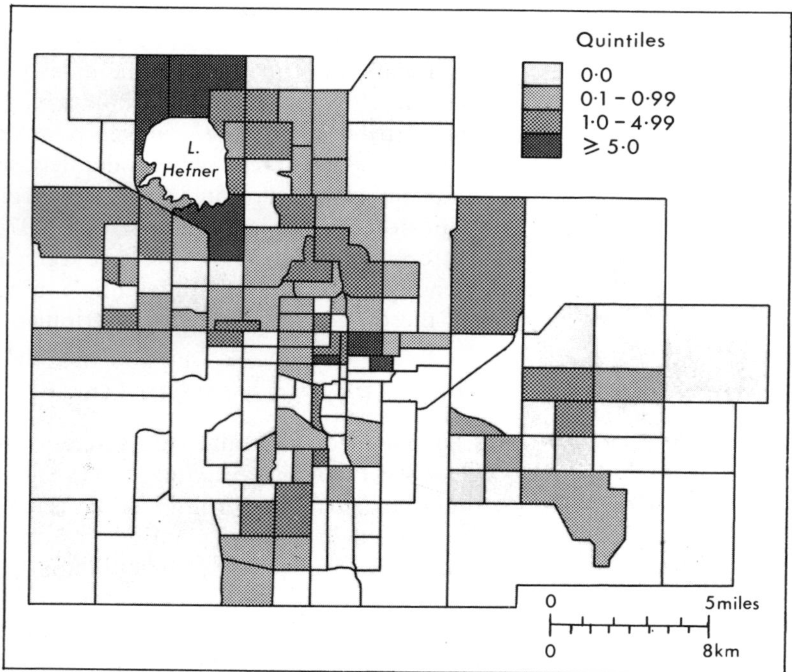


Figure 15.4 Per capita distribution of primary care physicians in Oklahoma City

had no physicians, and most were concentrated around the large hospitals (Figures 15.2 and 15.4). As a result, 64 per cent of all primary care physicians were located in six census tracts, four being close to the CBD. The largest concentration was associated with the medical complex at the University Health Science Center. In neighbourhoods more distant from the CBD, Baptist and Mercy hospitals were the foci for physicians.

Although hospital agglomerations dominated the distribution, a sectoral bias was also evident. The number of physicians in the north-west quadrant was much higher than in the other sectors and deficiencies were particularly evident in the south-west and south-east. Without the clustering of physicians around South Community hospital, the entire southern half of the city would have been critically under-served.

The clustering of physicians meant that many residents were not well situated to obtain primary care services. Whether this was true for the elderly was measured in two ways. First, the index of dissimilarity showed that the distribution of physicians was poorly matched to that of the elderly. To match the elderly distribution, 71 per cent of the physicians would have needed to be redistributed. This maldistribution of physicians was not, however, biased against the elderly, for the index for the younger population was also high (69).

Because census tracts rarely correspond to urban activity fields, an additional measure was employed to measure access in terms of travel. For each tract the numbers of physicians within 3- and 6-mile travel zones of its centroid were tabulated and physicians per capita (PCP) ratios calculated. The PCP ratios were classified in relation to the government standard of 1 : 3500. The number of persons aged 65 years or more and the number of younger people in each PCP category for each travel zone was tabulated (Table 15.1). For tracts on the boundary of the study area some underestimation of physicians was encountered because of the lack of information on physicians outside the area. Fortunately, most places beyond the study area were either rural or low-density residential distincts and had few physicians.

Approximately 30 per cent of the elderly population had no physician within 3 miles of their home tract, and 75 per cent lived in areas where the PCP ratio was less than the standard. In the 6-mile zone one-fifth lived in tracts with sub-standard ratios. Primary care quite obviously was not immediately accessible to most older residents of the city. In comparative terms, however, the elderly actually were in a slightly better situation than persons younger than 65. For this group, 82 per cent lived in substandard tracts in the 3-mile case and over half in the 6-mile zone.

Admittedly the analysis focused only on one aspect of access, proximity. Althouth proximity to physicians does not guarantee use or quality of care, inaccessibility indicates which elements of the urban population must expend more resources on travel in order to secure care. Because the mobility of many aged is restricted and personal incomes are lower, the time and cost

Table 15.1 The availability of primary health care physicians to the elderly and non-elderly populations of Oklahoma City

| Availability of physicians per capita (PCP). Ratio to national standard | Within 3 miles | | Within 6 miles | |
|---|---|---|---|---|
| | Elderly (%) | Non-elderly (%) | Elderly (%) | Non-elderly (%) |
| No primary care physicians | 29.5 (29.5)[a] | 38.2 (38.7) | 5.3 (5.3) | 7.6 (7.6) |
| Less than 0.5 | 28.8 (58.3) | 36.8 (75.5) | 20.3 (25.3) | 29.6 (37.2) |
| 0.5–0.99 | 17.4 (75.5) | 7.3 (82.8) | 21.5 (47.1) | 17.9 (55.1) |
| 1.0–1.99 | 10.5 (86.2) | 7.0 (89.8) | 20.8 (67.9) | 18.3 (73.4) |
| 2.0–3.99 | 4 0 (90.2) | 4.6 (94.4) | 7.9 (76.8) | 14.6 (88.0) |
| 4.0 or more | 9.8 (100) | 5.6 (100) | 24.2 (100) | 12.0 (100) |

[a] Cumulative percentages.
*Source*: Survey of Oklahoma City Hospital Emergency Rooms conducted by the authors.

constraints of travel are more important to this group, and different norms in terms of relative location must be applied.

## EMERGENCY ROOMS AS PRIMARY CARE SETTINGS

As noted earlier, emergency rooms are being used increasingly for primary care. A survey in New York substantiated high utilization levels by the elderly, for 43 per cent indicated that hospital out-patient clinics and emergency rooms were their first choices as primary care treatment settings. In the inner city the dependence reached 90 per cent, while the suburban percentage was considerably lower at 27 (Auerbach *et al.*, 1977). Much lower levels of use characterized the all-age population of Pittsburgh where only 22 per cent of the inner city residents used hospital services for primary care. In the suburbs the percentage was less than 2 (Solon and Rigg, 1972). Unfortunately neither study differentiated between emergency rooms and out-patient clinics so their relative contributions could not be estimated.

We have limited our analysis to emergency rooms to assess their role in primary care. In many respects emergency rooms are unlikely settings for the elderly's primary care; costs are high, even though most honour Medicare, the emergency room environment can be congested, disquieting and impersonal, and continuing care with the same physician is not guaranteed. Why then are such facilities used by the elderly? The inner city location of hospitals, the greater willingness of hospitals to honour third-party vendors, such as Medicare, and the ability to obtain service on a walk-in basis appear to be important.

To analyse the elderly's use of emergency rooms, a two per cent sample was taken of patients at Baptist, University and South Community hospitals in 1977 (Figure 15.2). Ten hospitals in the area provide emergency services, but these three admit 53 per cent of all emergency room patients in a year (Area Wide Health Planning Organization, 1975). Of the three hospitals, only University is located in the inner city, immediately to the east of the CBD in an older Black neighbourhood. As part of the teaching and research complex of the University of Oklahoma Health Sciences Center, it is only one of several hospitals in the immediate area. It has, however, the largest emergency room facility in the complex and admits more emergency patients than the others. Largely because Oklahoma County does not have a county hospital, University has assumed major responsibility for treating charity patients. Baptist is a large, church-affiliated hospital situated in the north-west of the city. The newest of the three, it enjoys a reputation as an innovative, efficient hospital with the latest technology. South Community is unique in that it was built and is maintained by a city trust to alleviate the shortage of health care facilities in the southern half of the city (Figure 15.4). Surrounding neighbourhoods are heterogenous in income and race, but most are older, working-class neighbourhoods.

Although we were prohibited from interviewing patients, information was obtained from written records on patient characteristics, type of complaint, personal physician, and place of residence. It is therefore possible to relate aspects of the spatial behaviour of patients to the type of service received. In analysing the emergency room information, however, a serious problem was encountered in classifying types of care. Emergency room personnel use the classification: non-urgent—disorder is minor or non-acute; urgent—disorder is acute but not necessarily severe; and emergent—disorder is acute and potentially threatens life or function (American Hospital Association, 1972). Although this is helpful the urgency criterion does not correspond perfectly with level of care. Many urgent cases, for example, could be considered as requiring primary care of a more serious nature.

Primary care was eventually determined as all non-urgent cases plus the urgent cases involving certain patient complaints. Patient complaints were used rather than physician diagnoses because the patient's perceptions influence their selection of a type of treatment centre (Ingram, Clarke and Murdie, 1978). Physicians were consulted to help with the screening of patient complaints. While we are confident of the validity of all cases classified as primary care, the procedure probably underestimates the total number of primary care patients.

If we assume that the proportions at other hospitals were similar to those in the sample, emergency rooms were used more by the elderly than by younger residents. In two hospitals, Baptist and University, the percentage of elderly emergency room patients was higher than the aged percentage for the study area (Table 15.2). Since all three hospitals were near neighbourhoods with concentrations of older persons, the high percentages were not as surprising as the low figure for South Community.

In all three hospitals the proportion of elderly patients that received primary care was lower than for younger patients (Table 15.2). Although these figures contradict earlier studies, this is more apparent than real. The elderly constitute a smaller percentage of the urban population but have a higher rate of use of the emergency rooms. The emergency room primary care percentage for the entire urban elderly population was estimated to be 4.6 but 1.8 for younger patients. This elderly rate was still well below the figure reported in the New York study, suggesting that out-patient clinics rather than emergency rooms were the principal source of care in hospitals. There were substantial differences between the hospitals in the proportion of their emergency room patients who were 65 years and over. Baptist serviced the majority of the elderly in the sample (62 per cent) with University second (24 per cent). The importance of Baptist to the elderly community throughout the city was evident from the geographical extent of its catchment area (Figure 15.5). Elderly patients came from all over the city to use the emergency room at Baptist and in so doing by-passed closer hospitals. As a result their mean travel distance was 4 miles greater than for University's elderly patients (Table 15.2). The comparable distance for South Community indicated that it was serving primarily the elderly population in the immediate neighbourhoods.

The pre-eminence of Baptist as a treatment location for the elderly was

Table 15.2 Selected characteristics of emergency room patients at three Oklahoma City hospitals

| Hospital | All patients (%) | | Receiving primary care (%) | | Without physician (%) | | Average distance travelled |
|---|---|---|---|---|---|---|---|
| | < 65 | ⩾ 65 | < 65 | ⩾ 65 | < 65 | ⩾ 65 | ⩾ 65 miles |
| University | 89.6 | 10.4 | 46.7 | 35.0 | 72.7 | 25.0 | 12.4 |
| Baptist | 87.9 | 12.1 | 43.4 | 39.0 | 56.8 | 76.7 | 16.3 |
| South Community | 94.0 | 6.0 | 41.5 | 36.3 | 45.3 | 15.0 | 6.2 |
| Average | 88.9 | 10.9 | 43.9 | 37.6 | 59.2 | 55.9 | 14.1 |

*Source*: Survey of Oklahoma City Hospital Emergency Rooms conducted by the authors.

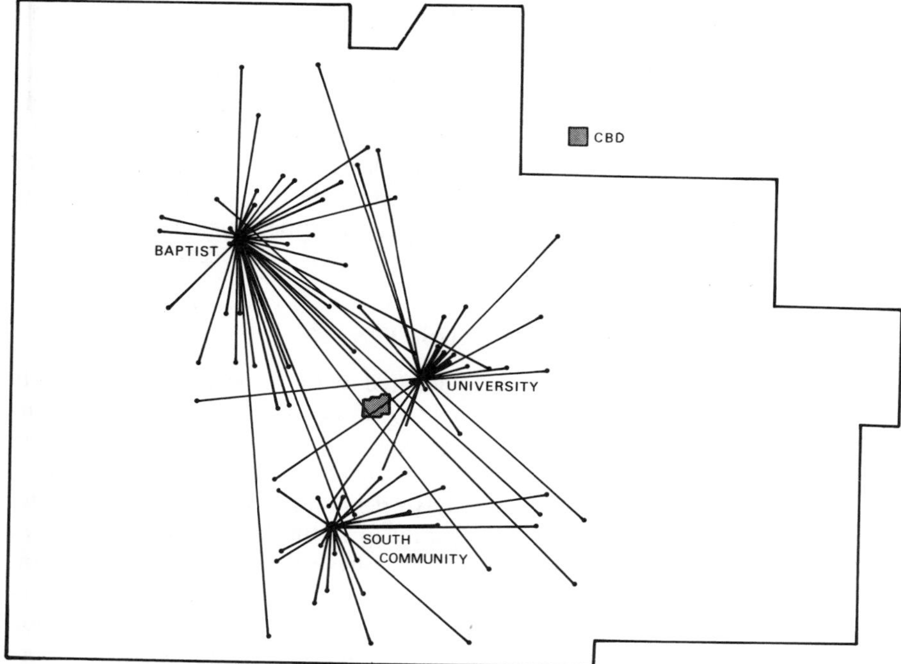


Figure 15.5 Travel to hospital emergency rooms by elderly patients. (*Note*: The lines connect the residences of the elderly patients with the place where emergency room services were obtained.)

surprising because University is more centrally situated and because of Baptist's situation in the middle–upper-income sector where one would anticipate greater utilization of private physicians. Several reasons can be offered for this, including its newness, its religious affiliation, and its reputation for innovation. In contrast, University hospital is situated among Black neighbourhoods and this probably deters many elderly. The size of this medical complex, and the congestion it creates, is confusing and makes it difficult to find the required facility. Finally, the 'charity' reputation of the University hospital concerns those elderly patients who do not wish to be supported by the county.

The possibility that the elderly selected a type and location of emergency room because other choices, particularly private physicians, were unavailable was also considered. Because of the absence of information on each individual's choice set the results were inconclusive, but it was clear that the location of physicians was not important since the majority were clustered around the three hospitals. Travel time would not generally have been reduced by consulting a private doctor. The more important dimension of access appeared to be the availability of a physician within a reasonable time, and in this respect emergency rooms had a decided advantage.

Data from the patients' records indicated that a majority of those using the emergency room for primary care did not have a personal physician (Table 15.2). At Baptist this applied to over three-quarters of the elderly patients, and to as many as 65 per cent of those receiving primary care. In the other two hospitals the percentages were smaller, particularly at South Community, but even so the lack of a personal physician did appear to be an important factor in the selection of emergency rooms.

## CONCLUSIONS

Primary care physicians were poorly located with respect to most elderly residents of the Oklahoma City area. The agglomeration of physicians means that most elderly people, like younger people, are distant from primary care physicians. As we have shown, many elderly turn to hospital emergency rooms to receive primary care. Few of them have personal physicians and they use emergency rooms instead. The reasons for the low utilization of other treatment facilities are unclear but it does appear that physical access is less important than anticipated. The elderly who used emergency rooms came long distances and thereby avoided more adjacent facilities. It appears that the reputation of the hospital and the character of the surrounding neighbourhoods were important factors influencing the selection of the hospital, but like the factors influencing the choice of a type of facility, they require further investigation.

Our analysis has focused on distance as a measure of access. It might be argued from a 'needs' perspective that in comparison to younger residents the elderly are in a worse position if their physical accessibility is the same. Their higher morbidity rates and longer periods of convalescence require more frequent use of primary care facilities. It will therefore be worthwhile to develop other measures of access which incorporate frequency as well the distance of travel. A needs element might show that the problem is worse than our results have suggested.

While Medicare and Medicaid have reduced the financial liabilities of professional medical services for many elderly persons, the costs associated with securing care, such as travel costs, still exist and continue to be borne by the individual. Such costs are strongly influenced by the spatial structure of primary care treatment facilities. It is obvious then that the spatial distribution of health facilities influences the quality of health care, and consequently, the quality of the lives of the aged living in urban areas. Unfortunately, the distribution of medical facilities within the city currently are influenced very little by the needs and demands of groups, such as the elderly, that have special continuing needs. As a consequence, the medical facilities are inaccessible and inconvenient for many who have the greatest need for care. If the inequities are allowed to persist, the consequences for the aged are intolerable. However, until more effort is put forth to find and apply practical measures for eliminating the existing inequities the *status quo* will persist, and the aged will continue to shoulder an unnecessary financial burden for health care.

## REFERENCES

American Hospital Association (1972). *Emergency Services.* AHA, Chicago.

Area Wide Health Planning Organization (1975). *Task Force Report on Emergency Medical Services.* AHPO, Oklahoma City.

Auerbach, M. I., Gordon, D. W., Ullmann, A., and Weisel, M. J. (1977). Health care in a selected urban elderly population. *Gerontologist*, **17**, 341–6.

Bashshur, R. L., Shannon, G. W., and Metzner, C. A. (1970). Application of three-dimensional analogue models to the distribution of medical care facilities. *Medical Care*, **8**, 395–407.

Cantor, M. (1975). Life space and the social support system of the inner city elderly of New York. *Gerontologist*, **15**, 26–7.

Cowgill, D. O. and Ostertag, S. F. (1962). *The People of Wichita, 1960.* Urban Studies Center, Wichita, Kansas.

Dear, M. and Wolch, J. (1979). The optimal assignment of human service clients to treatment settings. In Golant, S. M. (ed.), *Location and Environment of Elderly Population*, pp. 197–209. V. H. Winston & Sons, Washington, DC.

Department of Health, Education, and Welfare (1978). *Health Manpower Shortage Areas: Criteria for Designation.* Public Health Services, DHEW, Washington, DC.

DeVise, P. (1973). *Misused and Misplaced Hospitals and Doctors.* Commission on College Geography, Resource Paper, No. 22. Association of American Geographers, Washington, DC.

Earickson, R. (1970). *The Spatial Behaviour of Hospital Patients. A Behavioural Approach to Spatial Interaction in Metropolitan Chicago.* Dept. of Geography, Research Paper No. 124. University of Chicago, Chicago.

Giggs, J. A. (1979). Human health problems in urban areas. In Herbert, D. T. and Smith, D. M. (eds), *Social Problems and the City: Geographical Perspectives*, pp. 84–116. Oxford University Press, Oxford.

Golant, S. M. and McCaslin, R. (1979). A social indicator model of the elderly population's social welfare environment. In Golant, S. M. (ed.), *Location and Environment of Elderly Population*, pp. 181–96. V. H. Winston & Sons, Washington, D C.

Hodgart, R. L. (1978). Optimizing access to public services: a review of problems, models and methods of locating central facilities. *Progress in Human Geography*, **2**, 17–48.

Ingram, D. R., Clarke, D. R., and Murdie, R. A. (1978). Distance and the decision to visit an emergency department. *Social Science and Medicine*, **12**, 55–62.

Jonas, S. (1973). Some thoughts on primary care: problems in implementation. *International Journal of Health Services*, **3**, 176–80.

Jonas, S. and Rimer, B. (1977). Ambulatory care. In Jonas, S. (ed.), *Health Care Delivery in the United States*, pp. 120–63. Springer Publishing Company, New York.

Kennedy, J. M. and DeJong, G. F. (1977). Aged in cities: residential segregation in ten USA central cities. *Journal of Gerontology*, **33**, 97–102.

Knox, P. L. (1978). The intraurban ecology of primary medical care: patterns of accessibility and their policy implications. *Environment and Planning A*, **10**, 415–35.

Lewis, C., Rashi, F., and Mechanic, D. (1976). *A Right to Health: The Problem of Access to Primary Medical Care.* Wiley, New York.

Morrill, R. L., Earickson, R. J., and Rees, P. (1970). Factors influencing distances travelled to hospitals. *Economic Geography*, **46**, 161–71.

Mueller, M. S. and Gibson, R. M. (1975). Age differences in health care spending, fiscal year 1974. *Social Security Bulletin*, **38**, 3–16.

Neibanck, P. L. (1965). *The Elderly in Older Urban Areas: Problems of Adaption and the Effects of Relocation*. University of Pennsylvania, Institute for Environmental Studies, Philadelphia.

Noble, J. J., LaMontagne, M. E., Bellottic, C., and Wechsler, H. (1971). Variations in visits to hospital emergency care facilities: ritualistic and meteorological factors affecting supply and demand. *Medical Care*, **9**, 415–27.

Norman, J. C. (1969). *Medicine in the Ghetto*. Appleton-Century-Crofts, New York.

Oklahoma State Medical Association (1979). *OSMA Medical Directory*. OSMA, Oklahoma City.

Oktay, J. S. and Sheppard, F. (1978). Home health care for the elderly. *Health and Social Work*, **3**, 36–47.

Pinch, S. (1979). Territorial justice in the city: a case study of the social services for the elderly in Greater London. In Herbert, D. T. and Smith, D. M. (eds), *Social Problems and the City. Geographical Perspectives*, pp. 201–23. Oxford University Press, Oxford.

Phillips, D. R. (1979). Public attitudes to general practitioner services: a reflection of an inverse care law in intra-urban primary medical care. *Environment and Planning A*, **11**, 815–24.

Shanas, E. (1979). The family as a social support system in old age. *Gerontologist*, **19**, 169–74.

Shannon, G. W. and Dever, G. E. A. (1974). *Health Care Delivery. Spatial Perspectives*. McGraw-Hill, New York.

Shannon, G. W. and Spurlock, C. W. (1976). Urban ecological containers, environmental riskcells, and the use of medical services. *Economic Geography*, **52**, 171–80.

Shannon, G. W., Spurlock, C. W., and Skinner, J. L. (1975). A method of evaluating the geographic accessibility of health services. *Professional Geographer*, **27**, 30–6.

Solon, J. A. and Rigg, R. D. (1972). Patterns of medical care among users of hospital emergency units. *Medical Care*, **10**, 60–72.

Sommers, A. R. (1978). The high cost of health care for the elderly: diagnosis, prognosis, and some suggestions for therapy. *Journal of Health Politics, Policy and Law*, **3**, 163–79.

Timms, D. W. G. (1971). *The Urban Mosaic: Towards A Theory of Residential Differentiation*. Cambridge University Press, Cambridge.

Tobin, S. S. (1975). Social and health services for the future aged. *Gerontologist*, **15** (Supplement), 32–7.

Wiseman, R. F. (1978). *Spatial Aspects of Aging*. Association of American Geographers, Resource Paper No. 78–4, Washington, DC.

Geographical Perspectives on the Elderly
Edited by A. M. Warnes


Chapter 16

# Patterns of social service provision for the elderly:

## Variations between local authorities of England in 1975/76, 1977/78, and as forecast in 1979/80

*Andrew C. Bebbington* and *Bleddyn Davies*

### THE CURRENT PATTERN OF PROVISION

This chapter is concerned with the geographical distributions of a group of services used by old people which are provided by the social services departments of local authorities—residential homes, domestic help, day centres, and meals on wheels. They form part of a wider spectrum of welfare provision, mainly for the elderly, administered by a variety of agencies: local authorities also provide sheltered housing and minor services such as physical aids, housing adaptations, concessionary fares, free telephones and holidays; health services provide geriatric and psychogeriatric hospital services, home nursing and chiropody services; while voluntary organizations also play an important part in providing similar services.

Variation between local authorities in the provision of social services is notoriously large. For example, we estimate the social services current expenditure on the elderly in 1977/78 was less than £25 for each person aged over 65 in Devon and the Isle of Wight, while in the London Boroughs of Camden and Islington it was about £137. (Expenditures in 1975/76 and 1977/78 are determined from Department of Environment revenue out-turns for the personal social services. Recurrent expenditure only is examined throughout, defined as spending on manpower and running costs less fees and other income. Populations are mid-year estimates of the Office of Population Censuses and Surveys. Quantities of service provision are determined from *Department of Health and Social Security Personal Social Services Local Authority Statistics* for the year ending 31 March 1978.) This enormous range of variation has scarcely decreased since it was first described and examined a decade ago (see for example Davies, 1968; Davies *et al.*, 1971; Sumner and Smith, 1969).

Table 16.1 Levels of provision and current expenditure on services for the elderly in 1977/78 for each social services department in England, together with a need indicator for expenditure

| Local authority | Residential care[a] | Home helps[b] | Meals on wheels[c] | Day centres[d] | Expenditure for elderly.[e] | Needs indicator[f] |
|---|---|---|---|---|---|---|
| Camden | 370 | 151 | 97 | 195 | 137 | 103* |
| Greenwich | 179 | 126 | 105 | 69 | 78 | 64 |
| Hackney | 361 | 160 | 115 | 96 | 121 | 76* |
| Hammersmith | 272 | 107 | 121 | 67 | 102 | 87* |
| Islington | 354 | 99 | 115 | 228 | 137 | 96* |
| Kensington | 428 | 78 | 56 | 75 | 97 | 119* |
| Lambeth | 290 | 123 | 146 | 287 | 113 | 85 |
| Lewisham | 217 | 130 | 96 | 424 | 95 | 69 |
| Southwark | 291 | 133 | 107 | 356 | 97 | 83 |
| Tower Hamlets | 325 | 109 | 180 | 387 | 133 | 91 |
| Wandsworth | 248 | 102 | 123 | 233 | 96 | 79 |
| Westminster | 319 | 85 | 52 | 35 | 91 | 93* |
| Barking | 164 | 84 | 54 | 103 | 59 | 56 |
| Barnet | 207 | 42 | 35 | 73 | 51 | 60 |
| Bexley | 140 | 73 | 51 | 86 | 43 | 42 |
| Brent | 251 | 60 | 69 | 131 | 74 | 62 |
| Bromley | 185 | 49 | 36 | 99 | 45 | 56 |
| Croydon | 237 | 42 | 27 | 55 | 57 | 65 |
| Ealing | 264 | 63 | 102 | 57 | 71 | 67 |
| Enfield | 185 | 53 | 49 | 133 | 55 | 58 |
| Haringey | 212 | 144 | 135 | 58 | 85 | 83* |
| Harrow | 175 | 44 | 35 | 91 | 44 | 50 |
| Havering | 135 | 79 | 36 | 140 | 59 | 44 |
| Hillingdon | 173 | 71 | 59 | 78 | 62 | 44 |
| Hounslow | 176 | 44 | 73 | 128 | 53 | 61 |
| Kingston | 132 | 32 | 47 | 110 | 43 | 53 |
| Merton | 173 | 87 | 68 | 93 | 64 | 60 |
| Newham | 249 | 106 | 54 | 142 | 63 | 80* |
| Redbridge | 199 | 61 | 55 | 154 | 55 | 57 |
| Richmond | 186 | 36 | 41 | 260 | 45 | 59 |
| Sutton | 153 | 48 | 48 | 110 | 45 | 56 |
| Waltham Forest | 145 | 90 | 39 | 58 | 65 | 62 |
| Cleveland | 208 | 67 | 35 | 116 | 36 | 47 |
| Cumbria | 182 | 58 | 30 | 61 | 40 | 41 |
| Durham | 217 | 99 | 32 | 56 | 54 | 47 |
| Northumberland | 183 | 95 | 32 | 53 | 51 | 45 |
| Gateshead | 209 | 106 | 54 | 49 | 54 | 50 |
| Newcastle | 227 | 146 | 54 | 119 | 77 | 62 |
| North Tyneside | 170 | 85 | 50 | 63 | 53 | 46 |
| South Tyneside | 189 | 83 | 31 | 299 | 57 | 58 |
| Sunderland | 203 | 158 | 27 | 42 | 70 | 59 |
| Humberside | 198 | 74 | 30 | 90 | 48 | 47 |
| North Yorkshire | 198 | 47 | 24 | 66 | 32 | 48 |

(Contd.)

Table 16.1 (Contd.)

| Local authority | Residential care[a] | Home helps[b] | Meals on wheels[c] | Day centres[d] | Expenditure for elderly[e] | Needs indicator[f] |
|---|---|---|---|---|---|---|
| Barnsley | 168 | 117 | 35 | 93 | 61 | 49 |
| Doncaster | 194 | 86 | 36 | 165 | 69 | 44 |
| Rotherham | 160 | 129 | 20 | 263 | 66 | 45 |
| Sheffield | 200 | 94 | 12 | 78 | 67 | 60 |
| Bradford | 214 | 103 | 21 | 42 | 70 | 59 |
| Calderdale | 212 | 69 | 18 | 122 | 52 | 60 |
| Kirklees | 228 | 75 | 23 | 114 | 59 | 55 |
| Leeds | 203 | 84 | 17 | 86 | 48 | 56 |
| Wakefield | 188 | 108 | 27 | 298 | 75 | 52 |
| Cheshire | 144 | 67 | 24 | 51 | 41 | 43 |
| Lancashire | 176 | 62 | 21 | 54 | 37 | 49 |
| Bolton | 202 | 91 | 29 | 31 | 54 | 54 |
| Bury | 198 | 62 | 27 | 64 | 41 | 47 |
| Manchester | 285 | 106 | 130 | 217 | 82 | 68 |
| Oldham | 212 | 128 | 19 | 50 | 65 | 62 |
| Rochdale | 226 | 94 | 19 | 197 | 56 | 57 |
| Salford | 217 | 92 | 37 | 176 | 62 | 59 |
| Stockport | 157 | 64 | 35 | 31 | 43 | 45 |
| Tameside | 153 | 118 | 40 | 58 | 50 | 49 |
| Trafford | 166 | 88 | 24 | 47 | 41 | 45 |
| Wigan | 169 | 103 | 50 | 78 | 48 | 47 |
| Knowsley | 174 | 123 | 25 | 68 | 50 | 46* |
| Liverpool | 253 | 68 | 65 | 98 | 55 | 62 |
| Sefton | 192 | 80 | 22 | 63 | 52 | 62 |
| St Helens | 142 | 133 | 51 | 37 | 54 | 44 |
| Wirral | 258 | 62 | 27 | 84 | 50 | 54 |
| Hereford | 161 | 59 | 28 | 57 | 40 | 43 |
| Salop | 190 | 47 | 37 | 21 | 32 | 43 |
| Stafford | 160 | 76 | 39 | 77 | 41 | 44 |
| Warwickshire | 182 | 75 | 23 | 45 | 39 | 41 |
| Birmingham | 208 | 66 | 37 | 52 | 43 | 45 |
| Coventry | 160 | 99 | 57 | 76 | 55 | 47 |
| Dudley | 122 | 36 | 31 | 82 | 32 | 39 |
| Sandwell | 183 | 59 | 32 | 127 | 50 | 50 |
| Solihull | 161 | 51 | 21 | 82 | 25 | 36* |
| Walsall | 182 | 58 | 28 | 70 | 48 | 43 |
| Wolverhampton | 180 | 63 | 68 | 85 | 45 | 48 |
| Derbyshire | 167 | 63 | 35 | 68 | 41 | 46 |
| Leicestershire | 206 | 64 | 49 | 84 | 47 | 49 |
| Lincolnshire | 170 | 55 | 30 | 55 | 39 | 46 |
| Northamptonshire | 150 | 42 | 33 | 65 | 34 | 47 |
| Nottinghamshire | 144 | 78 | 60 | 107 | 47 | 47 |
| Bedfordshire | 193 | 56 | 52 | 265 | 48 | 43 |
| Berkshire | 147 | 70 | 49 | 66 | 41 | 47 |
| Buckinghamshire | 148 | 44 | 26 | 37 | 33 | 44 |

(Contd.)

Table 16.1 (Contd.)

| Local authority | Residential care[a] | Home helps[b] | Meals on wheels[c] | Day centres[d] | Expenditure for elderly[e] | Needs indicator[f] |
|---|---|---|---|---|---|---|
| Cambridgeshire | 112 | 56 | 36 | 115 | 36 | 46 |
| Essex | 187 | 52 | 28 | 22 | 35 | 47 |
| Hertford | 155 | 51 | 36 | 42 | 37 | 44 |
| Norfolk | 173 | 47 | 22 | 27 | 36 | 43 |
| Oxfordshire | 195 | 72 | 41 | 93 | 53 | 43 |
| Suffolk | 168 | 54 | 31 | 15 | 33 | 45 |
| Dorset | 145 | 32 | 23 | 89 | 30 | 49 |
| Hampshire | 169 | 47 | 30 | 30 | 34 | 46 |
| Isle of Wight | 142 | 22 | 13 | 0 | 20 | 42 |
| Kent | 139 | 42 | 22 | 24 | 36 | 52 |
| Surrey | 170 | 34 | 39 | 32 | 30 | 46 |
| East Sussex | 172 | 37 | 28 | 35 | 32 | 59 |
| West Sussex | 164 | 33 | 38 | 25 | 28 | 49 |
| Wiltshire | 154 | 56 | 26 | 65 | 30 | 41 |
| Avon | 195 | 72 | 68 | 76 | 54 | 51 |
| Cornwall | 148 | 39 | 17 | 43 | 27 | 41 |
| Devon | 148 | 41 | 24 | 46 | 24 | 46 |
| Gloucester | 161 | 59 | 25 | 18 | 35 | 45 |
| Somerset | 149 | 49 | 26 | 47 | 29 | 46 |

*Note*: As explained in the text, the value of the needs indicator is averaged across several separate needs indicators, using different need judgements (and other different assumptions), and scaled to correspond with 1977/78 expenditure. For the eleven asterisked values, there is considerable divergence among the individual needs indicators, and so the average must be treated with caution.

[a] Supported residents per 10,000 persons aged 65 + .
[b] No. of home helps per 10,000 persons aged 65 + .
[c] Meals delivered per 100 persons aged 65 + .
[d] Places (all types) per 10,000 persons aged 65 + .
[e] £ per person aged 65 + .
[f] £ per person aged 65 + .

Although costs are higher in certain parts of the country, particularly in the Greater London Area, this variation is primarily one of volume of services. Columns 2–5 of Table 16.1 show the amount of each service which was provided per elderly capita by each local authority social services department in England (excluding City of London and Isles of Scilly) in 1977/78. The home-help service and day centres are not provided exclusively for the elderly; nationally about seven clients out of eight of the home help services are elderly, as are slightly over one half of all day centre clients. Taking this into account, column 6 of Table 16.1 shows an estimated amount spent by each social service department on the elderly in 1977/78.

It would hardly be sufficient for us to point out the existence of such variations without inquiring further how they have arisen, and why they persist. A proper account of the reasons for these variations demands that we consider a wide range of specific circumstances. Historical factors, local political ideologies and policies, relative costs, and availability of alternative services are all relevant, but of paramount importance is the extent of need for services among the elderly population of an area.

The key question is, to what extent can the variation in provision of services be justified on the grounds of equity? To answer such a question requires that we confront fundamental issues relating to the definition of need. Yet we believe that in principle it should be possible to specify what would be the ideal distribution of resources in relation to needs, so as to study variations in standards of provision. This chapter will examine firstly, the problem of determining what constitutes territorial justice, that is equity between populations of individuals in territories; secondly, the extent to which actual variations in service provision are equitable as we define it; and thirdly, how far these variations appear to be influenced by other factors such as political and social conditions. First, the modern development of social services for the elderly is reviewed to account for historical circumstances which have led to the present situation.

A striking feature of the services under consideration is how unsettled has been the history of their development. All four owe their establishment in the public sector to specific legislation, and in each case there have been substantial changes in their administration, and their role. Residential homes, established under the National Assistance Act of 1948, were intended originally to be the major welfare provision for the elderly. The expectation was that they would provide for the relatively able-bodied aged unable to continue their own household management, in a manner which as far as possible would substitute for a normal home. Above all else, they should represent an approach to welfare which would be in complete contrast with the low standards which characterized much former Poor Law provision. For several reasons these high expectations were not realized, and the extent of their initial failure was documented dramatically by Townsend and Wedderburn (1965). The rapid expansion in levels of provision during the 1950s, coupled with limited capital expenditure, meant that many of the old institutions remained, and with them the Poor Law attitudes and institutionalism. Between 1948 and 1975 permanently supported elderly residents increased from 50,000 to 120,000; but since the early 1960s even this has probably not done more than keep up with the exceptional increase in the number of vulnerable elderly, which has outpaced the growth of the general elderly population. Pressure of demand on hospital services for the elderly has remained so acute that in practice the elderly infirm have always had priority for residential care. It is probable that the trend toward using homes for the chronically sick on the margin of need for hospital care has accelerated rapidly since the public expenditure cutbacks of the mid-1970s.

The shift in the role of residential care has been possible partly because of the changing role of domiciliary care, and partly because of the development of sheltered housing, which today often serves clients whose needs are similar to those for whom residential care was originally intended. Since the mid-1950s there has been steady and increasing pressure towards the care of the elderly in the community, encouraged both from those who have deprecated the continuing institutionalism of residential care, and from economic necessity. The home-help service, by far the most important of the domiciliary and day care services (at least financially), has had a particularly chequered career. Originally intended as a maternity service, from 1944 it was provided for the elderly, and by 1953 one-half of its clients were elderly. At present, seven clients out of eight are elderly. The number of cases of all ages visited has risen from about 120,000 to 750,000 per annum now, and about twice as many elderly persons are visited than were in the early 1960s (Bebbington, 1979). Yet even at this rate of expansion, the home-help service has struggled to meet the rising tide of need among the elderly in the community. This has been caused above all else by the increase in social isolation of the most vulnerable. Despite continued aspirations for an integrated community service for the elderly, it has increasingly been seen as an important aim of the home-help service to postpone the need for entry into residential care, although this goal has been inadequately pursued (see Davies, 1980). A further problem for its development has been its vulnerability to more general changes. For example, during the expenditure cutbacks of the mid-1970s, it was initially regarded as the easiest service to cut, but later this policy was reversed in favour of the apparently much more cost-saving measure of cutting residential accommodation. This last, and the fact that health services for the elderly (in particular health visitors and home nurses) have expanded only modestly, must undoubtedly mean that the home-help service is being provided to increasingly needy clients. Like residential care it must change its role; already a number of social services departments are experimenting with forms of the home-help service which are concerned with personal care as well as domestic duties.

Because these services for the elderly were established so recently and developed so quickly in the face of rising need and the mounting criticism of the quantity and quality of provision, it is not surprising that their distribution is now uneven. Furthermore, there have been a number of administrative problems which are perhaps the natural consequence of rapid expansion. For example, such growth has given special opportunities to those local authorities prepared to be most entrepreneurial in the development of capital stock. There is also evidence, and it was probably inevitable, that services were initially developed fastest in those areas where there was a relative shortage of provision by voluntary agencies and health services. Furthermore, by comparison with other forms of welfare provision, central control is weak. Guidance to local authorities by the Department of Health and Social Security (DHSS) on appropriate standards of all personal social services can best be described as 'persuasive' rather than 'directive'. A final problem has been that these services have undergone massive reorganizations both in 1971, when social service departments were established, often putting responsibility for administering services for the elderly into the hands of those who had worked solely with children; and in 1974 during local government reorganization when sometimes large bureaucracies were created under the direction of inexperienced administrators.

Table 16.1 illustrates part of the legacy of this development. The variations in quantities reported there conceal further variations which may affect the quality of provision. For residential care, for example, there is wide variation in the use of voluntary homes, which accommodate one in four of supported residents in London but less than one in ten elsewhere. Despite the pressure to build small homes of about 30–35 places, around half the residents of local authority homes in the inner London boroughs of Hackney, Islington, Lambeth, and Westminster are accommodated in homes of more than twice this size (compared with under 5 per cent elsewhere). At the time of the 1970 *Residential Census* (DHSS, 1975) the percentage of residents described as substantially dependent ranged from 4.7 in Bath to 35.2 in Islington. There was no correlation between levels of provision and the dependency of residents.

Over the country as a whole the provision of residential care is more evenly distributed (with a coefficient of variation of 28 per cent) than the domiciliary and day services for the elderly. Social services departments which are relatively low providers often tend to concentrate their provision on residential services. The proportion of expenditure on the elderly which is spent on residential services runs from 37 per cent in the London Borough of Greenwich to over 70 per cent in the counties of West Sussex, Surrey and the Isle of Wight. While these differences may in part be due to differing patterns of need and special problems of delivery of day services in rural areas, yet equally it is difficult to avoid the inference that those services with a comparatively short history of local authority delivery are now relatively underdeveloped in those areas where originally there was lowest demand.

Finally, we draw attention to other variations in the standards of domiciliary and day care. For example, not only does the home-help service vary widely between authorities (coefficient of variation, 42 per cent) from twelve per thousand elderly in inner London to under four in the south of England, but where the service is least well provided it is typically spread most thinly, ranging from an average of over 20 cases per home help per annum in Bromley, Harrow, Doncaster, Dudley and West Sussex, to about 12 in Northumberland, Gateshead, Sheffield, St Helens and Camden. Even wider variations occur for the meals on wheels service and day centre places, for both of which inner London departments provide over twice the national average (per elderly capita), and in the case of day centre places, more than five times that which is provided in the south of England. Table 16.2 summarizes the distribution of services between different types of authority. In addition, typically those authorities mak-

Table 16.2 The distribution of major personal social services for the elderly between different types of local authority in England

| | Residential care[a] | Home helps[b] | Meals on wheels[c] | Day centres[d] |
|---|---|---|---|---|
| 19 most sparsely populated Counties | 167 | 56 | 28 | 57 |
| 20 "urban" Counties | 170 | 57 | 36 | 63 |
| 36 Metropolitan County Districts | 193 | 91 | 36 | 103 |
| 20 Outer London Boroughs | 187 | 65 | 55 | 108 |
| 12 Inner London Boroughs | 305 | 117 | 109 | 204 |

[a] Supported residents per 10,000 persons aged 65 +.
[b] No. whole time equivalent (w.t.e.) per 10,000 persons aged 65 +.
[c] Meals delivered per 100 persons aged 65 +.
[d] Places (all types) per 10,000 persons aged 65 +.

ing high provision have very much higher unit costs. The average day centre place in London costs nearly twice as much to run as elsewhere, while the cost of providing meals is also very much higher (though both of these vary enormously between individual authorities). With each of these services, though these variations in standards may be the result of other factors, it is difficult to believe that there cannot also be considerable variations of quality.

## PROVISION AND 'NEED'

'*Need*' has been described as 'an incubus on the back of any serious student' (Culyer, 1976, p. ix). Feldstein (1963) argued that professionals talk about meeting needs 'when it would make a clearer analysis if they talked about optimising use of resources'. Culyer, Lavers and Williams (1972) thought that

> the word need ought to be banished from discussion of public policy, partly because of its ambiguity but also because...the word is frequently used in...'arbitrary' senses.... Indeed...in much public discussion it is difficult to tell, when some one says that society needs..., whether he means that *he* needs it, whether he means that society ought to get it in *his* opinion, whether a majority of the members of society want it or *all* of them want it. Nor is to clear whether it is needed *regardless* of the cost to society.

These authors are economists. The word is more often used by social administrators and fellow-travelling sociologists. Yet even an eminent social administrator, Nevitt (1977, pp. 125–7) wrote that 'need can only be a useful concept if it is equated to a demand by governments or individuals for goods and services', for otherwise 'the concept can have either theoretical nor empirical value, and it properly belongs not to the social sciences but to the vocabulary of political rhetoric'. Nevitt appears to advocate the withdrawal of the term '*need*' in favour of '*demand*'. It would then be recognized more clearly that the social changes required to achieve a more just and compassionate society are most appropriately brought about by treating social problems as matters of demand and supply of public goods in which it is considered desirable to change levels of public demand. Contemporary needs studies too often merely accumulate data on the availability or non-availability of a few selected services, with no consideration of the wider context of social planning in which benefits in any sector must take account of the consequences of their costs.

However, there are several reasons why the word *need* cannot be abandoned. The term is well established, and communication with policy-makers is not made easier if vocabulary is altered unnecessarily. Replacing one word with another does not side-step the intellectual problems of the arguments in which the concept is used. In particular, we do not believe that need and demand are simply interchangeable. Need has a number of aspects which make it distinct. It is true that need, like the demand function of economics, is an implicit judgement about priorities in the allocation of resources. The need judgement involves the evaluation of the expected consequences of alternative courses of action in relation to their costs, even though this is not often made explicit. Need is more obviously concerned with benefits than with goods and services as such. But what really distinguishes need from demand in the economist's sense is that need implies a societal rather than a private judgement—it is substantially a judgement about people who generally possess certain characteristics, not about oneself. As Williams (1974, p. 69) has suggested, it is this most of all which undermines the relevance of classical demand theory, which is based on the assumption of the sovereignty of each individual as he expresses his preferences in the market. Economists who couch problems of need in the language of demand theory are forced to introduce such concepts as 'externality' and 'merit good' to cover situations in which levels of demand are not solely determined by the purchasing power of the individual.

For these reasons, those who have recommended the expurgation of 'need' from argument have often had second thoughts. Indeed, Culyer (1976, p. ix) has written that exploration of the core ideas which relate to the concept of need amount to no less than a 'scientific research programme'.

## NEED JUDGEMENTS AND THE MEASUREMENT OF NEED

A crucial issue associated with notions of social rights and of social benefits is how societal judgements are constructed. Williams (1974, p. 71) argued that the various actors concerned; the consumers of services; the society at large; and the politicians, professionals, and experts who stand between them are required to play a variety of roles, according to rules whose terms of reference are themselves the outcome of social processes. However, there are other important issues relating to the definition of need which follow from the analysis of economists. Some are explained in a seminal paper by Culyer, Lavers and

Williams (1971). In this, the decisions of a minister, or supreme arbiter, stand proxy for this social process as a whole. The role of the arbiter is to make need judgements which will involve the allocation of a finite amount of resources to a consumer or consumer groups.

On what basis should these judgements be made? In allocating human services the arbiter should be concerned first and foremost with the production of outcome benefits, or those consequences valued in their own right (and not because they contribute to the production of other consequences), such as improvements in the quality of life of the recipient or of those close to the recipient. Secondly, in general a number of different benefits will be involved, and each benefit must be valued to compare the total utility of alternative strategies. Thirdly, the arbiter should consider the alternative strategies for the use of available resources; what packages of services will most efficiently produce different levels of benefits. As the characteristics of the recipients and of those performing the services affect outcomes greatly, non-resource factors also will have to be carefully considered.

An optimal judgement therefore requires a knowledge of how to produce benefits from inputs such as services in the most efficient way, bearing in mind that inputs are substitutable for one another in the production of benefits and that the relative prices of inputs vary through time and place. The arbiter must determine simultaneously the mix of benefits in the light of his relative valuation of each benefit. This prescription might discuss costs rather than inputs but would be essentially the same. It might also mention that costs and consequences occur through time and that they should be discounted to present value. In fact, the need judgement is essentially a cost–benefit judgement.

This conclusion has important consequences for empirical studies of need. Such studies ought to take into account the range of factors necessary for cost–benefit analysis, for without this they will lack a proper basis for drawing conclusions about policy, whether concerned with personal social services, housing or education. There ought to be more similarity between the factors studied in need surveys and those examined in the better studies of the effectiveness of services. Yet studies of need typically satisfy themselves with a survey of the incidence of a few broad personal characteristics (such as age, living conditions, and health) and an account of current service use. While such studies may be of use as the basis of management information systems, often one cannot help but be struck by the weakness of the link between the evidence and the conclusions about subsequent service development, and by how easy it has been for policy-makers to ignore or refute those conclusions, except when there have been strong external pressures for service expansion.

What factors did needs studies ought to examine? First, they should collect data in a systematic manner about all the consequences of provision which policy-makers consider important. In particular, they should attempt to measure benefits. If this information cannot be drawn from elsewhere, longitudinal surveys may have to be conducted to determine the consequences of specific types of service. Secondly, more attention must be paid to the priority that consumers and other beneficiaries attach to *alternative* types of service, otherwise need studies may support the fallacious argument that any beneficial consequence creates a need, even when that beneficial consequence is valued by consumers (or others) less than other benefits that have to be foregone. Few need studies assess different packages of services and it is a common assumption that no choice exists between alternative ways of achieving desired welfare consequences.

The task of assessing the consequences of alternative policies would be far simpler if evaluation studies of services were more uniform. It would be highly desirable for example if different studies adopted comparable criteria for determining outcome success. Also desirable would be more standardization in describing personal characteristics to permit cross-study inferences.

One effect of inadequate need studies is that local authorities often use standard packages of services which offer less variety than would be the case if they fully exploited the variations in the costs of alternatives. Indeed, many choices made by local authorities are clearly not cost-conscious. Such is the variation in the circumstances of welfare provision that the findings of national surveys can be greatly misleading for individual areas. For instance, it would be wrong to assume that the relative costs of providing additional units of each service vary in the same proportion in all areas. Because of this authorities should not aim to provide a uniform pattern of services, even if they are faced with uniform welfare short-falls.

The body of research into need has neglected, therefore, important features identified by the theory of the need judgement. The absence of a clear intellectual basis has left us without sufficient evidence for the normative analyses that would be useful for policy-making. In particular, need studies that showed more awareness of the implications, varying costs, and effectiveness of interventions would enable the development of guidelines for levels of service provision consistent with standard levels of benefits.

## A NEEDS INDICATOR FOR THE ELDERLY

The development of needs indicators, which are measures of the relative need of entire groups of individuals, are a special class of need study. Since an individual's need can be defined as the quantity of resources necessary to achieve in the most efficient manner a level of benefit judged appropriate by some arbiter, it follows that the needs indicator ought to take into account such factors as resources, services, and benefits. An essential criterion of a good needs indicator is that it is clearly linked to judgements about the use of resources. This is not the case with the majority of indicators which have been developed in the context of British social policy, although there are notable exceptions (see Bebbington and Davies, 1980a). Many examples used to compare the needs of different areas are little more than combinations of census counts constructed on the basis of empirical relationships amongst the variables computed by factor or cluster analysis. Even more so than with needs studies, it has proved difficult to determine what exactly they imply for actual policy-making.

At this point we move from the logic of what should underlie a needs judgement, to the rationale of the construction of a needs indicator. The relationship is established in two steps: first by relating the individual needs judgements to a hypothetical concept, the '*needs index*', and secondly by relating this hypothetical index to our actual needs indicator. These arguments have been elaborated by Davies (1977) and are simply summarized here.

The needs judgement can in principle be characterized by the cost of providing the required level of benefits by the most efficient means. If these costs can be measured in monetary terms, and if they refer to consistent needs judgements for a defined population, their aggregation constitutes a needs index for that population. This aggregation is usually—though not always—made for the population living within an area and is therefore a *territorial needs index*.

The needs indicator approximates the needs index and is employed because normally it is impractical to assess every eligible individual in several areas, unless these areas are very small. A survey within each area is possible but, for example, to compare the need of the elderly for personal social services in all local authorities in England would require effectively a separate survey in each authority. In any case the assessment of the most efficient method of allocating resources requires considerable further research, because variations in resource prices between local authorities affect the costs of achieving similar ends.

The needs indicator approach which we propose makes use of associations that can be established empirically between the specific characteristics of individuals (such as their physical condition) relevant to a need judgement, and other characteristics (such as their age) for which area data counts exists. This involves predicting the membership of a group with a particular combination of characteristics, using variables which have counterparts tabulated for areas in standard statistical reports, and applying these predictors to estimate the number in the population. This approach is well known among statisticians, and there have been a number of recent reviews of these methods (Gonzales and Hoza, 1978; Purcell and Kish, 1979).

The local authority needs indicator for personal social services for the elderly which is used here is based on this method and has been fully described elsewhere (Bebbington and Davies, 1980b). It postulates a number of 'target groups' of elderly persons whose needs for social services are likely to be broadly similar. Amongst the elderly living in the community throughout England, it is estimated that 9.5 per cent fall into the moderate need group, 5.3 in the considerable need group and 2.1 in the severe need group. The remainder have little or no need. The indicator is based on a set of need judgements to achieve levels of benefit constrained by budget limits; it is a statement of the resources needed to provide services such as home-helps, day centres, meals, and old people's homes. As mentioned, however, the lack of research on the costs of achieving given ends in different ways limits the present needs indicator. What has been done in practice is the definition of a package of services judged appropriate for the average member of each target group. Standard unit costs for services are applied, taking into account local factors such as wage rates, to produce a specific overall cost for each local authority. By allocating services regardless of location, the method does not respond to the local price of each service although it does reflect variations in prices between authorities. Also without being able to determine the locally most cost-effective set of needs judgements (given relative priorities for benefits of different kinds), the resulting need indicator does not point to the optimal use of resources. However, within the range of alternative needs judgements that approximates current practice, patterns of need within local authority areas of England are not sufficiently variable for different needs judgements to affect the variation in needs indicators, apart perhaps amongst inner London boroughs.

The number of elderly persons living in each local authority in each target group was estimated from a prediction equation using census and other variables. The equation was based on an examination of the characteristics of elderly persons in the target groups as revealed in a number of recent local and national surveys of the elderly. The need indicator (Table 16.1) was constructed for each local authority by combining the estimated number in each target group with estimates of the standard cost of services, and is expressed in monetary terms. In fact, the figure presented is an average across a number of needs indicators based on different need judgements. It has been scaled to make it comparable with expenditure on the elderly in 1977/78, but it must be noted for the purpose of making detailed comparisons that actual expenditures were partly estimated and that the indicator was based partly on 1971 Census data and may not reflect recent shifts in patterns of need.

## CAUSES OF VARIATIONS IN SPENDING

Needs indicators enable a detailed analysis of the relationship between apparent need and actual spending on the elderly by local authority social service departments. The dominant feature of spending patterns is the polarization between Inner London and the rest of England, and in order to explore the inter-relationship Inner London authorities have been excluded from subsequent analysis.

It may be readily ascertained that there is a relatively close and approximately linear relationship between the needs indicator per elderly capita and actual spending per capita in 1977/78. The correlation coefficient across all authorities excluding inner London is + 0.66, or, put another way, at least 44 per cent of the variation in spending per elderly capita is attributable to variation in expenditure need, which is need-adjusted for variations in prices. We say at least, because there is certain to be measurement error associated with the needs indicator, which most probably results in underestimation of the relationship. The slope of the regression line is also of interest because, under the assumption of a linear relationship between expenditure and the need indicator, it is a measure of the elasticity of supply of social services. If it were greater than unity, supply would be relatively high in authorities with high needs and low in those with low needs, and it could be said that authorities tended to be over-responsive to differences in need. If it were less than unity supply would be relatively high in authorities with low needs and *vice-versa*, and it could be said that authorities tended to be under-responsive to differences of need. The former situation might have arisen if those authorities which initially faced the highest levels of need had been quickest to develop services and then, having established a lead, retained it by incremental growth. Indeed, during periods of general growth, incrementalism will reinforce the lead of a high spending authority. The latter situation might have arisen if local authorities were sensitive to pressures which encourage conformity regardless of need. For instance, social services departments sometimes justify spending programmes partly by reference to trends within neighbouring authorities, or by citing DHSS guidelines which rarely discriminate between authorities. In fact, the slope of the regression line was 1.08 (not significantly different from unity), so the evidence was that authorities' patterns of spendings were indeed proportional to their degree of need.

Amongst the individual services, residential provision was most highly correlated with the need indicator, with $r = +0.62$; with home helps, $r = +0.33$; with meals on wheels, $r = +0.47$; and with day centre places, $r = +0.25$. Residential care was also the most evenly distributed of the services. This tends to confirm that it has benefited from its relatively settled development in comparison with other personal social services. However, one must be wary of too firm a conclusion because the smaller services substitute and interweave with one another.

Simple correlations of provision with our needs indicator do not distinguish the impact of either the size of populations in the target groups or cost-raising factors. Our analysis does not throw light on the relative importance of economic efficiency and pure equity considerations. Both are important features of the territorial justice argument. Secondly, the correlations tell us nothing about the impact of trends in needs on spending. It is important to know not only how well spending is adjusted to needs at a point in time, but also how far trends in spending are correlated with trends in needs. Thirdly, correlations do not allow us to comment on the basis of other normative criteria such as the influence of spending on relative degrees of environmental deprivation. Fourthly, the correlations do not investigate the degree to which trends in spending adjust to trends in social conditions. Such adjustment may be of particular interest at a time when the worsening economic circumstances weaken the informal support of the aged by relatives and increase the demands on local authority services.

The remainder of this section assesses the effect of needs, prices, and other factors on spending and trends in spending. Our assessment extends the range of evaluative criteria and so blurs the distinction between an account of the causes of variation and a normative evaluation of spending patterns. We excuse ourselves on the grounds that this distinction is frequently blurred in social policy analysis, but the reader should be alerted to the possible confusion (Pinker, 1971, p. 97).

Two expenditure patterns have been analysed: spending on the elderly by social services departments in 1975/76 and 1977/78, and forecasted change in expenditure from 1975/76 to 1979/80, as indicated by the local authority planning returns of 1977 (DHSS, 1978). To ensure that the regression analysis was not unduly affected by extreme values on any variable, a further ten local authorities were excluded leaving 83 in the analysis. This ensured that no variable was either leptokurtic or highly skewed. Graphical checks were used to eliminate the possibility of major non-linear relationships. The independent variables examined were:

(1) An Elderly Need Indicator, unadjusted for price variations. This was a different indicator from that used in the correlation analysis, because the intention was to separate the impacts on spending of the number of elderly persons in need from the cost of services. It was constructed from the estimated numbers of elderly in 'target groups' of need, but instead of weighting according to the relative cost of services in an authority, the unadjusted indicator used a weighting common to all local authorities.
(2) Labour Cost Index. This was used to measure the impact of cost-raising factors in spending for the elderly. We only took into account the compensation necessary for general variations in the price level of services, not the relative prices of specific inputs. This index was developed by the Department of the Environment for use in allocating the Rate Support Grant.
(3) Social Conditions Index. This index was chosen to determine the influence of the environmental deprivation particularly associated with older and decayed parts of towns and cities. It is a weighted combination of four social indicators from the 1971 census; households lacking basic amenities, one-parent families, single-pension households and overcrowded households. Imber (1976, p. 9) has argued that 'high values on these variables are indicative of the older parts of towns and cities where the elderly have been left

behind and where one-parent families are able to find cheap accommodation and possibly employment'.

(4) Change in Number of Elderly. Unfortunately, it is not yet feasible to estimate the changed number in each 'target group' and hence the change in the elderly needs indicator, and the nearest approximation to an indicator of change in need is the change in the total number of the elderly. Changes in the proportions of elderly in the populations of local authority areas are available for 1971–75, 1975–77, and 1977–79.

(5) Change in Unemployment. In the short term increases of unemployment are likely to affect the capacity of friends and relatives to cope unaided, and hence to increase pressure on social services. In the long term unemployment encourages the deterioration of social conditions, and so makes more desirable a systematic attempt to compensate for variations in local poverty by means of the multiplier effect of local social spending. Changes in unemployment (as a proportion of the population) are available for 1971–75 and 1975–77.

(6) Labour Party Representation. In a democratic system the choice of ruling party is determined by the preferences of the citizen and hence, in part, by the nature of local needs including those of the elderly. It is no surprise that there is considerable correlation between levels of need and party control. The question asked here is whether the party in control exerts an influence on expenditure over and above levels of need, either because there are territorial variations in the value systems of citizens or because of ideological inflexibility. The variable is the percentage of Labour-held seats on the local authority at May 1976.

(7) Ratepayers Price Index. Local responsibility is associated not only with the meeting of local needs, but with local financial constraints and the ability of areas to pay for services. This ability may be measured by local income or by rateable values, but previous studies have found these proxies unsatisfactory. Jackman and Sellars (1978) have suggested that less resistance to expenditure increases will be met where the domestic ratepayer is responsible for a relatively low proportion of rate-based income. This index is calculated as domestic rateable value as a proportion of total rateable value, which includes the local deficiency in rateable value where this is non-zero. The national average (excluding Inner London) is about 38 per cent.

## SOCIAL SERVICES RECURRENT SPENDING ON THE ELDERLY IN 1975/76

The influence of each of the above factors on the pattern of social services departments spending on the elderly per capita in 1975/76 excluding inner London authorities has been examined by multiple regression analysis. The explained variance was 71 per cent and the standardized regression coefficients (Table 16.3) indicate each variable's contribution to the variation in expenditure (Wright, 1960). It may be seen that the elderly need, social conditions, and labour price indexes were very similar in their impact on levels of expenditure on the elderly: the degree of urban malaise within an authority was as important as the number of elderly persons with specific needs. The significance of these three variables can be gauged from their elasticity coefficients. For both the needs indicator and the social conditions index these coefficients were around 0.7; significantly less than unity. Although spending was primarily related to levels of need, authorities with high levels of need were not spending as much extra as required. In the case of the labour price index, it is clear that authorities facing high costs (particularly in the south-east of England) spent more on the services. But the elasticity coefficient in this case was 3.4, much higher than unity, so that unless the labour price index underestimates the variation in the

Table 16.3 A regression analysis of variations in social services departments' current expenditure on the elderly in 1975/76, changes between 1975/76 and 1977/78, and forecast changes between 1975/76 and 1979/80

| Variable | Expenditure 1975/76 | Change 1975/76–1977/78 | Forecast change 1975/76–1979/80 |
|---|---|---|---|
| Elderly need indicator, unadjusted for price variations | 0.44* | 0.26* | 0.18* |
| Social conditions index | 0.44* | 0.11 | 0.36* |
| Interaction of social conditions and elderly need | 0.15* | 0.13 | 0.11 |
| Rise in proportion of elderly population, 1971–75 | 0.13 | –0.13 | –0.16 |
| Rise in proportion of elderly population, 1975–77 | — | –0.24* | — |
| Forecast rise in proportion of elderly population, 1975–79 | — | — | –0.12 |
| Rise in unemployment rate, 1971–75 | –0.05 | 0.10 | 0.16 |
| Rise in unemployment rate, 1975–77 | — | –0.03 | — |
| Labour price index | 0.42* | 0.02 | 0.39* |
| Labour Party representation on local council | 0.25* | –0.03 | 0.02 |
| Domestic ratepayers index | –0.23* | 0.23* | 0.06 |
| Variance explained ($R^2$) | 0.71 | 0.49 | 0.44 |

*Note:* The analysis is of 83 local authorities in England, excluding Inner London and 10 other authorities. The table gives standardized regression coefficients for each of the three analyses. An asterisk denotes coefficients significantly different from zero (at the 10% level).

prices of services, then authorities facing high prices are spending at a level over and above the difference in prices. So it seems that spending on services for the elderly is under-responsive to need, but over-responsive to price. These results confirm that Labour-dominated authorities tended to spend more regardless of levels of need, and that authorities where the domestic ratepayer was responsible for a relatively high proportion of the rate-based income tended to spend less.

## CHANGES SINCE 1975 IN SOCIAL SERVICES RECURRENT SPENDING ON THE ELDERLY

The last two columns of Table 16.3 show, by the same method, the effects of the factors on changes in spending between 1975/76 and 1977/78, and planned changes (in mid-1977) between 1975/76 and 1979/80. These are changes after deflation to a common cost level. In both cases rather less than half the variation in changes can be explained in terms of the variables we have studied. Nonetheless the results offer some interesting insights about the mechanisms behind long-term planning. The territorial justice model implies that the primary determinant of expenditure ought to be need: changes in expenditure should follow closely on changes in levels of need. But for a long period up to 1975/76 social services departments attracted rapidly expanding resources—a world indeed of the 'institutionalist' rather than the 'residualist' in which the aim was to grow towards a level of provision at which some absolute amount of 'need' could be met. This view was probably encouraged by the DHSS's promotion of 10 year plans and its publication of guidelines for services well above current levels of provision. Although growth was considerably curtailed by 1977, local authorities were still planning for a 17 per cent growth in real terms between 1975/76 and 1979/80 in spending on the elderly. The continued belief in the desirability of growth suggests that there is a consensus within social services departments that levels of provision still do not match levels of need: that our society should devote more of its resources to the personal social services. Under these circumstances individual departments will wish to expand according to their perception of the gap between current provision and need. Although changes in these levels of need are continually taking place, they will be regarded as only incidental to the central problem of raising resource levels, and we would expect to find little responsiveness to these changes, at least in the short term. In fact, this agrees well with the empirical results, in which it is those authorities with the highest levels of elderly need and adverse social conditions which wish to continue to expand, while changes in the numbers of elderly and of unemployment have zero or even negative effects on spending.

A picture emerges of a system of local government spending which is largely incremental. Indeed, there is a positive correlation of 0.22 between level of expenditure in 1975 and planned increase up to 1979/80 on the elderly. Even though incrementalism has been practically institutionalized through the rate support grant, it is not entirely the largely ungoverned incrementalism seen by American commentators of modern bureaucratic organizations in which changes in expenditure in any year are determined by expenditure in the previous year (Davis, Dempster and Wildavsky, 1966; Crecine, 1969). Rather, it is a pattern of growth which originated partly in long-term patterns of need and is sustained by the expectations of administrators and practitioners.

## SUMMARY

This chapter has examined the considerable variation in levels of provision and recurrent spending on present social services for the elderly. The rapid growth of these services and frequent administrative upheavals underlie an unsettled history over the last 30 years. In these circumstances it is not surprising that the questions have been asked about the equity of distribution. However, investigations have been hampered because '*need*' has been inadequately conceptualized and measured. We have developed a normative definition which expresses need as a cost–benefit concept. From this we have determined that while the current pattern of provision shows considerable responsiveness to the pattern of need, it does not produce territorial justice.

Various hypotheses about other influences on social services department spending on the elderly have been examined. It has been argued that authorities have gradually adjusted their expenditure in a manner compatible with their long-term pattern of needs. This conclusion is in sharp contrast to the many anecdotal accounts of the idiosyncratic behaviour of individual authorities. However, the pattern of provision has been responsive not only to the number of elderly in need but also to general social conditions and the cost of providing services. It is noteworthy that not only are those authorities which face above-average costs spending disproportionately more on the elderly, but that this trend is continuing to advance. It is suspected that the recent method of distributing the needs element of the rate-support grant, which linked levels of spending within one year with allocation in the next, may be at least partly responsible. No relation has been found between short-term changes in need and changes in expenditure on the elderly. Independent of need, certain political factors influenced the level of spending. It was relatively high in areas of high Labour Party representation and was low where the domestic ratepayer was responsible for a relatively large proportion of any marginal change in the rates bill. These suggest that local values' systems and local responsibility remains an important component in the pattern of provision for the elderly.

## REFERENCES

Bebbington, A. C. (1979). Changes in the provision of social services to the elderly in the community over fourteen years. *Social Policy and Administration*, **13**, 111–23.

Bebbington, A. C. and Davies, B. P. (1980a). Territorial need indicators: a new approach, part I. *Journal of Social Policy*, **9**(2), 145–68.

Bebbington, A. C. and Davies, B. P. (1980b). Territorial need indicators: a new approach, part II. *Journal of Social Policy*, **9**(4), 433–62.

Crecine, J. P. (1969). *Government Problem Solving*. Markham, Chicago.

Culyer, A. J. (1976). *Need and the National Health Service*. Martin Robertson, London.

Culyer, A. J., Lavers, R. J., and Williams, A. (1971). Social indicators: health. *Social Trends*, **2**.

Davies, B. P. (1968). *Social Needs and Resources in Local Services*. Michael Joseph, London.

Davies, B. P. (1977). *Need*. Personal Social Services Research Unit, Paper 69. University of Canterbury, Kent.

Davies, B. P. (1980). Strategic goals and piecemeal innovation. In Goldberg, E. N. (ed.), *Retrenchment in the Social Services*. Policy Studies Institute, London.

Davies, B. P., Barton, A. V., McMillan, I. S., and Williamson, V. K. (1971). *Variations in Services for the Aged*. Bell, London.

Davis, A., Dempster, M. A. H. and Wildavsky, A. (1966). A theory of the budgetary process. *American Political Science Review*, **60**, 529–47.

Department of Health and Social Security (1975). *The Census of Residential Accommodation 1970*. HMSO, London.

Feldstein, M. S. (1963). Economic analysis, operational research and national health service efficiency. *Oxford Economic Papers*, **1**, 19pp.

Gonzales, M. E. and Hoza, C. (1978). Small area estimation with application to unemployment and housing estimates. *Journal of the American Statistical Association*, **73**, 7–15.

Imber, V. (1976). *A Classification of the English Personal Social Services Authorities*. HMSO, London.

Jackman, R. and Sellers, M. (1978). Local expenditure and local discretion. *Centre for Environmental Studies Review*, **3**, 63–73.

Nevitt, D. A. (1977). Need and demand. In Heisler, H. (ed.), *Foundation of Social Administration*, chapter 8. Macmillan, London.

Pinker, R. (1971). *Social Theory and Social Policy*. Heinemann, London.

Purcell, N. J. and Kish, L. (1979). Estimation for small domains. *Biometrics*, **35**, 365–84.

Sumner, G. and Smith, R. (1969). *Planning Local Authority Services for the Elderly*. Allen & Unwin, London.

Townsend, P. and Wedderburn, D. (1965). *The Aged in the Welfare State*. Bell, London.

Williams, A. (1974). 'Need' as a demand concept. In Culyer, A. J. (ed.), *Economic Policies and Social Goals*. Martin Robertson, London.

Wright, S. (1960). Path coefficients and path regressions. *Biometrics*, **16**, 189–202.

Geographical Perspectives on the Elderly
Edited by A. M. Warnes


# Chapter 17

# Home-based mental health care for the elderly

*Christopher J. Smith*

The geographer's role in investigating social problems is usually limited to that of a consultant. Only rarely do we make or take the opportunity to get involved in the actual delivery of services that are designed to alleviate social problems. When such an opportunity arises it is instructive to reflect on some of the actual and potential contributions the geographer can make. This chapter describes the author's involvement in a community-based project in Oklahoma City that is currently attempting to improve the quantity and quality of services for the elderly mentally ill. The project involves some non-traditional roles for a geographer, including: advocacy for disadvantaged persons; community development for preventive mental health services; and the formation and extension of indigenous care systems that utilize non-professional personnel and local resources.

As the project evolved it was evident that the geographer's contribution could be useful in a number of ways. The simplest geographical contributions, such as mapping 'high-risk' areas of the city, and illuminating spatial variations in city-wide patterns of service delivery, were provided while the project was still embryonic. At other times the contributions were informal observations or suggestions about how spatial variables might help or hinder the development of informal services for needy populations (C. J. Smith, 1980a). At the time of writing the project is still only half-completed, so it is inappropriate to attempt an evaluation either of the geographical contributions or of the overall goals. This chapter begins, therefore, by putting the project into context—which involves a brief description of the history of mental health care for the elderly in the United States.

## CHANGING PATTERNS OF CARE FOR THE ELDERLY MENTALLY ILL

Mental hospitals first appeared in the United States in the early part of the nineteenth century. At the time they represented a well-meaning attempt to provide an orderly environment for the mentally ill. According to the pioneers, the 'asylum' could provide a shelter from the chaos and disorder of post-Revolutionary society (Rothman, 1971). By the 1860s it was clear, even to some of the original champions of asylums, that hospitalization alone was not an effective form of treatment for mental illness. Admission rates accelerated as the country became more urbanized, and as increasing numbers of immigrants arrived (Grob, 1973). Most observers agree that the hospitals were bound to fail from the outset because they were never able to control their admissions. They soon became hopelessly overcrowded, particularly with chronic patients for whom effective treatment was not, and in many cases still is not, available.

By the beginning of the twentieth century mental hospitals were also being used to house increasing numbers of elderly people (Grob, 1980). This continued throughout the first half of the century, and by 1940, age-specific admission rates to mental hospitals for men over 60 were 279.5 per 100,000 population, and 223.0 for women; compared with rates of 70.4 and 65.5 in 1885 (Goldhammer and Marshall, 1958). The mental hospital had become a last, and in some cases, the only, resort for the elderly. The simplest explanation for this phenomenon is that during this period the elderly became a much larger group in both absolute and relative terms. As Grob (1980) has noted, the over-65s numbered about 76 million in 1900, or 4.1 per cent of the population; but by 1940 there were more than 131 million elderly, representing 6.8 per cent of the total population. The obvious conclusion from these data would be that increased admissions to mental hospitals occurred because there were more elderly people *and* perhaps also because the elderly experience more than their share of mental health problems. In fact this conclusion may be only partly true, because many of those admitted to hospitals had nowhere else they could possibly go as they grew older and became less able to look after themselves. In many cases simply being old justified commitment to a mental hospital. As the superintendent of a hospital in New York remarked:

> A little mental confusion, forgetfulness, and garrulity are sometimes the only symptoms exhibited, but the patient is duly certified to us as insane and has no one at home capable... to care for him. We are unable to refuse these patients without creating ill-feeling in the community where they reside, nor are we able to assert that they are not insane within the meaning of the statute, for many of them, judged by the ordinary standards...cannot be regarded as entirely sane (Grob, 1980, p. 25).

For most of this century it has also been argued that mental hospitals could not provide adequate treatment for many of their inmates (Mechanic, 1969).

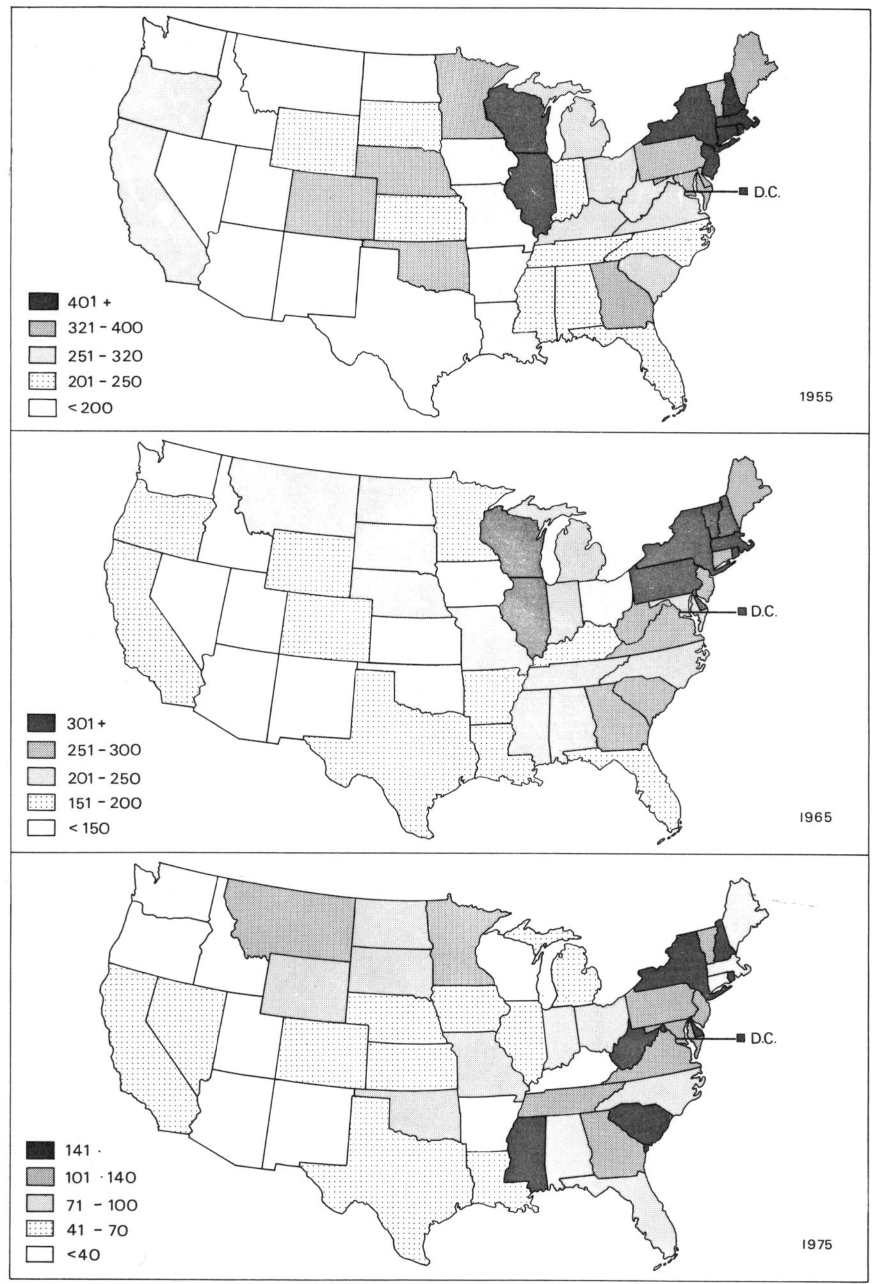


Figure 17.1 Resident patients in public mental hospitals per 100,000 civilian population, 1955, 1965, 1975. (*Note*: The maps show a sharp drop in the numbers of patients residing in mental hospitals 1955–75; but the *patterns* have stayed remarkably similar, in that the highest *rates* still tend to occur in the north-eastern states, and the lowest still in the western, south-western and mountain states.)

For a variety of reasons, however, it was not until the late 1950s and early 1960s that a widespread attempt was made to provide non-hospital care alternatives for the mentally ill (Scull, 1977; Rothman, 1971). In the United States as a whole the net effect of speeding-up discharge rates and shortening the average length of stay was a 60 per cent reduction in the number of resident patients, from close to a half-million in 1955, to 180,000 in 1978 (Bassuk and Gerson, 1978; see Figure 17.1). The shift away from hospital care has become widely known as *deinstitutionalization* (Bachrach, 1976), and the literature suggests several reasons why the policy was initiated, and why it has been implemented so vigorously (Chu and Trotter, 1974; Bradley, 1979). Community treatment was thought to be cheaper and more effective than hospital care; and an additional advantage, one that was to become crucial in the 1970s, was that community care does not infringe a patient's civil rights, as is often the case with involuntary commitments. The use of psychotropic drugs after the 1950s was also thought to be a major factor, because it was demonstrated that many patients could function adequately in the community if they adhered to a regimen of medication. The literature, however, overlooks the fact that much of the sharp decline in the number of inmates resulted from the shift of elderly patients out of hospitals into nursing homes. Many elderly people who would otherwise have been admitted to hospitals went directly into nursing homes; and at the same time nursing homes became popular for elderly patients who were being discharged from hospitals. The net effect is that the number of inmates over 65 years old has dropped noticeably in many states (Table 17.1). Although the actual reduction has varied from one state to another, depending on their specific policies (Aviram, Syme and Cohen, 1976), the total number of elderly people in mental hospitals fell from 135,322 in 1969 to 59,685 in 1974, a reduction of more than 50 per cent. In relation to the total number of patients in mental hospitals, the elderly in 1974 amounted to less than 25 per cent, compared with 32 per cent in 1969.

Most critical evaluations of this shift point out that a move from a hospital to a nursing home is often nothing more than a change of address (Lamb and

Table 17.1 Elderly patients in mental hospitals: selected states

| State | Patients aged 65 Years or More | | Percentage change 1969–74 |
|---|---|---|---|
| | 1969 | 1974 | |
| Alabama | 2646 | 639 | − 76 |
| California | 4129 | 573 | − 86 |
| Illinois | 7263 | 1744 | − 76 |
| Massachusetts | 8000 | 1050 | − 87 |
| Wisconsin | 4616 | 96 | − 98 |

*Source*: United States of America, Senate (1976), p. 719.

Goertzel, 1971). People may be living 'in the community', but in many cases nursing-home life is indistinguishable from hospital life (Glasscote, Gudeman and Miles, 1977). Most of the patients are still dependent on the home for all their essential services, and some observers have concluded that deinstitutionalization, at least for the elderly mentally ill, has been achieved largely by a policy of *reinstitutionalization* (Rose, 1979; Chase, 1973; Aviram and Segal, 1973).

## THE GEOGRAPHY OF SERVICE DELIVERY TO THE ELDERLY

Senator Frank Moss (1976) has summarized some of the most unfortunate aspects of what appears to many to have been a too-rapid shift of elderly mental patients from hospitals to nursing homes:

Patients are often discharged wholesale and indiscriminantly, with minimal screening to determine which ones are ready to leave.

Follow-up is rare once the patients arrive in the nursing homes.

Many homes are ill-equipped to handle large numbers of elderly patients. Often no psychiatric services are available, and few attempts are made to rehabilitate patients.

Severely ill patients are housed with others who are much less ill, which is detrimental to their self-esteem.

Few, if any, recreational or activity programmes are provided.

There is often a heavy use of drugs to help manage the patients, particularly in homes that are understaffed.

The list of complaints about individual nursing homes could continue, but it is important to remember that any publicity nursing homes receive is usually bad; few newspapers or television stations feature homes that are clean, well run, and provide a therapeutic environment for their clients (Glasscote, Gudeman and Miles, 1977). But even if the criticisms are exaggerated, it is still puzzling why deinstitutionalization, a movement that promised so much, has become little more than a geographical 'numbers game' in which the driving force more often than not has been a desire to move patients out of hospitals as quickly as possible (Chu and Trotter, 1974; Talbott, 1979). Critics have asked, 'Where have all the patients gone?', and often the answer is that they have been abandoned (Chase, 1973; Gruenberg and Archer, 1979). Once they leave, the hospital mental health departments are no longer responsible for them and they become wards of the welfare department (Wolpert and Wolpert, 1976). It is also apparent that many patients are discharged 'in the absence of consensus' before they are ready or willing to leave and before their communities are ready or willing to accept them (Armstrong, 1976; Scherl and Macht, 1979; C. J. Smith, 1980b; Smith and Smith, 1978a).

To understand why community treatment for the elderly mentally ill is still inadequate, it is necessary to consider the original goals of the deinstitutionalization movement. From the beginning, deinstitutionalization was intended to be much more than a simple shift in the geographical pattern of service delivery. Bachrach (1976) has argued, for example, that deinstitutionalization was meant to include two basic elements;

> the removal of persons who have already been hospitalized. . . and their transfer into the community; and the prevention of hospitalization of those persons who might be considered potential candidates for institutionalization (p. 2).

By the end of the 1970s the geographical element of deinstitutionalization had been achieved successfully. Most of the mentally ill, including the elderly, are now living outside institutions. Unfortunately the quality of care in most communities leaves much to be desired. The gap between the demand for services and their supply was quickly perceived by private-sector property owners. Former patients who do not have a home to return to are usually forced to look for inexpensive quarters in hotels, hostels, and boarding homes normally operated by private individuals. For elderly patients nursing homes are often more appropriate placements, and the drop in the percentage of elderly in mental hospitals accounts for much of the substantial recent increase in the nursing home industry (Table 17.1 and 17.2). One of the major concerns about the quality of care in nursing homes is exemplified in these data: between 1963 and 1964 there was a 22.7 per cent increase in the number of nursing homes in the United States; but during the same period the number of residents increased by 135.4 per cent. The occupancy rate of nursing homes has almost doubled, and there is a lack of qualified aides. From most accounts nursing homes in the 1970s are experiencing some of the same problems that faced mental hospitals in the 1870s; 'as with all social institutions that undergo enormous expansion in a very short time, there are inevitably various significant problems' (Glasscote, 1976, p. 147).

For the elderly, perhaps more than for any other group of the mentally ill,

Table 17.2 Recent trends in nursing home care in the United States

| Characteristics | 1963 | 1969 | 1974 | Percentage change |
|---|---|---|---|---|
| Nursing homes | 12,800 | 15,700 | 15,700 | + 22.7 |
| Residents | 457,050 | 778,290 | 1,075,800 | + 135.4 |
| Admissions | 358,480 | 946,020 | 1,110,800 | + 209.9 |
| Discharges | 339,260 | 872,250 | 1,077,500 | + 217.6 |
| Beds per home | 39.9 | 55.7 | 74.8 | + 87.5 |
| Residents >65 years per 100 US population >65 years | 2.3 | 3.6 | 4.6 | + 100.0 |

*Source*: Adapted from Ingram and Barry (1977), p. 304.

it is evident that most states have considered the geographical element of deinstitutionalization to be their only goal. Once this has been achieved, they have often become complacent, and the secondary objective of preventing hospitalization has been neglected. Bachrach (1980) has observed that the most frequent criticism of deinstitutionalization programmes is their inability or unwillingness to create a continuum of community-based services to meet the needs of the chronically mentally ill. In addition, community mental health professionals have been almost totally unresponsive to the increased demand for mental health services amongst the elderly. The percentage of mental illness 'episodes' treated outside institutions has increased sharply in the last 20 years (Bassuk and Gerson, 1978), but the representation of elderly people has hardly risen at all. Cohen (1976) estimated that in 1975 fewer than 4 per cent of the psychiatric out-patients of private practice and community mental health centres were over 65 years old. This finding was supported by the results of a survey conducted by the Neighborhood Exchange staff prior to the start of the training project in Oklahoma City. The low representation is even more surprising given that the elderly (over 65) now comprise more than 10 per cent of the United States population, and that they experience more mental health problems than any other section of the population (Butler and (Lewis, 1973; Harbert and Ginsberg, 1979).

It is difficult to explain why more out-patient mental health resources are not directed towards the elderly: some argue that the major problem is poor accessibility; others think that professionals choose not to treat the elderly for personal reasons (Cohen, 1976). Much of the blame, however, has been placed on the new community mental health centres (Chu and Trotter, 1974). Evidently many centres have concentrated on the provision of mental health services for a previously unserved element in the population, one which is considered to be more responsive to treatment than chronic patients, including the elderly, who have been discharged from hospitals. The effect is that mental health centres have created new demands, and the needs of many elderly patients have remained unserved.

A third reason why mental health services for the elderly have fallen far short of the demand is that locally based preventive services have not been expanded. When mental hospitals began to close their doors to all but the most seriously mentally ill, it was apparent that, at least in the short run, *in-situ* preventive services would be needed. In this respect there is evidence that most American communities lag far behind their British counterparts (Austin, 1976). The Neighborhood Exchange project is one attempt to remedy this situation.

## THE NEIGHBOURHOOD EXCHANGE PROJECT

In 1979 the author spent 12 months working with the Oklahoma County Mental Health Association, studying the problems associated with the deinstitutionalization of the mentally ill in Oklahoma County. The County contains the state's capital city, Oklahoma City, and within its boundaries live almost one-quarter of the state's total population. Approximately 75 per cent of the patients who are discharged from Central State Hospital (20 miles away in Norman) return to Oklahoma County. It has been recognized for some time that community services for the mentally ill in Oklahoma County have not kept pace with the extra demands that have occurred as a result of deinstitutionalization policies. In 1955 Central State Hospital housed almost 3000 patients, but by 1979 the number had dropped to 640. Similar declines have occurred at the other two state hospitals and in other states during the last two decades (Figure 17.2). While mental hospitals have increased their discharge rates and reduced their inmate populations considerably, until recently admission rates generally have been increasing (and in Oklahoma they continued to increase until 1976). This phenomenon reflects the absence or inadequacy of community facilities offering a viable alternative to hospital treatment. In Oklahoma County, as in almost all areas where deinstitutionalization has been implemented, readmission rates are high (C. J. Smith, 1978b; Bachrach, 1976). Mental patients return to the community, but after a short stay as many as half of them find it necessary to return to the hospital. In spite of the increasing admission rates, the overall number of hospitalized patients has declined steadily, mainly because the

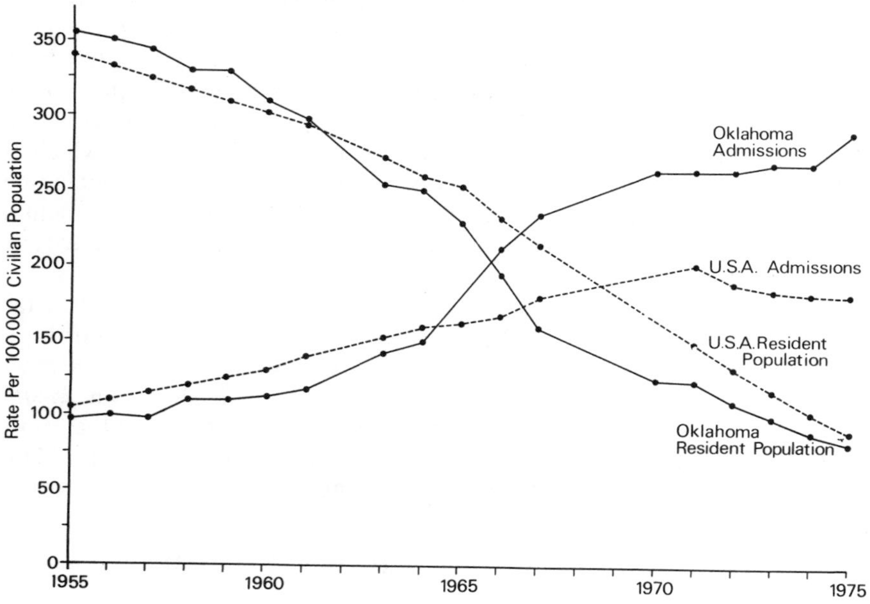


Figure 17.2 Oklahoma vs. United States: admissions and total inmate populations in public mental hospitals, 1955–75

average length of stay has been shortened. In Oklahoma, for example, in the late 1940s, the average stay was close to 10 years (Gorman, 1948); whereas in 1979 the average was slightly less than 3 weeks. On a typical day in 1979 the State Hospital in Norman admits an average of four new patients, but more than twice that number return as readmissions. During the year the resident population has remained stable because an average of 13 patients are discharged each day. Thus anywhere from 90 to 100 patients return to the community every week.

In 1978 the Mental Health Association established deinstitutionalization as one of its primary concerns for the next few years. Among the most urgently required tasks were an assessment of the needs of the mentally ill currently living in the community, and the development of strategies to prevent institutionalization whenever possible and desirable. In the early part of 1979 an inter-agency subcommittee, sponsored by the local Areawide Aging Agency, had also begun to consider some of the strategies for assessing mental health needs amongst the non-institutionalized elderly. The Federal Council on the Aging had recommended in 1975 that all disabled elderly people should be entitled to a minimum set of services, regardless of their ability to pay. These services should include professional psycho/social environmental assessment; skilled advocacy to ensure that the elderly receive the services and benefits they are entitled to; and the physical presence of at least one 'significant other' to help them cope with daily problems. This would represent a minimum level of services that could make the differences between 'a life that is basically satisfying and one that is not'; and between staying in the community and being institutionalized (Glasscote, Gudeman and Miles, 1977, p. 10).

Most of the available literature supports the general view that the elderly have a higher than average incidence of both 'low-level' emotional problems and the functional and organic disorders that are classified as mental illnesses (Butler and Lewis, 1973). For example, a subcommittee of the United States Senate Special Committee on Aging (1976, p. 706) reported that 'between 14 and 25 percent of our 22 million older Americans suffer from some degree of mental impairment...[and]...about 8 percent...are impaired to the point of needing protective (psychiatric) services'. Another study, reported in the same source, estimated that approximately 3 million non-institutionalized elderly people require mental health services, but fewer than 20 per cent have their needs met through existing resources.

As elsewhere in the United States, by the mid-1970s in the Oklahoma City metropolitan area, the elderly mentally ill were not receiving the recommended minimum level of sources. It was to investigate this situation, and to develop a strategy for improving the delivery of services, that the Areawide Aging subcommittee and the Mental Health Association combined in new initiatives including a training project called Neighborhood Exchange. With the help of federal funding and a 1-year 'on-site co-ordinator' position funded by the

Areawide Aging Agency, the project has begun to train residents as paraprofessional care-givers in Metro Park, a neighbourhood of Oklahoma City. The neighbourhood was selected because it has a relatively high proportion of elderly residents (close to 40 per cent), and because it has an active and enthusiastic neighbourhood association that was willing to host the project.

As stated in the initial request for funding, the purpose of the project is:

> 'To train a small group of [neighborhood] residents to perform a variety of services on behalf of elderly residents in their neighborhoods; in order to keep the at-risk elderly population in their homes whenever and wherever this is possible. . . or in the least restrictive environment available to them'.

At the end of the training the residents will hopefully be able to perform the following functions:

(1) identify and expand existing resources in the community, and match up the available services with the assumed needs of the elderly;
(2) establish links between informal resource providers and formal service agencies external to the neighbourhood, and arrange for service delivery when appropriate;
(3) work to improve local acceptance of the elderly mentally ill;
(4) assess the health and mental health needs of the non-institutionalized elderly;
(5) advocate for improved mental health and allied services for the elderly;
(6) monitor the quality of care provided to the elderly;
(7) train other residents to function as informed helpers and service providers (long-term objective).

## NEIGHBOURHOOD SERVICE DELIVERY: SOME UNDERLYING PRINCIPLES

The major goal of the Neighborhood Exchange project was to utilize the human and non-human resources of the Metro Park neighbourhood to provide, or provide access to, mental health care services for the elderly. This goal is consistent with the original goals of the deinstitutionalization movement, and with the overwhelming preference expressed by elderly people to remain in their own homes whenever possible (Shanas, 1972; Maguire, 1979). It should be recognized that some critics of attempts to keep people in their own homes point out that only 5 per cent of the elderly are institutionalized (1 per cent in hospitals; 4 per cent in nursing homes); and that in all probability many more could benefit from institutional life. The Neighborhood Exchange project staff prefer to keep an open mind on this issue. Obviously, if the comprehensive assessments clearly indicate institutional care, then such care will be recommended. This should be considered as one of the successes of the project rather than a failure to keep an individual out of the institution. The most important question for the Neighborhood Exchange staff, and for staff of all similar projects, is whether the neighbours are willing and able to offer the range of services needed to prevent institutionalization. This is possible in many neighbourhoods and many innovative attempts have been made to provide preventive mental health services at the local level (Collins and Pancoast, 1976; S. A. Smith, 1975). It is also obvious that many neighbourhoods are less fortunate. One of the traditional barriers to the development of 'primary preventive' services has been the assumption that until discrete aetiological factors have been identified, interventions cannot effectively eliminate the problems at their source (Mechanic, 1969). As an alternative, primary prevention attempts to improve healthy functioning wherever possible: by reducing stressful events in living and working environments; providing emergency (crisis) intervention services; and by educating people about mental health in general. As has been observed:

> Avoidance of precise causative targets does not render these preventive efforts random, nor their benefits to a population serendipitous. If the education, guidance, stress reducing, and crisis intervention experiences afforded to the community . . . are: (1) in keeping with the needs of a defined population; (2) culturally, financially, geographically, and procedurally accessible to that population; and (3) delivered in a form that can be readily used by the population in need, then their impact may reduce the number of individuals defined as emotionally ill and subsequently enrolled in the treatment population. Prevention, in effect, is of deterioration of adaptation and functioning, rather than of the emergence of a precise disorder and related set of symptoms (Saunders, 1979, p. 70).

Echoing this optimistic note, C. J. Smith (1980c) has suggested that neighbourhoods can potentially provide three interrelated sources of informal support for needy individuals:

(1) a favourable local 'climate' for healthy behaviour and help-seeking;
(2) the provision of informal services and resources; and
(3) improved access to external services and resources.

### The local 'climate' of opinion

If a neighbourhood is to provide what will ultimately be a comprehensive range of informal mental health services, the minimum requirement is a passive acceptance by neighbourhood residents of the elderly. This is a necessary condition if the neighbourhood is to continue to be home for the individuals in question. At the very least they must not be actively discriminated against in the streets and in the local shops; and the majority of residents must be willing to accept them as near-neighbours. Two recent studies give cause for both optimism and pessimism in this respect (Smith and Hanham, 1980a,

1980b). The first, a study of attitudes towards the mentally ill, indicated that people who lived close to a large mental health facility were rarely bothered by either the building or its clients. It appears that prolonged contact with and proximity to the mentally ill are associated with more positive attitudes, as measured on a social distance scale (Kirk, 1974). Other results were less promising; for example, there was evidence of a negative relationship between the respondent's age and his or her acceptance of mental illness, which suggests that the elderly themselves are less tolerant than younger people of other elderly people with mental health problems. It was also suggested that proximity to mental illness softens only some aspects of public attitudes. Residents of the neighbourhood adjacent to the facility were more tolerant than residents in a control neighbourhood, but the greater differences were evident in the relatively impersonal interactions (Table 17.3). In other words, it appeared that people are willing to have the mentally ill as neighbours and workmates (items 3, 7, and 9), but they prefer not to develop close relationships. The fact that residents are willing to have the mentally ill as neighbours does imply the existence of the passive acceptance that was posited earlier as the minimum requirement for a therapeutic community—but a substantial improvement in attitudes is obviously still needed. From previous educational attempts it is clear that we should not expect too much too soon in this direction (Baron and Rutman, 1979; Segal, 1978).

In the second study (Smith and Hanham, 1980b) a group of 90 respondents were asked to evaluate the similarities between a variety of public facilities, including mental health services and nursing homes for the elderly. The respon-

Table 17.3 Mean item scores: social rejection index (serious case)

| Item description | Mean scores | |
|---|---|---|
| | Hospital neighbourhood | Control neighbourhood |
| 1. Would you hire her in your own store? | 2.51 | 2.71 |
| 2. Would she make a good boss? | 2.68 | 2.91 |
| 3. Would you work with her on a neighbourhood project? | 1.97 | 2.50* |
| 4. Would you ask her to babysit? | 2.54 | 2.82 |
| 5. Would you rent her a room in your house? | 2.35 | 2.59 |
| 6. Would your rent her a house next door to you? | 1.70 | 1.91 |
| 7. Would you let her join your favourite club? | 1.67 | 2.18* |
| 8. Would you vote for her in political office? | 2.59 | 2.89 |
| 9. Would you work in a regular job with her? | 1.54 | 2.03* |
| 10. Would you let your children marry her? | 2.35 | 2.47 |

*Source*: Author's unpublished data.
*Notes*: *Differences significant at the $p = 0.01$ level.
Mean scores: 1 = Yes, 2 = Uncertain, 3 = No.

dents were asked to select the facilities they believed were about equally repellent or 'noxious', which was defined as 'undesirable, unpleasant, and unwholesome'. The data were subjected to a multidimensional scaling algorithm (INDSCAL), and a three-dimensional solution accounted for a satisfactory percentage of variance in the similarities data. The first two dimensions are illustrated in Figure 17.3, where clusters of facilities have been labelled and boundaries drawn (for purposes of clarity only). The illustration shows, again, that there is cause for both cheer and gloom. Evidently the respondents feel that nursing homes for the elderly are neither very desirable nor very noxious, which accounts for the location of the *community treatment* cluster close to the vertical axis. Nursing homes are grouped with other service facilities for so-called normal population groups, and the cluster includes general hospitals, health clinics, and planned parenthood clinics. These facilities were clearly separated from

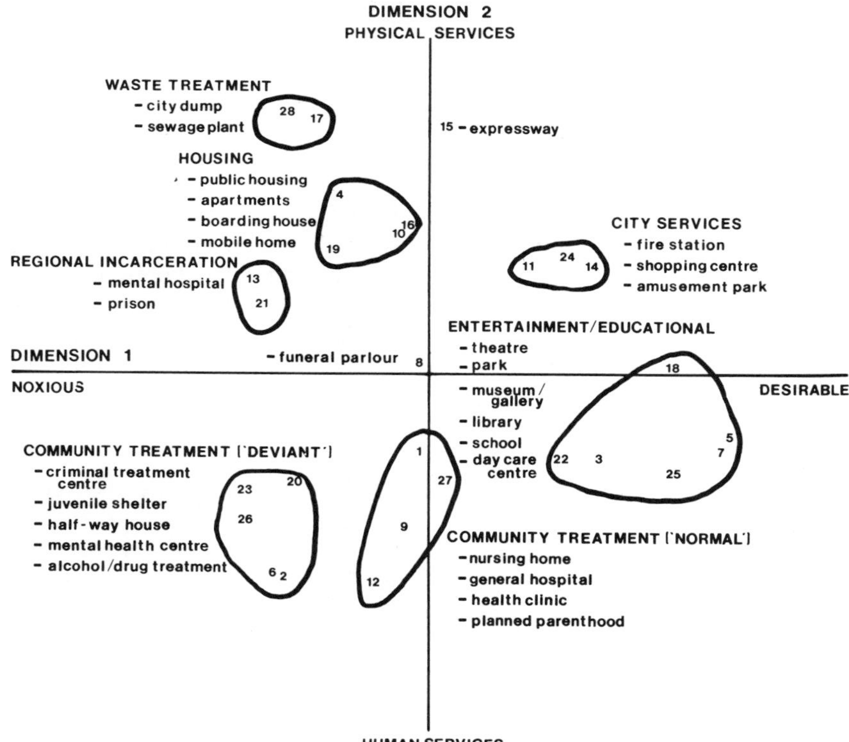


Figure 17.3 INDSCAL facility space. (*Note*: The illustration shows seven clusters of facilities; labels are assigned intuitively by considering (a) the facility types in each cluster and (b) facility scores on the two dimensions—noxious/desirable, and physical/human services.)

another cluster that included criminal treatment centres, juvenile shelters, mental health centres, and alcohol- or drug-treatment clinics. Herein, of course, lies the other side of the coin—that mental health facilities, both the small local ones and the larger hospitals, are considered by the respondents in this study to be highly undesirable as residential neighbours. One can only speculate what would have happened if the respondents had been asked to evaluate 'nursing homes that house former mental patients', but the responses would probably not have been favourable. It is unwise to infer from this experimental study that the majority of community residents are unwilling to accept the mentally ill as neighbours. On the other hand, we must be concerned that mental illness (but not necessarily old age) is still regarded in a generally negative fashion, and that given the choice most people would prefer not to have contact with the mentally ill. One optimistic sign, however, is that once a contact is made, attitudes tend to improve with the passage of time. It would appear, therefore, to be desirable to organize and through education promote increased interactions between the non-elderly and the elderly, including those with mental health problems.

## Informal service provision

In addition to developing a favourable 'climate' of opinion within the neighbourhood, if the elderly are to continue to live at home active acceptance is also required. Residents must do more than simply accept the presence of their elderly neighbours; they must volunteer their time and provide help to those who are in need. The provision of such informal services represents what might be a sufficient condition for keeping the elderly out of institutions in the absence of professional helping services. In many neighbourhoods in Oklahoma City, for example in Metro Park, this informal service provision is already occurring.

When an individual needs help, many different services are theoretically available, ranging from extremely informal conversations with friends and relatives, to the formal services provided by professional care-givers. Warren (1978) has estimated that up to 50 per cent of the people who experience psychological impairments that normally require treatment, seek help only from individuals in their church, their families, or their neighbourhood. Help of this type has become known as an individual's 'social support system' (Caplan, 1974, p. 7), and the notion of informal or locally based support system has caught on so rapidly in the mental health professions that it has been described as a 'third revolution' in mental health care, following successively the rise then the demise of the asylum (Stein, 1979; Turner and TenHoor, 1978). Neighbours are a particularly important element in an elderly person's support system, because in many cases the elderly are immobile. If family members and friends are either unable or unwilling to provide help, then an additional responsibility falls on the neighbours. It is implicit from this discussion that the notion of being 'only a neighbour' and therefore a person of limited importance beyond possibly borrowing the proverbial cup of sugar, needs to be revised substantially. Neighbours can provide a range of essential services, both tangible and intangible, to persons in need. We would expect a neighbour's role in primary prevention to be most effective in helping with everyday problems; problems that are not yet very serious, but which could deteriorate rapidly if left unattended. Such problems typically require what Warren (1980) has referred to as a low level of 'invoked expertise' for their solution. In fact, for this reason many professionals may be unwilling and/or unable to help with such problems, so the neighbours may be the best as well as the only solution. To provide effective support, at least some of the neighbourhood residents must have the following prerequisites: (1) proximity, (2) time to spare, (3) motivation, (4) knowledge of the neighbourhood and its resources, and (5) knowledge of the location of and routes to services elsewhere in the city. For neighbours who do not have the latter two categories of knowledge, much can be learned quickly and easily; it does not require a college degree or a professional training. In the Neighborhood Exchange project we were looking for people who were already providing informal help, but we hoped that the initial core of volunteers would disseminate by word of mouth the news about the training programme, and involve others.

The neighbourhood services provided for an elderly person will depend partly on the relationship between the helper and the person being helped, as well as on the type of service that is needed and the helper's ability. In this regard, four general categories of services have been identified: (1) the alleviation of social isolation, (2) emotional support, (3) communication activities, and (4) problem-centred services. This classification can be reduced to differentiate social support activities from problem- or crisis-centred services (S. A. Smith, 1975; see Table 17.4).

Although it is not possible to identify an evolutionary sequence of helping relationships, in many cases the people providing services to the elderly are themselves elderly, which raises the issue of mutuality. In most studies of informal helping, it is found that a large proportion of the people providing help also receive help at various times. It is almost a truism that most individuals assume they can best be helped by people who have experienced similar situations, and it is precisely this tendency that is at the root of the 'self-help' or 'mutual-aid' groups that have mushroomed in recent years (C. J. Smith, 1978a). Mutual aid ranges from the informal give-and-take that occurs within a residential neighbourhood, to quasi-institutional groups like Alcoholics Anonymous and Recovery, Inc. (for former mental patients). The only thing these groups have in common is mutuality—their members have, or have had, similar problems, although usually the individuals who provide help are not currently suffering from their particular affiliction. In an attempt to explain the

Table 17.4 Selected informal services for the elderly

| Social support activities | Problem-centred services |
|---|---|
| *Alleviating social isolation* | |
| Visiting, dropping in | Minor and major home repairs |
| Telephone calls | Transportation |
| Escorting/accompanying | Shopping, delivering groceries |
| Making introductions | Writing letters |
| Making invitations | Reading TV schedules, newspapers, books, magazines |
| Organizing activities | Housework |
| Meetings | Counselling |
| Sharing keys, food | Outreach/finding |
| Joint shopping trips | Cooking |
| *Emotional support* | Nursing/caregiving |
| Remembering at holidays, birthdays, special occasions | Picking up and supervising |
| Encouragement | Medication |
| Reassurance | Selling of house/real estate dealings |
| Watching out for | Getting rid of unwanted possessions |
| Looking in on | Taking care of business/finances etc. informally or formally |
| *Communication activities* | Finding companions, room-mates |
| Sharing general information | Information and referral to lawyers, doctors, dentists, nursing homes, welfare, mental health |
| Being a confidante | Walking and feeding pets |
| Listening | Lawn work |
| Giving opinions and advice | Sharing garden pools |
| Answering questions | |

*Source*: Adapted from S. A. Smith (1975), pp. 30–2.

phenomenal growth in mutual-aid groups at all levels of formality, Borman (1975) has suggested that the reasons:

> range from lack of confidence in, inadequate access to, or exorbitant costs of existing systems of service. For many conditions around which mutual-aid groups form, such as child abuse, alcoholism, obesity, mental illness, drug addiction, family problems, chronic disabilities and prison release, there appears to be a lack of professional programs of service to deal effectively with these issues. Accordingly these groups fill a vacuum.... Some suggest that these areas of distress can only be relieved by the personal involvement and commitment that is encouraged and sustained by a network of peers similarly afflicted (p. 333).

In many circumstances then, mutual-aid groups offer an effective complement to the activities of formal service agencies; in others, they provide services where formal provision does not exist. The advantages of mutual-aid groups in the provision of locally based mental health services have been noted by Reissman (1976) and C. J. Smith (1978a).

The importance of mutuality in the provision of services to the elderly person with mental health problems cannot be overstated. For example, of the 15 or so initial volunteers in the Neighborhood Exchange programme, 10 were themselves over 65 years old. However, it is important to stress that for the development of effective helping relationships, mutuality and not similarity is the most important ingredient. To provide help to another person, an individual does not need to have experienced an identical problem or to be similar in age or other characteristics. A helping relationship can develop between two people if they share common or overlapping needs and if they expect that their help will be reciprocated. An older person can interact usefully with a younger couple if the interaction satisfies some of the needs felt by both parties. The usual requirement for the development of a mutually trusting relationship is the existence of 'horizontal' interaction, in which the parties have approximately equal power, and help flows both ways (Shapiro, 1977; see figure 17.4). These relationships are usually nurtured over a long period of time, which explains why they are most typical of spouse or 'bosom-buddy'

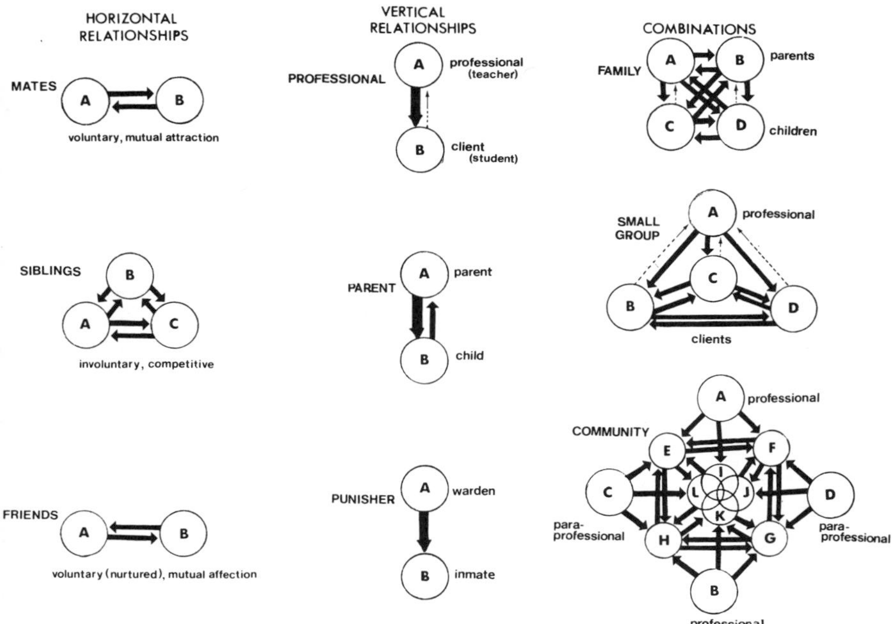


Figure 17.4 Mutuality configurations: horizontal and vertical relationships. (*Note*: The direction of the relationships is indicated by arrows; and the amount of reciprocity is indicated, crudely, by the thickness of the arrows. A thin, or absent, arrow indicates that a relationship is not reciprocal (e.g. warden–inmate).)

interactions. In the case of the older person and his younger friends, they are simulating the symmetry that is more commonly found between the parties of such closely tied relationships. They have reciprocal needs, which make them, at least temporarily, structurally equal in their relationship (Wellman, 1979; C. J. Smith, 1980d). In these circumstances there is no disadvantage from the disparity in ages and life cycle stage which normally implies an unbalanced or "vertical" interaction, as with the parent-child or teacher-student type relationship (Shapiro, 1977). In fact it is an advantage, for example, when an older person babysits for a young couple, and reactivates his grandparent or parent roles while allowing the couple some extra freedom (Smith, 1980a).

**Access to external services and resources**

The development of neighbourhood-based mental health services for the elderly should not replace the professional services provided by official agencies. A major purpose is to provide linkages between the two systems, so that what is lacking in one system can be located in the other. Ultimately, the two systems should complement each other in a more effective pattern of service delivery, but this is difficult to achieve (Gottlieb, 1977). Professionals often feel threatened by the presence of volunteers, either because the latter are believed to lack the necessary skills, or because of a fear that the non-professionals can do a better job. The volunteers may also resent the intrusion of the professionals, particularly if they tell them how to do what they believe they are already doing effectively. It is essential, therefore, to develop working relationships between the two systems and to ensure that their respective strengths are dovetailed. If this is achieved, the potential for extending and improving services is huge. There may never be enough professionals to meet all the mental health needs of a community, but if they train and supervise volunteers it is possible to spread the available resources more equitably throughout the community (Sarason *et al.*, 1977). In the Oklahoma City Neighborhood Exchange Project and similar programmes is the hope that the first volunteers will eventually train a new group of volunteers. To use an allegorical example: if we give a hungry person a fish he will eat today; if we teach him how to fish he will eat for the rest of his life! In the Oklahoma City neighbourhood we hope that neighbours will ultimately replace the outsiders wherever and whenever possible.

When formal services are unavailable or inaccessible, neighbours may offer indirect help by connecting residents with the information and services they need. This function is similar to that of a 'gatekeeper' (Snyder, 1976) or a 'hop-skipper' (Jacobs, 1961), who performs a bridging function to the larger community outside the neighbourhood. Two key determinants of the efficiency of this bridging function are the connectedness and the plexity of the social networks within the neighbourhood (C. J. Smith, 1980c). Connectedness is the number of neighbours who know each other. In a highly connected neighbourhood, information about who needs help travels quickly, and the help, if it is available, can be dispatched efficiently. The plexity of relationships within a neighbourhood measures how many different types of ties residents have with each other. Thus, if individual *A* knows almost all his neighbours, but most of them only in one context, he is likely to have access to more outside resources through their help and advice than if he just knows a few people very well. The opposite of uniplexity is multiplexity, a situation in which people know each other in a variety of contexts; they work, play, worship, and drink together (Mitchell, 1969). In the development of neighbourhood helping services, connectedness and plexity can be both advantageous and disadvantageous.

A high level of connectedness between a small number of residents is usually an advantage for informal service provision (Stack, 1974); but for linking up with city-wide services it may be better to know a large number of people in just one context, than a small number in many contexts. This was illustrated by Horwitz (1977) in his study of the influence of two structural variables on the decision to seek psychiatric help. One was a measure of the cohesiveness of an individual's kinship network; and the other was the openness of the friendship network, the number of an individual's friends who did not know each other. The results have suggested that while individuals with cohesive kin networks and closed friendships take advantage of informal services and mutual supportiveness, because they receive so much informal help, they may be hesitant to seek formal help even when their problems are serious. Consequently, by the time they go for help, their problems can be more serious than if informal help was unavailable. On the other hand, individuals with weaker kinship networks and open friendships are often unable to find informal help, but because they know a wider range of people they tend to have better access to external resources. On balance these people tend to seek out professional help earlier and with less serious symptoms than the others. Evidently, close kinship ties can provide a supportive milieu, but there may be a tendency to allow serious problems to compound and this may make the eventual treatment more difficult.

If Horwitz's results can be generalized, we may conclude that the social network characteristics of a neighbourhood exert a powerful influence on the creation of informal support systems. On the one hand, close ties promote informal help-seeking or the demand for services, and they also facilitate the supply of informal services. On the other hand, closeness may limit one's range of contacts, which is a handicap in a search for help with unusual or serious problems (Smith and Smith, 1978b).

From this discussion it is apparent that although a neighbourhood lacking in internal cohesiveness has some disadvantages, it does not necessarily follow that effective mental health services for the elderly and other groups cannot be provided. Trute and Segal (1976) have demonstrated, for example, that former hospital patients are able to reintegrate more effectively into community life in areas that are mid-way between the extremes of cohesiveness and disorganization. For many patients the optimum setting is a neighbourhood with a substantial proportion of non-nuclear family-oriented residents. This is an optimistic conclusion for mentally ill persons in general, and for the elderly in particular, because they so often have weak and disrupted social networks; and also because the neighbourhoods they live in are often socially disorganized (C. J. Smith, 1978b). On balance it may be advisable for community workers to spend at least some time developing these loose or 'weak' ties between neighbours (Granovetter, 1973), because in the long run this may turn out to be a more effective strategy than trying to foster interval cohesiveness and close social ties. In this light, the conclusion that neighbourhood residents do not appear willing to develop intimate ties with mentally ill people can be interpreted in a more positive fashion (Smith and Hanham, 1980a).

## SUMMARY

This chapter has briefly described a neighbourhood-based attempt to provide preventive mental health services for the elderly. The need for individual neighbourhoods to develop indigenous support services was highlighted by reviewing some of the inadequacies in the formal and institutional responses to mental illness amongst the elderly. A loose theoretical framework for building up neighbourhood-based service systems was outlined, but because at the time of writing the project is still in progress, firm conclusions and policy suggestions are impossible. It is worthwhile, however, to reiterate the optimistic philosophy underlying the Neighborhood Exchange project and many similar programmes that have been started in other cities in the United States. Keeping people in their own homes whenever possible, and utilizing informal services provided by neighbourhood paraprofessionals, will serve not only to improve the quality and quantity of the services provided; it will also, in the long run, help to strengthen neighbourhood life. Institutionalization will always be necessary and desirable for some elderly residents, but the Neighborhood Exchange staff hope to create a local awareness that alternatives are available. Preventive mental health requires that informal help is provided long before problems reach a critical level, but the provision of help is only a partial solution. People in need must learn how to ask for help, and a prerequisite for this is the knowledge or the expectation that one's request will be heard. In this sense, a neighbourhood that is defined by objective criteria (e.g. hospital admission rates) as 'pathological' or 'high-risk', may also be one in which the residents have developed an impressive repertoire of informal helping skills, and a willingness to seek help before it is too late. Active reporting of problems and an equally active set of informal responses may indicate healthy signs in what otherwise appears to be an unhealthy neighbourhood.

## ACKNOWLEDGEMENTS

In addition to the author, the staff of the Neighborhood Exchange project were: Sandi Behrens, Sandy Ingraham, and Jane Carney. They are to be complimented for their enthusiasm and commitment to the project. We are obviously indebted to Harold Earp and the residents of Metro Park, and we hope the project justifies their commitment to it. The author would also like to thank Carolyn Smith and Tony Warnes for their adroit and critical comments on earlier versions of this chapter.

When this chapter was written the author was on leave from his position in the Department of Geography at the University of Oklahoma. The project described in the chapter is funded by a Department of Health, Education and Welfare Contract No. R6–108–79. The author's leave was funded by the National Foundation's Public Service Science Residency Program. Neither HEW nor NSF are responsible for the views expressed in the chapter.

## REFERENCES

Armstrong, B. (1976). Preparing the community for the patient's return. *Hospital and Community Psychiatry*, **27**, 349–56.

Austin, M. J. (1976). Network of help for England's elderly. *Social Work*, **21**, 114–20.

Aviram, U. and Segal, S. P. (1973). Exclusion of the mentally ill. *Archives of General Psychiatry*, **29**, 126–31.

Aviram, U., Syme, S. L., and Cohen, J. B. (1976). The effects of policies and programs on reduction of mental hospitalization. *Social Science and Medicine*, **10**, 571–7.

Bachrach, L. L. (1976). *Deinstitutionalization: An Analytical Review and Sociological Perspective*. National Institute of Mental Health, Series D, No. 4, Rockville, Md.

Bachrach, L. L. (1980). Deinstitutionalization: a sociological perspective. In Smith, C. J. (ed.), *A Place to Call Home: Perspectives on Deinstitutionalization of the Mentally Ill*, pp. 41–68. Mental Health Association in Oklahoma County, Oklahoma City.

Baron, R. C. and Rutman, I. D. (1979). *These People: A Citizen Education Project Examining Public Response to Community Care for the Mentally Disabled.* Horizon House Institute for Research and Development, Philadelphia.

Bassuk, E. L. and Gerson, S. (1978). Deinstitutionalization and mental health services. *Scientific American*, **238**, 46–53.

Borman, L. D. (1975). *Explorations in Self-Help and Mutual Aid.* Center for Urban Affairs, Northwestern Univ., Evanston, Ill.

Bradley, V. J. (1979). Deinstitutionalization: social justice or political expedient? *Advocacy Now*, **1**, 104–10.

Butler, R. N. and Lewis, M. I. (1973). *Aging and Mental Health: Positive Psychosocial Approaches.* C. V. Mosby, St Louis, Missouri.

Caplan, G. (1974). *Support Systems and Community Mental Health.* Behavioral Publications, New York.

Chase, J. (1973). Where have all the patients gone? *Human Behavior*, October, pp. 14–21.

Chu, F. D. and Trotter, S. (1974). *The Madness Establishment.* Grassman, New York.

Cohen, G. D. (1976). Mental health services and the elderly: needs and options, *American Journal of Psychiatry*, **133**, 65–8.

Collins, A. H. and Pancoast, D. L. (1976). *Natural Helping Networks: A Strategy for Prevention*. National Association of Social Workers, Washington, DC.

General Accounting Office (1977). *Returning the Mentally Disabled to the Community: Government Needs to Do More*. Government Printing Office (HRD-76–152), Washington, DC.

Glasscote, R. M. (1976). *Old Folks at Homes: A Field Study of Nursing and Board-and-Care Homes*. American Psychiatric Association, Washington, DC.

Glasscote, R. M., Gudeman, J. E., and Miles, D. G. (1977). *Creative Mental Health Services for the Elderly*. American Psychiatric Association, Washington, DC.

Goldhammer, H. and Marshall, A. W. (1958). *Psychosis and Civilization: Two Studies in the Frequency of Mental Disease*. The Free Press, New York.

Gorman, M. (1948). Oklahoma tackles its snake pits. *Readers Digest*, **53**, (September) pp. 139–60.

Gottlieb, B. H. (1977). The primary group as supportive milieu: applications to community psychology. Paper presented at the American Psychological Association Meetings, San Francisco, August.

Granovetter, M. S. (1973). The strength of weak ties. *American Journal of Sociology*, **78**, 1360–80.

Grob, G. N. (1973). *Mental Institutions in America: Social Policy to 1875*. The Free Press, New York.

Grob, G. N. (1980). Psychiatry and mental hospitals in modern America: myths and realities. In Smith, C. J. (ed.), *A Place to Call Home: Perspectives on Deinstitutionalization of the Mentally Ill*, pp. 11–33. Mental Health Association in Oklahoma County, Oklahoma City.

Gruenberg, E. M. and Archer, J. (1979). Abandonment of responsibility for the seriously mentally ill. *Milbank Memorial Fund Quarterly*, **57**, 485–506.

Harbert, A. S. and Ginsberg, L. H. (1979). *Human Services for Older Adults: Concepts and Skills*. Wadsworth, Belmont, Calif.

Horwitz, A. (1977). Social networks and pathways to psychiatric treatment. *Social Forces*, **56**, 86–105.

Ingram, D. K. and Barry, J. R. (1977). National statistics on deaths in nursing homes: interpretations and implications. *The Gerontologist*, **17**, 303–8.

Jacobs, J. (1961). *The Death and Life of Great American Cities*. Random House, New York.

Kirk, S. A. (1974). The impact of labeling on rejection of the mentally ill: an experimental study. *Journal of Health and Social Behavior*, **15**, 108–17.

Lamb, H. R. and Goertzel, V. (1971). Discharged mental patients—are they really in the community? *Archives of General Psychiatry*, **24**, 29–34.

Maguire, G. A. (1979). Volunteer program to assist the elderly to remain in home settings. *The American Journal of Occupational Therapy*, **33**, 98–101.

Mechanic, D. (1969). *Mental Health and Social Policy*. Prentice-Hall, Englewood Cliffs, NJ.

Mitchell, J. C. (1969). The concept and use of social networks. In Mitchell, J. C. (ed.), *Social Networks in Urban Situations*, pp. 1–50. Manchester University Press, Manchester.

Moss, F. E. (US Senator) (1976). Where have all the patients gone? In *The Role of Nursing Homes in Caring for Discharged Mental Patients*. Supporting Paper No. 7, prepared by the Subcommittee on long-term care, of the Special Committee on Aging, US Senate, p. 728. Government Printing Office, Washington, DC.

Reissman, F. (1976). How does self-help work? *Social Policy*, **7**, 41–45.

Rose, S. M. (1979). Deciphering deinstitutionalization: complexities in policy and program analysis. *Milbank Memorial Fund Quarterly*, **57**, 429–60.

Rothman, D. J. (1971). *The Discovery of the Asylum: Social Order and Disorder in the New Republic*. Little, Brown & Co., Boston, Mass.

Sarason, S. B. *et al.* (1977). *Human Services and Resource Networks*. Jossey-Bass, San Francisco.

Saunders, S. (1979). Primary prevention from a neighborhood base: a working model. *American Journal of Orthopsychiatry*, **49**, 69–80.

Scherl, D. J. and Macht, L. B. (1979). Deinstitutionalization in the absence of consensus. *Hospital and Community Psychiatry*, **30**, 599–604.

Scull, A. T. (1977). *Decarceration: Community Treatment and the Deviant*. Prentice-Hall, Englewood Cliffs, NJ.

Segal, S. P. (1978). Attitudes toward the mentally ill: a review. *Social Work*, **23**, 211–17.

Shanas, E. (1972). *The Health of Older People: A Social Survey*. Harvard University Press, Cambridge, Mass.

Shapiro, B. Z. (1977). Mutual helping: a neglected theme in social work practice and theory. *Canadian Journal of Social Work Education*, **3**, 33–44.

Smith, C. A. and Smith, C. J. (1978a). Learned helplessness and preparedness in discharged mental patients. *Social Work Research and Abstracts*, **14**, 21–27.

Smith, C. A. and Smith, C. J. (1978b). Locating natural neighbors in the urban community. *Area*, **10**, 102–110.

Smith, C. J. (1976). Residential neighborhoods as humane environments. *Environment and Planning A*, **8**, 311–26.

Smith, C. J. (1978a). Self-help and social networks in the urban community. *Ekistics*, **65**, 106–16.

Smith, C. J. (1978b). Recidivism and community adjustment amongst former mental patients. *Social Science and Medicine*, **12**, 17–27.

Smith, C. J. (1980a). Urban structure and the development of natural support systems for dependent populations. Unpublished paper (mimeo).

Smith, C. J. (1980b). Optimum living environments for discharged mental patients. In *Optimizing Environments: Research, Practice, and Policy*. Proceedings of the Environmental Design Research Association (EDRA) 11th Annual Conference, Charleston, South Carolina.

Smith, C. J. (1980c). Neighborhood effects on mental health. In Johnston, R. J. and Herbert, D. T. (ed.), *Geography and the Urban Environment*, vol. 3, pp. 363–415. Wiley, London.

Smith, C. J. (1980d). Social networks as metaphors, models, and methods. *Progress in Human Geography*, **4**, 500–24.

Smith, C. J. and Hanham, R. Q. (1980a). Proximity and the formation of public attitudes towards mental illness. Unpublished paper (mimeo.)

Smith, C. J. and Hanham, R. Q. (1980b). Any place but here! Mental health facilities as noxious neighbors. Unpublished paper (mimeo).

Smith, S. A. (1975). *Natural Systems and the Elderly: An Unrecognized Resource*. Portland State University, School of Social Work, Portland, Oregon.

Snyder, P. Z. (1976). Neighborhood gatekeepers in the process of urban adaptation. *Urban Anthropology*, **5**, 35–52.

Stack, C. B. (1974). *All Our Kin: Strategies for Survival in a Black Community*. Harper & Row, New York.

Stein, L. I. (ed.) (1979). *Community Support Systems for the Long-term Patient*. Jossey-Bass, San Francisco.

Talbott, J. A. (1979). Deinstitutionalization: avoiding the disasters of the past. *Hospital and Community Psychiatry*, **30**, 621–4.

Trute, B. and Segal, S. P. (1976). Census tract predictors and the social integration of sheltered care residents. *Social Psychiatry*, **11**, 153–61.

Turner, J. C. and TenHoor, W. J. (1978). The NIMH community support program: pilot approach to a needed social reform. *Schizophrenia Bulletin*, **4**, 319–44.

United States of America, Senate (1976). *The Role of Nursing Homes in Caring for Discharged Mental Patients.* Supporting paper No. 7, prepared by the Subcommittee on Long-term Care of the Special Committee on Aging, US Senate, Government Printing Office, Washington, DC.

Warren, D. I. (1978). The neighborhood factor in problem coping, help seeking and social support: research findings and suggested policy implications. Paper presented at the 55th Annual Meeting of the American Orthopsychiatric Association, San Francisco, March.

Wellman, B. (1979). The community question: the intimate networks of east Yorkers, *American Journal of Sociology*, **84**, 1201–31.

Wolpert, J. and Wolpert E. (1976). The relocation of released mental hospital patients into residential communities. *Policy Sciences*, **17**, 31–51.

PART 5

# OVER VIEWS PLANNING AND GEOGRAPHICAL RESEARCH CONTRIBUTIONS

Geographical Perspectives on the Elderly
Edited by A. M. Warnes


Chapter 18

# The implications of an ageing population for land-use planning

*Lawrence Greenberg*

*The views expressed in the chapter are the author's own and not those of the Department of the Environment*

There is a growing appreciation of the realities of old age, both of its problems and the opportunities it offers. This awareness is accompanied by a questioning of traditional attitudes and practices and an increasing pressure to take positive account of the needs and wants of elderly people. Where these emerge as demands for changes in land-use they impinge on the planning system and influence policies and decisions. The relationship also holds in reverse: planning action can affect the elderly. Where the results are severe they may, in in part, be due to insufficient understanding of the way old people live and how they use their environment.

'Town and country planning is essentially a matter of resolving conflicts and seeing that the many and various demands that we make upon our limited stock of land are met in an orderly fashion' (Ardill, 1974). It is a political activity and thus entails balancing interests, reaching compromises, and determining priorities. The benefits will not always be evenly distributed. It is essential to look at the elderly in this context to establish the implications of an ageing population and to enable the interests of the elderly to be given due weight in the planning process. It should be explained that throughout this chapter 'planning' is used as a shorthand term for 'land-use planning' and 'planners' for 'land-use planners'.

## THE CHARACTERISTICS OF THE ELDERLY AS THEY RELATE TO PLANNING

The elderly are the same as the rest of us—but older: 'except for the inevitable changes in biology and health, older people are the same as middle-aged people with essentially the same psychological and social needs' (Havighurst, 1968).

The elderly share most of their characteristics with people of all ages and it is important to recognize and absorb this to design optimal environments for the old (Carp, 1976).

In common with any other age group, the elderly vary greatly one from another: their age span can range from the newly retired to their parents. Many people in their 60s may suffer the illnesses associated with ageing, but some of the very old are virtually free of ill health; and whilst a large proportion of old people are poor, about one-fifth of marketable wealth is owned by people over 65. So the elderly are by no means a homogeneous group and to assume 'homogeneity may have unfortunate consequences. . . programmes successful in one location may not be successful elsewhere' (Beckham and Kart, 1977).

The problems of older people are generally those faced by the rest of the population but exacerbated by the effects of ageing: no-one likes loneliness but the elderly feel it more keenly; the closure of a local shop is inconvenient to all in the neighbourhood but the elderly are the least able physically and financially to go elsewhere; poor housing conditions cause widespread distress but the elderly are least tolerant of cold and damp. The elderly may find themselves disadvantaged on two aspects in particular: health and income.

## Health

Old age is frequently accompanied by a decline in sensory acuity, strength, and agility leading to impaired perception, slower reactions, and difficulty in getting around (Carp, 1976). With the increasing average age of elderly people these difficulties are likely to become more widespread and severe (Personal Social Services Council Policy Group, 1979). It has further been suggested that, age for age, incapacity is becoming more prevalent (Bebbington, 1978). Appreciable numbers of the younger elderly suffer the illnesses usually associated with greater age (Hunt, 1977). Planners can thus expect there to be more people who cannot carry out personal or household tasks and who are unable to walk easily or carry heavy loads. The facilities they use will have to be carefully designed and located. This is especially important for the medical facilities most used by the elderly, the more so as they get older (Central Policy Review Staff, 1977; Hunt, 1977; Wroe, 1973).

## Income

Notwithstanding the wide variation of wealth to be found amongst the elderly as a whole, most retired people have about 20 per cent less disposable income than those who are still working. Income tends to diminish with age and that of the over-85s is markedly lower than those who have recently retired (Age Concern, 1977; Central Statistical Office, 1977; Hunt, 1977; Department of Employment, 1978). This significantly affects spending patterns for elderly people spend up to two-thirds of their income on basics, compared to 40 per cent for other households whose total outgoings are on average two or three times higher (Central Statistical Office, 1977; Department of Employment, 1978). Those with the lowest incomes have less choice of housing and little to spend on leisure pursuits and fares. They may find themselves unable to move from no-longer-suitable dwellings in neighbourhoods where they are forced to travel at high cost to shops, chemists, and hospitals. The spread and increasing real value of pension schemes could alleviate the financial problems of age, but it is unlikely that their relative standard of living will rise sufficiently to match that of the working population.

The elderly also find it difficult to adapt to external and involuntary change. Age is generally accompanied by an increasing reliance on the people, places and routines which are most familiar. Eighty per cent of the elderly have lived in the same district for at least 10 years (Hunt, 1977), giving them a local knowledge which reduces uncertainty and helps them to cope despite failing abilities. Change, on the other hand, engenders unfamiliarity, heightens uncertainty, and lessens confidence in the capacity to manage, and often leads to increased dependence. For instance, a blind person may be quite mobile and independent in accustomed surroundings but totally lost in a new setting. The relocation of older people without their express wish, as can happen during housing rehabilitation or urban redevelopment, breaks long-established patterns and results directly in a heightened demand for domiciliary and residential services (Personal Social Services Council Policy Group, 1979).

It is more difficult for the very old to remain in familiar surroundings because they are the most dependent on help and support from others. Age does not lessen the will to remain in the community (Bennett, 1974): of the over-85s in London in 1971, 80 per cent lived in private households (Permanand, 1977). They rely on their social network—which is strongly related to neighbourhood—for help, companionship, and support as they are often lonely and in poor health (Abrams, 1978; Age Concern, 1977; Hunt, 1977). Amongst the most important factors determining social contact and friendship for older people—and thus the degree of help—are proximity, length of residence, and the number of other elderly people in the same area (Newcomer and Bexton, 1978). Environmental change and particularly redevelopment may often act to alter these factors to the detriment of the very old. Even if they do not move, they may lose familiar shops and faces and the support and security they provide.

The elderly tend to be satisfied with their present circumstances. They are more content than younger people with their standard of living, despite having relatively lower incomes. They tend to express greater satisfaction with their homes and do not miss or require features which others may regard as essential (Abrams, 1978; Age Concern, 1974). Change may not appear to them to bring any advantages. The kind of change sought by other sections of the community in pursuit of a better quality of life, such as the greater usage of private transport or the wider availability of low-priced goods in large self-service stores, are of little value to those prevented by declining mobility or income from sharing the benefits. Indeed, the elderly often see change as positively harmful; the loss of a corner shop or of a local bus service may be more damaging than to more active and better-off people who are more able to change their behaviour. But change is not always harmful for the elderly. Moving house can bring considerable benefits, for instance where an older person makes a deliberate choice to move to a new dwelling to be closer to friends or relatives (Carp, 1976). Those who migrate on retirement usually do so in a positive search for a different and more suitable environment and these moves are normally successful. It is where change is involuntary or beyond their control that it tends to be damaging.

The difficulties of older people are often compounded, with the key factors being income, health, and mobility. Needs are greatest when the ability to satisfy them is least, and the effect may be a downward spiral to isolation, incapacity, and dependence. For instance those who are poor and ill tend to be the least able to look after themselves without help (Hunt, 1977). The least mobile frequently need regular medical attention but find it most difficult to reach hospitals and general practitioners (Skelton, 1978). The increasing separation of the elderly from the rest of the community faces them with the need to find a new way of life at a time when resilience and health are weakening—many find themselves living alone for the first time in their lives. The compounding of difficulties is most acute for the very old who are more likely to be living alone, in relatively poor conditions. They are the least able to get out of the house but tend to receive fewer visits from their friends or relatives (Department of the Environment, 1980).

The elderly are not only more vulnerable to the effects of major changes than other people, but are also worse affected by small ones. Declining health, fading energy, decreasing income, and diminishing time tend to constrain their opportunities and abilities. The world shrinks, giving a greater weight to the details that others take in their stride: the precise siting of a bus stop, the provision of shelters or benches, the loss of a zebra crossing, the time taken to alleviate damp. Greater awareness of the importance of details in the design and location of facilities for the elderly could bring about significant improvements in the their environment and their ability to manage for themselves.

It would be wrong to apply these generalizations to all elderly people. Owner-occupiers, whose income is generally higher than people in other forms of tenure (Office of Population Censuses and Surveys, 1979), usually enjoy better health and mobility and more informal social contact (Department of the Environment, 1980). Those who are physically and financially able to run a car can easily exploit the advantages of one-stop shopping.

There are many difficulties which are shared by old people and other groups.

The young disabled must face the consequences of immobility; children have no option but to use public transport; the unemployed have much spare time and little money to make use of it. Any success in alleviating the environmental disadvantages associated with age would be of widespread benefit.

There are two main conclusions for planners to draw from this brief discussion of the relationship between the environment and the elderly:

(1) The elderly are essentially the same as the rest of us but have difficulty in remaining part of the community. Planning decisions and policies should not act to reinforce existing barriers but attempt to dismantle them.
(2) Besides the overall similarities there are important differences between older and younger people to which planners should be sensitive if they are not to disadvantage the elderly further. Old people would not be the only beneficiaries of such an approach.

## FACILITIES FOR THE ELDERLY

Age does not obviate the desire or necessity to go shopping, see the doctor, visit friends, and undertake other everyday activities—but it may alter the method and frequency with which they are done. It is important to appreciate how far the elderly are distinctive and to reflect their special needs in planning the location of housing and services for them, if the elderly are to be helped to live independently for as long as possible.

### Housing

'The most widespread features of elderly residential behaviour are inertia and under-occupation' (Barnard, 1979). Most people stay on in the family house after retirement even though it may no longer fully meet their needs: two-thirds of elderly people have lived in the same house for 20 years or more (Central Statistical Office, 1977). Elderly households are rarely overcrowded. The average number of persons per room is about 30 per cent lower than for the population as a whole (Office of Population Censuses and Surveys, 1974). The housing conditions of elderly people tend to be poorer than for most other groups. Relatively few live in sub-standard housing, but a considerable number live in houses that lack some basic amenities. The worst-off tend to be those who are over 85, private tenants, and the more infirm (Hunt, 1977; Wroe, 1973). It is expected that the number of elderly people's houses lacking basic amenities will decline, partly as a result of housing improvements and partly through the higher expectations of subsequent generations of the retired.

For planners these general circumstances raise the issue of the distribution of the housing stock. The extent of under-occupation means that the system has to work harder to produce family dwellings. Clearly it would be easier if people could be encouraged to move from larger dwellings to smaller ones as their family circumstances change, particularly at a time when in terms of people and dwellings there is a crude balance between supply and demand. Local authorities are rightly opposed to enforced transfers, and the private sector has yet to provide, on a large scale, small dwellings of a kind and in a location that would tempt elderly people to dispose of their family homes.

Policies of rehabilitation and improvement also raise difficulties. Elderly people often become used to living without some amenities or in houses in poor repair and may not see any advantage in improvement schemes, however much their particular needs may be accommodated. They find it difficult to deal with the upheaval of building works and to pay the cost. Relocation may exacerbate the upheaval and injure their health (Howell, 1976). However, if the property is not maintained it may deteriorate to the point where it damages the physical well-being of its occupants, giving rise to greater demands for medical and social service attention (Personal Social Services Council Policy Group, 1979). Thus there is a dilemma, for both action and inaction to maintain or improve the dwellings of older people can be damaging.

Not all elderly people want to continue living in an unmodified family house, particularly if they cannot cope with its upkeep. Some wish to remain in familiar surroundings by converting their property into flats or maisonettes, keeping one for themselves and selling or renting the rest. Others move into a smaller dwelling altogether, and people seek different types of property to meet their own needs. The problem for planners is to keep abreast of changing preferences and to persuade both public and private builders to satisfy them. Whether elderly people are able to move depends variously on age, income, and current tenure. Those who own their own homes and are moving into cheaper property face few financial problems, but retired tenants often find it difficult to become first-time owner-occupiers because they tend to be low-income households with a short life-expectancy and are thus regarded as a high financial risk (Barnard, 1979). Many elderly people live in privately rented accommodation because it was widely available when they set up home, but their numbers can be expected to decline as a greater proportion of subsequent generations will be owner-occupiers. Planners would be well advised to anticipate a bigger role for the private sector in providing housing for the elderly.

At the moment most housing specifically for old people is provided by the public sector (Housing Corporation, 1976). Local authorities and housing associations build many small units which can be used by the elderly and have the power to re-allocate vacancies for re-letting to older people. An imbalance between the average size of households and the average size of dwellings remains despite the considerable efforts made to redress it by local authorities and housing associations with government encouragement. It is unfortunately exacerbated by the fact that even when small homes become available they are frequently not where the elderly want or need them. The importance of an appropriate location in fostering independence when health and mobility decrease cannot be over-emphasized.

## Travel and transport

The ability of the elderly to live a full life is circumscribed by restrictions on their travel. Walking is the most common means of covering short distances but one-fifth of the non-housebound reported difficulty in walking fast or far and the incidence increases with age (Hunt, 1977). Hardship increases where the journey entails climbing hills, crossing busy roads, using ramps, or coping with narrow or uneven pavements. Difficulties in walking may inhibit use of public transport either because it is beyond walking range, although the majority live within 10 minutes' walk of a bus or train, because it requires waiting for lengthy periods without shelter or seats, or because the vehicles are too difficult to mount (Hopkin, Robson and Town, 1978; Norman, 1977). The cost and frequency of the service may further constrain usage. The problems may be particularly acute in rural areas where services have been curtailed in recent years (Clark and Smith, 1978; Moseley *et al.*, 1976). One-third of elderly households own or can use a car, but this usage decreases with age as many owners find themselves forced to give up their vehicle due to cost or illness (Norman, 1977). The change is important because households with a car-driver make 25 per cent more journeys than those without a car or those relying on someone outside the household for a lift (Hopkin, Robson and Town, 1978).

The ascendancy of the private car over public transport results mainly from factors beyond the control of planners. The forces involved are in the realms of a lifestyle that sees no reason to forego private transport. However, it is the planners' responsibility to consider alternatives to the car, particularly in view of the uncertain cost and availability of petrol in the future. A return to a more compact urban form in which houses, shops, and places of employment are grouped more closely together would not only aid the conservation of energy but would also be to the advantage of the less mobile members of the community.

## Shopping

The elderly are less likely to buy consumer durables and luxury items, but otherwise want access to the same choice of goods and retailers as the rest of the population (Bruce, 1974). Older people tend to make greater use of small, local outlets—particularly for regular purchases such as food, medicines, and newspapers. These shops are conveniently situated for the elderly who generally shop more often, prefer to buy in small amounts, and are inclined to seek help from the neighbourhood shopkeeper on a wide variety of non-retail matters (Housing Corporation, 1976; Roberts, 1974; Sherman and Britten, 1973).

The number of local shops is declining due to changes in the economics of retailing and the habits of the shopping public. This is likely to produce more disadvantages for the elderly than for younger adults, as the elderly frequently have the most severe constraints on their mobility and are thus unable to choose shopping centres on the basis of price advantage (Hopkin, Robson and Town, 1978). Older people are less able to make the longer and costlier journeys to distant supermarkets and are often frightened and confused by the bustle in larger shops (Roberts, 1974; Sherman and Britten, 1973). The demise of local shops may be even more damaging to the elderly in rural areas where distance or the lack of public transport limits access to other retailers (Clark and Smith, 1978; Harman, 1977). Planning powers in respect of shopping are limited. While local planning authorities can control the siting of new shops they cannot prevent closures. Their role is mainly restricted to trying to influence and respond to private-sector initiatives which are themselves largely conditioned by economic considerations in which the needs of the elderly will only play a small part.

## Medical facilities

Elderly people are the heaviest users of medical facilities but it is often harder for them to get to doctors and clinics. With the trend for general practitioners to associate in group practices, surgeries are fewer and farther between and require longer journeys to reach. Old people who have difficulty in walking are more likely both to require medical attention and to visit doctors' surgeries more often. It has been observed that the most frequent visitors also take the longest time to reach the surgery (Hopkin, Robson and Town 1978). In rural areas few villages have sufficient population to support a pharmacy, and about half the general practitioners practising in rural areas also dispense medicines to patients.

Journeys to hospitals can also pose problems. In Guildford, the old people who travelled to hospital most frequently were those who had most difficulty in walking, and over two-thirds of the journeys were made on foot, by bus, or by ambulance (Hopkin, Robson and Town, 1978). A patient may have no choice of destination for a particular specialist. As hospitals are increasing in size but declining in number, they are tending to serve an ever-wider catchment area. Regular out-patients may thus have a long and difficult journey every week. Large hospitals can also be redoubtable and forbidding, deterring elderly out-patients and visitors by their complex layout and the distances that have to be covered to reach wards and clinics.

The growth of community care is based partly on the recognition that hardship can be caused to elderly people by institutional treatment. Day centres provide medical care and also act as a social focus for the more active elderly, helping them to make and retain the personal contacts so important for continued independence. In some areas there are plans to offer similar facilities to the more frail (London Borough of Wandsworth, 1977). The increase of community care does not obviate, however, the need for more residential establishments since the need to replace obsolete institutions and the pressures created by the increasing numbers of the very old continue to generate demands for greater provision (Personal Social Services Council Policy Group, 1979).

### Leisure

Retirement does not normally mean that people lose their previous interests but the extent to which they can continue actively to pursue them depends, once again, on health and income. Education is also an important factor in determining the range of interests (Rapoport and Rapoport, 1975). Involvement in physically active or costly pursuits tends to decrease with age and to be replaced by the more passive pleasures of reading and watching television (Age Concern, 1977; Greater London Council, 1975; Haynes and Raven, 1961; Hunt, 1977). Recent surveys have established that the only common active outside leisure pursuit is trips to urban parks and into the countryside, while 'idleness and contemplation are common ways of passing the time for the very old' (Hendricks and Hendricks, 1977). Few elderly people belong to social or special-interest clubs, and most only leave their homes regularly to go shopping, to attend to personal business, or to visit friends and relatives (Abrams, 1978; Age Concern, 1974; Hearnden and Fujishin, 1974; Hunt, 1977).

Little attempt has been made to explore or to promote the recreational abilities and potential of older people, despite the fact that they have more leisure time than most others. The private sector has only just begun to appreciate the possibilities—through SAGA holidays for retired people, for instance—and concentrates primarily on facilities for younger, more able car-users (Hillman and Whalley, 1977). Local authority centres tend to provide for active sports and are of limited use to older people. Where leisure provision is specifically made for the elderly it is generally based on a very narrow view of their potential and often assumes that they are all needy and have undifferentiated tastes. Future generations will be better-educated, with higher expectations, and are unlikely to be satisfied with current standards of provision. This is another area in which the private sector could have a large and profitable role to play.

### Employment

About 30 per cent of those reaching retirement age each year continue to work part-time, commonly in semi- or unskilled jobs for about 5 years after retirement

(Age Concern, 1977; Wroe, 1973). A substantial proportion of the retired would have wanted to carry on in employment for as long as possible (Central Statistical Office, 1978) but firm estimates of this latent demand for work do not exist. Those who continue tend to be better off than those who do not (Hunt, 1977). The ability to go on working varies with the availability of acceptable full- or part-time jobs, individual education and experience, the value of other sources of income, and the relative flexibility of attitudes towards retirement. Those whose skills are in short supply have a greater likelihood of being kept on, possibly in the sheltered workshops that some employers have provided. The role of planning in generating employment prospects for the elderly is limited to general support for industrial development.

### Relative accessibility to facilities

The provision of facilities used by the elderly is frequently to their disadvantage. Houses of suitable size are rarely available in the right place in sufficient numbers; transport arrangements favour the better-off and more able-bodied; changes in shopping patterns most benefit those who can buy and carry in bulk; the siting of medical facilities is often inconvenient for the chronically sick; leisure possibilities are rarely practical or attractive; and pensioners seem only to be able to carry on working if they are indispensable. In many ways the current level and standards of provision would appear to accentuate differences between the elderly and the rest of the population by ignoring their special requirements and failing to support those who attempt to retain their independence. Clearly this is not just a planning matter, nevertheless the planning system can ameliorate or accentuate the difficulties caused, and that in itself might make an impact on the independence of old people.

## WHERE THE ELDERLY LIVE

Knowledge of where the elderly live now, and how this is likely to change, is a prerequisite for the provision of appropriate facilities at the right time. 'It is a poor assumption, explicit or implicit, to think that the elderly of the future will locate where the elderly of the past did' (Sclar and Lind, 1976). Over most of England and Wales the elderly approached one-fifth of the population but the distribution is far from even and there are distinctive levels of representation and environmental conditions in different types of area.

### Inner cities

The elderly constitute both a higher and a faster-growing proportion of the population in metropolitan areas as a whole than in most other parts of the country (Association of Metropolitan Authorities, 1978). The declining population of the inner cities results primarily from young families moving out to the suburbs and low rates of in-migration. Older people are generally more reluctant to move and thus form a larger element of the remaining population. Their inertia also means that they tend to be found in old dwellings; often in fact the houses into which they moved on marriage and which may now need improvements or repairs they cannot afford or are unwilling to contemplate. The elderly are not always concentrated in the poorer parts of the inner city, and there is no positive ecological correlation between deprivation and the elderly among metropolitan districts. Affluence characterizes numerous central London locations that house large numbers of the elderly. This is not to contradict studies showing that many inner city elderly people live in poor conditions, but to illustrate that in high-density, high-population urban areas the living conditions of elderly people can vary considerably. Nevertheless, given the size of modern cities there can be no doubt that large numbers of elderly inner area residents are deprived and in need of support. The deterioration of urban areas has brought to light serious deficiencies in some aspects of life for older people. These include 'social isolation, increased vulnerability to traffic hazards, loss of security against personal assault and robbery, and difficulties in alerting and communicating with others in time of need' (Bromley, 1977). One advantage of their location is that public transport tends to be more widely available in inner cities than elsewhere.

## Outer suburbs and urban hinterlands

The rate of absolute growth in the elderly population was relatively high on the edge of the conurbations over the period 1951–71. It was particularly noticeable in some rural communities and market towns within easy reach of Manchester, Merseyside, Bristol, Birmingham, Leeds, Newcastle and Middlesbrough; in the Home Counties; and in some outer suburbs of London such as Barking, Havering and Hillingdon. It was not as prominent in other outer metropolitan areas. This growth arises partly from the decentralization of families to burgeoning suburbs before the Second World War, and the ageing of this population *in situ*. Those who could afford it sought to buy their own houses; others went to live on large local authority estates such as Wythenshawe (Manchester) and Hainault (London) (Department of the Environment, 1978). Another reason for this growth may be short-distance moves made on or before retirement. Small towns and rural communities are attractive to elderly people and a growing focus of retirement migration, and those close to conurbations and large towns offer the opportunity to retain links with family and friends relatively easily (Law and Warnes, 1980). This may not wholly be the case in the market towns which have traditionally been comparatively self-contained. Elderly people and commuters have only recently begun moving to them in any strength. The greater population of the elderly in market towns might be more a result of their being left behind after the outward movement of younger people seeking jobs.

In suburban and semi-rural areas the elderly tend to be widely distributed through lower-density development and there are few concentrations. Given the present distribution of the middle-aged the numbers of elderly people in these areas will grow. Concentrations may be found on those estates occupied on their completion by couples in a single age group but by and large the elderly will continue to be dispersed. This spread of elderly people over a wide area makes questionable the viable provision of specialist facilities. The small centres typical of these areas are unlikely to have all the services required and access to larger centres may be difficult. Changes in shopping patterns may result in the decline of smaller centres with resulting problems for those dependent on shops within walking distance. In the more recent suburbs and estates designed for heavy car usage and lacking alternative transport services, the elderly may become nearly as isolated as those living in purely rural areas once they have given up their cars.

### Small industrial towns

Many small towns with declining industries, such as the Lancashire cotton towns, display similar characteristics to the inner cities. Younger people have tended to move away and the elderly represent a rising proportion of a falling population. Again, they tend to live in the older neighbourhoods. These towns generally display common features of decline: high unemployment, poor housing amenities, lower income. The lack of younger people means an absence of formal and informal support which cannot easily be rectified. There is little point in providing services if there is no-one willing to staff them. Not all industrial settlements present this gloomy picture and some, for instance Skipton and Yeovil, show greater prosperity. Their socio-economic status is higher and the availability of cheap modern housing has ensured a greater degree of owner-occupation. The population as a whole may be more stable and this will be of benefit to its older members (Department of the Environment, 1979).

### Areas of post-war development

In the new towns such as Harlow, Crawley and Peterlee, and in other areas where development has been predominantly post-war, the percentage of older people is below the national average. Most of the early residents were young skilled workers and have yet to reach retirement. They will do so increasingly over the next decades and the proportion of elderly people in these areas will consequently rise sharply (Department of the Environment, 1978). The second generation often finds it difficult to acquire housing within the new towns and have moved away. The new towns are thus likely to be faced with concentrations of largely unsupported elderly people. However, these areas may be better able than older urban centres to accommodate the needs of their ageing population due to the flexibility inherent in their development.

## Rural areas

Scenically attractive rural hinterlands of the popular resorts have drawn retirement migrants, as in the New Forest and the Sussex Downs. They also attract people in late middle age, some of whom may be preparing for retirement or retiring early. Some small towns and villages close to pleasant countryside are also popular, although to a lesser extent, as evidenced by the increase in the numbers of elderly people in Richmond and Northallerton (North Yorkshire), Shropshire, and Bedfordshire (Department of the Environment, 1978). It is the existence of a small, sheltered and integrated community that has a particular appeal for some older people (Lemon, 1973).

Many rural areas, as in Wales and parts of the South-West, have a growing percentage of older people in a shrinking population. More active people have been attracted to larger centres which offer better-paid, non-agricultural employment, so leaving low numbers of the elderly scattered through the smaller towns and villages. Where a few elderly people are dispersed over large rural areas, they face similar problems to those of their contemporaries in the cities. But their difficulties are often exacerbated by the lesser availability of many services and facilities and by the transport problems which have been described above.

It has been argued that the elderly in particular need ready access to shops, post offices, and doctors but that these services are disappearing from many villages (Clark and Smith, 1978). The elderly are even affected by the closure of village schools, partly because they make greater uses of the hall than other groups and partly because of the psychological loss of a symbol and focus of the village community. Facilities may even decline in those villages gaining population through an influx of commuters or retired people, for the newcomers are often car-owners who have no need to make regular use of them. The withdrawal of essential services does prompt some younger families to move away, particularly from the more remote areas, reducing further the support from more active people necessary to counteract the loss of facilities.

It is expected that the number of elderly people in rural areas will increase. Not only is retirement migration to the countryside gaining in popularity, but also commuters in late middle age are finding it an attractive location. Many second homes and weekend cottages have been bought with a view to retirement in a rural retreat. However, this trend may be stemmed in some parts of the country, e.g. Gwynedd or the Lake District, by local antagonism resulting in the adoption of restrictive policies on second home development (White, 1978). The likely extra number of elderly people will not necessarily be a burden upon local authorities and may be a positive asset. In-migration can help to stabilize the population and to ensure a steady demand for declining services such as public transport and village shops. While the authorities will be faced with a need to ensure the provision of specialized facilities, this could generate new sources of local employment which will give young people an incentive to stay.

## Resorts

The growing phenomenon of retirement migration to seaside resorts is as yet confined to a relatively small proportion of the elderly population who have the means and the will to undertake it. It is generally founded on affluence: most migrants are from the professional, managerial, and other white-collar occupations and own their own homes. They also tend to take a positive view of retirement and like the idea of spending it in healthier and warmer surroundings among people with a similar lifestyle. They are generally younger than the indigenous elderly (Gordon, 1975; Karn, 1977). It seems likely that in the future more people will be in a position to move on retirement to both the coast and the countryside. A minority of retirement migrants are less well off and in most resorts there is an area around the town centre of rooming houses and shared dwellings occupied by people on small, fixed pensions. Many hotels are virtually old people's homes. It is frequently the oldest, sickest, and poorest who live in the least suitable conditions (Karn, 1977).

The effects of retirement migration on resorts have generally been regarded as being undesirable, particularly by the local authorities concerned (Blagden, 1976; West Sussex County Council, 1978). It is argued that the ability of older people to out-bid young local residents for the purchase of small dwellings forces the latter to leave, and that new employment opportunities are restricted by the migrants' unwillingness to contemplate new industrial or even holiday development. Recreation and shopping facilities are also believed to be constrained by the limited interests and spending power of the elderly, and migrants are said to make high demands on local health and social services to the detriment of other ratepayers. In most cases this is far from a complete or fair analysis. The competition for small dwellings is not only between the oldest and the youngest but involves all age groups: 50 per cent of the population are in one- and two-person households (Central Statistical Office, 1977). House prices are inflated more often by the presence of commuters than by the elderly; the employment problems of resorts are related to their specialized nature and are similar to those of all towns dominated by specific or seasonal employments; there is no evidence to suggest that retirement areas are deficient in leisure and retailing facilities; and welfare provision in retirement areas has been traditionally low with the cost of services for the elderly only partly met by local funds. It is also the case that retirement migration offers positive advantages to a district, most generally by bolstering local demand and employment. There is no reason why the adoption of a retirement function should not provide a viable economic basis for resorts, as it offers a year-round demand for leisure, shopping, and other facilities. It is pertinent to contrast the argument that elderly in-migrants are low spenders and a drain on local rates with the view that their affluence allows them to out-bid local people in the purchase of housing. The 'problem' may arise less from the migrants themselves than local perceptions.

## Concentrations of elderly people

A common reaction to a concentration of elderly people is disfavour, pointedly so in areas popular with retirement migrants. From the planner's point of view it is worth inquiring why there should be such general animosity, and whether this is a factor in considering the provision of facilities. Also important is whether there are 'agglomeration' advantages for the elderly themselves. Sometimes younger people tend to the extreme view of elderly communities as geriatric ghettoes displaying passivity, dependence, and decay (Ross, 1977). Strong negative reactions to concentrations of the elderly may be because they are a forceful reminder of our own ageing and mortality (West Sussex County Council, 1978). If old people do present such a potent image of decline, one must ask how far our attitude towards them has magnified that situation, as for instance in increasing the elderly's difficulties with housing and shopping. If a concentration has been produced by migration, a more objective assessment would contradict many stereotypes of old age and would recognize the positive attitudes of the enterprising movers. The decision to move reflects a willingness to take risks and an ability to cope with changed circumstances, and therefore demonstrates psychological and often physical health (Grant, 1971). In practice negative attitudes may reflect elements of resentment; not only are the elderly unproductive and hence in aggregate a burden, but when they migrate they take and enjoy opportunities for leisure not open to the rest of us (Karn, 1977; West Sussex County Council, 1978). Migrants create a lifestyle appropriate to their new status, and often of course are those that have above-average achievements in material and perhaps even personal terms. In an elderly community no-one has to justify being retired and living out their days in a leisurely fashion. Being amongst others in the same situation enhances mutual respect, aid and support and hence security and independence. Greater morale, friendships and help, and a corresponding reduction in the usage of welfare services, have been consistently observed in settings where the elderly are available to each other as neighbours and potential friends. 'Any recipe that the elderly discover for continuing life satisfaction in societies that surround them with extraordinary obstacles should be taken seriously, even if it contradicts assumptions and values that are difficult to let go' (Ross, 1977).

While local authorities may feel that the presence of large groups of elderly people 'unbalances' the population, to the planner their needs may be most efficiently met when they are concentrated in particular places. The opportunity to provide facilities specially for the elderly, or to ensure that detailed design of the environment meets their needs, is easier where substantial numbers of old people live in the same area. Conversely, when they are dispersed they may experience greater difficulties in gaining access to centres with the services they need and, most important in a period of exceptionally scarce resources, it is more difficult to help them.

## THE PLANNING SYSTEM: ENGLAND AND WALES

Having considered some of the specific problems and issues in contrasting areas, the more general role of physical planning in responding of the elderly can be considered. It might be a helpful preface to give a brief, and necessarily generalized, sketch of the planning system in Great Britain. While it was established formally and comprehensively by the 1947 Town and Country Planning Act, the control of building had been evolving for almost a century since the Victorian Public Health Acts. The system was modified in 1968 to give it greater flexibility and to encourage wider public participation. The cornerstone is the control of development. Before there can be any new building or major modification to the structure or use of an existing building, formal permission must be granted by a local authority. Its purpose is to ensure that development is carried out in an orderly way and in the public interest. Development control operates with a framework provided by development plans. These consist, for each area, of a Structure Plan prepared by the county authority and a Local Plan usually prepared by the district. The Structure Plan is primarily a written statement of policies and proposals for major change, while Local Plans are concerned with the more detailed implementation and will also reflect the particular concerns of the area. Both will be augmented by a number of *ad hoc* policies dealing with specific or urgent matters.

## PLANNING POLICIES, POWERS AND ACTION

The planning-related problems of older people can be tackled in a variety of ways and the methods used will be influenced by the far-reaching changes in the nature and discharge of public services now under consideration. Not all the problems of the elderly require or would be amenable to planning action: equally, the environmental difficulties faced by the elderly may be open to a variety of solutions, including measures outside planning control, such as providing home-help services or mobile libraries. Frequently the action will be more effectively taken by the private sector or voluntary bodies, subject to planning permission where appropriate. Effective measures to assist the elderly require co-operation and consultation over and within a wide range of authorities and institutions. The suggestions made in this section concern what can be done within the purview of the planning system in England and Wales, but will be relevant in those countries with comparable systems of planning.

## Central government

At central government level policies are general, and mainly aim to help the bodies most closely involved with the elderly's problems. For instance, old people (and others) living in inner city areas should benefit from the government's inner cities policies both within main programmes of expenditure and through the Urban Programme. These policies will bring improvements to the environmental, social and economic conditions in inner urban areas. Some measures in the Inner Area Programmes are being drawn up for areas of the worst urban deprivation and will be specifically directed towards the needs of the elderly.

In the areas of depopulation, where characteristically the relative presence of the elderly is growing, the government's policy has been to try to stem decline by creating more jobs through the advance factory programme of the Development Commission, and supporting the services of the Council for Small Industries in Rural Areas, and their Welsh equivalents. The benefits that this can bring to these areas will help to ease the position of all who live in them, including the elderly. The future of these communities, and hence the elderly people within them, will depend on the availability of rural services. To a large extent this will be determined by demand and the ability of people to pay for such services; the influence of the planning system is limited to helping meet—rather than creating—the necessary demand.

## Local government and development plans

Local authorities have a considerable responsibility for establishing and meeting the needs of the elderly in which the planning process can play a useful role. The preparation of development plans requires the collection and analysis of a wide array of data. This is updated and the plans reviewed periodically. Local authorities can thus monitor changes in the numbers, location and condition of their elderly residents and make provision accordingly. Planners have helped to develop appropriate techniques. For instance, recent research has shown that it is possible to identify different groups of the elderly sharing common characteristics. These groups can be associated with different packages of needs. Thus where local authorities know the extent to which each group is represented in the population in their area they will have a clearer idea of the type and degree of provision necessary in the light of their own policies and resources (Department of the Environment, 1980).

Structure and local plans deal with the development and use of land in the interests of the public as a whole and they seldom contain policies or proposals especially intended to benefit a particular group. However, local authorities are aware that their policies will have a differential impact and it is open to them to take this into account in the planning process. For instance, in the interests of the whole community rural settlement policies may be adopted which encourage the concentration of facilities at 'key villages'. Elderly residents in other villages might be deprived as a result. This could be taken into account by modifying the balance between public and private sector transport to increase bus services; adopting a policy of encouraging the construction of small dwellings in the key villages; or referring to non-planning powers and policies such as the provision of mobile facilities. If the consequent deprivation seemed sufficiently serious the local authority could reconsider the original policy.

Local authorities are increasingly aware of the impact upon them of the elderly. A growing number of plans consider the effects of the changing size, structure, and location of the elderly population and take account of the problems that arise, e.g. the lack of facilities for the many elderly people with high social need in inner city areas. Local plans can be used to allocate sites for particular uses benefiting the elderly, such as day centres and sheltered housing schemes. Structure and local plans could help to channel retirement migration in the long term by encouraging suitable development in currently underdeveloped resorts and rural areas. They are also amongst the mechanisms local authorities can use to promote the positive side of retirement migration, e.g. by extending the local economic base. The preparation of structure and local plans must include opportunities for public participation. This is particularly valuable to the elderly for not only can the process bring out their views on matters of importance to them, but it also enhances their self-esteem, morale and hence independence (Carp, 1976). Many methods of participation require the public to take the initiative, e.g. by attending public meetings and exhibitions. Elderly people are frequently unable to do this and special exercises need to be mounted so that their needs and aspirations can be registered.

### Local government and development control

When making a decision on a planning application the local authority exercises its powers on behalf of the whole community. It would be wrong to seek the promotion or protection of the interests of only one section of the population. All the interests involved must be carefully balanced and it is inevitable that some decisions will not benefit the elderly. The situation is somewhat different when the proposed development is specifically for elderly people. Their interests must be given particular weight if the proposal is to achieve its desired effects. Before reaching a decision local authorities will need to consult the public and private agencies that provide individual services to ensure that location, design, and service delivery are closely co-ordinated to ensure maximum access by those elderly people for whom the facility is intended.

The private sector provides a number of facilities and services used by the elderly, and local planning authorities have only limited power to control or encourage them. For the most part the authority can only respond to initiatives and decisions of the private sector which will normally be determined by economic considerations related to the whole population rather than just the elderly. Local authorities have restricted influence over the type of housing built by the private sector. They have been asked by the government to do what they can to stimulate the development of smaller, lower-priced housing through land-use policies amongst other mechanisms. For instance, they can influence the number and size of private dwellings through the terms of disposal when making land in their ownership available for private development. Where small dwellings are in short supply planning authorities should continue to give sympathetic consideration to applications for conversion of larger houses to smaller units, especially in areas where there is a continuing demand. Local authorities of course have no control over occupancy in the private market in which the elderly compete with single people, young and childless couples to purchase or rent small homes. Even in areas of restraint on development, planning authorities cannot restrict the occupancy of private housing through planning conditions on the development: in these areas the difficulties of the elderly may be exacerbated.

**Implementation in detail**

It is at the level of detail prompted by the implementation of plans and policies that local planning authorities may find that they have the greatest impact on the lives of older people. Greater sensitivity to the fine grain of location and design can significantly improve the ability of the elderly to manage on their own. Design is an important factor in encouraging health and activity. Older people are better able to look after themselves in warm and well-designed dwellings and will make fewer demands on welfare services. Movement, interest, and outside activity can be promoted by an environment designed to provide variety in what its elderly users see and do. If the concept is introduced at an early stage in the design process its beneficial effects can be gained at no extra cost. This should be borne in mind for the very old. The growth in their numbers will require an increase in developments catering for the more passive elderly. 'Care should be taken to introduce activity for them to observe; for example, even in a very cramped inner city street scheme, [the London Borough of]

Hammersmith has been able to provide a miniature fish pool, an aviary and raised flower beds' (Fox, 1979).

The importance of variety does not only apply to design. The elderly are not all the same and therefore they do not all want the same kind of shopping, housing, or leisure opportunities. This diversity of interests should be reflected in a concomitant variety of services and facilities—policies and plans do not have to be implemented in the same way throughout. More positively, detailed action could be a vehicle for helping and encouraging elderly people to develop a lifestyle appropriate to their circumstances, rather than one deemed suitable by younger people.

The tendency for the elderly to continue living in houses that are too big or difficult to manage is reinforced by the problems they face in moving. A greater variety of suitable housing in a greater variety of places might be an incentive to move, particularly if they could be helped by specially tailored arrangements for financing. Bearing in mind the fact that people become less well, and worse off, as they get older, these dwellings must be cheap and easy to run if individual independence is to be maintained for as long as possible. Housing likely to be occupied by the elderly should have good access to centres containing the facilities they visit frequently. In urban areas these should be within short walking distance as far as possible; elsewhere they should be linked by convenient public transport. If health, social, or recreational facilities are located in or near these centres, this may reduce the number of journeys the elderly have to make and possibly help them to join in social and leisure activities from which, through relative immobility, they might otherwise be excluded. Wherever possible, new small homes and grouped or sheltered housing should be sited where the journey between the home and the centre does not involve the need to walk uphill or cross very busy roads. If this is not possible appropriate measures should be taken to ameliorate the locational disadvantages—e.g. provision of pedestrian-controlled traffic lights, speed restrictions and amended bus services. Where a major loss of shops occurs the local authority may need to consider a re-alignment of public transport routes to improve access to the nearby shopping centres that remain.

In certain circumstances services for the general public could be incorporated in a facility specially designed for the elderly—such as a bank in a sheltered housing scheme or a creche next to a day centre—to help reduce the tendency for older people to be segregated from the rest of the community. Some housing developments for the elderly in other countries offer a wide range of activities: supermarkets, bars, restaurants, cinemas, laundrettes and libraries (Hazel, 1974). Similar advantages can be gained by locating old people's dwellings in a town centre.

It is in such ways that the details of design and location help the elderly to remain part of the community without their being too exposed. Housing for the elderly should not be inward-looking and screened from view, as this prevents the residents from indulging in the enjoyable pastime of watching the hustle and bustle of everyday life and reinforces a sence of separation (Lawton, 1976). 'The isolation of the elderly from visual or physical interaction with other generations may mean loss of meaningful contact with the real world as it changes about them' (Howell, 1976). Nevertheless, their housing should not be too exposed to activities that may distress them, such as children's noisy play or the insecurity engendered by unknown callers. Small improvements to the external environment can help to keep the elderly active and independent, including:

(1) detailed attention to the layout of footpath and open areas in new housing schemes and improvement areas, to offer easy access to nearby facilities;
(2) the increased provision of benches and shelters along footpaths, at bus stops and in local centres so they can rest when they wish;
(3) the provision of ramps as well as steps and angled kerbs, to lessen the effects of physical obstacles;
(4) greater consideration of the precise location of bus stops to assist use of public transport;
(5) the provision of public conveniences close to shops and small open spaces utilized by the elderly, to provide reassurance if lengthy absences from home are planned;
(6) the provision of clearly named and lettered street and building signs, and of plentiful and well-illuminated signposts to help people whose sight, memory or orientation are failing (Lawton, 1970).

The Chronically Sick and Disabled Persons' Act 1970 requires the provision of access for disabled people to new public buildings 'where reasonable and practicable'. It will be of particular benefit to the elderly who are either seriously physically handicapped or just frail if buildings which are in everyday use by the community are easily accessible and usable, e.g. phone boxes low enough for wheelchair-users, spaces for wheelchairs in auditoria, toilets for the disabled, seats in open and waiting areas, and doors that respond to a light touch. Detailed action can also be taken to ease the transport difficulties of older people. The Orange Badge Scheme exempts disabled people from certain parking restrictions and is valuable to those elderly impaired people who still drive, and public transport concessionary fares do increase use. Considerable research has been carried out recently to modify the design of buses, and particularly their entrances.

There would frequently be advantage from gathering the opinions or elderly people about environmental or building proposals. For instance local authorities should take special care to consider the views of elderly occupants in Housing Action Areas, General Improvement Areas and other area-wide programmes, and to provide them where necessary with additional professional advice and financial assistance. The additional effort involved would be worthwhile because many of the needs presented to social service departments and voluntary organizations would be avoided or ameliorated (National Corporation for the Care of Old People, 1979). Adoption of a sensitive and individual approach to older people in these areas would lessen the disruptiveness of renewal and rehabilitation programmes.

There are undoubtedly many other matters where detailed modification to planning action could increase the mobility and independence of the elderly. It is for the authorities and institutions concerned to determine their response in the light of prevailing needs and circumstances. None of these should involve any extra claim on resources—rather, an application of existing resources with a greater sensitivity to the needs to the elderly. Much can be done during the process of maintenance and improvement, and in the design of new buildings special features should be incorporated from the beginning of a project.

## THE FUTURE

The time-span of the planning process requires planners to base their policy and proposals on what seems likely to happen in the foreseeable future. It can be anticipated that demands for services by the elderly will probably increase. Although the overall numbers of people over retirement age will fall slightly over the next 20 years, the population of those aged 75 and over will continue to rise and with it the need for welfare facilities. At the other end of the elderly age range, any tendency for people to retire earlier will effectively inflate the elderly population. Increasing pressure on the facilities used by the more active elderly, in particular, can be anticipated. The scale of future demand for services will vary from area to area. The majority will probably stay where they have lived most of their lives and thus areas with high concentrations of people in middle age—such as the new towns—can expect to have concentrations of the elderly in the future. Conversely there could be a decline in the elderly population of the inner cities. The problems of elderly people isolated in the countryside or in rural communities with contracting services are unlikely to to abate. The attraction of seaside and rural locations will probably continue. It is possible that there will be a shift to some sort of regionalism or local autonomy with central government less concerned to set detailed standards. This could lead to wide geographical differences in provision for the elderly (Bromley, 1977). It also seems likely that future generations of elderly people will have higher expectations. They will have been better educated, had more possessions, and been more widely travelled. Many services now regarded as benefaction will be seen as rights by those who grew up after the establishment of the welfare state. More generally we should be prepared for a gradual shift of political strength to middle-aged and older people and possibly for more explicit intergenerational political dispute (Bromley, 1977).

## CONCLUSIONS

The elderly are fundamentally the same as the rest of us but much of the provision for them tends to put them apart from other people and to reinforce the differences and difficulties brought about by advanced age. In a limited way planning can help break down the barriers to give the elderly improved opportunities to enjoy the same quality of life as the remainder of the community. Planning cannot achieve this alone. Even to take action to improve the environment of the elderly requires a more positive attitude to old age and an acknowledgement that old age should not bar access to services and facilities which the rest of us take for granted. It will not always be possible to strike a balance between the needs of the elderly and the wider public interest—generally desirable development must go forward—but without a greater appreciation of what it is like to be old the elderly are always likely to be unnecessarily disadvantaged. The more they are disadvantaged, the less they will be able to cope and the more dependent they will become. Changes that benefit the younger and more able-bodied need not be at the expense of the elderly.

None of the suggestions made in this chapter involve bold new measures whose value and efficacy may be in doubt. They rely instead on a widespread increase in our awareness and understanding of how the elderly live and in particular the use they make of the physical environment, which could be taken into account not only in making physical planning policies and decisions but in other spheres as well. With more thought and greater sensitivity much can be achieved to enable elderly people to live independently and to the full. If society can create an environment which they can use easily, nobody else is likely to have any trouble with it.

## REFERENCES

Abrams, M. (1978). *Beyond Three Score Years and Ten.* Age Concern, Mitcham, Surrey.

Age Concern (1974). *Attitudes of the Retired and Elderly.* Age Concern, Mitcham, Surrey.

Age Concern (1977). *Profiles of the Elderly:* 1, *Who Are They? etc.*, Age Concern, Mitcham, Surrey.

Ardill, J. (1974). *New Citizens Guide to Town and Country Planning.* Town and Country Planning Association, London.

Association of Metropolitan Authorities (1978). *Services for the Elderly: a Metropolitan View.* AMA, London.

Barnard, K. C. (1979). Retirement housing in England and Wales. Unpublished paper to the Institute of British Geographers Annual Conference, University of Manchester.

Bebbington, A. C. (1978). *The 'Elderly at Home' Survey: Changes in the Provision of Domiciliary Services to the Elderly over Fourteen Years.* Discussion Paper No. 87. Personal Social Services Research Unit, University of Kent, Canterbury.

Beckham, B. L. and Kart, C. S. (1977). The heterogeneity of large metropolitan areas. *Urban Affairs Quarterly*, **13**, 233–42.

Bennett, L. C. (1974). Housing for the elderly and disabled. *Housing*, **9**, 8–13.
Blagden, C. (1976). Planning for the Retired. Unpublished PhD thesis, University of London, London.
Bromley, D. B. (1977). Speculations in social and environmental gerontology. *Nursing Times*, **73**, 53–6.
Bruce, A. (1974). Facilities required near home. *Built Environment*, **3**, 290–1.
Carp, F. M. (1976). Urban lifestyle and lifestyle factors. In Lawton, M. P., Newcomer, R. J., and Byerts, T. O. (eds), *Community Planning for an Aging Society*, pp. 19–40. Dowden, Hutchinson & Ross, Stroudsburg, Penn.
Central Policy Review Staff (1977). *Population and the Social Services*. HMSO, London.
Central Statistical Office (1978). *Social Trends 8, 1977*, HMSO, London.
Clark, D. and Smith, M. (1978). *The Decline of Rural Services*. Standing Committee of Rural Community Councils, London.
Department of Employment (1978). Family expenditure survey and the annual revision of weights for retail price indices. *Department of Employment Gazette*, **86**, 305–9.
Department of the Environment (1978). The changing distribution of the elderly in England and Wales. Unpublished paper, DOE, London.
Department of the Environment (1979). Characteristics of areas with large concentrations of the elderly. Unpublished paper, DOE, London.
Department of the Environment (1980). Planning and the elderly: a multivariate analysis. Unpublished paper, DOE, London.
Fox, D. (1979). The housing needs of the elderly. *Housing*, **7**, 5–7.
Gordon, I. R. (1975). *Retirement to the South West*. HMSO, London.
Grant, W. (1971). Old people's towns. *New Society*, **17**, 13 May, 816–8.
Greater London Council (1975). *Greater London Recreation Study*. GLC, London.
Harman, A. J. (1977). *Local Shops in Rural Norfolk*. Centre for East Anglian Studies, University of East Anglia, Norwich.
Havighurst, R. J. (1968). Personality and the patterns of aging. *Gerontologist*, **8**, 20–3.
Haynes, K. J. and Raven, J. (1961). *The Living Patterns of Some Elderly People*. Building Research Station, Garston, Watford.
Hazel, N. (1974). Residential provision for the elderly in Switzerland and Germany. *Social Work Today*, 16 May.
Hernden, J. and Fujishin, B. (1974). *Membership of Old People's Clubs*. Centre for Urban and Regional Studies, University of Birmingham, Birmingham.
Hendricks, J. and Hendricks, C. D. (1977). *Aging in a Mass Society: Myths and Realities*. Winthrop, Cambridge, Mass.
Hillman, M. and Whalley, A. (1977). *Fair Play for All*. Broadsheet 571, Political and Economic Planning, London.
Hopkin, J., Robson, P., and Town, S. W. (1978). *The Mobility of Old People: A Study in Guildford*. Transport and Road Research Laboratory, Crowthorne, Berkshire.
Housing Corporation (1976). The role of the housing association movement in housing elderly people. Unpublished paper, Housing Corporation, London.
Howell, S. C. (1976). Site selection and the elderly. In Lawton, M. P., Newcomer, R. J., and Byerts, T. O. (eds), *Community Planning for an Aging Society*, pp. 181–94. Dowden Hutchinson & Ross, Stroudsburg, Penn.
Hunt, A. (1977). *The Elderly at Home*. HMSO, London.
Karn, V. A. (1977). *Retiring to the Seaside*. Routledge & Kegan Paul, London.
Law, C. M. and Warnes, A. M. (1980). The characteristics of retirement migrants. In Herbert, D. T. and Johnston, R. J. (eds), *Geography and the Urban Environment*, vol. 3, pp. 175–222. Wiley, Chichester.
Lawton, M. P. (1970). Planning environments for elderly people. *Journal of the American Institute of Planners*, **36**, 124–9.

Lawton, M. P. (1976). Homogeneity and heterogeneity in housing for the elderly. In Lawton, M. P., Newcomer, R. J., and Byerts, T. O. (eds), *Community Planning for an Aging Society*, pp. 173–80. Dowden, Hutchinson, & Ross, Stroudsburg, Penn.

Lemon, A. (1973). Retirement and its effects on small towns. *Town Planning Review*, **44**, 254–62.

London Borough of Wandsworth (1977). *Services for the Elderly*. London Borough of Wandsworth, Wandsworth.

Moseley, M. J., Harman, R. G., Coles, O. B., and Spencer, M. B. (1976). *Rural Transport and Accessibility*. Centre for East Anglian Studies, University of East Anglia, Norwich.

National Corporation for the Care of Old People (1979). Response to *A Happier Old Age*. Unpublished paper. NCCOP, London.

Newcomer, R. J. and Bexton, E. F. (1978). Aging and the environment. In Hobman, D. (ed.), *The Social Challenge of Aging*, pp. 73–116. Croom Helm, London.

Norman, A. (1977). *Transport and the Elderly*. National Corporation for the Care of Old People, London.

Office of Population Censuses and Surveys (1974). *Census of England and Wales Population 1971: Age, Marital Condition and General Table*. HMSO, London.

Office of Population Censuses and Surveys (1979). *General Household Survey 1977*. HMSO, London.

Permanand, R. (1977). *London's Institutional Population: A Look at the Future*. Research Memorandum 521, Greater London Council, London.

Personal Social Services Council Policy Group (1979). Response to *A Happier Old Age*. Unpublished paper. PSSCPG, London.

Rapoport, R. and Rapoport, R. N. (1975). *Leisure and the Family Life Cycle*. Routledge & Kegan Paul, London.

Roberts, E. (1974). *The Retired as Consumers*. Age Concern, Mitcham, Surrey.

Ross, J. K. (1977). *Old People: New Lives*. University of Chicago Press, Chicago.

Sclar, E. D. and Lind, S. D. (1976). Aging and residential location. In Lawton, M. P., Newcomer, R. J., and Byerts, T. O. (eds), *Community Planning for an Aging Society*, pp. 266–81. Dowden, Hutchinson & Ross, Stroudsburg, Penn.

Sherman, E. M. and Britten, M. A. (1973). Contemporary food gatherers. *Gerontologist*, **13**, 358–64.

Skelton, N. (1978). Understanding travel. In *Mobility for the Elderly and Handicapped*. Proceedings of the International Conference on Transport for the Elderly and Handicapped, Cambridge, 4–7 April.

West Sussex County Council (1978). *Retirement Migration*, Technical Paper 18, County Structure Plan. West Sussex CC, Chichester.

White, D. (1978). Have second homes gone into hibernation? *New Society*, 10 August pp. 286–8.

Wroe, D. C. L. (1973). The elderly. *Social Trends*, **4**, 23–34.

Geographical Perspectives on the Elderly
Edited by A. M. Warnes


Chapter 19

# British research on social gerontology and its relevance to policy: towards a geographical contribution

*Hedley Taylor* and *Hilary Todd*

In the 30-plus years that have elapsed since the establishment of the welfare state in Britain, statutory and voluntary bodies have pioneered a multitude of health and social services for elderly people which still provide a model for much of the rest of the world. Paradoxically, this concern for the welfare of the elderly has not been matched by a comparable interest amongst the academic community in researching the many issues relating to the place of elderly people in society. Until comparatively recently, British research on old age was dominated by the efforts of medical practitioners, whilst a smaller number of biologists have been studying the biological bases of the ageing process. Social research, however, remains an underdeveloped field. Britain is alone amongst developed nations in having no institute for the study of social gerontology and, at the time of writing, no academic journal devoted to the subject. Indeed, the very phrase 'social gerontology' would barely be recognized in British universities and research institutes, and only through the Open University is it possible to take a course on 'An Ageing Population'. This situation is in stark contrast to the United States, for example, where despite comparatively primitive welfare services for older people, research on ageing is a considerable industry.

In this chapter we aim to do three things. Firstly, to review general directions in British research on social gerontology over the last 10 years, with particular reference to policy-relevant studies. Secondly, to examine in greater detail those areas likely to be of special interest to geographers; to note instances where geographers have already undertaken important work and to assess its significance for policy-makers. Finally, to suggest the contribution which geographers might usefully make to policy-relevant research and generally to social research on ageing.

## RESEARCH AND POLICY: A REVIEW OF TRENDS

Social research on ageing in Britain does not have a long history, nor until very recently was there a body of work of any considerable proportion. Even now, after 10 years of steadily increasing interest in age research, a glance through *Old Age: A Register of Social Research* (Centre for Policy on Ageing (CPA), annual) suggests that the concern of most researchers, in the first place at least, is with the wider aspects of social policy and that the study and sometimes concentration on ageing issues has grown out of this. This accords with the generally accepted principle of social gerontologists that the elderly should not be 'labelled' as a special problem, but should be studied in the context of ageing in society. There is a strong tradition of such broader social research in this country, from the early Booth (1892–97) and S. Rowntree (1902) studies to the government-initiated surveys under the Chronically Sick and Disabled Persons Act in the early 1970s and Townsend's (1979) monumental *Poverty in the United Kingdom*. While not 'gerontological' works, since their findings cover all sections of the population, they have all identified the elderly as one of the most vulnerable groups, with enormous implications for social policy.

Against a general paucity of age-focused research until the 1970s, the works of Rowntree (1947), Sheldon (1948), Shenfield (1957), Townsend (1957, 1962), Townsend and Wedderburn (1965), Tunstall (1966) and Harris (1968) stand out prominently. Their outstanding features are a practical, problem-oriented approach, an emphasis on the circumstances and needs of the elderly, and their utility to policy-makers. Townsend's volumes have been striking examples of research influencing not only social policy, but also public attitudes regarding the needs of the elderly and the ways in which they should be met. The two main concerns of social policy for the elderly—to support them in their own homes for as long as possible, where it is assumed that they want to remain, and to improve the quality of care for the minority who require institutional provision—can be traced in large part to the influence of these works. Of the above-mentioned studies only Tunstall's *Old and Alone* and Townsend's *Family Life of Old People* have a sociological as opposed to a social policy orientation.

During the 1950s and 1960s, then, two features emerged which most distinctly characterize research on ageing in Britain; its empirical problem-oriented nature, and its primary concern with social policy, particularly in relation to service provision. In the last decade research has increased markedly, but the emphasis has remained on information surveys, policy-evaluation studies, and monitoring exercises at the expense of theory (Abrams, 1978a). The few theoretical perspectives are derived from the United States where social gerontology is a multi-disciplinary pursuit in dozens of institutes and university departments. A slight growth of interest in the sociology of ageing in this country can be perceived, most notably at the Medical Research Council Medical Sociology Unit at Aberdeen. Only six of the 154 entries in the current CPA register (1978–79) have a discernible theoretical orientation; but rather more encouraging have been the seminars convened since 1978 by the Social Science Research Council (SSRC) to promote research in this field. Similarly, recent annual conferences of the British Society of Gerontology (formerly the British Society of Social and Behavioural Gerontology) have placed more emphasis on the sociology of ageing. These trends are welcomed, for the development of theory in regard to the social processes of ageing would provide a much-needed framework for evaluating and guiding empirical study.

The imbalance between theoretical and practical studies is reflected in research methods, for the interview survey and secondary analysis of existing data dominate over non-quantitative and experimental methods. Some social gerontologists, such as Johnson (1976), cast doubt on the ability of conventional tools of social analysis, particularly the survey questionnaire, to provide an accurate picture of the circumstances of old people as perceived by themselves. Social survey techniques, it is argued, impose the researcher's categories, concepts, and values on the respondents—and these may not truly express the reality of older people. Hence, any theoretical framework based on this methodology is suspect. Such criticism echoes a more general debate about the epistemological base of sociology, which, if more sociologists showed interest in ageing, could stimulate and inform research in social gerontology.

Theoretical weaknesses are paralleled by the spread of research amongst a large number of institutions and individuals, each pursuing its own interest, apparently with little attention to work elsewhere.

> The most obvious example of this is the work undertaken in the research sections of Social Services Departments. Many Departments have carried out surveys of the welfare needs of their own population, usually without any attempt to co-ordinate methods of data collection or compare findings with other areas. As a result, the opportunity which was presented, at the same time as assessing needs to explore how different community structures and the services available within them affect the lives of old people, has been lost (Taylor, 1978).

The absence of an institute of social gerontology or comparable organization further hampers the development of age research. The British Society of Gerontology (BSG), whose small membership is drawn mostly from the social and behavioural sciences, lacks both independent finance and permanent staff. Voluntary bodies are the only organizations in the country with a permanent interest and expertise in the subject of old age. Age Concern is primarily concerned with direct services to elderly people through its nationwide local groups, but it has recently established a small research unit, commissioned a major survey of the elderly, *Beyond Three Score and Ten* (Abrams, 1978b, 1980), and published several *Profiles* (Age Concern, 1977– ) which collate data on the elderly population. The Centre for Policy on Ageing (CPA, formerly the National Corporation for the Care of Old People) commissioned research during its period as a grant aid organization (e.g. Harris, 1968) and is now establishing an in-house research team. Since 1955 it has published an annual research register, it maintains a reference library on social aspects of old age, and is sponsoring the journal, *Ageing and Society* (to be published in spring 1981). Both Age Concern and the CPA are, however, registered charities with limited resources, and both inevitably concentrate on research which has immediate relevance to policy and practice.

The lack of interest of British social scientists in age research, the duplication in some areas and neglect in others, and the absence of a cumulative approach produce a 'destructive incoherence' (Norris, 1976) which stems largely from the nature of funding. Over 50 per cent of studies in 1978–79 were financed by central and local government and the health authorities (and often carried out by them) and were mainly problem-oriented and short-term. One result is the slight encouragement for researchers to contact others and exchange ideas; another is that neither time nor resources are available to explore the findings of other studies. When the research is completed and funds run out, the findings are commonly 'lost' because they are not related to a wider body of work. Even universities and institutes rely heavily on short-term grants which often demand proof of the immediate utility of research. The extent of SSRC funding remains disappointingly small despite the initiatives already referred to; in 1978–79 it supported only 8 per cent of the registered projects. Postgraduate research is often innovative and informative but unfortunately is rarely published or presented at seminars and conferences. Until the value of existing research is realized, the general public have good reason to be sceptical as to its value—and this attitude appears to affect researchers themselves.

As regards the topics within social gerontology which have been studied in Britain, a preponderance of national and local fact-finding surveys of the circumstances and needs of elderly people has been noted. They cover basic demographic characteristics, the presence of family support, and social and physical morbidity. In contrast we know little about the lifestyles and activities of the elderly, and still less about either their perceptions of old age or the problems and opportunities of enforced economic inactivity in a society which equates status with the nature of one's job.

In addition to clinical research, the medical profession has contributed a great deal of information on general morbidity and on specific health problems such as falls, hypothermia and nutrition. Research on health services has tended to concentrate on hospital services, though there are studies of most of the community health services and on innovatory forms of health care such as 'hospital at home'. Very little research addresses terminal care, even though the taboos on death, dying, and bereavement are at last being lifted. The psychology of ageing is an under-researched field in Britain, though interest can now be discerned. Although it has been known for some 15 years that the incidence of mental illness is appallingly high in old people, mental disorder has received little attention until recently. Undoubtedly a major task facing researchers and policy-makers is to find ways of supporting elderly people suffering from dementia—which is not yet treatable; another task is to establish the origins of the many other mental illnesses which are probably socially determined.

Research on retirement has focused on individual adjustment to this transition, but a wider sociological analysis of retirement (Phillipson, 1977) highlights the general lack of interest amongst sociologists in this important phase in the life-cycle. A new area of investigation is the value of pre-retirement courses; and retirement activities which have been studied include education, employment, and watching television.

Social services for the elderly have attracted most research, with emphases on personal social services and housing, but little attention to income maintenance. Major studies exist on every form of support yet devised—day care, residential care, fostering schemes, the home-help services, meals services, volunteer care, often in isolation rather than on the whole care package. Housing has recently been a favoured topic, but the popularity of sheltered housing studies has been to the detriment of work on accommodation problems of the majority, i.e. those living in ordinary housing. While the economic circumstances of elderly people are fairly well known from general surveys and poverty studies, and despite public concern about the growing financial burden of pensioners, few economists appear to be working in this field. The extent to which higher income in retirement might mitigate the causes and effects of dependency is a subject ripe for investigation.

Notable gaps in research have already been referred to, and also include the history of the aged in society, the circumstances of ethnic minorities reaching old age, and cultural definitions of old age. Cross-national and cross-cultural studies are extremely rare, only two examples being known to the authors; i.e. those by Shanas (1968) and the work in progress at the Institute of Psychiatry.

Given its practical and policy orientation, the question arises how successful research has been in informing social policy. British policy with regard to the elderly has its roots in two responses to destitution—the old age pension (1908) and the workhouse (1601–1948). Pensions remain unchanged in their basic purpose; the workhouse gave rise in 1948 to residential homes, by which time (1946) the National Health Service had also come into being. Thus, by the time researchers began to investigate the needs of the elderly, the basic structure of the welfare state was established and they could at best relate the needs they discovered to an existing framework.

Subsequent influences on social policy have been many and varied. The post-war years spawned both CPA and Age Concern who were able to experiment, innovate, promote, and persuade. At the same time the welfare state gave rise to new groups of professionals in local and health authorities with a wealth of practical experience and reasonable freedom under existing legislation to experiment. More recently 'old age pensioners' have become a fashionable concern of the major political parties, trades unions, and the media, and individual writers also have campaigned on policy issues. *Sans Everything* (Robb, 1967), which described the low quality of life in long-stay hospitals exemplifies the books which had an enormous impact on public thinking.

Researchers, then, have competed with many other interested parties in their attempts to influence policy. The role they have established successfully is that of evaluating and promoting policies which have arisen, without explicit reference to the research community, in response to practical difficulties at field level. Research tends to follow in the trail of innovation in social care, but nevertheless can be very influential in shaping opinion about policy options, and in raising the general level of awareness. The major shift in emphasis from residential to domiciliary care of the early 1960s owed much to the work of Townsend, who in *The Last Refuge* criticized homes for their institutional qualities, and demonstrated that most residents could be supported in special housing. The benefits of domiciliary services, day care, and sheltered housing are now widely recognized and monitored. Many of the design features of sheltered and other special housing have been considerably refined as a result of studies like *New Housing for the Elderly* (Page and Muir, 1971); whilst more recently the benefits of group living in residential homes have been monitored, which will doubtless help to promote this important innovation.

Researchers are inclined to be sceptical about their achievements, especially when they measure their influence by increases in provision and improved quality of practice. These are severe tests, however, which ignore the changes in attitudes and aims both at policy and field level achieved through research influence. Perhaps the most valuable contribution that researchers can continue to make is to heighten public awareness and to raise the level of public debate without which social policy will be based on political dogma, expediency, or both.

## RESEARCH TOPICS

### Demography

To those working in the field of social gerontology or service provision for the elderly, the basic demographic characteristics of Britain's retired population have been well known for at least 30 years. The decennial censuses and the Registrar General's annual population estimates and projections have been reworked by almost every researcher since Rowntree (1947). Demographers themselves, however, have only recently identified older age groups as a subject for analysis. Only with the 1971 census did the Office of Population Censuses and Surveys (OPCS) collate in one volume some data on retired people. Further analyses by demographers have appeared in *Social Trends* (Wroe, 1973) and *Population Trends* (Davis, 1976; Hunt, 1978a): scant attention indeed.

Social gerontologists have supplemented the basic data with at least 33 national, regional, and local surveys since 1947 (CPA, 1980). Collectively they contain a wealth of (often repetitive) demographic data; many have been linked to the need for health and social services (Gruer, 1975; Harris, 1968); some have focused on morbidity (Harris, 1971; Miller, 1963); and others on family life (Bracey, 1966; Townsend, 1957). The majority, however, also enquired widely over housing, finance, employment, leisure and mobility (Abrams, 1978b, 1980; Glyn-Jones, 1975; Hunt, 1978b; Shanas *et al*, 1968). Longitudinal surveys in this field are rare, though Abrams hopes to re-interview his sample.

The value of these studies to the policy-maker has been self-evident since the Rowntree committee (1947) expressed its concern about the financial burden of an increasing group of pensioners on a decreasing proportion of workers. More recently the concern of policy-makers has been with the disproportionate demands on the health and social services by older people, and indeed the projected large increase in the number of people aged 75 and over has led central government to publish a consultative document, *A Happier Old Age*, with the promise of a white paper to follow (Department of Health and Social Security, 1978).

Despite these studies there are some neglected demographic issues, some of particular interest to geographers—for instance the ageing of ethnic minorities. Hunt (1978b) surveyed 2500 people aged 65 or more, and found that only 2.8 per cent were born outside the United Kingdom and only 1.4 per cent were non-white immigrants. In 20 years' time, however, the situation may be completely different and policy-makers cannot ignore the specific needs of various ethnic groups. Both CPA and Age Concern are hoping to commence work in this field.

A further unexplored issue is the formation of elderly households. While OPCS publish projections of population by age for the next 40 years, it would be helpful also to estimate household characteristics. The exhortations of successive governments that people should do more for their elderly relatives have failed to appreciate that many elderly people have no surviving family members. For these people state services may be crucial. Already over one-third of the over-75s live alone, and demographic trends suggest that single-person elderly households will increase.

The distribution of elderly people seems an obvious subject for both researchers and policy-makers, but work is still under-developed. Although it has long been recognized that certain environmentally attractive areas have high proportions of retired people, a study by geographers of the national distribution did not emerge until 1976 (Law and Warnes, 1976). Long-distance migration is one component in the uneven distribution of elderly people, but other influences such as the operation of housing markets have also been studied (Barnard, Chapter 7 of this book). Information about the distribution of older age groups is confined to the local authority scale and no investigations have been published on the patterns within local authority boundaries. It is widely assumed that elderly people are concentrated in the older, inner suburbs of towns and in smaller, decaying rural communities characterized by the out-migration of working age groups. A great deal more research is required to confirm or refute these ideas. As will be demonstrated, the location of elderly people, at both the national and neighbourhood level, is of more than academic interest.

The gaps in our knowledge of the demography of pensionable age groups are surprising given the data resources. The census is under-used in social gerontology, even though it dates quickly, and there is little take-up of the special tabulations OPCS can supply. Similarly, the data from other national enquiries, like the Family Expenditure Survey and the General Household Survey, and even some *ad hoc* surveys like that of Hunt (1978b), only rarely provide a basis for secondary analysis.

## Retirement migration

Policy-makers regard retirement migration as one cause of the much-publicized difficulties of providing adequate levels of service in the receiving areas, where retired people commonly make up one-third of the population. Retirement migration is directed towards the resort towns and environmentally attractive areas where the paucity of industry means that the cost of local services falls mainly on domestic ratepayers. Many retirement areas fall considerably below government norms for geriatric hospital beds, home-help services and the like, and there seems little likelihood of substantial improvement until the rate-support grant and health services financing adequately reflect the problems of these areas. There are also difficulties in recruiting staff to man the services, partly because of competition from the private sector in areas of affluent elderly in-migrants. Underlying all these difficulties is the failure to anticipate the effects of housing policies, since large private bungalow estates have been permitted by planning departments with inadequate consideration of the likely occupants and their needs.

Research has been carried out both on migration *per se* and on its impact, though the latter has been relatively neglected, no doubt because of its complexity. Geographers have been foremost amongst social scientists in studying migration, and although the total number of studies is still small, they have contributed a great deal to our understanding not just of spatial patterns of migration but also of the characteristics and motivations of migrants. Early studies were based largely on analyses of census data (Mellor, 1962; Lemon, 1973; Law and Warnes, 1975) and provided broad outlines of the origin and destination of migrants with some discussion of the policy implications. More recently a wider range of issues have been investigated, including the attitudes of migrants to retirement and to their old and new environments, the nature and importance of financial and family factors, migrants' perceptions of potential locations, and previous links with the area of their choice, and the nature of social support networks in retirement communities (Karn, 1973, 1977; Law and Warnes, 1973, 1977, 1980). The applied value of these studies is in identifying implications for the provision of services. A large proportion of migrants, for example, have no children, and whilst there is support from neighbours, this inevitably wanes when the community is ageing together. It is also evident that the wealth of migrants has been over-stressed because most are owner-occupiers, but the capital value of a house does not pay for assistance. These studies also predict both increasing migration because of the growing numbers of owner-occupiers in metropolitan areas, and changes in retirement destinations.

As regards the issues facing the areas receiving retired migrants, researchers might address themselves to: first, how best to utilize financial and manpower resources to provide services for elderly people; and second, the more complex issue of whether retirement communities should be allowed to develop at all. Most research has been concerned with the former at a local level (East Sussex County Council, 1975; Glyn-Jones, 1975; West Sussex Area Health Authority, 1979; Worthing District Community Health Council, 1977).

There is a disappointing lack of evidence on the advantages and disadvantages of retirement communities. Karn (1977) concluded that most migrants were satisfied with their situation but, since the opinions of indigenous people and of elderly people no longer living in their own homes were not sought, this view can only be partial. The one study by economists (South West Economic Planning Council, 1975) was concerned solely with the economic benefits accruing from the 'retirement industry', but these do need to be weighed against the costs of providing support services. A great deal more research is required on retirement communities; meanwhile, their development continues and service providers have to cope as best they can.

It should also be noted that despite the emphasis on migration to resort towns, the problems may be much more acute in rural areas. Little is known of the scale of retirement migration into rural areas, its relationship with the out-migration of young people, or the extent to which indigenous elderly people compete for scarce resources with newcomers. That outsiders can usually outbid local people for housing is well known. Second-home ownership is increasing and generates substantial controversy, yet nothing is known about its relationship to retirement migration, whilst the problems of service delivery in rural areas may be exacerbated by an influx of retired people. Clearly there are still many aspects of retirement migration which deserve attention.

## Housing

In the field of housing for the elderly more than any other, the absence of any major influence on central and local government policy by the research community is most notable and regrettable. The major innovations in policy have taken place as a response to practical demands and problems and not as a reaction to research evidence. The latter has followed in the trail of innovation in practice rather than identifying the need for it, and it is only in the last 12 years that researchers have begun seriously to investigate this area. If, as Fox asserts (1978), the development of special housing for the elderly is one area in which housing authorities have reason to be proud of their contribution, then it is clear that this success owes little to the work of social researchers.

Housing policy has not, however, developed entirely within an information vacuum, for various surveys have generated information about the housing circumstances of the elderly (Gruer, 1975; Harris, 1968; Hunt, 1978b; Rowntree, 1947). They reveal the generally inferior housing situation of the retired in comparison with the rest of the population; that their property is likely to be older, in need of repair and lacking adequate heating and other facilities; and that elderly people disproportionately occupy the private rented sector.

The need for more adequate housing for the retired was identified as long ago as 1947 (Rowntree, 1947). The Phillips Committee (1954) advocated special housing of various types, together with a range of co-ordinated services to provide a supportive environment, and the same points were emphasized by major committees of enquiry on social services (Seebohm, 1968) and on housing (Cullingworth, 1969). Special housing for the elderly has its roots in the almshouse trusts, some dating from medieval times (Housing Centre, no date), but sheltered housing began in the late 1940s. It was encouraged by successive governments; by CPA which financed various housing innovations that culminated in 1963 in the Hanover Housing Association, the first national body of its kind; and by Townsend (1962) who urged that it replace most residential care. Since then, research on housing has burgeoned, the main focus being on special housing.

The Ministry of Housing and Local Government (1962) conducted a survey of tenants' views on sheltered housing, with particular reference to design features, and a similar exercise was carried out for Hanover schemes (Page and Muir, 1971). Both studies demonstrated the high levels of satisfaction with the accommodation provided. Alarm systems were identified as a feature central to the concept of sheltered living and were the subject of a later study (Attenburrow, 1976). Despite the growing interest in sheltered housing, the amount and distribution of such housing was not known until early 1980 (Department of the Environment, 1980).

Researchers at the University of Aston have undertaken a number of important studies of practice in regard to design, location and management of sheltered housing, including wardens, alarm systems, space requirements, noise, safety, and communal facilities, and surveys of tenants and individual schemes (Rose, 1978; Rose and Bozeat, 1980). The value of this research lies in its accumulation of knowledge about the design and organization of sheltered housing rather than the analysis of its role in housing policy and other social welfare provision for the elderly. Other studies have, however, been addressed to these issues. A project on the characteristics of tenants in relation to the stated objectives of sheltered housing has highlighted the difficulties which occur as tenants become more frail (Boldy, Abel and Carter, 1973). Bytheway and James (1978) have argued that instead of providing accommodation for the more able-bodied elderly as originally intended, sheltered housing 'has slowly but surely been drifting towards residential accommodation in the needs it attempts to meet'. A major study is in progress at the University of Leeds (Butler, 1979) to examine and assess the role and contribution of sheltered housing in England over the last 10 years, an enquiry complemented by other studies in Scotland and Wales. Many local authority research departments have evaluated their own sheltered housing, and some have recently experimented with what is inelegantly known as 'very sheltered housing', which has additional services to support tenants who might otherwise enter residential homes (Hampshire County Council, 1978; Warwickshire County Council, 1979).

In contrast to the emphasis on sheltered housing, there has been relatively little work on the needs of the elderly in ordinary housing, though a shift of focus is now discernible. Tinker (1977) has questioned the assumption that special housing is always necessary and pointed out that local authorities possess powers to assist with improvements and adaptations to enable elderly people to remain in their own homes (Tinker and White, 1979). Having the requisite powers is not, however, the same as having the necessary resources, even though a Department of the Environment (1978) experiment to improve heating and insulation in privately owned houses demonstrated that comparatively small expenditure can make a substantial difference. Tinker's research has focused on supportive environments for elderly people other than sheltered housing. Her evaluation of 'granny annexe' schemes, whereby elderly people live as a separate household linked to a family home, demonstrates their success, both in providing help and in releasing under-occupied houses (Tinker, 1976). A second study, concerned with local authority and housing association practice in respect of rehousing elderly people near relatives, concluded that 'there is a clear demand from elderly people to move near relatives (and vice versa)' and that such moves would be advantageous but required the relaxation of residential qualification rules in allocating tenancies (Tinker, 1980).

Two other studies in progress at the University of Leeds and North Yorkshire Social Services Department concern arrangements whereby elderly (and handicapped) people are accommodated in private, non-related family homes, in much the same way as foster-homes for children. These apart, the main themes for research in the next few years are likely to be the role of sheltered housing; alternatives to sheltered housing such as warden schemes supporting those in their own homes; methods of financing and carrying out home improvements; and ways of facilitating beneficial changes of tenure.

Geographers have not yet added their perspective to the housing needs of retired people. Whilst Department of the Environment directives and some of the research mentions the need to locate housing in relation to other services, we have little detailed knowledge of spatial aspects of housing, though the subject is touched on in some mobility research. Sensible siting of housing is a major policy issue and merits closer examination. Geographers might ask: to what extent can well-sited housing contribute to the maintenance of an independent lifestyle for the elderly? Does badly sited housing precipitate dependency and the decision to become housebound? Are house-building trends influencing the location of the elderly? How are elderly people affected by housing renewal and development programmes?

## Personal social services

The assessment of need and the evaluation of social services delivery is a subject area in which social researchers can claim to have made a substantial impact on policy. Approximately one-third of recent research projects have been concerned with some aspect of personal social services; the following paragraphs describe only the major landmarks and trends, and their relation to policy.

Two major surveys of the social conditions and health circumstances of old people (Rowntree, 1947; Sheldon, 1948) were very influential in concentrating attention on the special problems posed by the elderly and may be regarded as the forerunners of social gerontological research in this country. A review of social provision for the elderly in Great Britain (Shenfield, 1957) coincided with Townsend's (1957) classic study of elderly people in Bethnal Green, which revealed that ties between the generations still provided the bulk of support to the elderly. A subsequent comparative study in Britain, Denmark and the United States refuted the chronic dependency of elderly people and established that while a minority were sick or disabled, the majority were able to look after themselves and only needed help with the heavier household tasks (Shanas *et al.*, 1968). It was, and is, those often of advanced old age who do not have an immediate family who are the main users of the social services.

In the 1960s attention was focused on the shortage of both residential and community care services and the close relationship between the two aspects of the welfare system. Efforts by the (then) Ministry of Health to initiate long-term planning of health and welfare services were heavily criticized because of their piecemeal approach and neglect of the interrelation between needs and services (Townsend, 1962, 1973; Townsend and Wedderburn, 1965).

The publication in 1963 of 10-year plans for community care services in England and Wales demonstrated the enormous variation in provision among local authorities unrelated to their demographic, economic or social characteristics, and stimulated CPA to fund two important studies of needs and provision. Harris (1968) surveyed 13 local authority areas in England, Wales and Scotland, and confirmed that the variation in services was not related entirely to 'need' but rather to local policies and lack of resources. Sumner and Smith (1969) concluded that there was a lack of effective planning and coordination of services for the elderly. Such evidence ensured that when, in 1971, local authority health, welfare and children's departments were integrated into Social Services Departments, the needs of the elderly were given greater initial emphasis.

At the present time, Social Services Departments undertake 14 per cent and fund 10 per cent of the research projects (excluding very minor studies) on social ageing in Britain. Most are published in the *Clearing House for Local Authority Social Services Research* which was established in 1972, and many, by examining the need for services and their delivery within a social services authority area, have a geographical orientation. Various environmental and demographic factors; e.g. urban/rural, inner city/suburban, social class, age composition; are used in order to explore variations in 'need', referral, and appropriate methods of delivery. An unfortunate concomitant of these characteristically independent research initiatives carried out in Social Services Departments is the lack of a cumulative approach.

Another important development has been the growing concern about handicapped people which culminated in the Chronically Sick and Disabled Persons Act 1970. This authorized local authorities to enquire into the numbers and needs of the disabled in their areas and to ensure that adequate provision was made. Harris (1971) estimated that nearly two-thirds of the over 3 million impaired persons in Great Britain were over retirement age, and attempted to define and measure degrees of impairment. Most local authorities responded to the Act by carrying out surveys of their own areas. Their value was unfortunately limited by the fact that the newly established Social Services Departments were already under severe pressure as a result of the public's heightened expectations, although they did demonstrate the amount of unmet need.

In recent years there has been a narrowing of focus on specific social policy issues. Chief amongst these has been residential care which continues to attract attention out of all proportion to its scale (Carstairs and Morrison, 1971; Department of Health and Social Security, 1975; DHSS Social Work

Service, 1979; Peace, Hall and Hamblin, 1979). There have also been studies of the home-help service (Howell, Boldy and Smith, 1979; Marks, 1975); day care (Carter, in press); the supply of aids and equipment (Keeble, 1979); and the role of professional social workers (Goldberg, 1970; Rowlings, 1978) and volunteers (Hadley, Webb and Farrell, 1975). Meacher's (1972) study of residential care for the mentally infirm, and Wicks's (1978) study of hypothermia consider the needs and circumstances of sub-groups within the elderly.

The main incidence of referrals for social services has been in urban areas, but rural authorities have begun to question the adequacy and justice of their generally low level of provision. Taylor's (1977) study of the welfare needs of households in a Herefordshire village based its recommendations for the effective delivery of services within the social, economic, and political structure of the village; and a major project is under way at the University College of North Wales to assess whether rural areas require special approaches to service delivery. In contrast, the report of a survey of housing and social services for the elderly in eight London boroughs does not treat the urban environment as a variable in itself (Plank, 1977). This is the case in all but a small number of inner-city based researches and territorial needs studies.

The elaboration of social need indicators to measure deprivation or shortfall in services and to evaluate or increase 'territorial justice' has exercised both sociologists and geographers (Davies *et al.*, 1971). Although 'territorial need indicators' have been developed, their application has been limited by the difficulty of establishing criteria for testing their validity (Bebbington and Davies, 1980). Pinch (1979) has compared social need indicators with the availability of local social services and found a 'relatively high degree of association between needs and services'. He points out, however, that 'the relatively large aggregate positive correlation conceals quite considerable variations in rates of social service provision amongst boroughs with similar conditions'—which would appear to be a fundamental weakness of this approach.

Although the hopes raised by the publication of *A Happier Old Age* (Department of Health and Social Security, 1978) have been postponed as a result of cuts in public expenditure, studies of personal social services have heightened consciousness of the many problems still to be resolved, and it seems likely that research into solutions will continue to attract reasonable support.

### Transport and mobility

Transport is not normally recognized as being as essential a service for the elderly as housing, health, and social services. Yet elderly people, commonly facing falling income coincident with decreasing physical abilities, still need mobility to reach shops, essential services, and social or recreational activities. The traditional concerns of transport policy-makers and researchers with mass movement of people and goods have been detrimental to the needs of the disadvantaged individual. It was not until 1970 that the Chronically Sick and

Disabled Persons Act enshrined the concepts of access and mobility in government thinking and attempted, amongst other things, to remove some of the barriers to the mobility of disabled people. In practice the Act was concerned mainly with improving access to public buildings and, even in association with other government policies on concessionary fares (which are neither uniform nor universal) and the mobility allowance (which is payable only to persons or working age), hardly amounts to a coherent strategy for meeting the mobility needs of elderly and disabled people. Many of these needs might, of course, be met by a more rational and co-ordinated approach to transport provision generally.

Policy-makers have consistently failed to grasp the facts that effective community care depends as much on transport as on any other resource, and conversely that transport cannot be considered in isolation from the locations of individuals. Changes in land-use patterns and retailing often penalize society's less mobile groups, and there are numerous examples of insensitive siting of old people's homes, housing, and health facilities. Research on transport and mobility reflects a variety of interests, from very specific features such as bus design to aggregate studies of old people's travel patterns, and most investigations have been problem oriented. Considerable opportunity exists to influence policy decisions, as demonstrated by the success of some pressure groups, particularly those representing the disabled.

The research emphasis on bus travel reflects the fact that elderly people comprise a large proportion of bus passengers, and a substantial majority depend on buses. Brooks *et al.* (1974) were concerned with those features of bus design which hamper older people's use of them, and design has also featured in wider mobility research, which shows that operating procedures, cost, reliability, and waiting time are all factors affecting the use of buses by older people (Feeney *et al.*, 1979; Hopkin, Robson and Town, 1978). A great deal of research has been carried out on unconventional bus services, such as rural postbuses and dial-a-ride schemes, although these rarely focus on any particular user group. Concessionary bus fares have been studied with respect to their influence upon travel patterns, but although they generate more confusion and injustice than any other aspect of transport for the elderly (Norman, 1977), the economic and political aspects of this example of 'territorial injustice' have not yet been fully explored.

Another subject which has been widely examined is safety. Elderly pedestrians are an extremely vulnerable group, and a study has recently been completed at Loughborough University on their behaviour and difficulties. A team at University College, London, has been studying the effects of ageing on drivers' awareness of traffic hazards. Both studies were commissioned by the Transport and Road Research Laboratory which has been associated with many of the studies in this field.

A detailed picture of the travel patterns of elderly people has emerged in the last 5 years. Few studies have focused solely on the elderly, most having considered the disabled, but there is, of course, a considerable overlap. In 1976 Political and Economic Planning (now the Policy Studies Institute) surveyed various groups, including the elderly, to gain insights into shopping and personal business travel, journeys to medical facilities, and for social purposes (Hillman, Henderson and Whalley, 1976). This drew attention to the importance of walking, and was followed by a specific examination of pedestrian travel (Hillman and Whalley, 1979). The difficulties experienced by disabled people in urban areas have been studied by Buchanan (1978), who is now replicating the work in a rural area. Another survey examined the mobility of older people in Guildford (Hopkin, Robson and Town, 1978) and, like the previous two projects, considered a wide range of influences on mobility: health, income, levels of car ownership, travel patterns, substitutes for personal mobility, and, not least, the location of respondents in relation to essential services. All have demonstrated the paradox that the more disabled the respondent, the greater the reliance on walking because of the unsuitability of public transport, yet one-half of the disabled in Buchanan's survey could walk no further than 100 yards. The concept of accessibility also underlines a study in East Anglia (Moseley *et al.*, 1977) which, although concerned with the needs of the whole community, is relevant to the problems of elderly and disabled people.

A small minority of old people are so severely disabled as to be virtually housebound (one-half of the respondents over 75 years old in Buchanan's survey could get no further than their garden gate). Many such people are aided by substitutes for personal mobility, such as home helps, meals on wheels, domiciliary nursing, and specialized door-to-door transport. The provision of specialized transport is a crucial but under-researched policy issue. It is not widely appreciated that the development of, for example, day care in hospitals, centres, and residential homes, is restricted not by the lack of places but by inadequate transport. CPA is currently investigating two forms of specialized, voluntary transport provision—minibuses and a voluntary car scheme, but there is scope for further work.

The main gaps in mobility research are an assessment of its role in the lifestyle and life-satisfaction of the elderly, and its relationship to physical and mental functioning. The ability to get out and about in late life may have an important therapeutic value, and while geographers will appreciate that this ability depends, to some extent, on the individual's location, to date there has been only one geographical study (Peace, 1977; and Chapter 12 of this book).

## Towards a geographical contribution

The main contribution geographers have made to British research in social gerontology has been their studies of retirement migration, but growing interests can be discerned in leisure, the delivery of personal social services, and housing. It is evident from this review, however, that many non-geographers have investigated aspects of the environments of older people and have touched on the significance of location. To emphasize one example, Abrams (1980) investigated the location of elderly people in relation to their family members, recognizing that the quantity and quality of family support depends to a large extent on physical proximity. Social scientists have already mapped out much of the territory and brought their own concepts to bear on locational problems. Many important gaps in our knowledge remain, however, which geographers are well qualified to investigate. Indeed, apart from Peace's (1977) work, the concept of environment has yet to be applied in British research on older people. Whilst some aspects of environment have been investigated at the micro-level, the totality of old people's environments has escaped analysis. It is perhaps worth reiterating that it is commonly overlooked that 'old people live in a community, the shape and nature of which largely determines the quality of their lives' (Taylor, 1978). A geographical contribution can only be welcomed; social gerontology is a subject which depends for its vitality on its ability to draw upon a wide range of disciplinary perspectives and tools of analysis.

In respect of policy there are two major areas in which there is a potential role for geographers. The first concerns the provision of appropriate services for elderly people in need. Geographers' interests in territorial justice in resource allocation and service delivery and with the location of housing, health, social and transport services are certainly appropriate in relation to a major user group, old people. An unfortunate weakness in our current approach to policy, practice, and research, however, is the emphasis on crisis support to the neglect of preventing the crisis in the first place. The maintenance of older people as independent members of the community ought to be the major goal of research. Independence in late life is a function of many variables, but one is undoubtedly environment. The planning and management of environments is well established in Britain, but the needs of older people are often overlooked, as with the wholesale destruction of communities in the name of housing improvement, and the promotion of private transport.

The limitations of interpreting environment solely in physical terms must, however, be recognized. Old people, like the rest of us, are located in a social network and it may be the quality of this which contributes most to successful ageing. The increasing geographical mobility of working age groups, the tendency of women to enter the labour market, and increasing marital breakdown, are but a few of the social trends conspiring to deprive the marginally competent old person of family or neighbour support, thus obliging the state to become a substitute family. Geographers who wish to study social policy must be, first and foremost, competent social scientists able to borrow appropriate findings and methods from other disciplines.

In conclusion, we must add that it is not enough for a researcher to select for investigation a policy-relevant topic and leave the rest to fortune. It is our belief that all social scientists have a responsibility beyond furthering their own disciplines. Perhaps one weakness of geography is its concentration on pursuing disciplinary ends to the neglect of explaining itself to other social scientists or of becoming involved in public debate on policy issues. Geographers who wish seriously to contribute to social policy for the elderly must be willing to make contact with statutory and voluntary agencies in the field, and to participate in multidisciplinary forums like the British Society of Gerontology, both to inform themselves of the issues with which policy-makers are grappling, and to promote their research findings. Human geography has grown enormously in stature in the last decade, but its integration into the policy process depends on geographers acquiring the confidence to promote themselves in non-geographical circles.

## REFERENCES


Abrams, M. (1978a). *The Elderly: an Overview of Current British Social Research.* NCCOP and Age Concern, London.

Abrams, M. (1978b). *Beyond Three Score and Ten: a First Report on a Survey of the Elderly.* Age Concern, Mitcham.

Abrams, M. (1980). *Beyond Three Score and Ten: a Second Report on a Survey of the Elderly.* Age Concern, Mitcham.

Age Concern (1977– ). *Profiles of the Elderly*, vols 1–5. Age Concern, Mitcham.

Attenburrow, J. (1976). *Grouped Housing for the Elderly: a Review of Local Authority Provisions and Practice with Particular Reference to Alarm Systems.* Department of the Environment Building Research Station, Garston.

Bebbington, A. C. and Davies, B. P. (1980.) Territorial need indicators: a new approach; Part 1. *Journal of Social Policy*, **9**(2), 145–68.

Boldy, D., Abel, A., and Carter, K. (1973). *The Elderly in Grouped Dwellings: a Profile.* University of Exeter, Exeter.

Booth, C. (1892–97). *The Life and Labour of the People of London.* Macmillan, London.

Bracey, H. E. (1966). *In Retirement: Pensioners in Great Britain and the United States.* Routledge & Kegan Paul, London.

Brooks, B. M., Ruffell Smith, H. P., and Ward, J. S. (1974). *An Investigation of Factors Affecting the Use of Buses by both Elderly and Ambulant Disabled Persons.* British Leyland Truck and Bus Division, Leyland.

Buchanan, J. M. (1978). *Survey of the Mobility of the Disabled in an Urban Environment.* Royal Association for Disability and Rehabilitation, London.

Butler, A. (1979). *Sheltered Housing for the Elderly: a Critical Review.* Department of Social Policy and Administration, University of Leeds, Leeds.

Bytheway, W. R. and James, L. (1978). *The Allocation of Sheltered Housing: a Study of Theory, Practice and Liaison.* Medical Sociology Research Centre, University College, Swansea.

Carstairs, V. and Morrison, M. (1971). *The Elderly in Residential Care: Report of a Survey of Homes and their Residents.* Scottish Home and Health Department, Edinburgh.

Centre for Policy on Ageing (annual). *Old Age: a Register of Social Research.* CPA, London.

Centre for Policy on Ageing (1980). *The Circumstances of Britain's Elderly: a Select List of Social Surveys.* CPA, London.

# Guide to further reading

A selected bibliography has been prepared from the relevant citations of the contributors and a small number of additional items. Its theme is the environmental and geographical aspects of the elderly, and as such it supplements recent literature lists in Wiseman (1978) and Warnes (1981).

For an introduction to the scope of social gerontology several authoritative readers and compendiums are available (Binstock and Shanas, 1977; Cowgill and Holmes, 1972; Lawton, Newcomer, and Byerts, 1976; Riley and Foner, 1968, 1969, 1972; Shanas and Sussman, 1977; Tibbitts and Donahue, 1962; Woodruff and Birren, 1975). Design and planning issues are particularly well covered by Lawton's several sole and joint publications. Specifically geographical volumes are confined to Wiseman (1978) and Golant (1979), although several monographs and special journal issues deal in an extended fashion with selected topics (*East Lakes Geographer*, 14(i) 1979; Golant, 1972; Paillat, 1979; *Research on Aging*, 2(ii), 1980; Rowles, 1978). Information concerning specifically British conditions is available (Age Concern, 1977; Carver and Liddiard, 1978; Hobman, 1978; Karn, 1977). The most convenient listings of new gerontological writing appear in each issue of *Journal of Gerontology*, and for Britain in the Centre for Policy on Ageing's bi-monthly *New Literature on Old Age*. A useful register of current social gerontological research in Britain is maintained by the annual publications from the Centre for Policy on Ageing.

## A SELECTED BIBLIOGRAPHY


Abrams, M. (1978). Time and the elderly. *New Society*, **46**, 685–6.

Abrams, M. (1978). *The Elderly : an Overview of Current British Social Research*. NCCOP and Age Concern, London.

Abrams, M. (1978). *Beyond Three Score and Ten : a First Report on a Survey of the Elderly*. Age Concern, Mitcham, Surrey.

Abrams, M. (1980). *Beyond Three Score and Ten : a Second Report on a Survey of the Elderly*, Age Concern, Mitcham, Surrey.

Age Concern (1973). *Age Concern on Transport*. Age Concern England, Mitcham, Surrey.

Age Concern (1974). *Attitudes of the Retired and Elderly*. Age Concern, Mitcham, Surrey.

Age Concern (1977). *Profiles of the Elderly 1, Who Are They? etc.*, Age Concern, Mitcham, Surrey.

Albrecht, R. (1980). Retirement hotels in Florida. In Osterbind, C. C. (ed.), *Feasible Planning for Social Change in the Field of Aging*, pp. 71–82. University of Florida Press, Gainesville, Florida.

Allon-Smith, R. D. (1978). Migration of the Elderly : a Study in Social Geography. Unpublished PhD thesis, University of Leicester, Leicester.

Anchor Housing Association (1977). *Caring for the Elderly in Sheltered Housing*. AHA, London.

Ashford, N. and Holloway, F. M. (1970). *The Effect of Age on Urban Travel Behaviour*. Florida State University, Transportation Centre Research Report 1, Tallahassee.

Association of Metropolitan Authorities (1978). *Services for the Elderly A Metropolitan View*. AMA, London.

Atchley, R. C. (1980). *The Social Forces in Later Life: An Introduction to Social Gerontology, Third Edition*. Wadsworth, Belmont, California.

Atchley, R. C. and Miller, S. J. (1979). Housing and households of the rural aged. In Byerts, T. O., Howell, S. C., and Pastalan, L. A. (eds). (1979), pp. 62–79.

Attenburrow, J. (1976). *Grouped Housing for the Elderly : a Review of Local Authority Provision and Practice with Particular Reference to Alarm Systems*. Department of the Environment Building Research Station, Garston, Watford, Hertfordshire.

Auerbach, M. I., Gordon, D. W., Ullmann, A., and Weisel, M. J. (1977). Health care in a selected urban elderly population. *Gerontologist*, **17**, 341–46.

Austin, M. J. (1976). Network of help for England's elderly. *Social Work*, **21**, 114–20.

Barker, J. and Bury, M. (1978). Mobility and the elderly: a community challenge. In Carver, V. and Liddiard, P. (eds) (1978), pp. 179–92.

Barnard, K. C. (1978). The Residential Geography of the Elderly: a Multiple-scale Approach. Unpublished PhD thesis, University of Southampton.

Barsby, S. L. and Cox, D. R. (1975). *Interstate Migration of the Elderly*. Heath-Lexington, Toronto.

Beattie, W. M. (1970). The design of supportive environments for the lifespan. *The Gerontologist*, **10**, 190–3.

Beattie, W. M. (1978). Aging: a framework of characteristics and considerations for cooperative efforts between the developing and developed regions of the world. Paper prepared for United Nations Expert Group Meeting on Aging, New York, 3–5 April, All-University Gerontology Center, Syracuse University, Syracuse, New York.

Beaver, M. L. (1979). The decision making process and its relationship to relocation adjustment in old people. *The Gerontologist*, **19**, 567–74.

Bebbington, A. C. (1979). Changes in the provision of social services to the elderly in the community over fourteen years. *Social Policy and Administration*, **13**, 111–23.

Bebbington, A. C. and Davies, B. P. (1980). Territorial need indicators: a new approach, part I. *Journal of Social Policy*, **9**(2), 145–68.

Bebbington, A. C. and Davies, B. P. (1980). Territorial need indicators: a new approach, part II. *Journal of Social Policy*, **9**(4), 433–62.

Bengston, V. L., Olander, E., and Haddad, A. (1975). The 'generation gap' and aged family members. In Gubrium, J. (ed.) (1974).

Bennett, L. C. (1974). Housing for the elderly and disabled. *Housing*, **9**, 8–13.

Benwell, M. (1976). Bus passes and the elderly—a need for more informed policy making? *Local Government Studies*, **2**, 51–57.

Benwell, M. (1977). *An Examination of the Extent and Welfare Implications of Bus Use by the Elderly in Harlow*. Memorandum 22, Centre for Transport Studies, Cranfield Institute of Technology, Cranfield, Bedfordshire.

Biggar, J. C. (1979). The sunning of America: migration to the sunbelt. *Population Bulletin*, **32**, 1–43.

Biggar, J. C. (1980). Reassessing elderly sunbelt migration. *Research on Aging*, **2**, 177–90.
Binstock, R. and Shanas, E. (1977). *Handbook of Aging and the Social Sciences*. Van Nostrand, New York.
Blagden, C. (1976). Planning for the Retired. Unpublished PhD thesis, University of London, London.
Blanchard, R. D., Bunker, J. B. and Wachs, M. (1977). Distinguishing aging, period and cohort effects in longitudinal studies of elderly populations. *Socio-Economic Planning Sciences*, **11**, 137–46.
Bohland, J. R. and Davis, L. (1978). Sources of residential satisfaction amongst the elderly: an age comparative study. Unpublished paper, Department of Geography, University of Oklahoma, Norman, Oklahoma.
Boldy, D., Abel, A., and Carter, K. (1973). *The Elderly in Grouped Dwellings: a Profile*. University of Exeter, Exeter.
Booth, C. (1894). *The Aged Poor in England and Wales*. Macmillan, London.
Bouvier, L., Atlee, E., and McVeigh, F. (1975). The elderly in America. *Population Bulletin*, **30**, 36pp.
Bracey, H. E. (1966). *In Retirement: Pensioners in Great Britain and the United States*. Routledge & Kegan Paul, London.
Britton, J. H. (1966). Living in a rural Pennsylvania community in old age. In Carp, F. M. and Burnett, W. M. (eds), *Patterns of Living and Housing of Middle-Aged and Older People*, pp. 99–105. Government Printing Office, Washington, DC.
Bromley, D. B. (1977). Speculations in social and environmental gerontology. *Nursing Times*, **73**, 53–6.
Brooks, B. M., Ruffell-Smith, H. P., and Ward, J. S. (1974). *An Investigation of Factors Affecting the Use of Buses by Both Elderly and Ambulant Disabled Persons*. Transport and Road Research Laboratory Contract Report. British Leyland UK Ltd, Leyland.
Bruce, A. (1974). Facilities required near home. *Built Environment*, **3**, 290–1.
Buchanan, J. M. and Chamberlain, M. A. (1978). *Survey of the Mobility of the Disabled in an Urban Environment*. The Royal Association for Disability and Rehabilitation, London.
Buchanan, J. M. and Chamberlain, M. A. (1978). Mobility of the disabled in an urban environment. In Ashford, N. and Bell, W. (eds), *Mobility for the Elderly and Handicapped*, pp. 239–242. Loughborough University of Technology, Loughborough.
Bultena, G. L. and Wood, V. (1969). The American retirement community: bane or blessing? *Journal of Gerontology*, **24**, 209–17.
Burgess, E. W. (1961). *Retirement Villages*. Division of Gerontology, University of Michigan, Ann Arbor.
Butler, A., Oldman, C., and Wright, R. (1978). *Sheltered Housing for the Elderly: A Critical Review*. University of Leeds, Leeds.
Butler, R. N. (1974). Mobile homes—stop gaps or permanent shelters? Public interest report no. 12. *International Journal of Aging and Human Development*, **5**, 213–14.
Butler, R. N. (1975). *Why Survive?: Being Old in America*. Harper & Row, New York.
Butler, R. N. and Lewis, M. I. (1973). *Aging and Mental Health: Positive Psychosocial Approaches*. C. V. Mosby, St Louis.
Byerts, T. O., Howell, S. C., and Pastalan, L. A. (eds) (1979). *Environmental Context of Aging: Life-styles, Environmental Quality, and Living Arrangements*. Garland, New York.
Bytheway, W. R. (1973). *Suggestions for Sheltered Housing*. Centre for Social Science Research, University of Keele, Keele.
Bytheway, W. R. (1974). *Possible Trends in Sheltered Housing*. Centre for Social Science Research, University of Keele, Keele.
Bytheway, W. R. and James L. (1978). *The Allocation of Sheltered Housing: A Study of*

*Theory, Practice and Liaison*. Report of Medical Sociology Research Centre, University College of Swansea, Swansea.

Cantor, M. (1975). Life space and the social support system of the inner city elderly of New York. *The Gerontologist*, **15**, 26–7.

Caplan, G. (1974). *Support Systems and Community Mental Health*. Behavioral Publications, New York.

Carp, F. M. (1966). Effects of impoverished housing on the lives of older people. In Carp, F. M. and Burnett, W. M. (eds), *Patterns of Living and Housing of Middle-aged and Older People*, pp. 147–67. Government Printing Office, Washington, DC.

Carp, F. M. (1966). *A Future for the Aged: Victoria Plaza and its Residents*. University of Texas Press, Austin.

Carp, F. M. (1968). Person–situation congruence in engagement. *The Gerontologist*, **8**, 184–8.

Carp, F. M. (1975). Impact of improved housing on morale and life satisfaction. *The Gerontologist*, **15**, 511–15.

Carp, F. M. (1974). Short-term and long-term prediction of adjustment to a new environment. *Journal of Gerontology*, **29**, 444–53.

Carp, F. M. (1976). Living environment of older people. In Binstock, R. H. and Shanas, E. (eds), *op. cit.*, pp. 244–71.

Carstairs, V. and Morrison, M. (1971). *The Elderly in Residential Care: Report of a Survey of Homes and Their Residents*. Scottish Home and Health Department, Edinburgh.

Carver, V. and Liddiard, P. (1978). *An Ageing Population: A Reader and Sourcebook*. Hodder & Stoughton in conjunction with The Open University Press, London.

Cavan, R. S., Burgess, E. W., Havighurst, R. J., and Goldhammer, R. (1949). *Personal Adjustment in Old Age*. Science Research Associates, Chicago.

Cebula, R. J. (1974). Interstate migration and the Tiebout hypothesis: an analysis according to race, age, and sex. *Journal of the American Statistical Association*, **69**, 876–9.

Cebula, R. J. (1974). The quality of life and migration of the elderly. *Review of Regional Studies*, **4**, 62–8.

Centre for Policy on Ageing (annual). *Old Age: a Register of Social Research*. CPA, London.

Centre for Policy on Ageing (1980). *The Circumstances of Britain's Elderly: a Select List of Social Surveys*. CPA, London.

Chapanis, A. (1974). Human engineering environments for the aged. *The Gerontologist*, **14**, 228–35.

Chevan, A. and Fischer, L. R. (1979). Retirement and inter-state migration. *Social Forces*, **57**, 1365–80.

Clark, M. (1971). Patterns of ageing among the elderly poor of the inner city. *The Gerontologist*, **11**, 59–66.

Cleland, C. B. (1965). Mobility of older people. In Rose, A. M. and Peterson, W. A. (eds), *Older People and Their Social World*, pp. 181–196. F. A. Davis, Philadelphia.

Cohen, C. I. and Sockolovsky, J. (1979). Health-seeking behavior and social networks of the aged living in single room occupancy hotels. *Journal of the American Geriatrics Society*, **27**, 270–8.

Cohen, G. D. (1976). Mental health services and the elderly: needs and options. *American Journal of Psychiatry*, **133**, 65–8.

Collins, A. H. and Pancoast, D. L. (1976). *Natural Helping Networks: A Strategy for Prevention*. National Association of Social Workers, Washington, DC.

Costa, F. J. and Sweet, M. (1976). Barrier-free environments for older Americans. *The Gerontologist*, **16**, 404–9.

Cowgill, D. O. (1974). The aging of populations and societies. *Annals of the American*

*Academy of Political and Social Science*, **415**, 1–18.
Cowgill, D. O. and Holmes, L. (eds) (1972). *Aging and Modernisation*. Appleton-Century-Crofts, New York.
Cribier, F. (1969). *La Grande Migration d'Eté des Citadins en France*. Centre National de la Recherche Scientifique (CNRS), Paris.
Cribier, F. (1973). Les rèsidences secondaires des citadins dans les campanges françaises. *Etudes Rurales*, No. 49–50, 181–204.
Cribier, F. (1975). *La Migration de Retraite des Parisiens*. Laboratoire de Geographie Humaine, Paris.
Cribier, F. (1975). Retirement migration in France. In Mansell Prothero, R. and Koszinski, E. (eds), *People on the Move*, pp. 360–73. Methuen, London.
Cribier, F. (1978). *Une Gènèration de Parisiens Arrive à la Retraite*. CNRS, Paris.
Cribier, F. (1977). La migration de retraite: dèfinitions et problèmes. *Gerontologie et Société*, No. **30**, 7–17.
Cribier, F. (1979). Relations à Paris et images de Paris: Les Parisiens qui se retirent en Province. In Frémont, A. (ed.), *L'Espace Vécu*, pp. 59–68. CNRS, Paris.
Cribier, F. (1980). A European assessment of aged migration. *Research on Aging*, **4**, 255–70.
Cribier, F., Duffau, M. L., and Kych, A. (1974). *La Migration de Retraite en France*, 2 vols. Laboratoire de Geographie Humaine, Paris.
Culyer, A. J. (1976). *Need and the National Health Service*. Martin Robertson, London.
Culyer, A. J., Lavers, R. J., and Williams, A. (1971). Social indicators: health. *Social Trends*, **2**.
Cumming, E. and Henry, W. E. (1961). *Growing Old: the Process of Disengagement*. Basic Books, New York.
Davies, B. P. (1968). *Social Needs and Resources in Local Services*. Michael Joseph, London.
Davies, B. P. (1977). *Need*. Personal Social Services Research Unit, Paper 69, University of Canterbury, Kent.
Davies, B. P. (1980). Strategic goals and piecemeal innovation. In Goldberg, E. N. (ed.), *Retrenchment in the Social Services*. Policy Studies Institute, London.
Davies, B. P., Barton, A. V., McMillan, I. S. and Williamson, V. K. (1971). Variations in *Services for the Aged*. Bell, London.
Davies, A., Dempster, M. A. H. and Wildavsky, A. (1966). A theory of the budgetary process. *American Political Science Review*, **60**, 529–47.
Davis, N. (1976). Britain's changing age structure, 1931–2011. *Population Trends*, **3**, 14–17.
Day, D. J. (1973). *1973 Concessionary Fares Survey*. Operational Research Report R200. London Transport Executive, London.
Dear, M. and Wolch, J. (1979). The optimal assignment of human service clients to treatment settings. In Golant, S. M. (ed.) (1979), pp. 197–209.
Department of Health and Social Security and Welsh Office (1973). *Residential Care for Elderly People*. Local Authority Building Note 2. HMSO, London.
Department of Health and Social Security (1975). *The Census of Residential Accommodation 1970: 1, Residential Accommodation for the Elderly and for the Younger Physically Handicapped*. DHSS, London.
Department of Health and Social Security (1978). *A Happier Old Age*. HMSO, London.
Department of Health and Social Security, Social Work Service, London Region (1979). *Residential Care for the Elderly in London*. DHSS, London.
Department of the Environment (1968). *Grouped Flatlets for Old People*, Design Bulletin 2. HMSO, London.
Department of the Environment (1970). *Housing for Old People*, HMSO, London.

Department of the Environment (1972). *Sheltered Housing for the Elderly*. HMSO, London.

Department of the Environment (1973). *Widening the Choice—The Next Step in Housing*. HMSO, London.

Department of the Environment (1975). *Housing Needs and Actions*. HMSO, London.

Department of the Environment (1975). *The Retirement Industry in the South West*, by I. R. Gordon. HMSO, London.

Department of the Environment (1980). *Report on a Survey of Housing Old People Provided by Local Authorities and Housing Associations in England and Wales*. Department of the Environment, London.

Department of the Environment, Housing Development Directorate (DOEHDD) (1976). *Housing the Elderly: How Successful are Granny Annexes?* DOEHDD, London.

DOEHDD (1978). *An Exploratory Project on Heating for the Elderly*. DOEHDD, London.

DOEHDD (1980). *Housing the Elderly Near Relatives: Moving and Other Options*. DOEHDD Occasional Paper 1/80. HMSO, London.

Department of Transport (1979). *Concessionary Fares For Elderly, Blind and Disabled People*, Cmnd. 7475. HMSO, London.

DeVise, P. (1971). Cook County Hospital: bulwark of Chicago's apartheid health system and prototype of the nation's public hospitals. *Antipode*, **3**, Part 1, 9–20.

DeVise, P. (1973). *Misused and Misplaced Hospitals and Doctors*, Commission on College Geography, Resource Paper, No. 22. Association of American Geographers, Washington, DC.

Donahue, W. (1960). Housing and community services. In Burgess, E. W. (ed.), *Aging in Western Societies*, pp. 106–55. University of Chicago Press, Chicago.

Donahue, W. (1966). Impact of living arrangements on ego development in the elderly. In Carp, F. M. and Burnett, W. M. (eds), *Patterns of Living and Housing of Middle-aged and Older People*, pp. 1–9. Government Printing Office, Washington DC.

East Sussex County Council Social Services Department (1975). *Survey on Ageing: Report on Findings*. East Sussex CC, Lewes, Sussex.

Eckerman, J. M. (1979). *An Exploratory Study of Age-integrated Retirement Communities in the Ozarks*. Unpublished MA thesis, Trinity University, San Antonio, Texas.

Feeney, R. J., Ashford, N. J., Morris, A., and Gazely, D. (1979). *Travel and the Handicapped: a Project Summary*, Supplementary Report 480, Transport and Road Research Laboratory, Crowthorne, Berkshire.

Fischer, D. H. (1977). *Growing Old in America*. Oxford University Press, New York.

Flynn, C. B. (1980). General versus aged interstate migration, 1965–1970. *Research on Aging*, **2**, 165–76.

Flynn, C. B., Biggar, J. C., Longino, C. F., and Wiseman, R. F. (1979). *Aged Migration in the United States, 1965–1975, Final Report*. National Institute on Aging, Washington, DC.

Fox, D. (1979). The housing needs of the elderly. *Housing*, **7**, 5–7.

Freeman, J. D. (1975). *Free Travel for the Elderly in Greater London—1974 Survey*. Operational Research Report R208. London Transport Executive, London.

Garden, J. (ed.) (1978). *Solving the Transport Problems of the Elderly: The Use of Resources*. Beth Johnson Foundation, Stoke-on-Trent.

Garden, J. (ed.) (1979a). *Social Services Transport and the Elderly*, The Beth Johnson Foundation, Stoke-on-Trent.

Garden, J. (1979b). A specialised vehicle for the transport of the elderly. In Garden, J. (ed.), *Social Services Transport and the Elderly*. The Beth Johnson Foundation, Stoke-on-Trent.

Gardner, M. and Donnan, S. (1978). Life expectations: variations among Regional Health Authorities. *Population Trends*, **10**, 10–12.

Gelwicks, L. E. and Newcomer, R. J. (1974). *Planning Housing Environments for the Elderly*. The National Council on the Aging, Inc., Washington.

Giggs, J. A. (1979). Human health problems in urban areas. In Herbert, D. T. and Smith, D. M. (eds), *Social Problems and the City: Geographical Perspectives*, pp. 84–116. Oxford University Press, Oxford.

Glasscote, R. M., Gudeman, J. E., and Miles, D. G. (1977). *Creative Mental Health Services for the Elderly*, American Psychiatric Association, Washington, DC.

Glyn-Jones, A. (1975). *Growing Older in a South Devon Town*. University of Exeter, Exeter.

Golant, S. M. (1972). *The Residential Location and Spatial Behaviour of the Elderly*. University of Chicago, Department of Geography, Research Paper No. 143, Chicago.

Golant, S. M. (1975). Residential concentration of the future elderly. *The Gerontologist*, **15**, 16–23.

Golant, S. M. (1978). Spatial context of residential moves by elderly persons. *International Journal of Aging and Human Development*, **8**, 279–89.

Golant, S. M. (1979). Central city, suburban, and nonmetropolitan area migration patterns of the elderly. In Golant, S. M. (ed.), (1979, pp. 37–54.

Golant, S. M. (ed.) (1979). *Location and Environment of Elderly Population*. V. H. Winston, Washington, DC.

Golant, S. M. (1980). Locational–environmental perspectives on old-age-segregated residential areas in the United States. In Johnston, R. J. and Herbert, D. T. (eds), *Geography and the Urban Environment*, vol. 3. Wiley, Chichester.

Golant, S. M. (1980). Future directions for elderly migration research. *Research on Aging*, **2**, 271–80.

Golant, S. M. and McCaslin, R. (1979). A social indicator model of the elderly population's social welfare environment. In Golant, S. M. (ed.) (1979), pp. 181–96.

Goldberg, E. M. (1970). *Helping the Aged: a Field Experiment in Social Work*. George Allen & Unwin, London.

Goldman, F. R. and Goldman, D. M. (1977). *Problems Brasileiros: Alguns Aspectos Sobre o Processo de Envelhecer*, Franciscana do Lar Franciscano de Menores, São Paulo.

Goldman, F. R. and Goldman, D. M. (undated). Gerontology in Brazil. Typescript at International Federation of Aging, Washington, DC.

Goldstein, S. (1967). Socio-economic and migration differentials between the aged in the labour force and in the labour reserve. *The Gerontologist*, **7**, 31–40.

Graff, T. O. and Wiseman, R. F. (1978). Changing concentrations of older Americans. *The Geographical Review*, **63**, 379–93.

Granovetter, M. S. (1973). The strength of weak ties. *American Journal of Sociology*, **78**, 1360–80.

Grob, G. N. (1980). Psychiatry and mental hospitals in modern America : myths and realities. In Smith, C. J. (ed.), *A Place to Call Home: Perspectives on Deinstitutionalization of the Mentally Ill*, pp. 11–33. Mental Health Association in Oklahoma County, Oklahoma City.

Gruenberg, E. M., and Archer, J. (1979). Abandonment of responsibility for the seriously mentally ill. *Milbank Memorial Fund Quarterly*, **57**, 485–506.

Gruer, R. (1975). *Needs of the Elderly in the Scottish Borders*. Scottish Home and Health Department, Edinburgh.

Gubrium, J. F. (1973). *The Myth of the Golden Years: A Socio-Environmental Theory of Aging*. Charles C. Thomas, Springfield, Massachusetts.

Gubrium, J. F. (1974). *Late Life: Communities and Environmental Policy*. Charles C. Thomas, Springfield, Massachusetts.

Gutman, G. M. (1978). Issues and findings relating to multilevel accommodations for seniors. *Journal of Gerontology*, **33**, 592–600.

Hadley, R., Webb, A., and Farrell, C. (1975). *Across the Generations: Old People and Young Volunteers*. George Allen & Unwin, London.

Hamovitch, M. B. (1968). Social and psychological factors in adjustment in a retirement community. In Carp, F. (ed.), *The Retirement Process*, pp. 53–65. Government Printing Office, Washington, DC.

Hamovitch, M. B., Peterson, J. A., and Larson, A. E. (undated). *Housing Needs of The Elderly*. Andrus Gerontology Center, University of Southern California, Los Angeles.

Hampshire County Council (1978). *Kinloss Court Sheltered Housing Scheme: A Report on the First Year's Monitoring*. Hampshire County Council, Social Services Department, Winchester.

Hansen, G. B. (1971). Meeting housing challenges: involvement—the elderly. In *Housing Issues. Proceedings of the Fifth Annual Meeting, American Association of Housing Educators*. University of Nebraska Press.

Hanson, P. (1977). The activity patterns of elderly households. *Geografiska Annaler*, **59B**, 109–24.

Harbert, A. S. and Ginsberg, L. H. (1979). *Human Services for Older Adults: Concepts and Skills*. Wadsworth, Belmont, California.

Harris, A. (1968). *Social Welfare for the Elderly: a Study in Thirteen Local Authority Areas in England, Wales and Scotland*, 2 vols. HMSO, London.

Harris, A. (1971). *Handicapped and Impaired in Great Britain*. HMSO, London.

Harris, L. and Associates (1975). *The Myth and Reality of Aging in America*. National Council on the Aging, Washington, DC.

Harrison, E., McKeown, M., and O'Shea, T. (1971). Old age in Northern Ireland—a study of the elderly in a seaside town. *Economic and Social Review*, **3**, 53–72.

Hauser, P. M. (1978). Aging and social structure. In Binstock, R. and Shanas, E. (eds) (1977), pp. 59–86.

Havighurst, R. J. (1968). Personality and the patterns of aging. *Gerontologist*, **8**, 20–3.

Haynes, K. J. and Raven, J. (1961). *The Living Patterns of Some Elderly People*. Building Research Station, Garston, Watford.

Hazel, N. (1974). Residential provision for the elderly in Switzerland and Germany. *Social Work Today*, 16 May.

Hearnden, J. and Fujishin, B. (1974). *Membership of Old People's Clubs*. Centre for Urban and Regional Studies, University of Birmingham, Birmingham.

Heintz, K. M. (1976). *Retirement Communities: For Adults Only*. Centre for Urban Policy Research, Rutgers, the State University, New Brunswick, New Jersey.

Hendricks, J. and Hendricks, C. D. (1977). *Aging in a Mass Society: Myths and Realities*. Winthrop, Combridge, Massachusetts.

Herbert, N. M. (1966). *The Older Adult: Life in a Retirement Community Compared to Life in a City*. Bureau of Community Research, Berkeley, California.

Hillman, M., Henderson, I., and Whalley, A. (1973). *Personal Mobility and Transport Policy*. Political and Economic Planning, Broadsheet 542, London.

Hillman, M., Henderson, I., and Whalley, A. (1976). *Transport Realities and Planning Policy*. Political and Economic Planning, Broadsheet 567, London.

Hillman, M. and Whalley, A. (1979). *Walking is Transport*. Policy Studies Institute, London.

Hiltner, J. and Smith, B. W. (1974). Intra-urban residential location of the elderly. *Journal of Geography*, **73**, 23–33.

Hobman, D. (ed.) (1978). *The Social Challenge of Ageing*. Croom Helm, London.

Hodgart, R. L. (1978). Optimizing access to public services: a review of problems, models and methods of locating central facilities. *Progress in Human Geography*, **2**, 17–48.

Hopkin, J. M., Robson, P., and Town, S. W. (1978). *The Mobility of Old People; a Study in Guildford.* Transport and Road Research Laboratory Report LR 850, Crowthorne, Berkshire.

Hopkin, J. W., Robson, P., and Town, S. W. (1978). *Transport and the Elderly: Requirements, Problems and Possible Solutions.* Transport and Road Research Laboratory Supplementary Report SR 419, Crowthorne, Berkshire.

Horwitz, A. (1977). Social networks and pathways to psychiatric treatment. *Social Forces*, **56**, 86–105.

Housing Centre (undated). *The London Almshouses: Six Centuries of Housing for the Aged.* Housing Centre, London.

Housing Corporation (1976). The role of the housing association movement in housing elderly people. Unpublished paper. Housing Corporation, London.

Housing Development Directorate (1976). The need for smaller homes. *The Architects Journal*, **164**, 925–30.

Howell, N., Boldy, D., and Smith, B. (1979). *Allocating the Home Help Services:* Bedford Square Press, London.

Howell, R. G. (1979). Planning in an ambulance service. In Garden, J. (ed.), *Social Services Transport and the Elderly.* The Beth Johnson Foundation, Stoke-on-Trent.

Howell, S. C. (1976). Site selection and the elderly. In Lawton, M. P., Newcomer, R. J., and Byerts, T. O. (eds) (1976), pp. 181–94.

Hoyt, G. C. (1954). The life of the retired in a trailer park. *American Journal of Sociology*, **59**, 361–70.

Hunt, A. (1978a). The elderly: age differences in the quality of life. *Population Trends*, **11**, 10–15.

Hunt, A. (1978b). *The Elderly at Home: a Study of People Aged 65 and Over Living in the Community in England in 1976.* HMSO, London.

Ingram, D. R., Clarke, D. R., and Murdie, R. A. (1978). Distance and the decision to visit an emergency department. *Social Science and Medicine*, **12**, 55–62.

Inwood, J. and Grayson, G. (1979). *The Comparative Safety of Pedestrian Crossings.* Laboratory Report 859, Transport and Road Research Laboratory, Crowthorne, Beshshire.

Jacobs, J. (1974). *Fun City: An Ethnographic Study of a Retirement Community.* Holt Rinehart & Winston, New York.

Johnson, M. (1976). That was your life: a biographical approach in later life. In Munnichs, J. M. A. and van der Heuvel, W. J. A. (eds), *Dependency or Interdependency in Old Age.* Martinus Nijhoff, The Hague.

Johnson, S. K. (1971). *Idle Haven: Community Building Among the Working-Class Retired.* University of California Press, Berkeley, California.

Jonas, S. (1973). Some thoughts on primary care: problems in implementation. *International Journal of Health Services*, **3**, 176–80.

Jonas, S. and Rimer, B. (1977). Ambulatory care. In Jonas, S. (ed.), *Health Care Delivery in the United States*, pp. 160–3. Springer, New York.

Kahana, E. (1980). A congruence model of person–environment interaction. In Lawton, M. P., Windley, P. G., and Byerts, T. O. (eds), *Aging and the Environment: Directions and Perspectives.* Garland, New York.

Karn, V. A. (1973). Retirement migration. In Mellor, H. (ed.), *Housing in Retirement: Some Pointers for Social Policy.* Bedford Square Press, London.

Karn, V. A. (1974). Retiring to the Seaside: a Study of Retirement Migration in England and Wales. PhD thesis, University of Birmingham, Birmingham.

Karn, V. A. (1977). *Retiring to the Seaside.* Routledge & Kegan Paul, London.

Kasschau, P. L. (1978). Developing gerontology in a developing country: the case of São Paulo, Brazil. *International Journal of Aging and Human Development*, **8**, 325–37.
Kennedy, J. M. and De Jong, G. F. (1977). Aged in cities: residential segregation in 10 USA central cities. *Journal of Gerontology*, **32**, 97–102.
Kerckhoff, A. C. (1965). Nuclear and extended family relationships: normative and behavioral analysis. In Shanas, E. and Streib, G. (eds), *op. cit.*, pp. 93–112.
Kleemeier, R. W. (1961). The use and meaning of time in special settings: retirement communities, homes for the aged, hospitals and group settings. In Kleemeier, R. W. (ed.), *Aging and Leisure*. Oxford University Press, New York.
Knox, P. L. (1978). The intraurban ecology of primary medical care: patterns of accessibility and their policy implications. *Environment and Planning A*, **10**, 415–35.
Lake, W. S. (1962). Housing preferences and social patterns. In Tibbitts, C. and Donahue, W. (eds) (1962), pp. 341–7.
Lamb, H. R. and Goertzel, V. (1971). Discharged mental patients—are they really in the community? *Archives of General Psychiatry*, **24**, 29–34.
Law, C. M. and Warnes, A. M. (1973). The movement of retired people to seaside resorts: a study of Morecambe and Llandudno. *Town Planning Review*, **44**, 373–90.
Law, C. M. and Warnes, A. M. (1975). Life begins at sixty: the increase in regional retirement migration. *Town and Country Planning*, **43**, 531–4.
Law, C. M. and Warnes, A. M. (1976). The changing geography of the elderly in England and Wales. *Institute of British Geographers, Transactions*, new series **1**, 453–71.
Law, C. M. and Warnes, A. M. (1977). *The Migration Decisions of Individuals at Retirement.* Final Report to the Social Science Research Council, London.
Law, C. M. and Warnes, A. M. (1980). The characteristics of retired migrants. In Herbert, D. T. and Johnston, R. J. (eds), *Geography and the Urban Environment*, vol. III, pp. 175–222. Wiley, Chichester.
Law, C. M. and Warnes, A. M. (1981). Planning and retirement migration. *Town and Country Planning*, **50**, 44–6.
Lawton, M. P. (1970). Ecology and ageing. In Pastalan, L. A. and Carson, D. H. (eds) (1970), pp. 40–67.
Lawton, M. P. (1970). Planning environments for older people. *Journal of the American Institute of Planners*, **36**, 124–9.
Lawton, M. P. (1975). *Planning and Managing Housing for the Elderly*. Wiley-Interscience, New York.
Lawton, M. P. (1976). Homogeneity and heterogeneity in housing for the elderly. In Lawton, M. P., Newcomer, R. J., and Byerts, T. O. (eds) (1976), pp. 173–80.
Lawton, M. P. (1976). The relative impact of congregate and traditional housing on elderly tenants. *The Gerontologist*, **16**, 237–42.
Lawton, M. P. (1977). The impact of the environment on aging and behavior. In Birren, J. E. and Schaie, K. W. (eds), *Handbook of the Psychology of Aging*, pp. 276–301. Van Nostrand Reinhold, New York.
Lawton, M. P. (1979). The housing status of the elderly: report on a national study. In Wagner, P. A. and McRae, J. M. (eds), *Back to Basics: Food and Shelter for the Elderly*. University of Florida Centre for Gerontological Studies and Programs, Gainesville.
Lawton, M. P. (1980). *Environment and Aging*. Brooks/Cole, Monterey, California.
Lawton, M. P. (in press). *Social and Medical Services in Housing for the Elderly*. Government Printing Office, Washington, DC.
Lawton, M. P. and Cohen, J. (1974). The generality of housing impact on the well-being of older people. *Journal of Gerontology*, **29**, 194–204.
Lawton, M. P. and Kleban, M. H. (1971). The aged resident in the inner city. *The Gerontologist*, **2**, 277–83.

Lawton, M. P. and Nahemow, L. (1973). Ecology and the aging process. In Eisdorfer, C. and Lawton, M. P. (eds), *The Psychology of Adult Development and Aging*. American Psychological Association, Washington, DC.

Lawton, M. P. and Nahemow, L. (1975). *Cost, Structure, and Social Aspects of Housing for the Aged. Final Report to the Administration on Aging, U. S. Department of Health, Education and Welfare*. Philadelphia Geriatric Center, Philadelphia.

Lawton, M. P., Nahemow, L., and Teaff, J. (1975). Housing characteristics and the well-being of elderly tenants in federally-assisted housing. *Journal of Gerontology*, **30**, 601–7.

Lawton, M. P., Newcomer, R. J., and Byerts, T. O. (eds) (1976). *Community Planning for an Aging Society: Designing Services and Facilities*. Dowden, Hutchinson & Ross, Stroudsburg, Pennsylvania.

Lawton, M. P. and Simon, B. (1968). The ecology of social relationships in housing for the elderly. *The Gerontologist*, **8**, 108–15.

Lemon, A. (1973). Retirement and its effect on small towns. *Town Planning Review*, **44**, 254–62.

Lewis, C. W. (1977). The role of age in the decision to migrate. *Annals of Regional Science*, **11**, 51–60.

Lewis, C., Rashi, F., and Mechanic, D. (1976). *A Right to Health: The Problem of Access to Primary Medical Care*. Wiley, New York.

Lipman, A. (1968). Public housing and attitude adjustment in old age. *Journal of Geriatric Psychiatry*, **2**, 88–101.

Litwak, E. (1960). Occupational mobility and extended family cohesion. *American Sociological Review*, **25**, 9–21.

Litwak, E. (1960). Geographic mobility and extended family cohesion. *American Sociological Review*, **25**, 385–94.

London Borough of Wandsworth (1977). *Services for the Elderly*. London Borough of Wandsworth, Wandsworth.

Long, L. H. and Hansen, K. A. (1979). Reasons for interstate migration. *Current Population Reports*, Series P–23. 81.

Longino, C. F. (1979). Going home: aged return migration in the United States 1965–70. *Journal of Gerontology*, **34**, 736–45.

Longino, C. F. Jr (1980). Residential relocation of older people: Metropolitan and Nonmetropolitan. *Research on Aging*, **2**, 205–16.

Longino, C. F. Jr (1980). The retirement community. In Bergho, F. J. and Schafer, D. E. (eds), *The Dynamics of Aging: Original Essays on the Experience and Process of Growing Old*. Westview Press, Boulder, Colorado.

Longino, C. F. Jr, McClelland, K. A., and Peterson, W. A. (1980). The aged subculture hypothesis: social integration, gerontophilia and self-regard. *Journal of Gerontology*, **34** (in press).

Lundy, G. R. (1978). Nonmetropolitan Migration: A Study of Age Specific Net Migration Rates in the Ozarks–Ouachita Area. Unpublished MSc. thesis, University of Oklahoma, Department of Geography.

MacGuire, J. (1977). The elderly in a new town: a case study of Telford. *Housing Review*, **6**, 132–6.

Maddox, G. (1963). Activity and morale—a longitudinal study of selected elderly subjects. *Social Forces*, **42**, 195–204.

Maddox, G. and Eisdorfer, C. (1962). Some correlates of activity and morale among the elderly. *Social Forces*, **60**, 254–60.

Maguire, G. A. (1979). Volunteer program to assist the elderly to remain in home settings. *The American Journal of Occuptional Therapy*, **33**, 98–101.

Mangum, W. P. (1971). Adjustment in Special Residential Settings for the Aged: An

Inquiry Based on the Kleemeier Conceptualization. Unpublished doctoral dissertation, University of Southern California, Los Angeles.

Mangum, W. P. (1973). Retirement hotels and mobile home parks as alternative living arrangements for older persons. In *Housing and Environment for the Elderly: Proceedings from a Conference on Behavioral Research Utilization and Environmental Policy, December, 1971, San Juan, Puerto Rico*. Gerontological Society, Washington.

Mangum, W. P. (1979). Retirement villages: past, present, and future issues. In Wagner, P. A. and McRae, J. M. (eds), *Back to Basics: Food and Shelter for the Elderly*, pp. 88–97. University of Florida Center for Gerontological Studies and Programs, Gainesville.

Markovitz, J. (1971). Transportation needs of the elderly. *Traffic Quarterly*, **25**, 237–53.

Marks, J. (1975). *Home Help: a Study of Needs, Management and Home Help Staff in a Local Authority*. Bell, London.

Marshall, V. W. (1975). Socialization for impending death in a retirement village. *American Journal of Sociology*, **80**, 1124–44.

Matalon, B. and Averous, B. (1978). The mobility of elderly people: the influence of retirement and former life style. In Ashford, N. and Bell, W. (eds), *Mobility for the Elderly and Handicapped*, pp. 122–9. Loughborough University of Technology, Loughborough.

McRae, J. (1975). *Elderly in the Environment of Northern Europe*. University of Florida Center for Gerontological Studies and Programs, Gainesville.

McTavish, A. D. and Mullen, P. (1977). *Survey of Concessionary Bus Fares for the Elderly, Blind and Disabled in England and Wales*. Local Transport Note 1/77, Department of Transport, London.

Mellor, H. (1962). Retirement to the coast. *Town Planning Review*, **33**, 40–8.

Mellor, H. W. (1973). Special housing for the elderly. In Mellor, H. W. (ed.), *Housing in Retirement*, pp. 15–26. National Corporation for the Care of Old People, London.

Messer, J. (1967). The possibility of an age-concentrated environment becoming a normative system. *The Gerontologist*, **7**, 247–51.

Ministry of Housing and Local Government (1957). *Housing Old People*. Circular 181/57. HMSO, London.

Ministry of Housing and Local Government (1962). *Grouped Flatlets for Old People: a Sociological Study*. HMSO, London.

Ministry of Housing and Local Government (1966). *Old People's Flatlets at Stevenage*. Design Bulletin 11. HMSO, London

Ministry of Housing and Local Government (1968). *Some Aspects of Designing for Old People*. Design Bulletin 1. HMSO, London.

Mitchell, C. G. B. and Town, S. W. (1977). *Accessibility of Various Social Groups to Different Activities*. Transport and Road Research Laboratory Supplementary Report SR 258, Crowthorne, Berkshire.

Moindrot, C. (1963). Les villes de retraités de la côte de Sussex. *Population*, **18**, 364–6.

Montgomery, J. E. (1972). The housing patterns of older families. *The Family Coordinator*, **21**, 37–46.

Morrill, R. L., Earickson, R. J., and Rees, P. (1970). Factors influencing distances traveled to hospitals. *Economic Geography*, **46**, 161–71.

Moseley, M. J. (1978b). The mobility and accessibility problems of the rural elderly: some evidence from Norfolk and possible policies. In Garden, J. (ed.) (1978), pp. 51–62.

Mueller, M. S. and Gibson, R. M. (1975). Age differences in health care spending, fiscal year 1974. *Social Security Bulletin*, **38**, 3–16.

Mumford, L. (1976). For older people: not segregation but integration. *Architectural Record*, **119**, 191–4.

Murphy, P. A. (1979). Migration of the elderly. *Town Planning Review*, **50**, 84–93.
National Council on the Aging (1969). *A National Directory on Housing for Older People.* The National Council on the Aging, New York.
National Council on the Aging, Inc. (1975). *The Myth and Reality of Aging in America.* The National Council on the Aging, Inc., Washington, DC.
Neibanck, P. L. (1965). *The Elderly in Older Urban Areas: Problems of Adaptation and the Effects of Relocation.* University of Pennsylvania, Institute for Environmental Studies, Philadelphia.
Newcomer, R. J. and Bexton, E. F. (1978). Aging and the environment. In Hobman, D. (ed.), *The Social Challenge of Ageing*, pp. 73–116. Croom Helm, London.
Norman, A. (1977). *Transport and the Elderly: Problems and Possible Action.* National Corporation for the Care of Old People, London.
Office of Population Censuses and Surveys (1974). *Census 1971: Great Britain: Persons of Pensionable Age.* HMSO, London.
Oktay, J. S. and Sheppard, F. (1978). Home health care for the elderly. *Health and Social Work*, **3**, 36–47.
Oram, J. (1979). Social services transport: efficient and effective use of resources. In Garden, J. (ed.), (1979a).
Page, D. and Muir, T. (1971). *New Housing for the Elderly: a Study of Housing Schemes for the Elderly Provided by the Hanover Housing Association.* National Council of Social Service for NCCOP, London.
Paillat, P. (ed.) (1979). Migrations de retraités. *Gérontologie et Société*, **8**, 213 pp.
Parsons, T. (1943). The kinship system of the contemporary United States. *American Anthropologist*, **45**, 22–38.
Parsons, T. (1949). The social structure of the family. In Anshen, R. N. (ed.), *The Family: Its Function and Destiny*, pp. 173–201. Harper, New York.
Parsons, T. (1963). Old age as a consumatory phase of life. *Gerontologist*, **3**, 53–4.
Pastalan, L. A. and Carson, D. H. (eds) (1970). *Spatial Behavior of Older People.* University of Michigan Press, Ann Arbor, Michigan.
Peace, S. M. (1977). *The elderly in an urban environment.* Unpublished PhD Thesis. University of Wales.
Peace, S. M., Hall, J. F., and Hamblin, G. (1979). *The Quality of Life of the Elderly in Residential Care.* Polytechnic of North London, Survey Research Unit, Research Report No. 1, London.
Peterson, J. A. and Larson, A. E. (1966). Social-psychological factors in selecting retirement housing. In *Patterns of Living and Housing of Middle Age and Older People*, US Government Printing Office, Public Health Service Publication No. 1496, Washington, DC.
Phillips, D. R. (1979). Public attitudes to general practitioner services: a reflection of an inverse care law in intra-urban primary medical care. *Environment and Planning A*, **11**, 815–24.
Pinch, S. (1979). Territorial justice in the city: a case study of the social services for the elderly in Greater London. In Herbert, D. T. and Smith, D. M. (eds), *Social Problems and the City: Geographical Perspectives*, pp. 201–23. Oxford University Press, Oxford.
Plank, D. (1977). *Caring for the Elderly: Report of a Study of Various Means of Caring for Dependent Elderly People in Eight London Boroughs.* Greater London Council, London.
Rigby, J. P. (1978). *Access to Hospitals: a Literature Review.* Transport and Road Research Laboratory Report LR 853, Crowthorne, Berkshire.
Riley, M. W. and Foner, A. (eds) (1968, 1969, and 1972). *Aging and Society*, 3 vols. Russell Sage, New York.

Rives, N. W. Jr (1980). Conducting research on the migration of the elderly: sources of statistical information. *Research on Aging*, **2**, 155–64.

Robbins, I. S. (1971). *Housing the Elderly: Background and Issues*. White House Conference on Aging, Washington.

Rose, E. A. (1978). *Housing for the Aged*. Saxon House, Farnborough.

Rose, E. A. and Bozeat, N. R. (1980). *Communal Facilities in Sheltered Housing*. Saxon House, Farnborough.

Rosow, I. (1967). *Social Integration of the Aged*. Free Press, New York.

Rowles, G. D. (1978). *Prisoners of Space? Exploring the Geographical Experience of Older People*. Westview, Boulder, Colorado.

Rowles, G. D. (1979). The last new home: facilitating the older person's adjustment to institutional space. In Golant, S. M. (ed.), (1979), pp. 81–94.

Rubenstein, J. M. (1979). Housing the elderly in Europe. *The East Lakes Geographer*, **14**, 50–9.

Rudzitis, G. (1979). Determinants of the central city migration patterns of older persons. In Golant, S. M. (ed.) (1979), pp. 55–63.

Schooler, K. K. (1969). The relationship between social interaction and morale of the elderly as a function of environmental characteristics. *The Gerontologist*, **9**, 25–9.

Schooler, K. K. (1970). Effect of environment on morale. *The Gerontologist*, **10**, 194–7.

Sclar, E. D. and Lind, S. D. (1976). Aging and residential location. In Lawton, M. P., Newcomer, R. J. and Byerts, T. O. (eds) (1976), pp. 266–81.

Serow, W. J. (1978). Return migration of the elderly in the USA: 1955–1960 and 1965–1970. *Journal of Gerontology*, **33**, 288–95.

Seymour, L. (1973). Social Interaction of Senior Citizens in St. Mary's Ontario. Unpublished MA thesis, University of Western Ontario, Ontario.

Shanas, E. (1972). *The Health of Older People: A Social Survey*. Harvard University Press, Cambridge, Mass.

Shanas, E. (1979). The family as a social support system in old age. *The Gerontologist*, **19**, 169–74.

Shanas, E. and Streib, G. (eds) (1976). *Social Structure and Family: Generational Relations*. Prentice-Hall, Englewood Cliffs, New Jersey.

Shanas, E. and Sussman, M. B. (eds) (1977). *Family, Bureaucracy and the Elderly*. Duke University Press, Durham, North Carolina.

Shanas, E., Townsend, P., Wedderburn, D., Friis, H., Milhøj, P., and Stehower, J. (1968). *Old People in Three Industrial Societies*. Atherton, New York.

Shannon, G. W. and Dever, G. E. A. (1974). *Health Care Delivery. Spatial Perspectives*. McGraw-Hill, New York.

Shannon, G. W., Spurlock, C. W. and Skinner, J. L. (1975). A method of evaluating the geographic accessibility of health services. *Professional Geographer*, **27**, 30–6.

Shannon, G. W. and Spurlock, C. W. (1976). Urban ecological containers, environmental risk cells, and the use of medical services. *Economic Geography*, **52**, 171–80.

Shapiro, B. Z. (1977). Mutual helping: a neglected theme in social work practice and theory. *Canadian Journal of Social Work Education*, **3**, 33–44.

Sheldon, J. H. (1948). *The Social Medicine of Old Age: Report of an Inquiry in Wolverhampton*. Oxford University Press, London.

Sherman, S. R. (1971). The choice of retirement housing among the well-elderly. *Aging and Human Development*, **2**, 118–38.

Sherman, S. R. (1972). Satisfaction with retirement housing: attitudes, recommendations and moves. *Aging and Human Development*, **3**, 339–66.

Sherman, S. R. (1975). Mutual assistance and support in retirement housing. *Journal of Gerontology*, **30**, 479–83.

Sherman, S. R., Mangum, W. P., Dodds, S., Walkley, R. P., and Wilner, D. M. (1968). Psychological effects of retirement housing. *The Gerontologist*, **8**, 170–5.

Sherwood, S., Morris, J. N., and Barnhart, E. (1975). Developing a system for assigning individuals into an appropriate residential setting. *Journal of Gerontology*, **30**, 331–42.

Siegel, J. S. (1978). Prospective trends in the size and structure of the elderly population, impact of mortality trends, and some implications. In US Bureau of the Census (1978), pp. 76–121.

Skelton, N. G. (1977). *Travel Patterns of Elderly People Under a Concessionary Fares Scheme*. Supplementary Report 280, Transport and Road Research Laboratory, Crowthorne, Berkshire.

Skelton, N. G. (1978). An Investigation into the Travel of Elderly People in Urban Areas. Unpublished PhD thesis, University of Newcastle upon Tyne.

Skrimshire, J. (1973). Retiring to the seaside. *Built Environment*, **2**, 494–5.

Smith, C. A. and Smith, C. J. (1978). Locating natural neighbours in the urban community. *Area*, **10**, 102–10.

Smith, C. J. (1976). Residential neighborhoods as humane environments. *Environment and Planning A*, **8**, 311–26.

Smith, C. J. (1978). Self-help and social networks in the urban community. *Ekistics*, **65**, 106–16.

Smith, C. J. (1980). Neighborhood effects on mental health. In Johnston, R. J. and Herbert, D. T. (eds), *Geography and the Urban Environment*, vol. 3, pp. 363–415. Wiley, London.

Smith, C. J. (1980). Social networks as metaphors, models, and methods. *Progress in Human Geography*, **4**, 500–24.

Smith, S. A. (1975). *Natural Systems and the Elderly: An Unrecognized Resource*. Portland State University, School of Social Work, Portland, Oregon.

Smith Blau, Z. (1973). *Old Age in a Changing Society*. Franklin Watts Inc., New Viewpoints, New York.

Soldo, B. J. (1978). Living arrangements of the elderly: future trends and implications. In United States Bureau of the Census, *Demographic Aspects of the Aging and the Older Population*. Joint Hearing before the Subcommittee on Population of the House of Representatives and Subcommittee on Aging, 95th Congress, 2nd session, 24 May, No. 9. vol 1, pp. 208–30.

Solon, J. A. and Rigg, R. D. (1972). Patterns of medical care among users of hospital emergency units. *Medical Care*, **10**, 60–72.

Sommers, A. R. (1978). The high cost of health care for the elderly: diagnosis, prognosis, and some suggestions for therapy. *Journal of Health Politics, Policy and Law*, **3**, 163–79.

South West Economic Planning Council (1975). *Retirement to the South West*. HMSO, London.

Stallybrass, A. (1976). Housing the elderly. *The Times*, 6 April. Special report.

Stehower, J. (1968). The household and family relations of old people. In Shanas, E. *et al.* (1968), pp. 177–226.

Streib, G. F. and Streib, R. B. (1975). Communes and the aging: utopian dream and gerontological reality. *American Behavioral Scientist*, **19**, 176–89.

Struyk, R. J. (1977). The housing situation of elderly Americans. *The Gerontologist*, **17**, 130–9.

Struyk, R. J. and Soldo, B. J. (1980). *Improving the Elderly's Housing: A Key to Preserving the Nation's Housing Stock and Neighborhoods*. Ballinger, Cambridge, Massachusetts.

Sumner, G. and Smith, R. (1969). *Planning Local Authority Services for the Elderly*. George Allen & Unwin, London.

Sussman, M. B. (1965). Relations of adult children with their parents in the United States.

In Shanas, E. and Streib, G. (eds) (1965), pp. 62–92.

Sussman, M. B. (1975). The family life of old people. In Binstock, R. and Shanas, E. (1977), pp. 218–43.

Svart, L. M. (1976). Environmental preference migration: a review. *The Geographical Review*, **66**, 314–30.

Taylor, H. (1978). Old age: a review of social research. In Todd, H. (ed.), *Old Age: a Register of Social Research 1977–8*. National Corporation for the Care of Old People, London.

Taylor, S. D. (1974). The Geography and Epidemiology of Psychiatric Illness in Southampton. Unpublished PhD thesis, University of Southampton, Southampton.

Tibbitts, C. and Donahue, W. (eds) (1962). *Social and Psychological Aspects of Aging*. Columbia University Press, New York.

Tinker, A. (1976). *Housing the Elderly: How Successful are Granny Annexes?* Department of the Environment, Housing Development Directorate, London.

Tinker, A. (1977). Can a case be made for special housing? *Municipal Review*, **47**, 314–15.

Tinker, A. and White, J. (1979). How can elderly owner occupiers be helped to improve and repair their own homes? *Housing Review*, **28**, 74–5.

Tinker, A. (1980.) *Housing the Elderly near Relatives: Moving and Other Options*. Department of the Environment, Housing Development Directorate, London.

Tobin, S. S. (1975). Social and health services for the future aged. *Gerontologist*, **15** (Suppl.), 32–7.

Townsend, P. (1957). *The Family Life of Old People*. Routledge & Kegan Paul, London; (1963 edn), Penguin, Harmondsworth, Middlesex.

Townsend, P. (1962). *The Last Refuge: a Survey of Residential Institutions and Homes for the Aged in England and Wales*. Routledge & Kegan Paul, London.

Townsend, P. (1979). *Poverty in the United Kingdom*. Allen Lane, London.

Townsend, P. and Wedderburn, D. (1965). *The Aged in the Welfare State*. Bell, London.

Tunstall, J. (1966). *Old and Alone*, Routledge & Kegan Paul, London.

United Nations (1977). *The Aging in Slums and Uncontrolled Settlements*. UNO, New York.

United States of America (USA), Bureau of the Census (1976). *Current Population Reports, Special Studies, Demographic Aspects of Aging and Older Population in the United States*. US Government Printing Office, Series P. 823, No. 59, Washington, DC.

USA, Bureau of the Census (1978). *Demographic Aspects of Aging and the Older Population*. Joint Hearing before the Select Committee on Population of the US House of Representatives and the Select Committee on Aging, 95th Congress, 2nd session, 24 May 1978, No. 9, vol. 1.

USA, Department of Health, Education, and Welfare (1978). *Health Manpower Shortage Areas: Criteria for Designations*. Public Health Services, Department of Health, Education, and Welfare, Washington, DC.

USA, Department of Health, Education, and Welfare (1978). *The Elderly Population: Estimates by County, 1976*. Administration on Aging, National Clearinghouse in Aging, US Department of Health, Education, and Welfare, Washington, DC.

USA, Department of Housing and Urban Development (1979). *Annual Housing Survey: 1973, Housing Characteristics of Older Americans in the United States*, US Government Printing Office, Washington, DC.

USA, Department of Housing and Urban Development (1979). *U. S. Housing Developments for the Elderly or Handicapped*, Office of Multifamily Housing Development. US Department of Housing and Urban Development, Washington, DC.

USA, Senate (1976). *The Role of Nursing Homes in Caring of Discharged Mental Patients*. Supporting paper No. 7, prepared by the subcommittee on long term care of the Special Committee on Aging. Government Printing Office, Washington, DC.

USA, Senate Special Committee on Aging (1979). *Developments in Aging, Part 1—1978.* Government Printing Office, Washington, DC.
USA, Senate Special Committee on Aging (1980). *Developments in Aging, Part 1–1979.* Government Printing Office, Washington, DC.
USA, White House Conference on Ageing (1971). *Housing the Elderly.* Government Printing Office, Washington, DC.
Urban Systems Research and Engineering, Inc. (1976), *Evaluation of the Effectiveness of Congregate Housing for the Elderly: Final Report.* Prepared for US Department of Housing and Urban Development, US Government Printing Office, Washington, DC.
Vivrett, W. K. (1960). Housing and community settings for old people. In Tibbitts, C. (ed.), *Handbook of Social Gerontology.* University of Chicago Press, Chicago.
Wachs, M. (1978). Lifestyles and changing transportation needs of the elderly in Los Angeles. In Ashford, N. and Bell, W. (eds), *Mobility for the Elderly and Handicapped,* pp. 130–9. Loughborough University of Technology, Loughborough.
Wachs, M. and Blanchard, R. D. (1975). *Lifestyles and Transportation Needs of the Elderly in the Future,* Report for the Urban Mass Transit Administration, Washington, DC.
Walker, J. and Price, K. (1975). Retirement choice and retirement satisfaction. *The Gerontologist,* **15**, 50.
Walkley, R. B., Mangum, W. P., Sherman, S. R., Dodds, S., and Wilner, D. M. (1966). The California survey of retirement housing. *The Gerontologist,* **6**, 28–34.
Warnes, A. M. (1981). Towards a geographical contribution to gerontology. *Progress in Human Geography,* **5**, 317–41.
Webber, I. L. and Osterbind, Carter (1961). Types of retirement villages. In Burgess, E. W. (ed.) (1961), **11**, 3–10
West Sussex County Council (1978). *Retirement Migration,* Technical Paper 18, County Structure Plan. WSCC, Chichester.
Wilner, D. M. and Walkley, R. P. (1966). Some special problems and alternatives in housing for older persons. In McKinney, J. C. and DeVyer, F. P. (eds), *Aging and Social Policy,* pp. 231–59. Appleton-Century-Crofts, New York.
Winiecke, L. (1973). The appeal of age-segregated housing to the elderly poor. *Aging and Human Development,* **4**, 293–306.
Wirz, H. (1977). Economics of welfare: the implications of demographic change for Europe. *Futures,* **9**, 45–51.
Wiseman, R. F. (1978). *Spatial Aspects of Aging,* Resource Paper 78–4. Association of American Geographers, Washington, DC.
Wiseman, R. F. (1979). Regional patterns of elderly concentration and migration. In Golant, S. M. (ed.) (1979), pp. 21–36.
Wiseman, R. F. (1980). Why older people move: theoretical issues. *Research on Aging,* **2**, 141–54.
Wiseman, R. F. and Roseman, C. C. (1979). A typology of elderly migration based on the decision-making process. *Economic Geography,* **55**, 324–37.
Woodruff, D. S. and Birren, J. E. (eds) (1975). *Aging: Scientific Perspectives and Social Issues.* Van Nostrand, New York.
Wroe, D. C. L. (1973). The elderly. *Social Trends,* **4**, 23–34.

# Author Index

# Subject Index